BEST LOVED HOTELS

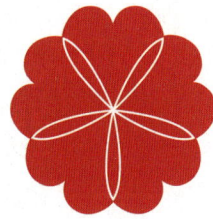

2005

ENGLAND · SCOTLAND
WALES · IRELAND

CONTENTS

PUBLISHED BY
World Media Publishing Limited
Suite 11, The Linen House
253 Kilburn Lane
London W10 4BQ
United Kingdom
T +44 (0)870 432 8700
F +44 (0)870 432 8770
mail@bestlovedhotels.com

*Book sales: See insert at back of book
or visit www.bestlovedhotels.com*

UNITED KINGDOM
Best Loved Hotels of the World
FREEPOST LON16342
London W10 4BR
T +44 (0)870 432 8700
F +44 (0)870 432 8770

UNITED STATES
c/o DDS, 20770 Westwood Drive
Strongsville, OH 44149
Administration: 440-572-7263
Book sales: 800-808-7682
Fax: 800-572-8131

PUBLISHER/FOUNDER
Jeffrey M Epstein

DEPUTY PUBLISHER
Emily J Evans

EDITOR
Jessica Schilling

DEPUTY EDITOR
Michelle Webb

COMMUNICATIONS DIRECTOR
Peter C H Jarvis

GENERAL MANAGER
Julie Pugh

ELECTRONIC SERVICES MANAGER
David Homof

SALES & MARKETING
Frida Andersson

DATA SOFTWARE
Collier Pickard Ltd

PRINTED BY
Pindar PLC, Scarborough

ADDITIONAL PHOTOGRAPHY
Britainonview.com
Fáilte Ireland

Typeset in Gill Sans, Trajan and Garamond

COVER IMAGE
Bolton Priory, Bolton Abbey, North Yorkshire
by Herbert Royle (1870-1958)
On display at the Devonshire Arms
(page 95)

*Ancient history meets modern vibrance and luxury
in this land of breathtaking Highlands, verdant
lowlands, sporting escapes and cultural delights.*

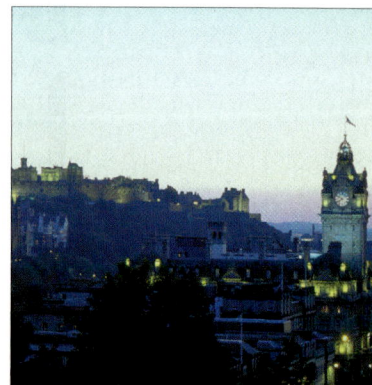

*Unmatched countryside offers a tranquil escape from the
everyday, with literary legends, Lakeland paradise,
outdoor attractions and city culture all within easy reach.*

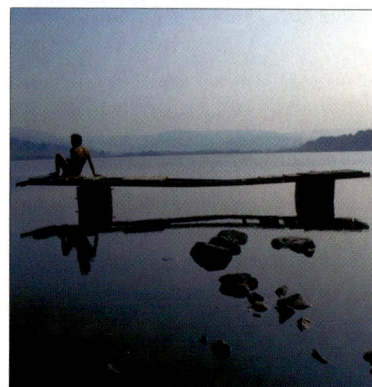

*From Snowdonia's majestic glories to a book-lover's
idyll at Hay-on-Wye, this land of scenery, poetry
and song offers something for all.*

*The Cotswolds, the Norfolk Broads,
Sherwood Forest, Oxford and Cambridge -
a wealth of experiences await to delight you.*

CONTENTS

WEST COUNTRY

From summertime fun on the English Riviera to blissful walks in Dartmoor and Exmoor, there's history and scenery to spare in the West.

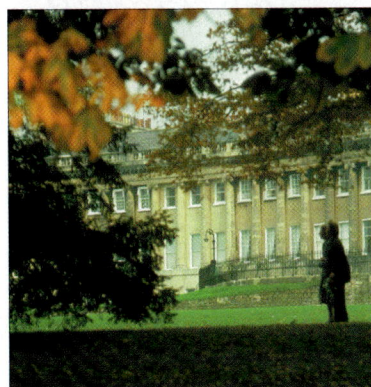

THE SOUTH

With London on your doorstep and Bath, Windsor and the New Forest within your grasp, the South is a showcase of delights.

LONDON

A city for all seasons and every reason, London has an irresistible pull, whether you're craving shopping, theatre, art or just a night on the town.

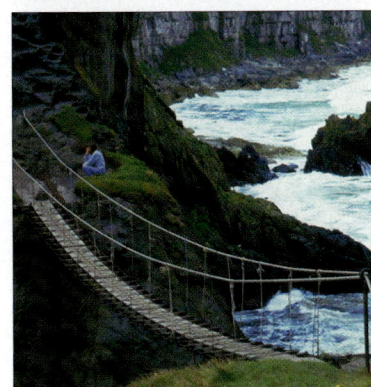

IRELAND

Legend, song and story mingle with city chic and top-class sport - guaranteeing an unforgettable escape, no matter your destination.

INDEX

A MESSAGE OF WELCOME

JEFFREY M EPSTEIN
PUBLISHER AND FOUNDER
BEST LOVED HOTELS

Welcome to your new edition of Best Loved Hotels! This 12th edition of our guide comes with a newly redesigned look, and we hope that our new format makes it even simpler for you to find the perfect place to stay. You'll notice, however, that while some things have changed, our goal - to present the finest of all places to stay in the United Kingdom and Ireland, for all needs and all price ranges - remains as consistent as the magnificent works of art that have graced our covers since our first edition. In many ways, the hotels in this book are works of art in themselves; and, like your favourite works of art, we like to think that these exquisite places to stay are also places you will want to revisit again and again.

A hotel for EVERY DAY in the year

If you are a veteran reader of Best Loved Hotels, we think you'll be pleased by the revised and expanded selection in this year's edition. Inside this book, you'll find a hotel for every day of the year, with stunning new additions ranging from the magnificent Bovey Castle in Devon (see page 249) to musical charm in Bath at Dorian House (page 255) and a warm Highland welcome at the Bridge Hotel in Sutherland (page 22). What's more, you'll notice that each of this book's United Kingdom hotels now features a national-rate number for reaching the hotel's reservations desk quickly and easily from within the UK.

Finally, we would also like to invite you to our newly redesigned and enhanced Web site, www.bestlovedhotels.com, where all the information in this book awaits, as well as interactive maps, cross-indexed search capabilities and a guide to thousands of things to do and places to see, wherever your Best Loved favourite may take you. We feel it's the perfect companion to this directory, and we hope you'll agree.

Best wishes.

A NOTE ON THE COVER

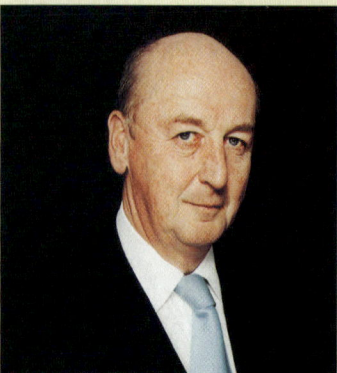

THE DUKE OF DEVONSHIRE CBE
CHAIRMAN
DEVONSHIRE HOTELS

The painting on the cover of this book, of Bolton Priory at Bolton Abbey, is one of a number of paintings by Herbert Royle on permanent display in the Devonshire Arms, which can be found on page 95. Many of the hotel bedrooms have original paintings, including a number by local artists. In addition, the hotel has a number of works of art from the Chatsworth Collection, including fine Neapolitan paintings by Raffaele Carelli and Gabrielle Carelli commissioned by the 6th Duke of Devonshire. There are also nine hand-coloured etchings by the contemporary artist Howard Hodgkin in the Devonshire Brasserie.

A GUIDE TO RATINGS

To provide a quick and simple assessment of the Best Loved hotels in the book, we have used ratings from regional tourist boards, the Royal Automobile Club (RAC), the Automobile Association (AA) and the Consumer Association's Good Food Guide and WHICH? Guide to Good Hotels, as well as a range of independent reviews and awards. All ratings and awards are supplied to us by the hotels and verified by Best Loved Hotels wherever possible.

However, remember that symbols are not everything! Some hotels are so new, they had not been rated at time of publication, while others are so non-conformist that they cannot satisfy the standard criteria but are certainly appealing places to stay. All the hotels in this book have been visited by at least one member of the Best Loved team, and we can confirm by the quotations at the top of every page in this book that each is best-loved by someone – and for a very good reason!

English Tourism Council

★★★★★ ◆◆◆◆◆

Gold Award

Ratings of one to five stars indicate a hotel's size and facilities; diamonds indicate the same for guest accommodation.

Gold or silver awards indicate the highest levels of quality.

BWRDD CROESO CYMRU WALES TOURIST BOARD

★ - Fair
★★ - Good
★★★ - Very Good
★★★★ - Excellent
★★★★★ - Exceptional

Establishment categories: hotel, country hotel, country house, guest house, lodge, B&B, farmhouse, inn and restaurant with rooms. Establishments should only be compared with others within their own category.

AA

★★★★★ 76% ◆◆◆◆◆

Ratings of one to five stars indicate a hotel's size and facilities; diamonds indicate the same for guest accommodation. Percentage ratings indicate the level of quality within each category.

★★★★★

Red Stars are given to the top 200 hotels considered to be the best in their star category.

❀❀❀❀❀

Rosettes range from one to five, denoting the quality of food.

Visit Scotland™

★ - Fair and Acceptable
★★ - Good
★★★ - Very Good
★★★★ - Excellent
★★★★★ - Exceptional

Establishment categories: small hotel, hotel, guest house, inn, restaurant with rooms and serviced apartments. Establishments should only be compared with others within their own category.

Fáilte Ireland APPROVED

Northern Ireland Tourist Board

★★★★★

Ratings of one to five stars indicate a hotel's amenities and quality.

RAC

★★★★★ ◆◆◆◆◆

Ratings of one to five stars indicate a hotel's size and facilities; diamonds indicate the same for guest accommodation.

Dining Award 1

For both hotels and guesthouses, dining quality is indicated by five levels of dining awards.

Gold Ribbon, Blue Ribbon & White Ribbon

The Gold Ribbon is the highest accolade, followed by the Blue Ribbon and White Ribbon.

Other awards for guest accommodation include:

Little Gem - for all-around quality
Sparkling Diamond - for hygiene
Warm Welcome - for hospitality

ACKNOWLEDGMENTS

We have used ratings from the following organisations where relevant and would like to thank each organisation's quality assurance departments for their assistance:

Automobile Association
Royal Automobile Club
VisitBritain
VisitScotland
Wales Tourist Board
Jersey Tourism and Guernsey Tourism
Northern Ireland Tourist Board
Fáilte Ireland

In addition we have acknowledged specific annual awards given by the following well-respected guides:

The Which? Guide to Good Hotels 2005
The Good Food Guide 2005

PLEASE NOTE

Every care has been taken in the compilation of this Directory. The hotels' factual information was supplied to us by the hotels themselves and is, to the best of our knowledge, accurate at the time of publication. The descriptive information is compiled by, and is the impression of, the Best Loved editorial team.

© 2005 World Media Publishing Limited

ISBN 1 898889 75 9

HOW TO USE THIS BOOK

This book is about places to stay in the United Kingdom and Ireland: castles, stately homes, country house hotels, city-centre hotels, townhouses, inns, resorts and spas. Each has its own page with comprehensive details and a recommendation in the form of a 'Best Loved' quotation from someone who has been there. When you plan a holiday, a friend's advice is always helpful; our aim is to provide that kind of information. The design of this book is aimed to make the business of making a choice as simple as possible - but if you need a bit of help finding somewhere to begin, read on.

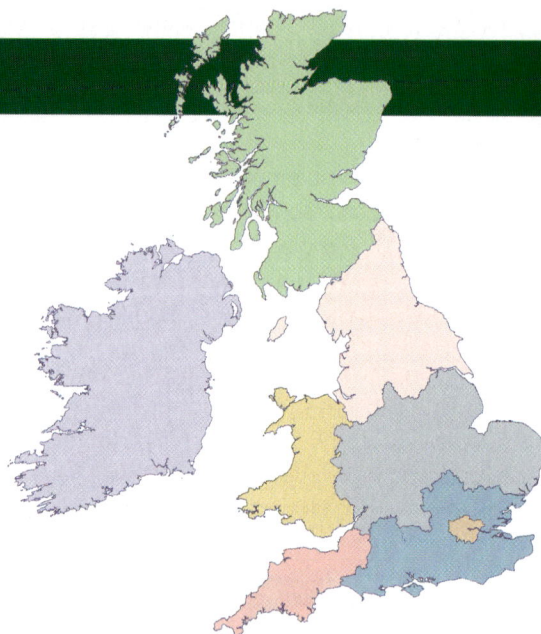

GENERAL STRUCTURE

The book is divided into eight regions (for an overview, see the map above), beginning with Scotland and moving south; Ireland is at the end the book. Within their regions, hotels are listed in alphabetical order.

Each region features a six-page introduction highlighting the best attractions and culinary delights the area has to offer - we hope it's a spark for ideas of your own!

If you're looking for specific attributes like golf courses, pet-friendly hotels or space for meetings, the indexes in the back of the book may be the best place to start. Or, if you're looking for a specific area in which to stay, check the detailed regional maps in the very back of this book.

HOTEL PAGES

Each hotel's page is packed with information to help you make the best choice:

Good-quality pictures to give you an idea of the look of the place.
Descriptive editorial to give you a feel for the character of the hotel and the people who run it.
A fact column that brings together all the information you need about the hotel, its facilities and how to make contact.
A green location guide tells how to find

the hotel, whether it's on a city street or tucked away on a country road.

ROUTE PLANNING MAPS

Regional route planning maps (pages 440-455) give you instant help in two ways:

Finding the nearest Best Loved hotel to where you want, or have, to be.
Finding a Best Loved hotel within a price band to suit your pocket or celebrate a special occasion.

All hotels are denoted by colour-coded rosettes, as shown to the right. Each colour represents a price band of room rates, including applicable taxes, as the average of the lowest to highest tariffs throughout the

year. For hotels that include meals, an adjustment has been used to arrive at the average rate.

These rosettes also include the hotel's page number, making it easy to flip to the hotel's page to discover more details.

REGIONAL INDEX

This index lists all the hotels in the book in an 'at-a-glance' guide to hotels by price and region. The same colour-coded rosettes are included, as well as the page number, county and map grid reference so you can find all your information quickly.

CHILDREN-FRIENDLY HOTELS

Hotels that accommodate children are annotated in the A - Z index beginning on page 426. Details also appear on the hotels' own pages.

KEY TO HOTELS

Rosettes indicate the page number of the hotel, with the colour a rough guide to the price of a twin or double room.

- Up to £95 per night
- £96 - £145 per night
- £146 - £195 per night
- £196+ per night

Base map © MAPS IN MINUTES™ 2004
© Crown Copyright, Ordnance Survey 2004
Design and modification
© 2005 Best Loved Hotels of the World

HOW TO USE THIS BOOK

PET-FRIENDLY HOTELS

Hotels that accommodate pets are indexed on page 438.

GENERAL FACILITIES

Although every hotel page itemises its facilities, you may prefer to look at our index of facilities, where we list hotels with swimming pools, health spas and tennis as well as those offering riding and other sport. The index starts on page 432.

MEETING FACILITIES

If an hotel has facilities for meetings (for 8 or more people), you will find details in the fact column on the hotel's page and in the index on page 434.

GOLF

Hotels with their own courses or with courses nearby are listed on page 436.

HELI-PADS

Many Best Loved hotels have landing facilities for helicopters - perfect for quick and convenient access directly to your favourite place to stay. Hotels with heli-pads are indexed on page 439.

OUT-OF-SEASON RESERVATIONS

Remember that even if a hotel closes for the winter season or the holidays, you can almost always still call to make a booking or get more information.

EXCHANGE RATES

Throughout England, Scotland, Wales and Northern Ireland, the currency is pounds sterling (£); in the Republic of Ireland, the currency is the Euro (€).

In January 2002, Ireland converted to the Euro; Irish Punts are no longer in circulation and are invalid.

At the time of going to press, the exchange rate was as follows:

£1 = €1.45
£1 = $1.79
€1 = £0.69
€1 = $1.23

Address, phone, fax and Web site so you can make your booking or get more information. Or, look for a reservation number below. In the UK, use the national-rate number to quickly and easily reach the reservations desk. **Always quote Best Loved** for the best rates.

E-mail will also help you find out more or make a booking.

Room rates estimate the lowest to highest seasonal rates. Most rates are per room per night for two people sharing, with a few exceptions where the rate is per person per night.

Credit/charge cards accepted by the hotel. Look for the American Express logo.

Other abbreviations indicate:
DC = Diners Club
MC = MasterCard
VI = Visa
JCB = Japan Credit Card

Ratings and awards are taken from the most recent published information from tourist boards, the Royal Automobile Club and the Automobile Association. For more information on ratings, see page 5. Awards from other industry-recognised organisations are also included where relevant and if permitted.

Affiliations. Some hotels belong to consortia or marketing groups, and many also provide toll-free reservations numbers (see below). Details of affiliations are given on page 8.

National rate and toll-free **reservations numbers** make the booking process easier, whether you're calling from within or outside of Britain or Ireland. **Always quote Best Loved.**

Access codes have relevance only to travel agents.

Port Appin, Argyll PA38 4DF
T (UK) 0870 432 8700
T 01631 730236
F 01631 730535
airds@bestloved.com
www.airds.bestloved.com

OWNERS
Shaun and Jenny McKivragan

ROOM RATES
Single occupancy £170 - £305
3 Doubles/Twins £230 - £280
8 Superior Doubles/Twins £250 - £320
1 Suite £280 - £360
Includes full breakfast, dinner and VAT

CREDIT CARDS
• JCB • MC • VI

RATINGS & AWARDS
VisitScotland ★★★★ Small Hotel
AA ★★★
AA Top 200 - 2004/2005

FACILITIES
On site: Garden, heli-pad, licensed for weddings
1 meeting room/max 12 people
Nearby: Golf, fishing, walking, climbing, cycling, sailing, riding, clay pigeon shooting, diving, skiing

RESTRICTIONS
Limited facilities for disabled guests
No children under 8 years in the restaurant
Smoking in conservatory and one lounge only
Pets by arrangement
Closed 5 - 26 January

ATTRACTIONS
Inverary Castle, Oban Sea Life Centre, Eilean Donan Castle, Oban Distillery, Torosay Castle, Duart Castle, Fort William, Isle of Mull, Glencoe, Nevis Gondola

NEAREST
CITY:
Oban - 19 miles/35 mins
Fort William - 29 miles/40 mins
AIRPORT:
Glasgow - 98 miles/2 ½ hrs
Edinburgh - 98 miles/2 ½ hrs
RAIL STATION:
Oban - 19 miles/26 mins
FERRY PORT:
Oban - 20 miles/27 mins

AFFILIATIONS
Independent

RESERVATIONS
National rate in UK: 0870 432 8700
Quote Best Loved

ACCESS CODES
AMADEUS UI ABCDEF
APOLLO/GALILEO UI 12345
SABRE/ABACUS UI 67890
WORLDSPAN UI 98765

AFFILIATIONS

A project of this scale and scope could not come together without the support of many organisations whose hotels appear in this book. We acknowledge them below, as well as in the fact columns of the pages dedicated to their hotels.

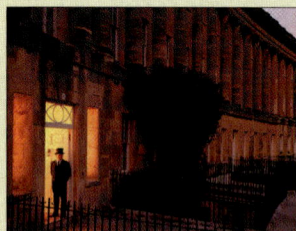

Royal Crescent Hotel, page 280

THE CELEBRATED HOTELS COLLECTION PRESTON'S GLOBAL HOTELS

Historic deluxe country house and city townhouse hotels that display traditional elegance and personal service reminiscent of a bygone age while providing for the needs of the modern sophisticated traveller.

US: 3816 Briar Oak Drive, Birmingham, AL 35243
US Toll Free (CHC): 800-322-2403 (PGH): 800-544-9993
T 205-967-7054: F 205-967-5192

UK: Suite 11, The Linen House
253 Kilburn Lane, London W10 4BQ
T 0870 432 8700   F 0870 432 8770

Grants Hotel, page 101

FINE INDIVIDUAL HOTELS

Havens of luxury for those who enjoy life with a certain style. These charming, per-sonally-managed hotels offer delightful accommodation, menus ranging from classical to contemporary, a connoisseur's wine list and courteous attention.
All reservations and enquiries should be made directly with each individual hotel.

Taplow House, page 333

GRAND HERITAGE HOTELS

A collection of hotels that are steeped in tradition, from manor houses through to palaces. Each hotel offers the best service, cuisine and comfort in order to make a journey an unforgettable experience.

1st Floor, Warwick House, 181-183 Warwick Road, London, W14 8PU
T 020 7244 6699 • F 020 7244 7799 • www.grandheritage.com
US Toll Free: 888-93-GRAND

Gregans Castle, page 397

IRELAND'S BLUE BOOK

High standards of accommodation, traditional hospitality and good food in the rural beauty of Ireland. Members of ICHRA offer an opportunity to enjoy quality that is fast disappearing. Guests are welcomed with 'céad mílle fáilte' at every door.

8 Mount Street Crescent, Dublin 2, Ireland
T +353 (0)1676 9914• F +353 (0)1631 4990 • www.irelandsbluebook.com
Toll free in US: 800-323-5463

AFFILIATIONS

MANOR HOUSE HOTELS OF IRELAND

Manor House Hotels are a superb collection of Irish country houses and castles in the most picturesque of locations. They consist of three- and four-star properties that are as unique as you are.

1 Sandyford Office Park, Foxrock, Dublin 18, Ireland
T +353 (0)1 295 8900 • F +353 (0)1 295 8940 • www.manorhousehotels.com

Cahernane House Hotel, page 387

PRIDE OF BRITAIN

This collection of privately-owned and owner-run country house properties offers a glimpse of style and tradition that is uniquely British. Each strives to produce extra-special hospitality for their guests.

Cowage Farm, Foxley, Wiltshire, SN16 0JH
Reservations: 0870 609 3012
T 01666 824666 • F 01666 825779 • www.prideofbritainhotels.com
US toll free: 800-98-PRIDE

Lewtrenchard Manor, page 269

SCOTLAND'S HOTELS OF DISTINCTION

Quality hotels and inns, all individually owned and managed. World-renowned hospitality, with highest standards of ambience and quality of food and service. A warm welcome, the finest Scottish cuisine and excellent value for money. UK reservations and enquiries should be made directly with each individual hotel.

www.hotels-of-distinction.com
US: McFarland Ltd, 185 Ponderosa Drive, Athens, GA 30605
US Toll Free: 800-437-2687 • Fax: 706-549-1515

Coul House Hotel, page 29

SMALL LUXURY HOTELS

The SLH stamp guarantees an unequalled level of privacy, luxury and exclusivity. These fine quality hotels embrace the sophistication of city centres and the glamour and charm of resorts, historic chateaux and country houses throughout the world.

James House, Bridge Street, Leatherhead Surrey KT22 7EP
T 01372 361873 • F 01372 361874 • www.slh.com
Toll free in US: 800-525-4800 • Fax in US: 212-953-0576

Mar Hall, page 64

WELSH RAREBITS

These hotels are all in interesting houses, in good locations, with superb food, imaginative décor and indefinable atmosphere. Wales's top country house hotels and traditional farmhouses, seaside hotels and historic inns are all included, and each in its own way is exceptional.

Prince's Square, Montgomery Powys SY15 6PZ
T 01686 668030 • F 01686 668029 • www.rarebits.co.uk

Castell Deudraeth, page 145

SCOTLAND

A COUNTRY HOUSE HOTEL
Lodge - Daviot Mains, Inverness-shire

A CITY HOTEL
The Scotsman, Edinburgh

A CASTLE
Culzean Castle, Ayrshire

REPRESENTING *the best of* SCOTLAND

A LUXURY TRAIN
The Royal Scotsman, Edinburgh

Best Loved Hotels offer the cream of the crop across Great Britain and Ireland - from stately palaces to welcoming inns - each the best of its kind within its locality and price range.

Whichever place you choose as your own place to stay, you'll find every hotel offers character, charm and the best delights and attractions of its region.

And each, in its own special way, is best-loved by someone who's been there.

A STATELY HOME
Cally Palace Hotel, Dumfries & Galloway

AN ISLAND HOTEL
Flodigarry Country House Hotel, Isle of Skye

A TOWNHOUSE
One Devonshire Gardens, Glasgow

A CITY HOTEL
Prestonfield, Edinburgh

AN IDEAL ESCAPE:
Scotland

BEST LOVED HOTELS
An ideal escape

FROM HIGHLAND SPLENDOUR to Edinburgh's bright city lights, Scotland offers something for everyone. Whether your interests run toward history, art or sport, you're sure to find a perfect escape for any season of the year.

Day One

A place of natural beauty with mountains, lochs, rivers and unspoilt countryside: No wonder one of the major reasons for visiting Scotland is its landscape. A great way to start off your visit to this stunning region is to explore the wilderness with a tour of one of Scotland's most famous settings – the legendary **Loch Ness**, home to fantastic vistas and, if you believe the tales, the famous Nessie. Beginning from Inverness, you have the choice of two routes: the remarkably wild scenery southeast of the loch, or the more popular northwest route.

The north side, following the A82, brings you to the village of **Drumnadrochit**, where you can learn more about Loch Ness and the legend of the Loch Ness Monster at the visitor centre, **Loch Ness 2000**. Continue south of Drumnadrochit and you'll come across the impressive ruins of **Urquhart Castle**. Built around 800 years ago, it's well worth finding out about the abandoned castle's rich history before seeing it yourself. With such a wonderful position overlooking the mysterious loch, you'll want to take some time to soak up the scenery and mystery!

Continuing further south, drive through **Fort Augustus**, named after William Augustus, son of George II. Why not stop here to take a relaxing stroll alongside the **Caledonian Canal** and locks? You're guaranteed to feel invigourated by the fresh air.

Urquhart Castle looks out over Loch Ness

Day Two

Your tour of the stunning scenery of the Highlands continues at **Fort William**, a popular town for its scenery, sports and leisure activities - and, of course, mountain climbing and skiing, being home to **Ben Nevis**, Britain's highest mountain. Ben Nevis itself is a sight to behold, whether you're viewing from inside hiking gear or behind a warm window, and the views from the mountain across the Highlands are said to be truly spectacular. For those with an interest in history, you might like to discover more about Highland life at the **West Highland Museum** at Fort William - it's a delightful look at the region's past.

If you're after some relaxation, it's certainly in your interest to take time to explore the beaches, rivers and nearby villages surrounding Fort William, including the charming

The views from BEN NEVIS are truly grand

village of **Inverlochy** (home to a real Highland castle where you can stay - see page 54). Further south, **Glencoe** village is the perfect example of unspoilt countryside – great for walks, cycling and just taking in the clean Highland air! A leisurely drive east to **St Fillans** will finish your village tour, taking in the spectacular scenery on the shores of Loch Earn.

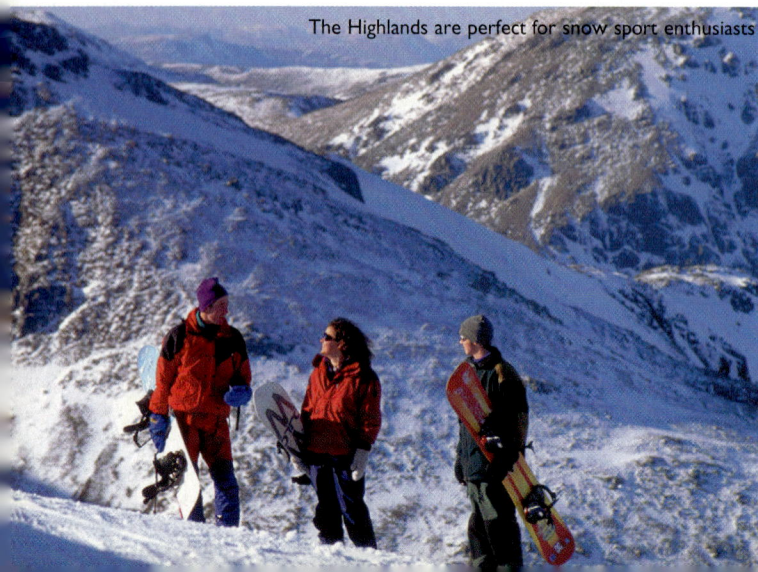
The Highlands are perfect for snow sport enthusiasts

Edinburgh Castle is an ever-present vista from the city, and is even more spectacular at night

Day Three

Now that you've explored some of Scotland's rich countryside, a drive to **Edinburgh** - only a bit over an hour - completes the experience. It is well worth visiting the city, if just to stroll past the beautiful blackened buildings in Princes Street. There are a multitude of attractions tucked away in Edinburgh, too - one favourite is the **Edinburgh Royal Botanic Gardens**, where you can explore a collection of around 16,000 species of plants **Edinburgh Zoo** is home to meerkats, hippos, snow leopards, tamarins and more. For families, **Edinburgh Butterfly and Insect World** has an impressive collection that includes crabs, spiders, scorpions, snakes and lizards - and of course, for those who aren't fond of creepy-crawlies, there are also some 40 species of tropical butterflies.

For art lovers, be sure to visit the **National Gallery of Scotland**, home to an incredible collection of European art; for another view, the **National Gallery of Modern Art** also makes a fun and refreshing outing.

Views of Ben Nevis are nearly as spectacular as views from the mountain itself

ESCAPE FROM YOUR DESKTOP

If you can't wait to get away, or if you'd simply like to do a little investigating before you make your Scotland holiday, browse the links below. Remember, too, that thousands of places to see and things to do await at Best Loved's Web site, **www.bestlovedhotels.com**.

Loch Ness 2000 exhibit
www.loch-ness-scotland.com

Loch Ness Monster legend
www.nessie.co.uk

Drumnadrochit visitors information
www.drumnadrochit.co.uk

Fort Augustus visitors information
www.fortaugustus.org

Fort William visitors information
www.visit-fortwilliam.co.uk

A guide to Perthshire
www.perthshire-scotland.co.uk

Glencoe visitors information
www.glencoe-scotland.net

Edinburgh Royal Botanic Gardens
www.rbge.org.uk

Edinburgh Zoo
www.edinburghzoo.org.uk

Edinburgh Butterfly and Insect World
www.edinburgh-butterfly-world.co.uk

National Gallery of Scotland and
National Gallery of Modern Art
www.nationalgalleries.org

A TASTE OF THE BEST
Scotland

THE IDEAL ACCOMPANIMENT to your perfect Scottish holiday, splendid dining awaits in this land of excellent seafood, beef and choice produce. Add in the creativity of a talented chef - like the ones below - and the possibilities are nearly endless.

Scallops are a choice dish at Prestonfield

course, make the most of fine Scottish produce and home-grown ingredients. Choose from a wide selection of the world's finest wines available from the castle's extensive cellars, and be sure to save room for one of the castle's indulgent puddings: Try specialties ranging from rhubarb soufflé with chocolate-coated natural yoghurt sorbet or lightly spiced pears poached in red wine with toasted fruit bread and natural yoghurt mousse. Of

A taste of the HOME-GROWN at Glenapp Castle

course, all of this is in a marvellous setting in which to dine, from the oak-panelled entrance hall to warm, gracious public areas granting an understated sense of luxury throughout.

FOUR SEASONS HOTEL ❀❀

There are two restaurants at the renowned Four Seasons Hotel - no matter which you choose, you'll have the benefit of this lovely house's spectacular forest setting on the shores of Loch Earn. Both the Meall Reamhar fine-dining restaurant and the less formal Tarken Room have magnificent views out to the loch, and serve fine Scottish produce from Orkney scallops and Loch Fyne mussels to East Coast halibut and Border lamb. A tempting choice of starters includes seared scallops or, for something a bit more hearty, ribbon pasta with clam and saffron cream mussels. There are plenty of delicious options for your main course, too, including as roast guinea fowl with buckwheat, corn kernels and a garlic and almond emulsion. You may want to sample a bit of it all after spending a day amongst the area's magnificent walking, fishing and other sport!

GLENAPP CASTLE ❀❀❀

At this fairytale Scottish baronial castle high above the village of Ballantrae, Head Chef Tristan Welch and his team produce cuisine that is equally as superb as the surroundings. Enjoy such treats as the castle's slowly-cooked fillet of Aberdeen Angus beef with truffled artichokes, castle garden potatoes and parmesan sauce - all, of

THE PEAT INN ❀❀❀

Just a short drive from St Andrews, The Peat Inn is well-known for its relaxed atmosphere and attitude - and even more renowned for its first-class cuisine prepared by Chef Laureate, Master Chef and Proprietor David Wilson. Creative dishes - such as medallions of monkfish and lobster with asparagus and wild mushroom in lobster sauce, or roast loin of Scotch pork with sausage, apricot and raisin stuffing - are irresistible, and accompanied by a well-chosen and varied wine list. You might also wish to sample their impressive, award-winning selection of champagne, for which the Peat Inn was voted one of the top six establishments in the UK.

At Glenapp Castle, the gardens are as delicious as they are beautiful

A TASTE OF THE REGION

Looking for even more to tempt your palate? There are a wealth of fantastic places to dine in Scotland, all within the covers of this book! Have a browse to whet your appetite, or jump to some of our own favourites:

INVERLOCHY CASTLE ❀❀❀

This enchanting castle in the foothills of Ben Nevis has three elegant dining rooms with period furnishings, including an elaborate carved breakfont sideboard presented to Inverlochy as a gift by the King of Norway. Fresh Scottish produce makes for an even more delightful dining experience.

ONE DEVONSHIRE GARDENS ❀❀

A stylish Glasgow hotel offering formal dining in their own 'No5' Restaurant, as well as classic cuisine with a contemporary twist in their eatery, Room Glasgow. Everything about this hotel has a fresh sense of individuality, and the dining is no different!

GLENMORISTON ARMS ❀❀

Glenmoriston Arms, situated close to Loch Ness, serves local game in season, quality Scottish beef and Highland lamb, as well as fresh seafood from the west coast and a variety of vegetarian dishes. One guest described their restaurant as 'one of the most superb culinary experiences in Scotland!'

Prestonfield's Rhubarb restaurant provides an opulent backdrop

PRESTONFIELD ❀❀

Gothic and lavishly decorated, a recent restoration at this splendid city hotel has attracted many celebrities from Joan Collins to Dido, as too has their celebrated Rhubarb Restaurant - so-called because Prestonfield was the first estate in Scotland to grow rhubarb. The striking restaurant has already received rave reviews! Gareth McLean from the Guardian described it as 'exquisite!' and celebrities such as J K Rowling and Minnie Driver have dined here - so, then, should you. There is a wealth of first-class cuisine to choose from: for a starter, you might choose pan-seared Isle of Skye scallops with horseradish potatoes, mustard oil and parsley juice, and for your main course, there are plenty of mouth-watering options, such as pumpkin gnocchi, smoked scarmoza cheese, cherry tomatoes and basil. There is also a set two-course menu available - but think carefully about skipping dessert, as it may just be the best part!

SUMMER ISLES ❀❀

Owned by Mark and Geraldine Irvine, this family-run restaurant with rooms offers a tasteful, healthy, top-quality menu created from a variety of fresh, home-produced or locally caught produce. Head Chef Chris Firth-Bernard's delectable fare has earned the restaurant a Michelin rosette, and for good reason! Locally caught produce appearing on their menu includes scallops, lobster, crab, halibut and salmon - a perfect complement to the hotel's wild setting.

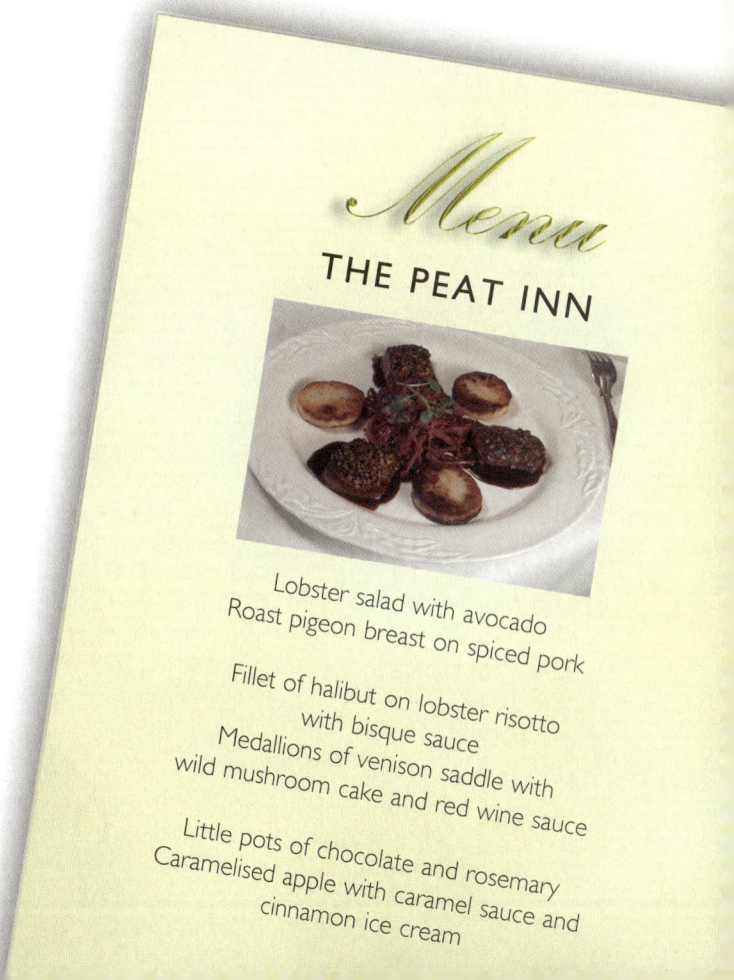

Menu

THE PEAT INN

Lobster salad with avocado
Roast pigeon breast on spiced pork

Fillet of halibut on lobster risotto
with bisque sauce
Medallions of venison saddle with
wild mushroom cake and red wine sauce

Little pots of chocolate and rosemary
Caramelised apple with caramel sauce and
cinnamon ice cream

> When life is black, I contemplate running away to three sanctuaries, and one of them is the Airds Hotel
>
> JANE GRIGSON

THE AIRDS HOTEL

Country hotel

Port Appin, Argyll PA38 4DF

T (UK) 0870 432 8516
T 01631 730236
F 01631 730535
airds@bestloved.com
www.airds.bestloved.com

OWNERS
Shaun and Jenny McKivragan

ROOM RATES
Single occupancy	£170 - £305
3 Doubles/Twins	£230 - £280
8 Superior Doubles/Twins	£250 - £320
1 Suite	£280 - £360

Includes full breakfast, dinner and VAT

CREDIT CARDS
JCB • MC • VI

RATINGS & AWARDS
VisitScotland ★★★★ Small Hotel
AA ★★★ ❀❀❀
AA Top 200 - 2004/2005

FACILITIES
On site: Garden, heli-pad, licensed for weddings
1 meeting room/max 12 people
Nearby: Golf, fishing, walking, climbing, cycling, sailing, riding, clay pigeon shooting, diving, skiing

RESTRICTIONS
Limited facilities for disabled guests
No children under 8 years in the restaurant
Smoking in conservatory and one lounge only
Pets by arrangement
Closed 5 - 26 January

ATTRACTIONS
Inverary Castle , Oban Sea Life Centre, Eilean Donan Castle, Oban Distillery, Torosay Castle, Duart Castle, Fort William, Isle of Mull, Glencoe, Nevis Gondola

NEAREST
CITY:
Oban - 19 miles/35 mins
Fort William - 29 miles/40 mins

AIRPORT:
Glasgow - 98 miles/2 hrs 30 mins
Edinburgh - 98 miles/2 hrs 30 mins

RAIL STATION:
Oban - 19 miles/26 mins

FERRY PORT:
Oban - 20 miles/27 mins

AFFILIATIONS
Celebrated Hotels Collection

RESERVATIONS
National rate in UK: 0870 432 8516
Toll free in US: 800-322-2403
Quote Best Loved

ACCESS CODES
Not applicable

A family atmosphere in a majestic west coast location

This family-run country hotel is a place of quiet and refuge that's also rich in wildlife and outdoor activities. The relaxed atmosphere does not discourage you to explore the nearby wildlife, such as the beautiful Atlantic Oakwoods, and the rich history of the area - castles and gardens are plentiful, and you can take the ferry to visit the islands of Mull, Iona and Lismore.

Airds is situated in the small village of Port Appin and enjoys fantastic views of the surrounding mountains, lochs and countryside. From entering the flower-filled conservatory to lazing in either of the two sitting rooms with blazing fires and piles of books and board games, the atmosphere here is cosy and informal. This extends to the 12 bedrooms, which are comfortable and elegant, with spacious bathrooms. Their restaurant is renowned for its fine food made from the very best fresh ingredients, and guests can enjoy this simply elegant dining whilst sampling one of Airds' many wines and admiring the incredible view.

Walking, fishing, riding, cycling, climbing and clay pigeon shooting are just some of the outdoor activities available, and numerous attractions, such as Iverary Castle, Oban Distillery and Glencoe, are all nearby.

LOCATION
From Crianlarich, take the A82 to Ballachulish. The hotel is 16 miles south of the Ballachulish Bridge. Follow signs to Port Appin from the A828.

> "Warm hospitality and great food - thank you!
>
> DAVID & TINA THOMPSON, EDINBURGH

17

Village hotel

ARCHIESTOWN HOTEL

This Whisky Trail haven offers hospitality for all tastes

Sightseeing and fly fishing, a cosy hearth and good food are just a few of the favourite things guests can enjoy on a visit to Archiestown Hotel. This delightful small property sits in the middle of its namesake village (founded by Sir Archibald Grant of Monymusk in 1760), and welcomes fishers, walkers, golfers, whisky enthusiasts and anyone else in search of traditional hospitality and atmosphere.

The hotel is personally run by Philip and Rosalind Lewis, whose reputation as superb hosts is legendary. As executive head chef, Philip, together with his team, provides daily changing menus specialising in the best local meat, game, fish and shellfish dishes, followed by sybaritic homemade treats such as rhubarb and strawberry crumble and crème brûlée figs and minted syrup. After dinner, relax by the fireside and enjoy a dram from one of the famous local distilleries while planning the next day's pleasures.

Archiestown is on the Whisky Trail and a short step from the Speyside Way. There are 15 golf courses within an hour's drive, as well as skiing in the Cairngorms, sailing on the Moray Firth - or venture no further than a stroll around the walled garden, where the hotel's fresh flowers and herbs are grown.

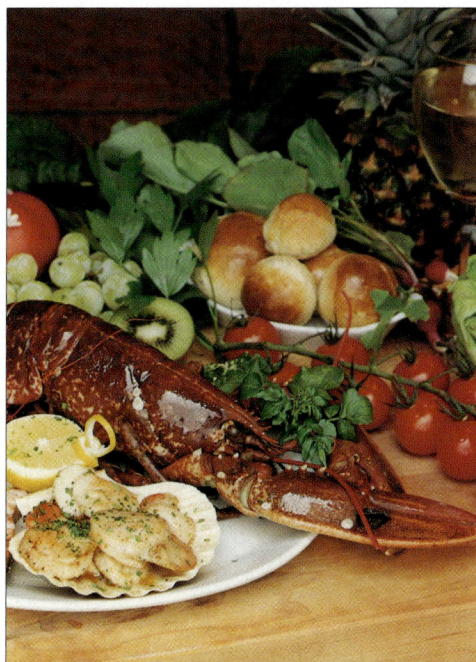

LOCATION

Take the A95 Spey Valley route between Grantown and Craigellachie. Archiestown is on the B9102 four miles from Craigellachie.

Archiestown, by Aberlour, Moray AB38 7QL

T (UK) 0870 432 8520
T 01340 810218
F 01340 810239
archiestown@bestloved.com
www.archiestown.bestloved.com

OWNERS
Philip and Rosalind Lewis

ROOM RATES
1 Single	£30 - £50
10 Doubles/Twins	£60 - £100

Includes full breakfast and VAT

CREDIT CARDS
AMERICAN EXPRESS • MC • VI

RATINGS & AWARDS
VisitScotland ★★★★ Small Hotel
AA ★★ ✿ 78%

FACILITIES
On site: Garden
1 meeting room/max 25 people
Nearby: Golf, tennis, riding, shooting, fishing, stalking, walking

RESTRICTIONS
No facilities for disabled guests
Smoking in lounge only

ATTRACTIONS
Malt Whisky Trail,
Moray Firth beaches and dolphins,
Loch Ness,
Balmoral and Cawdor castles,
Cairngorms, the Highlands,
Speyside Way

NEAREST
CITY:
Inverness - 50 miles/1 hr

AIRPORT:
Aberdeen - 59 miles/1 hr 15 mins
Inverness - 50 miles/1 hr

RAIL STATION:
Elgin - 16 miles/20 mins

AFFILIATIONS
Independent

RESERVATIONS
National rate in UK: 0870 432 8520
Quote Best Loved

ACCESS CODES
Not applicable

> **Ballathie is not just a fine hotel - it is a civilised haven of rural peace**
>
> SIR PATRICK CORMACK, FSA MP

BALLATHIE HOUSE HOTEL

Country house

Kinclaven by Stanley, Perth,
Perthshire PH1 4QN

T (UK) 0870 432 8525
T 01250 883268
F 01250 883396
ballathie@bestloved.com
www.ballathie.bestloved.com

GENERAL MANAGER
Christopher J Longden

ROOM RATES
6 Singles	£79 - £110
33 Doubles/Twins	£158 - £220
3 Suites	£228 - £250

Includes full breakfast and VAT

CREDIT CARDS
AMERICAN EXPRESS • DC • JCB • MC • VI

RATINGS & AWARDS
VisitScotland ★★★★ Hotel
AA ★★★ ❀❀
AA Top 200 - 2004/2005

FACILITIES
On site: Garden, heli-pad, fishing,
croquet, shooting
3 meeting rooms/max 60 people
Nearby: Golf, riding, castles, distillery

RESTRICTIONS
Limited facilities for disabled guests
No children under 5 years in
restaurant, high tea provided
Smoking in bar and hall only
Pets by arrangement

ATTRACTIONS
Scone Palace, Blair Castle, Perth,
Edinburgh, Glamis Castle

NEAREST
CITY:
Perth - 10 miles/15 mins

AIRPORT:
Edinburgh - 60 miles/1 hr

RAIL STATION:
Perth - 10 miles/15 mins

AFFILIATIONS
Independent Innkeepers
Scotland's Heritage Hotels

RESERVATIONS
National rate in UK: 0870 432 8525
Toll free in US: 800-934-6374
Quote Best Loved

ACCESS CODES
Not applicable

An enviable touring base on the River Tay in the heart of Perthshire

A winding driveway through the woodlands leads to Ballathie's handsome facade, crowned by a trio of pointy witches'-hat roofs. In spring, the woods are ablaze with rhododendrons, while in autumn the 1,500-acre estate is bathed in the red-gold of turning leaves.

This is a tranquil haven for all seasons that's ideally placed for sightseeing and sportsmen, who can fish for salmon on the Tay, shoot game in season and play a round or two of golf at the championship Rosemount course nearby (St Andrews and Carnoustie are also within easy reach). On the sightseeing front, Perth, the cathedral town of Dunkeld and Scone Palace are all within a 20-minute drive, while Edinburgh, Dundee, and the late Queen Mother's childhood home of Glamis Castle are under an hour away. Inverness and the West Coast can be reached on day trips.

After a busy day, Ballathie's welcoming country-house atmosphere beckons. The attractive bedrooms have been thoughtfully equipped and have lovely views, and the dining room has a reputation for fine Scottish cuisine accompanied by a wide-ranging wine list. After dinner, guests can settle in front of a log fire with a glass of malt to plan the next day's diversions.

LOCATION
From Perth, continue two miles north on the A9; then, take the B9099 through Stanley and turn right at the sign for Kinclaven and Ballathie.

> An **exceptional meal, beautifully presented, and all the staff so accommodating - it couldn't have been improved upon**
>
> WILLIE AND MARILYN HUNTER, EXETER

Country house

BANCHORY LODGE

SCOTLAND

First-class fishing fit for a king at this scenic anglers' paradise

Banchory Lodge is just 40 miles away from Balmoral Castle and set amongst breathtaking woodland and countryside - and once you see the scenery, you will undoubtedly come to understand why this remote corner of Scotland is so popular with the Queen and her family!

Situated on the banks of the Dee, renowned as one of the best salmon rivers in the world, this traditional, family-run hotel has its own beat, and as such is nothing short of an anglers' paradise. August sees the opening of the 'glorious 12th' season for grouse, and arrangements can be made for grouse, rough and pheasant shooting on nearby estates. Also within walking distance are two 18-hole golf courses, and anyone wishing to tour locally can do so on bicycles loaned by the hotel free of charge. The 22-bedroom lodge is conveniently located in the middle of three specialist trails: The Victorian Heritage Trail, the Castle Trail, which includes some 40 National Trust properties, and the Whisky Trail, which incorporates a mind-boggling 50 local distilleries.

Whether you spend the day standing waist-high in water or visiting historic sites, breakfast is a hearty Scottish affair; local game, Scottish salmon and Aberdeen Angus are also on the menu.

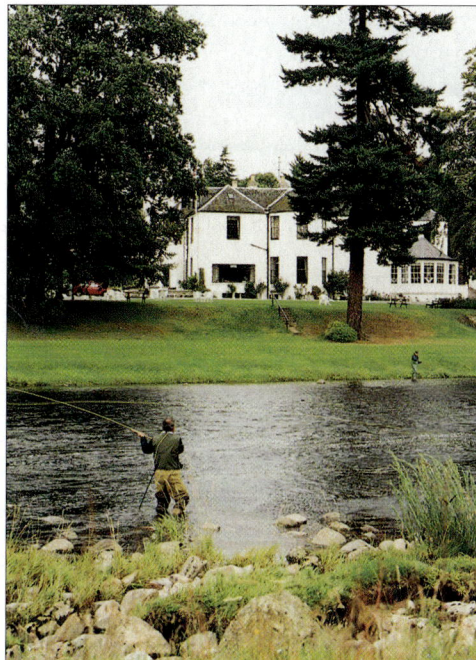

LOCATION

From Aberdeen, take the A93 to Banchory. In the town centre, turn left into Bridge Street; the hotel is well-signed.

Dee Street, Banchory, Kincardineshire AB31 5HS

T (UK) 0870 432 8526
T 01330 822625
F 01330 825019
banchory@bestloved.com
www.banchory.bestloved.com

OWNER
Margaret Jaffray

GENERAL MANAGER
Donald Law

ROOM RATES

2 Singles	£70 - £85
12 Doubles/Twins	£110
2 Four-posters	£110
6 Family Rooms	£110 - £130

Includes full breakfast and VAT

CREDIT CARDS

AMERICAN EXPRESS • DC • MC • VI

RATINGS & AWARDS
RAC Blue Ribbon ★★★
Dining Award 3
AA ★★★ ❀ 75%

FACILITIES
On site: Garden, river
2 meeting rooms/max 130 people
Nearby: Golf, fishing, riding, swimming, shooting

RESTRICTIONS
Limited facilities for disabled guests
Smoking in some bedrooms only

ATTRACTIONS
Balmoral and Crathes castles, Fettercairn and Royal Lochnagar distilleries, Victorian Heritage Trail, Whisky and Castles trails

NEAREST
CITY:
Aberdeen - 18 miles/30 mins

AIRPORT:
Aberdeen - 22 miles/35 mins

RAIL STATION:
Aberdeen - 18 miles/30 mins

AFFILIATIONS
Independent

RESERVATIONS
National rate in UK: 0870 432 8526
Quote Best Loved

ACCESS CODES
Not applicable

A breath of fresh air. The room and bathroom lovely, staff really friendly, food superb. A little jewel in the Scottish tourist industry!

MRS ALLEN, LANARK

THE BOAT HOTEL

Country house

Boat of Garten,
Inverness-shire PH24 3BH

T (UK) 0870 432 8539
T 01479 831258
F 01479 831414
boat@bestloved.com
www.boat.bestloved.com

OWNERS
Ian and Shona Tatchell

MANAGER
Jackie Robertson

ROOM RATES
Single occupancy	£70
19 Doubles/Twins	£119
6 Master Rooms	£139
1 Suite	£165
Includes full breakfast and VAT	

CREDIT CARDS
JCB • MC • VI

RATINGS & AWARDS
VisitScotland ★★★★ Hotel
AA ★★★ ❀❀ 72%
Scotch Beef Club
Investors in People
Hospitality Assured

FACILITIES
On site: Garden, snooker, golf (adjacent)
2 meeting rooms/max 80 people
Nearby: Skiing, fishing, riding, shooting,
off-roading, rafting, water sport

RESTRICTIONS
No facilities for disabled guests
Closed 7 - 31 Jan.

ATTRACTIONS
Cawdor Castle, Loch Ness,
Malt Whisky Trail, Fort George,
Rothiemurchus Sporting Estate,
Culloden Battlefield, Cairngorm
Mountains & Mountain Railway

NEAREST
CITY:
Inverness - 30 miles/40 mins

AIRPORT:
Inverness - 35 miles/45 mins

RAIL STATION:
Aviemore - 6 miles/10 mins

AFFILIATIONS
Independent

RESERVATIONS
National rate in UK: 0870 432 8539
Quote Best Loved

ACCESS CODES
AMADEUS HK INVBOA
APOLLO/GALILEO HT 37833
SABRE/ABACUS HK 60101
WORLDSPAN HKBOATH

All aboard for a Highland special firmly anchored in the Strathspey

In the heart of the Cairngorms National Park, Boat of Garten is a peaceful Highland village set amongst heather-clad hills. This was once a stop on the Great North of Scotland railway route, and The Boat occupies the fine old Victorian station hotel where anglers and other sporting types would install themselves for Highland holidays.

Fully restored to its Victorian splendour, complete with polished wooden floors, Oriental rugs and marble fireplaces, this hotel is a welcoming one; the bedrooms are comfortably traditional, while The Capercaillie restaurant has a bolder contemporary feel to match the chef's stylish cuisine. Signature dishes include a tian of home-cured salmon or Shetland crabmeat and Cairngorm beef fillet. Informal meals can also be taken in the relaxing lounge bar, and there is a lively and popular public bar with occasional live music.

The Boat's sporting pedigree lives on - adjacent to the hotel is the 18-hole Championship Boat of Garten golf course. Nearby Rothiemurchus Estate offers numerous outdoor activities and is home to a charming old shooting lodge, Drumintoul - a wonderful venue for weddings and conferences.

LOCATION

From the A9, take the A95 just north of Aviemore. Follow signs to Boat of Garten.

Townhouse

THE BONHAM

SCOTLAND

Voted one of the world's coolest hotels - and we're certain you'll agree

Without doubt, The Bonham belongs to the new, smart and creative generation of townhouse hotels. In fact, it was one of the first of this new breed to hit the scene back in 1998. More recently, the hotel was voted one of the world's 'coolest' hotels by Condé Nast Traveller magazine.

The interiors at The Bonham have been created by a leading designer and cleverly incorporate high contemporary style around the existing Victorian features. There is not a shred of chintz in sight: Spacious rooms, large windows and tall ceilings of the period accentuate the uncluttered and bright atmosphere. Colour schemes are fantastic, and the fabrics and furnishings are simply the epitome of modern luxury. Huge, colourful canvasses adorn the walls, making for a truly vibrant stay.

Whilst stylishly 'cool', there is certainly nothing pretentious about The Bonham. It is an exceptional place in every sense, run with expert professionalism with a wonderful team of staff. The restaurant is striking and lively, serving a grand mix of European-inspired dishes. Better still, The Bonham is located just five minutes' walk from Edinburgh's West End, which makes it a very central place to stay for both business and leisure travellers.

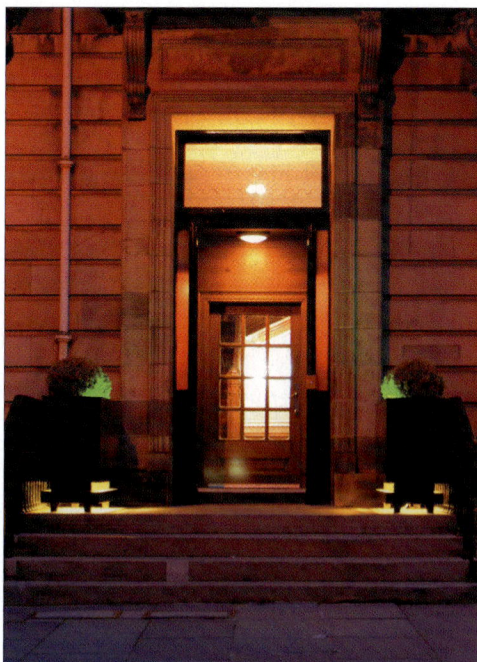

LOCATION

Five minutes' walk from Edinburgh's West End and city centre.

35 Drumsheugh Gardens,
Edinburgh EH3 7RN

T (UK) 0870 432 8541
T 0131 623 9301
F 0131 623 9306
bonham@bestloved.com
www.bonham.bestloved.com

OWNER
Peter Taylor

GENERAL MANAGER
Hans Rissmann

ROOM RATES
10 Single occupancy £108 - £165
36 Doubles/Twins   £127 - £225
2 Suites   £221 - £295
Includes continental breakfast and VAT

CREDIT CARDS
AMERICAN EXPRESS • DC • MC • VI

RATINGS & AWARDS
VisitScotland ★★★★ Hotel
AA ★★★★ ❀❀
AA Top 200 - 2004/2005
Which? Hotel of the Year 2000

FACILITIES
On site:
1 meeting room/max 70 people
Nearby: Golf, fitness centre

RESTRICTIONS
No pets; guide dogs only

ATTRACTIONS
Edinburgh Castle,
Royal Yacht Britannia,
Botanical Gardens, Edinburgh Castle,
Holyrood House, Royal Mile,
National Art Gallery of Scotland

NEAREST
CITY:
Edinburgh

AIRPORT:
Edinburgh - 6 miles/25 mins

RAIL STATION:
Waverley - 1 ½ miles/10 mins
Haymarket - ½ mile/5 mins

AFFILIATIONS
Preston's Global Hotels

RESERVATIONS
National rate in UK: 0870 432 8541
Toll free in US: 800-544-9993
Quote Best Loved

ACCESS CODES
AMADEUS HK EDIDRU
APOLLO/GALILEO HT 88207
SABRE/ABACUS HK 1451
WORLDSPAN HK DRUMS

"The tastes, the sounds and the traditions of the Highlands, wrapped in unique 21st-century style and comfort"

SHAHNAZ PAKRAVAN, BBC 'TOMORROW'S WORLD' PRESENTER

THE BRIDGE HOTEL & TACKLE SHOP Village hotel

Dunrobin Street, Helmsdale,
Sutherland KW8 6JA

T (UK) 0870 432 8543
T 01431 821100
F 01431 821101
bridge@bestloved.com
www.bridge.bestloved.com

DIRECTORS
Ralph and Maggie Klinkenberg

ROOM RATES
1 Single	£65 - £75
17 Doubles/Twins	£95 - £105
1 Suite	£145

Includes a glass of champagne,
full breakfast, service and VAT

CREDIT CARDS
AMERICAN EXPRESS • DC • MC • VI

RATINGS & AWARDS
Independent

FACILITIES
On site: Disabled room,
private parking, tackle & gift shop
Nearby: Salmon & trout fishing,
stalking, shooting, golf, bird watching,
nature walks

RESTRICTIONS
No smoking in dining room

ATTRACTIONS
Inverness,
Dornoch,
Dunrobin Castle,
Brora village and golf course,
beaches,
whisky distilleries

NEAREST
CITY:
Inverness - 70 miles/1 hr 30 mins

AIRPORT:
Inverness - 80 miles/1 hr 45 mins

RAIL STATION:
Helmsdale - ½ mile/5 mins

AFFILIATIONS
Independent

RESERVATIONS
National rate in UK: 0870 432 8543
Quote Best Loved

ACCESS CODES
Not applicable

A sportsman's home from home with memorable dining to match

The Bridge Hotel is almost a legend in itself: Built nearly 200 years ago as a central stop in Helmsdale village square, this remarkable area landmark has enjoyed life as a focus point for sportsmen and travellers passing through (it is, after all, a central stop between Caithness and Sutherland) for nearly its entire existence. Extensively renovated beginning in 1999, it re-opened in September 2004, and its new zest for life is evident at every turn.

An ideal stop on the way to the North, or simply a fantastic haunt for fishing fans and sportsmen, the hotel is pleasingly atmospheric, with 19 spacious bedrooms and décor themed to sporting pursuits. Every night at seven, resident piper Donnie Mackay welcomes the end of the day; with any luck, you'll be around to sample his music along with a complimentary glass of champagne in front of a roaring fire in the residents' lounge. The food, as you might expect, is dedicated to game and seafood from this 'Larder of Europe' - whether salmon, deer, hare, pheasant or duck, all is expertly prepared and sure to please.

Outdoors, all manner of attractions await, including golf, visits to castles and distilleries or even gold panning! Of course, fishing and stalking are available in the area, and the hotel is complete with a well-stocked tackle and gift shop.

LOCATION
From the A9 coastal road, take the first turn into Helmsdale; as you come over the old bridge, the hotel is straight ahead in front of you.

Stately home

BUNCHREW HOUSE HOTEL

Timelessness and tranquillity by the banks of the Beauly Firth

Steeped in history and tradition, this beautiful 17th-century Scottish mansion stands in 20 acres of landscaped gardens with a wall lapped by the sea in the Beauly Firth. Bunchrew House was built by Simon Fraser, the eighth Lord Lovat, whose marriage to Jean Stewart in 1621 is commemorated by a stone marriage lintel above the fireplace in the drawing room.

Magnificent views from the hotel include the Black Isle and Ben Wyvis, while the dining room - filled with contemporary paintings of the Frasers - overlooks the sea. Traditional cuisine includes prime Scottish beef, fresh lobster and langoustines, local game and venison and fresh vegetables cooked with herbs from the hotel's own herb garden. These superb dishes are complemented by a comprehensive wine list.

Fourteen comfortable guest rooms include two with luxurious four-posters and one with a sumptuous half-tester; all rooms are furnished to an extremely high standard. And for recreation, Bunchrew House offers many options; the area boasts a number of outdoor sporting activities, a diversity of castles, glens, gardens, and, of course, the intriguing legend of the Loch Ness Monster.

LOCATION

A short distance from both Inverness Airport and railway station, off the A862 between Inverness and Beauly.

Bunchrew, Inverness,
Inverness-shire IV3 8TA

T (UK) 0870 432 8549
T 01463 234917
F 01463 710620
bunchrew@bestloved.com
www.bunchrew.bestloved.com

OWNER
Terry Mackay

MANAGER
Gillian Omand

ROOM RATES
Single occupancy   £90 - £128
12 Doubles/Twins   £130 - £195
2 Four-posters   £160 - £210
Includes full breakfast and VAT

CREDIT CARDS
AMERICAN EXPRESS • JCB • MC • VI

RATINGS & AWARDS
VisitScotland ★★★★ Small Hotel
AA ★★★ ❀❀ 74%
Scotch Beef Club

FACILITIES
On site: Garden, heli-pad, fishing
3 meeting rooms/max 100 people
Nearby: Golf, riding, fishing, shooting, skiing, walking

RESTRICTIONS
No smoking in dining room
No pets in public rooms
Closed 24 - 27 Dec.

ATTRACTIONS
Loch Ness, Culloden Battlefield, Glens of Affric, Cawdor Castle, Strathfarrar and Strathglass, Cannich, Isle of Skye

NEAREST
CITY:
Inverness - 3 miles/10 mins

AIRPORT:
Inverness - 13 miles/20 mins
Edinburgh - 150 miles/2 hrs 30 mins

RAIL STATION:
Inverness - 3 miles/10 mins

AFFILIATIONS
Independent

RESERVATIONS
National rate in UK: 0870 432 8549
Quote Best Loved

ACCESS CODES
AMADEUS UI INVBUN
APOLLO/GALILEO UI 41478
SABRE/ABACUS UI 62868
WORLDSPAN UI 42581

The best features are the relaxing atmosphere, space and good service - and the marvellous surroundings

G D ENTWHISTLE, DERBY

SCOTLAND

CALLY PALACE HOTEL

Stately home

Gatehouse of Fleet,
Dumfries & Galloway DG7 2DL

T (UK) 0870 432 8553
T 01557 814 341
F 01557 814 522
callypal@bestloved.com
www.callypal.bestloved.com

PROPRIETOR
Mr H C McMillan

GENERAL MANAGER
Douglas McDavid

RATES PER PERSON
Single occupancy   £123 - £144
41 Doubles/Twins   £97
9 Family Rooms   £104
5 Suites   £108
Includes full breakfast, dinner and VAT

CREDIT CARDS
AMERICAN EXPRESS • MC • VI

RATINGS & AWARDS
VisitScotland ★★★★ Hotel
AA ★★★★ ❀ 71%

FACILITIES
On site: Fishing, croquet, golf, tennis, indoor pool, private golf course, swimming pool, Jacuzzi, sauna
1 meeting room/max 30 people
Nearby: Riding, fishing, sailing, hunting/shooting

RESTRICTIONS
Limited facilities for disabled guests
Smoking in Louis Lounge and bar only
No pets
Closed 3 Jan. - early February

ATTRACTIONS
Whithorn,
Creetown Gem Rock Museum,
Mill on the Fleet,
Tolbooth and Stewartry Museum,
Cream of Galloway,
Drumlanrig Castle, Wigtown,
Galloway Forest Park

NEAREST
CITY:
Glasgow - 90 miles/2 hrs

AIRPORT:
Prestwick - 65 miles/1 hr 30 mins
Glasgow - 90 miles/2 hrs

RAIL STATION:
Dumfries - 30 miles/30 mins

AFFILIATIONS
Independent

RESERVATIONS
National rate in UK: 0870 432 8553
Quote Best Loved

ACCESS CODES
Not applicable

An opulent country mansion with its own private golf course

Built in 1763, this beautiful converted country mansion opened as a hotel in 1934. Today, present-day owners the McMillans have succeeded in retaining the hotel's historic elegance whilst returning it to its former glory - a fact that's immediately evident upon entering and taking a glance at the entrance hall, flanked with marble pillars and leading into the Bow Lounge, complete with gilded cupola ceiling.

But it's not just the elegant interior that will warm your heart. The McMillans' vibrant Scottish hospitality will positively woo you, as will any one of the 55 spacious en-suite bedrooms and first-class cuisine featuring the freshest Galloway produce. Dinner is accompanied by music from the house pianist, lending an even more elegant air to the occasion - and to add to the atmosphere, gentlemen are asked to wear jacket and tie in the evenings.

Still, be prepared to shed the evening dress and head out for the links; after all, Cally Palace offers its own 18-hole golf course for the exclusive use of hotel guests. Other attractions include the artists' town of Kirkcudbright and Wigtown, the book town of Scotland.

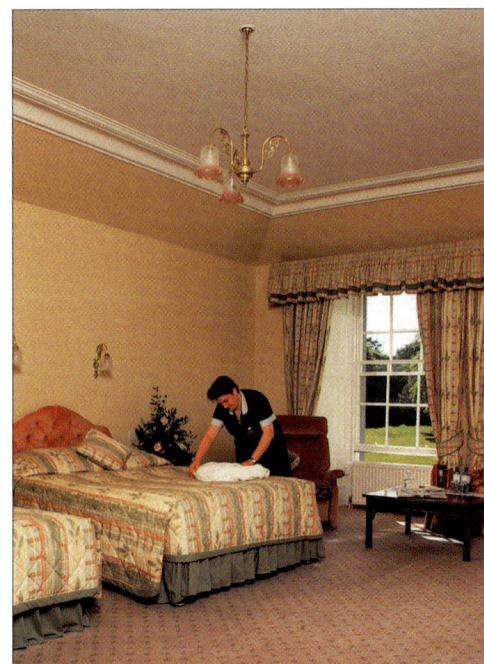

LOCATION
Thirty miles west of Dumfries on the A75; turn for Gatehouse of Fleet, and the hotel's drive is just before the village.

Country house

CASTLETON HOUSE HOTEL

SCOTLAND

Glamis, Angus DD8 1SJ
T (UK) 0870 432 8558
T 01307 840340
F 01307 840506
castleton@bestloved.com
www.castleton.bestloved.com

OWNERS
David Webster and Verity Nicholson

ROOM RATES
Single occupancy	£100 - £140
4 Standard Doubles	£140
1 Superior Double	£150
1 Four-poster	£180
Includes breakfast and VAT	

CREDIT CARDS
AMERICAN EXPRESS • MC • VI

RATINGS & AWARDS
VisitScotland ★★★★ Small Hotel
AA ★★★ ✿✿✿
AA Top 200 - 2004/2005

FACILITIES
On site: Nine-hole putting green,
in-room spa treatments upon request
3 meeting rooms/max 40 people
Nearby: Fishing, golf, country sport
centre, riding, shooting, walking

RESTRICTIONS
No facilities for disabled guests
Pets welcome; £7 surcharge

ATTRACTIONS
Glamis Castle, Angus Folk Museum,
J M Barrie's birthplace, Scone Palace,
Royal Research Ship Discovery,
House of Dunn, St Andrews,
Blair Castle

NEAREST
CITY:
Perth - 15 miles/30 mins
Dundee - 15 miles/30 mins

AIRPORT:
Edinburgh - 70 miles/1 hr 15 mins

RAIL STATION:
Perth - 15 miles/30 mins
Dundee - 15 miles/30 mins

AFFILIATIONS
Celebrated Hotels Collection

RESERVATIONS
National rate in UK: 0870 432 8558
Toll free in US: 800-322-2403
Quote Best Loved

ACCESS CODES
Not applicable

A first choice for luxurious accommodation and thoughtful, personalised service

When it comes to this splendidly-appointed Victorian estate nestled in prime Scottish scenery, small truly is beautiful. At just six bedrooms - perfect for both a comfortably private stay or a full-house family gathering - Castleton House Hotel is a treat for all seasons, from a peaceful, snowy winter (with skiing at nearby Glenshee!) to the brilliantly-coloured blooms of spring, summer's lazy allure and autumn's blazing scenery. In fact, Castleton House is a glorious retreat for all outdoor interests, whether it's croquet on the lawn, a bit of nearby fishing, a nature walk or a round of golf at any one of a handful of nearby golf courses.

When you're ready for repast, dining at Castleton House is itself a memorable occasion, with a variety of locally-sourced delights and selections from the hotel's own vegetable garden and poultry yard. After dinner, treat yourself to an evening in nearby Perth or Dundee - or simply settle in to one of the delightful individually-decorated bedrooms and enjoy comfortable beds, luxurious antiques and a host of personal touches.

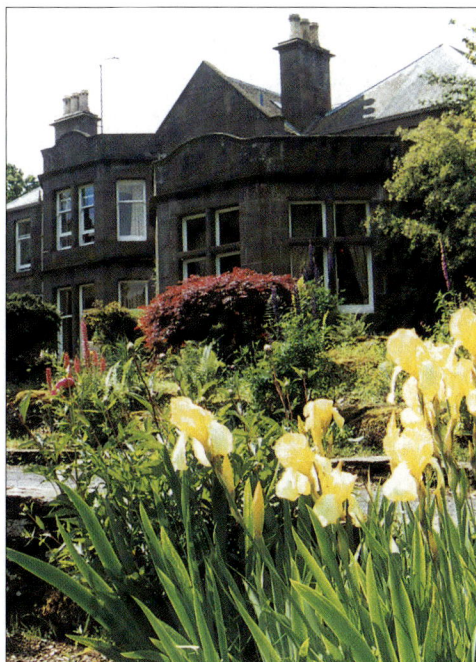

LOCATION
Take the A90 to Forfar; then, take the A94 for six miles. The hotel is between Glamis and Meigle.

> "There's good food, fine wine, a beautiful setting and a warm and friendly atmosphere. When it's done this well, what more could you want?"
>
> ALAN WILKINSON, GLASGOW HERALD

CAVENS COUNTRY HOUSE HOTEL

Country house

Cavens, Kirkbean,
Dumfries & Galloway DG2 8AA

T (UK) 0870 432 8559
T 01387 880234
F 01387 880467
cavens@bestloved.com
www.cavens.bestloved.com

OWNERS
Angus and Jane Fordyce

ROOM RATES
Single occupancy   £100
7 Doubles/Twins   £125 - £160
Includes full breakfast and VAT

CREDIT CARDS
AMERICAN EXPRESS • JCB • MC • VI

RATINGS & AWARDS
VisitScotland ★★★★ Small Hotel
AA ★★ ❀ 79%

FACILITIES
On site: Garden, fishing, croquet
1 meeting room/max 100 people
Nearby: Golf, shooting, fishing, riding

RESTRICTIONS
No facilities for disabled guests
Smoking in sitting room only
No pets; kennels available

ATTRACTIONS
Threave Garden and Estate,
Shambellie House,
Burns Cottage and Museum,
The Tam O'Shanter Experience,
Drumlanrig Castle,
John Paul Jones Cottage

NEAREST
CITY:
Dumfries - 13 miles/15 mins

AIRPORT:
Glasgow - 100 miles/2 hrs

RAIL STATION:
Dumfries - 13 miles/15 mins

AFFILIATIONS
Independent

RESERVATIONS
National rate in UK: 0870 432 8559
Quote Best Loved

ACCESS CODES
Not applicable

A spacious and gracious garden retreat in the heart of Burns Country

Cavens was built by tobacco baron Sir Richard Oswald in 1752 as the centrepiece of his extensive Dumfriesshire estates. The influential Oswalds were friends of Benjamin Franklin through their American connections and also contemporaries of Scottish poet Robert Burns, who wrote an 'Ode sacred to the memory of Mrs Oswald' upon her death. Tranquil, relaxing and surrounded by mature parkland gardens, Cavens is now home to Angus and Jane Fordyce.

Angus, who spent 20 years working in top London hotels, is responsible for most of the cooking. The four-course dinner menu features the best of local produce, from smoked salmon, venison and Highland beef to delicious Scottish cheeses. The house is marked a marvellous sense of space, so guests never feel crowded. The comfortable bedrooms are particularly generously proportioned; one has a six-foot bed, while the Oswald Room has its own veranda overlooking the garden.

Cavens is a great base for touring Burns Country, and golfers will find 12 golf courses nearby, including the renowned Southerness just a mile away. Travellers heading north will find Cavens an excellent stopover, and the house is also available for exclusive house parties of 16-18 guests.

LOCATION
Follow the A710 south from Dumfries 12 miles, passing through New Abbey to Kirkbean. From Kirkbean village, the hotel's driveway is signposted on the left.

Townhouse

CHANNINGS

SCOTLAND

You'll be charmed by the staff at this country-style townhouse

Situated in the cobbled streets of 'old' Edinburgh, this four-star hotel provides country-style ambience and pace within the centre of a vibrant, thriving city. What makes this hotel even more distinctive, however, is a team of outstanding staff who are collectively responsible for the Channings moniker of 'Edinburgh's friendliest hotel'.

The 46 bedrooms are up-to-the-minute and have been designed with great expertise using a collection of striking fabrics in bold colour combinations. Ideal for romantic getaways, some rooms have roll-top or double-sized Jacuzzi baths, as well as great views across the historic skyline. Impressively, all rooms are equipped with international modem points, voice mail, 55 cable channels, television with Internet access, DVD, video, games and hi-fi systems. Channings Restaurant has long since been regarded as one of the city's premier eateries, and hot on the scene is the hotel's Ochre Vita, which offers a taste of the Mediterranean in colourful surroundings.

Unlike many hotels, Channings really does cater appropriately for both the leisure and business customer, and the Library and Kingsleigh Suites (located in a part of the building that was once home to explorer Ernest Shackleton) are ideal for conferences, meetings and other corporate events.

LOCATION

Half a mile from the city centre (10 minutes' walk) and 20 minutes from the airport by taxi.

12-16 South Learmonth Gardens,
Edinburgh EH4 1EZ

T (UK) 0870 432 8560
T 0131 623 9302
F 0131 623 9306
channings@bestloved.com
www.channings.bestloved.com

OWNER
Peter Taylor

GENERAL MANAGER
Duncan Johnston

ROOM RATES
5 Singles	£101 - £160
37 Doubles/Twins	£131 - £225
1 Four-poster	£157 - £230
3 Suites	£187 - £260

Includes full breakfast and VAT

CREDIT CARDS
AMERICAN EXPRESS • DC • MC • VI

RATINGS & AWARDS
VisitScotland ★★★★ Hotel
RAC White Ribbon ★★★★
Dining Award 1
AA ★★★★ ✿✿ 79% Town House
AA Top 200 - 2004/2005

FACILITIES
On site: Garden, patio, Channings Restaurant, Ochre Vita Mediterranean Food and Wine Bar 2 meeting rooms/max 35 people
Nearby: Golf, fitness centre

RESTRICTIONS
No facilities for disabled guests
Smoking in some bedrooms only
No pets; guide dogs only

ATTRACTIONS
Dynamic Earth, Royal Yacht Britannia, Botanical Gardens, Edinburgh Castle, Holyrood House, Royal Mile, National Art Gallery of Scotland

NEAREST
CITY:
Edinburgh

AIRPORT:
Edinburgh - 6 miles/20 mins

RAIL STATION:
Waverley - 1½ miles/5 mins
Haymarket - 1½ miles/5 mins

AFFILIATIONS
Preston's Global Hotels
Classic British Hotels

RESERVATIONS
National rate in UK: 0870 432 8560
Toll free in US: 800-544-9993
or 800-437-2687
Quote Best Loved

ACCESS CODES
AMADEUS UI EDICHA
APOLLO/GALILEO UI 22312
SABRE/ABACUS UI 22560
WORLDSPAN UI 14126

"Better food than some of the top London restaurants and a view to die for"

THE MIRROR

CORRIEGOUR LODGE HOTEL

Lakeside hotel

SCOTLAND

Loch Lochy, By Spean Bridge,
Inverness-shire PH34 4EB

T (UK) 0870 432 8571
T 01397 712685
F 01397 712696
corriegour@bestloved.com
www.corriegour.bestloved.com

OWNERS
Christian and Ian Drew

RATES PER PERSON
2 Singles £80 - £95
9 Doubles/Twins £80 - £110
Includes full breakfast, dinner and VAT

CREDIT CARDS
AMERICAN EXPRESS • DC • JCB • MC • VI

RATINGS & AWARDS
VisitScotland ★★★★ Small Hotel
Hotel Review ✿✿✿✿

FACILITIES
On site: Garden, fishing
Nearby: Riding, shooting, walking, climbing, pony trekking, sailing, cycling, fishing, whitewater rafting, abseiling

RESTRICTIONS
No facilities for disabled guests
No children under 8 years
Smoking in bar only
No pets

ATTRACTIONS
Eilean Donan Castle, Glencoe, Urquhart Castle, Culloden Battlefield, Isle of Skye, Blair Castle, Glenfinnan, Loch Ness

NEAREST
CITY:
Inverness - 58 miles/1 hr 30 mins

AIRPORT:
Inverness - 66 miles/1 hr 45 mins
Glasgow - 110 miles/3 hrs

RAIL STATION:
Fort William - 12 miles/ 20 mins

AFFILIATIONS
Independent

RESERVATIONS
National rate in UK: 0870 432 8571
Quote Best Loved

ACCESS CODES
Not applicable

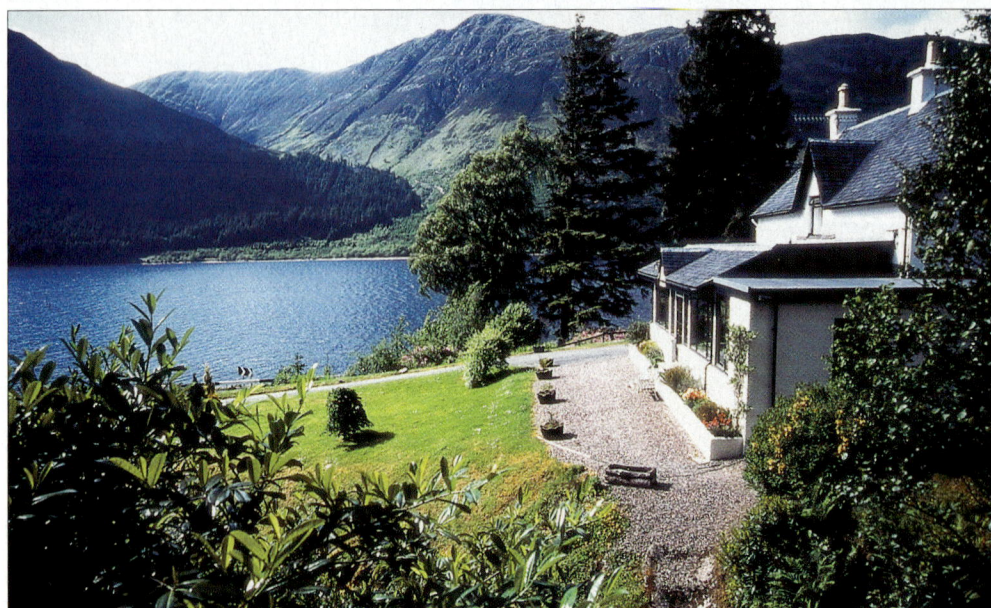

An experience to savour amidst the dramatic scenery of the Great Glen

One of the first things to say about Corriegour Lodge is that it is situated in one of the finest and most dramatic settings in the Great Glen - an area famed for its outstanding natural beauty.

The location is something the owners, Ian and Christian Drew, enthuse about with a great passion - a passion, incidentally, that is apparent in every aspect of their business. Refreshingly, their aim is to provide guests with the modern comforts of today and the standards and service of yesteryear - without charging a premium for it. They describe the hotel as a 'total experience', a retreat where guests can come and relax and enjoy the sheer beauty and tranquillity of the area.

An integral part of this experience is the dining, which by all accounts is showstopping. Head Chef Ian is one of Scotland's youngest, most talented chefs and he is, of course, spoilt by the abundance and quality of the area's natural larder. And the finale? Guests may be treated to a rare sighting of Lizzie, distant cousin of Nessie, who is believed to lurk in the loch below (or is it perhaps a case of just one whisky too many?)

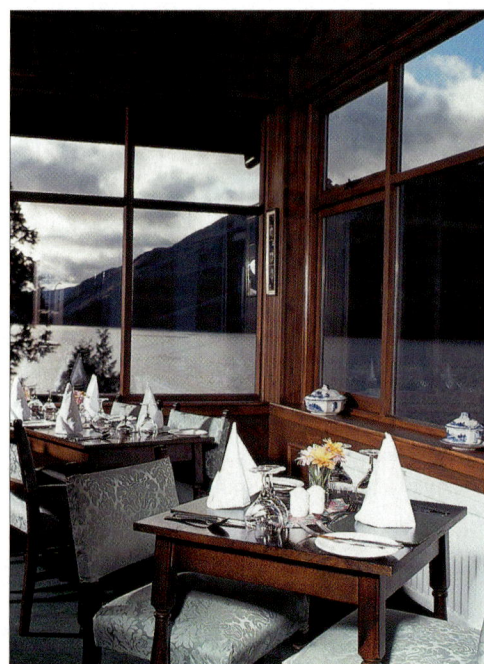

LOCATION
From Edinburgh, exit the A9 at Dalwinnie and follow signs for Spean Bridge. From Glasgow, follow the A82 to Crianlarich/Fort William, then signs to Spean Bridge. The hotel is on the Inverness road, on the right.

> **Very much the country house with a relaxed and welcoming atmosphere, and refreshingly unpretentious**
>
> D J ROBERTSON, AA INSPECTOR

Country house

COUL HOUSE HOTEL

Contin, by Strathpeffer,
Near Inverness,
Ross-shire IV14 9ES

T (UK) 0870 432 8575
T 01997 421487
F 01997 421945
coulhouse@bestloved.com
www.coulhouse.bestloved.com

SCOTLAND

So much to see and enjoy in such a perfect Highland setting

Built in 1821 for Sir George Stuart Mackenzie as a traditional hunting lodge, Coul House is now a beautiful country house hotel with stunning views over the Strathconon Valley and the Achilty Mountains beyond. Quite simply, this is the perfect place to base oneself to rediscover the romance and beauty of the highlands - guests can easily cruise Loch Ness, visit Macbeth's Cawdor Castle, or even sail to the Orkney Isles and still be back in time for dinner in the hotel's restaurant, a unique octagonal dining room that offers contemporary gourmet cuisine.

There are activities for everyone to enjoy, whether it's a stroll around the hotel's own eight acres of mature woodland (complete with private nine-hole pitch and putt course) or attractions further afield, including the Glen Ord & Glenmorangie whisky distilleries, fly fishing, clay pigeon shooting, stalking, rough hunts, world-class golf at Nairn or Royal Dornoch, hiking, biking, pony trekking and dolphin watch cruises.

With so much to see and do, Coul House is certainly a destination one should plan on enjoying for more than just a couple of nights!

LOCATION

From the south, bypass Inverness and continue on the A9 over Moray Firth Bridge. After five miles, take the A835 to Contin; the hotel's drive is on the right.

OWNERS
Stuart and Susannah Macpherson

ROOM RATES
2 Singles	£55 - £75
6 Doubles/Twins	£78 - £118
1 Superior Single	£69 - £89
7 Superior Doubles/Twins	£98 - £138
3 Family Rooms	£123 - £163
1 Master Suite	£130 - £170

Includes full breakfast and VAT

CREDIT CARDS
AMERICAN EXPRESS • MC • VI

RATINGS & AWARDS
VisitScotland ★★★ Hotel
AA ★★★ 71%

FACILITIES
On site: Garden, pitch and putt
3 meeting rooms/max 80 people
Nearby: Golf, fishing

RESTRICTIONS
None

ATTRACTIONS
Strathpeffer Spa Victorian Village,
Loch Ness, Strathconon,
Cromarty Firth,
Loch Achonachie salmon lift,
Rogie Falls and Torrachilty Forest Trail,
Beauly Priory, Castle Leod

NEAREST
CITY:
Inverness - 20 miles/30 mins

AIRPORT:
Inverness - 25 miles/35 mins
Glasgow - 180 miles/4 hrs

RAIL STATION:
Inverness - 20 miles/30 mins

AFFILIATIONS
Scotland's Hotels of Distinction

RESERVATIONS
National rate in UK: 0870 432 8575
Quote Best Loved

ACCESS CODES
Not applicable

CRAIGELLACHIE HOTEL OF SPEYSIDE Country house

SCOTLAND

Craigellachie, Speyside,
Banffshire AB38 9SR

T (UK) 0870 432 8579
T 01340 881204
F 01340 881253
craigellachie@bestloved.com
www.craigellachie.bestloved.com

GENERAL MANAGER
Duncan Elphick

ROOM RATES
12 Doubles/Twins   £130
8 Superior Doubles/Twins £145
5 Deluxe Doubles/Twins   £165
Includes full breakfast and VAT

CREDIT CARDS
AMERICAN EXPRESS • DC • JCB • MC • VI

RATINGS & AWARDS
VisitScotland ★★★★ Hotel
AA ★★★ ❀❀ 78%

FACILITIES
On site: Garden, tennis, bicycles
3 meeting rooms/max 70 people
Nearby: Golf, fishing, riding, cycling,
off-road driving

RESTRICTIONS
Limited facilities for disabled guests
No smoking in bedrooms
or restaurant

ATTRACTIONS
Loch Ness, the Highlands,
Balmoral Castle, Malt Whisky Trail,
Culloden Battlefield, Cairngorms

NEAREST
CITY:
Inverness - 50 miles/1 hr

AIRPORT:
Aberdeen - 55 miles/1 hr

RAIL STATION:
Elgin - 12 miles/20 mins

AFFILIATIONS
Scotland's Hotels of Distinction
Celebrated Hotels Collection
Grand Heritage Hotels

RESERVATIONS
National rate in UK: 0870 432 8579
Toll free in US: 800-322-2403
or 888-93-GRAND
Quote Best Loved

ACCESS CODES
AMADEUS UI ABZCRG
APOLLO/GALILEO UI 33029
SABRE/ABACUS UI 56409
WORLDSPAN UI 42062

Boundless Highland hospitality on the banks of the River Spey

The Craigellachie Hotel occupies a pre-eminent position crowning a low rise above lawns leading down to the banks of the River Spey. The fast-flowing Spey is one of Scotland's top salmon fishing rivers and a magnet for keen anglers, while the surrounding countryside is great for guests who want to enjoy some of the Highlands' finest scenery.

Generously proportioned rooms give a welcome sense of space and provide quiet corners for reading a good book by the fire, having a game of snooker or sitting to chat over tomorrow's touring plans. The elegant yet unfussy décor blends cleverly with the period of the building and extends to the charming bedrooms, decorated with subtle combinations of colours and fabrics.

At the very heart of the Malt Whisky Trail, Craigellachie's highly acclaimed Quaich Bar - the best whisky bar in the world, according to Scottish Veal magazine - serves over 500 single malts and is a celebration of the hotel's many world-famous neighbours. Whisky tasting and nosings can be arranged for up to 20 people; when it comes time to dine, modern Scottish cuisine with an international twist is the order of the day in the ambient Ben Aigan restaurant - and after dinner, what better way to spend the rest of the evening than sampling a dram or two!

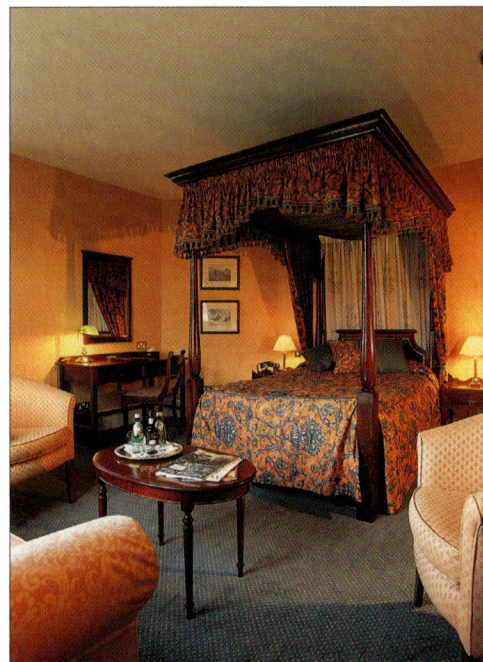

LOCATION
Near the junction of the A95/A941
Aviemore/Elgin road 12 miles south of Elgin.

Country house

CRINGLETIE HOUSE

SCOTLAND

Peebles, Borders EH45 8PL

T (UK) 0870 432 8582
T 01721 725750
F 01721 725751
cringletie@bestloved.com
www.cringletie.bestloved.com

PROPRIETORS
Jacob and Johanna van Houdt

ROOM RATES
1 Single   £95 - £120
13 Doubles/Twins   £115 - £260
Includes full breakfast and VAT

CREDIT CARDS
AMERICAN EXPRESS • MC • VI

RATINGS & AWARDS
VisitScotland ★★★★ Small Hotel
AA ★★★ ⊗⊗ 80%
Best Restaurant Meal in the Borders 2003

FACILITIES
On site: Garden, heli-pad, tennis,
licensed for weddings
4 meeting rooms/max 80 people
Nearby: Golf, riding, fishing

RESTRICTIONS
No smoking in restaurant or
bedrooms
No pets in public rooms;
£10 per dog per night
Closed early January - early February

ATTRACTIONS
Edinburgh,
Abbey Trail,
Dawyck Botanic Garden,
Abbotsford House,
Neidpath Castle,
Traquair House

NEAREST
CITY:
Edinburgh - 20 miles/35 mins

AIRPORT:
Edinburgh - 25 miles/45 mins

RAIL STATION:
Edinburgh - 20 miles/35 mins

FERRY PORT:
Rosyth - 40 miles/1 hr

AFFILIATIONS
Pride of Britain

RESERVATIONS
National rate in UK: 0870 432 8582
Toll free in US: 800-98-PRIDE
Quote Best Loved

ACCESS CODES
Not applicable

Splendidly romantic - and the food comes highly recommended

Cringletie House is a romantically splendid Victorian baronial mansion set in 28 acres of gardens and woodland in the beautiful rolling hills of the Scottish Borders. Just half an hour's drive from Edinburgh, this beautiful hotel's location makes it a convenient base for visiting the city but returning to peaceful rural surroundings.

Originally opened as a hotel in 1966 and fresh from a total renovation in the spring of 2004, Cringletie retains the atmosphere of a private country house whilst catering fully for all guests, including a full wheelchair access and a lift. Outside, there's a lovely 17th-century walled garden, which provides Cringletie's kitchen with a tempting variety of homegrown produce, no doubt contributing to the excellent ratings received by the hotel's chef, Paul Hart. Whether a traditional Sunday lunch in the Sutherland Room or the superb seven-course gourmet tasting menu (the contents of which are always a surprise, as the chef chooses the best local produce available that day!), dining is sure to delight, and all is accompanied by a well-chosen wine list.

Outdoors, there's much to do, from a world of beautiful walks (and the hotel can plan a picnic for you!) to notable golfing, cycling and fishing.

LOCATION

20 miles from Edinburgh, two miles north of Peebles on the A703.

CROMLIX HOUSE

Country house

Kinbuck by Dunblane,
Near Stirling, Perthshire FK15 9JT

T (UK) 0870 432 8583
T 01786 822125
F 01786 825450
cromlix@bestloved.com
www.cromlix.bestloved.com

OWNERS
David and Ailsa Assenti

ROOM RATES
Single occupancy £125 - £190
6 Doubles/Twins £225 - £275
8 Suites £260 - £390
Includes full breakfast and VAT

CREDIT CARDS
AMERICAN EXPRESS • DC • MC • VI

RATINGS & AWARDS
VisitScotland ★★★★★ Small Hotel
AA ★★★ ⊛⊛
AA Top 200 - 2004/2005
AA Top 10 Hotels in Scotland 2003

FACILITIES
On site: Garden, heli-pad,
fishing, croquet
3 meeting rooms/max 50 people
Nearby: Golf, riding,
salmon and trout fishing, tennis

RESTRICTIONS
No facilities for disabled guests
No children under 8 years in
restaurant, high tea provided
Smoking in some public rooms only
Pets by arrangement;
no pets in public rooms
Closed 2-25 January

ATTRACTIONS
Stirling Castle, Scone Palace,
Glenturret Distillery, the Trossachs

NEAREST
CITY:
Glasgow - 30 miles/35 mins
Edinburgh - 38 miles/55 mins

AIRPORT:
Edinburgh - 35 miles/40 mins
Glasgow - 40 miles/55 mins

RAIL STATION:
Dunblane - 4 miles/10 mins

AFFILIATIONS
Celebrated Hotels Collection
Pride of Britain

RESERVATIONS
National rate in UK: 0870 432 8583
Toll free in US: 800-322-2403
or 800-98-PRIDE
Quote Best Loved

ACCESS CODES
Not applicable

An absolute treasure
close to Edinburgh and Glasgow

Built in 1874 as the family home in a 2,000-acre estate, Cromlix House retains its original character and features, including a charming chapel perfect for weddings. The imposing exterior belies a comfortable and homely interior, and inside, the feeling is that of a relaxing, much-loved home. In the true traditions of country house hospitality, nothing is too precious or pretentious; everything about Cromlix is genuine, including the sense of history.

As you would expect, Cromlix is furnished throughout with antiques, fine furniture and paintings; the six bedrooms and eight very spacious suites with private sitting rooms offer comfort and luxury, and two of the five public rooms are typical of a Victorian shooting lodge. Dining at Cromlix, too, is an experience to be savoured. The award-winning staff prepare a fresh menu daily, and vegetarian, special and lighter diets are readily catered for.

Country pursuits include fishing, shooting or simply enjoying the wildlife. Trout and salmon fishing, sporting and clay shooting are available by advance arrangement, and 10 golf courses are nearby.

LOCATION
Five minutes off the A9 on the B8033, north of Dunblane and through Kinbuck village.

> **A wonderful place to unwind with superb food and excellent wines**
>
> MR & MRS ELLISON, EDINBURGH

Country house

CULDEARN HOUSE

Wonderful food and hospitality in the heart of Speyside

This small, privately-owned hotel, built in 1860, is situated in the glorious area of Speyside and is the ideal base for touring the Highlands and islands of Scotland. The perfect place to unwind at the end of a busy day, Culdearn's elegant lounge provides a peaceful setting in which to meet other guests or relax with a wee dram - or settle into one of the seven bedrooms, all of the highest standard.

In the hotel's renowned restaurant, locally-sourced fare includes excellent Scottish game and seafood. Guests might try the scallops set on an asparagus trellis with an arbroath smokie sauce, or roasted venison with a red wine and bitter chocolate jus. All this is accompanied by an impressive wine list and an extensive selection of malt whiskies are also available.

There is plenty to do in this picturesque area - fishing, golf, shooting, bird watching, hill and mountain walking are all nearby. Culdearn is also on the Whisky Trail, with many distilleries in the surrounding area offering a taste for the connoisseur and newcomer alike.

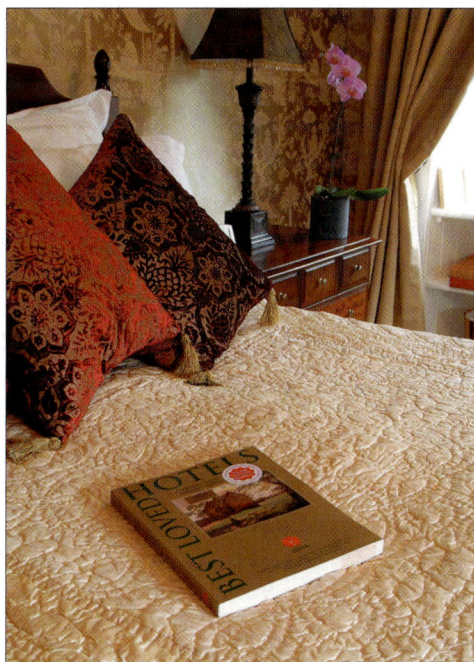

LOCATION

Approach Grantown from the southwest on the A95 and turn left at the '30 mph' sign. Culdearn faces you.

Woodlands Terrace,
Grantown-on-Spey,
Moray PH26 3JU

T (UK) 0870 432 8587
T 01479 872106
F 01479 873641
culdearn@bestloved.com
www.culdearn.bestloved.com

OWNERS
Sonia & William Marshall

RATES PER PERSON
Single occupancy £85
6 Doubles/Twins £85
1 Suite £90 - £95
Includes full breakfast, dinner and VAT

CREDIT CARDS
MC • VI

RATINGS & AWARDS
VisitScotland ★★★★ Small Hotel
RAC ★★ Dining Award 3
AA ★★ ✿ 77%
RAC Small Hotel of the Year
Scotland 1996/1997
Green Tourism Business -
Gold Award
Scotch Beef Club

FACILITIES
On site: Garden
Nearby: Golf, fishing, riding,
birdwatching

RESTRICTIONS
Limited facilities for disabled guests
No children under 10 years
No smoking throughout
No pets; guide dogs only
Closed December - mid-February

ATTRACTIONS
Ballindalloch,
Cawdor and Brodie castles,
Culloden Battlefield,
malt whisky distilleries

NEAREST
CITY:
Inverness - 30 miles/35 mins

AIRPORT:
Edinburgh - 140 miles/2 hrs 30 mins
Inverness - 35 miles/40 mins

RAIL STATION:
Aviemore - 15 miles/20 mins

AFFILIATIONS
Independent

RESERVATIONS
National rate in UK: 0870 432 8587
Quote Best Loved

ACCESS CODES
Not applicable

> "Princes past and present have enjoyed the ambience and hospitality of this elegant Palladian mansion"
>
> CAPTAIN EDMUND BURT, LETTERS FROM A GENTLEMAN IN THE NORTH OF SCOTLAND, C. 1730

CULLODEN HOUSE

Country house

Culloden, Inverness,
Inverness-shire IV2 7BZ

T (UK) 0870 432 8504
T 01463 790461
F 01463 792181
cullodenhse@bestloved.com
www.cullodenhse.bestloved.com

GENERAL MANAGER
Stephen Davies

ROOM RATES

3 Singles	£135 - £160
17 Doubles/Twins	£199 - £249
8 Suites	£249 - £279

Includes full breakfast, newspaper and VAT

CREDIT CARDS
AMERICAN EXPRESS • DC • JCB • MC • VI

RATINGS & AWARDS
VisitScotland ★★★★ Hotel
AA ★★★★ ❀❀ 71%
The Guardian Top 60 Independent
UK Restaurants
Der Feinschmecker Top 200
European Golfing Hotels

FACILITIES
On site: Garden, heli-pad, croquet, tennis, boules, sauna, golf driving net, putting green
3 meeting rooms/max 100 people
Nearby: 35 golf courses, fishing, riding, fitness centre, tennis, yachting

RESTRICTIONS
No facilities for disabled guests
No children under 10 years
Smoking in bar only
Pets by arrangement
Closed early January - early February

ATTRACTIONS
Cawdor Castle, Clava Cairns, Loch Ness, Caledonian Canal, Fort George, Aviemore, 21 distilleries, Culloden Battlefield

NEAREST
CITY:
Inverness - 3 miles/10 mins

AIRPORT:
Inverness - 3 miles/10 mins

RAIL STATION:
Inverness - 3 miles/10 mins

AFFILIATIONS
Celebrated Hotels Collection
Scotland's Heritage Hotels

RESERVATIONS
National rate in UK: 0870 432 8504
Toll free in US: 800-322-2403
Quote Best Loved

ACCESS CODES
Not applicable

Princely Palladian hospitality in a very special Highland setting

Culloden House is a gracious Georgian mansion refurbished in 1788 and incorporating a fortified mid-16th century castle set in 40 acres of stately parkland. As early as 1730, the resident Forbes family established a tradition of hospitality that lives on to this day: On arrival, guests could refresh themselves with a pint of fine claret and stay the night if they chose to. They always chose to.

The house's history features spies, sieges, proud Highland chieftains and romance. Bonnie Prince Charlie buckled his sword as he dashed from the house to fight his last battle, and the recent guest list includes politicians, film stars and royalty. The house is decorated and furnished in Palladian style; the main rooms feature ornate Adam plasterwork and fireplaces, and here you can listen to Scottish folk music played on pedal harp, bagpipes and clarsach. Bedrooms are appointed to a very high standard, many with four-poster beds or testers. Dinners are a delight, featuring fresh and smoked Scottish game, meat, fowl and produce cooked and presented imaginatively.

Close by are Culloden Battlefield, the Highland glens, Cawdor Castle, Clava Cairns, the Caledonian Canal and 35 golf courses. Dolphins wait near Inverness harbour ... and so may something else in Loch Ness!

LOCATION

From the A96 one mile from Inverness, turn right for Culloden; the hotel is signposted one mile on.

> "This is a place I can relax"
>
> DWIGHT D EISENHOWER, FORMER PRESIDENT OF THE USA

Castle

CULZEAN CASTLE - EISENHOWER APARTMENT

Rooms with a view atop one of Scotland's premier tourist attractions

Possibly one of the grandest bachelor pads ever constructed, Culzean Castle perches on the Ayrshire sea cliffs, commanding views across the water to the mountains of Arran and the Mull of Kintyre. Until the latter part of the 18th century, Culzean was a relatively modest castle keep belonging to the Kennedy family. Enter David Kennedy, the newly succeeded 10th Earl of Cassillis, who commissioned the great Scottish architect Robert Adam to provide him with a fabulous bachelor abode where he could entertain his friends in high old style. Adams obliged, creating his final masterpiece, completed in 1792.

In 1945, the Kennedys donated their home to the National Trust for Scotland, but not before gifting a six-bedroom apartment on the top floor of the castle to General Eisenhower as a 'thank you' to the wartime hero from the Scottish nation. During his retirement, Eisenhower spent time painting and walking in the castle grounds. Today, the self-contained Eisenhower Apartment is available to discerning guests, elegantly furnished in country-house style with a cosy dining room where guests enjoy fine Scottish food and a round drawing room offering spectacular sea views.

LOCATION

From Maybole, take the B7023 and then the A719, signed Turnberry. Culzean is on the right four miles from Maybole.

SCOTLAND

Maybole, Ayrshire KA19 8LE

T (UK) 0870 432 8589
T 01655 884455
F 01655 884503
culzean@bestloved.com
www.culzean.bestloved.com

PROPERTY MANAGER
Mike Schafer

ROOM RATES
Single occupancy   £140 - £250
4 Doubles/Twins   £225 - £275
1 Four-poster   £325
1 Eisenhower Suite   £375
Includes full breakfast, afternoon tea, complimentary drinks and VAT

CREDIT CARDS
MC • VI

RATINGS & AWARDS
Independent

FACILITIES
On site: Garden, shoreline and woodland walks
Nearby: Golf, shooting, fishing

RESTRICTIONS
Limited facilities for disabled guests
Children by arrangement
No smoking throughout
No pets

ATTRACTIONS
Culzean Castle,
Turnberry & Royal Troon golf courses,
Isle of Arran, Isle of Arran Distillery,
Tam O'Shanter Experience,
Ayr Racecourse

NEAREST
CITY:
Glasgow - 45 miles/1 hr

AIRPORT:
Prestwick - 15 miles/30 mins
Glasgow - 47 miles/1 hr

RAIL STATION:
Ayr - 12 miles/20 mins

AFFILIATIONS
Independent

RESERVATIONS
National rate in UK: 0870 432 8589
Quote Best Loved

ACCESS CODES
Not applicable

> ## "To all, to each, a fair good-night, and pleasing dreams, and slumbers light!"
> SIR WALTER SCOTT, WHILST STAYING AT DALHOUSIE IN 1808

DALHOUSIE CASTLE & SPA

Castle

Bonnyrigg, Edinburgh EH19 3JB
T (UK) 0870 432 8591
T 01875 820153
F 01875 821936
dalhousie@bestloved.com
www.dalhousie.bestloved.com

GENERAL MANAGER
Chris Ling

ROOM RATES
Single occupancy   £120 - £140
18 Doubles/Twins   £120 - £195
3 Triples/Quads   £235 - £260
14 Themed Rooms   £255 - £300
2 Themed Suites   £325
Includes full breakfast and VAT

CREDIT CARDS
AMERICAN EXPRESS • DC • JCB • MC • VI

RATINGS & AWARDS
VisitScotland ★★★★ Hotel
AA ★★★ ❀❀ 75%

FACILITIES
On site: Heli-pad, health & beauty, licensed for weddings, spa, falconry, archery, private chapel
5 meeting rooms/max 120 people
Nearby: Fishing, clay shooting, golf, riding, fitness, tennis, off-road driving

RESTRICTIONS
Limited facilities for disabled guests
No smoking in bedrooms or restaurant

ATTRACTIONS
Edinburgh City and Castle, Edinburgh Crystal, Holyrood House, Royal Yacht Britannia, Glenkinchie Distillery, Glasgow

NEAREST
CITY:
Edinburgh - 7 miles/20 mins

AIRPORT:
Edinburgh - 14 miles/30 mins

RAIL STATION:
Waverley - 7 miles/20 mins

AFFILIATIONS
von Essen Hotels
Preston's Global Hotels
Grand Heritage Hotels

RESERVATIONS
National rate in UK: 0870 432 8591
Toll free in US: 800-544-9993
or 888-93-GRAND
Quote Best Loved

ACCESS CODES
AMADEUS YX EDIDCH
APOLLO/GALILEO YX 78139
SABRE/ABACUS YX 30846
WORLDSPAN YX 40637
PEGASUS YX EDIDAL

A 13th-century castle with a state-of-the-art spa

The Ramsays of Dalhousie laid the foundations of their family seat more than 700 years ago, and its ancient stones have witnessed a fascinating procession of historical events and famous guests, from Edward I and Oliver Cromwell to Queen Victoria and Sir Walter Scott. However, the new millennium has probably heralded the most revolutionary development in the Castle's long and distinguished history with the arrival of the Aqueous Spa.

A short drive south of Edinburgh, Dalhousie Castle is set in its own estate of forest and parkland. Fourteen of its 27 luxuriously furnished and thoughtfully-equipped bedrooms are historically themed (for example, the Sir William Wallace Room), and there are a further six rooms in the century-old Lodge a two-minute walk away overlooking the South Esk River.

The Aqueous hydrotherapy spa is the first of its kind in Scotland, offering invigorating and rejuvenating hydrotherapy facilities combined with relaxing treatments to reduce stress and promote a healthy body and mind. Spa packages or individual treatments are available. Adjacent to the spa, the Orangery offers a Scottish-Mediterranean menu with light and healthy options as a counterbalance to the traditional Scottish-French cuisine served in the more formal, vaulted Dungeon Restaurant.

LOCATION
From Edinburgh, take the A7 south through Newtongrange; exit right for the B704. The hotel's entrance is half a mile along on the right.

> Amid tall trees on a hillside, the Darroch Learg is everything a Scottish country house hotel should be

GILBERT SUMMERS, FODOR'S

Country house

DARROCH LEARG

SCOTLAND

Braemar Road, Ballater,
Aberdeenshire AB35 5UX

T (UK) 0870 432 8594
T 013397 55443
F 013397 55252
darroch@bestloved.com
www.darroch.bestloved.com

PROPRIETORS
Nigel and Fiona Franks

ROOM RATES
15 Doubles/Twins   £145 - £175
2 Four-posters   £160 - £175
Includes full breakfast and VAT

CREDIT CARDS
AMERICAN EXPRESS • DC • JCB • MC • VI

RATINGS & AWARDS
VisitScotland ★★★★ Small Hotel
RAC Blue Ribbon ★★★ Dining Award 3
AA ★★★ ✿✿✿
AA Top 200 - 2004/2005

FACILITIES
On site: Garden
1 meeting room/max 40 people
Nearby: Golf, fishing, riding, tennis,
gliding, climbing

RESTRICTIONS
Limited facilities for disabled guests
Smoking in Smoke Room only
No pets in public rooms
Closed 19 - 29 Dec. and 10 - 31 Jan.

ATTRACTIONS
Balmoral Castle, Crathes,
Drum and Craigievar castles,
whisky distilleries,
Victorian Heritage trails,
Grampian Mountains

NEAREST
CITY:
Aberdeen - 42 miles/1 hr

AIRPORT:
Aberdeen - 42 miles/1 hr

RAIL STATION:
Aberdeen - 42 miles/1 hr

AFFILIATIONS
Scotland's Heritage Hotels

RESERVATIONS
National rate in UK: 0870 432 8594
Quote Best Loved

ACCESS CODES
Not applicable

A relaxing country house on Royal Deeside

The Darroch Learg truly is everything a Scottish country house hotel should be: relaxing and regal, the house was built in 1888 as a country residence on Royal Deeside, and stands in four acres of tall trees on the side of a rocky hill dominating the charming town of Ballater. This vantage point gives panoramic views over the golf course, the River Dee and the Balmoral estate to the Grampians and Lochnagar.

Another five bedrooms are in the adjacent mansion of Oakhall, built in Scottish baronial style in 1880 and perfect for exclusive use or parties. All are individually decorated and furnished to give each its own character. The dining room and spacious conservatory offer a wonderful outlook to the hills of Glen Muick. When it's time to dine, enjoy a modern Scottish dinner menu created using the finest fresh ingredients - Aberdeen Angus beef, Scottish lamb, local game, fresh fish and seafood. The award-winning wine list is exceptional, too, with more than 200 bins to choose from!

Outdoor activities in the area includes bird watching, clay pigeon and game shooting, gliding, golf, hang gliding, hill walking, riding and pony trekking, loch and river fishing, mountain biking and skiing. The area is also justly famous for its castles, the Highland Games, Royal Deeside and Balmoral Castle.

LOCATION

From the A93 to Ballater, the hotel is at the western edge of the town, on the main road to Braemar.

SCOTLAND

No other hotel in the British Isles has so invariably combined caring service and beautiful cooking, all in a completely relaxed atmosphere

SONIA & PATRICK STEVENSON

DUNAIN PARK HOTEL

Country house

Inverness,
Inverness-shire IV3 8JN

T (UK) 0870 432 8602
T 01463 230512
F 01463 224532
dunain@bestloved.com
www.dunain.bestloved.com

OWNERS
Ann and Edward Nicoll

ROOM RATES
3 Doubles/Twins   £138 - £178
2 Superior Doubles   £218
6 Suites   £218
2 Cottages   £178
Includes full breakfast and VAT

CREDIT CARDS
DC • JCB • MC • VI

RATINGS & AWARDS
VisitScotland ★★★★ Small Hotel

FACILITIES
On site: Garden, croquet,
indoor pool, sauna
Nearby: Golf, fishing, riding, walking

RESTRICTIONS
Limited facilities for disabled guests
Children by arrangement
No smoking in dining room or
bedrooms
Pets by arrangement
Closed 5-20 Jan.

ATTRACTIONS
Loch Ness, Cawdor Castle,
Culloden Battlefield, Whisky Trail,
Eden Court Theatre

NEAREST
CITY:
Inverness - 2 miles/5 mins

AIRPORT:
Inverness - 8 miles/30 mins
Glasgow - 188 miles/3 hrs 45 mins

RAIL STATION:
Inverness - 2 miles/5 mins

AFFILIATIONS
Independent

RESERVATIONS
National rate in UK: 0870 432 8602
Quote Best Loved

ACCESS CODES
Not applicable

A seasoned traveller's delight just outside of Inverness

Located just three miles from Loch Ness, Dunain Park Hotel was originally a shooting lodge, built in Georgian times by the Duke of Gordon and extended in Victorian times. Edward and Ann Nicoll have owned and run Dunain Park as a hotel for the past 19 years, and during their tenure have upgraded and refurbished it to the highest standard.

The five original bedrooms, all with private facilities, were complemented by a more recent addition of six deluxe king-bedded suites. Open fires in the main lounges help to create a welcoming atmosphere in which guests can relax. The two garden cottages, overlooking the walled garden, are fully serviced and furnished to the same high standard as the main building. Dunain Park's six acres of gardens and woodlands feature an explosion of colour in the form of thousands of bulbs, trees and shrubs, guaranteeing a glorious display during your stay.

Mrs Nicoll is in charge of the kitchen, and produces an à la carte menu that changes daily and uses the best local produce, including treats like salmon, venison and Highland beef. Accompanied by soft fruits, lettuce, vegetables and herbs from the kitchen garden, as well as homemade jams, jellies and chutneys, the meals prove to be innovative and irresistible.

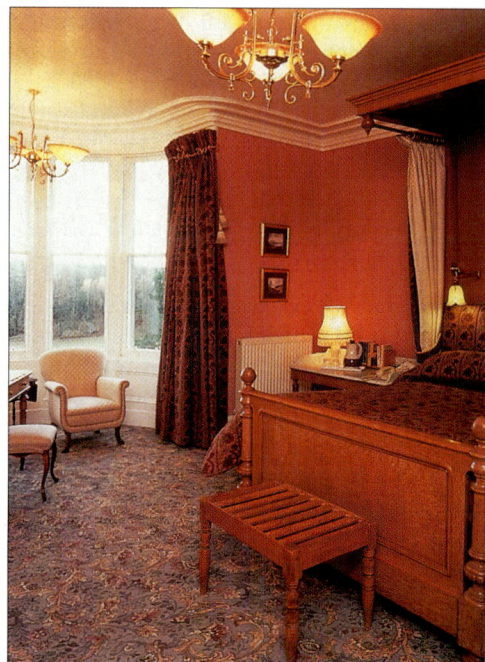

LOCATION
Heading west from Inverness on the A82, the hotel is one mile from the town boundary on the left.

Village hotel

THE DUNALASTAIR HOTEL

A fairytale location in idyllic Highland 'adventureland'

So, you fancy getting away from it all! The Dunalastair Hotel should be your destination, especially if you also fancy the great outdoors. Start the adventure on your journey to Dunalastair. In spite of its remoteness, an overnight Perth-London sleeper train can drop you at Pitlochry, just a taxi ride from the hotel or, from Glasgow, a branch line - is this the last one left? - will take you through breathtaking scenery right to Loch Rannoch on one of Europe's greatest train journeys.

The little village, snuggled beneath mountains at the end of the loch with its burn flowing under the bridge, was surely the inspiration for Brigadoon. Dominating the village square, with its small shops and cottages, is the hotel, where you can be absolutely sure of a tremendous Highland welcome. The Edwards family are wildly enthusiastic about all the Highlands have to offer and will be happy to spirit you away - if you can be persuaded from your spot beside the roaring log fires and a heart-warming selection of whiskies.

If you can resist the call to fishing, hill-walking, orienteering, mountain biking, sailing, whitewater rafting and various extreme sports, you will find a kaleidoscope of delights within this well-run Victorian sporting lodge.

LOCATION

Take the A9 to Pitlochry, then the B8019 via 'Queens View' to Kinloch Rannoch. The hotel is in the village square.

The Square, Kinloch Rannoch, Perthshire PH16 5PW

T (UK) 0870 432 8603
T 01882 632323
F 01882 632371
dunalastair@bestloved.com
www.dunalastair.bestloved.com

MANAGING DIRECTOR
Paul Edwards

ROOM RATES
2 Singles	£40 - £50
15 Doubles/Twins	£75 - £95
5 Superior Doubles/Twins	£85 - £105
4 Four-posters	£95 - £115
2 Deluxe Rooms	£105 - £130

Includes full breakfast and VAT

CREDIT CARDS
AMERICAN EXPRESS • MC • VI

RATINGS & AWARDS
VisitScotland ★★★ Hotel
Walkers Welcome
Cyclists Welcome

FACILITIES
On site: 3 meeting rooms/max 70 people
Nearby: Golf, fishing, riding, shooting, biking, whitewater rafting, off-roading, water sport on Loch Rannoch, walking, quad biking

RESTRICTIONS
Limited facilities for disabled guests
Children by arrangement
Pets by arrangement
Smoking in Whisky Bar only

ATTRACTIONS
Blair Castle, Scone Palace, West Highland Railway tour, House of Bruar, Pitlochry Theatre, outdoor activity centre, distillery tours

NEAREST
CITY:
Perth - 46 miles/1 hr 15 mins

AIRPORT:
Edinburgh - 87 miles/2 hrs
Glasgow - 90 miles/2 hrs

RAIL STATION:
Pitlochry - 18 miles/30 mins
Rannoch - 18 miles/30 mins

AFFILIATIONS
Independent

RESERVATIONS
National rate in UK: 0870 432 8603
Quote Best Loved

ACCESS CODES
AMADEUS HK DNDDUN
APOLLO/GALILEO HT 43977
SABRE/ABACUS HK 22476
WORLDSPAN HK DUNAL

THE EDINBURGH RESIDENCE

Apartments

SCOTLAND

7 Rothesay Terrace,
Edinburgh EH3 7RY

T (UK) 0870 432 8606
T 0131 226 3380
F 0131 226 3381
edinburghres@bestloved.com
www.edinburghres.bestloved.com

MANAGER

Ngaire Abbott

ROOM RATES

9 Classic Suites   £150 - £200
12 Grand Suites   £195 - £265
8 Townhouse Apartments £260 - £395
Includes full breakfast and VAT

CREDIT CARDS

AMERICAN EXPRESS • MC • VI

RATINGS & AWARDS

VisitScotland ★★★★★ Hotel

FACILITIES

On site: 1 meeting room/max 12 people
Nearby: Golf, tennis, fitness centre

RESTRICTIONS

No pets

ATTRACTIONS

Edinburgh Castle,
Edinburgh Festival,
Royal Yacht Britannia,
Holyrood Palace,
National Art Gallery of Scotland,
Scottish Parliament

NEAREST

CITY:
Edinburgh

AIRPORT:
Edinburgh - 10 miles/20 mins

RAIL STATION:
Waverley - 1 mile/5 mins

AFFILIATIONS

Celebrated Hotels Collection

RESERVATIONS

National rate in UK: 0870 432 8606
Toll free in US: 800-322-2403
Quote Best Loved

ACCESS CODES

Not applicable

Your own private apartment in the Georgian centre of Edinburgh

In most cases, when compared to their country counterparts, city hotels lose out when it comes to bedroom sizes - after all, in cities, the emphasis is normally on location first. However, this notion is turned on its head at the Edinburgh Residence.

Well located in Edinburgh's Georgian West End overlooking a leafy crescent, the Residence is a restored mansion and former home of the Lord Advocate of Scotland. Today, it's a collection of huge private suites, each one imaginatively and elegantly furnished. Everything appears oversized, from the armchairs and sofas to the king-sized beds - but even so, the overall effect is warm and welcoming. The suites are perfect for families, with several bedrooms accommodating a total of four people. Each suite has an entertainment centre with large-screen TV, CD player and stereo.

In keeping with the opulence of the suites, the bathrooms appear to have been designed for royalty and include Jacuzzi baths and high-powered showers. The staff here are committed to making your stay enjoyable; you really feel as though you have been lent a luxury flat by a generous friend. Ordinary city hotels are one thing; the Edinburgh Residence is quite another!

LOCATION

Located in the West End, just seven minutes walk' from Edinburgh centre and 20 minutes from the airport by car.

DR & MRS CARRUTHERS, NEW YORK

Country house

ENTERKINE COUNTRY HOUSE

A small and exclusive Ayrshire retreat for business and pleasure

A winding avenue of mature trees leads visitors up to Enterkine House, providing a gentle transition between the hustle and bustle of the real world and the serenity of this secluded country house retreat. The house dates from the 1930s, when it was built as a private residence, and with just six bedroom suites it still maintains an intimate ambience while providing a luxurious degree of comfort and service for individuals and small groups. For even greater privacy, choose from a further four en-suite bedrooms in the newly-opened farmhouse, or two in the cottage.

Enterkine is beautifully positioned in its own 310-acre estate with views over woodland, meadows and the Ayr valley. The attractive guest rooms are very comfortable and particularly spacious. Guests have a choice of three elegant reception rooms, the oval book-lined library for a quiet read and two dining rooms, where first-class cuisine is prepared by the head chef.

This corner of Ayrshire offers plenty of sporting and sightseeing diversions. Both Glasgow and Edinburgh are within easy driving distance, while golfers will find seven Championship courses (including Turnberry, Royal Troon, Western Gailes and Prestwick) no more than 30 minutes away. The hotel can also arrange game shooting and fishing on request.

LOCATION

From the A77, take the B742 (Annbank). The entrance to the estate is on the B742, 50 metres past Annbank.

Annbank, By Ayr,
Ayrshire KA6 5AL

T (UK) 0870 432 8609
T 01292 520580
F 01292 521582
enterkine@bestloved.com
www.enterkine.bestloved.com

GENERAL MANAGER
Louis MacCallum

RATES PER PERSON
6 Suites £45 - £95
Includes full breakfast, dinner and VAT

CREDIT CARDS
AMERICAN EXPRESS • MC • VI

RATINGS & AWARDS
VisitScotland ★★★★★ Small Hotel
RAC Blue Ribbon ★★★
Dining Award 3
AA ★★★ ⊛⊛ 76%

FACILITIES
On site: Garden, croquet,
licensed for weddings, putting green,
clay pigeon shooting
1 meeting room/max 24 people
Nearby: Golf, shooting, fishing, riding

RESTRICTIONS
Limited facilities for disabled guests
Children by arrangement
Pets by arrangement
Smoking in limited areas

ATTRACTIONS
Culzean Castle, Robert Burns Country,
Royal Yacht Britannia Excursions,
The Burrell Collection, Glentrool,
Royal Troon, Turnberry,
Western Gailes and
Prestwick golf courses,
Isle of Arran

NEAREST
CITY:
Glasgow - 38 miles/50 mins

AIRPORT:
Prestwick - 8 miles/12 mins
Glasgow - 42 miles/55 mins

RAIL STATION:
Ayr - 5 miles/10 mins

AFFILIATIONS
Preston's Global Hotels
Grand Heritage Hotels

RESERVATIONS
National rate in UK: 0870 432 8609
Toll free in US 888-93-GRAND
or 800-544-9993
Quote Best Loved

ACCESS CODES
AMADEUS UI PIKKIN
APOLLO/GALILEO UI 37468
SABRE/ABACUS UI 59801
WORLDSPAN UI 42460

> **It is worth beating a path to Flodigarry, which enjoys one of the finest situations of any country house in Scotland**
>
> NEIL MACLEAN, SUNDAY TIMES

FLODIGARRY COUNTRY HOUSE HOTEL   Country house

Staffin, Isle of Skye IV51 9HZ

T (UK) 0870 432 8615
T 01470 552203
F 01470 552301
flodigarry@bestloved.com
www.flodigarry.bestloved.com

OWNER
Robert Cairns

ROOM RATES
Single occupancy	£58 - £99
13 Doubles/Twins	£116 - £120
4 Family Rooms	£116 - £140
2 Four-posters	£116 - £170

Includes full breakfast and VAT

CREDIT CARDS
AMERICAN EXPRESS • MC • VI

RATINGS & AWARDS
VisitScotland ★★★★ Small Hotel
Macallan Country House Hotel of the Year
Talisker Awards for Best Service
and Best Accommodation

FACILITIES
On site: Garden, heli-pad, fishing,
croquet, licensed for weddings,
guided walks, music nights
1 meeting room/max 40 people
Nearby: Yachting, fishing,
water sport, riding

RESTRICTIONS
Limited facilities for disabled guests
Smoking in lounge and bar only

ATTRACTIONS
Dunvegan Castle, Quiraing,
Talisker Distillery, Old Man of Storr,
Trotternish ridge walk,
Skye Museum of Island Life,
boat trips to Outer Hebrides

NEAREST
CITY:
Inverness - 120 miles/3 hrs

AIRPORT:
Glasgow - 250 miles/5 hrs
Inverness - 120 miles/3 hrs

RAIL STATION:
Kyle of Lochalsh - 50 miles/1 hr

FERRY PORT:
Uig - 8 miles/20 mins

AFFILIATIONS
Independent

RESERVATIONS
National rate in UK: 0870 432 8615
Quote Best Loved

ACCESS CODES
Not applicable

A magical visual and culinary experience on the beautiful Isle of Skye

The quintessential escapist's dream, Flodigarry is set amidst one of the most stunningly beautiful and dramatic landscapes in the British Isles. Nestling beneath the towering pinnacles of the Quiraing Mountain in the remote northeast of Skye, the hotel overlooks the magnificent broad sweep of Staffin Bay, one of the most beautiful on the island.

Unspoilt by progress, the area is steeped in history from the Vikings to the more recent Jacobite rising of 1745; the family home of Highland heroine Flora MacDonald stands in the hotel grounds. But Flodigarry is more than just history; the comfortable public rooms and cosy bedrooms all enjoy superb views over the mountains and sea. In addition, there are seven luxury bedrooms in Flora's cottage, all lovingly restored and refurbished.

Winning awards for both fine cuisine and accommodation, Flodigarry prides itself on the warmth of its old-fashioned Highland hospitality, a sense of Victorian ease without stuffiness. Bide a while and soak up the wonderfully timeless atmosphere, the superb panoramic views and the Gaelic charm of this island gem.

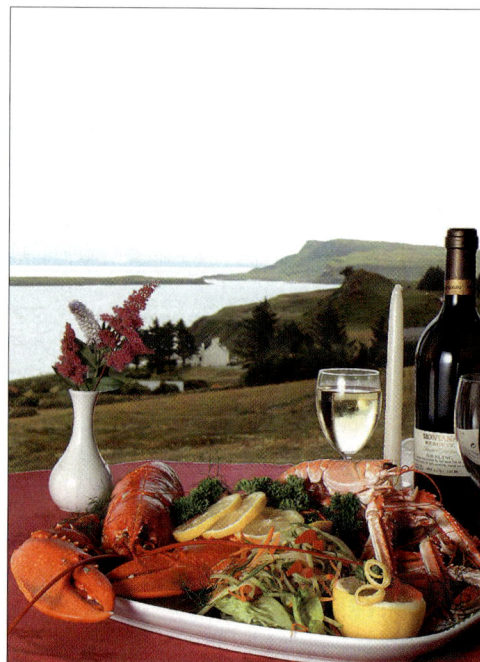

LOCATION
From Portree, take the A855 north 20 miles to Staffin. The hotel is four miles further north on the right.

"I always thought that Scotland held way too many beautiful places to discover to ever need to revisit the same place - until the Four Seasons"

AILEAN GRAHAM, ABERDEEN

Country house

THE FOUR SEASONS HOTEL

St Fillans, Perthshire PH6 2NF

T (UK) 0870 432 8617
T 01764 685333
F 01764 685444
fourseasons@bestloved.com
www.fourseasons.bestloved.com

OWNER
Andrew Low

MANAGER
Mary McDiarmid

ROOM RATES
Single occupancy   £44 - £88
12 Doubles/Twins   £82 - £106
Includes full breakfast and VAT

CREDIT CARDS
MC • VI

RATINGS & AWARDS
VisitScotland ★★★ Small Hotel
RAC ★★★ Dining Award 3
AA ★★★ ⊛⊛ 68%

FACILITIES
On site: Garden, fishing
3 meeting rooms/max 140 people
Nearby: Golf, fishing, riding, shooting,
mountain biking, water sport

RESTRICTIONS
Limited facilities for disabled guests
Smoking in some rooms only
Closed 3 Jan. - 3 March

ATTRACTIONS
Edinburgh, Scone Palace,
Devil's Cauldron, Rob Roy's Grave,
Mull & Iona, Loch Tay Crannog

NEAREST
CITY:
Perth/Stirling - 30 miles/45 mins

AIRPORT:
Edinburgh - 60 miles/1 hr 15 mins

RAIL STATION:
Perth/Stirling - 30 miles/45 mins

AFFILIATIONS
Independent

RESERVATIONS
National rate in UK: 0870 432 8617
Quote Best Loved

ACCESS CODES
Not applicable

An inspiring lochside setting with spectacular views and food to match

Set against a steep, forested backdrop on the shores of Loch Earn, the Four Seasons occupies one of the most enviably picturesque locations in the whole of Scotland, accompanied by a varied history: The main house was built in the early 1800s for the manager of the local limekilns, and later, it served a term as a schoolmaster's house before being gradually extended into a small and comfortable hotel.

The view from the Four Seasons stretches southwest down the loch and can honestly be described as magnificent. Spectacular sunsets, mist-wreathed mornings and the snow-covered Bens exercise a mesmeric fascination.

Perhaps one of the best places to watch the ever-changing scenery is from one of the hotel's two restaurants. Both offer the temptations you dream of: Orkney scallops, Loch Fyne mussels, Tweed Valley partridge, East Coast halibut and Border lamb. Nearby, there are all sorts of day trips to choose from, including the steam train to Mallaig on the West Coast, a visit to Scotland's smallest whisky distillery, a day's fishing and sailing or, for hill walkers, a Munro or two.

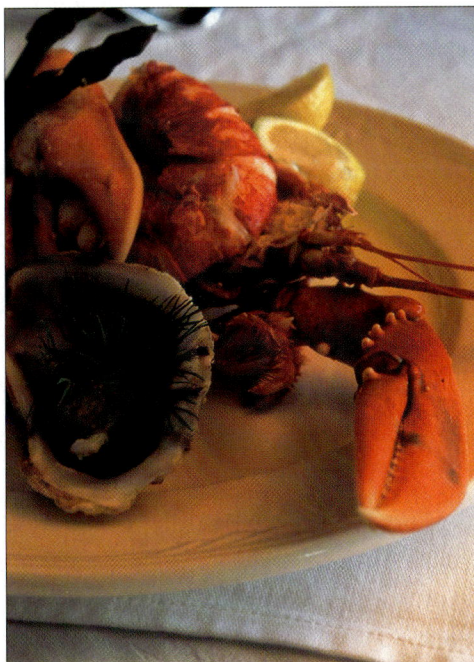

LOCATION

On the northeast edge of Loch Earn on the A85 Comrie to Lochearnhead road.

The food and wine were first-class, and we left feeling absolutely spoilt rotten

MR & MRS IAIN STODDART, DUNFERMLINE

GARVOCK HOUSE HOTEL

Country house

SCOTLAND

St John's Drive, Transy,
Dunfermline, Fife KY12 7TU

T (UK) 0870 432 8622
T 01383 621067
F 01383 621168
garvock@bestloved.com
www.garvock.bestloved.com

OWNERS
Rui and Pamela Fernandes

ROOM RATES
Single occupancy   £75
12 Doubles/Twins   £95 - £120
Includes full breakfast and VAT

CREDIT CARDS
MC • VI

RATINGS & AWARDS
VisitScotland ★★★★ Small Hotel
AA ★★★ 75%
Investors in People

FACILITIES
On site: Garden,
licensed for weddings
4 meeting rooms/max 150 people
Nearby: Golf, fishing, go-karting,
rally driving, sports centre,
health & beauty

RESTRICTIONS
Limited facilities for disabled guests
Smoking in lounges and bar only
Pets by arrangement

ATTRACTIONS
Dunfermline Abbey, Abbott House,
Dunfermline Palace and Monastery,
Andrew Carnegie Birthplace Museum,
St Margaret's Cave, Edinburgh,
Stirling, St Andrews

NEAREST
CITY:
Edinburgh - 18 miles/25 mins
Perth - 28 miles/30 mins

AIRPORT:
Edinburgh - 15 miles/20 mins
Glasgow - 48 miles/1 hr

RAIL STATION:
Dunfermline - ½ mile/5 mins

AFFILIATIONS
Independent

RESERVATIONS
National rate in UK: 0870 432 8622
Quote Best Loved

ACCESS CODES
Not applicable

A peaceful family-run Georgian house in the ancient capital of Scotland

Dunfermline was the capital of Scotland until 1603, and the abbey and palace ruins still lie at its heart bordering Pittencrieff Park. In 1902, this huge open space was bought by Andrew Carnegie, 'the richest man in the world', and gifted to his hometown. Set in its own grounds just a few minutes from Dunfermline's historic town centre, Garvock House was a private residence until 1996, when the handsome Georgian home was sympathetically transformed into one of West Fife's leading small hotels.

Twelve attractive and thoughtfully-equipped bedrooms await in a modern annex; upon arrival, warm scones and coffee are served in the lounge while luggage is whisked away to your room. Take time to relax, take in the fresh cut flowers and note the beautiful old oak floor that was serendipitously discovered during the renovations.

When it comes time to dine, the restaurant enjoys an excellent reputation and guests are encouraged to discuss their preferences with the chef. Dinner-menu temptations might include pan-fried wild trout with smoked salmon risotto or honey- and ginger-glazed duck breast with spiced cous cous. Garvock House also caters for a wide variety of private and corporate events in its impressive function rooms.

LOCATION
Exit 3 on the M90 for Dunfermline town centre. Turn left at the mini-roundabout onto Garvock Hill, then right onto St John's drive; the hotel is 500 metres on the right.

> "Fabulous - stunning attention to detail and most comfortable bed ever! I will be back"
>
> GARY SCHUMAN, WASHINGTON USA

Map p. 440, grid G10

City hotel

THE GLASSHOUSE

SCOTLAND

A cutting-edge window on the world in central Edinburgh

Sophisticated, luxurious and architecturally striking, The Glasshouse is an exciting new addition to the Edinburgh hotel scene. The hotel is superbly located at the foot of Calton Hill in an eye-catching development right at the heart of the historic Scottish capital just a few steps from Princes Street and Edinburgh Castle.

From the main entrance, which juxtaposes the 150-year-old facade of Lady of Glenorchy Church with a contemporary six-storey glass edifice, to the calm haven of the rooftop garden, The Glasshouse is a masterclass in stylish contemporary design. The glass theme has been enthusiastically embraced in the bedrooms and suites, which are all on the top two floors of the building to maximise the views over the city. There are floor-to-ceiling windows, and many rooms feature a terrace or patio overlooking the roof garden. Stunning glass bathrooms and an overall sensation of space and light combine with furnishings in rich, spicy tones complete the look.

The hotel also offers state-of-the-art meeting rooms and smaller purpose-built syndicate rooms for business travellers. And there's one final surprise - amongst the sleek and the chic, guests can enjoy a couple of welcome home-from-home touches such as an honesty bar and seriously good homemade breakfasts.

LOCATION

Located on Greenside Place a few yards from Princes Street and within easy reach of Edinburgh Castle.

2 Greenside Place,
Edinburgh EH1 3AA

T (UK) 0870 432 8624
T 0131 525 8200
F 0131 525 8205
glasshouse@bestloved.com
www.glasshouse.bestloved.com

GENERAL MANAGER
Daniel Pereira

ROOM RATES
40 Deluxe Doubles/Twins	£195
7 Executive doubles	£215
16 Suites	£295
2 Deluxe suites	£375
Includes VAT	

CREDIT CARDS
AMERICAN EXPRESS • DC • JCB • MC • VI

RATINGS & AWARDS
Awards Pending

FACILITIES
On site: Garden
3 meeting rooms/ max 36 people
Nearby: Health & beauty,
leisure centre

RESTRICTIONS
No pets

ATTRACTIONS
Edinburgh Castle,
Edinburgh Playhouse,
National Portrait Gallery,
Carlton Hill,
The Observatory,
Princes Street

NEAREST
CITY:
Edinburgh

AIRPORT:
Edinburgh - 8 miles/15 mins

RAIL STATION:
Edinburgh - 6 miles/5 mins

AFFILIATIONS
The Eton Group
Celebrated Hotels Collection

RESERVATIONS
National rate in UK: 0870 432 8624
Toll free in US: 800-322-2403
Quote Best Loved

ACCESS CODES
AMADEUS XL EDIGE
APOLLO/GALILEO XL 55179
SABRE/ABACUS XL 50465
WORLDSPAN XL EDIGE

Absolutely dreadful! How do we go to any other hotel after this? To sample perfection is a curse - we will never be satisfied again

D & R, GLASGOW

GLENAPP CASTLE

Country house

SCOTLAND

Ballantrae, Ayrshire KA26 0NZ

T (UK) 0870 432 8626
T 01465 831212
F 01465 831000
glenapp@bestloved.com
www.glenapp.bestloved.com

OWNERS
Graham and Fay Cowan

ROOM RATES
13 Luxury Doubles/Twins £385
2 Luxury Suites £445
2 Master Rooms £515
Includes dinner, breakfast and VAT

CREDIT CARDS
AMERICAN EXPRESS • MC • VI

RATINGS & AWARDS
VisitScotland ★★★★★ Hotel
AA ★★★ ✿✿✿
AA Top 200 - 2004/2005
Andrew Harper's Recommended Hotels

FACILITIES
On site: Garden, heli-pad, croquet, tennis, falconry
3 meeting rooms/max 34 people
Nearby: Shooting, fishing, curling, walking, boat trips, golf

RESTRICTIONS
No children under 6 years in restaurant
Smoking in library only
Pets in some bedrooms only
No pets in public areas
Closed November - March
(except for exclusive use)

ATTRACTIONS
Culzean Castle & Country Park,
Logan Botanical Gardens,
Galloway Forest Park,
Ayrshire - Robert Burns country,
Castle Kennedy Gardens,
Mull of Galloway

NEAREST
CITY:
Glasgow - 70 miles/1 hr 30 mins

AIRPORT:
Glasgow Prestwick - 35 miles/50 mins

RAIL STATION:
Girvan - 13 miles/15 mins
Stranraer - 17 miles/20 mins

AFFILIATIONS
Celebrated Hotels Collection
Relais & Châteaux

RESERVATIONS
National rate in UK: 0870 432 8626
Toll Free in US: 800-322-2403
or 800-735-2478
Quote Best Loved

ACCESS CODES
AMADEUS WB GLAB26
APOLLO/GALILEO WB 41722
SABRE/ABACUS WB 05587
WORLDSPAN WB GB26

A magical experience in a fairytale Scottish castle

High above the village of Ballantrae looking out over the Irish Sea towards Ailsa Craig and the Mull of Kintyre, Glenapp Castle is indeed a magical sight. The ancestral seat of the Earls of Inchcape is now the home of the Cowan family, opened as a luxury hotel in April 2000. In order to preserve the peaceful ambience of a traditional country house, Glenapp Castle is open only to guests who have made an advance reservation. On arrival, you will find everything you could possibly wish for, including splendid three-AA-rosette meals prepared by head chef Tristan Welch and a comprehensive list of fine wines and spirits.

The interior of this spectacular Scottish baronial castle has been totally preserved, including the magnificent Austrian oak-panelled entrance hall and staircase. The bedrooms and suites are spacious, elegant and furnished with antiques and original oil paintings to provide an ambience of traditional luxury. The 30 acres of delightful gardens and woodland that surround the castle abound with specimen rhododendrons and many rare and unusual shrubs and trees. The showpiece walled garden boasts a 150-foot Victorian glasshouse.

The Cowans' intention was to create something unique at Glenapp. They have truly succeeded!

LOCATION
Fifteen miles north of Stranraer and 35 miles south of Ayr and Prestwick airport on the A77, near the village of Ballantrae.

> "Thank you for looking after me so very well during my stay. The ambience, hospitality and cooking were such that it will take little persuasion to come back"
>
> DEREK REID, FORMER CHAIRMAN, SCOTTISH TOURIST BOARD

Country house — GLENMORANGIE HIGHLAND HOME

SCOTLAND

Cadboll, Fearn, By Tain,
Ross-shire IV20 1XP

T (UK) 0870 432 8627
T 01862 871671
F 01862 871625
glenmorangie@bestloved.com
www.glenmorangie.bestloved.com

MANAGER
Helen McKenzie Smith

ROOM RATES
3 Cottage Rooms   £140
4 Doubles/Twins   £145
2 Master Doubles/Twins £185
Includes full breakfast and VAT

CREDIT CARDS
AMERICAN EXPRESS • JCB • MC • VI

RATINGS & AWARDS
VisitScotland ★★★★★ Small Hotel
AA ★★ ⊛⊛
AA Top 200 - 2004/2005

FACILITIES
On site: Garden, heli-pad, croquet,
falcon and clay pigeon shooting,
archery, husky racing
1 meeting room/max 12 people
Nearby: Golf, fishing, tennis,
fitness centre, hunting, riding

RESTRICTIONS
Limited facilities for disabled guests
No children under 12 years
No smoking in bedrooms
Pets by arrangement
Closed 4-23 Jan.

ATTRACTIONS
Glenmorangie and
Glen Moray distilleries,
Urquhart and Dunrobin castles,
Loch Ness, dolphin watching,
beaches and coastal walks,
Tain and Dornoch golf courses,
Harrods at the Falls of Shin

NEAREST
CITY:
Inverness - 43 miles/45 mins

AIRPORT:
Inverness - 43 miles/45 mins
Edinburgh - 180 miles/3 hrs 30 mins

RAIL STATION:
Tain - 6 miles/10 mins

AFFILIATIONS
Pride of Britain

RESERVATIONS
National rate in UK: 0870 432 8627
Toll free in the US: 800-98-PRIDE
Quote Best Loved

ACCESS CODES
Not applicable

Let a famed distillery's 'Home in the Highlands' be your home!

If Scotland is famous for anything, it has to be whisky - and, for connoisseurs, the single malt varieties. Enthusiasts will already know that situated in Easter Ross, amongst the driest regions in the UK, is the famed Glenmorangie Distillery; what they may not know is that sixteen years ago, Glenmorangie made a corporate decision to convert a nearby 16th-century estate into a 'Home in the Highlands' for their best corporate clients and customers. The result was Glenmorangie Highland Home. In 1998, the policy of accepting guests was extended to the public.

What can you expect at this superb place to stay? Gorgeous panoramic views of the sea, log fires in the Morning Room and cosy Buffalo Room, a profusion of fresh flowers and memorabilia throughout. Sleeping arrangements are exceedingly comfortable and show no hint of pretension, whether in the main house or one of several cottages. Topping off your visit is the food. The kitchen at Glenmorangie Highland Home makes the best use of the freshest salmon, homegrown vegetables and herbs and local lamb and beef, creating classically-influenced modern cuisine that is both homely and delicious. With all this to offer, we're certain you'll be ready to toast your good fortune with a wee dram at Glenmorangie Highland Home.

LOCATION

From Inverness, take the A9, then the B9175 toward Nigg. After two miles, turn left toward Hilton. The hotel is five miles on the right, signposted.

GLENMORISTON ARMS HOTEL

Inn

SCOTLAND

Invermoriston, Near Loch Ness,
Inverness-shire IV63 7YA

T (UK) 0870 432 8628
T 01320 351206
F 01320 351308
glenmoriston@bestloved.com
www.glenmoriston.bestloved.com

OWNERS
Nik and Hazel Hammond

ROOM RATES
Single occupancy   £50 - £70
7 Doubles/Twins   £70 - £110
1 Four-poster   £90 - £130
Includes full breakfast and VAT

CREDIT CARDS
JCB • MC • VI

RATINGS & AWARDS
AA ★★ ✿✿ 77%

FACILITIES
On site: Garden, fishing, Jacuzzi, Bistro
1 meeting room/max 24 people
Nearby: Fishing, stalking, riding, golf,
boat trips, walking

RESTRICTIONS
No facilities for disabled guests
No smoking in bedrooms
No pets; guide dogs only
Closed January - February

ATTRACTIONS
Loch Ness, Isle of Skye, Ben Nevis,
Inner and Outer Hebrides,
Aonach Mor Ski Centre,
Culloden Moor Battlefield,
Urquhart and Eilean Donan castles,
Great Glen Way

NEAREST
CITY:
Inverness - 26 miles/35 mins

AIRPORT:
Inverness - 26 miles/35 mins

RAIL STATION:
Inverness - 26 miles/35 mins

AFFILIATIONS
Preston's Global Hotels

RESERVATIONS
National rate in UK: 0870 432 8628
Toll free in US: 800-544-9993
Quote Best Loved

ACCESS CODES
Not applicable

Character, comfort and creative cuisine just a short stroll from Loch Ness

Glenmoriston Arms Hotel lies close to Loch Ness at the foot of one of the most beautiful Highland glens. Every turn of the road brings fresh views of mystical mountains and lochs and ancient Caledonian forests - scenery that is literally breathtaking. Located in the very heart of Highland history, day trips from the hotel include the enchanting Isle of Skye, where you can visit Dunvegan Castle and the Clan Donald Centre. You can also follow the route of Bonnie Prince Charlie by visiting the Battlefield at Culloden, where, after his defeat, he escaped to Skye, passing through Glenmoriston en route.

When it comes to Glenmoriston Arms itself, well, it's a treat; '"small is beautiful" is certainly an appropriate way to describe this delightful hotel', according to one AA inspector. The atmosphere is a unique blend of warmth, elegance and informality, and with just eight bedrooms, each guest is welcomed as an individual. The feeling carries over to the hotel's restaurant, which was deemed recently by one guest as 'one of the most superb culinary experiences in Scotland'.

This is one of the last unspoilt regions of Europe, where fresh air is just one of many great simple pleasures and a wealth of surprises await - and one of the best is Glenmoriston Arms.

LOCATION
Off the A82, six miles north of Fort Augustus and 12 miles south of Drumnadrochit.

> **"** Long live Greywalls, so dear in our hearts **"**
>
> EDOUARD VAN VYVE, ANTWERP

Country house

GREYWALLS

Follow in the footsteps of Nicklaus, Faldo, Edward VII and King Hussein

Sir Edwin Lutyens, architect of the British Embassy in Washington and the Cenotaph in Whitehall, designed Greywalls in 1901. King Edward VII stayed here - you can write your postcards in the panelled library he loved - and King Hussein of Jordan was a more recent visitor.

Greywalls is also next to Muirfield golf course, and past guests including Arnold Palmer, Jack Nicklaus, Lee Trevino, Greg Norman and Nick Faldo are all part of the hotel's story.

Despite this lineage, however, the hotel still feels like a family home. The warmth of hospitality from Giles and Ros Weaver today makes guests feel like honoured family friends. There are 23 comfortable, cosy bedrooms, each with its own bathroom; many are furnished with antiques. In the public areas, revel in a Steinway grand piano, a sunny Edwardian tea room and a small bar with a fine stock of whiskies. When it's time to dine, the very best of local produce is used to create outstanding meals, from hearty breakfasts to fulsome dinners!

Outside, take time to explore the gardens that Lutyens himself helped to plan. There's much to do, too, only slightly further afield; within eight miles are 10 golf courses, long sandy beaches, nature reserves renowned for bird life and ancient ruined castles.

LOCATION

Link from the M8, M9 or M90 motorways to the A198 via the A720 Edinburgh city bypass.

Muirfield, Gullane,
East Lothian EH31 2EG

T (UK) 0870 432 8637
T 01620 842144
F 01620 842241
greywalls@bestloved.com
www.greywalls.bestloved.com

OWNERS
Giles and Ros Weaver

MANAGER
Sue Prime

ROOM RATES
4 Singles   £130 - £250
19 Doubles/Twins   £230 - £270
Includes full breakfast and VAT

CREDIT CARDS
AMERICAN EXPRESS • DC • MC • VI

RATINGS & AWARDS
VisitScotland ★★★★ Hotel
AA ★★★ ⊛⊛
AA Top 200 - 2004/2005

FACILITIES
On site: Garden, croquet, tennis, putting green
1 meeting room/max 50 people
Nearby: Golf, shooting, fishing, walking, beaches

RESTRICTIONS
Limited facilities for disabled guests
No smoking in dining room
No pets in public areas
Closed mid-October - mid-April

ATTRACTIONS
Tantallon Castle, Dirleton Castle,
Edinburgh and Edinburgh Castle,
Holyrood House,
Muirfield Golf Course

NEAREST
CITY:
Edinburgh - 18 miles/35 mins

AIRPORT:
Edinburgh - 25 miles/40 mins

RAIL STATION:
Drem - 2 miles/5 mins

AFFILIATIONS
Independent

RESERVATIONS
National rate in UK: 0870 432 8637
Quote Best Loved

ACCESS CODES
Not applicable

SCOTLAND

> **Still a great pleasure to stay at the best hotel in Skye - lovely welcome, gorgeous food and homely atmosphere**
>
> LADY CHRISTIAN INNES, ROSS-SHIRE

HOTEL EILEAN IARMAIN

Country house

Isle Ornsay, Sleat,
Isle of Skye IV43 8QR

T (UK) 0870 432 8652
T 01471 833332
F 01471 833275
eilean@bestloved.com
www.eilean.bestloved.com

OWNERS
Sir Iain and Lady Noble

ROOM RATES
Single occupancy   £90
9 Doubles/Twins   £120
1 Four-poster   £150
2 Triples   £160
4 Suites   £180 - £250
Includes full breakfast and VAT

CREDIT CARDS
AMERICAN EXPRESS • DC • MC • VI

RATINGS & AWARDS
VisitScotland ★★★ Small Hotel
RAC ★★ Dining Award 1
AA ★★ ✿✿ 74%
Joint winner, Les Routiers
Best Hotel of the Year 2001

FACILITIES
On site: Garden, heli-pad, fishing, shooting, stalking
2 meeting rooms/max 50 people
Nearby: Golf, riding, pool

RESTRICTIONS
Limited facilities for disabled guests
No smoking in bedrooms
Pets by arrangement

ATTRACTIONS
Armadale Castle & Gardens,
Dunvegan Castle,
Aros Heritage Centre,
Talisker Distillery,
Hotel Eilean Iarmain Art Gallery,
'Bella Jane' boat trips,
Serpentarian Reptile Centre

NEAREST
CITY:
Glasgow - 148 miles/4 hrs

AIRPORT:
Inverness - 93 miles/2 hrs

RAIL STATION:
Kyle of Lochalsh - 14 miles/30 mins

FERRY PORT:
Mallaig/Armadale - 8 miles/15 mins

AFFILIATIONS
Independent

RESERVATIONS
National rate in UK: 0870 432 8652
Quote Best Loved

ACCESS CODES
Not applicable

An enchanting atmosphere reflecting the legends and romance of Skye

   Built in 1888, this small, privately-owned hotel is situated on the small rocky bay of Isle Ornsay in the south of Skye, with expansive views over the Sound of Sleat to the Knoydart hills.

   This lovely house has certainly retained its Victorian charm and old-world character; the 16 bedrooms are decorated and furnished in traditional style and include four new suites housed in the restored stables, one of which is especially suitable for disabled guests. Each bedroom has its own charm, including the Tower Room, panelled in old pine, and the Leabaidh Mhor, with a canopied bed from nearby Armadale Castle. There are log fires in the reception rooms, and a panelled dining room where candlelit dinners can be enjoyed overlooking the bay.

   The dinner menu, a real temptation at five courses, combines imaginative cooking with a variety of fresh local produce, including fish and shellfish landed at the old stone pier, oysters and game from the estate and home-baked bread and oatcakes. The extensive wine list has been selected by the proprietors with the aim of offering some unusual wines with fascinating historical provenances as well as a very good range of more famous choices. And there's no need to rush to enjoy this relaxed hospitality; Hotel Eilean Iarmain is open year-round.

LOCATION
Approximately 20 minutes from Skye Bridge, 20 minutes from Kyle of Lochalsh rail station and 30 minutes from Kylerea ferry.

> **"** Absolutely fantastic in every way - many, many thanks **"**
>
> LADY CLARE MACDONALD, ISLE OF SKYE

City hotel

THE HOWARD

SCOTLAND

34 Great King Street,
Edinburgh EH3 6QH

T (UK) 0870 432 8657
T 0131 623 9303
F 0131 623 9306
howard@bestloved.com
www.howard.bestloved.com

OWNER
Peter Taylor

MANAGER
Johanne Falconer

ROOM RATES
2 Singles	£108 - £210
11 Doubles/Twins	£180 - £295
5 Suites	£243 - £47

Includes full breakfast and VAT

CREDIT CARDS
AMERICAN EXPRESS • DC • MC • VI

RATINGS & AWARDS
VisitScotland ★★★★★ Small Hotel
AA ★★★★ Town House
AA Top 200 - 2004/2005

FACILITIES
On site: Guests' dining room, car park
2 meeting rooms/max 18 people
Nearby: Golf, swimming pool,
cycling & jogging route

RESTRICTIONS
Limited facilities for disabled guests
Smoking in drawing rooms only
No pets; guide dogs only

ATTRACTIONS
Edinburgh Castle, Holyrood House,
National Gallery,
Edinburgh Festival & Military Tattoo,
Old Town and New Town,
Dynamic Earth, Royal Yacht Britannia

NEAREST
CITY:
Edinburgh

AIRPORT:
Edinburgh - 8 miles/15 mins

RAIL STATION:
Waverley - 1 mile/2 mins

AFFILIATIONS
Celebrated Hotels Collection
Small Luxury Hotels
The Small Hotel Company

RESERVATIONS
National rate in UK: 0870 432 8657
Toll free in US: 800-322-2403
or 800-525-4800
Quote Best Loved

ACCESS CODES
AMADEUS LX EDIHWO
APOLLO/GALILEO LX 96963
SABRE/ABACUS LX 8591
WORLDSPAN LX HOWAE

A place where elegance and discretion are watchwords

It has to be said that there is something distinctively different about The Howard. The first impression is that it's reminiscent of the townhouse residences of the late 1800s - ultimately elegant and unobtrusive. This is evident from the most discreet of check-ins to the dedicated butler service (upon arrival, bags are unpacked and tea is served in the Drawing Room) and the Floris toiletries in the bathroom.

However, it is important to note that there is nothing old-fashioned about The Howard, and it is the result of considerable skill that the hotel retains this genuine traditional air whilst providing guests with the most up-to-the-minute facilities. All rooms are fully equipped with every modern convenience, including international modem points, television, DVD, Internet access, a hi-fi system and games. Some rooms feature freestanding roll-top bathtubs, Jacuzzis or power showers.

The Howard's dining room, The Atholl, provides an unsurpassed five-star dining experience in lovely Georgian surroundings, but dinner can also be served in your room if you wish. The hotel has two private rooms ideal for holding small, high-level corporate events - in all, a truly spectacular pied á terre.

LOCATION
Travelling west along Queen Street, turn right into Queen Street Gardens East. Great King Street is the third on the right.

THE INN AT ARDGOUR

Inn

SCOTLAND

Ardgour, Fort William,
Inverness-shire PH33 7AA

T (UK) 0870 432 8660
T 01855 841225
F 01855 841214
ardgour@bestloved.com
www.ardgour.bestloved.com

OWNERS
The Alexander Family

ROOM RATES
8 Doubles/Twins   £60 - £100
2 Family rooms   £80 - £120
Includes full breakfast and VAT

CREDIT CARDS
JCB • MC • VI

RATINGS & AWARDS
VisitScotland ★★★ Small Hotel

FACILITIES
On site: Drying room, cycle storage
Nearby: Golf, fishing, water skiing, climbing, sailing

RESTRICTIONS
Limited facilities for disabled guests
No smoking in bedrooms or restaurant
Pets by arrangement

ATTRACTIONS
Ben Nevis, Glencoe, Sea Life Centre, Glenfinnan, Isle of Skye, Isle of Mull, Castle Tioram, cycle tours

NEAREST
CITY:
Glasgow - 95 miles/2 hrs 30 mins

AIRPORT:
Glasgow - 80 miles/2 hrs

RAIL STATION:
Fort William - 8 miles/15 mins

AFFILIATIONS
Independent

RESERVATIONS
National rate in UK: 0870 432 8660
Quote Best Loved

ACCESS CODES
Not applicable

This highest-rated Highland inn is bursting with personality

This welcoming old Highland hostelry lies at the mouth of the Great Glen on the shores of Loch Linnhe near Fort William. The oldest part of the inn, now the But 'n Ben restaurant, began life as cottages for the Corran ferrymen after Hanoverian troopers burned their homes to the ground after the 1746 rebellion. Today, every one of the cosy bedrooms is at the front of the inn to catch the spectacular mountain-framed view of the loch. In the foreground the ferry plies back and forth across the loch as it has done for many hundreds of years; after all, this is the original 'Road to the Isles'!

This is also the beginning of the Caledonian Canal, so many visiting yachts and fishing boats and even Scotland's last working paddle steamer, Waverley, can be spied. When you can finally bear to tear yourself away from this captivating view, the Western Highlands offer outdoor diversions from hiking and wildlife watching (otters, seals, golden eagle, red deer and wild goats) to day trips to the Hebridean islands of Mull, Iona and Skye. For duller days, the inn has a great selection of books in the library bar, where the craich (chat) is good and the whiskies plentiful.

LOCATION
From the A82 Onich to Fort William road, take the ferry (four minutes) across to Ardgour from Corran.

Restaurant with rooms

INN AT LATHONES

By Largoward, St Andrews,
Fife KY9 IJE

T (UK) 0870 432 8661
T 01334 840494
F 01334 840694
lathones@bestloved.com
www.lathones.bestloved.com

OWNERS
Nick and Jocelyn White

ROOM RATES
1 Single	£100
11 Doubles/Twins	£140
2 Master Rooms	£200

Includes full breakfast and VAT

CREDIT CARDS
AMERICAN EXPRESS • DC • MC • VI

RATINGS & AWARDS
VisitScotland ★★★★ Inn
AA ❀❀ 75% Restaurant with Rooms
Investors in People
Scotch Beef Club

FACILITIES
On site: Patio, outdoor play area
1 meeting room/max 60 people
Nearby: Golf, fishing, water skiing,
yachting, tennis, fitness centre, riding,
clay pigeon shooting

RESTRICTIONS
Smoking in lounge only
Pets by arrangement
Closed 3 - 17 January

ATTRACTIONS
Kellie Castle, Isle of May,
St Andrews Cathedral,
18-hole golf courses,
Sea-Life Centre, Secret Bunker,
Royal and Ancient Golf Museum

NEAREST
CITY:
St Andrews - 5 miles/10 mins

AIRPORT:
Edinburgh - 50 miles/1 hr 30 mins
Dundee - 10 miles/20 mins

RAIL STATION:
Leuchars - 7 miles/15 mins

AFFILIATIONS
Preston's Global Hotels
Grand Heritage Hotels

RESERVATIONS
National rate in UK: 0870 432 8661
Toll free in US: 800-544-9993
or 888-93-GRAND
Quote Best Loved

ACCESS CODES
AMADEUS UI ADXINN
APOLLO/GALILEO UI 27836
SABRE/ABACUS UI 52266
WORLDSPAN UI 41354

A first choice for gourmet and golfer alike

Fine food, great golf - and maybe even the odd ghost - all await visitors to the historic coaching Inn at Lathones. Situated just five miles from St Andrews and in the heart of Fife, home to more than 40 top-quality golf courses, this 400-year-old hotel is the ideal location for anyone who enjoys a round. Staff will be happy to arrange tee times, tuition and practice sessions, whatever your handicap, at the course that most suits you.

Easy access to first-class sporting facilities is matched by the Inn's highly regarded restaurant: Proprietors Nick and Jocelyn White and head chef Marc Guibert have always made it their business to hand-source all their local suppliers, from fishermen to organic farmers. The result is a regionally focused yet diverse menu that has earned the unique accolade of being the only four-star inn listed by the Scottish Tourist Board. Patrons have long enjoyed atmospheric hospitality at Lathones - and some, like The Grey Lady, have even been said to return from beyond the grave! The deluxe room named after her, as is typical of the hotel's high standards, boasts its own log fire, power shower and corner bath.

LOCATION
Five miles south of St Andrews on the A915, the main road between St Andrews and Leven.

INVERLOCHY CASTLE

Castle

SCOTLAND

Torlundy, Fort William, Inverness-shire PH33 6SN

T (UK) 0870 432 8664
T 01397 702177
F 01397 702953
inverlochy@bestloved.com
www.inverlochy.bestloved.com

GENERAL MANAGER
Norbert Lieder

ROOM RATES
14 Doubles/Twins   £290 - £395
3 Suites   £440 - £550
Includes VAT

CREDIT CARDS
AMERICAN EXPRESS • MC • VI

RATINGS & AWARDS
VisitScotland ★★★★★ Hotel
RAC Gold Ribbon ★★★★
Dining Award 4
AA ★★★★ ❀❀❀
AA Top 200 - 2004/2005

FACILITIES
On site: Garden, snooker, heli-pad, fishing, croquet
1 meeting room/max 25 people
Nearby: Golf, fishing, skiing, riding, stalking, guided hill walking, yachting, shooting, biking

RESTRICTIONS
No facilities for disabled guests
Smoking in Great Hall and drawing room only
Closed 4 Jan. - 3 Feb.

ATTRACTIONS
Glencoe, Glenfinnan, Culloden, Isle of Skye, Blair Castle

NEAREST
CITY:
Glasgow - 100 miles/2 hrs

AIRPORT:
Glasgow - 100 miles/2 hrs
Inverness - 70 miles/1 hr 30 mins

RAIL STATION:
Fort William - 4 miles/15 mins

AFFILIATIONS
Celebrated Hotels Collection
Connoisseurs Scotland
Relais & Châteaux

RESERVATIONS
National rate in UK: 0870 432 8664
Toll free in US: 800-322-2403
or 888-424-0106
Quote Best Loved

ACCESS CODES
AMADEUS WB FWMINV
APOLLO/GALILEO WB 14748
SABRE/ABACUS WB 40329
WORLDSPAN WB GB22

Peerless scenery and tasty food at this haunt of the rich and famous

The present-day Inverlochy Castle was built by the first Lord Abinger in 1863 near the site of the original 13th-century fortress. This remarkable building is set against some of the most magnificent scenery in the Western Highlands, and stands amongst the foothills of Ben Nevis in its own 500-acre estate surrounded by landscaped gardens and rhododendrons.

Inside, the baronial Great Hall has beautiful frescoed ceilings with crystal chandeliers and a handsome staircase. Fine decorations throughout befit the Victorian proportions of the rooms, lovingly renovated to include 17 individual suites and bedrooms with private bathrooms and all-modern facilities. In the dining room, there's an elaborate carved breakfont sideboard presented as a gift to Inverlochy by the King of Norway; on the table, the menu features a daily-changing menu of international cuisine with an emphasis on fresh Scottish produce.

Loch fishing and many beautiful walking paths are within the grounds. Highland scenic attractions and sport and leisure activities are situated within a short drive. Such is the reputation of Inverlochy that it is advisable to book well in advance!

LOCATION
From Fort William, take the A82 north for four miles; pass Fort William Golf Club, take the next left to Inverlochy and watch for the hotel's sign.

> **It was a great pleasure to stay in the Isle of Barra Hotel and enjoy the comfort and cuisine and the courtesy and friendliness of all of the staff**
>
> ALEX AND JOHN, CHESHIRE

Map p. 440, grid A7

Island hotel

ISLE OF BARRA HOTEL

SCOTLAND

The place to experience the natural beauty of the Western Isles

On sunny days, summer or winter, when the sky is a perfect cloudless blue, Barra's sandy shore dazzles bright white against the clear turquoise water. Minutes later, the scene could dramatically turn to great swells and sulking skies. A little poetical, perhaps, but the point is made that this is a place to witness natural beauty against the ever-changing elements.

The Isle of Barra Hotel, run by the Worthington family, has been designed with the great outdoors in mind, and the spacious public rooms have large picture windows to maximise the hotel's stunning setting on Halaman Bay. Bedrooms are comfortable and nicely furnished - but again, it is the view that forms the central feature. As you would expect, fresh local seafood is the speciality of the dining room, which has fresh Barra lamb and beef on the menu as well as an excellent wine list.

Barra is the most southerly of the Western Isles, but is still easily accessible, with flights from Glasgow Monday-Saturday on Cockleshell Strand. If that isn't romantic enough, the five-hour ferry crossing from Oban may give you a chance to see dolphins or even a whale! Either route offers a great introduction to the delights to follow.

LOCATION

Turn left at the top of the road from the pier onto Barra's main circular road, the A888. Continue up Heather Hill; the hotel is on the left before Borve, two miles from the pier.

Tangasdale Beach, Isle of Barra, Western Isles HS9 5XW

T (UK) 0870 432 8666
T 01871 810383
F 01871 810385
barrahotel@bestloved.com
www.barrahotel.bestloved.com

OWNER
Diane Worthington

RATES PER PERSON
Single occupancy   £48
4 Doubles   £42
26 Twins   £42
Includes full breakfast and VAT

CREDIT CARDS
MC • VI

RATINGS & AWARDS
VisitScotland ★★★ Hotel
AA ★★ 68%

FACILITIES
On site: Direct beach access
1 meeting room/max 50 people
Nearby: Swimming pool, sauna, gym, beach

RESTRICTIONS
No facilities for disabled guests
No smoking in lounge or restaurant
Closed 5 Oct. - Easter

ATTRACTIONS
Allt Chrisal Valley,
Iron Age wheelhouse, hill walks, cycling, Kisimul Castle, Cille Bharra, Barra Airport on Cockleshell Strand, An Dubhardaidh

NEAREST
CITY:
Glasgow - 95 miles / 7 hours
(1 hour by air)

AIRPORT:
Barra - 6 miles / 15 mins
Glasgow - 95 miles / 7 hours
(1 hour by air)

RAIL STATION:
Oban - 76 miles/5 hrs (ferry)

FERRY PORT:
Eriskay - 5 miles / 10 mins
Castlebay - 2 miles/5 mins

AFFILIATIONS
Independent

RESERVATIONS
National rate in UK: 0870 432 8666
Quote Best Loved

ACCESS CODES
Not applicable

"It's quirky and eccentric, but they really know about country living"

LORD LICHFIELD

ISLE OF ERISKA

Country house

SCOTLAND

Ledaig, Oban, Argyll PA37 1SD

T (UK) 0870 432 8667
T 01631 720371
F 01631 720531
eriska@bestloved.com
www.eriska.bestloved.com

OWNERS
The Buchanan-Smith Family

ROOM RATES
Single occupancy   £200
17 Doubles/Twins   £260 - £315
3 Spa Suites   £375
1 Two-bedroom Suite   £500
Includes full breakfast, complimentary newspaper, afternoon tea and VAT

CREDIT CARDS
AMERICAN EXPRESS • MC • VI

RATINGS & AWARDS
VisitScotland ★★★★★ Hotel
AA ★★★★ ✸✸✸
AA Top 200 - 2004/2005

FACILITIES
On site: Garden, gym, heli-pad, fishing, croquet, golf, tennis, indoor pool, health & beauty, sauna, sea fishing, 6-hole golf course
3 meeting rooms/max 40 people
Nearby: Golf, riding, river and lake fishing

RESTRICTIONS
Limited facilities for disabled guests
No pets in public areas
No smoking in dining room and drawing room
Closed 3 Jan. - 3 Feb.

ATTRACTIONS
Sea Life Centre, Glencoe, distilleries, Isle of Mull, Dunstaffnage Castle, Loch Linnhe

NEAREST
CITY:
Glasgow - 90 miles/2 hrs 30 mins

AIRPORT:
Glasgow - 90 miles/2 hrs 30 mins

RAIL STATION:
Oban - 12 miles/20 mins

AFFILIATIONS
Celebrated Hotels Collection
Pride of Britain

RESERVATIONS
National rate in UK: 0870 432 8667
Toll free in US: 800-322-2403
or 800-98-PRIDE
Quote Best Loved

ACCESS CODES
AMADEUS HK OBNERI
APOLLO/GALILEO HT 17678
SABRE/ABACUS HK 34098
WORLDSPAN HK ERISK

Its own private island, Eriska is all about fulfilling dreams

Eriska is a small, secluded island fewer than 100 miles from Glasgow and Edinburgh - and it's the only island in Britain solely devoted to the care and wellbeing of guests. Since 1973, Eriska has been owned by the Buchanan-Smith family. They set high priority on peace and tranquillity, and these qualities attract people back to the island again and again.

Eriska lives up to the Scottish country house requirement for 'a good table' throughout the day, from the delicious breakfasts to the acclaimed candlelit dinners. The Big House was built in 1884 at the height of Scottish baronial style. Blazing log fires in the burr-oak-panelled Hall make for a very Scottish holiday, as does a glass of malt whisky in the library.

Sporting facilities include a 6-hole golf course, 17-metre swimming pool, steam room, sauna, gymnasium, all-weather tennis court, croquet, golf putting and clay pigeon shooting - as well as a new spa wing with a relaxation room and a new range of pampering therapies. The island is virtually a nature reserve, with designated nature trails and seals, otters, badgers and roe deer all around. Eriska has its own road bridge to link with the mainland and is only 30 minutes from the seaport of Oban, whence steamers ply to Iona and Staffa. Mainland attractions include Glencoe and Inverary Castle, seat of the Clan Campbell.

LOCATION
From Edinburgh and Glasgow, drive to Tyndrum, then follow the A85 toward Oban. At Connel, take the A828 bridge four miles, north of Benderloch; the hotel is signposted.

Lakeside hotel

KILCAMB LODGE

Argyll, Highland PH36 4HY

T (UK) 0870 432 8670
T 01967 402257
F 01967 402041
kilcamb@bestloved.com
www.kilcamb.bestloved.com

OWNERS
David and Sally Fox

ROOM RATES
1 Single occupancy	£75
6 Garden View Rooms	£75 - £138
4 Loch View Rooms	£120 - £159
2 Suites	£187 - £220

Includes full breakfast and VAT

CREDIT CARDS
AMERICAN EXPRESS • JCB • MC • VI

RATINGS & AWARDS
VisitScotland ★★★★ Small Hotel
AA ★★ ⊛⊛
AA Top 200 - 2004/2005
AA Courtesy & Care Award
AA Best Breakfast Award
The Good Hotel Guide - Scottish
Hotel of the Year

FACILITIES
On site: Fishing,
licensed for weddings, sailing
1 meeting room/max 22 people
Nearby: Walking, fishing, cycling

RESTRICTIONS
No facilities for disabled guests
No children under 12 years
No smoking throughout
Pets by arrangement
Closed 2 Jan. - 12 Feb.

ATTRACTIONS
Isle of Skye, Isle of Mull, Isle of Staffa,
walking, fishing, cycling, diving,
extreme sport

NEAREST
CITY:
Inverness - 100 miles/2 hrs 30 mins
Glasgow - 100 miles/2 hrs 30 mins

AIRPORT:
Glasgow - 100 miles/2 hrs 30 mins
Edinburgh - 130 miles/3 hrs

RAIL STATION:
Fort William - 20 miles/30 mins
Inverness - 100 miles/2 hrs 30 mins

AFFILIATIONS
Independent

RESERVATIONS
National rate in UK: 0870 432 8670
Quote Best Loved

ACCESS CODES
Not applicable

Steeped in history and the beauty of an unparalleled natural setting

Kilcamb Lodge lies on the shores of Loch Sunart with lawns leading down to the water's edge and a backdrop of woodlands where guests might stumble upon rare wild orchids. To the west, the spectacular Ardnamurchan Peninsula teems with wildlife, including pine martens, wildcats, deer, golden eagles and otters.

Nestled amidst all this natural splendour, Kilcamb can lay claim to being one of the oldest stone houses in the west of Scotland. A barracks for soldiers searching for Bonnie Prince Charlie during the 1745 Jacobite uprising, it later became a shooting lodge and is currently a beautifully-restored country house run by resident owners Sally and David Fox.

It goes without saying that the cosy and attractive drawing room enjoys superb loch views, as do many of the bedrooms. There is a well-stocked bar, and head chef Neil Mellis cooks fine cuisine from the best local ingredients in the excellent restaurant. Dinner menu temptations might include roast loin of venison or Argyll lamb with a soft herb crust, and the Scottish breakfasts are historic - even the breakfast muslei is honey-roasted in-house!

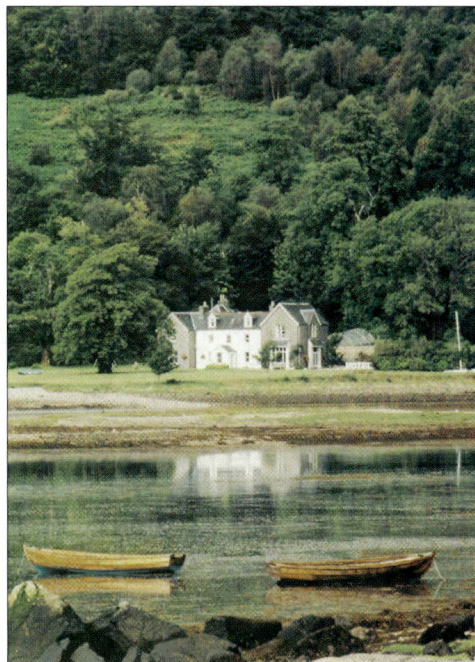

LOCATION

From the A82, take the Corran Ferry to Ardgour. On leaving the ferry, turn left for Strontian. Go through the village; the hotel is on the left after 300 yards.

> "The welcome is wonderfully warm, service is immaculate and discreet, comfort is considerable, and the food is famously good. Balm for body and soul"
>
> PHILIPPA DAVENPORT, FINANCIAL TIMES WEEKEND

KINLOCH LODGE

Country house

Sleat, Isle of Skye,
Highland IV43 8QY

T (UK) 0870 432 8671
T 01471 833214
F 01471 833277
kinlochlodge@bestloved.com
www.kinlochlodge.bestloved.com

OWNERS
Lord and Lady Macdonald

RATES PER PERSON
14 Doubles/Twins   £85 - £135
Includes full breakfast, dinner and VAT

CREDIT CARDS
AMERICAN EXPRESS • MC • VI

RATINGS & AWARDS
VisitScotland ★★★★ Small Hotel
Courvoisier's Book of the Best

FACILITIES
On site: Garden, heli-pad, fishing, stalking
Nearby: Golf, riding, boat trips

RESTRICTIONS
Limited facilities for disabled guests
Smoking in drawing rooms only
Pets by arrangement
Closed 20 - 28 Dec.

ATTRACTIONS
Isle of Skye, Clan Donald Centre, Inverewe Gardens, Dunvegan Castle

NEAREST
CITY:
Inverness - 100 miles/3 hrs 30 mins

AIRPORT:
Inverness - 100 miles/3 hrs 30 mins

RAIL STATION:
Kyle of Lochalsh - 12 miles/45 mins

FERRY PORT:
Kyle of Lochalsh - 12 miles/45 mins

AFFILIATIONS
Celebrated Hotels Collection
Relais du Silence
Great Little Hotels of Scotland

RESERVATIONS
National rate in UK: 0870 432 8671
Toll free in US: 800-322-2403
Quote Best Loved

ACCESS CODES
Not applicable

At home with Lord and Lady Macdonald in this lochside retreat

Kinloch Lodge is an elegant country house dating from the early 1600s whose gardens slope down to meet the sea loch, Na Dal, on the Isle of Skye. It is the ancestral home of Lord Macdonald of Macdonald, High Chief of Clan Donald, who runs it as a small, very personal hotel with his wife, world-renowned cookery writer Claire Macdonald. In 1998 the Macdonalds expanded to 15 bedrooms with a new house, known as Kinloch, adjacent to the Lodge and in similar style.

The setting is romantic, beautiful and incomparably peaceful. Secluded between a wooded hillside and the sea loch on two sides, the surrounding area is fascinating for those who love and appreciate nature, with a wealth of notable flowers and plants, golden eagles on the hill behind the house, seals galore and a colony of otters. The bird life is varied and plentiful.

Here, in view of Skye and the spectacular Cuillin Hills, the Macdonalds offer the warmest hospitality from their family home. The atmosphere is very relaxed, with comfortable rooms decorated in traditional country-house style, log fires and a five-course dinner that features the freshest of ingredients naturally available in season.

LOCATION

One mile off the A851, six miles south of Broadford and 10 miles north of Armadale.

Apartments

THE KNIGHT RESIDENCE

Stylish private apartments in the shadow of Edinburgh Castle

Serviced apartments offer increased privacy and the opportunity to relax as if you were at home without having to worry about keeping things in order when you're travelling on holiday or business. The Knight Residence takes this ethic and adds to it by offering a well-thought-out, attentive concierge service with a personal touch.

General Manager Colin Stone is proud of his team, who are all committed to this ethic of providing daily housekeeping and service that's efficient and friendly, yet unobtrusive. Each of the 19 apartments has its own kitchen and lounge and is equipped with cable TV, video and hi-fi with extension speakers into the bathroom; business facilities include fax, e-mail, Internet access and secretarial support.

Whether you are visiting for the Edinburgh Festival in August or at any other time, Scotland's capital city is renowned worldwide for its cultural heritage, and many tourist attractions are within easy reach. The Residence has a commitment to showcasing the work of local artists, and throughout the property original paintings, sculpture and designs are permanently on show. The best thing is if you fall in love with any particular piece, you can arrange to buy it and either take it home immediately or have it sent on!

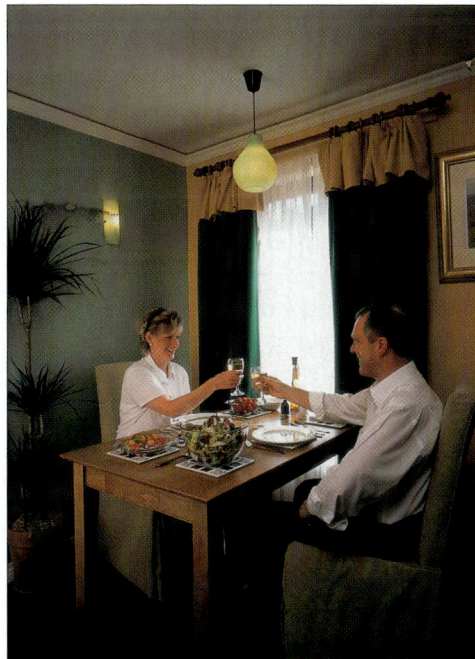

LOCATION

From Princes Street, turn into Lothian Road, left into King Stables Road, right onto the West Port and left into Lauriston Street.
The hotel is on the right.

---

12 Lauriston Street,
Edinburgh EH3 9DJ

T (UK) 0870 432 8672
T 0131 622 8120
F 0131 622 7363
knightres@bestloved.com
www.knightres.bestloved.com

GENERAL MANAGER
Colin Stone

ROOM RATES
Single occupancy	£90 - £145
9 One-bedroom Apts	£99 - £155
10 Two-bedroom Apts	£135 - £210
1 Three-bedroom Apts	£140 - £220
Includes VAT	

CREDIT CARDS
AMERICAN EXPRESS • DC • JCB • MC • VI

RATINGS & AWARDS
VisitScotland ★★★★★
Serviced Apartments
RAC ◆◆◆◆◆
RAC Warm Welcome,
Sparkling Diamond Awards

FACILITIES
On site: Private parking
Nearby: Golf, leisure centre

RESTRICTIONS
Limited facilities for disabled guests
No smoking throughout
Pets by arrangement

ATTRACTIONS
Edinburgh Castle , Holyrood House ,
Dynamic Earth, Royal Yacht Britannia,
National Gallery,
Edinburgh Festival and Military Tattoo

NEAREST
CITY:
Edinburgh

AIRPORT:
Edinburgh - 7 miles/20 mins

RAIL STATION:
Waverley - 1 ½ miles/5 mins

AFFILIATIONS
Independent

RESERVATIONS
National rate in UK: 0870 432 8672
Quote Best Loved

ACCESS CODES
AMADEUS IP EDI012
APOLLO/GALILEO IP 46358
SABRE/ABACUS IP 29353
WORLDSPAN IP 2900

SCOTLAND

KNOCKINAAM LODGE

Country house

SCOTLAND

Portpatrick, Near Stranraer,
Dumfries & Galloway DG9 9AD

T (UK) 0870 432 8674
T 01776 810471
F 01776 810435
knockinaam@bestloved.com
www.knockinaam.bestloved.com

OWNERS
David and Sian Ibbotson

RATES PER PERSON
Single occupancy   £125 - £165
4 Doubles/Twins   £105 - £140
5 Master Rooms   £130 - £185
Includes full breakfast, dinner and VAT

CREDIT CARDS
AMERICAN EXPRESS • MC • VI

RATINGS & AWARDS
VisitScotland ★★★★ Small Hotel
AA ★★★ ⊛⊛⊛
AA Top 200 - 2004/2005

FACILITIES
On site: Garden, heli-pad,
croquet, sea fishing
1 meeting room/max 40 people
Nearby: Fishing, shooting, golf, walking

RESTRICTIONS
No facilities for disabled guests
No children under 12 years in
restaurant for dinner, high tea provided
No smoking in bedrooms
Pets by arrangement

ATTRACTIONS
Logan, Ardwell and Glenwhan gardens,
Castle Kennedy, Culzean Castle,
Galloway Castle, Dunsky Gardens

NEAREST
CITY:
Stranraer - 8 miles/15 mins

AIRPORT:
Glasgow - 98 miles/2 hrs

RAIL STATION:
Stranraer - 8 miles/15 mins

FERRY PORT:
Stranraer - 8 miles/15 mins

AFFILIATIONS
Celebrated Hotels Collection
Pride of Britain

RESERVATIONS
National rate in UK: 0870 432 8674
Toll free in US: 800-322-2403
or 800-98-PRIDE
Quote Best Loved

ACCESS CODES
AMADEUS HK PIKKNO
APOLLO/GALILEO HT 80308
SABRE/ABACUS HK 07439
WORLDSPAN HKKNOCL

One of Churchill and Eisenhower's best-kept secrets

Secluded in a beautiful 30-acre setting beside the Irish Sea, Knockinaam enjoys one of Scotland's most romantic settings. Built in 1869 as a hunting lodge by Lady Hunter-Blair and extended to its present size in 1901, this hotel offers marvellous sea views and sunsets, gardens, public rooms with open log fires and 10 comfortable en-suite bedrooms. Knockinaam also has an international reputation for service, hospitality and attention to detail, and is the ideal place for a relaxing getaway: Sir Winston Churchill even chose Knockinaam as his secret meeting place with General Dwight D. Eisenhower during the Second World War.

The restaurant serves superbly delicious and innovative cuisine using only the freshest ingredients, including Scottish beef and lamb and local seafood. To complement the dining, the wine list has over 500 varieties on offer, and the hotel is noted for its display of over 124 malt whiskies - a pleasure for the connoisseur and an education for the novice!

There is superb fishing and shooting close by, and nearby golf clubs include Turnberry, Royal Troon, Prestwick, Brunston Castle, Southerness, Stranraer and Portpatrick.

LOCATION
Follow signs to Portpatrick from the A75 or A77. Two miles west of Lochans, turn left at sign to Knockinaam Lodge, pass Colfin Smokehouse and follow the signs to the lodge.

> "We had the opportunity to experience some very fine hotels in Scotland, but the most comfortable and cosy one was definitely Knockomie"
>
> ANNETTE & ROY SCWALBE, WEISSWASSER, GERMANY

Country house

KNOCKOMIE HOTEL

Pampered comfort surrounded by a wealth of sights and sport

Overlooking the Royal Burgh of Forres, Knockomie is ideally situated near castles, distilleries and golf courses, while salmon and deer await the keen sportsman. The front hall is panelled in Scots pine, while all 15 bedrooms are individually decorated with soft furnishings and period furniture. Some have four-poster or half-tester beds; others, with patios, are on the ground floor, including one with facilities for the disabled.

Knockomie House was built in 1821, added to in the Arts and Crafts style in 1914 and extended in 1993. The grill and bistro serve the best of Scottish produce to specialise in the Taste of Scotland, complemented by an extensive wine list and a large collection of malt whiskies.

Knockomie is an ideal location to visit the many castles in the area, including Cawdor, Brodie and Ballindalloch or the unique Whisky Trail in the Spey Valley. Loch Ness is less than an hour away, waiting to reveal its secret. Other opportunities include stalking and shooting in the glens or fishing in the lochs and rivers. Local golf courses include Lossiemouth, Hopeman, Forres, Nairn (Championship) and Dornoch (Championship).

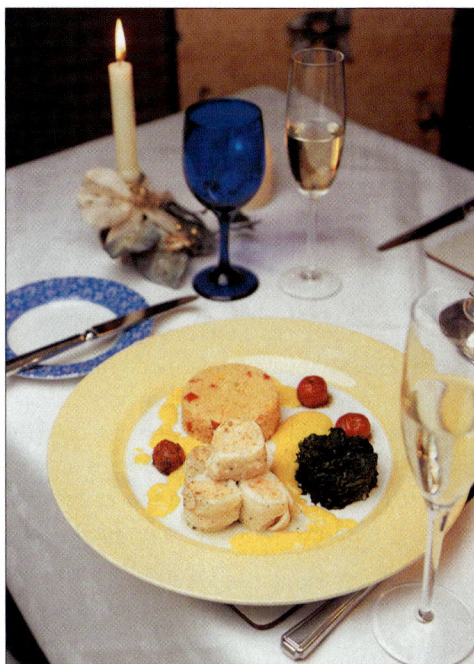

LOCATION

One mile south of Forres on the A940.

Grantown Road, Forres,
Moray IV36 2SG

T (UK) 0870 432 8675
T 01309 673146
F 01309 673290
knockomie@bestloved.com
www.knockomie.bestloved.com

DIRECTOR
Gavin Ellis

ROOM RATES
Single occupancy	£105 - £130
11 Doubles/Twins	£138 - £162
1 Family Room	£153
2 Four-posters	£180
Includes full breakfast and VAT	

CREDIT CARDS
AMERICAN EXPRESS • DC • JCB • MC • VI

RATINGS & AWARDS
VisitScotland ★★★★ Small Hotel

FACILITIES
On site: Garden, heli-pad, croquet
2 meeting rooms/max 70 people
Nearby: Golf, fishing, shooting, stalking, walking

RESTRICTIONS
Limited facilities for disabled guests
Smoking in bar only
Pets by arrangement

ATTRACTIONS
Brodie Castle, Cawdor Castle,
Ballindalloch Castle,
Benromach and Glen Grant distilleries,
Johnston's of Elgin,
Findhorn Foundation,
Malt Whisky Trail

NEAREST
CITY:
Inverness - 27 miles/30 mins

AIRPORT:
Inverness - 25 miles/30 mins
Aberdeen - 79 miles/2 hrs

RAIL STATION:
Forres - 1 mile/5 mins

AFFILIATIONS
Preston's Global Hotels
Grand Heritage Hotels

RESERVATIONS
National rate in UK: 0870 432 8675
Toll free in US: 800-544-9993
or 888-93-GRAND
Quote Best Loved

ACCESS CODES
AMADEUS UI FSSKNO
APOLLO/GALILEO UI 73447
SABRE/ABACUS UI 32407
WORLDSPAN UI 40671

SCOTLAND

> " Ladyburn exemplifies life as it used to be lived and ought to be lived "
>
> JACK MACMILLAN MBE, EDINBURGH

LADYBURN

Country house

by Maybole, Ayrshire KA19 7SG

T (UK) 0870 432 8678
T 01655 740585
F 01655 740580
ladyburn@bestloved.com
www.ladyburn.bestloved.com

OWNERS
David and Jane Hepburn

GENERAL MANAGER
Catriona Hepburn

ROOM RATES
Single occupancy   £60 - £95
3 Doubles/Twins   £110 - £180
2 Four-posters   £160 - £200
1 Two-bedroom Apartment £220
Includes full breakfast and VAT

CREDIT CARDS
MC • VI

RATINGS & AWARDS
RAC Blue Ribbon ★★ Dining Award 3
AA ★★ ⊛
AA Top 200 - 2004/2005

FACILITIES
On site: Garden, heli-pad, croquet
1 meeting room/max 20 people
Nearby: Golf, fishing, stalking,
clay pigeon shooting

RESTRICTIONS
Limited facilities for disabled guests
Children by arrangement
Smoking in library only
No pets; guide dogs only
Restricted opening November - April

ATTRACTIONS
Burns Centre,
Tam O'Shanter Experience,
Culzean Castle,
Glentrool, Crossraguel Abbey

NEAREST
CITY:
Glasgow - 45 miles/1 hr

AIRPORT:
Glasgow - 50 miles/1 hr 15 mins
Prestwick - 12 miles/30 mins

RAIL STATION:
Ayr - 12 miles/20 mins

AFFILIATIONS
Preston's Global Hotels

RESERVATIONS
National rate in UK: 0870 432 8678
Toll free in the US: 800-544-9993
Quote Best Loved

ACCESS CODES
Not applicable

Character, comfort and good food, tied with a Blue Ribbon of excellence

Ladyburn and Jane Hepburn are, as they say, an item! Indivisible. Praise one and you praise the other. It's not obvious from the picture above, but there is a clue in the fact column on this page: You will not find another Blue Ribbon (the second highest accolade the RAC can give) sitting next to only two stars (representing size and facilities).

Ladyburn is about as original as you can get! In service and comfort it could shame the best five-stars in the world. Ladyburn is a combination of irrepressible enthusiasm, total understanding of what people want when away from home and an instinctive genius for cooking. There are only five rooms in the house, but what rooms - what comfort! Real coffee on the side and, at bedtime, not just chocolates but a hot water bottle, too.

You will not find a menu in sight; Jane will ask you what you would like - making a suggestion or two, if you need a prompt - and then go out and buy whatever is necessary. The gardens, too, are more than worthy of a mention - recently accepted into Scotland's Garden Scheme, tours can be arranged between Ladyburn and other gardens throughout Ayrshire.

Ladyburn - there is nothing to match it!

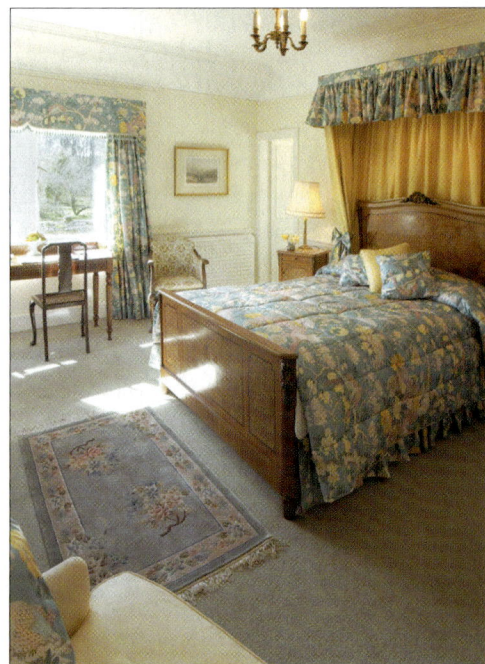

LOCATION

Take the A77 to Maybole; then, take the B7023 to Crosshill and a right at the War Memorial. Turn left after two miles; the hotel is three quarters of a mile on the right.

Hospitality of the highest order - we'll meet again

JEFF AND JEAN READER, LINCOLNSHIRE

A jewel in the crown of opulent Scottish retreats

Sharon Taylor

MAR HALL

Stately home

Earl of Mar Estate,
Bishopton, Near Glasgow,
Renfrewshire PA7 5PU

T (UK) 0870 432 8704
T 0141 812 9999
F 0141 812 9997
marhall@bestloved.com
www.marhall.bestloved.com

OPERATIONS DIRECTOR
Jeanette Montgomery

ROOM RATES
41 Doubles/Twins   £135 - £225
12 Suites   £245 - £495
Includes VAT

CREDIT CARDS
AMERICAN EXPRESS • DC • JCB • MC • VI

RATINGS & AWARDS
Awards Pending

FACILITIES
On site: Garden, gym, golf, tennis,
indoor pool, licensed for weddings,
Aveda spa, off-road driving,
laser clay shooting, yoga classes,
hair salon
7 meeting rooms/max 250 people
Nearby: Horse riding, fishing

RESTRICTIONS
Smoking in Cigar Bar only
Pets by arrangement

ATTRACTIONS
Paisley Abbey,
Scottish Exhibition Centre,
The Burrell Collection,
House for an Art Lover,
Glasgow Cathedral,
Kelvingrove Art Gallery

NEAREST
CITY:
Glasgow - 13 miles/20 mins

AIRPORT:
Glasgow - 6 miles/10 mins

RAIL STATION:
Glasgow - 13 miles/20 mins
Paisley - 7 miles/10 mins

AFFILIATIONS
Celebrated Hotels Collection
Small Luxury Hotels

RESERVATIONS
National rate in UK: 0870 432 8704
Toll free in US: 800-322-2403
or 800-525-4800
Quote Best Loved

ACCESS CODES
AMADEUS LX GLAMAHA
APOLLO/GALILEO LX 65994
SABRE/ABACUS LX 63384
WORLDSPAN LX GLAMH

A grand historic hall
just minutes from Glasgow

Spectacular Gothic architecture, graceful accommodation and impeccable service combine to make Mar Hall a world-class hotel. This impressive building, named after the 11th Earl of Mar, was built in 1840 and, following an extensive renovation, opened to guests in June 2004.

The hotel is surrounded by a stunning 240-acre estate and has wonderful views of the Kilpatrick Hills and River Clyde. Guests can stroll through the formal gardens and indulge in the state-of-the-art Aveda Concept Spa; for the sporting-minded, in 2006 Mar Hall will open its own Championship golf course.

Food enthusiasts are spoilt for choice, with The Cristal, their fine-dining restaurant, The Organic Diner, located in the spa, and the Grand Hall, which serves a selection of snacks throughout the day.

Located just a few miles from the cosmopolitan city of Glasgow, there is plenty to see and do in the surrounding area, with the Gallery of Modern Art, Glasgow Cathedral and much more just a short drive away.

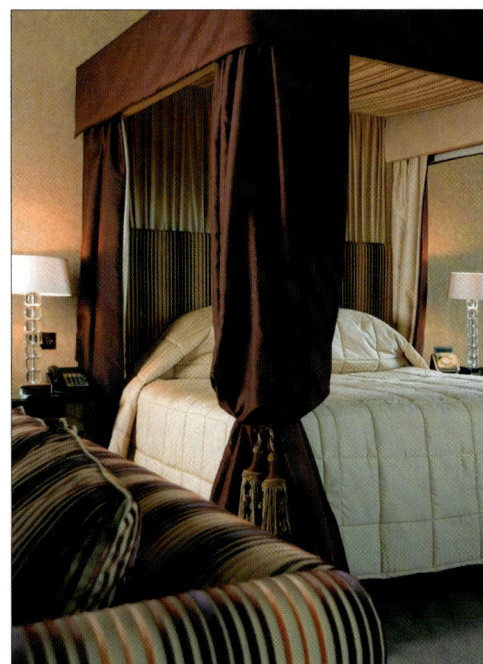

LOCATION

From Glasgow, take the M8 toward Greenock and exit at junction 30 (Erskine Bridge); then, exit for Bishopton (B815), take the first left at the roundabout, straight through the mini-roundabout and turn right at the gatehouse into the Earl of Mar Estate.

> **"** We were both so relaxed we were horizontal **"**
>
> BILLY & CATHY BEATON, GLASGOW

Lakeside hotel

MELFORT PIER & HARBOUR

Kilmelford, By Oban,
Argyll PA34 4XD

T (UK) 0870 432 8707
T 01852 200333
F 01852 200329
melfortpier@bestloved.com
www.melfortpier.bestloved.com

SCOTLAND

MANAGER
Sara Milton

RATES
3 One-Bedroomed Houses £80 - £170
8 Two-Bedroomed Houses £140 - £180
4 Three-Bedroomed Houses £160 - £210
Includes VAT (minimum two-night stay);
all houses self-catering

CREDIT CARDS
MC • VI

RATINGS & AWARDS
VisitScotland ★★★★★ Self-Catering
VisitScotland Scottish Thistle Award 2002
VisitScotland Category Two
Disabled Access
Cyclists Welcome/Walkers Welcome

FACILITIES
On site: Fishing, solarium, sauna,
spa bath, canoeing, rowboating, sailing,
swimming, diving, harbour berths,
swinging moorings
1 meeting room/max 12 people
Nearby: Golf, riding,
clay pigeon shooting, cycling,
hill walking, water sport, skiing,
islands, shopping and dining

RESTRICTIONS
None

ATTRACTIONS
Boat trips to islands, hill walking,
golf courses, Arduaine Gardens,
distilleries, castles, Isle of Mull,
Iona Abbey

NEAREST
CITY:
Oban - 15 miles/25 mins

AIRPORT:
Glasgow - 100 miles/2 hrs 30 mins

RAIL STATION:
Oban - 15 miles/25 mins

AFFILIATIONS
Independent

RESERVATIONS
National rate in UK: 0870 432 8707
Quote Best Loved

ACCESS CODES
Not applicable

A private luxury retreat on Scotland's stunning west coast

Arriving at Melfort Pier, you would be forgiven for thinking you had just arrived at a private retreat on a Norwegian fjord or a Canadian lakeside - but this beautiful idyll is just two hours north of Glasgow. Nestled into this lovely forested loch shore are 15 luxurious lochside houses; each one is well placed to ensure complete privacy and space and all are south facing with balconies.

The houses, varying from one to three bedrooms, are very Scandinavian in design. Open-planned and tiled throughout with under-floor heating, they are bright, fresh and spacious. In some, the bedrooms are upstairs and in others down - all in order to make the best of the views down Loch Melfort. Each house is also equipped with a 'serious' kitchen, sauna, spa bath, two televisions (including films and Sky Sports), e-mail hookups, a log fire and even a sunbed - this is Scotland, after all! Bed linen and towels are, of course, provided.

Perhaps the greatest thing about Melfort Pier is the flexibility - something not normally associated with self-catering accommodation. Your holiday or break can start on any day of the week, with the minimum stay being just two days. We think, however, that you will want to stay for longer!

LOCATION
Just off the A816, 16 miles south of Oban and north of Lochgilphead. Melfort Pier is well-signed.

SCOTLAND

MELVIN HOUSE HOTEL

Townhouse

3 Rothesay Terrace,
Edinburgh EH3 7RY

T (UK) 0870 432 8708
T 0131 225 5084
F 0131 226 5085
melvinhouse@bestloved.com
www.melvinhouse.bestloved.com

OWNERS
The McKenzie Family

ROOM RATES
Single occupancy   £79 - £115
10 Doubles/Twins   £140
6 Executive Rooms   £180
6 Family Rooms   £180
Includes full breakfast and VAT

CREDIT CARDS
AMERICAN EXPRESS • DC • MC • VI

RATINGS & AWARDS
VisitScotland ★★★ Hotel

FACILITIES
On site:
4 meeting rooms/max 100 people
Nearby: Golf, swimming

RESTRICTIONS
Limited facilities for disabled guests
Suitable for children over 12 years
Smoking in bar and foyer only
Pets by arrangement

ATTRACTIONS
Edinburgh Castle,
Holyrood House, Royal Mile,
National Art Gallery of Scotland,
Dynamic Earth, Royal Yacht Britannia

NEAREST
CITY:
Edinburgh

AIRPORT:
Edinburgh - 6 miles/25 mins

RAIL STATION:
Haymarket - 1/4 mile/10 mins

AFFILIATIONS
Preston's Global Hotels

RESERVATIONS
National rate in UK: 0870 432 8708
Toll free in US: 800-544-9993
Quote Best Loved

ACCESS CODES
Not applicable

Stop press! Excellent value in Edinburgh's fashionable West End

In 1766, 22-year-old James Craig won a public competition to design a New Town for Edinburgh that would expand the city beyond the confines of the rocky outcrop dominated by Edinburgh Castle. Craig's neoclassical plan extended north of Princes Street, and by the late 19th century the final piece of the New Town development, the West End, neared completion.

It was here in 1883 that John Ritchie Findlay, legendary owner of Scotland's national newspaper, The Scotsman, built himself a handsome terraced house, now transformed into this centrally-located hotel. Extensively restored, Melvin House remains full of grand Victorian character, intricate mouldings, dark wood panelling and imposing marble fireplaces in the public rooms. The generously sized bedrooms, which provide exceptional value-for-money family accommodation, boast views over the city to the castle or the ancient kingdom of Fife.

A short walk from Princes Street shops and major attractions such as the National Gallery of Scotland, Melvin House's location is hard to beat, and business travellers are well-placed for the city's financial and business communities - as well as the hotel's own conference rooms.

LOCATION
Enter Edinburgh city centre via Queensferry Road. Cross Dean Bridge; take the second right into Drumsheugh Gardens. The hotel is diagonally opposite on the corner.

"Exceptional hotel - not to be missed"

MR & MRS M J MCCARTHY, SUTTON COLDFIELD

Country house

OLD MANOR HOTEL

Lundin Links, Near St Andrews, Fife KY8 6AJ

T (UK) 0870 432 8723
T 01333 320368
F 01333 320911
oldmanor@bestloved.com
www.oldmanor.bestloved.com

OWNERS
The Clark Family

ROOM RATES
1 Single	£70 - £95
17 Doubles/Twins	£90 - £160
3 Superior Doubles/Twins	£150 - £190
2 Four-posters	£180 - £200

Includes full breakfast and VAT

CREDIT CARDS
AMERICAN EXPRESS • DC • JCB • MC • VI

RATINGS & AWARDS
VisitScotland ★★★★ Hotel
AA ★★★ ✿✿ 78%
Scotch Beef Club

FACILITIES
On site: Garden
3 meeting rooms/max 180 people
Nearby: Golf, fishing, riding, tennis, squash, bowls, beaches, walking

RESTRICTIONS
Limited facilities for disabled guests
No children under 10 years in the restaurant
No smoking in seaview rooms
No pets in public areas

ATTRACTIONS
Deep Sea World, Crail, Anstruther, St Andrews Cathedral, St Andrews Golf Course, Falkland Palace, Fife coastal path

NEAREST
CITY:
St Andrews - 12 miles/20 mins
Edinburgh - 38 miles/50 mins

AIRPORT:
Edinburgh - 35 miles/45 mins

RAIL STATION:
Markinch - 6 miles/10 mins
Kirkcaldy - 12 miles/20 mins

AFFILIATIONS
Scotland's Hotels of Distinction
Preston's Global Hotels
Les Routiers

RESERVATIONS
National rate in UK: 0870 432 8723
Toll free in US: 800-544-9993
or 800-437-2687
Quote Best Loved

ACCESS CODES
AMADEUS HK EDIOLD
APOLLO/GALILEO HT 28503
SABRE/ABACUS HK 53935
WORLDSPAN HK OLDMS

A country house where dining is excellent and golfers are spoilt for choice

This pleasant hotel is only 20 minutes from St Andrews itself, looking out onto the Lundin Links and Leven Open qualifying golf courses. Golf enthusiasts will enjoy the hotel's complimentary booking service: You can choose convenient tee times at over 30 courses within an hour's drive.

The Old Manor is a fine old country house situated in its own grounds with impressive views over Largo Bay. All of the public rooms are comfortably furnished to provide an easy place to relax. Many of the bedrooms have delightful sea views, several with balconies; all are en suite. Dining here is delightful, too. In the Terrace Brasserie and Grill, Chef James McKay and his team make imaginative use of local produce, game and seafood. At the popular Coachman's Grill, head chef Roberta Drummond offers fine chargrilled steaks and seafood in a less formal atmosphere with choice real ales and more than 100 malt whiskies.

In addition to such a rich golfing heritage; there's much to see in St Andrews, including beautiful beaches and Scotland's oldest university. The surrounding area has plenty of leisure parks, museums, castles, stately homes and gardens. With all this in mind, it's no wonder Old Manor Hotel is a wonderful venue for a wedding reception or a honeymoon.

LOCATION
Exit 2A from the M90 for the A92 (St Andrews); at the roundabout, exit for the A915 (St Andrews). The hotel is on the right as you enter Lundin Links.

SCOTLAND

ONE DEVONSHIRE GARDENS

Townhouse

1 Devonshire Gardens,
Glasgow G12 0UX
T (UK) 0870 432 8728
T 0141 339 2001
F 0141 337 1663
onedevonshire@bestloved.com
www.onedevonshire.bestloved.com

GENERAL MANAGER
Stephen G McCorkell

ROOM RATES
32 Doubles/Twins £145 - £285
3 Suites £355 - £485
Includes VAT

CREDIT CARDS
AMERICAN EXPRESS • DC • MC • VI

RATINGS & AWARDS
VisitScotland ★★★★★ Hotel
AA ★★★★ ⊛⊛
AA Romantic Hotel
AA Top 200 - 2004/2005

FACILITIES
On site: Gym, private dining room,
No5 Restaurant
3 meeting rooms/max 50 people
Nearby: Golf, riding, tennis

RESTRICTIONS
No facilities for disabled guests
No smoking in restaurant
Pets by arrangement

ATTRACTIONS
The Burrell Collection,
Kelvingrove Art Gallery,
Rennie Mackintosh's Hill House and
House for an Art Lover,
The Scottish Ballet,
Royal Scottish Opera,
Loch Lomond & The Trossachs

NEAREST
CITY:
Glasgow - 1 ½ miles/10 mins
AIRPORT:
Glasgow - 12 miles/20 mins
RAIL STATION:
Glasgow - 130 miles/10 mins

AFFILIATIONS
Celebrated Hotels Collection
Epoque Hotels

RESERVATIONS
National rate in UK: 0870 432 8728
Toll free in US: 800-322-2403
Quote Best Loved

ACCESS CODES
AMADEUS HK GLADEV
APOLLO/GALILEO HT 25902
SABRE/ABACUS HK 31789
WORLDSPAN HK DEVOS

Distinction and stylish splendour in Glasgow's West End

There is so much to say about One Devonshire Gardens, but to give too much away would spoil the overwhelming 'wow' factor. Located in Glasgow's fashionable West End, the hotel is housed within an elegant Victorian townhouse terrace and provides an exclusive temporary address in this exciting and progressive city.

The interiors are magnificent, with high ceilings, oak paneling, grand staircases and stained-glass windows. The bedrooms - ranging from Classic to Grand, some with four-posters - are spectacularly designed and furnished with widescreen televisions, CD systems, and DVD players. The bathrooms are very well appointed, with baths that are fathoms deep and a very generous supply of luxury toiletries. A recent refurbishment means even more sumptuous accommodation, plus a new luxury gym and state-of-the-art kitchen. The No5 Restaurant is fresh and spacious, serving innovative, award-winning cuisine, and the hotel's new eatery, Room Glasgow, offers classic cuisine with a contemporary twist.

The general tone of the hotel is discreet and unhurried. The overall attention to the smallest detail is impressive, as is the attentiveness and professionalism of the entire staff. All in all, a five-star experience in every way.

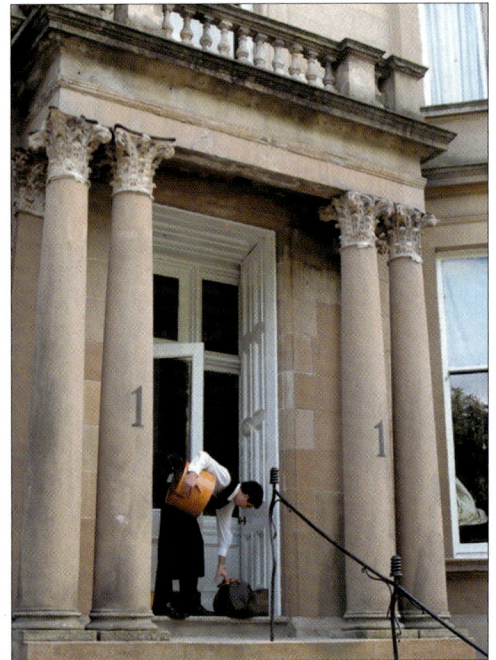

LOCATION

Exit 17 (right) off the M8 for the A82. After a mile, turn left at the traffic lights onto Hyndland Road; take the first right and a right at the roundabout, and the hotel is at the end of the road.

> **One of the most honest and enterprising restaurants in Britain**
>
> R W APPLE JR, THE NEW YORK TIMES

Restaurant with rooms

THE PEAT INN

SCOTLAND

Peat Inn, By Cupar,
Fife KY15 5LH

T (UK) 0870 432 8736
T 01334 840206
F 01334 840530
peat@bestloved.com
www.peat.bestloved.com

OWNERS
David and Patricia Wilson

ROOM RATES
8 Suites   £165 - £175
Includes continental breakfast and VAT

CREDIT CARDS
AMERICAN EXPRESS • MC • VI

RATINGS & AWARDS
VisitScotland ★★★★★
Restaurant with Rooms
AA ★★ ❀❀❀
AA Romantic Hotel
AA Top 200 - 2004/2005
Andrew Harper's Hideaway Report

FACILITIES
On site: Garden
1 meeting room/max 12 people
Nearby: Riding, golf, fishing, shooting

RESTRICTIONS
Limited facilities for disabled guests
Smoking in bedrooms only

ATTRACTIONS
St Andrews, East Neuk fishing villages,
Falkland Palace, Inchcolm Abbey,
Kellie Castle

NEAREST
CITY:
Edinburgh - 40 miles/1 hr
Dundee - 19 miles/30 mins

AIRPORT:
Edinburgh - 40 miles/1 hr

RAIL STATION:
Cupar - 6 miles/10 mins

AFFILIATIONS
Independent

RESERVATIONS
National rate in UK: 0870 432 8736
Quote Best Loved

ACCESS CODES
Not applicable

A celebrated restaurant
just a short drive from St Andrews

Food lovers the world over are attracted to The Peat Inn in the tiny rural village named after the inn itself. David Wilson, Chef Laureate, Master Chef and Proprietor, is well known as one of the nation's first TV chef celebrities, and is still active in encouraging high standards of cuisine and the use of the best Scottish produce.

As if the food and wine at The Peat Inn were not enough, the accommodation is the envy of many large country house hotels. Sympathetically designed by Patricia Wilson, seven of the suites are split-level, while one is single-level, and every suite features a marble bathroom, a pretty sitting room and welcome extras such as a selection of homemade cakes and fresh fruit.

St Andrews is, of course, synonymous with golf, but the area also offers plenty more to keep guests interested. The Kingdom of Fife is a land of contrasts, from the fishing villages of the East Neuk of Fife to Falkland Palace, country residence of the Stewart monarchs. Other attractions include Kellie Castle, Hill of Tarvit Mansion House and a wealth of interesting walks.

LOCATION
At the junction of the B940 and the B941, six miles southwest of St Andrews.

SCOTLAND

THE PLOCKTON HOTEL

Lochside hotel

Harbour Street, Plockton,
Wester Ross IV52 8TN

T (UK) 0870 432 8742
T 01599 544274
F 01599 544475
plockton@bestloved.com
www.plockton.bestloved.com

OWNERS
Dorothy, Tom and Alan Pearson

ROOM RATES
I Single	£45
13 Doubles/Twins	£90 - £100
I Family Room	£90 - £100

Includes full breakfast and VAT

CREDIT CARDS
AMERICAN EXPRESS • MC • VI

RATINGS & AWARDS
VisitScotland ★★★ Small Hotel
AA ★★ 71%
AA Scottish Pub of the Year 2004
Les Routiers Scottish Inn of the Year 2004

FACILITIES
Nearby: Golf, fishing, sailing

RESTRICTIONS
Smoking in bar only
No pets

ATTRACTIONS
Eilean Donan Castle, Isle of Skye,
Inverewe Gardens, Highland Games,
walking & climbing

NEAREST
CITY:
Inverness - 82 miles/2 hrs

AIRPORT:
Inverness - 82 miles/2 hrs

RAIL STATION:
Kyle of Lochalsh - 8 miles/15 mins

AFFILIATIONS
Independent

RESERVATIONS
National rate in UK: 0870 432 8742
Quote Best Loved

ACCESS CODES
Not applicable

An unsurpassed location and an outstanding reputation for seafood

Arriving at Plockton, it's quite possible that your breath will be taken away. To be truthful, it could happen several times on your journey trundling up through the West Highland Way past mirrored lochs, soaring mountains and palm trees! But still, Plockton, with its houses curving along the lochside, is a magnificent surprise, a hidden gem, located in a National Trust village - one of the most beautiful in Scotland and so close to Skye.

There is a hidden gem, too, in the form of the Plockton Hotel. Modest in scale, it was created from several fishermen's crofts, with the 13 charming bedrooms decorated in a delightful cottage style - but the restaurant is the jewel in the crown. With such access to seafood, it is not surprising that it specialises in delicious locally caught prawns, salmon and haddock, but for it to have been voted Best Seafood Pub in Scotland in 2002 is an added bonus.

The sentiments from the Plockton's visitor book really do say it all: 'If the big place in the sky is anything like this, then take me now - but just one more pickled herring before I go!' Almost too good to be true.

LOCATION
Located in the centre of the village facing the sea - and not to be confused with Plockton Inn.

City hotel

PRESTONFIELD

Priestfield Road,
Edinburgh EH16 5UT

T (UK) 0870 432 8746
T 0131 225 7800
F 0131 220 4392
prestonfield@bestloved.com
www.prestonfield.bestloved.com

OWNER
James Thomson

ROOM RATES
24 Luxury Doubles/Twins £195
2 Suites £250
Includes full breakfast, VAT and a
bottle of champagne upon arrival

CREDIT CARDS
AMERICAN EXPRESS • DC • JCB • MC • VI

RATINGS & AWARDS
VisitScotland ★★★★★ Hotel
AA ★★★★ ⊗⊗
AA Hotel of the Year 2004/2005
AA Top 200 - 2004/2005
Hotel Review Scotland
Romantic Hotel of the Year 2004
Tatler Top 20 2004

FACILITIES
On site: Garden, heli-pad, golf,
licensed for weddings,
Rhubarb restaurant
6 meeting rooms/max 1,000 people
Nearby: Riding, golf

RESTRICTIONS
No smoking in restaurant

ATTRACTIONS
Edinburgh Castle, the Royal Mile,
Palace of Holyrood House,
National Gallery of Scotland,
Museum of Scotland,
Royal Botanic Garden

NEAREST
CITY:
Edinburgh

AIRPORT:
Edinburgh - 10 miles/25 mins

RAIL STATION:
Edinburgh Waverley - 2 miles/7 mins

AFFILIATIONS
Celebrated Hotels Collection

RESERVATIONS
National rate in UK: 0870 432 8746
Toll free in US: 800-322-2403
Quote Best Loved

ACCESS CODES
Not applicable

A perfect location makes this Edinburgh's most indulgent retreat

Prestonfield is one of Scotland's finest historic mansions, situated in 20 acres of gardens yet just five minutes from Edinburgh's Princes Street. The mansion was built in 1687 for Sir James Dick, Lord Provost of Edinburgh, and succeeding generations of his family lavished their home with fine furnishings that can still be seen today.

This magnificent building has been recently refurbished to combine chic and luxurious accommodation with cutting-edge technology. Distinctively decorated bedrooms with Frette bed linen also discretely feature Bose sound systems, flatscreen televisions and high-speed wireless Internet connections, as well as air conditioning, for that little extra comfort. Original features of the building, such as the cherub ceiling in the grand hall, have also been restored in order to capture the absolute splendour of Prestonfield. The striking new Rhubarb restaurant has already gained a fine reputation for its cuisine and collection of fine wines. (The name Rhubarb was chosen because Prestonfield was the first estate in Scotland to grow the tangy treat!) Guests can also relax in the chic Whisky Room, the elegant Yellow Room or the historic Tapestry Room.

It would be difficult to match Prestonfield - recently voted by Tatler as one of the UK's top 20 hotels - for its comfort and lavish décor, combined with such an unbeatable city location.

LOCATION

Turn off the A7 Dalkeith road into Priestfield Road, just north of the Cameron Toll roundabout. The hotel is signposted.

SCOTLAND

ROMAN CAMP COUNTRY HOUSE　　Country house

Off Main Street, Callander,
Perthshire FK17 8BG

T (UK) 0870 432 8755
T 01877 330003
F 01877 331533
roman@bestloved.com
www.roman.bestloved.com

OWNERS
Eric and Marion Brown

ROOM RATES
2 Singles	£70 - £125
5 Doubles/Twins	£110 - £125
4 Superior Doubles	£165
3 Suites	£185

Includes full breakfast and VAT

CREDIT CARDS
AMERICAN EXPRESS • DC • MC • VI

RATINGS & AWARDS
VisitScotland ★★★★ Small Hotel
AA ★★★ ❀❀
AA Top 200 - 2004/2005

FACILITIES
On site: Garden, heli-pad, fishing
2 meeting rooms/max 100 people
Nearby: Golf, fishing, shooting

RESTRICTIONS
No smoking in restaurant
Pets by arrangement

ATTRACTIONS
Rob Roy country,
Trossachs National Park,
Inchmahome Priory, Stirling Castle,
Loch Lomond, Castle Campbell

NEAREST
CITY:
Edinburgh - 52 miles/1 hr

AIRPORT:
Edinburgh - 46 miles/50 mins

RAIL STATION:
Stirling - 17 miles/30 mins

AFFILIATIONS
Independent

RESERVATIONS
National rate in UK: 0870 432 8755
Quote Best Loved

ACCESS CODES
Not applicable

An historic house centrally situated for Callander and the Trossachs

Roman Camp Country House takes its name from earthworks to the east of its walled gardens, believed to be the site of a Roman fort. It was built originally as a hunting lodge in 1625 for the Dukes of Perth, and passed into the ownership of Viscount Esher in 1897; the turrets that give the building its unique character were added at that time. The house became a hotel in 1939, and remains a grand getaway to this day.

Each of the 14 bedrooms has its own distinctive style and character; some have coombed walls and furniture dating back 200 years! The library, panelled in 16th-century oak, has a log fire that's lit even in summer. The oval-shaped restaurant features tapestries of English cathedrals woven by Elizabeth Esher in the 1930s. Menus are prepared from local ingredients in season, and there are tasty à la carte and vegetarian menus.

Beyond the 20 acres of tranquil parkland and gardens with views of the River Teith are the Trossachs and the Highlands. This is a land of mountain and glen, rolling pasture and heather moor - a marvellous base for your Scottish holiday.

LOCATION
From the M9, exit 10 north on the A84 through Callander; turn left down the drive at the east end of Callander main street.

> What a joy it is for world-weary travellers to find an oasis of such calm and caring attention
>
> SARAH LORD, CALVIN KLEIN

Country house

ROYAL MARINE HOTEL

SCOTLAND

A place of comfort and calm in a wild and beautiful environment

The renowned Scottish architect Sir Robert Lorimer originally designed the Royal Marine Hotel as a private country house in the 1900s, and even after a thoroughly extensive renovation, features hearken back to an earlier day: a number of carved wooden fireplaces and an elegant stairway and reception foyer, all complemented by the chef's cuisine in the traditionally-styled dining room.

This charming hotel is especially attractive to sportsmen, too; nearby are several Championship links courses, including Brora, Golspie, Royal Dornoch and Tain. The Royal Marine also has its own boat on Loch Brora for fly fishing, and their on-site leisure centre offers a host of activities and facilities available to all residents.

Situated midway between Inverness and John O'Groats, Brora is ideal as a centre for touring the Northern Highlands and the Orkney Islands. This sparsely populated region abounds with birds and wildlife, and the rock formations are of particular interest to geologists and anyone tempted by excellent hill walking.

LOCATION

One hour north of Inverness just off the A9 and adjacent to James Braid's 18-hole links course.

Golf Road, Brora,
Sutherland KW9 6QS

T (UK) 0870 432 8760
T 01408 621252
F 01408 621181
royalmarine@bestloved.com
www.royalmarine.bestloved.com

MANAGING DIRECTOR
Robert Powell

ROOM RATES
Single occupancy	£75 - £95
18 Doubles/Twins	£120 - £130
2 Master Rooms	£130 - £150
1 Family Room	£130 - £150

Includes full breakfast and VAT

CREDIT CARDS

AMERICAN EXPRESS • DC • MC • VI

RATINGS & AWARDS
VisitScotland ★★★★ Hotel
AA ★★★ ❀ 72%

FACILITIES
On site: Garden, gym, snooker, indoor pool, curling, snooker, sauna, steam rooms, spa bath, solarium, disabled bedroom
2 meeting rooms/max 70 people
Nearby: Golf, fishing, tennis

RESTRICTIONS
Pets by arrangement
No smoking in restaurant

ATTRACTIONS
Dunrobin Castle, Orkney Islands, Clynelish Malt Whisky Distillery, Glenmorangie Whisky Distillery, Falls of Shin

NEAREST
CITY:
Inverness - 60 miles/1 hr

AIRPORT:
Inverness - 70 miles/1 hr 15 mins
Glasgow - 238 miles/4 hrs

RAIL STATION:
Brora - ¼ mile/2 mins

AFFILIATIONS
Classic British Hotels
Scotland's Hotels of Distinction

RESERVATIONS
National rate in UK: 0870 432 8760
Quote Best Loved

ACCESS CODES
Not applicable

SCOTLAND

THE ROYAL SCOTSMAN

Luxury train

46A Constitution Street,
Edinburgh EH6 6RS

T (UK) 0870 432 8762
T 0131 555 1021
F 0131 555 1345
royalscotsman@bestloved.com
www.royalscotsman@bestloved.com

COMMERCIAL MANAGER
Les Maitland

RATES PER PERSON
4 Singles   £610 - £4,680
16 Twins   £610 - £4,680
Includes accommodation, all meals,
drinks, visits and entertainment
from one to seven nights

CREDIT CARDS
AMERICAN EXPRESS • MC • VI

RATINGS & AWARDS
VisitScotland ★★★★★ Train

FACILITIES
On site: Two dining cars,
observation car, outside veranda

RESTRICTIONS
Limited facilities for disabled guests
Children by arrangement only
No smoking throughout
No pets
Closed November-March

ATTRACTIONS
Ballindalloch Castle, Isle of Skye,
Eilean Donan Castle, Glamis Castle,
Glen Grant Distillery , Plockton village,
Strathisla Distillery

NEAREST
CITY:
Edinburgh

AIRPORT:
Edinburgh - 8 miles/15 mins

RAIL STATION:
Edinburgh Waverley

AFFILIATIONS
Celebrated Hotels Collection
Pride of Britain
Connoisseurs Scotland

RESERVATIONS
National rate in UK: 0870 432 8762
Toll free in US: 800-322-2403
or 800-922-8625 or 800-323-7308
Quote Best Loved

ACCESS CODES
Not applicable

The ultimate
luxury train experience

A journey on The Royal Scotsman, considered to be the world's most luxurious train, is regarded as one of the great travel experiences. Enjoy exclusive visits to romantic castles, distilleries and private homes with a maximum of just 35 other guests as you explore Scotland's magnificent scenery and history. There are a variety of journeys available, from one to seven nights in duration; for those with a particular passion, why not join renowned hosts from the whisky world on a whisky adventure, or legendary chefs on a culinary delight?

Dinner is a treat, no matter your journey. Meals are prepared onboard using the freshest local ingredients and accompanied by fine wines. After dinner, relax with a rare malt in the stunning Edwardian Observation Car as your very own Highlander offers tales of life in Scotland in centuries gone by. Then, retire to your mahogany-adorned State Cabin, with private facilities, for a peaceful night's sleep as The Royal Scotsman slips quietly into a siding where it stables for the night.

All prices are per person and are fully inclusive of accommodation, meals, alcoholic and non-alcoholic beverages, entertainment and off-train visits, as well as the services of your onboard host, there solely to make your journey more enjoyable.

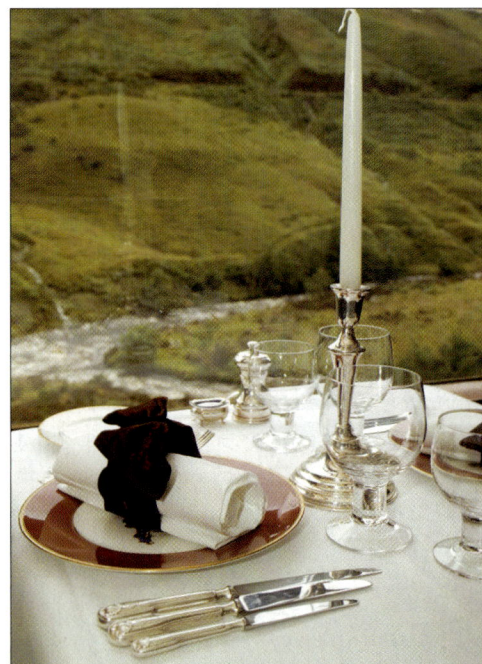

LOCATION
The train departs from Edinburgh Waverley station, located near the Scottish National Gallery on Princes Street.

"**Having entertained MTV guests Justin Timberlake and Pink, this fantastic five-star hotel brings glamour to Scotland's capital all year round**"

OUTLOOK MAGAZINE

City hotel

THE SCOTSMAN

Contemporary opulence between Princes Street and the Royal Mile

A contemporary hotel with an incredible Edinburgh location, The Scotsman has all you could need for business or leisure trips: opulent bedrooms, great meeting rooms and a state-of-the-art spa.

All 69 sumptuous bedrooms are designed for optimum comfort, containing hand-made beds, DVD and CD players, widescreen televisions and even Edinburgh Monopoly games! For business travellers, there is Internet access, printer and modem point, and all rooms have a privacy hatch, so that you can take advantage of room service without being disturbed.

The Scotsman is perfect for meetings and receptions - they have seven meeting rooms, including the Screening Room, which seats 46 in comfortable leather chairs, and where guests can have private viewings of classic films. And to de-stress after a meeting or a day's sightseeing in the city, the Escape Spa offers many relaxing treatments and a remarkable 16-metre stainless steel pool - perfect for relaxing before dinner in the luxuriously elegant Vermilion restaurant, built in 2002, or The North Bridge Brasserie, which has become a popular haunt in Edinburgh for its great food and relaxed atmosphere. And all of this is just a few minute's walk from Edinburgh's Princes Street and the Royal Mile!

LOCATION

A minute's walk from Waverley Station, on North Bridge.

20 North Bridge,
Edinburgh EH1 1YT
T (UK) 0870 432 8766
T 0131 556 5565
F 0131 652 3652
scotsman@bestloved.com
www.scotsman.bestloved.com

GENERAL MANAGER
Jonathan Dawson

ROOM RATES
12 Study Rooms	£250
32 Deluxe Rooms	£295
12 Editor Rooms	£350
12 Suites	£450 - £750
1 Penthouse	£1,200
Includes VAT	

CREDIT CARDS
AMERICAN EXPRESS • DC • JCB • MC • VI

RATINGS & AWARDS
VisitScotland ★★★★★ Hotel
AA ★★★★★ ⊛⊛
AA Town House
AA Hotel of the Year 2003
AA Top 200 - 2004/2005

FACILITIES
On site: Gym, indoor pool, health & beauty, sauna, steam room, Jacuzzi
7 meeting rooms/max 250
Nearby: Golf, riding

RESTRICTIONS
Smoking in some rooms only
Pets by arrangement

ATTRACTIONS
Edinburgh Castle, National Portrait Gallery, Princes Street, The Royal Mile, Palace of Holyrood House, Royal Botanic Garden

NEAREST
CITY:
Edinburgh

AIRPORT:
Edinburgh - 8 miles/20 mins

RAIL STATION:
Edinburgh Waverley - 100 yards/1 min

AFFILIATIONS
Leading Small Hotels

RESERVATIONS
National rate in UK: 0870 432 8766
Quote Best Loved

ACCESS CODES
AMADEUS LW EDI507
APOLLO/GALILEO LW 31499
SABRE/ABACUS LW 56195
WORLDSPAN LW 0507

"Thank you for a most relaxing stay ... Good food, good wine, good staff"

MR G MCINTYRE, GLASGOW

STONEFIELD CASTLE HOTEL

Castle

Tarbert, Argyll PA29 6YJ

T (UK) 0870 432 8780
T 01880 820836
F 01880 820929
stonefield@bestloved.com
www.stonefield.bestloved.com

GENERAL MANAGER
Alistair Wilkie

RATES PER PERSON
4 Singles	£85 - £145
25 Doubles/Twins	£85 - £100
4 Suites	£125

Includes dinner, breakfast and VAT

CREDIT CARDS
AMERICAN EXPRESS • DC • MC • VI

RATINGS & AWARDS
VisitScotland ★★★★ Hotel
RAC ★★★ Dining Award 2
AA ★★★ ❀ 71%

FACILITIES
On site: Garden, snooker, heli-pad
4 meeting rooms/max 200 people
Nearby: Golf, fishing, boating, riding,
swimming, tennis, walking,
sailing, shooting

RESTRICTIONS
No facilities for disabled guests
No smoking in bedrooms
Pets by arrangement

ATTRACTIONS
Inverary Castle,
Kilmartin House Museum,
Machrihanish Golf Course,
Achamore Gardens, Mount Stuart

NEAREST
CITY:
Glasgow - 95 miles/1 hr 45 mins

AIRPORT:
Glasgow - 92 miles/1 hr 45 mins

RAIL STATION:
Oban - 40 miles/1 hr

AFFILIATIONS
Independent

RESERVATIONS
National rate in UK: 0870 432 8780
Quote Best Loved

ACCESS CODES
Not applicable

Baronial elegance with an exotic touch of the Himalayas

High on the Kintyre peninsula with magnificent views over Loch Fyne, Stonefield Castle represents the epitome of baronial elegance rising gracefully from conifer woodlands. The castle was built in 1837 for the Campbell family, but its famous gardens were the work of Himalayan plant collector Sir Joseph Hooker.

Stonefield simply oozes character and a timeless ambience complemented by many original period furnishings. Guests will discover a beguiling serenity in the traditional wood-panelled lounges and comfortable country-house-style bedrooms. The restaurant is almost as renowned for its views as it is for the award-winning Scottish cuisine of head chef Angus Macfarlane, whose skills are brought to bear on the freshest local seafood, Loch Fyne oysters and Buccleuch beef accompanied by homegrown vegetables.

One of the most breathtaking sights here is the morning mist rising from the loch. Another is the woodland garden, where a century ago Sir Joseph planted the first seeds in what is now the finest collection of rhododendrons outside Kew Gardens. Here, winding paths thread through the woods in a scene more reminiscent of the Himalayan kingdom of Bhutan than Argyll!

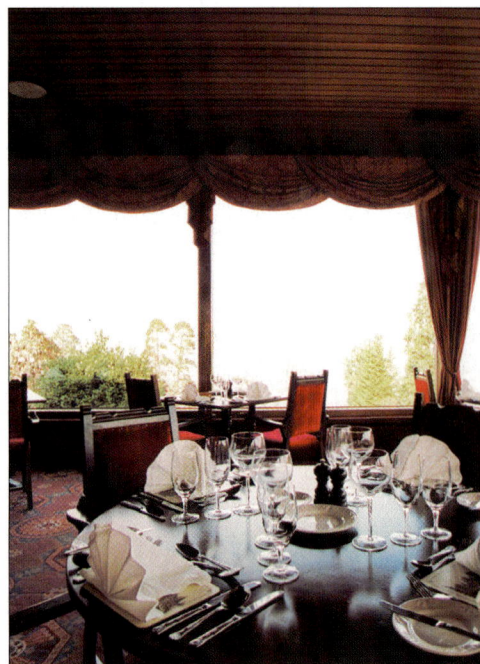

LOCATION
On the A83 between Ardrishaig and Tarbert; the hotel is two miles before Tarbert, on the left.

It is a simple, casually elegant place - with a chef who makes the most of local produce

JAN MOIR, THE TELEGRAPH

Inn

SUMMER ISLES

SCOTLAND

An oasis of civilisation in a wild, untouched landscape

Mark and Geraldine Irvine run this individual but sophisticated hotel, a family effort since the late 1960s. Since its opening, Summer Isles has established itself as an oasis of civilisation hidden away in a stunningly beautiful, but still wild and untouched, landscape.

Nearly everything you eat there is home-produced or locally caught: scallops, lobsters, langoustines, crabs, halibut, turbot, salmon, venison, big brown eggs, wholesome brown bread fresh from the oven - the list of real food is endless. Using such fresh ingredients, chef Chris Firth-Bernard provides the delicious, healthy fare that has earned the hotel a Michelin rosette.

Two more recent additions to the family of very finely appointed bedrooms are The Boathouse and William's Cottage, the latter sleeping four. Both are exquisite, with stunning views. After breakfast, Mark and Geraldine are happy to talk to you about fishing, walking or bird-watching. A local boat, the Hectoria, sails around the islands to show off seals and rare birds. You can also explore the scenery sub-aqua with the local diving school. Inverewe Gardens, Inverpolly Nature Reserve and the Sutherland coast are all within easy reach. In short, this place has a huge amount to offer!

LOCATION

In the village of Achiltibuie (accessible via the A835 or the A837), just past the post office.

Achiltibuie,
Ross-shire IV26 2YG

T (UK) 0870 432 8783
T 01854 622282
F 01854 622251
summer@bestloved.com
www.summer.bestloved.com

OWNERS
Mark and Geraldine Irvine

ROOM RATES
Single occupancy   £75 - £120
9 Doubles/Twins   £115 - £180
4 Suites   £180 - £235
Includes full breakfast and VAT

CREDIT CARDS
MC • VI

RATINGS & AWARDS
AA ✿✿ Restaurant with Rooms

FACILITIES
Nearby: Birdwatching, walking, fishing, scuba diving, sailing, beach

RESTRICTIONS
No facilities for disabled guests
No children under 8 years
Smoking in bar and lounge only
Pets by arrangement
Closed 17 October - 23 March

ATTRACTIONS
Inverewe Gardens,
Inverpolly Nature Reserve,
Sutherland coast, Western Isles,
the Highlands

NEAREST
CITY:
Inverness - 78 miles/1 hr 45 mins

AIRPORT:
Inverness - 78 miles/1 hr 45 mins

RAIL STATION:
Inverness - 78 miles/1 hr 45 mins

AFFILIATIONS
Independent

RESERVATIONS
National rate in UK: 0870 432 8783
Quote Best Loved

ACCESS CODES
Not applicable

TAYCHREGGAN

Country house

SCOTLAND

Kilchrenan, by Taynuilt,
Argyll PA35 1HQ

T (UK) 0870 432 8512
T 01866 833211
F 01866 833244
taychreggan@bestloved.com
www.taychreggan.bestloved.com

GENERAL MANAGER
Alistair Stevenson

ROOM RATES
13 Doubles/Twins   £127
6 Superior Doubles/Twins £198 - £237
Includes full breakfast and VAT

CREDIT CARDS
AMERICAN EXPRESS • JCB • MC • VI

RATINGS & AWARDS
VisitScotland ★★★★ Hotel
RAC ★★★ Dining Award 2
AA ★★★ ❀❀ 77%
Scotland The Brand
Investors in People

FACILITIES
On site: Garden, snooker, fishing
2 meeting rooms/max 30 people
Nearby: Walking, gliding

RESTRICTIONS
Limited facilities for disabled guests
No children under 14 years
Smoking in bar only
Pets by arrangement

ATTRACTIONS
Kilchurn Castle, Inveraray, loch cruises,
forest walks, gardens of Argyll

NEAREST
CITY:
Glasgow - 90 miles/2 hrs

AIRPORT:
Glasgow - 90 miles/2 hrs

RAIL STATION:
Taynuilt - 7 miles/15 mins

AFFILIATIONS
Preston's Global Hotels

RESERVATIONS
National rate in UK: 0870 432 8512
Toll free in US: 800-544-9993
Quote Best Loved

ACCESS CODES
Not applicable

Mountain grandeur, fascinating wildlife and lochside beauty

Surrounded by the grandeur of mountains, the house at Taychreggan has nestled on the shores of magnificent Loch Awe for the past 300 years. Originally a cattle drover's inn, this old stone house and its orangerie form the centrepiece of a beautiful hotel where the aim is to woo visitors into feeling like houseguests.

Most of the beautiful bedrooms overlook the loch; all offer high standards of quality, style and comfort. The friendly and experienced staff have received great trade and consumer recognition, and have scooped many prestigious awards. The magnificent view from the dining room is matched by superb Scottish cuisine, a comprehensive list of French wines and fine single malt whiskies.

From Taychreggan, you can visit historic places such as Inveraray or Kilchurn Castle, or choose from many outdoor activities. For hill walkers, there are 13 peaks over 3,000 feet within an hour's drive; for anglers, the hotel has its own fishing rights and boats. Birds of prey and rare species can be seen in these breathtaking surroundings, and horse riding, deer stalking, water sport, loch cruises, golf and rough shooting can all be arranged.

LOCATION
From Edinburgh, exit 10 on the M9 (Stirling), then the A84 (Callander), A85 (Crianlarich/Oban) and B845 (Taychreggan). The hotel is at end of this single-track road.

> "A warm welcome, the freshest local food and a great night's rest ...
> a charming hotel set in the most spectacular scenery"
>
> SIR CHRIS BONINGTON

Seaside hotel

TIGH AN EILEAN

SCOTLAND

A highland inn surrounded by dramatic sea and landscapes

Tigh an Eilean (House of the Island) stands in a 200-year-old seafront fishing village set in the Torridon Mountains, facing the Scottish National Trust's Isle of Pines and with glorious views over Loch Shieldaig to Loch Torridon and the open sea beyond.

Hoteliers Cathryn and Christopher Field greet you with a warm welcome into the two lounges and a cosy residents' honesty bar/library. Many of the en-suite bedrooms offer a sea view; in all, furnishings, prints and paintings lend character and charm. The dining room, looking across the sea, offers menus with produce from local sea, river and hill; specialities include seafood delivered direct from boat to kitchen door that day. The reasonably-priced wine list is short but thoughtfully chosen.

This is the great outdoors, where the aromatherapy of heather, Caledonian pines and the sea is free; here, the hill walker, angler and golfer will find paradise, and sightseers by car can take in the spectacular scenery - try the the Beinn Eighe Nature Reserve or the 2,000-foot Bealach na Bo pass to Applecross, with its views across the sea to Skye. Astronomers will find a soulmate in Christopher, whose telescope is set up in the garden. With so many attractions, the lure of Tigh an Eilean is ever-present; one visit is never enough.

LOCATION

Take the A832 from Inverness to Kinlochewe; exit for the A896 to Shieldaig.

Shieldaig, on Loch Torridon,
Ross-shire IV54 8XN

T (UK) 0870 432 8799
T 01520 755251
F 01520 755321
tighan@bestloved.com
www.tighan.bestloved.com

RESIDENT MANAGER
Christopher and Cathryn Field

ROOM RATES
3 Singles	£55
8 Doubles/Twins	£120
Includes full breakfast and VAT	

CREDIT CARDS
AMERICAN EXPRESS • MC • VI

RATINGS & AWARDS
VisitScotland ★★★★ Small Hotel
RAC ★ Dining Award 3
AA ★ ⊛⊛
AA Top 200 - 2004/2005

FACILITIES
On site: Fishing, boat hire, kayaks
Nearby: Hill walking, mountain climbing

RESTRICTIONS
Limited facilities for disabled guests
No smoking in dining room
No pets in public areas
Closed late November - late March

ATTRACTIONS
Applecross Peninsula,
Inverewe Gardens,
Torridon loch and mountains,
Beinn Eighe Nature Reserve,
Isle of Skye

NEAREST
CITY:
Inverness - 68 miles/1 hr 45 mins

AIRPORT:
Glasgow - 223 miles/4 hrs 45 mins
Inverness - 75 miles/2 hrs

RAIL STATION:
Strathcarron - 12 miles/30 mins

AFFILIATIONS
Independent

RESERVATIONS
National rate in UK: 0870 432 8799
Quote Best Loved

ACCESS CODES
Not applicable

A truly remarkable find

GORDON WALKER, INVERNESS

THE WOODSIDE HOTEL

Country house

Aberdour, Fife KY3 0SW

T (UK) 0870 432 8823
T 01383 860328
F 01383 860920
woodside@bestloved.com
www.woodside.bestloved.com

OWNERS
Martin and Liz McIlrath

ROOM RATES
1 Single	£60
17 Doubles/Twins	£60 - £88
1 Family Room	£75 - £95
1 Four-poster Suite	£100 - £125

Includes full breakfast and VAT

CREDIT CARDS
AMERICAN EXPRESS • JCB • MC • VI

RATINGS & AWARDS
VisitScotland ★★★ Small Hotel
AA ★★★ ✿ 65%

FACILITIES
On site:
2 meeting rooms/max 100 people
Nearby: Golf, tennis, fitness, yachting,
fishing, riding, shooting

RESTRICTIONS
Limited facilities for disabled guests
No smoking in restaurant
Pets by arrangement

ATTRACTIONS
St Andrews town & golf course,
Edinburgh city & castle,
award-winning beach,
Deep Sea World, Glasgow,
Stirling Castle, Blair Castle,
Bells Whisky Distillery

NEAREST
CITY:
Edinburgh - 15 miles/25 mins

AIRPORT:
Edinburgh - 13 miles/20 mins

RAIL STATION:
Aberdour - ¼ mile/10 mins

AFFILIATIONS
Independent

RESERVATIONS
National rate in UK: 0870 432 8823
Quote Best Loved

ACCESS CODES
Not applicable

Modern comforts, good food and a warm welcome in an historic mansion

The influence of the sea can be felt throughout this warm and friendly hotel. The original owner's great-grandfather founded the Russian Navy, but the elaborate mahogany and glass ceiling in the smoking lounge - brought to the hotel in 1926 from the steamship Orontes, which sailed between Australia and the UK - grabs the most attention.

Woodside is located in the centre of the picturesque town of Aberdour, and keeping with the local theme, each of the hotel's bedrooms is decorated and furnished in a very individual style and is named after a Scottish clan. The Rennie Room, for example, is an apartment with four-poster bed and private sitting room, while the Thomson Room is a luxury family room with views across the Firth of Forth to Edinburgh. There's another local influence, too: Fresh fish are taken directly to the hotel's excellent restaurant from the local harbour quayside. A bar bistro offers lighter variations of the fare you can enjoy in the fine dining room.

Aberdour has the distinction of being the only Scottish beach to have been awarded Blue Flag status, just one of many attractions that make Woodside an ideal touring base for Edinburgh and beyond.

LOCATION
Exit 1 on the M90 from Forth Road Bridge; turn right under the M90 to Kirkcaldy. Aberdour is after five roundabouts; the hotel is on the left after a garage.

PRESENT PERFECT

MAR HALL, NEAR GLASGOW (PAGE 64)

Give your friends or family memories they'll cherish for a lifetime ... a great meal or a stay at a Best Loved Hotel.

The **Best Loved Hotels Gift Voucher Package** includes

- The latest 456-page Best Loved Hotels - UK/Ireland full-colour directory, packed with enticing travel ideas
- £100 gift certificate valid for accommodation or dining
- One year's free membership in the Red Rosette Travel Club
- All beautifully gift-wrapped with your special message and sent to the address of your choice

Only £149.95, including VAT, postage and packing

Already have a copy of the book? Vouchers alone are available in values of £50, £100, £150 and up.

Or, give a perfect present in pocket size - the **Little Gold Book Gift Voucher Package** for just £129.95, including VAT, postage and packing. Includes a £100 voucher, a year's membership in the Red Rosette Travel Club, gift wrapping and a copy of the Best Loved Hotels Little Gold Book, packed with special offers at more than 350 great places to stay throughout the UK and Ireland.

LLANGOED HALL, BRECON, POWYS (PAGE 152)

COTTAGE HOTEL, BROCKENHURST (PAGE 304)

Call today for a gift that won't soon be forgotten!

NORTH

A COUNTRY HOUSE HOTEL
Miller Howe Hotel, Cumbria

A TOWNHOUSE
Eleven Didsbury Park, Manchester

A SPA HOTEL
Seaham Hall Hotel & Serenity Spa, Co Durham

REPRESENTING
the best of the
NORTH

A COUNTRY HOUSE HOTEL
The Devonshire, North Yorkshire

Best Loved Hotels offer the cream of the crop across Great Britain and Ireland - from stately palaces to welcoming inns - each the best of its kind within its locality and price range.

Whichever place you choose as your own place to stay, you'll find every hotel offers character, charm and the best delights and attractions of its region.

And each, in its own special way, is best-loved by someone who's been there.

A LAKELAND HOTEL
The Samling, Cumbria

A CITY HOTEL
Quebecs, Leeds

A CONTEMPORARY ISLAND HOTEL
Sefton Hotel, Isle of Man

A COACHING INN
The White Swan, Yorkshire

AN IDEAL ESCAPE:
The North

INSPIRATION on a grand scale is the hallmark of the North, and from the peaceful grandeur of the Lake District to the hills and dales that inspired so many great writers and artists, the region is home to sights certain to delight.

Day One

The **Lake District** is one of the most beautiful parts of the North, with magnificent views from the hilly landscape down to **Lake Windermere**. The drive up to the Lake District is in itself a treat; take your time and enjoy the twists and turns whilst taking in the views. Whether you climb one of the peaks, take a relaxing walk or enjoy a boat trip, it is simply breathtaking, and Lake Windermere alone is certainly worth an entire morning, especially in good weather. For some particularly colourful scenery, take time to visit **Holehird Gardens**, where a wonderful variety of plant species is set in 10 acres with great views of the surrounding area.

Such scenery has inspired many poets and authors over the years - perhaps it may just inspire your own flights of fancy? For inspiration, take a peek into the life and history of William Wordsworth with a visit to the writer's pretty **Dove Cottage** and the accompanying **Wordsworth Museum** in **Grasmere**. Visitors can look through the cottage and discover just what it was like to be in William Wordsworth's study, where he is said to have written much of his poetry, and in the guest bedroom, where visitors Sir Walter Scott and Samuel Taylor Coleridge probably slept.

Or, if your literary interest doesn't include the Romantics, another writer inspired by the Lake District is Beatrix Potter - it was here that stories of such characters as Peter Rabbit were created. You can learn more about the tales and the author's life at the **World of Beatrix Potter**, a delightful attraction that's perfect for the entire family. Children can come face to face with Peter Rabbit, Mrs Tiggy-winkle and a whole host of favourites, and for all, the spirit of Potter's work is certainly contagious!

History at the Brontë Parsonage Museum

Grandeur at Bolton Abbey

Day Two

Another area of incredible beauty is the **Yorkshire Dales**. Why not explore the vast green dales, working your way down to **Bolton Abbey**? The 3,000-acre estate of woodland, moorland, rivers and medieval buildings is home to the Duke and Duchess of Devonshire, and includes magnificent grounds and an equally magnificent hotel (see page 95).

Again, the wonderful scenery of the North has been an inspiration to writers, as well as a wealth of painters including the Romantic landscape and marine artist J M W Turner. For those who have not yet had their fill of literary inspiration, you're also now not too far from **Brontë Country**. Explore the countryside

The North has been INSPIRATION for great artists

that inspired Wuthering Heights - a walk around these landscapes can be stunningly evocative - and visit the **Brontë Parsonage Museum** in **Haworth**. Once the Brontë family home, this fascinating museum is where much of the sisters' literature was written. The museum also offers a variety of talks, concerts, workshops and other events throughout the year, with many geared toward families.

Lake Windermere is home to great views, but perhaps the best way to experience them is on the water itself

Day Three

Harrogate is home to many attractions – the **Valley Gardens** are charming, and include activities such as tennis, mini golf and pitch and putt. Or, visit the **Royal Pump Room Museum** to learn about the history of Harrogate and how it became a spa town. This exhibit of the 'Queen of the Inland Spas' includes artefacts ranging from ancient Egypt to the twentieth century.

After so much exploring and sight-seeing (and perhaps a spot of shopping!) you might be in need of a different form of relaxation: the **Turkish Baths and Health Spa** in Harrogate, perfect for any aching feet. Experience the steam room, plunge pool, hot room chambers and relaxation room, and emerge as good as new. It is recommended that you allow yourself around two and a half hours for a truly relaxing and rejuvenating experience!

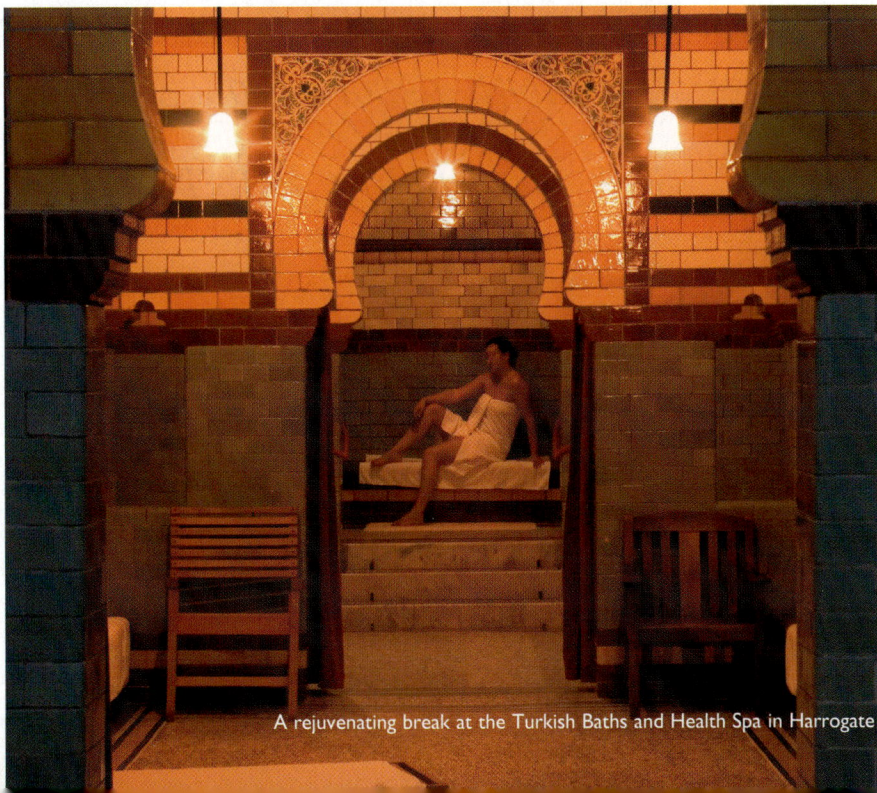

A rejuvenating break at the Turkish Baths and Health Spa in Harrogate

ESCAPE FROM YOUR DESKTOP

If you can't wait to get away, or if you'd simply like to do a little investigating before you make your holiday to the North, browse the links below. Remember, too, that thousands of places to see and things to do await at Best Loved's Web site, **www.bestlovedhotels.com**.

Lake District visitors guide
www.lake-district.gov.uk

Lake Windermere boating
www.windermere-lakecruises.co.uk

Holehird Gardens
www.holehirdgardens.org.uk

The Wordsworth Trust
www.wordsworth.org.uk

World of Beatrix Potter
www.hop-skip-jump.com

Yorkshire Dales visitors guide
www.yorkshire-dales.com

Bolton Abbey
www.boltonabbey.com

Haworth visitors guide
www.haworth.yorks.com

Brontë Parsonage Museum
www.bronte.org.uk

Harrogate visitors guide
www.harrogate.gov.uk

Turkish Baths and Health Spa
www.harrogate.gov.uk/turkishbaths

A TASTE OF THE BEST

The North

CULINARY DIVERSITY is a theme running through Best Loved's Northern favourites: Ranging from fine country-house cuisine to breathtakingly innovative juxtaposition and deliciously authentic Oriental cuisine, you're sure to find something to delight.

THE DEVONSHIRE ARMS ✿✿✿

At this elegant country house set in the Yorkshire Dales, Michael Wignall, executive chef of their Michelin-starred Burlington Restaurant, produces outstanding cuisine for an innovative daily-changing menu. Some tempting starters that might appear during your visit include veal sweetbreads with onion confit, truffle gnocchi and asparagus or a divine assiette of salmon that's a must-try. The main menu offers an ever-changing and mouth-watering selection of venison, lamb, brill, pigeon and sea bass dishes - varieties might include sea bass with roasted artichokes or poached brill in red wine. Better still, there is a delicious choice of desserts on offer, ranging from Bramley apple mousse and Granny Smith sorbet to rum pannacotta and gratin of berries.

The exciting food is complemented by a stunning wine list, or for informal dining, try The Devonshire Brasserie and Bar with its vibrant contemporary decor - not to be missed!

THE FEVERSHAM ARMS ✿

The Feversham Arms has recently been transformed by award-winning hotelier Simon Rhatigan into an utterly sumptuous and modern retreat. And dining here is equally luxurious - the restaurant's award-winning cuisine has an emphasis on game, lamb and seafood from nearby Whitby. The menu comprises delicious and good-value dishes, including a delightful starter of smoked duck breast with celeriac remoulade, and perhaps lobster, seafood and saffron risotto with rocket salad for a main course. As if that isn't appetising enough, the food here is complemented by a fine wine collection of more than 100 bins, meaning you're certain to find something you'll enjoy.

Vibrant dining at the Feversham Arms

L'ENCLUME ✿✿✿

With a beautiful setting in the historic village of Cartmel, L'Enclume is a charming restaurant with rooms and a gastronomic experience to remember. Culinary marvel Simon Rogan

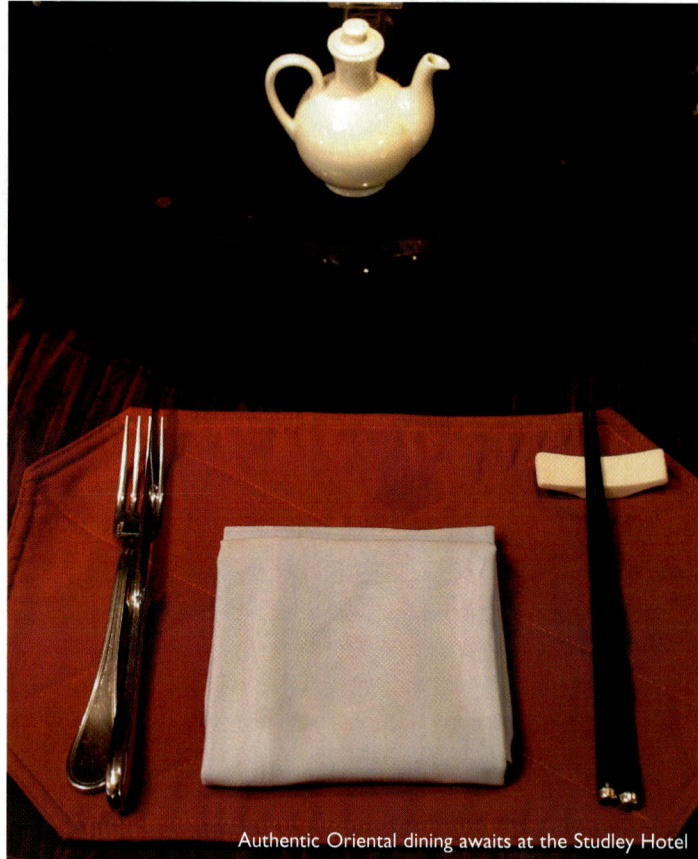

Authentic Oriental dining awaits at the Studley Hotel

A menu devoted to TASTE & TEXTURE *delights at L'Enclume*

serves fresh and exciting cuisine which experiments with contrasting tastes and textures. More adventurous diners will try the Taste and Texture Menu, which features peppered parmesan French fries with pineapple and thyme, or crab with warm jelly, a hint of woodruff and sweet pistachio fudge! From the à la carte menu, enjoy a wide selection of imaginative treats such as loin of venison with speck croustillant, deep-fried grapes and mugwort broth. Desserts are just as much an adventure, with upside-down coconut soufflé, spiced pineapple and mango chutney ice cream. Or, try the hot chocolate mousse with eucalyptus foam, smoked paprika ice cream and stem ginger. It's not surprising that their culinary rule is that rules are there to be broken!

Burnt cream pots - with a creative twist! - at L'Enclume

MIDDLETHORPE HALL & SPA ✿✿✿

In the elegant panelled dining rooms of this beautifully restored hall, diners can enjoy wonderfully imaginative fare from the three- or four-course seasonally-varied menus, on which you'll find such creations - made with local and home-produced ingredients - as tian of Whitby crab and tranche of Scarborough cod. Head chef Lee Heptinstall also produces a variety of vegetarian options, including simple salad of Middlethorpe herbs, and roast asparagus with a poached egg, rocket and hazelnut vinaigrette. One of their celebrated breakfasts comes highly recommended, too, before you leave to explore the nearby sights!

STUDLEY HOTEL

A great location in the spa town of Harrogate is reason enough to visit the Studley Hotel, but an even better incentive is its wonderful restaurant, The Orchid, which serves Oriental cuisine in a beautifully elegant and modern setting. Authentic Thai, Malaysian, Indonesian, Japanese and Philipino dishes include starters such as tempura tiger Prawns (light and crispy tiger prawns or assorted vegetables served with a seaweed-based sauce), and there is a diverse choice of main dishes ranging from pork Tonkatsu (deep-fried marinated loin of pork with a dip of lemon juice based Tonkatsu sauce) to Seven Jewels (stir-fried vegetables with a choice of soy, garlic or chilli sauce). Diners can also choose from The Orchid's set menus, Jasmine or Lotus, which demonstrate their variety of innovative cuisine.

Devonshire chef Michael Wignall's signature assiette of salmon

A TASTE OF THE REGION

Looking for even more to tempt your palate? There are a wealth of fantastic places to dine in the North, all within the covers of this book! Have a browse to whet your appetite, or jump to some of our own favourites:

NORTHCOTE MANOR ✿✿✿

Northcote's award-winning, Michelin-starred restaurant is renowned for its innovative recreation of traditional local dishes, resulting from chef proprietor Nigel Haworth's love of traditional Lancashire cooking.

SWINTON PARK ✿✿

At this stately home near the Yorkshire Dales, fruit and vegetables grown in the walled garden are used in the Samuels Restaurant, as well as at their cookery school run by celebrity chef Rosemary Shrager.

CREWE HALL ✿✿

The oak-panelled Ranulph Restaurant at this stunning Jacobean mansion serves fine, traditional English cuisine, whilst the Café Bar Brasserie serves international food.

LINTHWAITE HOUSE ✿✿

This Lake District Victorian country house serves a variety of fresh, modern British food in a relaxed setting. The views from Linthwaite are not to be missed!

Menu

MIDDLETHORPE HALL & SPA

Diver-caught scallops with bacon crème caramel, squash puree and fresh pea vinaigrette

Roast quail with Bayonne ham, black cherries, celeriac remoulade and hazelnut oil

Roast asparagus with warm poached egg, rocket and hazelnut vinaigrette

Roast loin of Swaledale lamb with purple potatoes, ratatouille, courgette en fleur and summer garlic

Eaton Mess - Yorkshire clotted cream and strawberry cordial

Roast white peach with vanilla waffle and lavender ice cream

"A house of perfect and irresistible atmosphere"

HUGH WALPOLE

ARMATHWAITE HALL HOTEL

Country house

Bassenthwaite Lake,
Cumbria CA12 4RE

T (UK) 0870 432 8570
T 017687 76551
F 017687 76220
armathwaite@bestloved.com
www.armathwaite.bestloved.com

OWNERS
The Graves Family

ROOM RATES
4 Singles   £75 - £129
34 Doubles/Twins   £150 - £258
2 Four-posters   £258 - £298
2 Studio Suites   £298
Includes full breakfast and VAT

CREDIT CARDS
AMERICAN EXPRESS • DC • MC • VI

RATINGS & AWARDS
AA ★★★★ ❀ 72%

FACILITIES
On site: Garden, heli-pad, fishing, croquet, tennis, indoor pool, licensed for weddings, sauna, spa, steam room, gym, beauty salon, wildlife park, archery, clay shooting, quad bike safaris by arrangement
4 meeting rooms/max 80 people
Nearby: Golf

RESTRICTIONS
Limited facilities for disabled guests
No smoking in restaurant, spa and Lake View Lounge

ATTRACTIONS
Beatrix Potter Museum & House, William Wordsworth's homes, Rheged Discovery Centre, Hadrian's Wall, Roman wall and forts, Trotters World of Animals

NEAREST
CITY:
Carlisle - 20 miles/40 mins
Newcastle - 70 miles/1 hr 30 mins

AIRPORT:
Manchester - 120 miles/2 hrs 30 mins
Newcastle - 79 miles/1 hr 50 mins

RAIL STATION:
Penrith - 17 miles/20 mins
Carlisle - 20 miles/40 mins

AFFILIATIONS
Independent

RESERVATIONS
National rate in UK: 0870 432 8570
Quote Best Loved

ACCESS CODES
Not applicable

NORTH

A stately home that will appeal to sportsman and connoisseur alike

Armathwaite Hall is set in a magnificent private estate encompassing parks, woodlands and lake frontage. The present hall, part of which dates from 1650, stands on the site of an ancient manor owned by Sir Adam de Bassenthwaite in the reign of Edward II.

The Hall is run personally by the owners, who pursue the continuing development of their hotel and its leisure and conference facilities with painstaking regard for the warm, elegant nature of this genuinely English stately home.

Connoisseurs of fine cuisine will find much to appreciate at Armathwaite Hall. Master Chef Kevin Dowling takes full advantage of a wealth of local seasonal produce and Cumbrian specialities to create a variety of gastronomic delights.

Management training, personnel motivation courses and corporate hospitality days are popular with delegates and guests, making full use of the extensive sports and leisure facilities available on the estate. One interesting feature is a safari on quad bikes in an area famed for its spectacular views. In short, Armathwaite Hall is the perfect centre to explore the Lake District for either business or pleasure.

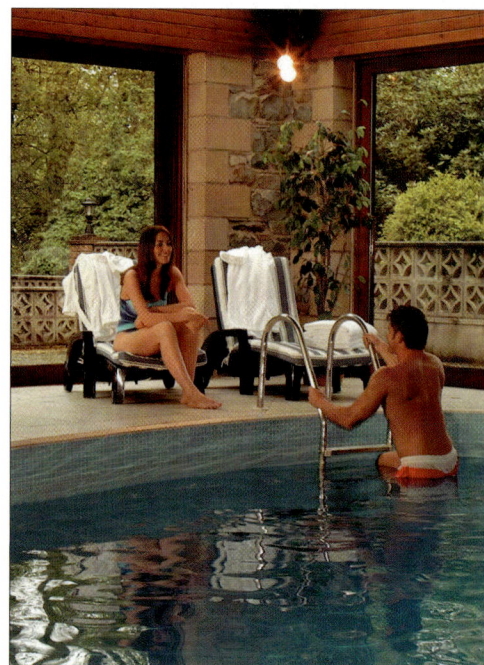

LOCATION
Leave the M6 at exit 40 and follow the A66 to the Keswick roundabout; take the A591 to Carlisle for eight miles and turn left at Castle Inn. The hotel is 300 yards ahead.

> "A very special stay - excellent food, service and comfort"
> NICOLA AND ROBERT DUNN

Map p. 442, grid D6

Inn

THE BLUE LION

The perfect base for English country sport and leisure

Fishing, walking, shooting, racing - experience the simple pleasures of the Yorkshire Dales from one of only three Best Loved Hotels in the region, a welcoming 18th-century coaching inn made even better by an extensive yet sympathetic renovation. Wensleydale may be famous the world over for its deliciously crumbly cheese, but a stay at the The Blue Lion in East Witton will reveal a host of additional local treasures, whether culinary, equine or pedestrian! The historic ruins of Jervaulx Abbey are certainly worth a visit; Catterick, Wetherby, Ripon and York race tracks are all within an hour's drive, and the nearby town of Middleham is making its name as the 'Newmarket of the North'. For those with outdoors inclinations, other activities available include golf, tennis and pony trekking.

Upon your return from an evening stroll along the riverbank - or, if you prefer, a taxing 10-mile challenge hike - you may decide to put up your aching feet and order dinner at the hotel. If so, you can choose the flag-stoned bar, with its open fire and ample selection of hand-pulled beers, or the warm and inviting restaurant. Either way, local game and fish - all procured from one of three provincial estates - should be available.

LOCATION

From the A1, take the B6267 toward Masham; then, follow the A6108 to East Witton. The hotel is on the right soon into the village.

East Witton, Near Leyburn,
North Yorkshire DL8 4SN

T (UK) 0870 432 8538
T 01969 624273
F 01969 624189
bluelion@bestloved.com
www.bluelion.bestloved.com

OWNERS
Paul and Helen Klein

ROOM RATES
Single occupancy £54
11 Doubles/Twins £69 - £89
1 Family Room £89 - £105
Includes full breakfast and VAT

CREDIT CARDS
MC • VI

RATINGS & AWARDS
Independent

FACILITIES
On site: Garden
2 meeting rooms/max 50 people
Nearby: Tennis

RESTRICTIONS
Limited facilities for disabled guests

ATTRACTIONS
Bolton Castle,
Jervaulx Abbey,
Raby Castle,
Fountains Abbey & Studley Royal,
York,
Yorkshire Moors

NEAREST
CITY:
Harrogate - 29 miles/45 mins

AIRPORT:
Leeds/Bradford - 40 miles/1 hr

RAIL STATION:
Northallerton - 25 miles/30 mins

AFFILIATIONS
The Great Inns of Britain

RESERVATIONS
National rate in UK: 0870 432 8538
Quote Best Loved

ACCESS CODES
Not applicable

NORTH

BORROWDALE GATES

Country house

NORTH

Grange-in-Borrowdale, Keswick, Cumbria CA12 5UQ

T (UK) 0870 432 8542
T 017687 77204
F 017687 77254
borrowdale@bestloved.com
www.borrowdale.bestloved.com

GENERAL MANAGER
Helen Patterson

RATES PER PERSON
3 Singles   £65 - £90
26 Doubles/Twins   £65 - £90
Includes full breakfast, dinner and VAT

CREDIT CARDS
AMERICAN EXPRESS • MC • VI

RATINGS & AWARDS
ETC ★★★ Silver Award
RAC White Ribbon ★★★
Dining Award 2
AA ★★★ ❀❀ 79%
Which? Hotel of the Year 2003

FACILITIES
On site: Garden
Nearby: Fishing, riding, golf, boating, cycling, hiking, climbing

RESTRICTIONS
Limited facilities for disabled guests
No children under 7 years
No smoking in restaurant
No pets
Closed 5 Jan. - 1 Feb.

ATTRACTIONS
Borrowdale Valley, Cockermouth, Grasmere, Wordsworth's birthplace and Dove Cottage, Carlisle Castle, Muncaster Castle, Hadrian's Wall

NEAREST
CITY:
Carlisle - 30 miles/45 mins

AIRPORT:
Manchester - 120 miles/2 hrs
Glasgow - 145 miles/2 hrs 30 mins

RAIL STATION:
Penrith - 22 miles/30 mins

AFFILIATIONS
Independent

RESERVATIONS
National rate in UK: 0870 432 8542
Quote Best Loved

ACCESS CODES
Not applicable

A rich stroke of fortune amongst the majestic Lakeland mountains

Baddeley's Guide to the English Lakes says: '... there can be no doubt that Borrowdale holds the first position amongst [the Lake District's] valleys'. In the north of the valley is Derwentwater, 'The Queen of the Lakes', and all around are the majestic Lakeland mountains, changing colour with the weather and the seasons.

Within this idyllic picture is Borrowdale Gates, secluded in its own two acres of wooded gardens. The house was built in 1860 as a private residence, and its air of comfortable informality continues; this is a wonderful place to shed one's cares and release one's tensions. The furniture and fabrics contribute to the feeling of mellow good living, and antiques and fresh flowers add a personal touch. The bedrooms (10 on the ground floor) make the most of the breathtaking views, as do the lounges and restaurant with their picture windows.

The restaurant, which has won critical acclaim from numerous food guides, serves award-winning meals from a daily-changing menu inspired by the finest local produce.

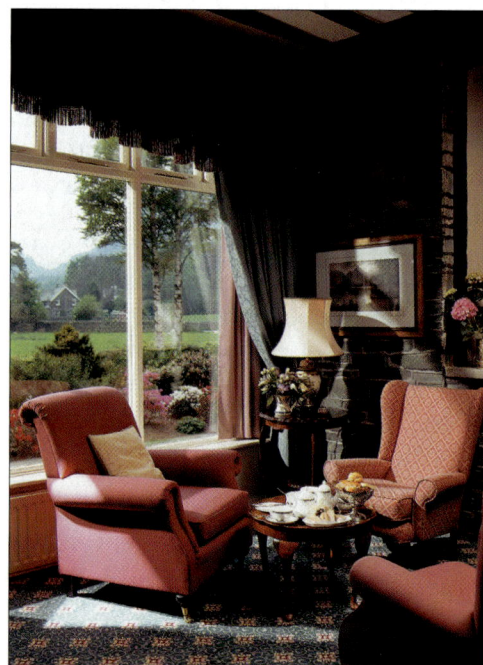

LOCATION
Exit 40 off the M6, A66 to Keswick; then, take the B5289 four miles and turn right at the double humpback bridge into Grange. The hotel is a quarter of a mile past the village, on the right.

Country house

BROXTON HALL

NORTH

A historic house of character just a league or so from Roman Chester

Built in 1671, Broxton Hall is a black-and-white half-timbered Tudor house set in five acres of grounds and extensive gardens. The historical walled city of Chester, famed for its Roman and medieval remains and buildings, is less than 10 miles away.

The hotel provides modern comfort, yet retains the ambience of a bygone age: The reception area reflects this character in the furnishings, mahogany-panelled walls, carved mahogany staircase and a massive Jacobean fireplace, where a welcoming log fire burns most evenings. All 10 bedrooms are beautifully furnished with antiques and offer every facility for your comfort including, of course, full central heating. The Cestria restaurant overlooks the fountain terrace and gardens, and is much praised by regular diners. Internationally-inspired cuisine is served throughout the year, with local game in season and freshly caught fish.

Broxton Hall is ideally placed for visiting the delightful North Wales seaside and the dramatic scenery of Snowdonia. There are excellent golf courses locally, and for the racing enthusiast, Chester and Bangor-on-Dee races are nearby.

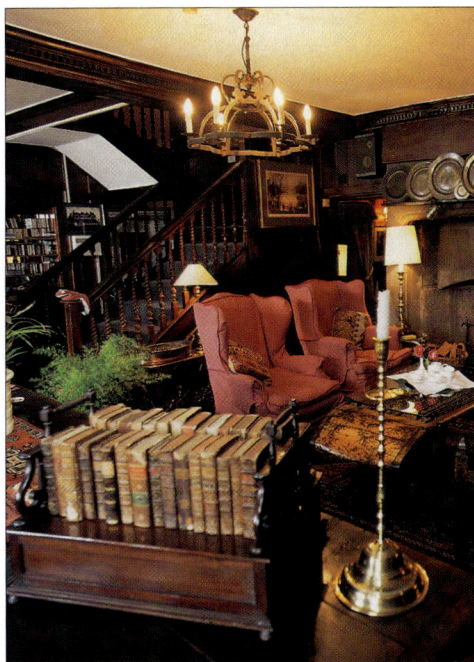

LOCATION
From Chester, take the A41, signposted to Whitchurch. The hotel is nine miles on, shortly after the A534 junction, on the left.

Whitchurch Road, Broxton, Chester, Cheshire CH3 9JS

T (UK) 0870 432 8547
T 01829 782321
F 01829 782330
broxton@bestloved.com
www.broxton.bestloved.com

OWNERS
Angela and John Ireland

ROOM RATES
Single occupancy   £75
8 Doubles/Twins   £90
1 Four-poster   £110
1 Junior Suite   £130
Includes full breakfast and VAT

CREDIT CARDS
AMERICAN EXPRESS • DC • MC • VI

RATINGS & AWARDS
RAC ★★★ Dining Award 2

FACILITIES
On site: Garden, heli-pad, licensed for weddings
1 meeting room/max 45 people
Nearby: Golf, riding, fishing

RESTRICTIONS
Limited facilities for disabled guests
Children by arrangement
No smoking in restaurant
Pets by arrangement

ATTRACTIONS
Peckforton and Beeston castles, Snowdonia National Park, Chester, Erdigg Hall, Staveley Water Gardens, Chester and Bangor-on-Dee racecourses

NEAREST
CITY:
Chester - 10 miles/15 mins

AIRPORT:
Manchester - 30 miles/40 mins
Liverpool - 25 miles/35 mins

RAIL STATION:
Chester - 10 miles/15 mins
Crewe - 12 miles/15 mins

AFFILIATIONS
Independent

RESERVATIONS
National rate in UK: 0870 432 8547
Quote Best Loved

ACCESS CODES
Not applicable

To say I was stunned by the place would be an understatement ...
Everything was perfect - we couldn't fault the arrangements in any way

JAYNE FERGURSON, LEICESTER

CREWE HALL

Stately home

Weston Road, Crewe,
Cheshire CW1 6UZ

T (UK) 0870 432 8581
T 01270 253333
F 01270 253322
crewehall@bestloved.com
www.crewehall.bestloved.com

GENERAL MANAGER
James Harding

ROOM RATES
Single occupancy	£177 - £397
39 Doubles/Twins	£219
13 Superior Doubles/Twins	£249
8 Four-posters	£274
5 Suites	£359 - £439
Includes full breakfast and VAT	

CREDIT CARDS
AMERICAN EXPRESS • DC • MC • VI

RATINGS & AWARDS
RAC ★★★★ Dining Award 3
AA ★★★★ ⊛⊛ 75%
Cheshire Life Hotel of the Year

FACILITIES
On site: Garden, croquet, tennis,
football pitch
17 meeting rooms/max 350 people
Nearby: Golf

RESTRICTIONS
Limited facilities for disabled guests
No pets
No smoking in restaurant

ATTRACTIONS
Arley Hall & Gardens, Beeston Castle,
Biddulph Grange, Chester,
the Potteries, Tatton Park,
Bridgemere Garden World

NEAREST
CITY:
Chester - 20 miles/40 mins
Manchester - 35 miles/40 mins

AIRPORT:
Manchester - 35 miles/30 mins

RAIL STATION:
Crewe - 2 miles/5 mins

AFFILIATIONS
Grand Heritage Hotels
Marston Hotels

RESERVATIONS
National rate in UK: 0870 432 8581
Toll free in UK: 0845 1300 700
Toll free in US: 888-93-GRAND
Quote Best Loved

ACCESS CODES
AMADEUS UI XVCCWE
APOLLO/GALILEO UI 24840
SABRE/ABACUS UI 49965
WORLDSPAN UI 41056

A stately home that sets a truly luxurious standard

Looks are deceiving at Crewe Hall, an imposing Jacobean pile that was built in 1615 and refurbished in 1866 by architect Edward Barry, who worked on the Houses of Parliament. The exterior is everything you would expect from a significant stately home, but the addition of a contemporary building known as the West Wing concludes a long tradition of blending the old and new. There are 26 superior rooms in the original Hall, including 10 four-posters, and 39 new accommodations with air conditioning and modern furnishing throughout. Connected to the old hall via a glass link and rotunda with pleasing views of the gardens, they benefit from ample proportions, even by four-star standards.

The reception is light and airy, with limestone flooring and a feature glass-and-brushed-steel staircase. Similar contrast is achieved in the dining options: The oak-panelled Ranulph Restaurant offers traditional English cuisine amidst roaring log fires, whereas an inventive international menu is the order of the day at the sleek and sophisticated brasserie. Conference facilities are first-class, and corporate guests will impress their clients if they take them to the aptly-named πr^2 - a revolving bar that offers a gradually-revealed indoor panorama.

LOCATION

Exit the M6 at junction 16 and follow the A500 toward Crewe; at the first roundabout, take the last exit. At the next roundabout, take the first exit. The hotel is a few hundred yards on the right.

NORTH

Country house

CROSBY LODGE

The splendours of good living on the picturesque Scottish border

This splendidly romantic Georgian house, home of the Sedgwick family, stands high above the village of Low Crosby, surrounded by wooded areas and parkland and with a marvellous view of the River Eden. The house, built in 1802 and altered some years later to the castellated appearance of today, is beautifully furnished with family antiques complemented by stunning flower arrangements.

Perfectionist and chef Roger Herring and his young team serve up deliciously exciting menus featuring authentic Continental cuisine and the very best of traditional British fare. (The Crosby Lodge sweet trolley, along with their homemade bread and preserves, is renowned far and wide!) Patricia looks after the front of the house and will greet you personally. The wine list, written and supplied by daughter Philippa and stored in their courtyard wine warehouse, is exceptional.

The house has 11 bedrooms tastefully designed by Patricia. The friendly, efficient staff make this the ideal venue for a peaceful holiday, short break, shooting party or golfing holiday.

LOCATION
Situated just off the A689 five miles east of Carlisle. Three and a half miles from junction 44 on the M6, on the right, just through Low Crosby.

High Crosby, Crosby-on-Eden, Carlisle, Cumbria CA6 4QZ

T (UK) 0870 432 8584
T 01228 573618
F 01228 573428
crosby@bestloved.com
www.crosby.bestloved.com

OWNERS
Patricia and Michael Sedgwick

ROOM RATES
Single occupancy	£90
6 Doubles/Twins	£140
2 Four-posters	£140 - £180
3 Family Rooms	£160 - £185

Includes full breakfast and VAT

CREDIT CARDS
AMERICAN EXPRESS • JCB • MC • VI

RATINGS & AWARDS
ETC ★★★ Silver Award

FACILITIES
On site: Garden
2 meeting rooms/max 14 people
Nearby: Golf, fishing, shooting

RESTRICTIONS
Limited facilities for disabled guests
Smoking in bar only
Pets by arrangement

ATTRACTIONS
Hadrian's Wall, the Lake District, Carlisle Castle and Cathedral, Wetheral Woods, Penrith Castle, Lanercost Priory, Brougham Castle

NEAREST
CITY:
Carlisle - 5 miles/8 mins

AIRPORT:
Newcastle - 58 miles/1 hr
Glasgow - 100 miles/1 hr 30 mins

RAIL STATION:
Carlisle - 5 miles/15 mins

AFFILIATIONS
Independent

RESERVATIONS
National rate in UK: 0870 432 8584
Quote Best Loved

ACCESS CODES
Not applicable

NORTH

"A little bit of heaven at the foothills of Helvellyn"

JOHN AND HELEN, HAMPSHIRE

DALE HEAD HALL

Country house

NORTH

Lake Thirlmere, Keswick,
Cumbria CA12 4TN
T (UK) 0870 432 8590
T 017687 72478
F 017687 71070
dalehead@bestloved.com
www.dalehead.bestloved.com

OWNERS
Alan and Shirley Lowe

GENERAL MANAGER
Hans Bonkenburg

RATES PER PERSON
Single occupancy   £110
6 Doubles/Twins   £85 - £95
3 Superior Doubles/Twins £100
3 Four-posters   £100
Includes full breakfast, dinner and VAT

CREDIT CARDS
AMERICAN EXPRESS • JCB • MC • VI

RATINGS & AWARDS
ETC ★★★ Gold Award
AA ★★★ ✿✿ 75%
Which? Hotel of the Year 2003

FACILITIES
On site: Garden, fishing, croquet
Nearby: Golf, sailing, canoeing, riding

RESTRICTIONS
Limited facilities for disabled guests
No children under 10 years in the
restaurant, high tea provided
Smoking in bar only
No pets; guide dogs only
Closed 1 Jan. - 3 Feb.

ATTRACTIONS
Wordsworth's Dove Cottage,
Beatrix Potter's museum and house,
Cumbrian fells, Ruskin's Brantwood

NEAREST
CITY:
Carlisle - 40 miles/45 mins

AIRPORT:
Manchester - 100 miles/2 hrs

RAIL STATION:
Penrith - 10 miles/20 mins

AFFILIATIONS
Independent

RESERVATIONS
National rate in UK: 0870 432 8590
Quote Best Loved

ACCESS CODES
Not applicable

Blissful solitude on the lush, green shores of Lake Thirlmere

Next to Lake Thirlmere, surrounded by lush woodland, stands this glorious 16th-century house. Rich green lawns sweep towards the water, and the tranquillity of the location cannot be surpassed, since the house stands alone on the shores of the three-and-a-quarter-mile lake.

The Leathes family came to Dale Head Hall in 1577; in 1877, lake and hall were purchased by the city of Manchester to provide the city with clean drinking water and successive Lord Mayors with an idyllic summer retreat. Today, Alan and Shirley Lowe and their family offer exceptional accommodation and service. In restoring the hall, they set high priority on recreating its 16th-century authenticity. The bar and lounge are also delightful. The five-course table d'hôte dinner is served in the oak-beamed Elizabethan dining room, which has an inglenook fireplace. The food is fresh and imaginatively prepared, and is complemented with a good choice of fine wines.

All the splendours of the Lake District are adjacent; Helvellyn is on the doorstep, and Borrowdale is close by. Fishing, sailing and canoeing can all be enjoyed - so please be sure to take your own equipment, as this cannot be supplied by the hotel.

LOCATION
On the A591 halfway between Keswick and Grasmere. The hotel is situated along a quarter of a mile of private driveway overlooking Lake Thirlmere.

This is a hotel experience exceeded by no other in this country

BRIAN HARGREAVES, FOOD AND WINE EDITOR, LIFE MAGAZINES

Country house

THE DEVONSHIRE

Bolton Abbey, Near Skipton,
North Yorkshire BD23 6AJ

T (UK) 08700 432 8595
T 01756 710441
F 01756 710564
devonskip@bestloved.com
www.devonskip.bestloved.com

OWNERS
Duke and Duchess of Devonshire

MANAGING DIRECTOR
Jeremy Rata

ROOM RATES

Single occupancy	£160 - £330
28 Doubles/Twins	£220
9 Four-posters	£260 - £330
3 Suites	£380

Includes full breakfast,
daily newspaper and VAT

CREDIT CARDS

AMERICAN EXPRESS • DC • MC • VI

RATINGS & AWARDS
RAC Gold Ribbon ★★★
Dining Award 4
AA ★★★ ⊛⊛⊛
AA Top 200 - 2004/2005
International Wine Spectator
Best of Excellence Award

FACILITIES
On site: Garden, heli-pad, fishing,
croquet, tennis, indoor pool, gym,
sauna, solarium, spa, steam room,
beauty therapy, licensed for weddings
4 meeting rooms/max 120 people
Nearby: Golf

RESTRICTIONS
No smoking in Burlington Restaurant

ATTRACTIONS
Brontë Parsonage, Bolton Priory,
Skipton Castle, Castle Howard,
Fountains Abbey, Harewood House,
Newby Hall

NEAREST
CITY:
Leeds - 17 miles/30 mins

AIRPORT:
Manchester - 60 miles/1 hr 15 mins
Leeds/Bradford - 12 miles/20 mins

RAIL STATION:
Ilkley - 5 miles/10 mins

AFFILIATIONS
Small Luxury Hotels
Pride of Britain
Celebrated Hotels Collection
The European Connection

RESERVATIONS
National rate in UK: 0870 432 8595
Toll free in US: 800-544-9993
or 800-525-4800 or 800-98-PRIDE
Quote Best Loved

ACCESS CODES
AMADEUS LX MANDCH
APOLLO/GALILEO LX 44518
SABRE/ABACUS LX 11172
WORLDSPAN LX MANDC

NORTH

Fabulous facilities in the breathtaking Yorkshire Dales

Everyone who comes to Wharfedale for the first time is struck by the beauty of the countryside. The 30,000 acre Bolton Abbey Estate is owned by the Duke of Devonshire and there are 80 miles of footpaths along the riverbank to the spectacular ruins of the 12th-century Bolton Priory, through woodland and over the moors. All this is on the doorstep of the hotel, originally a 17th-century coaching inn.

The hotel reveals a wonderfully warm and welcoming interior furnished and decorated using antiques and fine paintings from the family home at Chatsworth in Derbyshire. Understated elegance best describes the comfortable lounges and exquisitely appointed bedrooms which include nine romantic four-poster rooms.

Michael Wignall is Head Chef of The Michelin-starred Burlington Restaurant where guests are treated to outstanding cooking and service. The stunning wine list has over 2,000 bins including 60 'house wines'. The Devonshire Brasserie and Bar provides a lively and less formal alternative. A converted 17th-century barn is home to the leisure facilities of the Devonshire Club, where guests can use the gym, pool, steam room, sauna, and tennis court or enjoy a relaxing therapy treatment. Luxury spa days are available, which include a consultation and full use of the facilities.

LOCATION

On the B6160 to Bolton Abbey, 250 yards north from its roundabout junction with the A59 Skipton to Harrogate road.

NORTH

ELEVEN DIDSBURY PARK

Townhouse

11 Didsbury Park,
Didsbury Village,
Manchester M20 5LH

T (UK) 0870 432 8505
T 0161 448 7711
F 0161 448 8282
11didsbury@bestloved.com
www.11didsbury.bestloved.com

OWNER
Eamonn O'Loughlin

ROOM RATES
Single occupancy   £81 - £145
13 Doubles/Twins   £81 - £145
4 Junior Suites   £105 - £175
Includes service and VAT

CREDIT CARDS
AMERICAN EXPRESS • DC • JCB • MC • VI

RATINGS & AWARDS
Sunday Times Top Five
Hotel Town Houses

FACILITIES
On site: Garden, gym, croquet
2 meeting rooms/max 20 people
Nearby: Tennis, entertainment centre

RESTRICTIONS
Limited facilities for disabled guests
No smoking throughout
No pets; guide dogs only

ATTRACTIONS
Lowry Centre, Bridgewater Hall,
Old Trafford,
Manchester United Museum,
The Opera House, Lyme Park

NEAREST
CITY:
Manchester - 3 ½ miles/10 mins

AIRPORT:
Manchester - 4 miles/10 mins

RAIL STATION:
Stockport - 3 miles/10 mins

AFFILIATIONS
Independent

RESERVATIONS
National rate in UK: 0870 432 8505
Quote Best Loved

ACCESS CODES
Not applicable

A stylish urban retreat reflecting Manchester's newfound dynamism

Prosperous mill owners and industrialists founded the exclusive south Manchester suburb of Didsbury in the 1850s. Just 15 minutes from the city centre, this leafy neighbourhood of imposing Victorian homes has metamorphosed into a cosmopolitan enclave brimming with hip restaurants and bars.

Eamonn and Sally O'Loughlin have transformed a series of outbuildings arranged around a Victorian walled garden into a classic townhouse hotel. There is not a shred of chintz or an over-stuffed armchair in sight, but instead a vision of artful contemporary chic and the odd quirky feature - such as the Chinese sideboard that serves as a bar. Sally's work as a TV make-up artist may account for her creative flair with colours. Eamonn's innate sense of Irish hospitality is echoed by the boy Fergal the tabby cat - just so long as you don't sit on His chair.

The O'Loughlins offer a scrumptious breakfast, and there are plenty of restaurants nearby for dining out (and a courtesy four-wheel-drive to take you, when available). There is also a small conference room for up to 15 people. Additionally, just 100 metres down the road is Eleven Didsbury Park's new sister hotel, Didsbury House, complete with beauty spa and gym.

LOCATION

From the M60, take the A34; turn left onto the A5145 and continue down Wilmslow Road. Turn right into Didsbury Park opposite The Towers Business Park. The hotel is halfway down on the left.

> **Always one of our favourite places - it gets better every time we stay! Thanks for looking after us so well**
>
> SUSIE & DAVID HAWKE

Inn

THE FEVERSHAM ARMS

A Yorkshire inn with a refreshing new look by an award-winning hotelier

If you haven't paid a visit to the Feversham Arms in a while, you are urged to renew your acquaintance with this historic North Yorkshire Inn. The Feversham has welcomed travellers to Helmsley since 1855, but in the last few months has undergone a transformation by award-winning hotelier Simon Rhatigan - no doubt a reason for the hotel's inclusion in this year's Good Food Guide and Which? Guide to Good Hotels!

From the minute you cross the threshold, The Feversham promises stylish relaxation. Deep sofas in subtly-lit lounges invite guests to sink in mellow comfort before open log fires. Each bedroom has its own character and country-chic décor, including a Bang & Olufsen TV with integral DVD/CD. Rooms have a DVD/CD library; every bathroom pampers you with Molton Brown toiletries and big, soft bathrobes.

The food is deeply rooted in the national park that surrounds the hotel, with an emphasis on game, lamb and seafood from nearby Whitby - all complimented by a wine list of more than 100 bins. The hotel has a strong following of guests who enjoy a variety of country pursuits, but many come simply to relax and escape from reality - some, in fact, never leave their rooms (don't ask!). Others make the most of the gym, tennis and pool and explore the myriad of interesting shops and sights on offer within a short drive.

LOCATION

From York, take the A19 to Thirsk, then the A170 (Scarborough). Helmsley is 14 miles along the A170 and the hotel is just off the market square.

NORTH

Helmsley,
North Yorkshire YO62 5AG

T (UK) 0870 432 8506
T 01439 770766
F 01439 770346
feversham@bestloved.com
www.feversham.bestloved.com

OWNER
Simon Rhatigan

ROOM RATES
Single occupancy	£120 - £190
12 Doubles/Twins	£130 - £160
5 Suites	£200

Includes morning hot drink, newspaper, full breakfast and VAT

CREDIT CARDS
AMERICAN EXPRESS • MC • VI

RATINGS & AWARDS
RAC ★★★ Dining Award 2
AA ★★★ ✿ 77%

FACILITIES
On site: Garden, gym, outdoor pool, riding, golf, tennis, pool terraces, walking trails, shooting, mountain biking
1 meeting room/max 30 people
Nearby: Riding, shooting

RESTRICTIONS
No smoking in bedrooms
Pets by arrangement

ATTRACTIONS
Helmsley Castle, Duncombe Park, Rievaulx Abbey, Castle Howard, Jorvik Viking Centre, York, Yorkshire Moors

NEAREST
CITY:
York - 22 miles/30 mins

AIRPORT:
Leeds/Bradford - 50 miles/1 hr 15 mins

RAIL STATION:
York - 22 miles/30 mins

AFFILIATIONS
Independent

RESERVATIONS
National rate in UK: 0870 432 8506
Quote Best Loved

ACCESS CODES
Not applicable

> "Standards are as high as ever and, if anything, seem to have improved"
>
> TIM & HEATHER ERRIDGE, LANCASHIRE

THE GENERAL TARLETON INN

Inn

Boroughbridge Road, Ferrensby,
Knaresborough,
North Yorkshire HG5 0PZ

T (UK) 0870 432 8623
T 01423 340284
F 01423 340288
tarleton@bestloved.com
www.tarleton.bestloved.com

OWNERS
John and Claire Topham

ROOM RATES
Single occupancy   £85
14 Doubles/Twins   £97 - £120
Includes full breakfast and VAT

CREDIT CARDS
AMERICAN EXPRESS • MC • VI

RATINGS & AWARDS
ETC ★★★ Hotel
AA ★★★ ✿✿ 68%
Yorkshire Life Dining Pub of
the Year 04/05

FACILITIES
On site: Garden,
licensed for weddings
1 meeting room/max 40 people
Nearby: Golf, riding, fishing

RESTRICTIONS
No facilities for disabled guests
No smoking in bedrooms
Pets by arrangement

ATTRACTIONS
City of York, spa town of Harrogate,
Fountains Abbey, Harewood House,
Ripon Cathedral, Beningborough Hall

NEAREST
CITY:
York - 16 miles/30 mins

AIRPORT:
Leeds/Bradford - 16 miles/25 mins

RAIL STATION:
Harrogate - 6 miles/20 mins

AFFILIATIONS
Independent

RESERVATIONS
National rate in UK: 0870 432 8623
Quote Best Loved

ACCESS CODES
Not applicable

Delicious food, a lovely coaching inn and proprietors with a magic touch

This 250-year-old coaching inn surrounded by beautiful, unspoilt Yorkshire countryside, is owned by John and Claire Topham, who have turned it into a charming hotel with pretty, top-quality bedrooms and an outstanding reputation for good food.

John Topham leads a kitchen brigade that takes food seriously and has been showered with awards to prove it. From traditional dishes such as sausage and mash - featuring Lishman's of Ilkley prize-winning sausages - to carpaccio of beef or seared sea bass on a tomato tart, everything is sourced with the utmost care and loyalty to local suppliers. Choose from the intimate restaurant, the covered courtyard for al fresco eating or the oak-beamed bar with its nooks and crannies and log fires for a less formal atmosphere. The General Tarleton is perfect for visiting historic York, elegant Harrogate and bustling Leeds - all of which are within a half hour's drive of the hotel. It is also ideal for touring the Yorkshire moors and dales.

LOCATION
Exit the A1(M) at junction 47 onto the A59 to Knaresborough; then take the A6055 to Ferrensby.

Country house

GILPIN LODGE HOTEL

A true gourmet retreat amidst idyllic Cumbrian scenery

Troutbeck and Patterdale, Kentmere and Crook are just some of the names of the 14 romantic bedrooms at Gilpin Lodge, reflecting the profusion of beauty spots close to this gem of a hotel near Lake Windermere. Set in 20 tranquil acres of woodland, moors and country gardens, the hotel is just 12 miles from the M6, almost opposite Windermere golf course and at the heart of the Lake District's wealth of sightseeing, history and activities.

At the end of each day's exploration, the promise of extreme luxury and comfort awaits. The elegant lounges and dining rooms invite relaxation; real fires blaze on chilly days; fresh flowers and picture-lined walls abound. The sumptuous bedrooms are thoughtfully furnished and equipped, some with four-poster beds, whirlpool baths and patios leading onto the gardens. The breakfast menu here is sybaritic, and dinner - a modern interpretation of classical cuisine - will undoubtedly be the highlight of the day. The wine list (a copy awaits in your room) merits deliberation.

Gilpin Lodge is meticulously run by the Cunliffe family and a team of dedicated and long-serving staff whose experience shows in every corner. What's more, there are no conferences or weddings to distract you from your peace - in short, Gilpin Lodge is the art of relaxation, perfected.

LOCATION
Leave the M6 at exit 36 and take the A590/591 to the roundabout north of Kendal; then take the B5284 for five miles.

Crook Road, Windermere,
Cumbria LA23 3NE

T (UK) 0870 432 8890
T 015394 88818
F 015394 88058
gilpin@bestloved.com
www.gilpin.bestloved.com

OWNERS
John and Christine Cunliffe

DIRECTORS
Richard Marriott and Barney Cunliffe

RATES PER PERSON
9 Doubles/Twins   £110 - £145
5 Four-posters   £125 - £145
Includes full breakfast, dinner and VAT

CREDIT CARDS
AMERICAN EXPRESS • DC • JCB • MC • VI

RATINGS & AWARDS
ETC ★★★ Gold Award
RAC Gold Ribbon ★★★
Dining Award 4
AA ★★★ ❀❀
AA Top 200 - 2004/2005
AA Top 10 - 2004

FACILITIES
On site: Garden, croquet
Nearby: Golf, riding, tennis, fishing

RESTRICTIONS
Limited facilities for disabled guests
No children under 7 years
Smoking in one lounge only
No pets

ATTRACTIONS
Wordsworth's Dove Cottage,
World of Beatrix Potter,
Lake Windermere, Holker Hall,
Levens Hall,
Blackwell Arts & Crafts House

NEAREST
CITY:
Manchester - 80 miles/1 hr 15 mins

AIRPORT:
Manchester - 90 miles/1 hr 45 mins

RAIL STATION:
Windermere - 2 miles/10 mins

AFFILIATIONS
Celebrated Hotels Collection
Pride of Britain

RESERVATIONS
National rate in UK: 0870 432 8890
Toll free in US: 800-322-2403
or 800-98-PRIDE
Quote Best Loved

ACCESS CODES
Not applicable

NORTH

Map p. 442, grid E7

THE GRANGE HOTEL

Townhouse

NORTH

1 Clifton, York,
North Yorkshire YO30 6AA

T (UK) 0870 432 8631
T 01904 644744
F 01904 612453
grange@bestloved.com
www.grange.bestloved.com

OWNER
Jeremy Cassel

GENERAL MANAGER
Graham Usher

ROOM RATES
3 Singles   £110
24 Doubles/Twins   £140 - £200
2 Four-posters   £200
1 Suite   £250
Includes full breakfast and VAT

CREDIT CARDS
AMERICAN EXPRESS • DC • JCB • MC • VI

RATINGS & AWARDS
ETC ★★★ Gold Award
RAC Blue Ribbon ★★★ Dining Award 3
AA ★★★ ⊕⊕
AA Top 200 - 2004/2005

FACILITIES
On site: Licensed for weddings
2 meeting rooms/max 100 people
Nearby: Golf, fitness,
use of private leisure club

RESTRICTIONS
Limited facilities for disabled guests
No smoking in restaurant
Pets by arrangement

ATTRACTIONS
York Minster, The Shambles,
National Railway Museum,
Castle Howard, York Racecourse,
Yorkshire Moors & Dales

NEAREST
CITY:
York

AIRPORT:
Leeds/Bradford - 30 miles/50 mins

RAIL STATION:
York - 1 mile/10 mins

AFFILIATIONS
Celebrated Hotels Collection
Grand Heritage Hotels

RESERVATIONS
National rate in UK: 0870 432 8631
Toll free in US: 800-322-2403
or 888-93-GRAND
Quote Best Loved

ACCESS CODES
AMADEUS UI LQQYGRA
APOLLO/GALILEO UI62076
SABRE/ABACUS UI26908
WORLDSPAN UI 43146

Luxury, fine cuisine and all the splendours of York and the Dales

Given its history of conquerors (Roman, Saxon, Viking and Norman), it is not surprising that York boasts of being one of Britain's most interesting cities - and you would be hard pressed to find anywhere more convenient or comfortable for its exploration than The Grange. Within walking distance are the minster (dating from 1100) and its remarkable stained glass, the City Walls, the Jorvik Viking Centre, the National Railway Museum and the medieval Shambles. Within easy driving distance are stately homes, the Yorkshire Dales and the renowned York Racecourse.

The Grange itself is a listed Regency townhouse built in 1834 and carefully restored to create a luxurious 30-bedroom hotel. Light streams down the vine-leaf cast-iron staircase, which leads from finely-decorated bedrooms. English chintz and fine antiques pervade, and all rooms offer satellite television.

Not only is the hotel ideally situated for the explorer, the gourmet has a choice of three restaurants, from the elegance of the award-winning Ivy Restaurant, mixing classic French and modern British cuisine, to the Seafood Bar and the relaxed Brasserie, converted from the old brick-vaulted cellars. Eat, drink, relax, explore - The Grange Hotel conquers all.

LOCATION

About 500 yards from York city centre on the
A19 York - Thirsk road.

Map p. 442, grid D7

Townhouse

GRANTS HOTEL

Swan Road, Harrogate,
North Yorkshire HG1 2SS

T (UK) 0870 432 8632
T 01423 560666
F 01423 502550
grants@bestloved.com
www.grants.bestloved.com

MANAGING DIRECTOR
Pam Grant

ROOM RATES
13 Singles	£75 - £114
26 Doubles/Twins	£95 - £148
1 Four-poster	£115 - £160
2 Suites	£120 - £170

Includes full breakfast and VAT

CREDIT CARDS
AMERICAN EXPRESS • DC • JCB • MC • VI

RATINGS & AWARDS
ETC ★★★ Silver Award
RAC ★★★ Dining Award 1
AA ★★★ 74%

FACILITIES
On site: Garden, patio gardens
5 meeting rooms/max 80 people
Nearby: Golf, health & leisure club,
riding, fishing

RESTRICTIONS
Limited facilities for disabled guests
No smoking in bistro
Pets by arrangement

ATTRACTIONS
Fountains Abbey,
Middleham and Bolton castles,
Herriot Country, Yorkshire Dales,
York, Harrogate

NEAREST
CITY:
Leeds - 15 miles/25 mins

AIRPORT:
Leeds/Bradford - 12 miles/20 mins

RAIL STATION:
Harrogate - ½ mile/5 mins

FERRY PORT:
Hull - 70 miles/1 hr 30 mins

AFFILIATIONS
Fine Individual Hotels
Preston's Global Hotels

RESERVATIONS
National rate in UK: 0870 432 8632
Toll free in UK: 0800 371343
Toll free in the US: 800-544-9993
Quote Best Loved

ACCESS CODES
APOLLO/GALILEO RM 48485
SABRE/ABACUS RM 04297

Elegant and individual hospitality in the heart of historic England

Harrogate is a beautiful spa and floral town in the heart of an area rich in English history. James Herriot, the world's most celebrated veterinarian, was a regular weekly visitor for many years, finding a convivial refuge from the nearby Yorkshire Dales, scene of his adventures.

Within a short distance is the Roman city of York, with its Jorvik Viking Centre. Alternatively, visit Fountains Abbey, England's largest Cistercian monastery which was disestablished by Henry VIII and now preserved as a World Heritage Site.

You can explore Middleham Castle, home of Richard III and immortalised by William Shakespeare, visit Bolton Castle where Mary, Queen of Scots was imprisoned, or see Haworth, home to the Brontë family.

Grants is a family-run hotel with a reputation for quality service, combining modern efficiency with old-fashioned hospitality. Each of the tastefully decorated bedrooms offers a full range of facilities, and a lift serves all floors. Chimney Pots Bistro provides an imaginative menu in an elegant air-conditioned atmosphere and is a firm favourite with local gourmets.

LOCATION
From the M1 or M62 at Leeds, take the A61 to Harrogate, then the second left after The Royal Hall traffic lights into Swan Road.

NORTH

Map p. 442, grid B8

GREEN BOUGH HOTEL

Townhouse

NORTH

60 Hoole Road, Chester,
Cheshire CH2 3NL

T (UK) 0870 432 8635
T 01244 326241
F 01244 326265
greenbough@bestloved.com
www.greenbough.bestloved.com

OWNERS
Janice & Philip Martin

GENERAL MANAGER
Wendy Smith-Williams

ROOM RATES
Single occupancy   £90 - £180
8 Doubles/Twins   £125 - £165
7 Suites   £185 - £250
Includes full breakfast and VAT

CREDIT CARDS
AMERICAN EXPRESS • DC • MC • VI

RATINGS & AWARDS
ETC ★★★ Gold Award
RAC Blue Ribbon ★★★ Dining Award 3
North West Tourist Board -
Small Hotel of the Year 2003
England In Excellence Award Finalists 2003

FACILITIES
On site: Rooftop garden, bicycles,
private dining room
1 meeting room/max 24 people
Nearby: Golf, fishing, tennis, leisure
centre with swimming pool and gym

RESTRICTIONS
Limited facilities for disabled guests
No children under 12 years
No smoking throughout
No pets; guide dogs only

ATTRACTIONS
Snowdonia, Lake District,
Historic Chester, Chester Zoo,
National Trust and English Heritage
properties and gardens,
Liverpool, Manchester

NEAREST
CITY:
Chester
Liverpool - 25 miles/30 mins

AIRPORT:
Manchester - 40 miles/40 mins
Liverpool - 25 miles/30 mins

RAIL STATION:
Chester - ½ mile/5 mins
Crewe - 20 miles/30 mins

FERRY PORT:
Hollyhead - 40 miles/1 hr 30 mins
Liverpool - 25 miles/30 mins

AFFILIATIONS
Independent

RESERVATIONS
National rate in UK: 0870 432 8635
Quote Best Loved

ACCESS CODES
Not applicable

Savour an award-winning combination of accommodation and food

Named as one of the 50 Best Winter Escapes in the World in the travel pages of a leading national newspaper, the Green Bough Hotel seems set to continue from strength to strength. Its location on a leafy avenue a few minutes' walk from the walled Roman city of Chester makes a great base for touring the beautiful Cheshire countryside, and within an hour's drive you can be immersed in the dramatic landscapes of North Wales, Snowdonia and the Lake District.

From the moment you walk through the hotel's impressive oak doors, you know you've come to the right place. The welcome is warm and friendly; the Champagne Bar Lounge is a marvellous synergy of comfortable couches, a grand Charles II carved wooden fireplace and original oils depicting scenes from a bygone Roman era, emulating a truly exclusive ambience. This same attention to detail is reflected in the soothing tones and understated luxury of the bedrooms.

The Olive Tree Restaurant is a showcase for Savoy-trained chef patron Philip Martin's exceptional cuisine. Together with the hotel's professional, attentive but unobtrusive service, the award-winning restaurant offers a sophisticated dining experience in a relaxed environment.

LOCATION

From the M53, junction 12, take the A56 to Chester; the hotel is one mile on the right.

> "So very nice to be back - thanks to everyone for looking after us so well"
> MR & MRS HORTON-RICK

Country house HOB GREEN HOTEL, RESTAURANT & GARDENS

An elegant country house surrounded by award-winning gardens

When the Hutchinson family lovingly converted this charming country house set in beautiful Yorkshire countryside into an elegant hotel and restaurant, they clearly had the optimum comfort and relaxation of guests in mind - the graceful drawing room is scattered with comfy sofas and chairs, whilst the traditionally styled bedrooms (including a romantic four-poster room and spacious junior suite) have been individually decorated with antique furnishings. The rooms have wonderful views, either over the two and a half acres of gardens or across the lawns to the valley beyond.

The restaurant has a mouthwatering menu that features such dishes as whole roast partridge with black cherry and cassis sauce, or Pacific oysters grilled with pancetta, red peppers and pesto sauce. Fresh ingredients are sourced from small local businesses or grown in the hotel's own kitchen garden. Head gardener Sheila Johnson and head chef Chris Taylor work together to grow fruit and vegetables to be used both for the daily-changing menus and for homemade jams and chutneys.

Situated close to Harrogate, the antiques centre of the north, the ancient city of Ripon and the Yorkshire Dales, Hob Green is an ideal base for sight seeing - the world heritage sight of Fountains Abbey and Studley Royal Park is on the doorstep.

LOCATION
From Harrogate, take the A61 (Ripon), then at Ripley the B6165 (Pateley Bridge). After 500 yards, turn right onto Scarah Bank. After two miles, turn right at the Drovers Inn. The hotel is one mile along, on the right.

Markington, Harrogate, Yorkshire HG3 3PJ

T (UK) 0870 432 8643
T 01423 770031
F 01423 771589
hobgreen@bestloved.com
www.hobgreen.bestloved.com

OWNERS
Mr and Mrs Hutchinson

ROOM RATES
1 Single   £90 - £110
9 Doubles/Twins   £110 - £165
1 Four-poster   £130 - £170
1 Junior Suite   £135 - £180
Includes VAT

CREDIT CARDS
AMERICAN EXPRESS • DC • MC • VI

RATINGS & AWARDS
RAC ★★★ Dining Award 2
AA ★★★ 77%
AA Country House

FACILITIES
On site: Garden, licensed for weddings
1 meeting room/max 12 people
Nearby: Golf, walking, riding

RESTRICTIONS
Limited facilities for disabled guests
Smoking in designated areas only
Pets by arrangement

ATTRACTIONS
Fountains Abbey and Studley Royal, Ripon Cathedral, Ripon Races, Newby Hall, York, Mother Shipton's Cave, spa town of Harrogate, Ripley Castle, Yorkshire Dales

NEAREST
CITY:
Ripon - 6 miles/10 mins
York - 26 miles/45 mins
AIRPORT:
Leeds/Bradford - 18 miles/30 mins
RAIL STATION:
Harrogate - 7 miles/15 mins

AFFILIATIONS
Independent

RESERVATIONS
National rate in UK: 0870 432 8643
Quote Best Loved

ACCESS CODES
Not applicable

NORTH

NORTH

HOLBECK GHYLL HOTEL & SPA Country house

Holbeck Lane, Windermere,
Cumbria LA23 1LU

T (UK) 0870 432 8644
T 015394 32375
F 015394 34743
holbeck@bestloved.com
www.holbeck.bestloved.com

OWNERS
David and Patricia Nicholson

ROOM RATES
18 Doubles/Twins £150 - £260
2 Four-posters/Suites £170 - £270
Includes full breakfast and VAT;
enquire for 5-course dinner-inclusive rates

CREDIT CARDS
AMERICAN EXPRESS • DC • JCB • MC • VI

RATINGS & AWARDS
ETC ★★★ Gold Award
RAC Gold Ribbon ★★★
Dining Award 4
AA ★★★ ❀❀❀
AA Top 200 - 2004/2005

FACILITIES
On site: Garden, croquet, tennis,
health & beauty, licensed for
weddings, health spa, woodland walks,
cycling, putting green
2 meeting rooms/max 65 people
Nearby: Golf, riding, fishing

RESTRICTIONS
Limited facilities for disabled guests
Smoking in main house rooms only
Pets by arrangement

ATTRACTIONS
Wordsworth's Dove Cottage,
Beatrix Potter's home, lake cruises,
Holker Hall, Levens Hall

NEAREST
CITY:
Manchester - 90 miles/1 hr 30 mins
AIRPORT:
Manchester - 90 miles/1 hr 30 mins
RAIL STATION:
Windermere - 3 miles/5 mins

AFFILIATIONS
Celebrated Hotels Collection
Small Luxury Hotels
Pride of Britain

RESERVATIONS
National rate in UK: 0870 432 8644
Toll free in US: 800-322-2403
or 800-525-4800 or 800-98-PRIDE
Quote Best Loved

ACCESS CODES
AMADEUS LX VEMHGC
APOLLO/GALILEO LX 21650
SABRE/ABACUS LX 31195
WORLDSPAN LX BWFHG

A connoisseur's hotel with sensational views of Lake Windermere

Back in 1888, Lord Lonsdale (of boxing's Lonsdale Belt fame) was so taken by the views across Lake Windermere and the Langdale Fells that he bought Holbeck Ghyll for use as his hunting lodge. His idea of the perfect country residence has made a lasting impression on the property's style and appearance. More than 100 years on, the view has hardly altered at all, but the house is now a hotel of outstanding character. Our congratulations go to David and Patricia Nicholson, whose quest for excellence has made this charming hotel such a pleasure to visit.

The interiors are styled in the manner of Charles Rennie Mackintosh, with a wealth of oak panelling and stained glass. Into this magnificence are interwoven the luxuries of a first-class hotel and a connoisseur's clutter of a home: antiques, original paintings, flowers, really comfortable furniture ... Six luxury lakeview rooms also await in The Lodge, only 45 metres from the old house itself.

Part of the Holbeck experience is the five-course dinner, which features dishes classically prepared and artistically presented in the English style with just a hint of France. Exciting and unusual vegetarian items are also included in every course. Gourmets should go for the inclusive rate that includes dinner; they won't be disappointed.

LOCATION
Take the M6, exit 36, to Windermere and pass Brockhole Visitor Centre; after half a mile, turn right into Holbeck Lane (signed Troutbeck). The hotel is a half mile on the left.

> **"** Wonderful ambience, fantastic food, helpful staff. We'll be back **"**
>
> MRS R DARLING, SUSSEX

Country house

HORTON GRANGE

Seaton Burn, Newcastle upon Tyne,
Tyne & Wear NE13 6BU

T (UK) 0870 432 8648
T 01661 860686
F 01661 860308
horton@bestloved.com
www.horton.bestloved.com

OWNERS
Geoff Dobson and Gary Speed

ROOM RATES

Single occupancy	£95
9 Doubles	£105

Includes full breakfast and VAT

CREDIT CARDS

AMERICAN EXPRESS • MC • VI

RATINGS & AWARDS
ETC ★★

FACILITIES
On site: Garden, licensed for weddings
3 meeting rooms/max 150 people
Nearby: Golf, fishing, riding, swimming,
walking, gym

RESTRICTIONS
Limited facilities for disabled guests
No smoking throughout
No pets; guide dogs only

ATTRACTIONS
Northumbrian coastline,
Newcastle Castle, Hadrian's Wall,
Angel of the North, Bamburgh Castle,
Gateshead Millennium Bridge

NEAREST
CITY:
Newcastle-upon-Tyne - 9 miles/15 mins

AIRPORT:
Newcastle - 8 miles/10 mins

RAIL STATION:
Newcastle-upon-Tyne - 9 miles/15 mins

AFFILIATIONS
Independent

RESERVATIONS
National rate in UK: 0870 432 8648
Quote Best Loved

ACCESS CODES
Not applicable

NORTH

Good food is a vital ingredient at this charming country house hotel

Just eight miles north of Newcastle's vibrant city centre, Horton Grange offers a wonderfully quiet and relaxing escape from the hurly burly. The handsome Victorian stone house is set in its own peaceful tree-lined grounds, and owners Geoff Dobson and Gary Speed have decorated the interior with a seamless blend of traditional and contemporary furnishings. The result is an engaging home-from-home ambience boasting rather more than the usual range of creature comforts.

Chief amongst these is the restaurant, a light and airy space overlooking the soothing Japanese garden. The imaginative 'modern classic' menu showcases the finest local produce, including Scotch beef and Tweed salmon from across the border. Other favourites to look out for are the crab timbale, roast saddle of rabbit with wild garlic mash and woodland mushrooms and a hot apple and walnut crumble tart with vanilla bean ice cream. The guest bedrooms in the main house are spacious and attractively finished, and there are four delectable cottage garden rooms with original beams and stone floors.

Local diversions range from shopping in Newcastle to exploring Roman forts on Hadrian's Wall; also worth a visit is the open-air Beamish Museum, Newcastle Racecourse, Alnwick Gardens and glorious walks along the North Tyneside coast.

LOCATION

Exit A19 from the A1; take the first exit at the roundabout signed Morpeth. Turn left towards Ponteland and Dinnington; the hotel is two miles along, before Ponteland.

NORTH

JUDGES COUNTRY HOUSE HOTEL — Country house

Kirklevington, Yarm,
North Yorkshire TS15 9LW

T (UK) 0870 432 8668
T 01642 789000
F 01642 782878
judges@bestloved.com
www.judges.bestloved.com

OWNERS
Michael and Shirley Downs

GENERAL MANAGER
Tim Howard

ROOM RATES
Single occupancy   £134 - £148
18 Doubles/Twins   £159 - £174
3 Four-posters   £159 - £174
Includes full breakfast and VAT

CREDIT CARDS
AMERICAN EXPRESS • DC • MC • VI

RATINGS & AWARDS
RAC Blue Ribbon ★★★
RAC Dining Award 3
AA ★★★ ❀❀❀
AA Top 200 - 2004/2005

FACILITIES
On site: Garden, gym, croquet,
licensed for weddings, Jacuzzi,
bowls, mountain biking
7 meeting rooms/max 600 people
Nearby: Golf, tennis, riding, fishing,
swimming, health & beauty

RESTRICTIONS
Limited facilities for disabled guests
No smoking in restaurant
No pets; guide dogs only

ATTRACTIONS
Whitby Abbey, Yorkshire Moors,
Rievaulx Abbey, High Force Falls,
Pickering Castle, HM Bark Endeavour

NEAREST
CITY:
Middlesborough - 8 miles/20mins

AIRPORT:
Teeside - 5 miles/15 mins

RAIL STATION:
Yarm - 1 mile/5 mins

AFFILIATIONS
Pride of Britain

RESERVATIONS
National rate in UK: 0870 432 8668
Toll free in the US: 800-98-PRIDE
Quote Best Loved

ACCESS CODES
AMADEUS YX MMEJCH
APOLLO/GALILEO YX 51228
SABRE/ABACUS YX 64360
WORLDSPAN YX 42867

The verdict is unanimous approval for this former judges' lodging

Judges Country House was built on the edge of the North Yorkshire moors in 1881 as a family residence for the Richardsons of Hartlepool, prosperous engineering entrepreneurs. In the 1970s, the building was transformed into a country lodging for circuit court judges - hence the name.

The carefully restored house, replete with glossy Victorian woodwork, has a comfortably clubby atmosphere that is known to play havoc with guests' short-stay plans! Ingredients in this charm are the lovely garden with its sunny terraces, the Victorian walled garden, where fruit and vegetables are grown for the kitchens, and the extensive woodland walkways.

Judges is a delightful getaway for families, couples and business travellers alike. A variety of special breaks on offer involve health treatments, tickets to local attractions and other great treats. Other breaks include the Wine Appreciation Weekend, Golfing Break or the Helicopter Flying Experience.

A terrific base for exploring the moors, visiting the ancient abbeys of Rosedale and Rievaulx or Mount Grace Priory - or heading to the coast for Whitby, where Bram Stoker wrote 'Dracula', fossil-hunting is a must and Captain Cook is celebrated with his own museum and monument.

LOCATION
From the A19, take the A67 towards Yarm. The hotel is on the left just after Kirklevington.

Restaurant with rooms

L'ENCLUME

A connoisseur's delight in a charming historic village

If you are looking for a unique gastronomic experience, L'Enclume is the ideal place. This restaurant with rooms is nestled in the historic village of Cartmel by the famous Cartmel Priory, and owners Simon Rogan and Penny Tapsell have made their hotel an 'experience for all the senses', with exciting menus, chic accommodation and great views out to the Priory - not to mention the garden, designed by Christopher Halliday.

Guests can sample the à la carte menu, or if you're feeling adventurous, their Taste and Texture Menus range from 'An Introduction' of eight courses, to 'Gourmand', with no less than 23. Their food, which makes great use of herbs and flowers, is fresh and exciting - not surprising as their culinary rule is that 'rules are there to be broken'! The two restaurant areas are light and contemporary, with fine art adorning the walls. And in the summer, you can dine al fresco on the terrace.

Guests can stay in one of the seven elegant bedrooms in the main house, or for groups and business meetings, the nearby Bluebell House has four double bedrooms, a private courtyard and can accommodate private dining for up to 20 people.

LOCATION

From the M6, exit 36 for the A591, then exit for Newby Bridge on the A590. Follow signs for Cartmel Priory; in Cartmel, take the first available right. Turn the corner at the church; the hotel is on the left.

Cavendish Street, Cartmel, Grange-over-Sands, Cumbria LA11 6PZ

T (UK) 0870 432 8676
T 015395 36362
F 015395 38907
lenclume@bestloved.com
www.lenclume.bestloved.com

OWNERS
Simon Rogan and Penny Tapsell

ROOM RATES
7 Doubles   £110 - £200

CREDIT CARDS
AMERICAN EXPRESS • DC • MC • VI

RATINGS & AWARDS
AA ❀❀❀ Restaurant with Rooms

FACILITIES
On site: Garden
1 meeting room/max 25 people
Nearby: Golf, fishing, swimming, gym, paragliding, corporate and leisure centre

RESTRICTIONS
Limited facilities for disabled guests
Children by arrangement
No smoking throughout
Pets by arrangement

ATTRACTIONS
Lake Windermere,
Beatrix Potter's House,
Wordsworth's Dove Cottage,
Cartmel Priory,
Sizergh Castle and Garden,
Stagshaw Garden

NEAREST
CITY:
Manchester - 84 miles/1 hr 30 mins

AIRPORT:
Manchester - 90 miles/1 hr 40 mins

RAIL STATION:
Windermere - 16 miles/30 mins

AFFILIATIONS
Independent

RESERVATIONS
National rate in UK: 0870 432 8676
Quote Best Loved

ACCESS CODES
Not applicable

LINDETH HOWE COUNTRY HOUSE — Country house

NORTH

Longtail Hill,
Bowness-on-Windermere,
Cumbria LA23 3JF

T (UK) 0870 432 8687
T 015394 45759
F 015394 46368
lindeth@bestloved.com
www.lindeth.bestloved.com

MANAGING DIRECTOR
Stephen Broughton

ROOM RATES
5 Singles	£54 - £115
2 Family Rooms	£108 - £198
17 Doubles	£108 - £190
12 Twins	£132

Includes full breakfast and VAT

CREDIT CARDS
AMERICAN EXPRESS • JCB • MC • VI

RATINGS & AWARDS
ETC ★★★ Hotel
AA ★★★ ❀ 79%
AA Country House

FACILITIES
On site: Garden, indoor pool, sauna, solarium, fitness, sightseeing tours 2 meeting rooms/max 30 people
Nearby: Leisure centre, angling, walking, cycling, sailing, golf

RESTRICTIONS
No children under 7 in restaurant
Smoking in bar lounge and some bedrooms only
No pets; guide dogs only
Closed 7-13 Jan.

ATTRACTIONS
Windermere lake cruises, Holker Hall, World of Beatrix Potter, Lakeside Aquarium, Muncaster Castle, La'al Ratty Steam Railway

NEAREST
CITY:
Manchester - 90 miles/1 hr 45 mins
Carlisle - 60 miles/1 hr 15 mins

AIRPORT:
Manchester - 100 miles/1 hr 50 mins
Leeds-Bradford - 90 miles/1hr 40 mins

RAIL STATION:
Oxenholme - 12 miles/25 mins
Windermere - 3 miles/10 mins

FERRY PORT:
Liverpool - 100 miles/2 hrs
Newcastle - 120 miles/2 hrs

AFFILIATIONS
Classic British Hotels

RESERVATIONS
National rate in UK: 0870 432 8687
Quote Best Loved

ACCESS CODES
Not applicable

The tranquil lakeland retreat where Beatrix Potter created Timmy Tiptoes

Set on a gentle slope overlooking Lake Windermere, Lindeth Howe was built as a holiday home for a wealthy mill owner in 1879. The house was often rented out to family and friends, among them the Potter family. Between 1905 and 1913, Beatrix Potter was a regular visitor and wrote and illustrated several of her children's stories here, including Timmy Tiptoes (1911) and Pigling Bland (1913).

Today, holidaymakers can still delight in the spectacular views from Lindeth Howe's sunny terrace. The peace and quiet is as relaxing and reviving as ever, but now guests can also enjoy the hotel's 21st-century comforts, subtly blended into the traditional fabric of the house. Bedrooms range from comfy singles through to spacious doubles, twins and family rooms, as well as honeymoon suites with half-tester beds and stunning lake views. There is a fine restaurant, comfortable lounge and separate reading room, and leisure facilities including an indoor pool, sauna and fitness room. For getting out and about, mountain bike rentals, golf reservations and fishing permits can all be arranged by the hotel. Lindeth Howe also works closely with The Mountain Goat tour company, offering full and half-day sightseeing tours of the Yorkshire Dales and Lake District - a great opportunity to explore further the world of Beatrix Potter!

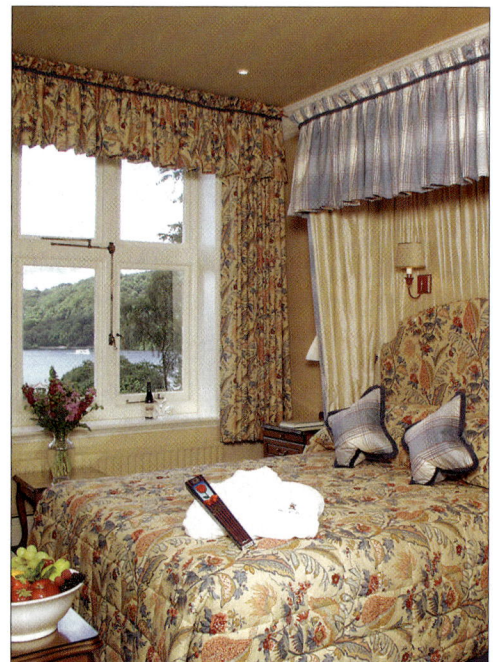

LOCATION

Longtail Hill is just off the A592, half a mile south of Bowness-on-Windermere.

Country house

LINTHWAITE HOUSE

NORTH

Crook Road, Windermere,
Cumbria LA23 3JA

T (UK) 0870 432 8688
T 015394 88600
F 015394 88601
linthwaite@bestloved.com
www.linthwaite.bestloved.com

OWNER
Mike Bevans

ROOM RATES

1 Single	£115 - £125
9 Doubles/Twin	£150 - £180
4 Superior Doubles/Twins	£190 - £220
12 Lake/Garden Views	£220 - £270
1 Suite	£250 - £295

Includes full breakfast and VAT

CREDIT CARDS
AMERICAN EXPRESS • DC • JCB • MC • VI

RATINGS & AWARDS
ETC ★★★ Gold Award
RAC Blue Ribbon ★★★ Dining Award 3
AA ★★★ ⊛⊛
AA Top 200 - 2004/2005

FACILITIES
On site: Garden, fishing, croquet,
licensed for weddings, bicycles
3 meeting rooms/max 60 people
Nearby: Golf, riding, tennis,
water sport, leisure spa

RESTRICTIONS
Limited facilities for disabled guests
Smoking in bar only
Pets by arrangement

ATTRACTIONS
Beatrix Potter's Home & Museum,
Wordsworth's Dove Cottage,
Lake Windermere, Sizergh Castle,
Levens Hall & Topiary Gardens

NEAREST
CITY:
Manchester - 95 miles/1 hr 45 mins

AIRPORT:
Manchester - 95 miles/1 hr 45 mins

RAIL STATION:
Windermere - 3 miles/10 mins

AFFILIATIONS
Celebrated Hotels Collection
Grand Heritage Hotels

RESERVATIONS
National rate in UK: 0870 432 8688
Toll free in US: 800-322-2403
or 888-93-GRAND
Quote Best Loved

ACCESS CODES
AMADEUS UI CAXLHH
APOLLO/GALILEO UI 48735
SABRE/ABACUS UI 35752
WORLDSPAN UI 40645

A relaxing break amongst the hills and valleys of the Lake District

Situated in 14 acres of glorious hilltop gardens overlooking Lake Windermere and 'Coniston Old Man', Linthwaite House is a haven for those with distinctive tastes who appreciate the finer things in life. Breathtaking sunsets, superb scenery and a multitude of places of special interest lie within easy reach, including historic houses, theatres and cinemas, museums and galleries and the homes of William Wordsworth and Beatrix Potter. Sweeping fells and Lakeland villages have been the source of inspiration for poets and writers alike since time began.

Good food and fine wine served in a relaxed, unstuffy atmosphere and unpretentious surroundings combine to give you a rewarding break in the heart of the Lake District.

There are 27 rooms, some with lake views, and a garden suite with separate lounge. Each has an en-suite bath/shower, bathrobes, direct-dial telephone, radio, trouser press, hair dryer, tea/coffee-making facilities and stereo/CD player.

Whatever the occasion, whatever the season, Linthwaite House will be there to pamper you.

LOCATION

On the eastern side of Lake Windermere. Exit 36 on the M6 and A591 for eight miles; take the first left at roundabout onto the B5284 to Crook. The hotel is seven miles on the left, past Windermere Golf Club.

Map p. 442, grid C5

LOVELADY SHIELD

Country house

NORTH

Nenthead Road, Alston,
Cumbria CA9 3LF

T (UK) 0870 432 8694
T 01434 381203
F 01434 381515
lovelady@bestloved.com
www.lovelady.bestloved.com

OWNERS
Peter and Marie Haynes

RATES PER PERSON
9 Doubles/Twins   £90 - £110
1 Four-poster   £110
Includes full breakfast, dinner and VAT

CREDIT CARDS
AMERICAN EXPRESS • JCB • MC • VI

RATINGS & AWARDS
ETC ★★ Silver Award
AA ★★ ⊛ 77%

FACILITIES
On site: Garden, heli-pad, croquet,
licensed for weddings
2 meeting rooms/max 45 people
Nearby: Golf, fishing, shooting,
riding, walking

RESTRICTIONS
No facilities for disabled guests
No children under 7 in the restaurant
No smoking in restaurant
No pets in public rooms

ATTRACTIONS
Lake District, Hadrian's Wall,
Holy Island, High Force Waterfall,
Barnard Castle, Durham Cathedral

NEAREST
CITY:
Penrith - 19 miles/30 mins

AIRPORT:
Newcastle - 42 miles/1 hr

RAIL STATION:
Penrith - 19 miles/30 mins

AFFILIATIONS
Fine Individual Hotels

RESERVATIONS
National rate in UK: 0870 432 8694
Toll free in US: 800-544-9993
Quote Best Loved

ACCESS CODES
Not applicable

Hidden atop the Pennine moors is a guestbook swelling with compliments

At Alston, you are at a watershed. As England's highest market town, it stands amongst the moors and fells of the North Pennines, located in a heatherclad wilderness with a choice of the Lake District, Yorkshire Dales or Border Forest to explore. Indecision has its own rewards: Simply by staying put, you'll discover prolific wildlife and heritage galore (for example, the South Tyneside narrow-gauge railway starts here).

At Lovelady Shield, the pleasures start even before you arrive - winding through scenery reminiscent of the south of France, the drive up to the house is truly one of the most beautiful in Europe. Once there, first impressions are to be trusted. Lovelady, nestled in three acres of garden upon a wooded hillside on the banks of the Nent, looks an absolute gem of a place - and it is. The guestbook positively swells with compliments, particularly about the friendliness of the owners, Peter and Marie Haynes, and their staff. Highly complimented, too, is the food, which owes everything to master chef Barrie Gordon. Alas, Lovelady Shield is a secret that's hard to keep - but who could deny a friend such pleasure?

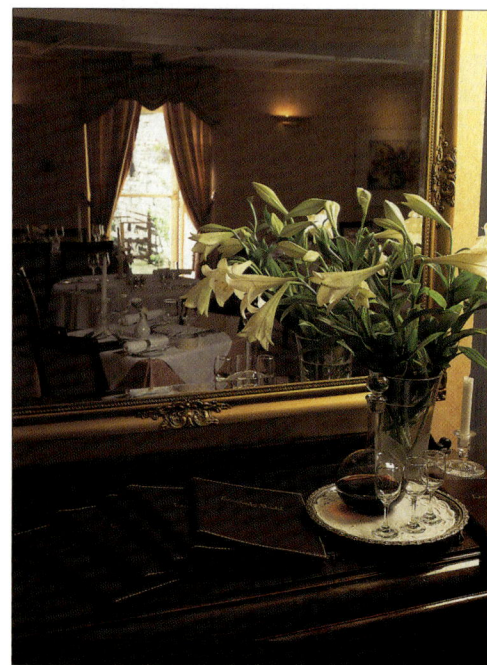

LOCATION
Two and a quarter miles east of Alston; the drive is at the junction of the A689 and the B6294.

Country house

MATFEN HALL

Matfen,
Near Newcastle-upon-Tyne,
Northumberland NE20 0RH

T (UK) 0870 432 8705
T 01661 886500
F 01661 886055
matfenhall@bestloved.com
www.matfenhall.bestloved.com

OWNERS
Sir Hugh and Lady Blackett

GENERAL MANAGER
David Hunter

NORTH

ROOM RATES
Single occupancy   £102 - £145
51 Doubles/Twins   £140 - £220
2 Four-posters   £235
Includes full breakfast and VAT

CREDIT CARDS
AMERICAN EXPRESS • MC • VI

RATINGS & AWARDS
ETC ★★★★
AA ★★★★ ❀❀ 77%
Investors in People
Excellence in England Award for
Tourism 2002 Gold Winner

A magnificent Northumberland landmark with something for everyone

As soon as you enter Matfen Hall's impressive two-mile driveway, you just know that you are going to find something special at the end. Sir Hugh and Lady Blackett have carefully restored the Hall into a magnificent country house hotel set in some of Northumberland's most stunning countryside.

Nestled alongside the extremely pretty village of Matfen, with an equally pretty pub where guests can become temporary 'regulars', Matfen Hall is finished to exacting standards. Each of the bedrooms is wonderfully opulent, but traditionally so, and at the same time, all the modern amenities are there. Great care has been taken to preserve many original features, such as the ornate ceilings, drawing room fireplace and library, now a cosy, book-lined dining room. The quite magnificent Great Hall, with its massive pillars, is a breathtaking venue for private dining, wedding receptions and corporate use.

Matfen's highly-rated golf course boasts a variety of teasing water features and several holes where dry stone ha-ha walls add a distinctly local note to the proceedings. Their brand-new leisure club offers a fantastic array of facilities, including a swimming pool, fitness studio and Pamper Suite.

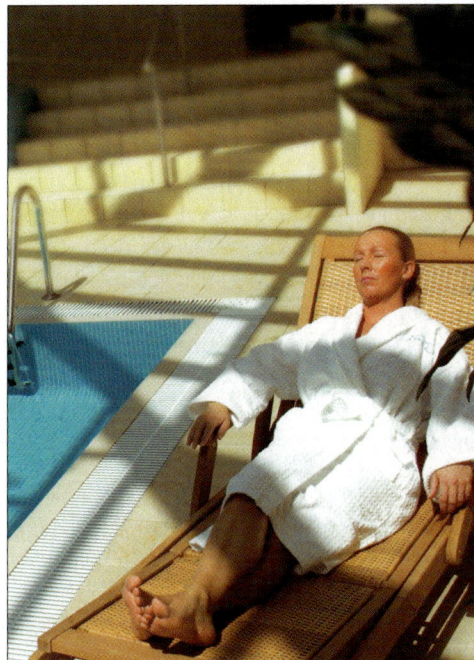

FACILITIES
On site: Garden, heli-pad, croquet, golf, licensed for weddings, leisure club 8 meeting rooms/max 150 people
Nearby: Riding, fishing

RESTRICTIONS
Limited facilities for disabled guests
Smoking in some rooms only
Pets by arrangement

ATTRACTIONS
Alnwick Castle & Gardens,
Millennium Bridge, Centre of Life,
Angel of the North,
Baltic Centre for Contemporary Art,
Bamburgh Castle, Hadrian's Wall

NEAREST
CITY:
Newcastle - 15 miles/20 mins

AIRPORT:
Newcastle - 8 miles/15 mins

RAIL STATION:
Newcastle - 15 miles/20 mins

AFFILIATIONS
Independent

RESERVATIONS
National rate in UK: 0870 432 8705
Quote Best Loved

ACCESS CODES
AMADEUS HK NCLMAT
APOLLO/GALILEO HT 22362
SABRE/ABACUS HK 49495
WORLDSPAN HK MATFE

LOCATION

From the A1, take the A69, signposted Hexham and Carlisle. At Heddon on the Wall, take the B6318 toward Chollerford. The hotel is on the right after seven miles.

MIDDLETHORPE HALL AND SPA
Country house

NORTH

Bishopthorpe Road, York,
North Yorkshire YO23 2GB

T (UK) 0870 432 8710
T 01904 641241
F 01904 620176
middlethorpe@bestloved.com
www.middlethorpe.bestloved.com

GENERAL MANAGER
Lionel A Chatard

ROOM RATES
4 Singles	£109 - £115
15 Doubles/Twins	£160 - £210
2 Four-posters	£275
8 Suites	£230 - £360

Includes continental breakfast, service and VAT

CREDIT CARDS
MC • VI

RATINGS & AWARDS
RAC Gold Ribbon ★★★
Dining Award 4
AA ★★★ ❀❀❀
AA Top 200 - 2004/2005

FACILITIES
On site: Garden, heli-pad, croquet, indoor pool, health & beauty
2 meeting rooms/max 60 people
Nearby: Golf, riding, tennis

RESTRICTIONS
No children under 8 years
Smoking in library and some bedrooms only
No pets; guide dogs only

ATTRACTIONS
Castle Howard, Fairfax House, Newby Hall, Fountains Abbey, National Railway Museum, Castle Museum, York Racecourse, York Minster

NEAREST
CITY:
York - 2 miles/5 mins

AIRPORT:
Manchester - 84 miles/1 hr 30 mins
Leeds/Bradford - 25 miles/40 mins

RAIL STATION:
York - 2 miles/5 mins

AFFILIATIONS
Pride of Britain
Grandeur
Celebrated Hotels Collection
Historic House Hotels

RESERVATIONS
National rate in UK: 0870 432 8710
Toll free in US: 800-322-2403
or 800-98-PRIDE
Quote Best Loved

ACCESS CODES
AMADEUS YX QQYTHO
APOLLO/GALILEO YX 14942
SABRE/ABACUS YX 4540
WORLDSPAN YX GB17

An impeccable William III country residence overlooking York racecourse

'Tis a very pretty place', wrote the diarist Lady Mary Wortley Montagu, who made her home here in the early 18th century - and she would probably feel quite at home revisiting Middlethorpe today. The beautifully restored hall dates from 1699, and antique furnishings and paintings have been carefully selected to blend with their period surroundings. The public rooms are decorated in mellow tones, with fresh garden flowers lending a charmingly informal note. In particular, the pale yellow drawing room has a marvellously relaxing and timeless feel, as do the comfortable guest rooms, which are divided between the main house and an adjoining courtyard.

Middlethorpe is set in 20 acres of parkland and gardens, where guests can stroll in the glorious rose garden and admire the magnificent cedar of Lebanon standing sentinel behind the house. They can also enjoy a gentle game of croquet or a session in the well-equipped health and fitness spa, with its large indoor pool, sauna and steam rooms, gym and beauty salons. In addition to its prime location for racing enthusiasts, Middlethorpe is ideally placed for visiting the historic city of York. Further afield are ancient abbeys, Castle Howard and the Yorkshire Dales.

LOCATION
From the A64, follow signs to York West (A1036), then signs to York Racecourse and Bishopthorpe. The hotel is on the right just before the racecourse.

Map p. 442, grid B6

113

Country house

MILLER HOWE HOTEL

Priceless views and a peerless restaurant overlooking Lake Windermere

Charles Garside is so taken with the magical view from Miller Howe that he has a camera linked to his Web site so browsers can enjoy the remarkable changing lakeland vista several times a day. This is typical of Garside's enthusiastic approach to running one of the Lake District's most renowned hotel-restaurants. A former international newspaper editor, Garside returned to his Cumbrian roots in 1998 and relishes every aspect of his role here, from cherishing his superb long-time staff to entertaining his guests.

Miller Howe began as a restaurant with rooms founded by celebrated chef John Tovey. However, the handsome Edwardian hotel is a destination in its own right, stylishly furnished with oodles of antiques, paintings and objets d'art. The country house bedrooms have fabulous new bathrooms and are thoughtfully equipped with music centres, books, games and even umbrellas! The delectable Cottage at Miller Howe is close to the herb garden and has three suites, a kitchen and patio - ideal for private get-togethers.

LOCATION
Off the A592 between Windermere and Bowness.

Rayrigg Road, Windermere,
Cumbria LA23 1EY

T (UK) 0870 432 8712
T 015394 42536
F 015394 45664
millerhowe@bestloved.com
www.millerhowe.bestloved.com

OWNER
Charles Garside

RATES PER PERSON
5 Standard Doubles/Twins £100 - £120
6 Master Doubles/Twins £110 - £140
1 Mini Suite £105 - £125
3 Cottage Suites £110 - £175
Includes full breakfast, dinner and VAT

CREDIT CARDS
AMERICAN EXPRESS • DC • MC • VI

RATINGS & AWARDS
RAC Gold Ribbon ★★
Dining Award 3
AA ★★ ❀❀
AA Top 200 - 2004/2005
Courvoisier's Book of the Best

FACILITIES
On site: Garden, heli-pad, croquet,
licensed for weddings
2 meeting rooms/max 40 people
Nearby: Golf, riding, fishing
(permits provided), complimentary
use of leisure club

RESTRICTIONS
Limited facilities for disabled guests
No children under 8 years
No smoking in restaurant
No pets in public areas

ATTRACTIONS
Lake District National Park,
Beatrix Potter's home and museum,
Steamboat Museum,
Wordsworth's Dove Cottage,
Holehird Gardens

NEAREST
CITY:
Manchester - 90 miles/1 hr 30 mins

AIRPORT:
Manchester - 100 miles/1 hr 30 mins

RAIL STATION:
Windermere - 1 mile/5 mins

AFFILIATIONS
Celebrated Hotels Collection

RESERVATIONS
National rate in UK: 0870 432 8712
Toll free in the US: 800-322-2403
Quote Best Loved

ACCESS CODES
Not applicable

NORTH

MONK FRYSTON HALL

Stately home

Monk Fryston, Near York,
North Yorkshire LS25 5DU

T (UK) 0870 432 8713
T 01977 682369
F 01977 683544
fryston@bestloved.com
www.fryston.bestloved.com

OWNER
Lord Edward Manners

GENERAL MANAGER
Pam Smith

ROOM RATES
Single occupancy   £92 - £102
27 Doubles/Twins   £116 - £136
2 Four-posters   £146 - £171
Includes full breakfast and VAT

CREDIT CARDS
AMERICAN EXPRESS • DC • MC • VI

RATINGS & AWARDS
ETC ★★★
AA ★★★ 70%

FACILITIES
On site: Garden, croquet,
licensed for weddings
3 meeting rooms/max 80 people
Nearby: Golf, riding, flying

RESTRICTIONS
Limited facilities for disabled guests
Smoking in restaurant only

ATTRACTIONS
City of York,
York, Doncaster and
Pontefract racecourses,
Castle Howard, Harewood House,
Yorkshire Dales,
National Trust properties,
Royal Armouries

NEAREST
CITY:
York - 15 miles/30 mins
Leeds - 14 miles/30 mins

AIRPORT:
Leeds/Bradford - 18 miles/40 mins
Manchester - 75 miles/1 hr 30 mins

RAIL STATION:
Selby - 7 miles/15 mins
Leeds - 14 miles/30 mins

AFFILIATIONS
Rutland Hotels Ltd

RESERVATIONS
National rate in UK: 0870 432 8713
Quote Best Loved

ACCESS CODES
Not applicable

NORTH

Heritage and hospitality close to historic York

This 17th-century hall is built on a site that dates back to the time of William the Conqueror. It was purchased in 1954 by the late 10th Duke of Rutland and recently celebrated its 50th year as a hotel, under the ownership of the Duke's youngest son Lord Edward Manners. Grey stone walls, mullioned windows and the coat of arms above the doorway certainly give the appearance of a gracious manor house.

The gardens feature wisteria and rambling rose, and an ornamental lake and fountain. For all the grandeur of this Grade 11 listed building, it is by no means stuffy; the overall atmosphere is very relaxed. The staff are efficient, but friendly. The bedrooms are elegantly styled with homely touches and have modern facilities, including modems in most rooms.

Guests can enjoy a variety of modern, internationally influenced cuisine on a monthly changing à la carte menu, and have the choice of a one, two or three course lunch or dinner. The cheese menu is a treat and includes some local favourites. All manner of snacks are available, too - something that is welcomed by corporate visitors - and can be enjoyed on the terrace balcony. All these things, plus its accessible location, make Monk Fryston a great base for both business and leisure guests.

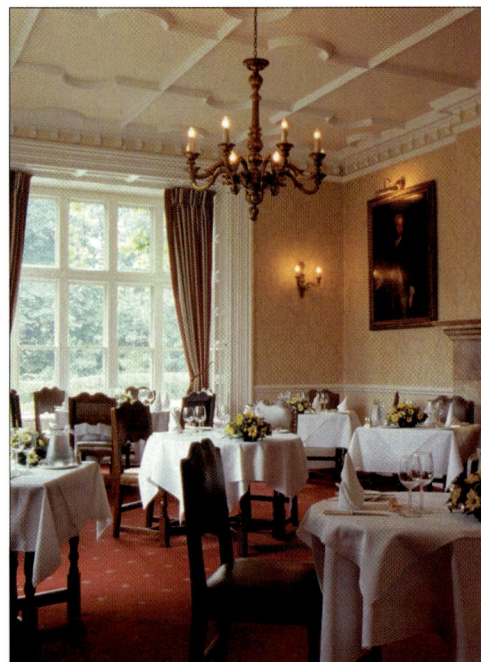

LOCATION
Situated on the A63 three miles east of the A1.

> **The food was so fantastic that the Palace would have approved and the atmosphere so relaxed I kicked off my shoes**
>
> CAROL CHESTER, TRAVEL WRITER

Country house

NORTHCOTE MANOR

Northcote Road, Langho,
Near Blackburn,
Lancashire BB6 8BE

T (UK) 0870 432 8719
T 01254 240555
F 01254 246568
northcote@bestloved.com
www.northcote.bestloved.com

OWNERS
Craig Bancroft and Nigel Haworth

ROOM RATES
Single occupancy   £110 - £145
13 Doubles/Twins   £140 - £175
1 Four-poster   £175
Includes full breakfast and VAT

CREDIT CARDS
AMERICAN EXPRESS • MC • VI

RATINGS & AWARDS
ETC Restaurant with Rooms Silver Award
RAC Gold Ribbon ★★★
Dining Award 3
AA Restaurant with Rooms ❀❀❀ 74%

FACILITIES
On site: Garden, heli-pad,
licensed for weddings
1 meeting room/max 100 people
Nearby: Golf, fishing

RESTRICTIONS
Limited facilities for disabled guests
No smoking in restaurant
No pets

ATTRACTIONS
Ribble Valley, Clitheroe,
Stonyhurst College, Whalley Abbey,
Pendle Witches, Ribchester

NEAREST
CITY:
Manchester - 28 miles/40 mins

AIRPORT:
Manchester - 40 miles/45 mins
Blackpool - 29 miles/35 mins

RAIL STATION:
Preston - 11 miles/20 mins

AFFILIATIONS
Independent

RESERVATIONS
National rate in UK: 0870 432 8719
Quote Best Loved

ACCESS CODES
Not applicable

Lovers of fine food and wine may want to stay forever

Located in the Ribble Valley, one of the great beauty spots of England, Northcote Manor is owned and run with great talent by partners Craig Bancroft and Nigel Haworth. Together, they have built up this small hotel to become one of the most successful in the country.

Northcote Manor is best known for its outstanding food and award-winning restaurant and was awarded its first Michelin star in 1996. Chef Nigel Haworth has a special love of traditional Lancashire cooking, and he has recreated many of those dishes in a very different style, including a sticky toffee pudding that has been voted one of the best in the country! While Nigel cooks and presides over the kitchen, Craig looks after the guests' needs in the restaurant and rooms. His special love is wine, and he delights in personally matching food and wine for the guests.

There are 14 bedrooms and one four-poster. Games, books, interesting ornaments and tea- and coffee- making facilities add to the home-from-home atmosphere. The very comfortable beds have even prompted many visitors to ask where they can buy them! On a final note, their policy regarding children reads 'all welcome to experience fine dining' - admirable and refreshing, we think!

LOCATION

Exit 31 off the M6 and take the A59 towards Clitheroe. Langho is close to the junction with the A666.

NORTH

NUNSMERE HALL

Country house

Tarporley Road, Oakmere,
Near Chester,
Cheshire CW8 2ES

T (UK) 0870 432 8720
T 01606 889100
F 01606 889055
nunsmere@bestloved.com
www.nunsmere.bestloved.com

OWNERS
Malcolm and Julie McHardy

ROOM RATES
Single occupancy   £125 - £145
29 Doubles/Twins   £175 - £195
3 Four-posters   £250 - £350
4 Junior Suites   £325 - £350
Includes VAT

CREDIT CARDS
AMERICAN EXPRESS • DC • MC • VI

RATINGS & AWARDS
Independent

FACILITIES
On site: Garden, snooker, croquet,
licensed for weddings, snooker
4 meeting rooms/max 100 people
Nearby: Golf, riding, fitness,
tennis, racing

RESTRICTIONS
Limited facilities for disabled guests
No children under 12 years
in restaurant after 7 p.m.
No smoking in dining room
and some bedrooms
No pets

ATTRACTIONS
Chester, The Potteries,
Stapeley Water Gardens,
Delamere Forest, Lake District,
North Wales,
Aintree and Haydock racecourses,
Oulton Park racing circuit

NEAREST
CITY:
Chester - 12 miles/20 mins

AIRPORT:
Manchester - 20 miles/30 mins

RAIL STATION:
Hartford - 5 miles/10 mins

AFFILIATIONS
Independent

RESERVATIONS
National rate in UK: 0870 432 8720
Quote Best Loved

ACCESS CODES
AMADEUS HK CEGNUN
APOLLO/GALILEO HT 26042
SABRE/ABACUS HK 51639
WORLDSPAN HK NUNSM

The style of a great transatlantic liner in the idyllic Cheshire countryside

The Brocklebanks shipping company dates back to the early 1700s. In the 20th century, Sir Aubrey Brocklebank designed the Queen Mary, and his son Sir John designed the QEII and became chairman of Cunard. It was Sir Aubrey who built Nunsmere Hall as his family home in 1898. Today, Nunsmere Hall echoes the style and eminence of the great transatlantic liners. The setting is idyllic: This exquisite manor house is surrounded on three sides by a lake in its own wooded grounds. It has 36 comfortable bedrooms, an elegant lounge, a fine wood-panelled cocktail bar and a library.

The Garden Restaurant overlooks the sunken garden and in every way matches the quality of the house. Owners Malcolm and Julie McHardy are determined to achieve excellence, and have won a high reputation for exceptional country house food with a modern Mediterranean influence. Service by their young team is impeccable and the wine list is a classic.

Nunsmere Hall is close to North Wales, the historic Roman city of Chester and Manchester Airport. Liverpool, the Lake District, Stoke and the other Potteries towns are all easily reached by motorway.

LOCATION

On the A49 at Oakmere near Northwich. From the north, leave the M6 at exit 19. From the south, leave the M6 at exit 18.

NORTH

> Since 1970 we have met annually at venues throughout the country and I cannot recall having received warmer hospitality than at your hotel
>
> JAMES HILTON

Country house

PHEASANT HOTEL

An historic blacksmith's cottage gets a new lease on life

The Pheasant Hotel, established from what was at one time the village blacksmith's two cottages and shop, has been renovated and extended to make a very comfortable country hotel with 12 bedrooms, all with private bathrooms. All bedrooms face either south or southwest, with some overlooking the village pond and mill stream, the remainder the courtyard and walled garden.

There is a small oak-beamed bar with a log fire and a large drawing room which, together with the dining room, open onto the stone-flagged terrace looking over the mill stream. In the kitchen, the best of English food is produced under the supervision of Tricia Binks. Ample car parking is also provided.

Harome is a small village less than three miles from the attractive market town of Helmsley and the North York Moors National Park; it is unspoilt, still retaining six thatched cottages (probably more than any village in North Yorkshire). There are seven farms, an inn and both a church and chapel.

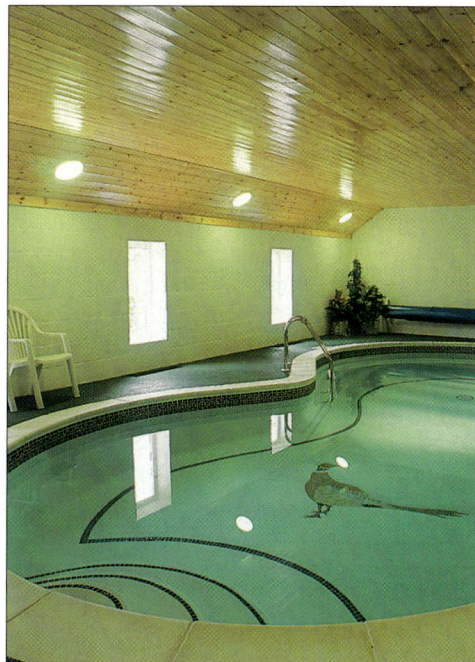

LOCATION

Leave Helmsley on the A170 (Scarborough); after a quarter of a mile, turn right for Harome. The hotel is near the church in the centre of the village.

NORTH

Harome, Helmsley,
North Yorkshire YO62 5JG

T (UK) 0870 432 8740
T 01439 771241
F 01439 771744
pheasant@bestloved.com
www.pheasant.bestloved.com

OWNERS
The Binks Family

RATES PER PERSON
2 Singles   £75 - £77
8 Doubles/Twins   £75 - £77
1 Thatched Cottage   £75 - £77
Includes full breakfast, dinner and VAT

CREDIT CARDS
AMERICAN EXPRESS • DC • JCB • MC • VI

RATINGS & AWARDS
ETC ★★★
RAC ★★★
AA ★★★ 71%

FACILITIES
On site: Garden, indoor pool
Nearby: Golf, riding, swimming, fishing

RESTRICTIONS
Limited facilities for disabled guests
No children under 7 years
No smoking in dining room
Pets by arrangement
Closed mid-December - mid-March

ATTRACTIONS
Castle Howard, Rievaulx Abbey,
North York Moors National Park,
Byland Abbey, Nunnington Hall

NEAREST
CITY:
York - 22 miles/40 mins

AIRPORT:
Manchester - 90 miles/2 hrs 30 mins
Leeds/Bradford - 55 miles/1 hr 30 mins

RAIL STATION:
York - 22 miles/40 mins

AFFILIATIONS
Independent

RESERVATIONS
National rate in UK: 0870 432 8740
Quote Best Loved

ACCESS CODES
Not applicable

Quebecs will be my home from home in the north of England!

PETER CARRAUD, DONALD RUSSELL

QUEBECS

Townhouse

9 Quebec Street,
Leeds, Yorkshire LS1 2HA

T (UK) 0870 432 8750
T 0113 244 8989
F 0113 244 9090
quebecs@bestloved.com
www.quebecs.bestloved.com

GENERAL MANAGER
Margaret Kavanagh

ROOM RATES
5 Singles	£125
5 Doubles/Twins	£135
13 Deluxe Doubles/Twins	£155
9 Executive Doubles/Twins	£170
4 Studio Suites	£185
9 Suites	£195

Includes service and VAT

CREDIT CARDS
AMERICAN EXPRESS • DC • JCB • MC • VI

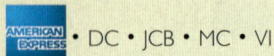

RATINGS & AWARDS
Which? Hotel of the Year 2003

FACILITIES
On site:
3 meeting rooms/max 6 people
Nearby: Golf, leisure club

RESTRICTIONS
Limited facilities for disabled guests
No smoking in the breakfast room

ATTRACTIONS
The Royal Armouries,
Leeds City Centre Art Gallery,
Yorkshire Sculpture Park,
Harewood House, York,
Bolton Abbey, The Dales,
Harvey Nichols, Victorian Quarter

NEAREST
CITY:
Leeds

AIRPORT:
Leeds/Bradford - 10 miles/20 mins

RAIL STATION:
Leeds - ½ mile/2 mins

AFFILIATIONS
Summit Hotels & Resorts
The Eton Group

RESERVATIONS
National rate in UK: 0870 432 8750
Toll free in US: 800-457-4000
Quote Best Loved

ACCESS CODES
AMADEUS XL LBALEE
APOLLO/GALILEO XL 29470
SABRE/ABACUS XL 54498
WORLDSPAN XL 41590

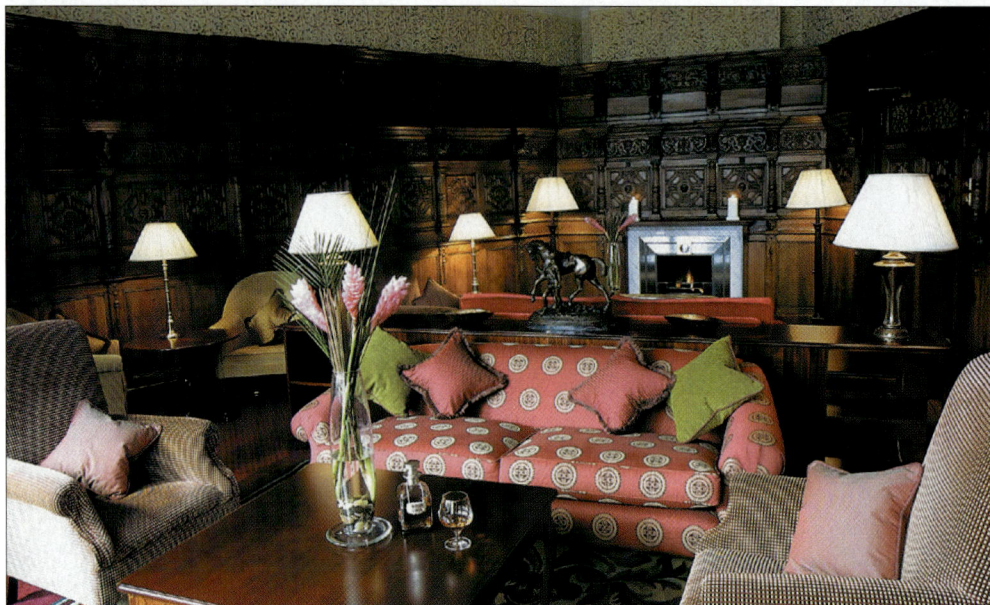

Leeds city centre's favourite boutique hotel is a Liberal success

Nothing confirms the rejuvenation of a city centre better than the opening of a first-class boutique hotel. Quebecs is a member of The Eton Collection, who also own boutique hotels in Edinburgh and London, including The Academy and The Colonnade.

Quebecs, opened in February 2002, is located in the former Leeds and County Liberal Club, a handsome high Victorian building right in the heart of town. The city square, central station, and the business and fashionable shopping districts are a few minutes' walk away. The historic red-brick building has been completely renovated from top to bottom and the original Victorian features immaculately restored. The magnificent main staircase, constructed of dark polished oak, is lit by stained glass panels depicting the Three Ridings of Yorkshire, and the first-floor Oak Room is a work of art, decorated with delicately carved oak panels. Each of the supremely comfortable bedrooms features controllable air conditioning, a CD player and music library, satellite television and full communications hookups for the business traveller, including personal voicemail. Beds are made with crisp Egyptian cotton bedlinen and fresh fruit, tea and coffee are provided as part of the 24-hour room service.

LOCATION
Upon entering the city centre, follow signs for the railway station. Join the loop road, which is clearly signed and leads into Quebec Street.

> " By the finest stretch of river, fell and moorland scenery in Yorkshire "
>
> BING CROSBY

Inn

THE RED LION HOTEL & RESTAURANT

An historic ferryman's stopover with an inspiring riverside view

Roaring log fires, hearty beamed ceilings, creaky oak floors and a true Yorkshire welcome - what more could you want? Well, chances are that if you can think of anything at all, the Red Lion probably offers it. This converted 16th-century ferryman's inn, now a cosy hotel with adjacent holiday cottages, positively oozes heritage; from its vantage point on the riverbank, you can almost feel the centuries speed by, and the intriguing mix of ancient and modern in the bedrooms and public areas leave plenty of wandering room for the imagination.

In the kitchen, there's something to tempt everyone, from full English breakfast to traditional pub meals, fresh fish, game in season and a tempting pudding menu - and, of course, a fine selection of cask-conditioned real ales, wines and an extensive brasserie menu in the bar. Business travellers will appreciate the newly refurbished Terrace room, suitable for private functions or business gatherings, while all can enjoy the wealth of attractions in the area, including the hotel's own shooting expeditions on the nearby Grimwith Estate. And if, while you're exploring, you get the feeling that it all looks slightly familiar - well, you've probably seen the Red Lion in the hit film Calendar Girls!

LOCATION

From Harrogate or Skipton, take the A59 to the B6160 at Bolton Abbey. From Leeds, take the A65 to Ilkley, turning toward Bolton Abbey just through the town.

By the Bridge at Burnsall, Burnsall, North Yorkshire BD23 6BU

T (UK) 0870 432 8753
T 01756 720204
F 01756 720292
redlionbur@bestloved.com
www.redlionbur.bestloved.com

OWNERS
Andrew and Elizabeth Grayshon and family

ROOM RATES
1 Single	£58
6 Standard Doubles	£115
4 Superior	£140
Includes full breakfast and VAT	

CREDIT CARDS
AMERICAN EXPRESS • DC • JCB • MC • VI

RATINGS & AWARDS
AA ★★ ✿ 72%

FACILITIES
On site: Licensed for weddings
2 meeting rooms/max 80 people
Nearby: Fell walking by River Wharfe

RESTRICTIONS
Limited facilities for disabled guests
No smoking in bedrooms
Pets by arrangement

ATTRACTIONS
Grassington, Dickensian Weekends, Harrogate - spa, Skipton, Jorvik Viking Centre

NEAREST
CITY:
Leeds - 30 miles/45 mins
Harrogate - 20 miles/30 mins

AIRPORT:
Leeds/Bradford - 8 miles/25 mins

RAIL STATION:
Skipton - 8 miles/20 mins
Ilkley - 8 miles/20 mins

AFFILIATIONS
Independent

RESERVATIONS
National rate in UK: 0870 432 8753
Quote Best Loved

ACCESS CODES
Not applicable

NORTH

ROTHAY MANOR

Country house

NORTH

Rothay Bridge, Ambleside,
Cumbria LA22 0EH

T (UK) 0870 432 8757
T 015394 33605
F 015394 33607
rothay@bestloved.com
www.rothay.bestloved.com

OWNERS
Nigel and Stephen Nixon

ROOM RATES
1 Single   £72 - £90
13 Doubles/Twins £120 - £155
3 Suites   £165 - £180
Includes full breakfast and VAT

CREDIT CARDS
AMERICAN EXPRESS • DC • MC • VI

RATINGS & AWARDS
ETC ★★★ Silver Award
RAC ★★★ Dining Award 2
AA ★★★ ❀ 78%

FACILITIES
On site: Garden, croquet
1 meeting room/max 34 people
Nearby: Golf, fishing, free use of
local leisure club, sailing, walking

RESTRICTIONS
Limited facilities for disabled guests
No children under 7 years in
dining room for dinner
No pets; guide dogs only
Closed 3 Jan. - 6 Feb.

ATTRACTIONS
Wordsworth's homes at
Rydal Mount & Dove Cottage,
World of Beatrix Potter,
Lake Windermere, Holker Hall,
Levens Hall, lake cruises

NEAREST
CITY:
Carlisle - 50 miles/1 hr

AIRPORT:
Manchester - 95 miles/1 hr 30 mins

RAIL STATION:
Windermere - 4 miles/10 mins

AFFILIATIONS
Fine Individual Hotels
Preston's Global Hotels

RESERVATIONS
National rate in UK: 0870 432 8757
Toll free in the US: 800-544-9993
Quote Best Loved

ACCESS CODES
Not applicable

Relax and enjoy a Regency gem in the heart of Wordsworth country

William Wordsworth described the Lake District as 'the loveliest spot that man has ever known'. He shared his passion for its inspirational landscape of rugged mountains, reflective lakes, doughty stone villages and valleys with fellow poets and artists - as well as generations of visitors who come here to hike, sail, fish or just admire their surroundings from a lake cruise.

A quarter of a mile from the head of Lake Windermere and within a short walk of Ambleside, Rothay Manor is a wonderful base for exploring the region. The elegant Regency house is set in its own peaceful grounds and has been personally managed by the Nixon family for more than 35 years (brothers Nigel and Stephen are currently at the helm). There is a real sense of family pride in the hotel's warm and welcoming style, the thoughtfully-decorated bedrooms and the imaginative and beautifully presented food in the restaurant. Guests can pick up a free fishing permit or use the pool, sauna and steam room at a nearby leisure club without charge. The Nixons also offer a programme of special interest breaks between October and May, ranging from painting and photography to walking, gardening and bridge.

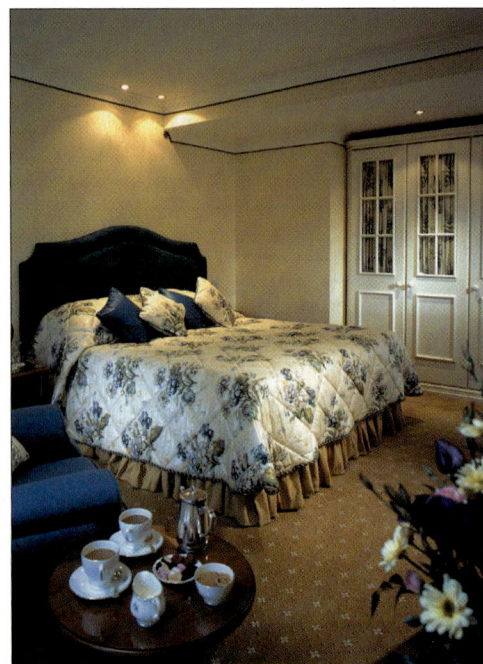

LOCATION
A quarter mile from Ambleside on the B5286 Coniston road or the B5285 from Windermere. The A593 passes by the hotel.

Country house

THE SAMLING

An idyllic Lakeland hideaway with inspirational views

A few hundred feet above the shores of Lake Windermere, The Samling nestles amongst woodlands and landscaped gardens overlooking one of the finest vistas in Cumbria. The house was built for its views some 200 years ago, and the timeless majesty of the scenery remains as magical as ever. Some things, however, are a little different, and although this is the heart of Beatrix Potter and Wordsworth country, do not expect to find anything twee or 'olde-worlde' about The Samling!

A hotel in the country that is emphatically not a country house hotel, The Samling combines the informality of a private house with profound comfort and thoughtful yet unobtrusive service that hints at telepathy. There are 10 suites divided between the house and adjacent buildings set into the hillside. A deep bath, power shower, television with VCR, CD player, phone and fax machine come as standard; all rooms have seating areas, and some have sitting rooms and open fires. Guests can relax in the drawing room with a drink, enjoy light and delicious cuisine and sample the excellent wine cellar. The Samling was also designed with house parties in mind, and can be taken in its entirety for 24 hours or longer.

LOCATION

Between Windermere and Ambleside. From Windermere, pass the Low Wood Hotel and take the next right.

Ambleside Road, Windermere, Cumbria LA23 1LR

T (UK) 0870 432 8765
T 015394 31922
F 015394 30400
samling@bestloved.com
www.samling.bestloved.com

GENERAL MANAGER
Nigel Parkin

ROOM RATES
Single occupancy	£195 - £415
11 Suites	£195 - £415

Includes early morning tea, full breakfast, newspaper and VAT

CREDIT CARDS
AMERICAN EXPRESS • DC • MC • VI

RATINGS & AWARDS
RAC Gold Ribbon ★★★
Dining Award 3
AA ★★★ ❀❀❀
AA Top 200 - 2004/2005

FACILITIES
On site: Garden
1 meeting room/max 18 people
Nearby: Leisure centre, golf

RESTRICTIONS
No facilities for disabled guests
No smoking in restaurant
Pets by arrangement

ATTRACTIONS
Wordsworth's Dove Cottage, World of Beatrix Potter, Lake Windermere, Holker Hall, Levens Hall & Topiary Gardens

NEAREST
CITY:
Manchester - 90 miles/1 hr 30 mins

AIRPORT:
Manchester - 90 miles/ 1 hr 30 mins

RAIL STATION:
Windermere - 3 miles/5 mins

AFFILIATIONS
Pride of Britain

RESERVATIONS
National rate in UK: 0870 432 8765
Toll free in US: 800-98-PRIDE
Quote Best Loved

ACCESS CODES
Not applicable

NORTH

SEAHAM HALL HOTEL & SERENITY SPA — Spa hotel

NORTH

Lord Byron's Walk, Seaham,
Co Durham SR7 7AG

T (UK) 0870 432 8767
T 0191 516 1400
F 0191 516 1410
seaham@bestloved.com
www.seaham.bestloved.com

CEO
Tom Maxfield

HOTEL MANAGER
Graham Bradford

ROOM RATES
Single occupancy   £195 - £525
18 Suites   £195 - £435
1 Penthouse   £525
Includes early morning hot drinks,
continental breakfast and VAT

CREDIT CARDS
AMERICAN EXPRESS • DC • MC • VI

RATINGS & AWARDS
ETC ★★★★ Gold Award
RAC Gold Ribbon ★★★★
Dining Award 4
AA ★★★★ ❀❀❀
AA Top 200 - 2004/2005
AA Hotel of the Year 2003/2004
Which? Newcomer of the Year 2003
Pride of Northumbria Small Hotel of
the Year 2003

FACILITIES
On site: Garden,
licensed for weddings, Serenity Spa
4 meeting rooms/max 120 people
Nearby: Golf, riding, tennis,
leisure centre

RESTRICTIONS
No smoking in restaurant
No pets

ATTRACTIONS
Durham Castle, Durham Cathedral,
Crook Hall and Gardens,
Hadrian's Wall, Newcastle,
Newcastle & Quayside,
Alnwick Gardens

NEAREST
CITY:
Newcastle-upon-Tyne - 18 miles/25 mins

AIRPORT:
Newcastle-upon-Tyne - 18 miles/25 mins

RAIL STATION:
Durham - 14 miles/25 mins

AFFILIATIONS
Pride of Britain

RESERVATIONS
National rate in UK: 0870 432 8767
Toll free in US: 800-98-PRIDE
Quote Best Loved

ACCESS CODES
Not applicable

Contemporary luxury and supreme indulgence

Romantic, state-of-the-art and unashamedly luxurious, Seaham Hall stands poised above the rugged North Sea coast and offers a sensational take on the hotel scene. The house where 'mad, bad and dangerous to know' poet Lord Byron married is a truly contemporary chintz-free zone where the queue for reception has been replaced by a personal greeting at the door and guests can enjoy levels of comfort that verge on the decadent.

Each stylish suite is equipped with mood lighting, open fires, high-speed Internet connection ports and entertainment systems complete with Bang & Olufsen TVs and extensive music libraries. Most have fantastic sea views as well. In the generous bathrooms, baths are big enough for two and hands-free phones actually filter out water noises. Breakfast in bed, needless to say, is de rigueur. An award-winning restaurant and four meeting rooms equipped with the latest technology complete the picture.

Follow the sound of water through the beautiful underground walkway to the Serenity Spa, where the business of feeling good is actually good for you. Oriental in style and designed along Feng Shui principles, it's the ultimate pamper zone and offers over 80 different treatments for men and women.

LOCATION

From junction 62 of the A1M, take the A690 towards Sunderland. At the A19 junction, turn right for Seaham.

"A marvel of modern design"

PAUL MANSFIELD, THE TELEGRAPH

Contemporary hotel

SEFTON HOTEL

Harris Promenade, Douglas,
Isle of Man IM1 2RW

T (UK) 0870 432 8768
T 01624 645500
F 01624 676004
sefton@bestloved.com
www.sefton.bestloved.com

MANAGING DIRECTOR
Chris Robertshaw

ROOM RATES
8 Singles   £74 - £96
80 Doubles/Twins   £81 - £115
2 Suites   £130 - £150
Includes full breakfast and VAT

CREDIT CARDS
JCB • MC • VI

RATINGS & AWARDS
AA ★★★★ ❀ 72%

FACILITIES
On site: Indoor pool, health & beauty,
spa pool, two saunas and steam
rooms, gym, indoor water garden,
library, private car park
3 meeting rooms/max 80 people
Nearby: Golf, conference centre, gardens

RESTRICTIONS
No children
Smoking in library, bar
and some bedrooms only
No pets; guide dogs only

ATTRACTIONS
'Story of Man' heritage sites,
Victorian rail system,
hill, glen and coastal walks

NEAREST
CITY:
Liverpool - 70 miles/25 mins (air)
or 2 hrs 45 mins (ferry)

AIRPORT:
Isle of Man

FERRY PORT:
Isle of Man

AFFILIATIONS
Independent

RESERVATIONS
National rate in UK: 0870 432 8768
Quote Best Loved

ACCESS CODES
Not applicable

A hotel for the green at heart where guests are cosseted like prize blooms

The Isle of Man, renowned for its rugged beauty, unique presentation of its history and fine walking, can now add a notable contemporary hotel to its charms - and one with a most unusual interior! The Sefton overlooks Harris Promenade at the heart of the island capital, Douglas. Its wonderfully ornate cream façade is a Victorian classic, but behind the stucco visitors are greeted by an explosion of greenery flourishing beneath the glass roof of the Atrium Water Garden.

The Water Garden is intrinsic to the ethos of the hotel, a conscious rejection of the sealed windows, dry air and constant hum of many modern buildings. Instead, elegant palm fronds and lily ponds, ferns and luxuriant creepers create a fantastically soothing atmosphere and state-of-the-art technology allows nature itself to dictate the optimum conditions for hotel guests and plants alike. Tranquil bedrooms overlook the atrium or spectacular Douglas Bay. Friendly staff are happy to advise on anything from golfing (there are eight courses all within 10 miles of the hotel) to exploring the island by electric tram, and the fine Gallery Restaurant and the Wallbery Bar offer good food and a relaxing retreat. For business-minded visitors, the hotel also provides free wireless Internet throughout.

An excellent experience - and one made all the better by its convenience of online booking, recommended for ease and better value!

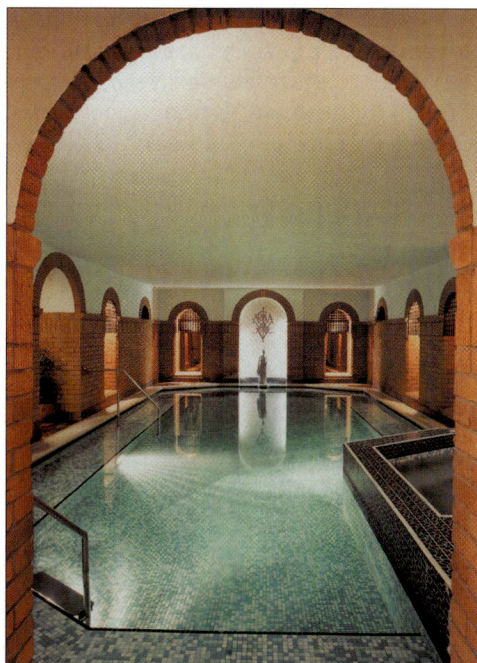

LOCATION

A central position on the capital's main promenade.

STUDLEY HOTEL

Townhouse

Swan Road, Harrogate,
North Yorkshire HG1 2SE

T (UK) 0870 432 8782
T 01423 560425
F 01423 530967
studleyhtl@bestloved.com
www.studleyhtl.bestloved.com

OWNER
Chan Bokmun

ROOM RATES
11 Singles   £69 - £90
23 Doubles/Twins   £85 - £120
2 Suites   £100 - £140
Includes full breakfast and VAT

CREDIT CARDS
AMERICAN EXPRESS • DC • MC • VI

RATINGS & AWARDS
AA ★★★ 67%

FACILITIES
On site: Orchid Restaurant
1 meeting room/max 50 people
Nearby: Golf, swimming, leisure centre

RESTRICTIONS
No facilities for disabled guests
Pets by arrangement

ATTRACTIONS
Fountains Abbey, Harewood House,
Yorkshire Dales, Herriot Country,
York, Ripley Castle, horse racing

NEAREST
CITY:
Leeds - 16 miles/30 mins

AIRPORT:
Manchester - 78 miles/1 hr 30 mins
Leeds/Bradford - 15 miles/30 mins

RAIL STATION:
Harrogate - 3 miles/5 mins

AFFILIATIONS
Independent

RESERVATIONS
National rate in UK: 0870 432 8782
Quote Best Loved

ACCESS CODES
Not applicable

NORTH

Lift the lid off an Oriental taste sensation in deepest Yorkshire

Adjacent to the beautiful 120-acre Valley Gardens and a convenient stone's throw from Harrogate's International Conference Centre, popular sightseeing and shopping opportunities, the Studley rejoices in one of the best locations in town. The hotel occupies a traditional Yorkshire townhouse and is well-known to discerning travellers - owner Bokmun Chan has used his international experience and flair to make this hotel an extraordinary asset to the area.

The Orchid is their first-class Oriental restaurant, where you can see the chefs cooking and order from a menu that reads like a gourmet journey through the Far East. In a clean-cut modern setting, authentic Thai, Malaysian, Indonesian, Japanese and Philipino dishes are skillfully prepared and presented. If the choice seems a little overwhelming, the staff are more than willing to discuss your personal food preferences before making their recommendations. The comfortable guest rooms have been spruced up, too. Traditional bedrooms have been renovated to become light and airy, with a Continental look and feel - and for business travellers, there's the added perk of wi-fi access.

Harrogate offers a busy year-round calendar of events and there are many places of interest in the vicinity - and curists can still enjoy a Turkish bath!

LOCATION
30 minutes from York, Leeds, the M1 and the M62, and 20 minutes from the A1.

> "My wife lectures in tourism and marketing, and she feels that your hotel displays levels of customer service that the rest of the industry should aspire to"
>
> MR DAVID ABBOTT, MANCHESTER

Country house

THE SWAN HOTEL

Newby Bridge, Near Ulverston, Cumbria LA12 8NB

T (UK) 0870 432 8511
T 015395 31681
F 015395 31917
swancumbria@bestloved.com
www.swancumbria.bestloved.com

GENERAL MANAGER
Paul Roebuck

ROOM RATES
Single occupancy	£103
2 Singles	£83
47 Doubles/Twins	£166
6 Suites	£204
Includes full breakfast and VAT	

CREDIT CARDS
AMERICAN EXPRESS • JCB • MC • VI

RATINGS & AWARDS
ETC ★★★★
AA ★★★★ ❀❀ 75%

FACILITIES
On site: Garden, fishing, indoor pool, spa, sauna, steam room, fitness studio, fishing, marina
3 meeting rooms/max 150 people
Nearby: Golf, pony trekking, hot-air ballooning, clay pigeon shooting

RESTRICTIONS
Limited facilities for disabled guests
Smoking in some rooms only
No pets; guide dogs only

ATTRACTIONS
Lake Windermere,
Wordsworth's Dove Cottage,
Beatrix Potter's House, Levens Hall,
Lakeside Aquarium,
National Park Visitor Centre,
Holker Hall

NEAREST
CITY:
Manchester - 80 miles/1 hr 30 mins

AIRPORT:
Manchester - 90 miles/1 hr 30 mins

RAIL STATION:
Grange-over-Sands - 6 miles/10 mins
Oxenholme - 12 miles/20 mins

AFFILIATIONS
Independent

RESERVATIONS
National rate in UK: 0870 432 8511
Quote Best Loved

ACCESS CODES
Not applicable

NORTH

A well-equipped Lakeland hotel for all seasons

The River Leven begins its short journey to the sea from the southern tip of Lake Windermere. A few miles from its source, the river flows past the landmark Swan Hotel, a former 17th-century coaching inn by Newby Bridge. Today, the Swan has emerged as one of the most comfortable and well-equipped hotels in the region.

Very much an antidote to the classic country house hotel, the Swan offers all the facilities and service of a city centre hotel, yet in a beautiful setting. Guests can still enjoy cosy traditional lounges with roaring log fires, the traditional décor and beamed ceilings of Revells Restaurant and charming, thoughtfully appointed guest rooms. However, the superb spa facilities are strictly 21st-century and include a pool, sauna, steam room and a state-of-the-art gym.

Nestled in the gateway to the Lake District National Park, the Swan is set in 14 acres. At the adjacent Swan Marina, there are peaceful waterfront pathways inviting a gentle stroll, and more active guests can participate in water sports and outdoor activities from golf and pony trekking to hot-air ballooning.

LOCATION

At Newby Bridge on the A590 Kendal to Barrow-in-Furness road, approximately 20 minutes from junction 36 of the M6.

SWINTON PARK

Country house

NORTH

Masham, Near Ripon,
North Yorkshire HG4 4JH
T (UK) 0870 432 8784
T 01765 680900
F 01765 680901
swintonpark@bestloved.com
www.swintonpark.bestloved.com

OWNERS
The Cunliffe-Lister Family

ROOM RATES
Single occupancy   £120
26 Doubles/Twins   £120 - £250
4 Suites   £250 - £350
Includes full breakfast and VAT

CREDIT CARDS
AMERICAN EXPRESS • DC • MC • VI

RATINGS & AWARDS
ETC ★★★★ Silver Award
AA ★★★★ ⊛⊛
AA Top 200 - 2004/2005
Excellence in England
Hotel of the Year 2004
Yorkshire Tourist Board
Hotel of the Year 2003
Yorkshire Tourist Board Outstanding
Customer Services Award 2003

FACILITIES
On site: Garden, heli-pad, fishing,
croquet, riding, golf, cricket, health &
beauty, shooting, walking trails, model
boat racing, boules, bowls, mountain
biking, falconry, off-road driving,
licensed for weddings
5 meeting rooms/max 150 people

RESTRICTIONS
No smoking in bedrooms
or dining room
Pets by arrangement

ATTRACTIONS
Brewery tours, Wensleydale,
Ripon Cathedral, Herriot Centre,
Fountains Abbey, Jervaulx Abbey,
Newby Hall, Harewood House

NEAREST
CITY:
Leeds - 35 miles/50 mins
York - 35 miles/50 mins

AIRPORT:
Leeds/Bradford - 33 miles/50 mins

RAIL STATION:
Northallerton - 14 miles/25 mins

AFFILIATIONS
Celebrated Hotels Collection

RESERVATIONS
National rate in UK: 0870 432 8784
Toll free in US: 800-322-2403
Quote Best Loved

ACCESS CODES
Not applicable

A country-house experience par excellence in the Yorkshire Dales

Swinton Park is positioned in a stunning 200-acre park with lakes and gardens and fascinating areas to explore, from the Quarry Gill Bridge to Druid's Seat. The building has been developed over the years as a Victorian 'castle' with the addition of battlements, turrets and enormous reception rooms. For that real 'castley' feel, choose the Turret Room, with its steep stairs, or one of the vast suites on both floors with fabulously draped half-tester beds.

Elegant bedrooms are equipped with modem points, CD players and satellite television, and there is wi-fi access throughout the hotel. The gracious reception rooms are lavishly furnished with open fires, antiques and ancestral portraits. The hotel also has a spa, a wide choice of massage and beauty treatments, private cinema, boot room and snooker room. The superb Samuels Restaurant enjoys sweeping views over the surrounding parkland, and serves a contemporary menu with an emphasis on game, venison and fresh produce from the surrounding family estate and walled garden.

Celebrity chef Rosemary Shrager runs a cookery school in the converted Georgian stables, with a wide choice of hands-on day and residential courses to choose from throughout the year.

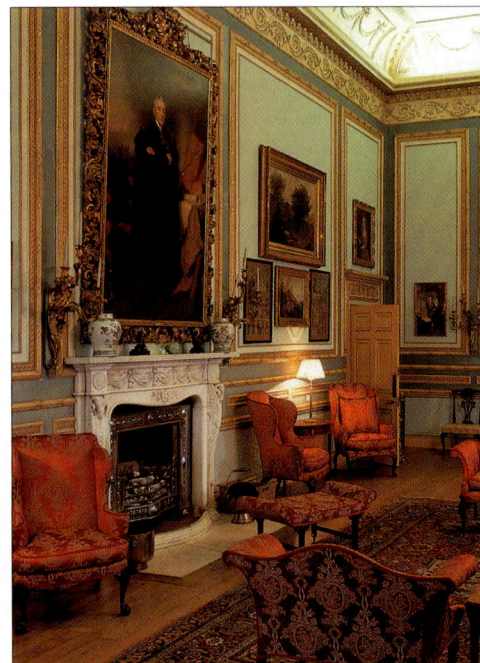

LOCATION
From the A1, take the B6267 to Masham. Drive through town and follow the signs for Swinton.

> The food was excellent, staff pleasant and welcoming, the room a good mix of modern and traditional. Ambience very comfortable and relaxing throughout. Highly recommended!
>
> CARLIE AND PAUL S, PREVIOUS GUESTS

Country house

THE TRADDOCK

Austwick, Via Lancaster,
North Yorkshire LA2 8BY

T (UK) 0870 432 8802
T 015242 51224
F 015242 51796
austwick@bestloved.com
www.austwick.bestloved.com

OWNERS
Bruce & Jane Reynolds

ROOM RATES
2 Singles £50 - £75
10 Doubles/Twins £100 - £140
Includes full breakfast and VAT

CREDIT CARDS
AMERICAN EXPRESS • MC • VI

RATINGS & AWARDS
RAC ◆◆◆◆◆ Dining Award 1
RAC Warm Welcome

FACILITIES
On site: Garden, heli-pad, croquet
1 meeting room/max 30 people
Nearby: Golf, riding, fishing

RESTRICTIONS
Limited facilities for disabled guests
Smoking in bar only

ATTRACTIONS
Yorkshire Dales National Park,
Bolton Abbey, Skipton Castle,
Ingleborough Cave, Kirkby Lonsdale,
the Lake District,
Fountains Abbey and Studley Royal Park

NEAREST
CITY:
Lancaster - 16 miles/25 mins
Leeds - 56 miles/1 hr 30 mins

AIRPORT:
Leeds/Bradford - 48 miles/1 hr 15 mins

RAIL STATION:
Settle - 5 miles/10 mins

AFFILIATIONS
Independent

RESERVATIONS
National rate in UK: 0870 432 8802
Quote Best Loved

ACCESS CODES
Not applicable

NORTH

Relax and recharge in a truly majestic moorland setting

Way back in the 1700s, an elegant Georgian residence was constructed overlooking a paddock where the Dales village of Austwick hosted a horse trading market. It must have seemed only natural to name the house after the neighbouring 'trading paddock', hence the Traddock - a name that this lovely hotel's owners have readopted, much to the delight of the villagers.

Jane and Bruce Reynolds have created a tremendously engaging fusion of traditional country-house comfort and style, complete with English antiques and log fires and just the right touch of sophistication to create a more intimate ambience in the attractive bar area. The garden decking for sunny summer days is another bonus. In the pretty bedrooms, the look is crisp but cosy, and there are some fabulous antique beds. The restaurant is Jane's domain, loosely modern British with an emphasis on seasonal local and organic produce.

Austwick itself is astonishingly unspoilt, and the magnificent walking country encompassed by the Yorkshire Dales National Park literally begins at the Traddock's front door. Scenic railways, limestone caves and the tourist delights of York and Fountains Abbey are within easy reach.

LOCATION
A mile off the A65 between Skipton and Kendal; approximately two miles northwest of Settle and 13 miles southeast of Kirkby Lonsdale.

UNDERSCAR MANOR

Country house

Applethwaite, Near Keswick,
Cumbria CA12 4PH

T (UK) 0870 432 8804
T 017687 75000
F 017687 74904
underscar@bestloved.com
www.underscar.bestloved.com

OWNERS
Pauline and Derek Harrison
Gordon Evans

ROOM RATES
Single occupancy   £120
11 Doubles/Twins   £90 - £140
Includes full breakfast, dinner and VAT

CREDIT CARDS
AMERICAN EXPRESS • MC • VI

RATINGS & AWARDS
AA ⊛⊛ Restaurant with Rooms

FACILITIES
On site: Garden, indoor pool,
health spa,
1- ,2- and 3-bedroom luxury apartments
Nearby: Golf, riding, fishing, walking

RESTRICTIONS
No facilities for disabled guests
No children under 12 years
No smoking in dining rooms
No pets

ATTRACTIONS
Lake District National Park,
Castlerigg Stone Circle,
Beatrix Potter's House,
Wordsworth's Dove Cottage,
Brougham Castle, Penrith Castle

NEAREST
CITY:
Manchester - 120 miles/2 hrs

AIRPORT:
Manchester - 120 miles/2 hrs

RAIL STATION:
Penrith - 17 miles/20 mins

AFFILIATIONS
Independent

RESERVATIONS
National rate in UK: 0870 432 8804
Quote Best Loved

ACCESS CODES
Not applicable

NORTH

History repeats itself
in these beautiful accommodations

'Today my companion and I took tea with the Oxleys at their exquisite house, Underscar. The house has been constructed on one of the most breathtaking locations that I have ever seen; set against the slopes of Skiddaw, and overlooking the tranquil Derwentwater. A lush garden surrounds the house filled with flowers and shrubs; with places to sit and admire the view. As I sipped my tea in the drawing room, a gem with its ornate plaster-work ceiling, I gazed down towards the lake and watched the sun setting on the water; it was a moment of rare, joyous beauty and I wish I could have stayed at Underscar forever.'

'The Diary of a Victorian Country Gentlewoman',
11th May 1860

Today, 145 years on, Underscar Manor is a family-owned and operated country house in the experienced and caring hands of Pauline and Derek Harrison. Its beautiful Victorian restaurant provides award-winning fine cuisine and a breathtaking location in the Lake District National Park, designated an Area of Outstanding Natural Beauty.

The house, including luxurious self-catering apartments, is surrounded by 40 acres of gardens and woodland walks by a cascading stream - among which you are likely to see a few of the famous red squirrels that roam the grounds.

LOCATION
Exit 40 off the M6 onto the A66 toward Workington for 17 miles. At the large roundabout, take the third exit and turn immediately right up the lane signposted 'Underscar'. The drive is ¾ mile on the right.

> "Expect and receive the best accommodation, dining and service in the city
> CORPORATE ENTERTAINER MAGAZINE

Contemporary hotel

VERMONT HOTEL

NORTH

A blissful contemporary getaway in bustling Newcastle

Vibrant, unique and impeccably stylish, the Vermont Hotel is a fantastic vantage point from which to view Newcastle's attractions, history and social scene. Nestled near the Quayside in a superb central Newcastle location, the Vermont, with its 101 bedrooms and suites in an impressive 12-storey Manhattan-style tower, offers something for everyone - from the unrivalled scenic setting next to Castle Garth to its proximity to world-class attractions and entertainment. This tastefully decorated hotel offers rooms both contemporary and traditional, many with splendid views.

The Vermont is a boon for business travellers, too. All rooms have three telephones, a computer/modem/fax port, a well-equipped work desk, complimentary tea and coffee facilities and electrical points with conversion fittings for world travellers. But even with a sterling business pedigree, extraordinary meeting rooms and a fantastic ballroom, you'll never feel like just another conference guest - the Vermont is staffed with friendly folk who'll remember your every need.

Whether you're visiting for business or pleasure, there's a wide variety of after-hours pursuits, from Newcastle's lively night life to the hotel's Bridge restaurant (with spectacular views of Tyne Bridge) and the luxurious Blue Room, home to refined contemporary and classical dishes. The two bars, too, offer a welcoming place to relax, and the Redwood Bar remains open until very late.

LOCATION

Enter the city centre on the A695. Turn right onto Westgate Road, left onto Collingwood Street, right at the lights and left into Castle Garth just after the Castle Keep. The hotel is straight ahead.

Castle Garth,
Newcastle upon Tyne,
Tyne & Wear NE1 1RQ

T (UK) 0870 432 8806
T 0191 233 1010
F 0191 233 1234
vermont@bestloved.com
www.vermont.bestloved.com

GENERAL MANAGER
Teresa Brown

ROOM RATES
7 Singles	£125 - £140
80 Doubles/Twins	£135 - £140
6 Junior Suites	£240
6 Executive Suites	£360 - £550
Includes VAT	

CREDIT CARDS
AMERICAN EXPRESS • DC • MC • VI

RATINGS & AWARDS
RAC ★★★★ Dining Award 2
AA ★★★★ ❀ 76%
AA Courtesy & Care Award

FACILITIES
On site: Fitness centre, solarium
7 meeting rooms/max 250 people
Nearby: swimming pool, gym, walking

RESTRICTIONS
Smoking in restaurant and some bedrooms only

ATTRACTIONS
Theatre Royal,
Baltic Contemporary Art,
Theatre for Life, Hancock Museum,
Tyne and Millennium bridges,
Newcastle Cathedral and Castle,
Quayside, St James' Park

NEAREST
CITY:
Newcastle
Durham - 20 miles/20 mins

AIRPORT:
Newcastle - 8 miles/20 mins

RAIL STATION:
Newcastle - 1/4 mile/5 mins

FERRY PORT:
North Shields - 8 miles/10 mins

AFFILIATIONS
The European Connection

RESERVATIONS
National rate in UK: 0870 432 8806
Quote Best Loved

ACCESS CODES
Not applicable

A real gem!

WAREN HOUSE HOTEL

Country house

Waren Mill, Belford,
Northumberland NE70 7EE

T (UK) 0870 432 8810
T 01668 214581
F 01668 214484
warenhse@bestloved.com
www.warenhse.bestloved.com

OWNERS
Anita and Peter Laverack

ROOM RATES
8 Doubles/Twins   £130 - £150
1 Four-poster   £150 - £175
4 Suites   £175 - £205
Includes full breakfast and VAT

CREDIT CARDS
AMERICAN EXPRESS • DC • JCB • MC • VI

RATINGS & AWARDS
ETC ★★★
RAC ★★★ Dining Award 1
AA ★★★ 72%

FACILITIES
On site: Garden
1 meeting room/max 20 people
Nearby: Golf, riding

RESTRICTIONS
Limited facilities for disabled guests
No children under 14 years
Smoking in library only
Pets by arrangement

ATTRACTIONS
Bamburgh Castle, Holy Island,
Alnwick Castle & Gardens,
Farne Islands

NEAREST
CITY:
Edinburgh - 70 miles/1 hr 30 mins
Newcastle-upon-Tyne - 45 miles/1 hr

AIRPORT:
Newcastle - 45 miles/45 mins

RAIL STATION:
Berwick-upon-Tweed - 15 miles/20 mins

FERRY PORT:
Newcastle - 40 miles/45 mins

AFFILIATIONS
Independent

RESERVATIONS
National rate in UK: 0870 432 8810
Quote Best Loved

ACCESS CODES
Not applicable

A charming country house amongst the treasures of the North East

England's most northerly Best Loved hotel, Waren House is the home of Anita and Peter Laverack, who during the last 16 years have renovated and restored this lovely old house into an elegant 'Country Inn'. Set in six acres of mature grounds and walled garden, the hotel looks out over Budle Bay towards the Holy Island of Lindisfarne, reached only by causeway at low water.

This is the least populated part of the United Kingdom, and even at the height of summer you can walk on miles of deserted golden beaches; visit ancient castles, including Bamburgh, Alnwick, Lindisfarne and the ruins at Dunstanburgh; clamber over battlements including Hadrian's Wall; or have a round of golf on one of the numerous nearby courses before returning to Waren House, where a warm welcome, elegant accommodation, excellent food and a choice of over 250 wines awaits. For an extended stay, there are four suites; one, the Edwardian, looks out over the walled garden and Cheviot Hills. The Rose Suite is wheelchair accessible.

Waren House is within five miles of Northumberland's three main attractions: Farne Islands, Bamburgh Castle and Holy Island.

LOCATION
2 miles east of the A1 on the coast just south of Holy Island, with advance signs from both north and south. Take the B1342 to Waren Mill. The hotel (floodlit at night) is two miles from Bamburgh.

> **11 out of 10. That's not *just* an assessment, but our number of visits in a decade**
>
> MR G SIMMONS, GLOUCESTERSHIRE

Inn

THE WHITE SWAN

Luxuriously comfortable, unfussy and delightful

A warm welcome, luxuriously comfortable beds and service so personalised you'll feel as if the whole place is yours - such is the experience at the White Swan, a 16th-century coaching inn at the gateway of the North Yorkshire Moors.

One look at the decadently relaxing bedrooms, the sparkling white bathrooms and Penhaligon toiletries and you'll realise the place really is a home away from home. Relax in big comfy sofas while you mull over dinner plans, or just move straight for the restaurant, where a roaring fire in winter and a menu overflowing with good things await. The bar is, as they put it, a 'proper bar' and includes Yorkshire real ales, a generous wine list and a good selection of whiskies - and, if they're missing your favourite, they'll do their best to have it for you for next night's dinner. The food itself is unfussy and delightful. Head chef Darren Clemmit sources more than 80% of his ingredients from Yorkshire sources, and the result is splendid, whether you choose a full-on feast or even ask for something that isn't on that night's menu - it's all homemade, right down to the chutney.

Of course, there's no shortage of things to do in the area, from a walk along the beach at Whitby to a visit to Castle Howard, setting from 'Brideshead Revisited', or a trip along the North York Moors Steam Railway, home to some of the fantastic vistas from the 'Harry Potter' films.

LOCATION
Pickering is on the junction of the A169 and A170 Helmsley-Scarborough road. The hotel is in the marketplace.

The Market Place, Pickering,
Yorkshire YO18 7AA

T (UK) 0870 432 8816
T 01751 472288
F 01751 475554
whiteswan@bestloved.com
www.whiteswan.bestloved.com

OWNERS
The Buchanan Family

ROOM RATES
Single occupancy   £80 - £105
11 Doubles/Twins   £100 - £140
1 Suite   £160 - £180
Includes full breakfast and VAT

CREDIT CARDS
AMERICAN EXPRESS • MC • VI

RATINGS & AWARDS
ETC ★★ Silver Award Hotel
AA ★★ ❀ 76%

FACILITIES
On site: Garden, dogs welcome
1 meeting room/max 20 people
Nearby: Golf, riding, fishing, shooting, mountain biking, outdoor activities, paragliding, gliding

RESTRICTIONS
Smoking in bar only

ATTRACTIONS
North York Moors Railway,
Pickering Castle,
York Minster,
Castle Howard,
Rievaulx Abbey,
The Races,
outdoor pursuits

NEAREST
CITY:
York - 26 miles/40 mins

AIRPORT:
Leeds/Bradford - 60 miles/1 hr

RAIL STATION:
York - 26 miles/30 mins
Malton - 8 miles/15 mins

AFFILIATIONS
Independent

RESERVATIONS
National rate in UK: 0870 432 8816
Quote Best Loved

ACCESS CODES
Not applicable

NORTH

NORTH

WILLINGTON HALL

Country house

Willington, Tarpoley,
Cheshire CW6 0NB

T (UK) 0870 432 8818
T 01829 752321
F 01829 752596
willington@bestloved.com
www.willington.bestloved.com

OWNERS
Stuart and Diana Begbie

ROOM RATES
1 Single   £70
9 Doubles/Twins   £100 - £120
Includes full breakfast and VAT

CREDIT CARDS
AMERICAN EXPRESS • DC • MC • VI

RATINGS & AWARDS
ETC ★★★ Hotel
RAC ★★★ Dining Award 1
AA ★★★ 68%

FACILITIES
On site: Garden,
licensed for weddings
4 meeting rooms/max 180 people
Nearby: Golf, riding

RESTRICTIONS
Limited facilities for disabled guests
Children by arrangement
Smoking in bar only
Pets by arrangement
Closed 25 - 27 Dec.

ATTRACTIONS
Chester, Beeston Castle, Tatton Park,
Erdigg Hall, Delamere Forest,
Staveley Water Gardens,
Tabley - Tirley Garth,
Oulton Park Race Circuit

NEAREST
CITY:
Chester - 7 miles/15 mins

AIRPORT:
Manchester - 28 miles/40 mins

RAIL STATION:
Chester - 7 miles/15 mins

AFFILIATIONS
Independent

RESERVATIONS
National rate in UK: 0870 432 8818
Quote Best Loved

ACCESS CODES
Not applicable

The personal touch at this scenic Cheshire hotel makes for a memorable stay

Willington Hall enjoys a truly wonderful position at the foot of the Willington Hills, with views that stretch across miles of unspoilt Cheshire countryside to the Welsh mountains in the distance. The Elizabethan-style brick house was actually built in 1829 and remained in the same family for over 170 years before it was bought by Diana and Stuart Begbie.

The Begbies have done a splendid job of rejuvenating the interior whilst preserving the integrity of the house. The traditionally-decorated, comfy bedrooms offer oodles of space, and large windows allow the light to pour in (together with those lovely views!). The restaurant is open for lunch and dinner, and there are bars in the study and drawing room; in warmer weather, drinks can be taken out on the terrace.

One of Willington Hall's chief charms is the relaxed and friendly atmosphere created by the Begbies and their staff, which makes it a particular favourite with guests who value the personal touch. Peace and quiet is ensured by the rural setting and 17 acres of gardens and parkland, but Willington is also conveniently located for road, rail and air connections. The historic city of Chester is nearby, and North Wales and the Peak District are easily accessible for day trips.

LOCATION

Take the A51 from Tarporley to Chester and turn right at the Bull's Head at Clotton. Willington Hall is one mile ahead on the left.

> " Gracious service, courtesy, consideration and attention to detail "
>
> P HEAL

Country house

THE WORDSWORTH HOTEL

You'll wax poetic after staying at this lovely Lakeland beauty

In the very heart of English Lakeland and the centre of one of its loveliest villages, The Wordsworth combines the sophistication of the first-class hotel with the magnificence of the surrounding countryside. Situated in two acres of landscaped grounds next to the churchyard where William Wordsworth is buried, the hotel's name honours the memory of the area's most famous son. The scenery that so inspired the Lake Poets can be enjoyed from the peaceful lounges, furnished with fine antiques, or in the conservatory and cocktail bar with the aid of a favourite aperitif or specially mixed drink.

The two suites and 37 bedrooms combine great character with comfort. There is also an attractive indoor pool with Jacuzzi and mini-gym.

The Prelude Restaurant, named after Wordsworth's well-known poem, is the place to enjoy lighter or more substantial meals, skillfully prepared from a variety of fresh produce. 24-hour room service is available, and the hotel has its own charming pub, The Dove and Olive Branch, a friendly meeting place for a traditional beer or tasty snacks.

The Wordsworth, known for its welcome, is very convenient for Lakeland's principal beauty spots and places of interest.

LOCATION

Exit 36 on the M6 northbound (A591) and follow the A591 past Kendal, Windermere and Ambleside. Four miles north of Ambleside, turn left into Grasmere; the hotel is on right next to the church.

Grasmere, Cumbria LA22 9SW

T (UK) 0870 432 8825
T 015394 35592
F 015394 35765
wordsworth@bestloved.com
www.wordsworth.bestloved.com

GENERAL MANAGER
J G van Stipriaan

ROOM RATES
4 Singles	£55 - £70
28 Doubles/Twins	£130 - £180
3 Four-posters	£160 - £180
2 Suites	£195 - £225

Includes full breakfast and VAT

CREDIT CARDS
AMERICAN EXPRESS • DC • MC • VI

RATINGS & AWARDS
RAC ★★★★ Dining Award 2
AA ★★★★ ❀❀ 70%

FACILITIES
On site: Garden, gym, heli-pad, fishing, croquet, indoor pool, solarium, sauna, Jacuzzi, licensed for weddings
3 meeting rooms/max 120 people
Nearby: Golf, riding, sailing, walking, fishing

RESTRICTIONS
Limited facilities for disabled guests
No smoking in restaurant and one lounge
No pets; guide dogs only

ATTRACTIONS
Wordsworth's Dove Cottage and museum, John Ruskin's home, Levens Hall,
Hilltop - Beatrix Potter's home, Castlerigg Stone Circle, Keswick, Brougham, Penrith and Sizergh castles

NEAREST
CITY:
Manchester - 95 miles/1 hr 30 mins

AIRPORT:
Manchester - 100 miles/2 hrs

RAIL STATION:
Windermere - 9 miles/20 mins

AFFILIATIONS
Preston's Global Hotels

RESERVATIONS
National rate in UK: 0870 432 8825
Toll free in US: 800-544-9993
Quote Best Loved

ACCESS CODES
Not applicable

NORTH

THE YORKE ARMS

Restaurant with rooms

Ramsgill-in-Nidderdale,
Pateley Bridge, Near Harrogate,
North Yorkshire HG3 5RL

T (UK) 0870 432 8827
T 01423 755243
F 01423 755330
yorke@bestloved.com
www.yorke.bestloved.com

PROPRIETORS
Bill & Frances Atkins

GENERAL MANAGER
John Tullett

RATES PER PERSON
3 Singles   £105 - £125
5 Doubles/Twins   £100 - £125
5 Superior Rooms   £130 - £170
Includes full breakfast, dinner and VAT

CREDIT CARDS
AMERICAN EXPRESS • DC • MC • VI

RATINGS & AWARDS
AA ✿✿✿ Restaurant with Rooms
AA Top 200 - 2004/2005

FACILITIES
On site: Garden, heli-pad
2 meeting rooms/max 25 people
Nearby: Riding, fitness, shooting

RESTRICTIONS
No children under 12 years
No smoking in bedrooms or dining rooms
Pets by arrangement

ATTRACTIONS
Ripon Cathedral, Harrogate,
Ripley Castle,
the Nidderdale Reservoirs,
Fountains Abbey, Yorkshire Dales

NEAREST
CITY:
Harrogate - 20 miles/35 mins

AIRPORT:
Leeds/Bradford - 25 miles/45 mins

RAIL STATION:
Harrogate - 20 miles/35 mins

AFFILIATIONS
Independent

RESERVATIONS
National rate in UK: 0870 432 8827
Quote Best Loved

ACCESS CODES
Not applicable

A culinary marvel at work deep in the glorious Yorkshire Dales

Snuggled into the Nidderdale Valley, Ramsgill enjoys one of the loveliest settings in the Yorkshire Dales and also harbours one of Britain's leading restaurants with rooms. Since 1997, when chef Frances Atkins and her husband Bill took over The Yorke Arms, this creeper-covered old shooting lodge has featured regularly in any list of Britain's prominent restaurants.

The Yorke Arms has evolved into an outstanding Michelin-starred restaurant with rooms, yet still retains the atmosphere and character of a country inn, from the comfortable bedrooms upstairs to the warm glow of log fires in the lounge and dining room. The nerve centre of the operation is Frances's kitchen; recently doubled in size and refurbished with the best equipment, it has enabled her to raise the standard of her elegant but uncomplicated culinary style. Her food is ably complimented by Bill's excellent wine list.

Ramsgill is perfectly positioned for superb walks and exploring the beauties of the Dales. Further afield, favourite attractions include Fountains Abbey, the gardens at Newby Hall and the spa town of Harrogate.

LOCATION
In Ramsgill on the northwestern tip of Gouthwaite Reservoir, on the Low Wath Road 4 miles north of Pateley Bridge.

PERFECT ON THE GO

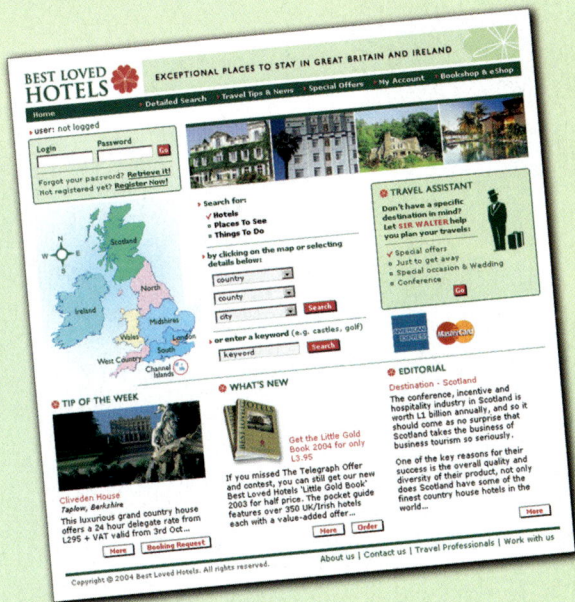

CHASE HOTEL, ROSS-ON-WYE (PAGE 179)

PARK HOTEL KENMARE & SÁMAS SPA, CO KERRY (PAGE 414)

Travelling light? You've always got Best Loved Hotels at your fingertips. Our newly enhanced and redesigned Web site, **www.bestlovedhotels.com**, offers the best of the book - and more, including ...

- Photos, descriptions and guest quotes from more than 350 member hotels - literally somewhere new to stay for every day of the year!

- Full details on room rates, facilities and area attractions, including easy-to-use, detailed maps to help you find attractions and points of interest close to your chosen hotel

- Our unique Travel Assistant, Sir Walter, at your service to help you find your perfect place to stay, whether for leisure, business, sport or festivities. Search by location on our user-friendly maps, or look for your favourite hotel by on-site facilities, nearby amenities, meeting capabilities or pet- and child-friendly options

- Online booking request capabilities - it's easy to get in touch via our e-mail enquiries centre

PRESTONFIELD, EDINBURGH (PAGE 71)

Explore today at www.bestlovedhotels.com

ORDERS/INFO: 0870 432 8700 (UK) OR +44 208 962 9555   E-MAIL ORDERS@BESTLOVED.COM

OR USE THE FREEPOST ORDER/INFORMATION FORM LOCATED IN THE BACK OF THIS BOOK

WALES

A COUNTRY HOUSE HOTEL
Palé Hall Country House, Gwynedd

A FARMHOUSE
Parva Farmhouse Hotel & Restaurant, Gwent

A CONTEMPORARY HOTEL
Castell Deudraeth, Gwynedd

REPRESENTING *the best of* WALES

A SPA HOTEL
Bodysgallen Hotel and Spa, Conwy

Best Loved Hotels offer the cream of the crop across Great Britain and Ireland - from stately palaces to welcoming inns - each the best of its kind within its locality and price range.

Whichever place you choose as your own place to stay, you'll find every hotel offers character, charm and the best delights and attractions of its region.

And each, in its own special way, is best-loved by someone who's been there.

A LAKESIDE HOTEL
Lake Vyrnwy Hotel, Montgomeryshire

A COUNTRY HOUSE HOTEL
Llansantffraed Court Hotel, Monmouthshire

A CONTEMPORARY COUNTRY HOUSE
Bae Abermaw, Gwynedd

A RESORT
Osborne House, Conwy

AN IDEAL ESCAPE:

Wales

BEST LOVED HOTELS · An ideal escape

SEASIDE DELIGHT and mountain reverie: Wales has much to offer, from Victorian coastal pastimes to bracing hill walks and strolls round gardens galore. Bring your walking shoes and make room for your camera - you'll want to remember every detail.

Day One

A charming seaside resort, **Llandudno** has as much to offer visitors as it must have in its heyday during the late 1800s, when the Victorian seaside holiday trend made the coastal town a must-visit. It is well worth taking some time to stroll along the sandy beaches, but be sure, too, to take some time to browse the shops in the **Victoria Shopping Centre**. If simply walking around the area doesn't give you a taste of what it might have felt like as a genteel Victorian traveller, take an hour's detour to the **Llandudno Museum** and get a better feel for the town and its history - it's worth it if only to get an idea of the life of its founder, artist F E Chardon. Stop for a moment in a reconstruction of the kitchen in his Snowdonia cottage, and think of the 'good old days' - perhaps giving thanks for modern-day comforts!

The nearby **Great Orme Country Park** makes a great afternoon out. Situated on limestone cliffs with fantastic sea views, the two-mile long park is full of interesting wildlife. Incidentally, the Great Orme region gives Llandudno its name; in the sixth century, St Tudno began a monastic group in the area, lending it his name as well as his legacy. Within Great Orme, visitors can also step into the Bronze Age with a tour of the **Great Orme Mines** - a perfect outing if you're bringing any little explorers along on your trip. The only Bronze Age copper mine in Europe open to the public, the site is today home to an underground tour that's interesting for all ages.

Whether or not you have children in tow, you need no excuse to visit the **Alice in Wonderland Centre** for a bit of a getaway. Alice Liddell, the girl who inspired Lewis Carroll's Alice in Wonderland, spent her childhood in Llandudno and the Centre exhibits life-sized scenes from the tale as you walk through Carroll's fantastic adventure for yourself. Curiouser and curiouser ...

A cable-car journey in Llandudno

Green at Bodnant Gardens

Day Two

Snowdonia is spectacularly beautiful, with its mystical mountains, charming towns and villages and, of course, the many castles. Why not take a day to tour of some of the castles here, such as **Beaumaris**, which means 'beautiful marsh', **Castell y Bere**, which lies above the Dysinni Valley, and **Caernarfon Castle**, birthplace of Edward II.

The walled town of **Conwy** has a castle of its own, and is a perfect stop for lunch or afternoon tea. Backing onto forested land and flanked by a nearly-complete town wall, Conwy is bursting with a beautiful mix of medieval and Victorian architecture - and, of course, a very tempting range of shops. Have a bit of a walk, and if the town takes your eye, there are plenty of Best Loved hotels in the area that are well worth a look.

Have a taste of WONDERLAND in Llandudno

If you have a little time to spare, **Bodnant Garden** is beautiful. Separated into two sections, the gardens offer contrast in the lower 'Dell' and the formal gardens above, which have great views over across Snowdonia.

Beaumaris Castle is a beautiful mix of historical interest and waterside scenery

Day Three

The private Italianate village of **Portmeirion** is truly enchanting. Created by Sir Clough Williams-Ellis, the village contains restored buildings, cottages, shops and restaurants with a colourful mix of architectural styles, all joined together by a lingering Italian flavour. Take the morning to stroll through the **Plas Brondanw Gardens** and **Gwyllt Woodlands**, and relax by the lakes to take in some of the scenery. After lunch, you may want to take a stroll round the shops - characteristic floral Portmeirion china is a colourful souvenir - and enjoy this unusual and idyllic village a bit more before heading off for a tour of the stunning **Snowdonian coastline**. Just be sure to take your time - in fact, this pretty coast is so alluring you may want to schedule an extra day!

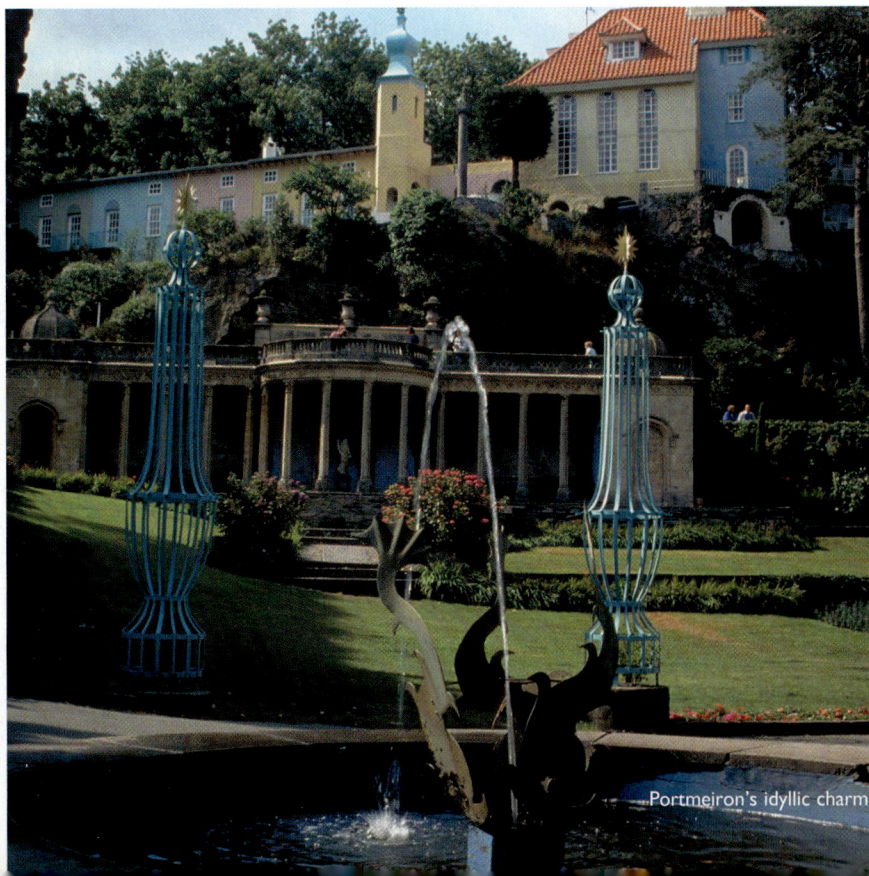

Portmeiron's idyllic charm

ESCAPE FROM YOUR DESKTOP

If you can't wait to get away, or if you'd simply like to do a little investigating before you make your holiday in Wales, browse the links below. Remember, too, that thousands of places to see and things to do await at Best Loved's Web site, **www.bestlovedhotels.com**.

Llandudno visitors guide
www.llandudno-tourism.co.uk

Llandudno Museum
www.llandudno-tourism.co.uk/museum

Great Orme Mines
www.greatorme.freeserve.co.uk

Alice in Wonderland Centre
www.wonderland.co.uk

Guide to castles in Wales
www.castlewales.com/listings.html

Caernarfon Castle
www.caernarfon.com/

Bodnant Garden
www.bodnantgarden.co.uk

Portmeirion visitors guide
www.portmeirion-village.com

Conwy visitors guide
www.conwy.gov.uk

A TASTE OF THE BEST

Wales

STUNNING VISTAS AND CHARMING SCENES aren't all on offer at Best Loved hotels in Wales; there's unforgettable dining, too, whether your tastes run toward hearty traditional fare or modern, creative cuisine.

BODYSGALLEN HALL & SPA ❀❀

Bodysgallen Hall has been awarded the title of 'Wales Commended' by the Which? Good Food Guide 2005. This 17th-century country house with views over Snowdonia has two dining rooms overlooking the gardens serving high-quality, creative fare made from the freshest ingredients – including vegetables grown in their own kitchen garden. Sample such delights as fillet of Welsh Black beef glazed with wild mushrooms and parmesan and tarragon polenta, followed by fig and brandy delice with marinated baby figs and a spiced biscuit. Traditional Welsh afternoon tea is also served in the public rooms - a real delight!

A taste of Bodysgallen's finest

LAKE COUNTRY HOUSE ❀❀

This elegant Victorian country house where guests can enjoy afternoon tea in front of a cosy log fire is also noted for its contemporary cuisine. Fine Welsh produce is used to create such delectable creations as galia and watermelon with a compote of wild berries and honey and yoghurt dressing; for a main course, try leg of Middlewood lamb with fondant potato, confit provencal vegetables, aubergine caviar and black olive sauce. For dessert, there are a number of enticing options, including a

Dine looking over GREAT VIEWS of Snowdonia

magnificent baked dark chocolate tart with vanilla ice cream - excellent fuel for a stroll round the hotel's 50 acres of parkland.

LLANSANTFFRAED COURT HOTEL ❀❀

The Court Restaurant is a great part of the charm that surrounds this country hotel with stunning views. At Llansantffraed, they are great believers in the saying that 'good food is the central element in any Welsh home', and it shows! Daily-changing menus offer such dishes as seared fillet of Welsh beef with fondant potato, glazed shallots and rich red wine jus or fillet of Swansea sea bass with peas and broad beans 'a la Francaise', as well as a wealth of other local delights. All this is, of course, a perfect setting for group dining - and a lovely backdrop for weddings, receptions and conferences.

TAN-Y-FOEL COUNTRY HOUSE ❀❀

Janet Pitman – a Master Chef of Great Britain – creates outstanding cuisine with an Oriental influence at this comfortably small five-star country house in Snowdonia. Local and organic ingredients are combined to create an excellent daily-changing menu, so no two meals are ever quite the same! Favourites in Janet's restaurant, which received the Dining Out in Wales Gold Award for 2004, include Welsh Black beef, organic Welsh mountain lamb and fresh turbot or sea bass. You might try the loin of Bryn Dowsi organic mountain lamb with mint and lemon, accompanied by aromatic fruited cous cous, sweet potato puree, beans and red wine minted jus. And don't forget to sample one or two options from Janet's stunning wine list!

Main dishes at Bodysgallen make fine use of Welsh beef

A TASTE OF THE REGION

Looking for even more to tempt your palate? There are a wealth of fantastic places to dine in Wales, all within the covers of this book! Have a browse to whet your appetite, or jump to some of our own favourites:

THE BELL AT SKENFRITH ❀❀

Fine cuisine is created by Head Chef Kurt Fleming, and served in an informal atmosphere at this 17th-century inn on the Welsh/English border. A stylish country escape!

LAKE VYRNWY HOTEL ❀❀

Enjoy stunning moorland and lake views, as well as top-quality, hearty cuisine at this Victorian country house. The hotel also has a small farm, and much of the lamb used in the kitchen is from the estate itself.

PALÉ HALL COUNTRY HOUSE ❀❀

Palé Hall is renowned for the kitchen's creative use of fresh and natural produce used to create their seasonal table d'hôte menu. The desserts are particularly eclectic, and worth a taste!

Choice ingredients, well presented, are a hallmark of Tan-y-Foel

WOLFSCASTLE COUNTRY HOTEL ❀❀

Recipients of the Dining Out in Wales Silver Award, Wolfscastle has built a reputation for good, high-quality fare. Dishes at this charming country house make great use of fresh Welsh ingredients and are accompanied by a wine list of more than 60 bins. From their à la carte menu, you might choose homemade cream of tomato and tarragon soup with puff pastry fleurons, or a honeydew melon, orange and ruby grapefruit cocktail with homemade citrus granite. Delicious main options include roast Pembrokeshire Gressingham duck on a bed of red cabbage with orange stuffing and Bigerade sauce, and pan-fried sea bass served on a bed of Chinese leaves with crème fraiche, Parma ham and tomato.

The restaurant at Wolfscastle is warm and inviting

Menu
LAKE COUNTRY HOUSE

Tian of Brandon roast smoked salmon and crayfish with pink fir apples
Tomato and mozzarella salad with basil pesto

Saddle of Beacons venison with braised red cabbage, cumin roasted squash, confit potatoes and beetroot puree
Fillet of cod with herb crust served with dauphinoise potatoes, roasted garlic chantrelle mushrooms, shallots and a roast fish reduction

Granny Smith bavarois served with kiwi and lime sorbet
Griottine cherry clafoutis with toffee ice cream

A secret place to be

BAE ABERMAW

Contemporary hotel

Panorama Hill, Barmouth,
Gwynedd LL42 1DQ

T (UK) 0870 432 8523
T 01341 280550
F 01341 280346
baeabermaw@bestloved.com
www.baeabermaw.bestloved.com

OWNERS
Richard and Connie Drinkwater

ROOM RATES
Single occupancy   £73 - £103
10 Doubles/Twins   £104 - £152
2 Mini-suites   £106 - £155
2 Family Rooms   £104 - £152
Includes full breakfast and VAT

CREDIT CARDS
AMERICAN EXPRESS • MC • VI

RATINGS & AWARDS
WTB ★★★★ Hotel
RAC Blue Ribbon ★★★
RAC Dining Award 2
AA ★★★ 68%

FACILITIES
On site: Garden, croquet,
licensed for weddings
1 meeting room/max 100 people
Nearby: Golf, fishing, cycling trails,
walking, climbing, sailing

RESTRICTIONS
No facilities for disabled guests
Smoking in bar only
No pets; guide dogs only

ATTRACTIONS
Snowdonia & Cader Idris,
Harlech & Caernarfon castles,
Portmeirion Italianate village,
Ffestiniog Railway and Slate Mine,
Mawwdach Estuary and Bird Sanctuary

NEAREST
CITY:
Chester - 69 miles/1 hr 45 mins

AIRPORT:
Manchester - 100 miles/2 hrs 15 mins

RAIL STATION:
Barmouth - ¼ mile/5 mins

FERRY PORT:
Holyhead - 65 miles/1 hr 45 mins

AFFILIATIONS
Welsh Rarebits

RESERVATIONS
National rate in UK: 0870 432 8523
Quote Best Loved

ACCESS CODES
Not applicable

Contemporary style overlooking Cardigan Bay and Snowdonia

Considerable skill and vision has gone into transforming this old Victorian hotel into a superbly stylish contemporary property with a spectacular position above Cardigan Bay. Enormous care has gone into restoring the handsomely proportioned rooms, highly polished wood floors, and marble and slate open fireplaces. The colour scheme is white on white, but far from being intimidating, the effect is chic and fresh, and guests are positively encouraged to get out and explore Snowdonia National Park or the beach, returning muddy (or sandy!) and relaxed to enjoy deep baths and great food.

Food is a compelling reason to discover Bae Abermaw. The chefs are passionate about this corner of the world, and they bake their own traditional Welsh lava bread, catch local sea bass and other delicacies and grow their own herbs in the garden.

The national park literally begins at the back door, and all the staff will be very eager to pass on tips about the best local walks, from gentle rambles to challenging hikes up mountainous Cader Idris. Golfers can sample notable courses at Aberdovey and Royal St David's, while other sporting activities range from sailing to sport fishing, mountain biking and rock climbing.

LOCATION

From Dolgellau, take the A496 to Barmouth. At Barmouth, turn right, signposted Bae Abermaw. The hotel is 100 yards up the hill on the right.

Inn

THE BELL AT SKENFRITH

Skenfrith, Abergavenny,
Monmouthshire NP7 8UH

T (UK) 0870 432 8535
T 01600 750235
F 01600 750525
skenfrith@bestloved.com
www.skenfrith.bestloved.com

OWNERS
William and Janet Hutchings

ROOM RATES
Single occupancy   £75 - £110
5 Doubles/Twins   £95 - £170
3 Suites   £145 - £170
Includes breakfast, newspaper and VAT

CREDIT CARDS
AMERICAN EXPRESS • JCB • MC • VI

RATINGS & AWARDS
WTB ★★★★★ Inn
WTB Best Place to Stay in Wales 02/03
AA Restaurant with Rooms ✿✿ 75%
The Good Hotel Guide
Cesar Award 2004

FACILITIES
On site: Garden
1 meeting room/max 60 people
Nearby: Golf, fishing, clay shooting,
archery, quad biking, team building

RESTRICTIONS
Limited facilities for disabled guests
No smoking in bedrooms or restaurant
Pets by arrangement
Closed Mondays November - March
and 24 Jan. - 10 Feb.

ATTRACTIONS
Hereford Cathedral & Mappa Mundi,
Grosmont Castle, Monmouth,
Raglan Castle, White Castle,
Hay-on-Wye, Tintern Abbey

NEAREST
CITY:
Hereford - 16 miles/24 mins
Abergavenny - 12 miles/20 mins

AIRPORT:
Birmingham - 85 miles/1 hr 45 mins

RAIL STATION:
Hereford - 16 miles/25 mins
Abergavenny - 12 miles/25 mins

AFFILIATIONS
Independent

RESERVATIONS
National rate in UK: 0870 432 8535
Quote Best Loved

ACCESS CODES
Not applicable

WALES

This historic border inn offers stunning food and plenty of scenery

A traditional coaching inn located on the Welsh/English border combining beautiful countryside with plenty of history, this 17th-century gem sits on the banks of the River Monnow overlooking Skenfrith Castle and Mill.

Owners William and Janet Hutchings offer guests the very best of classic and modern comfort. The eight stylish and airy bedrooms include four-poster and beamed attic rooms (and there is no expense spared on the comfy mattresses!), and all rooms enjoy views of the Welsh hills or river. Fine food is served in an informal atmosphere, where head chef Kurt Fleming creates imaginative dishes, like a magnificent meal of seared scallops, chorizo and squid tagliatelle with blueberry maple vinaigrette. Dinner here is complemented by a stunning wine list, including a large range of delicious dessert wines. And local beer is a must-try!

In addition to the food, the Bell is in a great area for outside activities - walking, shooting, fishing, golf, archery, canoeing, cycling, hang-gliding, paint balling, quad biking and go-karting are all available, and many of these can be arranged through the hotel. Nearby attractions include Tintern Abbey and Hay-on-Wye, plus Hereford Cathedral and Mappa Mundi.

LOCATION
From Abergavenny take the B4521,
signed Skenfrith, for approximately 12 miles.
The hotel is on the right as you enter the village.

BODYSGALLEN HALL AND SPA

Country house

WALES

Llandudno, Conwy LL30 1RS

T (UK) 0870 432 8540
T 01492 584466
F 01492 582519
bodysgallen@bestloved.com
www.bodysgallen.bestloved.com

DIRECTOR AND GENERAL MANAGER
Matthew Johnson

ROOM RATES
3 Singles   £120 - £165
15 Doubles/Twins   £165 - £270
16 Cottage Suites £190 - £280
2 Four-posters   £220 - £270
Includes service and VAT

CREDIT CARDS
MC • VI

RATINGS & AWARDS
WTB ★★★★★ Country Hotel
RAC Gold Ribbon ★★★★
Dining Award 4
AA ★★★★ ❀❀
AA Top 200 - 2004/2005
Which? Hotel of the Year 2004

FACILITIES
On site: Garden, heli-pad, croquet,
tennis, indoor pool, health & beauty
3 meeting rooms/max 60 people
Nearby: Golf, sailing, water sport,
riding, fishing

RESTRICTIONS
Limited facilities for disabled guests
No children under 8 years
Smoking in Cottage Suites only
No pets

ATTRACTIONS
Caernarfon Castle, Bodnant Gardens,
Swallow Falls, Penrhyn Castle,
Snowdonia, Ffestiniog Railway

NEAREST
CITY:
Chester - 50 miles/55 mins

AIRPORT:
Liverpool - 60 miles/50 mins
Manchester - 85 miles/1 hr 30 mins

RAIL STATION:
Llandudno Junction - 1 mile/3 mins

AFFILIATIONS
Celebrated Hotels Collection
Pride of Britain
Welsh Rarebits
Historic House Hotels Ltd

RESERVATIONS
National rate in UK: 0870 432 8540
Toll free in US: 800-322-2403
or 800-735-2478
Quote Best Loved

ACCESS CODES
AMADEUS YX CEGOD
APOLLO/GALILEO YX 14944
SABRE/ABACUS YX 11426
WORLDSPAN YX GB16

Jewel-like gardens and a sumptuous spa vie for attention with spectacular views

One of the prime joys of handsome 17th-century Bodysgallen Hall is the 200-acre private parkland setting, nestled on a ridge with views stretching off to the rugged heights of Snowdonia. Arranged around the main house and enclosed by mellow stone walls, the lovely gardens include a rare and intricate parterre planted with sweet-smelling herbs, a rose garden and several follies, as well as a croquet lawn and tennis courts. The kitchen garden is also an important feature, contributing fresh ingredients for the dining room, a skillful showcase of the best of local produce.

The interior of the hall has been beautifully restored and furnished with an eye to both comfort and style. Of special note is the oak-panelled drawing room, with its tiled fireplaces and stone mullioned windows providing a relaxing and peaceful retreat for guests. There are 19 attractive and very comfortable bedrooms in the main house, and 16 cottages in the grounds for guests who prefer a greater degree of privacy. Several cottages are adjacent to the first-class spa, where guests enjoy unlimited use of the large indoor pool, spa bath, sauna, steam room and gym; six beauty salons also offer a range of treatments.

LOCATION
From Chester, take the A55 to junction 19, then follow the A470 toward Llandudno for two miles. The hotel is on the right.

> We had a wonderful weekend at Castell Deudraeth. The staff are all very friendly and helpful, and create a relaxing atmosphere
>
> ALAN JONES

Contemporary hotel

CASTELL DEUDRAETH

Sybaritic comfort and cutting-edge style in a romantic seaside idyll

Portmeirion occupies a magical peninsular setting jutting into Tremadog Bay. The enchanting private village was the realisation of a childhood dream created by architect Clough Williams-Ellis between 1926 and 1976, and its deft marriage of beautiful and eclectic restored buildings and Italianate decorative features lends it a distinctly otherworldly charm. In fact, it became famous as the fantasy backdrop for the cult 1960s British TV series The Prisoner.

Castell Deudraeth's 19th-century castellated battlements have a touch of toytown fortress about them. The vaulted porch is one of a number of handsome Gothic and Tudor architectural features, as is the panelled hall and stunning baronial fireplace. However, 21st-century comfort is assured in every detail, from the underfloor heating beneath Welsh oak and original slate floors to the spacious, supremely relaxing contemporary bedrooms equipped with DVD and CD surround-sound systems. The finest Welsh produce is served in the chic dining room, which is laid out in a Victorian solarium overlooking the gardens. Guests have access to 70 acres of grounds and facilities including golf, woodland walks, gardens and beaches. Popular excursions include Caernarfon Castle and the Ffestiniog Railway.

LOCATION

From the A487 (Porthmadog), take a left at Penrhyndeudraeth, signed for Portmeirion. The hotel is a mile and a half along.

Portmeirion, Gwynedd
LL48 6EN

T (UK) 0870 432 8555
T 01766 770000
F 01766 771771
castell@bestloved.com
www.castell.bestloved.com

GENERAL MANAGER
Honor Williams

ROOM RATES
Single occupancy   £162 - £227
7 Doubles/Twins   £199 - £264
4 Suites   £214 - £264
Includes full breakfast and VAT

CREDIT CARDS
AMERICAN EXPRESS • JCB • MC • VI

RATINGS & AWARDS
WTB ★★★★★
RAC ★★★ Dining Award 1
AA ★★★ ❀ 78%
AA Hotel of the Year 2003

FACILITIES
On site: Garden, outdoor pool, health & beauty, licensed for weddings
1 meeting room/max 30 people
Nearby: Golf, riding

RESTRICTIONS
Limited facilities for disabled guests
No smoking in bedrooms
No pets

ATTRACTIONS
Bodnant Garden,
Plas Newydd Gardens,
Ffestiniog Steam Railway,
Llechwedd Slate Cavens,
Harlech Castle, Caernarfon Castle,
Criccieth Castle

NEAREST
CITY:
Bangor - 28 miles/45 mins

AIRPORT:
Manchester- 100 miles/2 hrs 15 mins

RAIL STATION:
Bangor - 28 miles/45 mins

AFFILIATIONS
Welsh Rarebits

RESERVATIONS
National rate in UK: 0870 432 8555
Quote Best Loved

ACCESS CODES
Not applicable

WALES

CASTLE HOTEL

Townhouse

WALES

High Street,
Conwy LL32 8DB

T (UK) 0870 432 8557
T 01492 582 800
F 01492 582300
castleconwy@bestloved.com
www.castleconwy.bestloved.com

MANAGING DIRECTOR
Peter Lavin

ROOM RATES
4 Singles	£69 - £85
7 Standard Doubles/Twins	£90 - £120
12 Superior Doubles/Twins	£110 - £140
2 Family Rooms	£110 - £140
2 Deluxe Rooms	£130 - £160
1 Suite	£200 - £300

Includes full breakfast and VAT

CREDIT CARDS
AMERICAN EXPRESS • JCB • MC • VI

RATINGS & AWARDS
WTB ★★★★ Hotel
AA ★★★ ✿ 71%
AA Top Three Hotels in Wales 2004
True Taste Dining Out Award 2004

FACILITIES
On site:
2 meeting rooms/max 30 people
Nearby: Golf, sailing, riding,
cycling, walking

RESTRICTIONS
Limited facilities for disabled guests
Smoking in some areas only
Pets by arrangement

ATTRACTIONS
Conwy Castle, Llandudno,
Bodnant Gardens,
Snowdonia National Park,
Betws-y-Coed, Anglesea coastline,
Conwy Estuary, Portmeirion

NEAREST
CITY:
Llandudno - 4 miles/10 mins
Liverpool - 60 miles/1 hr

AIRPORT:
Manchester - 76 miles/1 hr 30 mins
Liverpool - 60 miles/1 hr

RAIL STATION:
Conwy - 1/4 mile/2 mins
Llandudno Junction - 1 mile/5 mins

FERRY PORT:
Holyhead - 30 miles/45 mins
Mostyn - 40 miles/1 hr 15 mins

AFFILIATIONS
Welsh Rarebits

RESERVATIONS
National rate in UK: 0870 432 8557
Quote Best Loved

ACCESS CODES
Not applicable

A palace in its own right in the shadow of Conwy Castle

One of Conwy's most photographed buildings, this old coaching inn stands on the site of a Cistercian abbey. Its fascinating past as a hotel includes visits by Telford, Stephenson, Wordsworth and a past queen of Romania.

The interior is charming, relaxed but fascinating; 28 bedrooms and suites await, including a particularly grand four-poster bed from 1570 - considered to have once played home to Charles I when he stayed with a prominent local family during the Civil War. Victorian illustrator John Dawon-Watson spent many of his last days at the Castle Hotel, and though it's not certain whether his paintings paid for his lodgings, the hotel is certainly filled with his work, including a series of scenes from Shakespeare that give the hotel's restaurant its name. Cooking here is brilliant, a mix of traditional and modern created by Chef/Director Graham Tinsley with an emphasis on local Welsh produce.

Centrally located in Conwy near the quay and the castle, the hotel is an ideal base for Welsh travels; choose between a visit to the coast, walking in Snowdonia National Park, sailing, riding, golf and much more.

LOCATION
Exit the A55 eastbound at J17 or J18 westbound for Conwy, using the castle as a landmark. In Conwy's one-way system, pass through town walls; High Street is the main road on the right, adjacent to the quay.

> "We thought everything about the hotel was wonderful, especially all the personal touches"
>
> IAN AND KATHY MADDON, CHESHIRE

Resort

THE EMPIRE

Church Walks, Llandudno,
Conwy LL30 2HE

T (UK) 0870 432 8608
T 01492 860555
F 01492 860791
empire@bestloved.com
www.empire.bestloved.com

OWNERS
Len and Elizabeth Maddocks

MANAGERS
Elyse and Michael Waddy

ROOM RATES
Single occupancy   £55 - £100
51 Doubles/Twins   £90 - £120
7 Suites   £115 - £150
Includes full breakfast and VAT

CREDIT CARDS
AMERICAN EXPRESS • DC • JCB • MC • VI

RATINGS & AWARDS
WTB ★★★★ Hotel
AA ★★★ ❀ 75%

FACILITIES
On site: Indoor heated pool, outdoor heated pool, sauna, steam room, whirlpool bath, health & beauty, roof garden
Nearby: Golf, riding, fishing, sailing

RESTRICTIONS
Limited facilities for disabled guests
No pets; guide dogs only
Closed 18 - 30 Dec.

ATTRACTIONS
Snowdonia National Park,
Conwy and Caenarfon castles,
Bodnant Gardens,
Portmeirion Italianate Village,
Ffestiniog Railway, Swallow Falls

NEAREST
CITY:
Chester - 50 miles/45 mins

AIRPORT:
Manchester - 85 miles/1 hr 30 mins
Liverpool - 60 miles/50 mins

RAIL STATION:
Llandudno Junction - 3 miles/10 mins

FERRY PORT:
Holyhead - 45 miles/45 mins

AFFILIATIONS
Independent

RESERVATIONS
National rate in UK: 0870 432 8608
Quote Best Loved

ACCESS CODES
Not applicable

WALES

Romantic, affordable luxury for all occasions

The privately-owned Empire, set near a picturesque Victorian promenade and pier, has been run by the Maddocks family for more than 50 years. Helping hoteliers Len and Elizabeth are daughter Elyse and her husband, Michael Waddy, who between them offer some of the kindest hospitality in the region. Amongst the family treasures are wonderful antiques and one of the largest private collections of artists' prints by Sir William Russell Flint. The generously appointed bedrooms are complete with marbled bathrooms, televisions and VCRs (the videos are free) and modem connections. Inside, there is an indoor heated pool with sauna, steam room and spa bath. Outside, there is another heated pool, around which you can recline on sun loungers amongst the flowers. If you feel the need for greater relaxation, there are a range of beauty treatments on offer, including aromatherapy, reflexology and Indian head massage.

Michael and his gifted team of young chefs serve innovative fresh food daily in the award-winning Watkins and Co restaurant. Do not overlook the homemade bread and the sinful desserts! Best still, if you find all these temptations too much for a single evening, the Empire offers special two-night breaks for guests who seek a longer stay.

LOCATION

Exit A55 at junction 19. Follow signs to Llandudno, then the town centre. Proceed along Mostyn Street; at the Millennium Clock roundabout take the second exit. The Empire is at the top facing the town.

> Single-handedly, Maes-y-Neuadd seems to embody the virtues of Good Hotel Guide Cesar Award winners
>
> SEAN NEWSOM, THE TIMES

HOTEL MAES-Y-NEUADD

Country house

Talsarnau, Near Harlech,
Gwynedd LL47 6YA

T (UK) 0870 432 8654
T 01766 780200
F 01766 780211
maes@bestloved.com
www.maes.bestloved.com

OWNERS
Doreen and Peter Payne
Lynn and Peter Jackson

ROOM RATES
1 Single   £75
12 Doubles/Twins   £165 - £220
1 Four-poster   £185
2 Suites   £195 - £210
Includes full breakfast and VAT

CREDIT CARDS
AMERICAN EXPRESS • DC • MC • VI

RATINGS & AWARDS
WTB ★★★★ Country Hotel
RAC Blue Ribbon ★★ Dining Award 3
AA ★★ ⊛⊛
AA Top 200 - 2004/2005
The Good Hotel Guide - Welsh
Country House Hotel of the Year 2003
Good Hotel Guide Cesar Award 2003

FACILITIES
On site: Garden, heli-pad, licensed for weddings, putting green
1 meeting room/max 16 people
Nearby: Golf, riding, fishing, shooting

RESTRICTIONS
Limited facilities for disabled guests
No children under 8 years in restaurant, high tea provided
Smoking in bar and conservatory only
Pets by arrangement

ATTRACTIONS
Mount Snowdon,
Portmeirion Italianate village,
Caernarfon and Harlech castles,
Royal St David's golf course,
Narrow Gauge Railway, Slate Caverns

NEAREST
CITY:
Bangor - 35 miles/1 hr
Chester - 70 miles/1 hr 30 mins

AIRPORT:
Manchester - 100 miles/2 hrs

RAIL STATION:
Harlech - 3 miles/10 mins

AFFILIATIONS
Celebrated Hotels Collection
Welsh Rarebits
Grand Heritage Hotels

RESERVATIONS
National rate in UK: 0870 432 8654
Toll free in US: 800-322-2403
or 888-93-GRAND
Quote Best Loved

ACCESS CODES
AMADEUS UI CEGMAE
APOLLO/GALILEO UI 34651
SABRE/ABACUS UI 31036
WORLDSPAN UI 42175

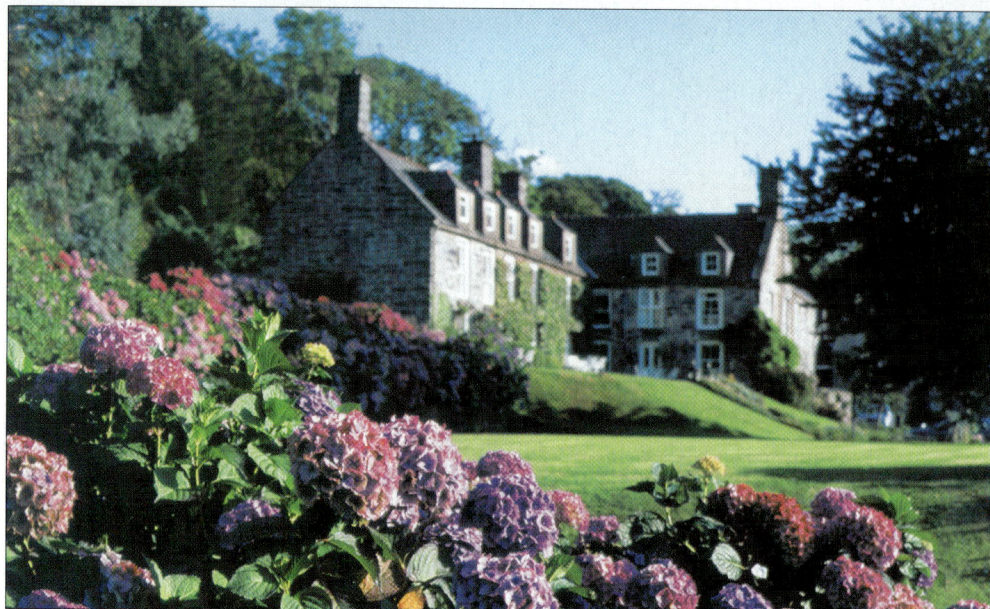

An elegant country house with sea and mountain views

Deep in Snowdonia amongst some of the most beautiful scenery in Britain, the manor house of Maes-y-Neuadd has watched over timeless, magnificent wilderness for more than 600 years. For centuries the home of one family, Maes-y-Neuadd is once again a family home, owned by two sisters and their husbands, Lynn and Peter Jackson and Doreen and Peter Payne. The couples have lovingly restored and refurbished the house, creating a warm and welcoming haven for travellers from all over the world. The rooms are furnished using the a seamless blend modern craftsmanship and fine antiques, as well as many paintings by local artists. The 75 acres of grounds reflect the beauty of the seasons, nurtured by the mild gulfstream climate.

Chef-proprietor Peter Jackson revels in the quality of the 'natural larder' on his doorstep. To complement the fine lamb, cheese, fish and game for which Wales is renowned, the hotel's garden features a fine assortment of vegetables, fruit and herbs.

The wealth of ancient language, culture and music set this area of Wales apart from the rest of Britain. But with so much to offer, the welcome 'Croeso' - for which Wales is so famous - is nowhere warmer than at Maes-y-Neuadd.

LOCATION
Located a mile and a half off the B4573, three and a half miles north of Harlech. Watch for the hotel's sign on the corner of the lane.

> " You can't really write about this place - you have to experience it
> KEITH JAMES, GREAT YARMOUTH "

Inn

THE INN AT THE ELM TREE

St Brides Wentlooge,
Near Newport,
South Wales NP10 8SQ

T (UK) 0870 432 8662
T 01633 680225
F 01633 681035
elmtree@bestloved.com
www.elmtree.bestloved.com

OWNER
Patricia Thomas

ROOM RATES
Single occupancy   £60 - £90
9 Doubles/Twins   £70 - £110
1 Four-poster   £110
Includes breakfast and VAT

CREDIT CARDS
AMERICAN EXPRESS • MC • VI

WALES

RATINGS & AWARDS
WTB ★★★★★ Inn
RAC ◆◆◆◆◆ Dining Award 2
RAC Sparkling Diamond,
Warm Welcome Awards
AA ◆◆◆◆◆ ❀
AA Premier Collection
Welcome Host Gold Award

Traditional hospitality and good food are the hallmarks of this appealing inn

Bordering the quiet marshland bird sanctuary of the Wentlooge Flats between Newport and Cardiff, The Elm Tree restaurant has enjoyed a fine reputation for almost two decades. In 2000, owners Mike and Patricia Thomas branched out and added rooms, transforming the property into a welcoming country inn where good food is still very much the order of the day - and so, now, is a really good night's sleep.

The Inn's bedrooms have each been individually designed and furnished in a variety of styles, from pretty country-style retreats with chunky pine furniture and patchwork quilts to the Fleur de Lys room, with its own waterbed. Romantics might be tempted by the four-posters in the medieval-styled Camelot room or the Cambridge honeymoon suite, which boasts its own Jacuzzi.

However, the one thing everybody is here for is the food. The emphasis is on modern British cuisine with a dash of European and Asian influence, and the Inn's chefs take their inspiration from Wales' best natural produce, sourced wherever possible from local organic farms. Specialities include Welsh Black beef, salt marsh lamb, lobster, oysters and game from local estates teamed with fine wines and an after-dinner selection of vintage ports and brandies.

FACILITIES
On site: Garden, croquet
2 meeting rooms/max 40 people
Nearby: Golf, riding, walking, fishing, shooting

RESTRICTIONS
Limited facilities for disabled guests
No children under 12 years
Smoking in bar and some bedrooms only
Pets by arrangement

ATTRACTIONS
Cardiff Bay,
Newport Transporter Bridge,
Tredegar House, Wye Valley,
Castell Coch, Roman town of Caerleon,
the Wentlooge Flats, sea wall

NEAREST
CITY:
Newport - 3 miles/10 mins

AIRPORT:
Cardiff - 27 miles/30 mins

RAIL STATION:
Newport - 4 miles/15 mins

AFFILIATIONS
Welsh Rarebits

LOCATION

Exit the M4 at junction 28 for the A48 toward Cardiff, signed Castleton. Follow signs for Dyffryn and St Brides Wentlooge.

RESERVATIONS
National rate in UK: 0870 432 8662
Quote Best Loved

ACCESS CODES
Not applicable

WALES

THE LAKE COUNTRY HOUSE

Country house

Llangammarch Wells,
Powys LD4 4BS

T (UK) 0870 432 8679
T 01591 620202
F 01591 620457
lakecountry@bestloved.com
www.lakecountry.bestloved.com

OWNERS
Jean-Pierre and Janet Mifsud

ROOM RATES
Single occupancy   £105 - £170
8 Luxury Doubles   £140
11 Suites   £200 - £240
Includes full breakfast and VAT

CREDIT CARDS
AMERICAN EXPRESS • DC • JCB • MC • VI

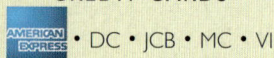

RATINGS & AWARDS
WTB ★★★★★ Country Hotel
RAC Gold Ribbon ★★★
Dining Award 3
AA ★★★ ⊛⊛
AA Top 200 - 2004/2005
AA Inspectors Selected Hotel

FACILITIES
On site: Garden, heli-pad, fishing,
croquet, tennis, licensed for weddings,
snooker, clay pigeon shooting,
salmon and trout fishing,
nine-hole par 3 golf course and
putting area, billiards room
3 meeting room/max 150 people

RESTRICTIONS
Limited facilities for disabled guests
No smoking in restaurant
Pets by arrangement

ATTRACTIONS
Powis Castle, The Elan Valley,
Brecon Beacons,
Hay-on-Wye's bookshops, Aberglasney,
National Botanical Gardens

NEAREST
CITY:
Hereford - 40 miles/45 mins

AIRPORT:
Cardiff - 60 miles/1 hr 15 mins

RAIL STATION:
Llangammarch Wells - 1 mile/5 mins

AFFILIATIONS
Pride of Britain
Welsh Rarebits

RESERVATIONS
National rate in UK: 0870 432 8679
Toll free in US: 800-98-PRIDE
Quote Best Loved

ACCESS CODES
AMADEUS HK SWSLAK
APOLLO/GALILEO HT 54137
SABRE/ABACUS HK 19413
WORLDSPAN HK LAKEW

If you can't relax here, you can't relax anywhere!

An air of elegance and calm informality pervades this exquisitely furnished Welsh country house. Warmly welcoming, this award-winning retreat stands serenely in 50 acres of parkland, including a large trout lake, a haven for fascinating wildlife. In such a setting, guests experience the true feeling of Wales.

One may enjoy a mouth-watering, traditional Welsh afternoon tea in front of log fires in the lounge or in the garden in summer. Dining by candlelight in the restaurant is a memorable experience, and the cuisine has won several prestigious awards for its excellence.

Suites and bedrooms are delightfully appointed, each having a private bathroom, television, direct-dial telephone, period furniture and fine pictures and books. For leisure, the hotel's billiards room is a popular evening venue. Excellent salmon and trout fishing is available on the rivers Wye and Irfon, as well as the hotel's own picturesque lake, which regularly yields trout of five pounds and over and has no closed season. Tennis, croquet, clay pigeon shooting and a nine-hole golf course are all on the grounds. There are four 18-hole courses in the vicinity, and for those with equestrian interests, pony trekking can be arranged.

LOCATION

Take the A40 to Abergavenny-Brecon; after Brecon, veer left onto the B4519, then left (Llangammarch Wells). Cross Mount Eppynt (6 miles) and left at the foot of the hill. Hotel is one mile along on the right.

> "It was indeed splendid. Everything was absolute perfection - the staff were wonderful and the food excellent"
>
> KATE DUNKLEY, CHESHIRE

Lakeside hotel

LAKE VYRNWY HOTEL

Lake Vyrnwy, Llanwddyn,
Montgomeryshire SY10 0LY

T (UK) 0870 432 8680
T 01691 870692
F 01691 870259
vyrnwy@bestloved.com
www.vyrnwy.bestloved.com

OWNERS
The Bisiker Family

ROOM RATES
34 Doubles/Twins   £120 - £190
1 Suite   £190
Includes full breakfast and VAT

CREDIT CARDS
AMERICAN EXPRESS • DC • MC • VI

RATINGS & AWARDS
WTB ★★★★ Country Hotel
AA ★★★ ✿✿ 73%

WALES

FACILITIES
On site: Garden, heli-pad, fishing, tennis,
licensed for weddings, fly fishing,
shooting, cycling, walking trails,
rowing, sailing, clay shooting
3 meeting rooms/max 130 people
Nearby: Whitewater rafting, canoeing,
walking trails

RESTRICTIONS
Limited facilities for disabled guests
No smoking in restaurant

ATTRACTIONS
Powis Castle,
Great Little Trains of Wales,
Vyrnwy Visitor Centre, Lake Vyrnwy,
Ffestiniog and Llanberis railways,
RSPB Hides,
hill and mountain walks

NEAREST
CITY:
Shrewsbury - 32 miles/45 mins
Chester - 43 miles/1 hr

AIRPORT:
Birmingham - 90 miles/1 hr 45 mins
Manchester - 90 miles/1 hr 45 mins

RAIL STATION:
Welshpool - 22 miles/30 mins
Shrewsbury - 32 miles/45 mins

AFFILIATIONS
Welsh Rarebits
Classic British Hotels

RESERVATIONS
National rate in UK: 0870 432 8680
Quote Best Loved

ACCESS CODES
Not applicable

A great sporting pedigree and magical views from the Roof of Wales

Set high on the slopes of the Berwyn Mountains with views stretching off across lakes and moorland to Snowdonia, the Vyrnwy really does sit atop the Roof of Wales. It is the centrepiece of the vast Vyrnwy Estate, which has its origins back in the late 19th century, when the city fathers of Liverpool dammed the Vyrnwy Valley to create a fresh water supply for the city. They ensured the water's purity by purchasing the surrounding 24,000-acre catchment area and transformed it into a sporting estate with a splendid lodge - the present-day hotel.

The former lodge has delighted countryside enthusiasts with its magnificent location, comfort and style for more than a century. The guest rooms are spacious and individually decorated; many are furnished with antiques, and some have four-poster beds, Jacuzzis and private balconies. The head chef takes pride in sourcing most of his ingredients from local suppliers, while the estate provides game in season.

Vyrnwy offers unrivalled opportunities for outdoor pursuits such as tennis, sailing, clay shooting, archery and trout fishing on the lake or walking, cycling and birdwatching around the estate. Further afield, Powis Castle, the Offa's Dyke Path and several great little mountain train rides are within easy reach.

LOCATION
Follow brown tourist signs for Lake Vyrnwy from Shrewsbury on the A458, or from Oswestry on the A5.

> What a delightful retreat! Thank you for the wonderful hospitality and kind service. We truly did feel as if we were in someone's beautiful home
>
> JANIS & JEFFREY RUBIN, CANFIELD, OHIO USA

LLANGOED HALL

Country house

Llyswen, Brecon,
Powys LD3 0YP

T (UK) 0870 432 8689
T 01874 754525
F 01874 754545
llangoed@bestloved.com
www.llangoed.bestloved.com

OWNER
Sir Bernard Ashley

ROOM RATES
Single occupancy	£140 - £320
11 Doubles/Twins	£180 - £315
7 Four-posters	£180 - £360
3 Suites	£340 - £360

Includes full breakfast and VAT

CREDIT CARDS
AMERICAN EXPRESS • DC • JCB • MC • VI

RATINGS & AWARDS
WTB ★★★★★ Country Hotel
RAC ★★★★ Dining Award 2
AA ★★★★ ✿✿ 74%

FACILITIES
On site: Garden, heli-pad, fishing, croquet, tennis, licensed for weddings, snooker, mountain bikes, clay pigeon shooting
3 meeting rooms/max 70 people
Nearby: Golf, shooting, riding, 4x4 driving, canoeing, gliding

RESTRICTIONS
Limited facilities for disabled guests
No children under 8 years
No smoking in dining rooms
No pets, kennels available

ATTRACTIONS
Brecon Beacons, Cardiff, Hay-on-Wye, Tintern Abbey, Powis and Raglan castles

NEAREST
CITY:
Cardiff - 55 miles/55 mins

AIRPORT:
Cardiff - 65 miles/1 hr 30 mins

RAIL STATION:
Abergavenny - 23 miles/40 mins

AFFILIATIONS
Celebrated Hotels Collection
Welsh Rarebits

RESERVATIONS
National rate in UK: 0870 432 8689
Toll free in UK: 0321 ASHLEY
Toll free in US: 800-322-2403
Quote Best Loved

ACCESS CODES
Not applicable

Designed by a distinguished architect, recreated by a great designer

Llangoed Hall may have been the legendary White Palace, home of the first Parliament at the dawn of Welsh history. In 560 AD, Prince Iddon donated it to the church in expiation of his sins. A mansion was built here in 1632; in 1912, the great architect Sir Clough Williams-Ellis designed it as a gracious country house, retaining the surviving Jacobean porch as part of the south wing.

Sir Bernard Ashley saw Llangoed Hall as the place where he could fulfil his ambition to recreate the atmosphere of an Edwardian house party. There is no reception desk, just friendly staff to carry the bags. In summer, the Great Hall's French windows are open so that guests can enjoy the garden. In winter, the huge stone fireplace has a merry log blazing. Fine portraits and works by Whistler and the Edwardians adorn the Picture Gallery's walls and bedrooms are decorated with furnishings from Sir Bernard's fabric company, Elanbach, situated in the hotel's grounds.

The dining room offers modern classical cooking, making the most of fresh local produce such as Welsh lamb, Wye salmon and laverbread.

The secluded Wye Valley and the Black Mountains are all around; the Brecon Beacons, Cardiff, Hay-on-Wye, Caerphilly, Raglan and Powis Castles and Tintern Abbey are nearby.

LOCATION
On the A470 9 miles southeast of Builth Wells and 10 miles northeast of Brecon.

> " Watching the fountain cascade into the lake whilst sipping a cool gin and tonic ... The sun setting on a clear blue evening was just magic "
>
> JOHN AND MARGARET KNAPP, CAMPBELLTOWN, AUSTRALIA

Country house   LLANSANTFFRAED COURT HOTEL

Delightful dining, panoramic views and so much to see at your door

The site of Llansantffraed Court dates to the 12th century, with the present house in William and Mary style standing in 19 acres of parkland. A hotel since the 1920s, it still holds true to old-fashioned standards of style and service. Inside, 21 individually-decorated bedrooms (some with oak beams and dormer windows!) offer a spacious charm graced by magnificent panoramic views; in the lounge, open fires await on cold days and on the terrace, afternoon teas delight in warmer weather.

Food is something taken quite seriously at Llansantffraed Court. Daily-changing menus take advantage of local delights, complemented by a wide-ranging wine-list; particularly tempting samples include Llansantffraed rabbit and hazelnut terrine wrapped in smoked bacon and a local goats' cheese, spinach and laverbread ravioli served with spicy sweet pepper compote. Weddings and conferences are a particular specialty, with meeting rooms catering for up to 200.

Outdoors, plenty awaits, whether on the grounds or nearby; on-site, enjoy archery, croquet, bowls, go-karting, putting, quad biking and fishing on the hotel's own lake; further afield, golfing abounds in Monmouthshire and all manner of sport is available in the Wye Valley, Brecon Beacons and the Forest of Dean.

LOCATION

Exit junction 24 on the M4 for the A449 (Abergavenny), then the A40 (Abergavenny). At the first roundabout, take the last exit (Clytha). The hotel's white gates are four miles along on the right.

Llanvihangel Gobion, Clytha, Abergavenny, Monmouthshire NP7 9BA

T (UK) 0870 432 8690
T 01873 840678
F 01873 840674
lcourt@bestloved.com
www.lcourt.bestloved.com

OWNERS
Mike and Heather Morgan

ROOM RATES
3 Singles   £86 - £165
16 Doubles/Twins   £112 - £185
1 Suite   £150
1 Four-poster   £170
Includes full breakfast and VAT

CREDIT CARDS
AMERICAN EXPRESS • DC • JCB • MC • VI

RATINGS & AWARDS
WTB ★★★ Country Hotel
AA ★★★ ✪✪ 70%

FACILITIES
On site: Heli-pad, croquet, licensed for weddings, archery, bowls, go-karting, putting, quad bikes, clay pigeon shooting, teambuilding, hot-air ballooning
3 meeting rooms/max 200 people
Nearby: Golf, fishing, badminton, riding, tennis, water sport

RESTRICTIONS
No facilities for disabled guests
No smoking in restaurant and some bedrooms

ATTRACTIONS
Raglan Castle, Grosmont Castle, Tintern Abbey, Hereford Cathedral & Mappa Mundi, White Castle, Monmouth, Hay-on-Wye

NEAREST
CITY:
Abergavenny - 5 miles/10 mins
Newport - 12 miles/20 mins

AIRPORT:
Bristol - 40 miles/1 hr
Birmingham - 90 miles/1 hr 50 mins

RAIL STATION:
Abergavenny - 5 miles/10 mins

AFFILIATIONS
Independent

RESERVATIONS
National rate in UK: 0870 432 8690
Quote Best Loved

ACCESS CODES
Not applicable

WALES

> "From the moment we walked in to Osborne House to when we left, you fulfilled in every way the expectation set out in your publicity"
>
> J P QUINN, HAGLEY, WEST MIDLANDS

OSBORNE HOUSE

Resort

Promenade, Llandudno,
Conwy LL30 2LP

T (UK) 0870 432 8729
T 01492 860330
F 01492 860791
osbornewales@bestloved.com
www.osbornewales.bestloved.com

OWNERS
Len and Elizabeth Maddocks

MANAGERS
Michael & Elyse Waddy

ROOM RATES
6 Suites   £150 - £250
Includes continental breakfast and VAT

CREDIT CARDS
AMERICAN EXPRESS • DC • JCB • MC • VI

RATINGS & AWARDS
WTB ★★★★★ Townhouse
RAC Gold Ribbon ★★★★
Dining Award 1
AA ★★★★ ❀ Town House
AA Top 200 - 2004/2005

FACILITIES
Nearby: Golfing, riding, fishing, sailing

RESTRICTIONS
No facilities for disabled guests
No children
No pets
Closed 18 - 30 Dec.

ATTRACTIONS
Snowdonia National Park,
Portmeirion Italianate village,
Bodnant Gardens,
Conwy and Caernarfon castles,
Ffestiniog and Llanberis railways,
Lechwedd Slate Caverns

NEAREST
CITY:
Chester - 50 miles/45 mins

AIRPORT:
Manchester - 85 miles/1 hr 30 mins
Liverpool - 60 miles/50 mins

RAIL STATION:
Llandudno Junction - 3 miles/10 mins

AFFILIATIONS
Independent

RESERVATIONS
National rate in UK: 0870 432 8729
Quote Best Loved

ACCESS CODES
Not applicable

Gloriously romantic and ludicrously spacious, with breathtaking sea views

For many visitors to Llandudno, the only address worth considering is The Empire, a stately and much-loved grande dame of a Victorian resort hotel owned and managed by the Maddocks family. Now, The Empire's faithful have been thrown into utter confusion by the arrival of The Osborne, a recent and splendiferous Maddocks venture that has seen a crumbling 1851 seafront property restored and refurbished in spectacular style and transformed into a stunning all-suites hotel.

To say that Len and Elizabeth Maddocks are excited about their hotel is something of an understatement. It has taken time to complete, as every huge, high-ceilinged room has been immaculately finished and furnished with antiques. The spacious bedrooms have fabulous views of Conwy Bay and Great Ormes Head, king-size brass beds and marble bathrooms (and each suite has its own parking bay at the rear of the property). Guests arrive to a cosy fire twinkling in the grate in winter. Downstairs, the newly-opened Cafe Bistro boasts impressively ornate ceilings, a large fireplace and a high quality brasserie menu served from 11 a.m. - 10 p.m.

Within easy reach of Llandudno are the wilds of Snowdonia, the lovely Bodnant Garden in the Vale of Conwy and Caernarfon.

LOCATION
Exit the A55 at Junction 19. Follow signs to Llandudno, then the Promenade. Osborne House is at the end of the Promenade and opposite the entrance to the pier.

> We found Palé Hall a haven of peace and tranquillity ... Good food and accommodation
>
> MR & MRS HOLMES, DERBYSHIRE

Country house

PALÉ HALL COUNTRY HOUSE

A magnificent house once graced by the presence of Queen Victoria

Palé Hall, a luxurious Victorian mansion set in acres of parkland, was built in 1870 for a wealthy Scottish gentleman and railway engineer. His brief to the architects was that 'no expense should be spared' in building this family home. This splendid house has stunning interiors, from the magnificent entrance hall with its lofty vaulted ceiling and galleried oak staircase to the boudoir with its handpainted ceiling and marble bar and fireplaces.

All bedrooms are individually decorated, with a commanding view of the gardens and surrounding panoramic scenery - including the entrance to the Queen's Walk, named after a stay by Queen Victoria in 1889. The original bath and half-tester bed used by Her Majesty during her stay are still available for the comfort of guests.

The restaurant is acclaimed for its food, including options for vegetarian and other diets as well as an emphasis on the fresh and natural marked by a regular change of menu. The restaurant possesses a restful, intimate atmosphere for dinner by candlelight - and when you're ready to explore a bit, Palé Hall is easily accessible by road and is an excellent base for touring. With the Land Rover Experience Centre based at Palé, the hotel offers guests the opportunity to drive off-road in a variety of current Land Rover models around 200 acres of rugged terrain in the Welsh mountainside.

LOCATION

The house is situated just off the B4401 Corwen to Bala road four miles from Llandrillo, and is signposted from the main road.

Palé Estate, Llandderfel, Bala, Gwynedd LL23 7PS

T (UK) 0870 432 8731
T 01678 530285
F 01678 530220
pale@bestloved.com
www.pale.bestloved.com

OWNERS
Saul and Judith Nahed

ROOM RATES
Single occupancy   £80 - £150
16 Doubles/Twins   £105 - £200
Includes full breakfast and VAT

CREDIT CARDS
JCB • MC • VI

RATINGS & AWARDS
WTB ★★★★ Country Hotel
AA ★★★ ✿✿ 78%

FACILITIES
On site: Garden, heli-pad, salmon and trout fishing, 4x4 off-road driving, walking 2 meeting rooms/max 40 people
Nearby: Hill and mountain walks, go-karting, water sport, clay and game shooting, pony trekking

RESTRICTIONS
No facilities for disabled guests
Children by arrangement
No smoking throughout
No pets

ATTRACTIONS
Snowdonia, Powis Castle & Gardens, Bodnant Gardens, Lechwedd Slate Caverns, Conwy and Penrhyn castles, Portmeirion, Erddig House, Chirk Castle, Pistyll Rhaeadr Waterfall

NEAREST
CITY:
Chester - 38 miles/50 mins

AIRPORT:
Manchester - 77 miles/1 hr 45 mins
Liverpool - 55 miles/1 hr 30 mins

RAIL STATION:
Welshpool - 30 miles/40 mins
Wrexham - 32 miles/45 mins

AFFILIATIONS
Independent

RESERVATIONS
National rate in UK: 0870 432 8731
Quote Best Loved

ACCESS CODES
Not applicable

WALES

Map p. 444, grid E6

Parva Farmhouse is busting out all over with old-fashioned charm and good humour

PADDY BURT, DAILY TELEGRAPH

PARVA FARMHOUSE HOTEL & RESTAURANT   Farmhouse

Tintern, Chepstow,
Gwent NP16 6SQ

T (UK) 0870 432 8733
T 01291 689411
F 01291 689557
parva@bestloved.com
www.parva.bestloved.com

OWNERS
Dereck and Vickie Stubbs

ROOM RATES
Single occupancy   £60 - £74
9 Doubles/Twins   £74 - £80
Includes full breakfast and VAT

CREDIT CARDS
AMERICAN EXPRESS • MC • VI

RATINGS & AWARDS
WTB ★★★ Hotel
AA ★★ ❀ 73%

FACILITIES
On site: Small garden
Nearby: Riding, fishing, clay shooting, walking in Wye Valley and Offa's Dyke

RESTRICTIONS
No facilities for disabled guests
No children under 4 years in the restaurant
No smoking in bedrooms and restaurant
Pets by arrangement

ATTRACTIONS
Tintern Abbey, Offa's Dyke, Wye Valley, Hay on Wye, Chepstow Racecourse, Royal Forest of Dean, Chepstow and Raglan castles

NEAREST
CITY:
Cardiff - 36 miles/45 mins

AIRPORT:
Cardiff - 50 miles/1 hr

RAIL STATION:
Chepstow - 5 miles/10 mins

AFFILIATIONS
The Circle Group

RESERVATIONS
National rate in UK: 0870 432 8733
Quote Best Loved

ACCESS CODES
Not applicable

Cottage charm and memorable meals in the picturesque Wye Valley

There are parts of this lovely old stone-built farmhouse that date back to the 16th century. Everywhere you look, low beamed ceilings, deep-set windows and a huge inglenook fireplace in the dining room bear testament to this hotel's venerable age and character. Just a mile from famous Tintern Abbey amidst the peaceful wooded surroundings of the Wye Valley, Parva is ideal for countryside enthusiasts, with glorious walking stretching off in all directions - including strolls along the River Wye itself, which runs through the bottom of the garden.

It comes as no surprise that owners Dereck and Vickie Stubbs have combined years of hotel experience to gauge just what guests want from a relaxing country break. Simple and pretty bedrooms are finished with designer fabrics, and most enjoy wonderful river views. The lounge is all beams and red leather Chesterfields. Guests can cosy up to the wood-burning stove in winter and help themselves to a drink from the honesty bar in anticipation of Dereck's four-course dinner menu. Generous and imaginative, it features local delicacies from Welsh game to Wye salmon, and the wine list includes a real Welsh wine made from grapes grown on the farm opposite.

To make it all the more tempting, special dinner, bed and breakfast rates are available for short breaks - call for more details!

LOCATION
When coming into Tintern on the A466 Chepstow-Monmouth road, the hotel is on the right toward the end of the village.

Country house

PENALLY ABBEY

All the beauty and drama of Britain's only coastal national park

Penally Abbey sits high above Carmarthen Bay, calmly surveying the easternmost portion of the spectacular Pembrokeshire Coast National Park from its lovely Gothic windows. This is a ringside seat for seascapes that change from hour to hour and season to season. In summer, warm, glittering seas beckon holidaymakers down to glorious sandy beaches, while spring and autumn are ideal for invigorating walks, a round at the Tenby golf course, horse riding or sailing. In the depths of winter, the best place to watch the elements battle it out over gale-swept seas is one of Penally's comfy armchairs, with a log fire crackling in the grate.

Little remains of the abbey's monastic origins, save a ruined chapel in the five-acre grounds. However, the listed house is full of character and elegant old-world charm. The bedrooms, both in the main house and adjoining coach house, have been furnished in period style (some have four-posters) and are equipped with every modern comfort. For evenings of fine weather, there is a outdoor terrace for drinks, and dinner is a romantic, candlelit affair in the dining room, where the emphasis is on delicious food created from local ingredients.

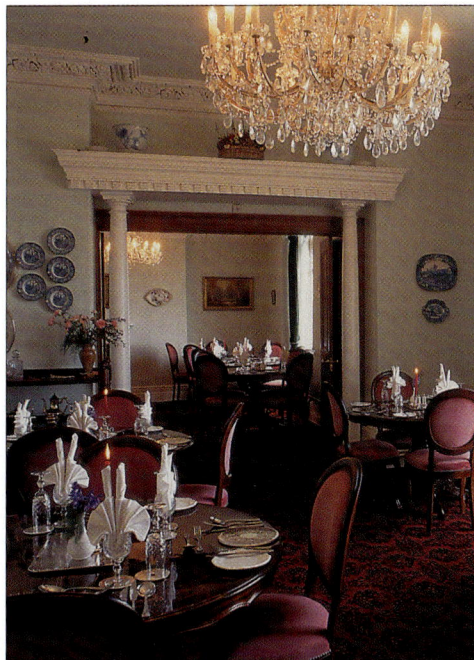

LOCATION
Adjacent to the 12th-century church on the village green in Penally, a mile and a half from Tenby off the A4139 Tenby-Pembroke coast road.

Penally, Near Tenby,
Pembrokeshire SA70 7PY

T (UK) 0870 432 8737
T 01834 843033
F 01834 844714
penally@bestloved.com
www.penally.bestloved.com

OWNERS
Stephen and Elleen Warren

ROOM RATES
Single occupancy	£104
5 Doubles/Twins	£128
7 Four-posters	£146

Includes full breakfast, newspaper and VAT

CREDIT CARDS
AMERICAN EXPRESS • MC • VI

RATINGS & AWARDS
WTB ★★★★ Country Hotel
AA ★★★ ✿ 76%

FACILITIES
On site: Garden, croquet, indoor pool, licensed for weddings, snooker
1 meeting room/max 20 people
Nearby: Golf, riding, fishing, clay pigeon shooting

RESTRICTIONS
No facilities for disabled guests
No children under 7 years in the restaurant for dinner
No smoking in restaurant
No pets

ATTRACTIONS
Tenby, Dylan Thomas's Boathouse, Pembroke Castle, Manorbier Castle, Pembokeshire National Park

NEAREST
CITY:
Cardiff - 90 miles/1 hr 45 mins

AIRPORT:
Heathrow - 250 miles/4 hrs
Cardiff - 90 miles/1 hr 45 mins

RAIL STATION:
Tenby - 1 ½ miles/5 mins

AFFILIATIONS
Welsh Rarebits

RESERVATIONS
National rate in UK: 0870 432 8737
Quote Best Loved

ACCESS CODES
Not applicable

WALES

> **"Every time we go down to Penbontbren, it's like visiting old friends"**
>
> A R, SOUTH ASCOT

PENBONTBREN FARM

Farmhouse

Near Glynarthen and Sarnau,
Cardigan, Ceredigion SA44 6PE

T (UK) 0870 432 8738
T 01239 810248
F 01239 811129
penbontbren@bestloved.com
www.penbontbren.bestloved.com

OWNERS
Jacky and Miles Glossop

ROOM RATES
Single occupancy   £63
10 Doubles/Twins   £96
Includes full breakfast and VAT

CREDIT CARDS
AMERICAN EXPRESS • MC • VI

RATINGS & AWARDS
WTB ★★★ Hotel
RAC ★★ Dining Award 1
AA ★★ 73%

FACILITIES
On site: Garden
1 meeting room/max 40 people
Nearby: Blue Flag beaches, walking,
riding, golf, fishing

RESTRICTIONS
No smoking in restaurant
No pets; guide dogs only
Closed Christmas and New Year

ATTRACTIONS
Cardigan Bay coastline,
seals and dolphins, New Quay,
Llangrannog and Mwnt ,
Llannerchaeron National Trust property,
Poppit Sands and Penbryn/Tresaith
beaches, famous sunsets at Penbryn

NEAREST
CITY:
Aberystwyth - 30 miles/1 hr
Carmarthen - 25 miles/45 mins

AIRPORT:
Cardiff International - 100 miles/2 hrs

RAIL STATION:
Aberystwyth - 30 miles/1 hr
Carmarthen - 25 miles/45 mins

FERRY PORT:
Fishguard - 19 miles/30 mins

AFFILIATIONS
Independent

RESERVATIONS
National rate in UK: 0870 432 8738
Quote Best Loved

ACCESS CODES
Not applicable

From secluded Victorian farm to charming rural retreat

Any guest staying at Penbontbren will instantly sense the warmth and genuineness of their hosts, Miles and Jacky, who make everyone feel thoroughly at ease. Enjoyment and relaxation is what they prescribe, and in large measures! The pair are also a fountain of local knowledge and will gladly come up with suggestions for great days out.

Nestled in a quiet valley a few miles inland from the coast, Penbontbren Farm dates from the mid-19th century. A sympathetic conversion saw the old buildings transformed into this delightful small hotel, with bedrooms laid out in the former stables, thrashing barn, granary and mill. The thick stone walls and hefty wooden beams make the perfect backdrop for cosy cottage-style décor, and each bedroom retains its own special character. Disabled access is throughout, including two especially disabled-friendly rooms.

Across the courtyard, the beamed restaurant presents a tempting à la carte menu, some of the dishes having been inspired by traditional Welsh recipes and ingredients.The serene countryside around Penbontbren is just begging to be explored, and there are fantastic beaches along Cardigan Bay just a short drive away.

LOCATION
9 miles north of Cardigan, just off the A487. The unclassified road to Penbontbren is between the villages of Sarnau and Tan-y-Groes and is well signed.

> "A little bit of heaven fell out of the sky and landed in Penmaenuchaf Hall"
>
> NICK AND WYN RYAN, IRELAND

Country house

PENMAENUCHAF HALL

An imposing and stylish find in the romantic foothills of Snowdonia

Cader Idris, the Chair of Arthur, stands 2,927 feet high amongst the peaks of Snowdonia, where folklore and legend intertwine with history in the romantic ruins that grace this spectacular part of Britain. Iron Age forts, Roman roads and fortresses and splendid Norman castles gather in haphazard profusion - altogether, a fascinating place to come for pony-trekking, walking and fishing.

And especially for the food! This stunning countryside sets the scene for some of the most memorable cuisine to be had in Wales. At Penmaenuchaf Hall, bass, lobster and crab, Welsh lamb, black beef and game, fresh fruit, vegetables and Welsh dairy products are all prepared with the authority and flair of an award-winning chef.

Penmaenuchaf Hall was built in 1860 and is set amidst 21 extensive acres of landscaped gardens and woodland with views of the Mawddach Estuary and the mountains beyond. Its dedicated owners have kept a family home atmosphere whilst indulging their guests in every way they can. Your room will be luxurious and well-appointed, and the hospitality as warm as the glowing oak and mahogany interiors and the crackling log fires of winter.

It's said that he who sleeps the night on Cader Idris will wake blind, mad or a poet. Not here; you will awake refreshed - and wiser, too, for having stayed at Penmaenuchaf Hall.

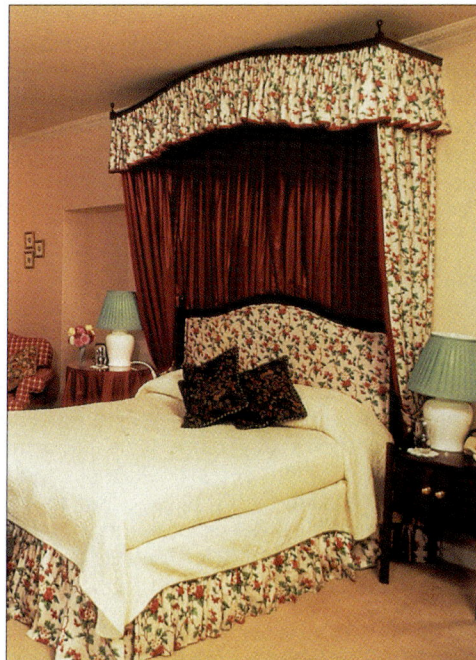

LOCATION

From the Dolgellau bypass (A470), take the A493 towards Tywyn and Fairbourne. The entrance is one mile on the left.

Penmaenpool, Dolgellau, Gwynedd LL40 1YB

T (UK) 0870 432 8739
T 01341 422129
F 01341 422787
penhall@bestloved.com
www.penhall.bestloved.com

OWNERS
Mark Watson and Lorraine Fielding

ROOM RATES
Single occupancy   £75 - £135
14 Doubles/Twins   £120 - £180
Includes full breakfast and VAT

CREDIT CARDS
DC • JCB • MC • VI

RATINGS & AWARDS
WTB ★★★★ Country Hotel
AA ★★★ ◎◎ 80%
Which? Hotel of the Year 2003

FACILITIES
On site: Garden, snooker, fishing, croquet, licensed for weddings
2 meeting rooms/max 50 people
Nearby: Riding, golf, clay pigeon shooting, quad biking, abseiling, mountain biking

RESTRICTIONS
Limited facilities for disabled guests
No children under 6 years
(does not apply to babes-in-arms)
Smoking in hall, bar and some bedrooms only
Pets by arrangement

ATTRACTIONS
Portmeirion, Harlech Castle, Ffestiniog Railway, Llechwedd Slate Caverns, Celtica: A Celtic Experience, Centre for Alternative Technology

NEAREST
CITY:
Chester - 69 miles/1 hr 15 mins

AIRPORT:
Manchester - 100 miles/2 hrs

RAIL STATION:
Fairbourne - 6 miles/10 mins

AFFILIATIONS
Welsh Rarebits

RESERVATIONS
National rate in UK: 0870 432 8739
Quote Best Loved

ACCESS CODES
Not applicable

WALES

WALES

> We were delighted to learn about your Booker Prize, which we know you earned through sheer hard work, warm hospitality and attention to detail

THE CONDRON FAMILY, NORTHAMPTON

SYCHNANT PASS HOUSE

Country house

Sychnant Pass Road, Conwy, Conwy LL32 8BJ

T (UK) 0870 432 8788
T 01492 596868
F 01492 596868
sychnant@bestloved.com
www.sychnant.bestloved.com

OWNERS
Bre and Graham Carrington-Sykes

ROOM RATES
3 Standard Doubles/Twins £80 - £90
3 Superior Doubles/Twins £100 - £110
4 Suites £120 - £150
Incudes full breakfast and VAT

CREDIT CARDS
MC • VI

RATINGS & AWARDS
WTB ★★★★ Country House
RAC ◆◆◆◆◆ Dining Award 1
RAC Warm Welcome,
Sparkling Diamond, Little Gem Awards
AA ◆◆◆◆◆
AA Premier Collection
AA Best Guest Accommodation for Wales 2004
Booker Prize for Excellence 2002 - Best Guesthouse

FACILITIES
On site: Garden, licensed for weddings, indoor heated pool and gym to open Easter 2005
Nearby: Golf, riding, walking, sailing, paragliding, bowling

RESTRICTIONS
Limited facilities for disabled guests
No smoking in bedrooms

ATTRACTIONS
Conwy Castle,
Pensychnant Nature Reserve,
Caernarfon Castle, Bodnant Gardens,
Swallow Falls, Penrhyn Castle,
Ffestiniog Railway

NEAREST
CITY:
Llandudno - 6 miles/15 mins
Chester - 48 miles/1 hr 10 mins

AIRPORT:
Liverpool - 69 miles/1 hr 30 mins
Manchester - 78 miles/ 1 hr 10 mins

RAIL STATION:
Llandudno Junction - 6 miles/15 mins
Conwy - 6 miles/15 mins

FERRY PORT:
Holyhead - 35 miles/40 mins

AFFILIATIONS
Welsh Rarebits

RESERVATIONS
National rate in UK: 0870 432 8788
Quote Best Loved

ACCESS CODES
Not applicable

Feel at home in this charming Snowdonia hideaway

This homely country house is run by resident owners Graham and Bre Carrington-Sykes, and you can immediately sense why they call it their home, too! The surrounding lawns here are teeming with wildlife, including herons, buzzards and foxes, and the hotel occupies an enviable location at the foothills of Snowdonia National Park, just over a mile from Conwy.

All 10 bedrooms, in keeping with the jovial atmosphere of the hotel, are named after a T S Eliot cat from 'Old Possum's Book of Practical Cats'. There's variety within, too: Some are suites and others have four-poster beds (including a Jacobean four-poster), and for guests who are less able to use stairs or those with pets there are two ground-floor rooms with French doors that open out onto pleasant decking. Antiques and ornaments feature throughout, adding to an atmosphere that's won a host of awards, including the only RAC Little Gem award issued to a Welsh country house - and for the fourth year running!

You can curl up here with a good book, explore the stunning countryside or enjoy wonderful food - Graham, with culinary training that includes the renowned Gleneagles, is in charge of the kitchen, creating country-house cuisine with an imaginative flair. Pets - and their people - will feel right at home, too, with the company of resident dogs Molly and Nellie, and of course Morris and Peter the cats.

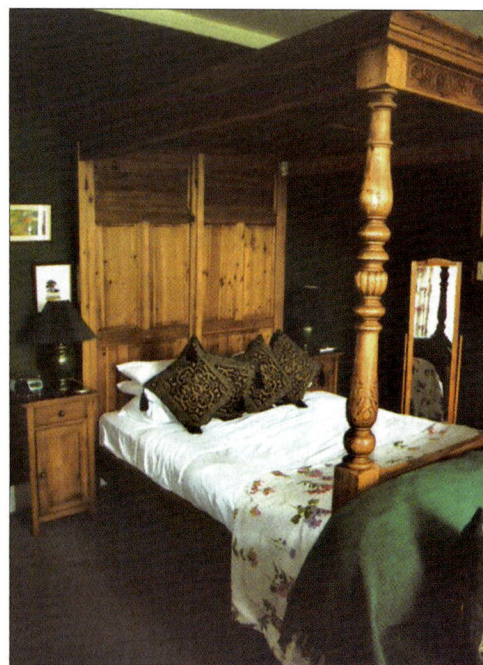

LOCATION
Exit the A55 at Llandudno for Conwy and follow signs for the town centre; pass the visitor centre, take the second left into Upper Gate Street and proceed for a mile out of Conwy. The hotel is on the right.

> **"** It was difficult to find - it was even more difficult to leave **"**
>
> GABRIEL PETY, BELGIUM

Country house
TAN-Y-FOEL COUNTRY HOUSE

An oasis of tranquillity and culinary excellence in Snowdonia

Tan-y-Foel means 'the house under the hillside', and perfectly describes this delectable hideaway set in eight acres of woodland and pasture with views stretching away to Snowdonia and the Conwy Valley. Garlanded with praise from all quarters, Tan-y-Foel is the only five-star country house in Snowdonia National Park; its six guest rooms have secured an Imaginative Bedroom Award from The Which? Hotel Guide, whilst Janet Pitman, a Master Chef of Great Britain, has earned a Restaurant of the Year Award from The Good Food Guide for her outstanding cuisine.

The awards offer a gentle hint as to what to expect. A traditional Welsh stone-built country house from the outside, Tan-y-Foel's contemporary interior design comes as a complete surprise. Earthy tones from beige and jute through to terracotta predominate, and dark teak ornaments suggest an Oriental influence that is echoed in Janet's cooking. Her signature dish is a superbly presented Welsh loin of pork with pakoras and an Oriental marinade, served with organic carrot and ginger sauce.

For visitors exploring the surrounding area, Conwy and Caernarfon castles are bastions of Welsh history; Bodnant Gardens are a must for garden lovers, and the wilds of Snowdonia beckon one and all.

LOCATION

From the A55, take the A470 to Llanrwst; keep on the A470 through Llanrwst, and after two miles, take the turning signposted 'Capel Garmon/Nebo'. The hotel is on the left after a mile and a half.

Capel Garmon, Betws-y-Coed, Conwy LL26 0RE

T (UK) 0870 432 8790
T 01690 710507
F 01690 710681
tanyfoel@bestloved.com
www.tanyfoel.bestloved.com

OWNERS
Peter and Janet Pitman

ROOM RATES
Single occupancy	£99 - £120
4 Doubles/Twins	£145 - £160
2 Four-posters	£145 - £160

Includes full breakfast and VAT

CREDIT CARDS
MC • VI

RATINGS & AWARDS
WTB ★★★★★ Country House
AA ★★ ✿✿✿
AA Top 200 - 2004/2005
Which? Hotel of the Year 2004

FACILITIES
On site: Garden
Nearby: Golf, fishing, riding, walking

RESTRICTIONS
No facilities for disabled guests
No children under 7 years
No smoking throughout
No pets
Closed Christmas and New Year

ATTRACTIONS
Snowdonia National Park,
Caernarfon Castle, Conwy Castle,
Plas Newydd, Chester,
Bodnant Gardens

NEAREST
CITY:
Chester - 50 miles/1 hr 15 mins

AIRPORT:
Manchester - 80 miles/1 hr 45 mins

RAIL STATION:
Llandudno Junction - 11 miles/25 mins

AFFILIATIONS
Welsh Rarebits

RESERVATIONS
National rate in UK: 0870 432 8790
Quote Best Loved

ACCESS CODES
Not applicable

WALES

"Wolfscastle is definitely a hotel I'll come back to ... and I don't say that about many of them"

PADDY BURT, THE DAILY TELEGRAPH

WOLFSCASTLE COUNTRY HOTEL | Country house

Wolf's Castle,
Near Haverfordwest,
Pembrokeshire SA62 5LZ

T (UK) 0870 432 8820
T 01437 741225
F 01437 741383
wolfscastle@bestloved.com
www.wolfscastle.bestloved.com

PROPRIETOR
Andrew Stirling

DIRECTOR
Sandy Falconer

ROOM RATES
Single occupancy   £55 - £75
19 Doubles/Twins   £79 - £107
Includes full breakfast and VAT

CREDIT CARDS
AMERICAN EXPRESS • MC • VI

RATINGS & AWARDS
WTB ★★★ Country Hotel
RAC ★★
AA ★★ ✿ 74%
Dining Out in Wales 2004 Silver Award

FACILITIES
On site: Garden, licensed for weddings
2 meeting rooms/max 180 people
Nearby: Riding, walking,
river and sea fishing

RESTRICTIONS
No facilities for disabled guests
Smoking in bar only
£5 surcharge for each dog
Closed Christmas and Boxing Day

ATTRACTIONS
Pembrokeshire Coast National Park,
St David's Cathedral,
Pembroke Castle,
Carew Castle, Manorbier Castle,
Oakwood Leisure Park

NEAREST
CITY:
Swansea - 60 miles/1 hr 30 mins

AIRPORT:
Cardiff - 100 miles/2 hrs

RAIL STATION:
Haverfordwest - 7 miles/10 mins

FERRY PORT:
Fishguard - 7 miles/10 minutes

AFFILIATIONS
Welsh Rarebits

RESERVATIONS
National rate in UK: 0870 432 8820
Quote Best Loved

ACCESS CODES
Not applicable

A fine country house in the centre of Pembrokeshire

This charming country house hotel has been under the same ownership since 1976, and the pride in this well-run former vicarage certainly shows! Located in the small village of Wolf's Castle midway between Fishguard and Haverfordwest, Wolfscatle Country Hotel is an ideal rural base for a Welsh holiday. If the region is for you a stop on a larger British Isles tour, it's worth noting the hotel is just 7 miles from the Fishguard Irish ferry port, too.

Recently-refurbished bedrooms make your stay a delight, combining a sense of period charm with modern amenities including Sky television, tea and coffee facilities and telephone. The second-floor bedrooms have wonderful views, too, looking out over Wolfscastle and Treffgarne rocks. The hotel has a well-deserved reputation for good food, making the most of Welsh produce, and a wine list of more than 60 bins awaits your choice. Conferences are a specialty at Wolfscastle, and the hotel's new function room can accommodate anything from a business meeting to wedding.

Outside, more than 200 miles of walks for every ability await on Pembrokeshire's stunning coastal path, as well as golf, water sport, fishing of all kinds and a wide range of historical sites and antique shops.

LOCATION
On the A40, midway between Fishguard and Haverfordwest.

A PERFECT MEETING

STAPLEFORD PARK, LEICESTERSHIRE (PAGE 226)

THE HOSTE ARMS, NORFOLK (PAGE 197)

Whether you're a professional conference planner or simply making plans for your company's next big event, Best Loved Hotels can help make organising your corporate needs a breeze. Call or e-mail to join our list of corporate professionals, and you're on your way to an event to remember!

- Receive our quarterly printed **Best Loved Hotels Corporate News**, packed with meeting ideas and a look at some of the best corporate and events venues in the UK and Ireland

- Our unique corporate e-newsletters highlight special promotions, notable offers and intriguing facilities - delivered right to your e-mail inbox

- Our newly-revamped Web site, **www.bestlovedhotels.com**, offers up-to-the-minute data on Best Loved hotels' meeting facilities, special accommodation offers, catering options and more - including special meetings and weddings search guides

HAYFIELD MANOR, CORK (PAGE 399)

Call today to become a Best Loved corporate professional!

ORDERS/INFO: 0870 432 8700 (UK) OR +44 208 962 9555   E-MAIL ORDERS@BESTLOVED.COM

OR USE THE FREEPOST ORDER/INFORMATION FORM LOCATED IN THE BACK OF THIS BOOK

MIDSHIRES

A FARMHOUSE
Dannah Farm, Derbyshire

AN HISTORIC TOWNHOUSE INN
Angel and Royal Hotel, Lincolnshire

A CASTLE
Thornbury Castle, South Gloucestershire

REPRESENTING *the best of the* MIDSHIRES

A RESTAURANT WITH ROOMS
Hotel des Clos, Nottinghamshire

Best Loved Hotels offer the cream of the crop across Great Britain and Ireland - from stately palaces to welcoming inns - each the best of its kind within its locality and price range.

Whichever place you choose as your own place to stay, you'll find every hotel offers character, charm and the best delights and attractions of its region.

And each, in its own special way, is best-loved by someone who's been there.

A STATELY HOME
Stapleford Park, Leicestershire

A COUNTRY HOUSE HOTEL
Le Manoir Aux Quat' Saisons, Oxfordshire

A RESTAURANT WITH ROOMS
Old Mill Hotel & Fusion Chino, Warwickshire

A SPA HOTEL
Calcot Manor, Gloucestershire

AN IDEAL ESCAPE:
The Midshires

FROM SHAKESPEARE'S BIRTHPLACE to the hallowed halls of Oxford and the mellow-stone cottages of the Cotswolds, the Midshires are an idyllic slice of Britain - and one you're sure to want to revisit again and again.

Day One

Oxford, famous for its university, is a charming city in which to spend a day at your own leisure. To begin with, get to know the city a little better at the **Story of Oxford Museum**, where you'll be taken on a 'dark ride' through the history of the university. The best thing is that after you're introduced to these people, places and events in Oxford's past, you'll be prepared to go out and explore them for yourself. Drink in the atmosphere and walk the same streets that have been home to legions of famous Oxonians, from Thomas More to Stephen Hawking, John Donne to C S Lewis. Between the honey-coloured stone buildings and the ivy-covered walls, Oxford truly is an inspiring place for a morning stroll.

A walk round the university is sure to inspire

With no end of shops, cafes and restaurants, lunchtime and a long afternoon in Oxford can easily pass by! But whatever your agenda, take time to stroll round one of the city's art galleries. **Inspires Art Gallery** exhibits contemporary art, from local notables as well as artists from around the world. Also well-recommended is **Modern Art Oxford**, with an ever-changing roster of exhibitions that guarantee a different experience every visit.

After dinner - and there's much to choose from, no matter your tastes - indulge your taste for drama with a show at **The Playhouse** or the **New Theatre**, both of which house a variety of theatre from drama to musicals and comedy. Best, though, to book tickets in advance, as shows can be very popular!

A show at the New Theatre comes highly recommended

Day Two

From Oxford, it isn't far to the many charming towns and villages of **the Cotswolds**. There are really too many to choose from, but one definite favourite is the lovely **Bourton-on-the-Water** – an idyllic village known as 'the Venice of the Cotswolds'. Better still, stop off at the nearby village of **Upper Slaughter** before travelling up to the historic market town of **Stow-on-the-Wold**, where rolling countryside surrounds the charming honey-coloured stone buildings and numerous antique shops. (In fact, be sure to leave a bit of extra space in your suitcase or your car - chances are, you'll come back with some treasures!) If you're in Stow in the evening, dining at the Grapevine Hotel (page 195) comes highly recommended - and highly sought-after, so be sure to make a reservation.

If shopping is what you're after, why not continue along to the Regency spa town of **Cheltenham**, with its elegant architecture, intriguing shops along the Promenade and numerous tempting restaurants. If you're in for a bit of pampering, one of Cheltenham's main attractions is the **Chapel Spa**, with six themed treatment rooms, a hydropool and steam room. For the more energetic, they also provide a range of exercise classes.

Shakespeare's birthplace is stunning in spring

The River Avon not only gives Stratford-upon-Avon its name, but also lends it a truly distinctive flavour

Day Three

Just north of the Cotswolds is Shakespeare's **Stratford-upon-Avon**, home to such a wealth of history that it's worth at least a day's visit. Visit the Henley Street house thought to be **Shakespeare's birthplace**, and other properties related to the playwright - you have plenty to choose from, including **Anne Hathaway's cottage**, home to Shakespeare's wife before they were married, or **Hall's Croft**, a striking Tudor house where Shakespeare's daughter lived with her husband John Hall.

For a relaxing afternoon, take a walk alongside the River Avon and watch the boats go by. Enjoy a leisurely dinner in the town centre, but make sure you're ready for curtain - after all, a visit to Stratford wouldn't be complete without seeing the Royal Shakespeare Company perform at the **Swan Theatre** or the **Royal Shakespeare Theatre**.

A walk through history at Anne Hathaway's cottage

ESCAPE FROM YOUR DESKTOP

If you can't wait to get away, or if you'd simply like to do a little investigating before you make your holiday in the Midshires, browse the links below. Remember, too, that thousands of places to see and things to do await at Best Loved's Web site, **www.bestlovedhotels.com**.

Oxford city guide
www.oxfordcity.co.uk

Modern Art Oxford
www.modernartoxford.org.uk

Oxford Playhouse
www.oxfordplayhouse.com

Oxford New Theatre
www.bbc.co.uk/oxford/stage/apollo.shtml

Stow-on-the-Wold visitors guide
www.stow-on-the-wold.com

Cheltenham visitors guide
www.visitcheltenham.com

Cheltenham Chapel Spa
www.chapelspa.co.uk

Shakespeare Birthplace Trust
www.shakespeare.org.uk

Stratford-upon-Avon visitors guide
www.stratford.co.uk

Royal Shakespeare Company
www.rsc.org.uk

A TASTE OF THE BEST
The Midshires

WHETHER YOUR TRAVELS bring you to Sherwood Forest or the Cotswolds, excellent dining in abundance is a hallmark of Best Loved hotels in the Midshires. From classic fine dining to inventive Oriental fusion, you're certain to discover a newfound favourite.

COCKLIFFE COUNTRY HOUSE HOTEL

The elegant Sherwood Restaurant is decorated in cool, relaxing colours, resulting in an endearing mix of classic and modern with patio doors leading out to the garden. You'll find a variety of delightful dishes on offer at this charming Nottinghamshire hideway, including such starters as chicken liver parfait with spiced roasted oranges or tender duck confit with wild asparagus and rocket salad. Delights on offer for your main course range from succulent fillet steak with wild mushroom ravioli and celeriac and mustard rosti to poached salmon and sole with asparagus and a tomato and keta caviar beurre blanc. Simply magical!

FOSSE MANOR ❀❀

At this welcoming hotel with views over rolling Cotswold hills, Executive Chef Tom Rains sources good local produce and ingredients for truly memorable dishes. Tom's loyalty to the best ingredients available in the area is evident in dishes ranging from slow-cooked shoulder of Cotswold lamb

A taste of the LOCAL at Fosse Manor

infused with mint with creamed potato and rosemary jus, to roast cutlet of Gloucester pork and confit belly, red cabbage and apple puree. Vegetarian options, such as roasted butternut squash and mushroom risotto with sage and parmesan, are also available - there's something for everyone, so bring a friend!

HOTEL DES CLOS ❀❀❀

The only recipient of a Michelin award in the county, Hotel des Clos is a treat not to be missed. This celebrated restaurant with rooms features master chef Sat Bains, who is incredibly passionate about food and quality of produce. This previous winner of the Roux Scholarship is currently refurbishing his renowned restaurant, and diners will be able to sample his exciting new menu from February

Understated glamour at the Old Mill

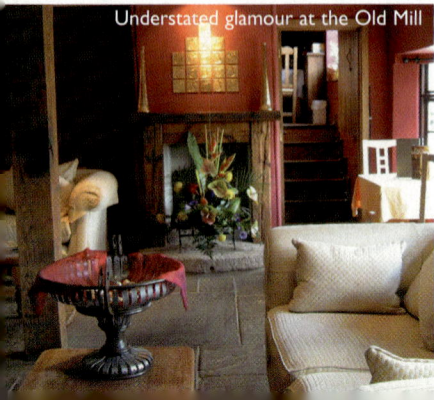
Elegance meets international flavour at the Peacock

2005 - we highly advise you mark it in your calendar now so as not to be disappointed.

LE MANOIR AUX QUAT' SAISONS ❀❀❀❀❀

This 15th-century manor in Oxford is home to Raymond Blanc's celebrated restaurant, the perfect setting for guests to relax in comfort and enjoy his first-class fare. The clean and fresh appearance of the restaurant is reflective of the modern French cuisine served here, and inventive dishes contain carefully chosen fresh organic vegetables and herbs from the hotel's two-acre kitchen garden. Diners can choose from an à la carte menu, a seven-course Menu Gourmand or three-course Menu du Jour. Dishes include such delights as braised Cornish turbot fillet and scallops with garden vegetables and wild mushrooms, or chive and lemon verbena scented jus. There is also a vegetarian à la carte menu and Menu Gourmand available, featuring wonderful options like roasted sweet Romano red pepper filled with taboulé artichoke confit and spiced pepper jus. The Times gave Raymond Blanc's cooking 10 out of 10 and rated it 'the best in Britain'.

A TASTE OF THE REGION

Looking for even more to tempt your palate? There are a wealth of fantastic places to dine in the Midshires, all within the covers of this book! Have a browse to whet your appetite, or jump to some of our own favourites:

BLENHEIM HOUSE HOTEL

Chef Proprietor Peter Simpson's Michelin-starred modern fare at this charming country house is based on classical European dishes.

TITCHWELL MANOR HOTEL ❀❀

A family-run Norfolk hotel where Eric Snaith runs a renowned seafood restaurant serving international cuisine influenced by his travels in Australia and the Far East.

THE ELMS ❀❀

This Queen Anne mansion's restaurant is celebrated for its fine cuisine created under the direction of Head Chef Daren Bale.

LANGAR HALL ❀❀

Country mansion and family home of Imogen Skirving, the dining room here is an elegant pillared hall where fresh, seasonal food is served with an emphasis on game in the winter and fish in the summer.

OLD MILL HOTEL & FUSION CHINO

The Old Mill Hotel is home to the innovative Fusion Chino Restaurant, which offers an exciting choice of Oriental cuisine. Dishes have a hint of French, Spanish and Thai influence, including a number of vegetarian options - creations vary from sea spiced pork or steamed whole sea bass with ginger and spring onion to soy 'beef' in black pepper and red wine sauce!

PEACOCK HOTEL

Offering a vibrant Eastern experience, the Peacock's award-winning Coconut Lagoon Restaurant serves tempting Southern Indian dishes with Portuguese and French influences. If you are dining with a group of four or more, why not try their specially created Pondichery or Bangalore Feasts? Located just down the road, their second restaurant, Raffles, is Britain's first colonial Malaysian restaurant - also a delectable experience.

Inventive and innovative cuisine at Mallory Court

MALLORY COURT HOTEL ❀❀❀

At Mallory Court, the only hotel in Warwickshire to be awarded a Michelin star, head chef Simon Haigh (who also gained a Michelin star during his time at Inverlochy Castle) and his team prepare excellent contemporary French and British cuisine. Many of the vegetables, fruit and herbs used in their kitchen are picked fresh from gardens in the hotel's 10 acres of grounds. There are some delicious options on their dinner menu, including a starter of lobster, avocado and mango salad and main courses such as pan-roast escalope of wild Cornish sea bass, or crispy goat cheese ravioli on a bed of ratatouille, spinach and new potatoes.

Menu

FOSSE MANOR

Seared scallops with smoked haddock and tomato fondue
Salad of crisp duck leg confit with orange and watercress salad

Breast of free range chicken with fondant potato,
Savoy cabbage and smoked bacon
Thyme grilled vegetable tart, wild rocket and balsamic

Vanilla mousse with mixed berry compote
Stilton and single Gloucester with celery and grapes

ABBEY HOTEL

Townhouse

10 Church Street, Wymondham,
Norfolk NR18 0PH

T (UK) 0870 432 8514
T 01953 602148
F 01953 606247
abbey@bestloved.com
www.abbey.bestloved.com

GENERAL MANAGER
Mark Richards

ROOM RATES
Single occupancy	£55
20 Doubles/Twins	£70 - £75
3 Superior Doubles	£80 - £85

Includes full breakfast and VAT

CREDIT CARDS

AMERICAN EXPRESS • JCB • MC • VI

RATINGS & AWARDS
AA ★★★ 68%

FACILITIES
Nearby: Leisure centre

RESTRICTIONS
No smoking in bedrooms or restaurant
No pets

ATTRACTIONS
Norfolk Broads, Tiffany Valley,
Sandringham, Mid Norfolk Railway,
Snetterton, nature reserves,
antiques hunting

NEAREST
CITY:
Norwich - 10 miles/20 mins

AIRPORT:
Stansted - 75 miles/1 hr 40 mins

RAIL STATION:
Wymondham - 1 mile/5 mins

AFFILIATIONS
Independent

RESERVATIONS
National rate in UK: 0870 432 8514
Quote Best Loved

ACCESS CODES
Not applicable

MIDSHIRES

Warmth, character and an unusual architectural pedigree

In a quiet quarter of Wymondham a stone's throw from the town centre, this welcoming small hotel faces its namesake 12th-century abbey across Church Street. The main building is a former private home dating from the 1880s, but over the years the hotel has been skilfully extended to incorporate a row of historic 16th-century cottages that once formed a timber framed baronial hall; the resulting winding corridors and the wealth of exposed beams have a particular charm.

The Abbey's accommodation includes spacious, relaxing rooms, some of which also offer a comfortable seating area; the double bedrooms benefit from marvellously comfortable king-sized beds. Under the experienced eye of the enthusiastic management team, all the rooms have been recently refurbished in a simple, traditional but chintz-free style with attractive handmade furnishings.

At the heart of the hotel, Cardinals Restaurant serves a delightful menu prepared from local ingredients. Guests can enjoy the chef's imaginative blend of modern English cuisine with an international flavour, and every dish is cooked to order. There is a fully licensed bar, too, and after-dinner coffee and liqueurs are served in the comfortable lounge.

LOCATION

Exit the A11 (Norwich-Thetford) for Wymondham; after the marketplace, turn left at the wooden town sign into Church Street. The hotel is opposite the abbey.

Map p. 446, grid F3

> "Thank you for a wonderful stay. The room was delightful, and we were treated like royalty"
>
> SAMANTHA AND TORY BOOMER, FLORIDA USA

Townhouse

ANGEL AND ROYAL HOTEL

England's oldest inn has a welcome that's as warm as ever

In medieval times, an angel atop a signpost signified a place to stay, welcome at the end of a day's journey. Today, the Angel and Royal offers the same sort of welcome, perfect for ending a day spent exploring the scenery of Lincolnshire and Nottinghamshire - and this hotel's history is no less impressive. Widely regarded as the oldest surviving inn in England, the original building was built circa 1203 as a hostel for the Brotherhood of the Knights Templar and visited by King John's royal court in 1213; the building standing today is some 600 years old, and itself offers more than its fair share of history!

Gleaming from a recent £2 million refurbishment, the Angel is a tasteful, luxurious home from home. Superb beds offer a relaxing night's sleep, and rooms feature the latest in DVD and CD players, valet centres, hospitality trays and generously fluffy towels! A delicious breakfast is on offer in the mornings, and Mondays through Thursdays, the hotel also offers special dinner, bed and breakfast rates from £85 per person per night. Dining is delightful; the King's Room Restaurant offers stone walls and an open fire as a backdrop to modern British cuisine, and the Angel Bar features an ancient fireplace with holes in the mantelpiece for hoisting grand spit roasts over the flame - though today, you'll find lovely lighter bites in the bistro, Simply Berties.

LOCATION

Grantham is easily reached from the A1; exit from the north for the A52 or, from the south, for the A607. The hotel is on the high street.

High Street, Grantham,
Lincolnshire NG31 6PN

T (UK) 0870 432 8519
T 01476 565816
F 01476 567149
angelroyal@bestloved.com
www.angelroyal.bestloved.com

GENERAL MANAGER
Diane Edwards

ROOM RATES

Single occupancy	£65 - £115
6 Standard Doubles/Twins	£105
7 Executive Doubles/Twins	£115
5 Superior Doubles/Twins	£140
3 Four-posters	£140
3 Junior Suites	£165

Includes full breakfast and VAT

CREDIT CARDS
AMERICAN EXPRESS • MC • VI

RATINGS & AWARDS
ETC ★★★
RAC ★★★ Dining Award 1
AA ★★★ ❀ 74%
Grantham Business of the Year 2003

FACILITIES
On site:
3 meeting rooms/max 65 people
Nearby: Golf

RESTRICTIONS
Limited facilities for disabled guests
Children by arrangement
Smoking in some rooms only
No pets; guide dogs only

ATTRACTIONS
Burghley House, Belton House,
Rockingham Castle,
Grimsthorpe Castle, Rutland Water,
historic town of Stamford,
Woolsthorpe Manor

NEAREST
CITY:
Nottingham - 24 miles/45 mins

AIRPORT:
Birmingham - 70 miles/1 hr 30 mins
Nottingham EMA - 25 miles/45 mins

RAIL STATION:
Grantham - ½ mile/5 mins

AFFILIATIONS
Independent

RESERVATIONS
National rate in UK: 0870 432 8519
Quote Best Loved

ACCESS CODES
AMADEUS HK XGMANG
APOLLO/GALILEO HK 53730
SABRE/ABACUS HK 36843
WORLDSPAN HK ANROY

MIDSHIRES

BEECHES HOTEL & VICTORIAN GARDENS   Townhouse

MIDSHIRES

2-6 Earlham Road, Norwich,
Norfolk NR2 3DB

T (UK) 0870 432 8534
T 01603 621167
F 01603 620151
beechesvic@bestloved.com
www.beechesvic.bestloved.com

GENERAL MANAGER
Mark Richards

ROOM RATES
8 Singles   £69 - £74
25 Doubles/Twins   £89 - £95
3 Superiors   £104 - £110
1 Four-Bedroom Apt   £200 - £250
Includes full breakfast and VAT

CREDIT CARDS
AMERICAN EXPRESS • JCB • MC • VI

RATINGS & AWARDS
ETC ★★★ Silver Award
AA ★★★ ⊛ 70%

FACILITIES
On site: Garden, gardens
1 meeting room/max 40 people
Nearby: Leisure centre

RESTRICTIONS
No children under 12 years
No smoking throughout
No pets

ATTRACTIONS
Norwich Castle, Anglican Cathedral,
Norfolk Broads,
Sandringham, Snetterton,
largest permanent market in England

NEAREST
CITY:
Norwich

AIRPORT:
Norwich - 10 miles/20 mins
Stansted - 85 miles/1 hr 50 mins

RAIL STATION:
Norwich - 4 miles/10 mins

AFFILIATIONS
Independent

RESERVATIONS
National rate in UK: 0870 432 8534
Quote Best Loved

ACCESS CODES
Not applicable

A trio of handsome 19th-century houses set in restored Victorian gardens

In 1856, successful cabinetmaker Henry Trevor built an attractive new family home, Plantation House, on the edge of a derelict chalk quarry a 10-minute stroll from the centre of Norwich. Over the next 40 years, he transformed the former quarry into the charming Plantation Gardens, a three-acre wooded hollow complete with terraces, decorative balustrades, mock ruins and a huge Gothic fountain.

Today, the gardens connect the three houses that make up this unusual hotel: the porticoed Plantation House, the Governors House (which once faced the old city gaol) and 1860 Beeches House, the hub of the group. It would take a number of visits to discover and enjoy the varied accommodation offered by these lovely old buildings and their modern annex, but the general impression is delightfully bright and airy and every effort has been made to preserve period features. Large sash windows overlook the garden, and some rooms offer memorable views of sunsets reflected in the stained-glass windows of the nearby cathedral.

The Beeches Restaurant serves an imaginative menu of modern English cooking with an international flavour, and guests will find the hotel's dedicated staff extremely welcoming and helpful.

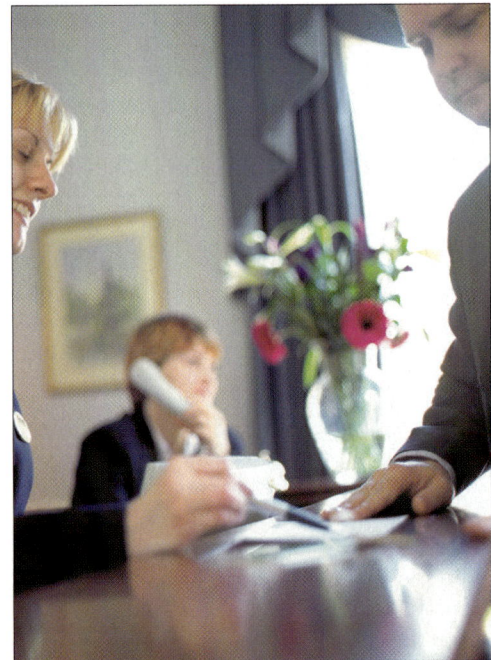

LOCATION
Exit the A11/A47 for the city ring road; then, exit for the B1108 and continue toward the city. The hotel is next to the cathedral.

Country house

THE BLENHEIM HOUSE HOTEL

Main Street, Etwall,
Derbyshire DE65 6LP

T (UK) 0870 432 8537
T 01283 732254
F 01283 733860
blenheim@bestloved.com
www.blenheim.bestloved.com

CHEF PROPRIETOR
Peter Simpson

ROOM RATES
1 Single		£60
6 Doubles		£75
2 Four - Posters		£110

Includes breakfast and VAT

CREDIT CARDS
MC • VI

RATINGS & AWARDS
Awards Pending

FACILITIES
On site: Licensed for weddings
2 meeting rooms/max 40 people
Nearby: Tennis, golf, horse riding,
shooting, health & beauty,
leisure centre, fishing

RESTRICTIONS
Limited facilities for disabled guests
No smoking in bedrooms
No pets; guide dogs only

ATTRACTIONS
Alton Towers, Chatsworth House,
Sudbury Hall, Haddon Hall,
Calke Abbey, the Peak District,
the Potteries

NEAREST
CITY:
Derby - 7 miles/15 mins

AIRPORT:
Nottingham EMA - 20 miles/30 mins

RAIL STATION:
Derby - 7 miles/15 mins

AFFILIATIONS
Independent

RESERVATIONS
National rate in UK: 0870 432 8537
Quote Best Loved

ACCESS CODES
Not applicable

MIDSHIRES

This personable country house is a must-see

Nestled in the village of Etwall, The Blenheim House Hotel is a warm, inviting country house that's as much of a favourite with locals as it is with visitors. An ideal destination for a weekend break or business conference alike, this small but personable village retreat welcomes with open arms, comfortable beds and magnificent food.

The Michelin-honoured restaurant features a modern menu based on classical European traditions, and makes the best of the area's bountiful local produce. Chef proprietor Peter Simpson is innovative and creative in his choices, whilst paying as much care to his guests as to his food! And when you're ready for a night's rest, take pleasure in one of the nine splendid individually-decorated bedrooms, each with their own signature style.

Area attractions have plenty to offer, whether you're visiting for a short holiday or a longer stay; for golfing enthusiasts, there are a whole handful of nearby courses to choose from - and need we even mention the glorious views and bracing walks of the Peak District?

LOCATION

Located in Etwall's main street, just off the A516 and easily accessible by the A50 and the A38.

BROCKENCOTE HALL

Country house

**Chaddesley Corbett,
Near Kidderminster,
Worcestershire DY10 4PY**

T (UK) 0870 432 8544
T 01562 777876
F 01562 777872
brockencote@bestloved.com
www.brockencote.bestloved.com

OWNERS
Alison and Joseph Petitjean

ROOM RATES
Single occupancy   £88 - £140
13 Doubles/Twins   £116 - £180
4 Four-posters   £144 - £180
Includes full breakfast and VAT

CREDIT CARDS
AMERICAN EXPRESS • DC • MC • VI

RATINGS & AWARDS
ETC ★★★ Gold Award Hotel
RAC Blue Ribbon ★★★ Dining Award 4
AA ★★★ ⊗⊗
AA Top 200 - 2004/2005
Heart of England Excellence in
Tourism Silver Award -
Small Hotel of the Year 2003
Taste of Worcestershire
Restaurant of the Year 2003/2004

FACILITIES
On site: Garden, fishing, croquet, tennis
2 meeting rooms/max 20 people
Nearby: Golf, riding, fishing, archery,
water sport, clay pigeon shooting

RESTRICTIONS
Smoking in lounges only
No pets; guide dogs only

ATTRACTIONS
Warwick Castle, Worcester,
Hereford Cathedral,
Stratford-upon-Avon,
Black Country Museum,
the Cotswolds, Ironbridge,
Cadbury World,
West Midlands Safari Park,
Harvington Hall

NEAREST
CITY:
Birmingham - 18 miles/30 mins

AIRPORT:
Birmingham - 20 miles/30 mins

RAIL STATION:
Kidderminster - 4 miles/10 mins

AFFILIATIONS
Preston's Global Hotels

RESERVATIONS
National rate in UK: 0870 432 8544
Toll free in US: 800-544-9993
Quote Best Loved

ACCESS CODES
AMADEUS UI BHXBHC
APOLLO/GALILEO UI 27837
SABRE/ABACUS UI 52406
WORLDSPAN UI 41367

MIDSHIRES

An authentic French enclave in the heart of Worcestershire

The builders of the original Victorian mansion that is now beautiful Brockencote Hall certainly knew a thing or two about finding a perfect place for relaxation. Nestled in the heart of the Worcestershire countryside, this glorious hotel is set in 70 acres of private parkland, yet is close to the motorway network and just half an hour from Birmingham - the perfect location for touring an area rich in history and culture. From here, you are equally well-placed to visit Shakespeare's Stratford-upon-Avon, Warwick Castle, the idyllic Cotswolds and the wonders of Wales.

Guests at Brockencote Hall will experience something else that is unique in the area: the hotel is renowned for its authentic French ambience. Proprietors Joseph and Alison Petitjean have created a charming Gallic oasis in the heart of England, combining traditional Continental comfort and friendliness with superb French cuisine. The hotel offers a choice of 17 superb bedrooms, all en-suite, including one especially designed to make stays comfortable for disabled guests.

LOCATION

Exit 1 on the M42 (westbound) or exit 4 on the M5. From Bromsgrove, take the A448 toward Kidderminster; the hotel is five miles along on the left.

> I am sure that when you decide to stay at the Brookhouse you will find comfort and relaxation
>
> D FOTHERINGHAM-KIDD

Country house

THE BROOKHOUSE

A house of character where dining is a pleasure and the beds are amazing

After the River Dove abandons the cascades of the Derbyshire Dales, it winds languorously through the fertile flatlands between Burton-on-Trent and Derby, an area of pastoral beauty barely touched by modern times. Rolleston-on-Dove is the quintessential Old English village, complete with thatched cottages and a babbling brook - The Dove, no less - running through it. This is the setting for The Brookhouse, a charming village character posing postcard-pretty by the river.

The Brookhouse has woven a kind of magic over the people who work there, and they are all local and as loyal as can be: Two of the staff have been there more than 20 years and the only new boy is the owner, John Westwood, who has been at The Brookhouse a mere 17 years! The service is nimble and comes wreathed in smiles and a winning country accent.

The restaurant has an excellent reputation for good food. Soft lights and candlelight reflect in silver and crystal; fresh flowers are everywhere. Freshness is the order of the day, and the wine list offers imaginative, rare and unusual wines. The bedrooms are splendidly appointed, but do ask to see them all; you'll find a truly remarkable collection of antique beds, all gorgeously caparisoned and notably comfortable.

LOCATION

Rolleston is just outside Burton-upon-Trent, between the A50 to Stoke-on-Trent and the A38 to Derby.

Brookside, Rolleston-on-Dove, Burton-upon-Trent, Staffordshire DE13 9AA

T (UK) 0870 432 8545
T 01283 814188
F 01283 813644
brookhouse@bestloved.com
www.brookhouse.bestloved.com

OWNER
John Westwood

ROOM RATES
7 Singles   £79 - £85
13 Doubles/Twins   £109 - £125
Includes full breakfast, newspaper and VAT

CREDIT CARDS
AMERICAN EXPRESS • DC • JCB • MC • VI

RATINGS & AWARDS
Independent

FACILITIES
On site: Garden
1 meeting room/max 20 people
Nearby: Golf, riding

RESTRICTIONS
Limited facilities for disabled guests
No children under 12 years
No smoking in restaurant
Pets by arrangement

ATTRACTIONS
Tutbury Castle, Tutbury Crystal, Haddon Hall, Keddleston Hall, Calke Abbey, Derbyshire Dales

NEAREST
CITY:
Derby - 8 miles/15 mins

AIRPORT:
Birmingham - 25 miles/40 mins
Manchester - 70 miles/1 hr 30 mins

RAIL STATION:
Burton-upon-Trent - 3 miles/10 mins
Derby - 9 miles/20 mins

AFFILIATIONS
Independent

RESERVATIONS
National rate in UK: 0870 432 8545
Quote Best Loved

ACCESS CODES
Not applicable

MIDSHIRES

> **Such a stylish and welcoming house, such friendly and professional hosts - what a combination**
>
> MICHAEL THOMPSON, CANFORD CLIFFS, DORSET

BURFORD HOUSE

Townhouse

99 High Street, Burford,
Oxfordshire OX18 4QA

T (UK) 0870 432 8550
T 01993 823151
F 01993 823240
burford@bestloved.com
www.burford.bestloved.com

OWNERS
Simon and Jane Henty

ROOM RATES
Single occupancy   £80 - £125
5 Doubles/Twins   £105 - £125
3 Four-posters   £140 - £155
Includes full breakfast and VAT

CREDIT CARDS
AMERICAN EXPRESS • JCB • MC • VI

RATINGS & AWARDS
ETC ◆◆◆◆◆ Gold Award
AA ◆◆◆◆◆
AA Premier Collection

FACILITIES
On site: Garden
Nearby: Golf, fishing, riding

RESTRICTIONS
No facilities for disabled guests
Smoking in sitting room only
No pets
Closed two weeks in January

ATTRACTIONS
Oxford, Bath,
Stratford-upon-Avon,
Blenheim Palace,
Warwick Castle

NEAREST
CITY:
Oxford - 18 miles/20 mins

AIRPORT:
Heathrow - 60 miles/1 hr 30 mins

RAIL STATION:
Kingham - 5 miles/10 mins
Charlbury - 10 miles/20 mins

AFFILIATIONS
Preston's Global Hotels
Cotswolds Finest Hotels

RESERVATIONS
National rate in UK: 0870 432 8550
Toll free in US: 800-544-9993
Quote Best Loved

ACCESS CODES
Not applicable

MIDSHIRES

Unashamed luxury on the doorstep of the Cotswolds

Said to be the gateway to the Cotswolds in the most beautiful countryside in England, Burford just goes on getting prettier and prettier as time matures the same golden Cotswold stone that built Blenheim Palace and St Paul's Cathedral. In the centre of town, built on a steeply sloping high street amongst quaint antique shops, tea rooms and traditional butchers and grocers, is Burford House, the focal point in a scene of rural peace and plenty.

Though the house dates back to Tudor times, owners Simon and Jane Henty bring a freshness to their special kind of hospitality, and already this gift has made many friends. It appears effortless - but that is the hallmark of professionals. Burford House is fast becoming a Cotswold landmark.

Described as a luxury bed-and-breakfast townhouse hotel, it is, indeed, very attractively furnished and decorated. Simon and Jane have made this their home - and it shows. The welcome is warm and friendly; the whole atmosphere is that of a private house. Four-poster beds and gleaming luxury bathrooms are there to indulge you, and a flower-filled courtyard and cosy sitting rooms refresh the flagging spirit.

LOCATION
Burford is just north of the junction of the A424 and the A40 Oxford to Cheltenham road. The hotel is on the high street in the middle of town.

Country house

CALCOT MANOR

Ancient and modern ...
an enduring family favourite

Calcot was originally converted in 1984 and is now run by hotelier Richard Ball. The hotel is located in an unspoilt part of the Cotswold Hills, well-placed for visiting Bath and within reach of the country's finest antique centres.

This charming manor house was originally a farmhouse dating back to the 15th century. Its beautiful stone barns and stables, now converted into further superb bedrooms, include a 14th-century tithe barn that was built by Cistercian monks in 1300 - amongst the oldest building of its kind in Britain. The hotel is beautifully furnished and the service is friendly and unobtrusive. In the award-winning restaurant, guests can linger over delicious meals whilst enjoying wonderful views of the countryside.

Calcot welcomes families and has a number of suites with sofa beds, toys and child-listening facilities. A new crèche is available for younger children, while the Mez has Playstations, Xboxes and a cinema to keep the older ones entertained. Additionally, guests can enjoy the use of Calcot Spa, incorporating a fitness studio, health and beauty treatments, sauna, steam room and hot tub. Outdoor facilities include a croquet lawn, tennis courts - and bicycles can also be provided for touring the famous Cotswold villages.

LOCATION

On the edge of the Cotswolds, 35 minutes north of Bath. Exit 18 off the M4; the hotel is 4 miles west of Tetbury at the junction of the A46 and the A4135.

Near Tetbury,
Gloucestershire GL8 8YJ

T (UK) 0870 432 8552
T 01666 890391
F 01666 890394
calcot@bestloved.com
www.calcot.bestloved.com

MANAGING DIRECTOR
Richard J G Ball

ROOM RATES
Single occupancy   £150 - £165
24 Doubles/Twins/Family   £175 - £215
4 Family Suites   £250 - £350
Includes full breakfast and VAT

CREDIT CARDS
AMERICAN EXPRESS • DC • MC • VI

RATINGS & AWARDS
ETC ★★★ Gold Award
RAC Gold Ribbon ★★★ Dining Award 3
AA ★★★ ⊛
AA Top 200 - 2004/2005

FACILITIES
On site: Garden, gym, heli-pad, outdoor pool, indoor pool, croquet, tennis, health & beauty, steam room, sauna, licensed for weddings
2 meeting rooms/max 100 people
Nearby: Golf, clay pigeon shooting, riding

RESTRICTIONS
Limited facilities for disabled guests
No pets

ATTRACTIONS
Westonbirt Arboretum, Bath, Badminton Horse Trails, the Cotswolds, Berkeley Castle, Slimbridge Wildfowl Trust, Cheltenham Racecourse

NEAREST
CITY:
Bath - 22 miles/35 mins

AIRPORT:
Heathrow - 100 miles/1 hr 30 mins
Bristol - 30 miles/45 mins

RAIL STATION:
Kemble - 15 miles/10 mins

AFFILIATIONS
Pride of Britain
Preston's Global Hotels

RESERVATIONS
National rate in UK: 0870 432 8552
Toll free in US: 800-544-9993
or 800-98-PRIDE
Quote Best Loved

ACCESS CODES
Not applicable

MIDSHIRES

"Charingworth Manor stands for unadulterated pleasure, and I am not ashamed to enjoy it"

PATRICK MACLAGAN, BERKSHIRE

CHARINGWORTH MANOR

Country house

Near Chipping Campden, Gloucestershire GL55 6NS

T (UK) 0870 432 8561
T 01386 593555
F 01386 593353
charingworth@bestloved.com
www.charingworth.bestloved.com

GENERAL MANAGER
Walter Fallon

ROOM RATES
Single occupancy   £115 - £180
21 Doubles/Twins   £150 - £235
2 Four-posters   £250
3 Suites   £275
Includes full breakfast, early morning tea or coffee, newspaper and VAT

CREDIT CARDS
AMERICAN EXPRESS • DC • MC • VI

RATINGS & AWARDS
RAC ★★★ Dining Award 3
AA ★★★ ✿✿ 78%

FACILITIES
On site: Garden, gym, heli-pad, croquet, tennis, indoor pool, licensed for weddings, sauna, steam room, solarium
3 meeting rooms/max 60 people
Nearby: Clay shooting, archery

RESTRICTIONS
No facilities for disabled guests
No children under 10 years in restaurant after 6:30 p.m.
Smoking in restaurant only
No pets; guide dogs only

ATTRACTIONS
The Cotswolds, Broadway, Warwick Castle, Oxford, Chipping Campden, Stratford-upon-Avon, Cheltenham Races, Silverstone Race Circuit, local historic houses & gardens

NEAREST
CITY:
Stratford-upon-Avon - 12 miles/30 mins

AIRPORT:
Birmingham - 36 miles/1 hr

RAIL STATION:
Moreton-in-Marsh - 8 miles/10 mins

AFFILIATIONS
Celebrated Hotels Collection
English Rose Hotels

RESERVATIONS
National rate in UK: 0870 432 8561
Toll free in UK: 0800 282811
Toll free in US: 800-322-2403
Quote Best Loved

ACCESS CODES
AMADEUS UI BHXCMH
APOLLO/GALILEO UI 35233
SABRE/ABACUS UI 57686
WORLDSPAN UI 40634

This ancient manor house is a perfect retreat from the 21st century

The ancient manor of Charingworth lies amidst the gently rolling Cotswold countryside three miles from Chipping Campden, often described as having the most beautiful high street in the whole of England. This 14th-century manor house is set in its own peaceful grounds of 50 acres and offers breathtaking views.

Inside Charingworth is an historic patchwork of intimate public rooms, with log fires burning during the colder months. The atmosphere is warm and relaxed and the service friendly and attentive, with a real focus on customer care. There are 26 bedrooms, all furnished with antiques and fine fabrics. For dining, the hotel's chefs create imaginative, award-winning dishes with great emphasis placed on local produce.

As if that weren't enticing enough, Charingworth Manor offers an elegant romanesque leisure spa entirely in keeping with the relaxed comfort found throughout the hotel; relax and enjoy the indoor heated pool, sauna, steam room, solarium and gym.

The hotel is also in excellent proximity to local tourist attractions - Cotswold villages, Warwick Castle and the famous gardens of Hidcote and Kiftsgate are very close by. Also easily reached are historic Stratford-upon-Avon and Oxford.

LOCATION

On the B4035 between Chipping Campden and Shipston-on-Stour, two and a half miles from the A429.

> "A real gem - so peaceful, with genuine, friendly, helpful staff and unobtrusive service"
>
> CLAIRE HOPLEY, NEW YORK USA

Country house

THE CHASE HOTEL

A Georgian country house in a pleasantly relaxed setting

Ross-on-Wye is a wonderfully picturesque market town overlooking the River Wye, rich in attractions, blossoming with antiques and steeped in fascinating stories. It's an excellent base for walkers, with Offa's Dyke and the Wye Valley at the doorstep, a relaxing stop for a weekend break or longer holiday and a pleasant escape for a business retreat or corporate get-together.

Perfect for all these is the Chase Hotel, a charming independently-owned hotel perched in its own 11 acres of grounds and landscaped gardens. Just a few minutes' walk from Ross-on-Wye, this Georgian country house still retains a wealth of period features, and the result is a relaxed, genial atmosphere that's well-matched by genuinely caring service. Thirty-six individually-decorated bedrooms offer something for all, including four-poster beds and views over the grounds in some; for business needs, there are five well-appointed meeting rooms with broadband wi-fi - and, of course, acres of grounds and nearby walks, perfect for team-building activities.

Dining is a treat, with the elegant Chase Restaurant offering superb traditional cuisine; for a lighter bite or a pre-dinner drink, there's the Chase Lounge and Bar, offering lovely views over the gardens.

LOCATION

From the end of the M50, take the first exit off the roundabout, then the relief road exit at the next roundabout and the second exit from the Hildersley roundabout. The hotel is on the left after half a mile.

Gloucester Road, Ross-on-Wye, Herefordshire HR9 5LH

T (UK) 0870 432 8562
T 01989 763161
F 01989 768330
chase@bestloved.com
www.chase.bestloved.com

GENERAL MANAGER
Colin Parcell

ROOM RATES
Single occupancy	£77
10 Standard Doubles	£89
20 Superior Doubles	£99
4 Executive Doubles	£109
2 Four-posters	£129

Includes full breakfast, newspaper and VAT

CREDIT CARDS
AMERICAN EXPRESS • DC • MC • VI

RATINGS & AWARDS
ETC ★★★ Silver Award Hotel
RAC ★★★ Dining Award 2
AA ★★★ ❀ 71%

FACILITIES
On site: Garden, heli-pad, licensed for weddings
5 meeting rooms/max 400 people
Nearby: Canoeing, fishing, golf, pony trekking, biking, quad biking, walking

RESTRICTIONS
Limited facilities for disabled guests
No smoking in restaurant and some bedrooms
No pets; guide dogs only
Closed 24 - 29 Dec.

ATTRACTIONS
Hereford Cathedral, Forest of Dean, Symonds Yat, Goodrich Castle, Gloucester

NEAREST
CITY:
Hereford - 14 miles/25 mins
Gloucester - 21 miles/30 mins

AIRPORT:
Birmingham - 65 miles/1 hr 15 mins
Bristol - 50 miles/1 hr

RAIL STATION:
Hereford - 14 miles/25 mins
Gloucester - 21 miles/30 mins

AFFILIATIONS
Classic British Hotels

RESERVATIONS
National rate in UK: 0870 432 8562
Quote Best Loved

ACCESS CODES
AMADEUS UZ GLOCHA
APOLLO/GALILEO UZ 58765
SABRE/ABACUS UZ 42063
WORLDSPAN UZ 43082

MIDSHIRES

Map p. 446, grid E3

The most amazing place! Everything was just perfect. Thank you
JON & HILARY ROWEL, SYDNEY

COCKLIFFE COUNTRY HOUSE HOTEL Country house

Burnt Stump Country Park,
Burnt Stump Hill, Nottingham,
Nottinghamshire NG5 8PQ

T (UK) 0870 432 8566
T 0115 9680179
F 0115 9680623
cockliffe@bestloved.com
www.cockliffe.bestloved.com

OWNERS
Dane and Jane Clarke

ROOM RATES
Single occupancy   £75
10 Doubles/Twins   £105 - £150
Includes full breakfast and VAT

CREDIT CARDS
AMERICAN EXPRESS • DC • MC • VI

RATINGS & AWARDS
Independent

FACILITIES
On site: Garden, heli-pad
1 meeting room/max 50 people
Nearby: Golf, riding, fishing,
fitness centre

RESTRICTIONS
Limited facilities for disabled guests
Pets by arrangement

ATTRACTIONS
Belvoir Castle, Chatsworth House,
Southwell Minster
and Lincoln Cathedral,
Sherwood Forest, Hardwick Hall,
Belton House, Haddon Hall

NEAREST
CITY:
Nottingham - 6 miles/10 mins

AIRPORT:
Nottingham EMA - 20 miles/25 mins

RAIL STATION:
Nottingham - 4 miles/10 mins

AFFILIATIONS
Independent

RESERVATIONS
National rate in UK: 0870 432 8566
Quote Best Loved

ACCESS CODES
Not applicable

MIDSHIRES

A secret hideout in Sherwood Forest - but with a modern slant

Romance is in the air at Cockliffe Country House Hotel, brought by the spirits of those romantic heroes Robin Hood and Lord Byron. A near neighbour to Newstead Abbey, Byron's family home, it is quite possible that that the poet was a frequent visitor - or that Robin Hood hid in this part of the mighty Sherwood Forest!

An intriguing building with half turrets at each corner, this 17th-century manor was rescued from neglect by owners Dane and Jane Clarke. Their affection for the house shows in their eclectic restoration, featuring items and styles from the past mixed with contemporary ideas in finishes and fabrics. The overall effect is stunning, and the comfortably appointed rooms delight even the most discerning guest.

Just six miles from Nottingham but secreted away down a tranquil country lane, Cockliffe is ideally placed for visiting the city's castle and widely-acclaimed interactive Galleries of Justice or, on a larger scale, the Peak District or the Lincolnshire Wolds. The location is so perfect for weddings that receptions are a speciality, as are conferences, which enjoy the benefit of the relaxing setting and high-tech facilities. And with the added allure of a newly-opened fine-dining restaurant, Cockliffe Country House Hotel makes the ideal hideout!

LOCATION
From Nottingham, take the A60 (Mansfield) through Arnold and the major roundabout. At the Seven Mile pub, turn right, signed 'Police HQ'. At the hilltop, take hidden right. Hotel is half a mile along on the right.

Country house

COLWALL PARK HOTEL

Colwall, Malvern,
Worcestershire WR13 6QG

T (UK) 0870 432 8568
T 01684 540000
F 01684 540847
colwallpark@bestloved.com
www.colwallpark.bestloved.com

OWNERS
Iain and Sarah Nesbitt

ROOM RATES
3 Singles	£70 - £80
17 Doubles/Twins	£110 - £130
2 Suites	£150
Includes full breakfast and VAT	

CREDIT CARDS
AMERICAN EXPRESS • MC • VI

RATINGS & AWARDS
ETC ★★★ Silver Award
AA ★★★ ❀❀ 75%
AA Courtesy & Care Award 2000

FACILITIES
On site: Garden, croquet, boules
4 meeting rooms/max 150 people
Nearby: Golf, riding, health club

RESTRICTIONS
Limited facilities for disabled guests
No smoking in bedrooms or restaurant
Children by arrangement
Pets by arrangement

ATTRACTIONS
Elgar Route,
Royal Worcester Porcelain,
shopping in historic Ledbury,
Eastnor Castle, the Cotswolds,
Hereford & Gloucester, Cheltenham

NEAREST
CITY:
Worcester - 12 miles/20 mins

AIRPORT:
Birmingham International - 40 miles/1 hr

RAIL STATION:
Colwall - 20 yds/1 min

AFFILIATIONS
Independent

RESERVATIONS
National rate in UK: 0870 432 8568
Quote Best Loved

ACCESS CODES
Not applicable

MIDSHIRES

Inspirational surroundings on the sunny side of the Malvern Hills

Long celebrated as one of Britain's most alluring landscapes, the Malvern Hills have inspired generations of artists and writers, most notably the composer Sir Edward Elgar. From the undulating ridge of the hills, the views stretch over 10 counties, east across the Cotswolds and west over the Severn Valley to the Welsh mountains. This is wonderful countryside to explore, full of interest and virtually untainted by tourism.

Nestled on the western flanks of the hills, Colwall Park combines high standards of traditional comfort and noticeably professional and efficient service in equal measure. The 22 bedrooms and suites are comfortable and prettily furnished, whilst downstairs guests can curl up in deep armchairs in the lounge. The oak-panelled Seasons Restaurant offers guests a range of classic modern British cooking and is a prior recipient of the prestigious Restaurant of the Year Award by the Birmingham Post and Mail.

Colwall Park offers instant access to the hills that inspired Elgar's 'Pomp and Circumstance' and the 'Enigma' Variations, and the Elgar Route leads you to both his birthplace and grave. Other popular side trips include Malvern, the Royal Worcester porcelain factory and Eastnor Castle.

LOCATION

In the centre of Colwall village, on the B4218 between Malvern and Ledbury.

"The epitome of the English country hotel
HILARY RUBINSTEIN, THE WHICH? GUIDE TO GOOD HOTELS"

CONGHAM HALL

Country house

Lynn Road,
Grimston, Kings Lynn,
Norfolk PE32 1AH

T (UK) 0870 432 8569
T 01485 600250
F 01485 601191
congham@bestloved.com
www.congham.bestloved.com

GENERAL MANAGER
Julie Woodhouse

ROOM RATES
2 Singles   £105
16 Doubles/Twins   £165
2 Suites   £250 - £285
Includes full breakfast and VAT

CREDIT CARDS
AMERICAN EXPRESS • DC • MC • VI

RATINGS & AWARDS
RAC Gold Ribbon ★★★
Dining Award 3
AA ★★★ ⊛⊛
AA Top 200 - 2004/2005

FACILITIES
On site: Garden, heli-pad, croquet,
tennis, licensed for weddings,
herb garden
1 meeting room/max 50 people
Nearby: Golf, fishing, riding,
shooting, sailing

RESTRICTIONS
Limited facilities for disabled guests
Smoking in hall & bar only
No pets; kennels available

ATTRACTIONS
Holkham Hall, Sandringham Estate,
Houghton Hall, RSPB Bird Reserves,
Newmarket Racecourse, ballooning

NEAREST
CITY:
Cambridge - 43 miles/1 hr
AIRPORT:
Stansted - 76 miles/1 hr 30 mins
RAIL STATION:
Kings Lynn - 6 miles/15 mins

AFFILIATIONS
von Essen Hotels
Pride of Britain
Preston's Global Hotels

RESERVATIONS
National rate in UK: 0870 432 8569
Toll free in US: 800-544-9993
or 800-98-PRIDE
Quote Best Loved

ACCESS CODES
AMADEUS HK KNFCON
APOLLO/GALILEO HT 41199
SABRE/ABACUS HK 34243
WORLDSPAN HK CONGH

A superb country-house experience that echoes the best of rural England

Not enough has been written extolling the virtues of Norfolk. In summer, acres of golden fields give way to the wilds of the Broads, a paradise to wildlife enthusiasts. In winter, the region's rugged coastline provides the perfect backdrop for reflective walks.

Another Norfolk virtue must be Congham Hall, the very essence of the country-house experience. Congham stirs up romantic images of a seemingly vanishing rural England - but here it is, thankfully as fresh as ever. The atmosphere here can be described as relaxed luxury. A member of staff is never far away to attend to your every need. Whether relishing a book in the potpourri-scented lounges or enjoying the pool, all has been designed to achieve an air of 'no hassle, no pressure, no noise!', as one guest put it. The spotless bedrooms are prettily furnished and exude a warmth and homeliness throughout; outside, the hotel's many acres of parkland include one of England's finest herb gardens.

If you come to Congham Hall in need of a good rest, your expectations will be met and exceeded. As a touring base for Norfolk and East Anglia, you will find no better choice of hotel.

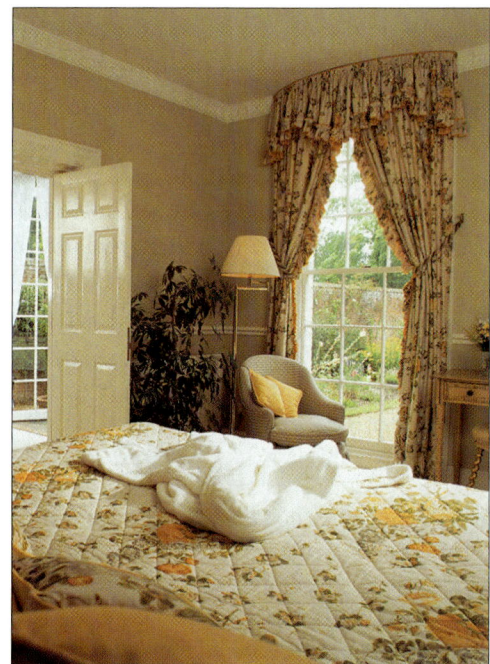

LOCATION
From the A148/A149 junction northeast of Kings Lynn, follow the A148 toward Cromer for 100 yards. Turn right for Grimston; the hotel is two and a half miles on the left.

Country house

COTSWOLD HOUSE HOTEL

A top-of-the-range hotel full of great surprises

This renowned Regency hotel with its trademark spiral staircase incorporates five luxury cottage rooms in the grounds, one with its own private garden and outdoor hot tub and another boasting a sitting room, log fire and private dining facilities. Here, as is the case throughout, sumptuous surroundings and décor are complemented by state-of-the-art technology - this means broadband Internet, Bang & Olufsen entertainment systems in the bedrooms and televisions in the bathrooms, where you can watch DVDs or listen to CDs at your leisure. Aromatherapy bath oils, along with pillows and bedding, are on a bespoke menu where you can select from a range that includes cashmere blankets and Frette linen sheets. Staff at this intimate country hotel, run by Ian and Christa Taylor, are dedicated to providing a truly individualised service that is sure to please even the most demanding guest.

Dining is, of course, equally sophisticated. Jamie Forman is the head chef, and his Juliana's Restaurant enjoys considerable acclaim. Here, elegance is not just confined to the dining room itself - which has French windows leading out onto the garden and terrace - but also extends to the food, which Jamie describes as 'modern, wholesome and seasonal'.

LOCATION

On the B4081, two miles north of the A44 between Moreton-in-Marsh and Broadway.

Chipping Campden,
Gloucestershire GL55 6AN

T (UK) 0870 432 8572
T 01386 840330
F 01386 840310
cotswoldhouse@bestloved.com
www.cotswoldhouse.bestloved.com

OWNERS
Ian and Christa Taylor

ROOM RATES
1 Single	£125
14 Deluxe Doubles/Twins	£185 - £295
5 Cottage Rooms	£295
1 2-Bedroom Suite	£550
Includes full breakfast and VAT	

CREDIT CARDS
AMERICAN EXPRESS • MC • VI

RATINGS & AWARDS
RAC Gold Ribbon ★★★ Dining Award 4
AA ★★★ ❀❀
AA Top 200 - 2004/2005

FACILITIES
On site: Garden, croquet
3 meeting rooms/max 80 people
Nearby: Golf, riding, fishing,
clay shooting, walking,
hot-air ballooning

RESTRICTIONS
No facilities for disabled guests

ATTRACTIONS
The Cotswolds, Stratford-upon-Avon,
Hidcote & Kiftsgate Gardens,
Warwick, Snowshill Manor,
Batsford Arboretum,
Berkeley & Sudeley castles

NEAREST
CITY:
Oxford - 33 miles/45 mins
Stratford - 10 miles/15 mins

AIRPORT:
Heathrow - 78 miles/1 hr 45 mins
Birmingham - 30 miles/30 mins

RAIL STATION:
Moreton-in-Marsh - 7 miles/10 mins

AFFILIATIONS
Celebrated Hotels Collection
Pride of Britain

RESERVATIONS
National rate in UK: 0870 432 8572
Toll free in US: 800-322-2403
or 800-98-PRIDE
Quote Best Loved

ACCESS CODES
AMADEUS YX 14869
APOLLO/GALILEO YX COTSW
SABRE/ABACUS YX 30593
WORLDSPAN YX BHXCOT

MIDSHIRES

Map p. 446, grid D5

COTTAGE IN THE WOOD

Country house

MIDSHIRES

Holywell Road, Malvern Wells,
Worcestershire WR14 4LG

T (UK) 0870 432 8574
T 01684 575859
F 01684 560662
cottagewood@bestloved.com
www.cottagewood.bestloved.com

OWNERS
The Pattin Family

ROOM RATES
Single occupancy   £79 - £99
31 Doubles/Twins   £99 - £170
Includes full breakfast and VAT

CREDIT CARDS
AMERICAN EXPRESS • MC • VI

RATINGS & AWARDS
ETC ★★★ Silver Award
AA ★★★ ◉◉ 74%
Taste of Worcestershire -
Highly Recommended

FACILITIES
On site: Garden
1 meeting room/max 14 people
Nearby: Golf, walking, shooting,
fishing, riding

RESTRICTIONS
Limited facilities for disabled guests
No smoking in restaurant and
some lounge areas
Pets by arrangement

ATTRACTIONS
Malvern Hills, Worcester Cathedral,
Warwick Castle, Stratford-upon-Avon,
Gloucester Cathedral, the Cotswolds,
Royal Worcester Porcelain, Elgar Trail,
Three Counties Showground,
Eastnor Castle

NEAREST
CITY:
Birmingham - 43 miles/1 hr

AIRPORT:
Birmingham - 48 miles/1 hr

RAIL STATION:
Great Malvern - 3 miles/5 mins

AFFILIATIONS
Independent

RESERVATIONS
National rate in UK: 0870 432 8574
Quote Best Loved

ACCESS CODES
Not applicable

Wine, dine and savour one of the finest views in England

High in the Malvern Hills lies the Cottage in the Wood, nestled in a secluded hideaway embraced by woodlands on three sides. The fourth is open to the view - a truly breathtaking vista that unfurls across the Severn Vale for 30 miles or more. There is no doubt that the Cottage occupies a magical position, but it also is notable as a delightful family-run hotel and restaurant spread over a trio of attractive buildings.

The Pattin family, headed up by John and Sue, are involved in every aspect of the hotel, creating a genuinely relaxed and welcoming atmosphere. A fine Georgian dower house is the heart of the hotel, containing the restaurant and a handful of bedrooms, while Beech Cottage offers homely accommodation and The Pinnacles contains sumptuous bedrooms traditionally styled with antique furnishings and commanding the finest views of all. Good food is assured in the dining room, and John has collected a superb wine list featuring more than 600 bottles and halves at astonishingly affordable prices.

Guests can enjoy bargain breaks year-round and discounted rates at the nearby Worcestershire Golf Course. Walks in the Malverns begin at the front door of the hotel, and sightseeing opportunities include three cathedral cities, Stratford-upon-Avon and the musical intrigue along the Elgar Trail.

LOCATION
10 miles from the M5. From the south, take Junction 8; from the north, Junction 7. The hotel is signposted three miles south of Great Malvern off the A449.

> "The welcome, comfort, service and food were second to none and I now have a new yardstick by which to judge other hotels"
>
> A POLLARD, SALISBURY

Country house

THE COUNTRY COTTAGE HOTEL

Impeccable hospitality with a touch of the Mediterranean

Under new ownership, The Country Cottage Hotel has been totally refurbished with delightful en-suite bedrooms. The hotel is formed by 17th-century cottages around a private, gated courtyard and walled garden, which make up this little haven, just a few minutes outside the cosmopolitan city of Nottingham.

You will appreciate this hotel's new personality, created by its owners, Julie Sturt and her son, Andrew. The bedrooms are all different in décor and benefit from the tremendous amount of thought that has gone into the choice of fabrics and colours, thus improving the space and feel of each and every room. The restaurant features a variety of continental dishes, including a healthy smattering of traditional English.

The charming lounge has a superb inglenook fireplace and a well-stocked wine cellar, which heighten the hotel's authentic character. 'The Country Cottage' is aptly named and oozes heritage: Cosy, wooden beams, and boundless hospitality, topped off with excellent facilities for conferences and weddings, this is one of those places that instantly makes you feel at home, whether on business or taking a leisure break.

LOCATION

Three miles south of Nottingham in Ruddington. Turn right off main A60, right into High Street and right again into Easthorpe Street. The hotel is 150 metres on the right.

Easthorpe Street,
Ruddington, Nottingham,
Nottinghamshire NG11 6LA

T (UK) 0870 432 8576
T 0115 984 6882
F 0115 921 4721
cottage@bestloved.com
www.cottage.bestloved.com

OWNER
Julie Sturt

ROOM RATES
1 Single		£65
12 Doubles/Twins		£95 - £145
3 Suites		£130
1 Four-poster		£120

Includes full breakfast and VAT

CREDIT CARDS
AMERICAN EXPRESS • JCB • MC • VI

RATINGS & AWARDS
Independent

FACILITIES
On site: Garden
4 meeting rooms/max 60 people
Nearby: Golf, tennis, water skiing, yachting, hunting/shooting, go-karting, fishing, riding

RESTRICTIONS
Limited facilities for disabled guests
Smoking in bar and lounge only
No pets

ATTRACTIONS
Nottingham City & Castle,
Belvoir Castle, Newstead Abbey,
Holmepierrepoint National
Watersports Centre, Wollaton Hall,
Robin Hood Experience

NEAREST
CITY:
Nottingham - 5 miles/10 mins

AIRPORT:
Heathrow - 130 miles/2 hrs 30 mins
Nottingham EMA - 13 miles/20 mins

RAIL STATION:
Nottingham - 5 miles/10 mins

AFFILIATIONS
Independent

RESERVATIONS
National rate in UK: 0870 432 8576
Quote Best Loved

ACCESS CODES
Not applicable

MIDSHIRES

THE CROWN AT BLOCKLEY

Inn

MIDSHIRES

High Street, Blockley,
Near Moreton-in-Marsh,
Gloucestershire GL56 9EX

T (UK) 0870 432 8586
T 01386 700245
F 01386 700247
crownblockley@bestloved.com
www.crownblockley.bestloved.com

OWNER
Dr Giovanni Testagrossa MHCIMA

ROOM RATES
Single occupancy	£55 - £85
18 Doubles/Twins	£90 - £130
4 Four-posters	£120 - £140
3 Suites	£120

Includes full breakfast and VAT

CREDIT CARDS
AMERICAN EXPRESS • MC • VI

RATINGS & AWARDS
RAC ★★★ Dining Award 2
AA ★★★

FACILITIES
On site: Car park
1 meeting room/max 50 people
Nearby: Golf, leisure centre,
clay pigeon shooting, archery, riding

RESTRICTIONS
Limited facilities for disabled guests
No smoking in restaurant

ATTRACTIONS
Broadway, Stratford-upon-Avon,
Warwick Castle, Oxford,
Cotswold villages, wildlife park

NEAREST
CITY:
Oxford - 25 miles/30 mins
Evesham - 11 miles/15 mins

AIRPORT:
Birmingham - 40 miles/1 hr

RAIL STATION:
Moreton-in-Marsh - 5 miles/10 mins

AFFILIATIONS
Independent

RESERVATIONS
National rate in UK: 0870 432 8586
Quote Best Loved

ACCESS CODES
Not applicable

A comfortable and traditional inn in a typical Cotswold village

This charming mellow-stone 16th-century coaching inn with its trademark archways is set in a picturesque village in the heart of the Cotswolds. The friendly staff are always on hand to make your stay memorable. The 24 well-equipped and tastefully furnished bedrooms are all en suite, with colour television and tea-making facilities.

In summer, the Crown, which is licensed for weddings and can cater for up to 50 guests (there's also a car park to fit 40 vehicles), provides the perfect setting to enjoy drinks and fine food under a cooling parasol on the patio or in the garden. On colder days you can relax and enjoy the traditional pub atmosphere of wooden beams, draught ale and quality bar food, in front of a log fire - there is also a very good chance you will meet one of the many local characters! The Rafters Restaurant has a fine menu of traditional English and European cuisine, with an interestingly laid out wine list to suit all tastes and aspirations.

For smaller business meetings, there is a conference room, making a highly desirable change from the office environment!

The Crown Hotel reflects the tranquil nature of the Cotswolds, with walks along tree-lined footpaths and horse riding from local stables. There is a golf club, and Batsford Arboretum is nearby.

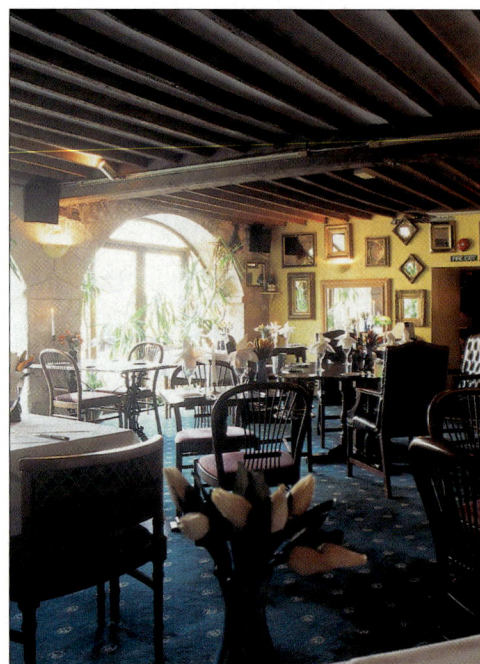

LOCATION
Three miles west of the A429
(Moreton-in-Marsh), off the A44 Evesham road.

> # "First-class as always - now even spectacular"
> JOAN & PETER GARRATT, SIDMOUTH, DEVON

Farmhouse

DANNAH FARM

Bowman's Lane, Shottle,
Near Belper, Derbyshire DE56 2DR

T (UK) 0870 432 8592
T 01773 550273
F 01773 550590
dannah@bestloved.com
www.dannah.bestloved.com

OWNERS
Joan and Martin Slack

ROOM RATES
Single occupancy   £65
5 Doubles/Twins   £85 - £120
3 Suites   £140 - £160
Includes full breakfast and VAT

CREDIT CARDS
MC • VI

RATINGS & AWARDS
RAC ♦♦♦♦♦ Dining Award I
RAC Warm Welcome,
Sparkling Diamond Awards
AA ♦♦♦♦♦
AA Premier Collection

FACILITIES
On site: Garden
I meeting room/max 15 people
Nearby: Golf, fishing, riding,
clay pigeon shooting

RESTRICTIONS
Limited facilities for disabled guests
Smoking in sitting room only
No pets; guide dogs only
Closed Christmas Eve - Boxing Day

ATTRACTIONS
Chatsworth House, Haddon Hall,
Bakewell, Blue John Mines,
Alton Towers, Dovedale,
Denby Pottery

NEAREST
CITY:
Derby - 9 miles/20 mins

AIRPORT:
Nottingham EMA - 23 miles/30 mins

RAIL STATION:
Derby - 9 miles/20 mins

AFFILIATIONS
Independent

RESERVATIONS
National rate in UK: 0870 432 8592
Quote Best Loved

ACCESS CODES
Not applicable

MIDSHIRES

A real working farm on the Chatsworth Estate

Wake up to a traditional country breakfast with homemade bread and free-range eggs on a real working farm that's also part of the Chatsworth Estate. Originally a royal deer park, Dannah is home to tenant farmers Joan and Martin Slack, who have a mixed working farm high above the Ecclesbourne valley.

Despite its rural isolation, this charming guesthouse is only 20 minutes from the M1 and very close to both Nottingham and Derby. It is also within easy reach of Derbyshire's many tourist attractions, including Bakewell, Haddon Hall (where the Brontë classic Jane Eyre was set) and Alton Towers. Despite its beauty, the area has fewer tourists than one might expect, with golf, fishing and riding nearby. It is ideal for those who love walking and touring, as well as families with children and the single business traveller who wants a few home comforts at the end of a long day.

Dinner is good, homemade food made from local produce, cooked and prepared by Joan Slack herself and served at 7 p.m. As the winner of a Best of Tourism Award, Dannah combines classic country (think cats, chickens, pigs and an English setter named Cracker) with a few little luxuries like four-poster beds and whirlpool baths thrown in.

LOCATION

From Belper, take the A517 (Ashbourne). Shortly after Blackbrook, turn right toward Shottle; the hotel is at the junction of Chequer Lane and Palace Lane.

MIDSHIRES

> "It is said to be a mistake to return - not here. Wonderful again"
>
> JENNY & COLIN, SURREY

THE DIAL HOUSE HOTEL

Village hotel

The Chestnuts, High Street,
Bourton-on-the-Water,
Gloucestershire GL54 2AN

T (UK) 0870 432 8596
T 01451 822244
F 01451 810126
dial@bestloved.com
www.dial.bestloved.com

OWNERS
Adrian and Jane Campbell-Howard

ROOM RATES
9 Doubles/Twins   £110
2 Four-posters   £160
1 Suite   £180
Includes full breakfast and VAT

CREDIT CARDS
• DC • JCB • MC • VI

RATINGS & AWARDS
ETC ★★ Silver Award Hotel
AA ★★ ❀❀ 77%
West Country Cooking
'Best Hotel in Gloucestershire 2002'

FACILITIES
On site: Garden, croquet,
putting lawn
1 meeting room/max 20 people
Nearby: Golf, riding, fishing

RESTRICTIONS
Limited facilities for disabled guests
No children under 10 years
No pets
No smoking throughout

ATTRACTIONS
The Cotswolds, Blenheim Palace,
Oxford, Sudeley Castle,
Hidcote Gardens, Stratford-upon-Avon

NEAREST
CITY:
Cheltenham - 17 miles/25 mins

AIRPORT:
Heathrow - 74 miles/1 hr 30 mins

RAIL STATION:
Moreton-in-Marsh - 9 miles/12 mins

AFFILIATIONS
Independent

RESERVATIONS
National rate in UK: 0870 432 8596
Quote Best Loved

ACCESS CODES
Not applicable

A secret, luxurious hideaway nestled in the Cotswolds

Imagine: it's a rare blue English summer's day, and you are lazing in the leaf-green walled garden of a classic Cotswold stone house. All is calm around you, and picture-postcard pretty; somewhere in the distance you can hear the gentle 'thwack' of croquet on the lawn. You are staying in the Dial House Hotel, and from the window by your four-poster bed you can see the River Windrush, which meanders right through the centre of a quintessentially English country village.

Known locally as the Venice of the Cotswolds, Bourton-on-the-Water is an idyllic, romantic location. In centuries past, Shakespeare himself might even have been inspired by its tranquil waters, as Stratford-upon-Avon is only half an hour's drive away. But here, just as in Italy, food is the music of love: the oak-beamed restaurant is well regarded by critics. The menu, created by head chef Daniel Bunce, is British with a modern European influence and includes local game and fish. With all these pleasures, it's hard to believe that London is just an hour and a quarter away!

LOCATION
In the centre of Bourton-on-the-Water,
set back behind the village green.

> *Everything and everyone was wonderful. We feel fortunate to have happened upon you*
>
> FRELING & LINDA SMITH, NEW YORK

Country house

DORMY HOUSE

A haven for Stratford-upon-Avon, the Cotswolds and Broadway itself

Dormy House is set high in the beautiful Cotswold countryside amidst picturesque medieval villages. Originally a 17th-century farmhouse, the hotel blends its historic past with 21st-century facilities and personalised service.

Each of the 48 bedrooms is beautifully decorated and provides every comfort for a good night's rest. The charming lounges, enhanced with bowls of fresh flowers, have deep armchairs in which to relax, and in winter roaring log fires provide a welcoming atmosphere. The candlelit dining room offers diners the choice of cosy alcoves in the old farmhouse or the elegant conservatory-style dining room. The food is of a truly international standard, and the freshest ingredients ensure an unforgettable experience. Lunch and evening meals are also served in the oak-beamed Barn Owl bar.

Surrounding the hotel on three sides is the Broadway Golf Club, where guests can play by arrangement. Alternatively, visitors can explore the numerous National Trust properties and gardens nearby, including Hidcote, Kiftsgate and the Brockhampton Estate. The friendly staff are a mine of information on the surrounding attractions, including Cotswold villages, Stratford's theatres and a variety of sporting facilities.

LOCATION

On the A44 atop Fish Hill, a mile and a half from Broadway. Turn for Saintbury and Picnic Area; after half a mile, fork left, and Dormy House is on the left.

Willersey Hill, Broadway, Worcestershire WR12 7LF

T (UK) 0870 432 8600
T 01386 852711
F 01386 858636
dormy@bestloved.com
www.dormy.bestloved.com

DIRECTOR
Ingrid Philip-Sorensen

GENERAL MANAGER
David Field

ROOM RATES
Single occupancy   £118
40 Doubles/Twins   £160 - £170
4 Four-posters   £195
4 Suites   £205
Includes full breakfast and VAT

CREDIT CARDS
AMERICAN EXPRESS • DC • MC • VI

RATINGS & AWARDS
ETC ★★★ Silver Award
RAC ★★★ Dining Award 3
AA ★★★ ❀❀ 78%

FACILITIES
On site: Garden, gym, croquet, licensed for weddings, putting green, sauna, billiards
5 meeting rooms/max 170 people
Nearby: Golf, riding, fishing, tennis, clay pigeon shooting, archery

RESTRICTIONS
Limited facilities for disabled guests
No smoking in restaurant
No pets in public rooms
Closed 24 - 27 Dec.

ATTRACTIONS
Warwick Castle, Blenheim Palace, Stratford-upon-Avon, the Cotswolds, Broadway, Chipping Campden, gardens of Hidcote and Kiftsgate

NEAREST
CITY:
Oxford - 40 miles/1 hr

AIRPORT:
Birmingham - 40 miles/1 hr
Heathrow - 90 miles/2 hrs

RAIL STATION:
Moreton-in-Marsh - 6 miles/10 mins

AFFILIATIONS
Independent

RESERVATIONS
National rate in UK: 0870 432 8600
Quote Best Loved

ACCESS CODES
Not applicable

MIDSHIRES

THE ELMS

Country house

Abberley,
Worcestershire WR6 6AT

T (UK) 0870 432 8607
T 01299 896666
F 01299 896804
elms@bestloved.com
www.elms.bestloved.com

MANAGER
Mark Green

ROOM RATES
2 Singles £90 - £110
14 Doubles/Twins £120 - £180
5 Double/Twin Coach Houses £110 - £120
Includes full breakfast and VAT

CREDIT CARDS
AMERICAN EXPRESS • DC • MC • VI

RATINGS & AWARDS
AA ★★★ ⚙️⚙️ 73%

FACILITIES
On site: Heli-pad, croquet, tennis
3 meeting rooms/max 50 people
Nearby: Golf, fishing, shooting, riding

RESTRICTIONS
None

ATTRACTIONS
Whitley Court and Baroque Church,
Worcester Cathedral,
Porcelain Museum, 'Black and White'
villages of Herefordshire,
the Cotswolds, Stratford-upon-Avon,
horse racing at Cheltenham
and Ludlow

NEAREST
CITY:
Worcester - 10 miles/20 mins
Ludlow - 10 miles/20 mins

AIRPORT:
Birmingham - 30 miles/45 mins

RAIL STATION:
Worcester - 10 miles/20 mins

AFFILIATIONS
von Essen Hotels

RESERVATIONS
National rate in UK: 0870 432 8607
Toll free in US: 800-525-4800
Quote Best Loved

ACCESS CODES
AMADEUS YX BHXTEH
APOLLO/GALILEO YX 523
SABRE/ABACUS YX 20362
WORLDSPAN YX BHXEL
PEGASUS YX BHXELM

MIDSHIRES

The Grande Dame
of the Severn Valley

The Elms graces the mellow farmland in the Teme Valley, like many classic British masterpieces. It was built by Gilbert White, a pupil of Sir Christopher Wren - but this lovely house is no museum; instead, it is a fine example of Britain's living heritage. The Elms was built in 1710 and was converted into a hotel in 1946. More than 50 years on, it has achieved international recognition for its service, comfort and food.

Antiques and comfortable furnishings adorn the public rooms of this Queen Anne mansion, which retains its original ornate plasterwork and other period touches. The bedrooms and suites each have their own character with views across the landscaped gardens and beyond. All are furnished with period antiques and have well-appointed bathrooms.

The restaurant, under head chef Daren Bale, has a reputation for the quality of its cuisine, its excellent cellar and the impeccable courtesies extended by the staff. The area is also rich in things to see and do, from good walking to cider tasting, lovely gardens to antique shops or simply exploring.

LOCATION
20 minutes from Worcester and the M5. The Elms is on the A443, two miles after Great Witley - but do not take the turning into Abberley.

"Not since Château de Bagnols in France has there been such attention to detail in an historic house hotel. It should be an inspiration to English hoteliers"

LYN MIDDLEHURST, GALLIVANTER'S GUIDE

Map p. 446, grid E5

191

Stately home

FAWSLEY HALL

Spend a little time living in the lap of history

Shakespeare's Cottage at Stratford-upon-Avon and the ancestral homes at Sulgrave Manor (George Washington) and Althorp (Diana, Princess of Wales) form a triangle (all within 30 minutes' drive) whose heart is Fawsley Hall. Each place marks an important aspect of England's colourful heritage.

In many respects, Fawsley Hall is as historically and architecturally important - and better yet, you can stay here! This 500-year-old stately house consists of four expertly and sensitively restored Tudor, Georgian, Victorian and modern classic wings, allowing the guest ample choice of historic accommodation. Topping off the house are the glorious Capability Brown-designed views. A more idyllic setting has rarely been realised. Luxury pervades every aspect of the Hall, from the decorative features to the staff's enthusiastic attentiveness, and you can easily begin to believe that you too are the lord of the manor.

While the décor is left to history, the restaurant provides a refreshing contemporary contrast. Here you will find cutting-edge European cuisine, excellently prepared and lovingly served. Additionally, the hotel's new spa in the Georgian cellar includes a beauty salon, fitness studio, steam room, sauna and spa bath. A splendid place for an intimate romantic getaway or a grand memorable gathering!

LOCATION

Exit 11 off the M40 for the A361 (Daventry). The hotel is located between Charwelton and Badby.

Fawsley, Near Daventry, Northamptonshire NN11 3BA

T (UK) 0870 432 8611
T 01327 892000
F 01327 892001
fawsley@bestloved.com
www.fawsley.bestloved.com

GENERAL MANAGER
Jeffrey Crockett

ROOM RATES

4 Standard	£140 - £150
24 Club Doubles/Twins	£175 - £190
5 Superior Rooms	£225 - £245
8 Luxury Doubles/Twins	£255 - £295
2 Suites	£340 - £390

Includes continental breakfast and VAT

CREDIT CARDS
AMERICAN EXPRESS • DC • MC • VI

RATINGS & AWARDS
AA ★★★★ ⊛⊛
AA Top 200 - 2004/2005

FACILITIES
On site: Heli-pad, tennis, health & beauty, licensed for weddings, fitness studio, spa
6 meeting rooms/max 200 people
Nearby: Golf, fishing, shooting, riding

RESTRICTIONS
Limited facilities for disabled guests

ATTRACTIONS
Althorp, Sulgrave Manor, Warwick Castle, Silverstone, Stratford-upon-Avon, Towcester Racecourse, designer shopping at Bicester Village

NEAREST
CITY:
Birmingham - 40 miles/1 hr

AIRPORT:
Birmingham - 35 miles/50 mins
Heathrow - 80 miles/1 hr 30 mins

RAIL STATION:
Northampton 15 miles/20 mins
Rugby - 18 miles/30 mins

AFFILIATIONS
Celebrated Hotels Collection

RESERVATIONS
National rate in UK: 0870 432 8611
Toll free in US: 800-322-2403
Quote Best Loved

ACCESS CODES
AMADEUS HK CVTFAW
APOLLO/GALILEO HT 33715
SABRE/ABACUS HK 56620
WORLDSPAN HK FAWSL

MIDSHIRES

BEST LOVED HOTELS

"Comfortable, charming and unpretentious ... it is one of the places to which I keep coming back"

ELIZABETH ORTIZ, GOURMET MAGAZINE

THE FEATHERS

Townhouse

Market Street, Woodstock,
Oxfordshire OX20 1SX

T (UK) 0870 432 8612
T 01993 812291
F 01993 813158
feathers@bestloved.com
www.feathers.bestloved.com

RESIDENT MANAGER
Jeremy Du Plessis

ROOM RATES
Single occupancy   £115 - £135
16 Doubles/Twins   £135 - £185
4 Suites   £240 - £290
Includes full breakfast and VAT

CREDIT CARDS
AMERICAN EXPRESS • DC • JCB • MC • VI

RATINGS & AWARDS
RAC Blue Ribbon ★★★ Dining Award 3
AA ★★★ ֎ 73%

FACILITIES
On site: Garden, courtyard garden,
mountain bikes
2 meeting rooms/max 50 people
Nearby: Golf, riding, fishing

RESTRICTIONS
No facilities for disabled guests
Pets by arrangement
No smoking in bedrooms
or restaurant

ATTRACTIONS
Blenheim Palace, Broughton Castle,
Oxford, Stratford-upon-Avon,
the Cotswolds, Silverstone

NEAREST
CITY:
Oxford - 8 miles/15 mins

AIRPORT:
Heathrow - 40 miles/1 hr

RAIL STATION:
Oxford - 8 miles/15 mins

AFFILIATIONS
Celebrated Hotels Collection
Grand Heritage Hotels

RESERVATIONS
National rate in UK: 0870 432 8612
Toll free in US: 800-322-2403
or 888-93-GRAND
Quote Best Loved

ACCESS CODES
AMADEUS UI OXFFEA
APOLLO/GALILEO UI 25900
SABRE/ABACUS UI 30576
WORLDSPAN UI 42150

Warmth and charm at the doorstep of Sir Winston Churchill's birthplace

This privately-owned 17th-century town hotel is located in the heart of picturesque Woodstock, which nestles by the gates of Blenheim Palace, the home of the 11th Duke of Marlborough and birthplace of Sir Winston Churchill. The Feathers offers the ideal base from which to explore the dreaming spires of the university city of Oxford and the beautiful Cotswolds - yet it is only an hour and a half from London!

The hotel has 16 individually designed rooms and four suites, all furnished with antiques, books and intriguing artwork. All rooms have private bathrooms, satellite television and direct-dial telephones.

In winter, log fires blaze in all the sitting rooms and the bar. In warmer months, the courtyard garden provides the ideal location to take a light meal or refreshment.

The well-renowned restaurant has received much critical acclaim. The interesting dishes on the menu are carefully but simply created using only the finest ingredients, and guests may select from the constantly changing à la carte menu.

LOCATION
From the south, take the A44 to Woodstock. After Blenheim Palace gates, take the first left after the traffic lights; the hotel is on the left.

> **Wonderful staff, superb cuisine, a delightful break - thank you**
> MR AND MRS SAWYER

Country house

FOSSE MANOR

Fosse Way, Stow-on-the-Wold,
Gloucestershire GL54 1JX

T (UK) 0870 432 8616
T 01451 830354
F 01451 832486
fosse@bestloved.com
www.fosse.bestloved.com

DIRECTOR
David Williams

FRONT OF HOUSE MANAGER
Clare Thomas

ROOM RATES
Single occupancy	£95
6 Standard Doubles/Twins	£130
10 Superior Doubles/Twins	£165
4 Suites	£225

Includes full breakfast and VAT

CREDIT CARDS
AMERICAN EXPRESS • MC • VI

RATINGS & AWARDS
ETC ★★★ Hotel
RAC ★★★ Dining Award 2
AA ★★★ ❀❀ 75%

FACILITIES
On site: Garden, croquet
1 meeting room/max 60
Nearby: golf, riding, shooting, fishing

RESTRICTIONS
Limited facilities for disabled guests
Smoking in bar and lounge only
Pets by arrangement

ATTRACTIONS
Batsford Arboretum,
Cotswold Wildlife Park and Gardens,
Cotswold Motoring Museum,
Bourton-on-the-Water Model Village,
Cotswolds Falconry Centre,
Cotswold Farm Park, Cheltenham,
Stratford-upon-Avon

NEAREST
CITY:
Gloucester - 35 miles/45 mins

AIRPORT:
Birmingham - 45 miles/1 hr
Gloucester - 35 miles/45 mins

RAIL STATION:
Moreton-in-Marsh - 5 miles/10 mins

AFFILIATIONS
Independent

RESERVATIONS
National rate in UK: 0870 432 8616
Quote Best Loved

ACCESS CODES
Not applicable

MIDSHIRES

A warm welcome in the heart of the Cotswolds

A contemporary haven in the heart of the Cotswolds sympathetically redesigned in 2004, Fosse Manor retains a delightful sense of warmth within its original architectural features. The hotel is spread between three buildings - the Old Rectory, Coach House and Lodge - offering 20 individually styled rooms, immaculately decorated in peaceful, pleasing natural tones and offering a good selection of games and films as well as either a DVD player or PlayStation in each.

Dining is also a treat; the recipient of two AA rosettes, the restaurant can cater for conferences and receptions as well as smaller parties or intimate dinners. The bar, green room and patio offer a more relaxed atmosphere and are all under the reign of executive chef Tom Rains, who has worked hard to source supplies of good local produce and ingredients. Views of the rolling Cotswold hills can be enjoyed from the bar or lounge, where comfy sofas and a roaring fire offer space to relax and unwind.

There is plenty to do in Stow and the surrounding area: Enjoy mellow Cotswold stone villages and legendary antique shops, the wonderful Batsford Arboretum, the Cotswold Falconry Centre and Cotswold Farm Park, a wealth of attractions in Bourton-on-the-Water and, a bit further afield, Oxford's academic atmosphere and the Regency spa town of Cheltenham, birthplace of Gustav Holst.

LOCATION

Adjacent to the A429 just south of Stow-on-the-Wold. From London, exit junction 8 off the A40/M40 for the A40 around Oxford; then, exit for the A429 (Stow-on-the-Wold). The hotel is signposted.

GRAFTON MANOR

Country house

MIDSHIRES

Grafton Lane, Bromsgrove,
Worcestershire B61 7HA

T (UK) 0870 432 8630
T 01527 579007
F 01527 575221
grafton@bestloved.com
www.grafton.bestloved.com

OWNER
The Lord of Grafton

MANAGER
Stephen Morris

ROOM RATES
1 Single		£85 - £95
5 Doubles/Twins		£105 - £125
1 Four-poster		£125 - £150
2 Suites		£150

Includes full breakfast and VAT

CREDIT CARDS
AMERICAN EXPRESS • DC • MC • VI

RATINGS & AWARDS
AA ❀ Restaurant with Rooms
Member of Master Chefs Institute

FACILITIES
On site: Garden, heli-pad, croquet,
licensed for weddings,
special wedding marquee
2 meeting rooms/max 180 people
Nearby: Golf, riding

RESTRICTIONS
No smoking in dining room
No pets

ATTRACTIONS
Stratford-upon-Avon, Worcester,
The Cotswolds, Warwick Castle,
Stourbridge Glass, Welsh Marches

NEAREST
CITY:
Birmingham - 17 miles/30 mins

AIRPORT:
Birmingham - 22 miles/30 mins

RAIL STATION:
Bromsgrove - 2 miles/5 mins

AFFILIATIONS
Independent

RESERVATIONS
National rate in UK: 0870 432 8630
Quote Best Loved

ACCESS CODES
AMADEUS HK BHXGRA
SABRE/ABACUS HK 36237
WORLDSPAN HK GRAFT

A great house with an illustrious past, now the epitome of modern elegance

The Manor of Grafton has an illustrious history: From its foundation before the Norman Conquest, Grafton has been recognised as one of Worcestershire's great historic houses. This splendid house, for centuries the home of king-makers, was opened as a hotel in 1980 by present owners John (now the Lord of Grafton) and June Morris, who, together with their family, ensure guests receive attentive, friendly service.

The elegant 17th-century dining room is the focal point of a visit to Grafton, with a fine wine list and imaginative menus created by Simon Morris and Tim Waldron, who aim to produce only the best for guests. Damask rose petal and mulberry sorbets are indicative of the inspired style of cuisine. The guest bedrooms have been painstakingly restored, introducing the comforts demanded today whilst retaining the grace and elegance of another age.

There is much to enjoy at Grafton: a superb formal Herb Garden in 26 acres of beautiful grounds, a two-acre lake, a 16th-century fish stew (a brick building in the stream) and a 15th-century private chapel. Further afield, Grafton Manor is an ideal base from which to explore the Worcestershire countryside.

LOCATION

Exit 5 from the M5 for the A38 toward Bromsgrove. Bear left at the second roundabout. Grafton Lane is the first left after half a mile.

> "The Grapevine mixes urban sophistication with reasonable prices, rural charm and intimacy. It's the best inn in town"
>
> FROMMERS GUIDES

Village hotel

GRAPEVINE HOTEL

A warm welcome and good food at the antiques centre of the Cotswolds

Set in the historic market town of Stow-on-the-Wold amidst the warm, honey-coloured Cotswold stone buildings and rolling countryside, the Grapevine has become justly renowned for its warm hospitality and fine dining, a fact that shines through at this beautifully appointed, award-winning 17th-century hotel and restaurant. The hotel is named after the ancient vine that shades the Conservatory Restaurant, where the atmosphere is relaxed but the catering is professional and imaginative, offering a delightfully modern interpretation of classic English and Mediterranean cooking. The Conservatory Restaurant and the hotel's two charming private dining rooms are open to non-residents all year round.

When it's time for a rest, the hotel's 22 highly individual bedrooms offer comfortable and peaceful accommodation, complete with all the necessary comforts or, if you're feeling particularly luxurious, even a four-poster bed. But you won't want to lie in for too long - after all, Stow-on-the-Wold offers a wealth of attractions and is an exquisite doorstep to the Cotswolds.

LOCATION

Off Fosse Way A429, take the A346 toward Chipping Norton; the Grapevine is 150 yards on the right facing a small green.

Sheep Street,
Stow-on-the-Wold,
Gloucestershire GL54 1AU

T (UK) 0870 432 8633
T 01451 830344
F 01451 832278
grapevine@bestloved.com
www.grapevine.bestloved.com

OWNERS
Mark and Janine Vance

ROOM RATES
Single occupancy	£85 - £95
10 Standard Doubles/Twins	£140
9 Superior Doubles/Twins	£160
1 Four-poster	£160
2 Family Rooms	£160

Includes full breakfast and VAT

CREDIT CARDS
AMERICAN EXPRESS • DC • JCB • MC • VI

RATINGS & AWARDS
RAC ★★★ Dining Award 1
AA ★★★ ❀ 72%

FACILITIES
On site: The Conservatory Restaurant, La Vigna Restaurant and Gigot Bar
2 meeting rooms/max 120 people
Nearby: Golf, riding, fishing, off-road driving

RESTRICTIONS
Limited facilities for disabled guests
Smoking in bar and lounge only
Pets by arrangement

ATTRACTIONS
Blenheim Palace, Hidcote, Warwick and Sudeley castles, Kiftsgate and Barnsley House Gardens, Oxford, Stratford-upon-Avon, Cheltenham, the Cotswolds

NEAREST
CITY:
Birmingham - 48 miles/1 hr
London - 85 miles/1 hr 45 mins

AIRPORT:
Birmingham - 45 miles/55 mins
Heathrow - 75 miles/1 hr 30 mins

RAIL STATION:
Kingham - 5 miles/10 mins

AFFILIATIONS
Independent

RESERVATIONS
National rate in UK: 0870 432 8633
Quote Best Loved

ACCESS CODES
Not applicable

MIDSHIRES

"It was a delight to be able to return to such a pleasant hotel"

THE RT HON JOHN MAJOR, FORMER PRIME MINISTER

THE GREENWAY

Country house

Shurdington, Cheltenham,
Gloucestershire GL51 4UG

T (UK) 0870 432 8636
T 01242 862352
F 01242 862780
greenway@bestloved.com
www.greenway.bestloved.com

GENERAL MANAGER
Andrew Mackay

ROOM RATES
1 Single   £99
18 Doubles/Twins   £150
1 Four-poster   £260
1 Suite   £280
Includes full breakfast and VAT

CREDIT CARDS
AMERICAN EXPRESS • DC • MC • VI

RATINGS & AWARDS
RAC Blue Ribbon ★★★
Dining Award 3
AA ★★★ ✿✿
AA Top 200 - 2004/2005

FACILITIES
On site: Garden, heli-pad, croquet,
licensed for weddings
2 meeting rooms/max 40 people
Nearby: Golf, fishing, clay pigeon
shooting, tennis, swimming, riding

RESTRICTIONS
Limited facilities for disabled guests
No smoking in restaurant
No pets in public areas

ATTRACTIONS
The Cotswolds, Stratford-upon-Avon,
Bath, Cheltenham Spa, Painswick,
Wye Valley, Sudeley Castle,
Forest of Dean, Cirencester Polo Park

NEAREST
CITY:
Cheltenham - 2 ½ miles/5 mins
Gloucester - 5 miles/15 mins

AIRPORT:
Birmingham - 60 miles/1 hr 30 mins
Bristol - 45 miles/50 mins

RAIL STATION:
Cheltenham - 2 ½ miles/5 mins

AFFILIATIONS
von Essen Hotels
Celebrated Hotels Collection
Grand Heritage Hotels

RESERVATIONS
National rate in UK: 0870 432 8636
Toll free in US: 800-322-2403
or 888-96-GRAND
Quote Best Loved

ACCESS CODES
AMADEUS UI GLOGRE
APOLLO/GALILEO UI 08838
SABRE/ABACUS UI 30477
WORLDSPAN UI 42525

A long-standing reputation for excellence in the Cotswolds

One of Britain's first country house hotels, The Greenway retains an enviable reputation for its peerless style and welcoming atmosphere. Guests can enjoy a genuine country-house experience with all the personalised attention to detail you would expect from the hostess of an elegant private home. The setting is glorious, too, with the Cotswold Hills for a backdrop and extensive gardens where the huge old yew hedges look like a scene straight out of Alice in Wonderland.

The Greenway's public rooms are delightfully furnished in fresh and pretty yellow and green tones. Gleaming antique furniture adds a mellow note, and there are cosy log fires in winter. In summer, there is a lovely indoor-outdoor feel as the bar opens onto the lawn, while the restaurant overlooks a sunken garden and lily pond. Bedrooms are generously proportioned and traditionally furnished, and are divided between the main house and a Georgian coach house, where original elements like the wooden beams and stalls have been cleverly incorporated in the design.

The Greenway is ideally placed for visiting the Cotswolds' numerous beauty spots, quaint villages and the spa town of Cheltenham, as well as Shakespeare's hometown, Stratford-upon-Avon.

LOCATION

Leave the M5 at exit 11A for the A417 (Cirencester). At the A46, turn left toward Cheltenham. The hotel is one mile on the right.

Map p. 446, grid H3

197

Village hotel

THE HOSTE ARMS

An exotic African twist amongst good food, drink and art

Of all Britain's villages, Burnham Market is arguably the most beautiful. In this time after the railways' departure from North Norfolk, the region's treasures and character happily coexist in unhurried peace - and this village is no exception, located in an area of Outstanding Natural Beauty with a fascinating coastline populated by all sorts of interesting gems. In the centre of Burnham Market is the Hoste Arms, once frequented by Lord Nelson and now thriving under the ownership of Paul Whittome.

The hotel's modern-day renaissance is in part due to a well-established reputation for good food, and the menu revels in temptation. The original bedrooms are pretty and well-appointed, but it is the intriguing South African wing that needs a special mention here; with eight bedrooms, including the penthouse and the Zulu Suite, there is something to lure every guest! Designed by Paul's South African wife, Jeanne, the rooms offer beds with leather headboards and zebra-print throws, ostrich-feather lampshades, walk-in wardrobes and televisions that appear at a flick of a switch - described by one critic as James Bond-esque.

'My aim has been to develop the Hoste to the most popular inn in England, combining my love of people, food, drink, music and art', says Paul. What a success he has made of it!

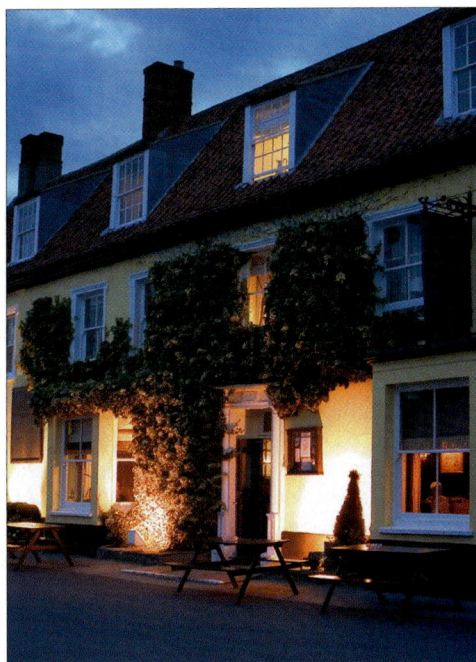

LOCATION

Located two miles from the A149, between Brancaster and Wells-next-the-Sea.

The Green, Burnham Market,
Norfolk PE31 8HD

T (UK) 0870 432 8649
T 01328 738777
F 01328 730103
hostearms@bestloved.com
www.hostearms.bestloved.com

OWNER
Paul Whittome

EXECUTIVE MANAGER
Emma Tagg

RATES PER PERSON
3 Singles   £78 - £138
19 Doubles/Twins   £54 - £103
4 Four-posters   £68 - £103
1 Penthouse   £84 - £118
Includes full breakfast and VAT

CREDIT CARDS
MC • VI

RATINGS & AWARDS
AA ★★ ❀❀ 77%

FACILITIES
On site: Garden
3 meeting rooms/max 80 people
Nearby: Golf, yachting, tennis, fitness centre, hunting/shooting, riding

RESTRICTIONS
Limited facilities for disabled guests
Pets by arrangement

ATTRACTIONS
Caithness Crystal, Holkham Hall, Pensthorpe Waterfowl Park, Sealife Centre, Sandringham, Norfolk Broads

NEAREST
CITY:
Norwich - 35 miles/45 mins

AIRPORT:
Norwich - 35 miles/45 mins
Stansted - 75 miles/1 hr 30 mins

RAIL STATION:
Kings Lynn - 22 miles/35 mins

AFFILIATIONS
The Great Inns of Britain

RESERVATIONS
National rate in UK: 0870 432 8649
Quote Best Loved

ACCESS CODES
Not applicable

MIDSHIRES

> His aim is to give diners new and enjoyable flavour combinations to encourage them to experiment and expand their gastronomic horizons
>
> MARTIN ISARK, WINE INTERNATIONAL

HOTEL DES CLOS

Restaurant with rooms

Old Lenton Lane, Nottingham, Nottinghamshire NG7 2SA

T (UK) 0870 432 8650
T 0115 986 6566
F 0115 986 0343
desclos@bestloved.com
www.desclos.bestloved.com

OWNER
Michael T Doak

ROOM RATES
Single occupancy	£100
4 Doubles/Twins	£110
5 Suites	£150

Excludes VAT and breakfast

CREDIT CARDS
AMERICAN EXPRESS • DC • MC • VI

RATINGS & AWARDS
AA ✿✿✿ Restaurant with Rooms
AA Top 200 - 2004/2005
Les Routiers Hotel of the Year 2003

FACILITIES
On site: Garden
1 meeting room/max 60 people
Nearby: Golf, fishing, swimming

RESTRICTIONS
Limited facilities for disabled guests
No children under 12 years
No pets; guide dogs only

ATTRACTIONS
Sherwood Forest,
Nottingham City and Castle,
Belvoir Castle, Newstead Abbey,
Wollaton Hall, Caves of Nottingham,
Angel Row Gallery

NEAREST
CITY:
Nottingham

AIRPORT:
Nottingham EMA - 13 miles/15 mins

RAIL STATION:
Nottingham - 3 miles/10 mins

AFFILIATIONS
Les Routiers

RESERVATIONS
National rate in UK: 0870 432 8650
Quote Best Loved

ACCESS CODES
Not applicable

MIDSHIRES

An incomparable hotel and dining experience bordering Nottingham city

The Hotel des Clos and Restaurant Sat Bains are conveniently situated on the banks of Nottingham's River Trent just five minutes from the city centre. Originally, the hotel was a dairy farm adjoining the breeding farm of Edward, Prince of Wales - who later chose Mrs Simpson and abdicated the throne. It is suggested that the Prince used to buy supplies from the farm for his house and cattle.

The hotel lives up to its claim of being 'not quite town' yet 'not quite country' - but one thing for sure, however, is that it is home to the only Michelin award in the county. The kitchen bakes fresh bread twice daily, and head chef Sat Bains, winner of the Roux Scholarship, is passionate about cooking and quality of produce. Above all, he endeavours to excite people with food, and his dinner menu includes such creations as carpaccio of tuna with candied violets and roast Cornish turbot with artichoke and wild asparagus.

A converted Victorian farm, the hotel encompasses nine elegant, stylishly decorated bedrooms with fine antiques and furnishings. This delightful establishment offers a peaceful ambience ensuring a memorable stay. The hotel boasts a stream of awards, including a Michelin star. For the business traveller, proximity to town makes this the ideal rest place, while the hotel's pretty courtyard gardens add the finishing touches to an intimate wedding celebration.

LOCATION
From the M1, exit junction 24 for the A453 (Nottingham), then the A52; take the first left, signed Lenton Lane Industrial Estate. At the roundabout, take the first exit (Boots), then a sharp left for 500 yards.

> " At last, a first-class luxury hotel in Cambridge "
>
> PRESTON EPSTEIN, CELEBRATED HOTELS COLLECTION

City hotel

HOTEL FELIX

Long-awaited contemporary luxury in historic Cambridge

Historic Cambridge has long lacked a stylish, privately-owned hotel, but all that changed with the opening of Hotel Felix in 2002. Originally built as a Victorian mansion in 1852, the hotel is now a chic and contemporary property, providing 52 wonderfully elegant bedrooms. For those in the know, this is the sister hotel of the luxury red-starred Grange Hotel in York.

Graffiti, the hotel's restaurant, serves excellent modern Mediterranean food in lovely surroundings where the walls are hung with large specially-commissioned canvasses. Tables overlook the terrace and gardens, where al fresco dining is available during the summer months. The adjoining bar is a relaxed and welcoming area for less formal dining and drinks, and there are also three connecting rooms ideal for private functions and meetings. All bedrooms are generously sized and gracefully styled, and for special occasions there is a sumptuous and very private suite up in the eaves.

Set in landscaped gardens and surrounded by fields, Hotel Felix is the perfect location from which to explore Cambridge and the surrounding countryside. It's less than a mile from the city centre and just 20 minutes' drive from the famous Newmarket racecourse, with ample car parking facilities.

LOCATION

Exit the M11 at junction 13 onto the A1303 for Cambridge; then follow signs for Huntingdon A14 to reach the A1307. Whitehouse Lane is halfway down the road on the right.

Whitehouse Lane,
Huntingdon Road, Cambridge,
Cambridgeshire CB3 0LX

T (UK) 0870 432 8653
T 01223 277977
F 01223 277973
felix@bestloved.com
www.felix.bestloved.com

OWNER
Jeremy Cassel

GENERAL MANAGER
Shara Ross

ROOM RATES
Single occupancy   £132 - £182
48 Doubles/Twins   £163 - £203
4 Junior Suites   £250 - £270
Includes continental breakfast and VAT

CREDIT CARDS
AMERICAN EXPRESS • DC • JCB • MC • VI

RATINGS & AWARDS
ETC ★★★★ Silver Award
AA ★★★★ ❀❀ 76%

FACILITIES
On site: Garden
4 meeting rooms/max 100 people
Nearby: Golf, riding

RESTRICTIONS
No pets in public rooms

ATTRACTIONS
King's College Chapel,
punting on the Cam,
Fitzwilliam Museum, Botanic Gardens,
Great St Mary's Church,
Houghton Mill,
Newmarket Racecourse

NEAREST
CITY:
Cambridge

AIRPORT:
Stansted - 30 miles/40 mins

RAIL STATION:
Cambridge - 1 mile/5 mins

AFFILIATIONS
Celebrated Hotels Collection
Grand Heritage Hotels
The European Connection

RESERVATIONS
National rate in UK: 0870 432 8653
Toll free in US: 800-322-2403
or 888-93-GRAND
Quote Best Loved

ACCESS CODES
AMADEUS UI CBGFEL
APOLLO/GALILEO UI 54800
SABRE/ABACUS UI 48639
WORLDSPAN UI 43006

MIDSHIRES

"The guide didn't do it justice! Perfection

MR & MRS TAYLOR, PENNSYLVANIA USA

HOTEL ON THE PARK

Townhouse

Evesham Road, Cheltenham,
Gloucestershire GL52 2AH

T (UK) 0870 432 8655
T 01242 518898
F 01242 511526
onthepark@bestloved.com
www.onthepark.bestloved.com

OWNER
Darryl Gregory

ROOM RATES
Single occupancy	£89
9 Doubles/Twins	£114 - £135
1 Junior Suite	£145
1 Four-poster	£164
1 Jacuzzi	£164

Includes VAT

CREDIT CARDS
AMERICAN EXPRESS • DC • MC

RATINGS & AWARDS
ETC ★★★ Gold Award Hotel
RAC Gold Ribbon ★★★ Dining Award 4
AA ★★★ ⊛⊛
AA Top 200 - 2004/2005

FACILITIES
On site: Garden,
'The Bacchanalian' Restaurant
1 meeting room/max 18 people
Nearby: Golf, riding, fishing

RESTRICTIONS
No facilities for disabled guests
No children under 8 years
No smoking in bedrooms
or restaurant
Pets by arrangement

ATTRACTIONS
The Cotswolds, Pittville Pump Room,
Gustav Holst's birthplace,
Sudeley Castle, Cheltenham Races

NEAREST
CITY:
Birmingham - 49 miles/1 hr

AIRPORT:
Birmingham - 49 miles/1hr

RAIL STATION:
Cheltenham - 2 miles/10 mins

AFFILIATIONS
Fine Individual Hotels
Preston's Global Hotels
Cotswolds Finest Hotels

RESERVATIONS
National rate in UK: 0870 432 8655
Toll free in US: 800-544-9993
Quote Best Loved

ACCESS CODES
Not applicable

Regency elegance in the centre of the Cotswolds

This beautifully restored Regency building is the finest townhouse hotel in the Cheltenham area, and is perfectly located for touring the Cotswolds and surrounding towns of interest, including historic Stratford-upon-Avon and Bath. It is in a superb position overlooking Pittville Park, yet only a short walk from Cheltenham town centre and the National Hunt Racecourse.

This exclusive privately-owned hotel has the air of a private club, yet offers welcoming and unstuffy hospitality. The bedrooms are individually designed and dressed with traditional fabrics, crisp Egyptian cotton sheets, fine antiques and porcelain, with original paintings adorning the walls.

All rooms feature en-suite bathrooms, some with ball-and-claw baths. There is an elegant candlelit drawing room and bar and an intimate library with a crackling log fire to read and relax in. The hotel is privileged to have as its restaurant The Bacchanalian; food is prepared by Lucy Hyder, whose modern British cuisine is highly acclaimed - she has won no fewer than 15 national awards.

LOCATION
In the Regency spa town of Cheltenham. Take the A435, signposted Evesham, from the town centre; the hotel is on the left opposite Pittville Park.

"As usual - elegance, style and homely attention. Everyone should know about you (or maybe not)!"

CAROLE SHADBOLT, OXFORD

Townhouse

KEGWORTH HOUSE HOTEL

Business or pleasure - just two minutes off the M1!

Owners Tony and Di Belcher have lovingly nurtured their relaxing village hotel to create wonderfully indulgent accommodation! A fresh appearance, spacious accommodation and a refreshingly light colour scheme combine to create a pleasant mix of traditional and modern; it all adds up to a homely feel, together with a real sense of history - some parts of the building are 350 years old. Their wonderful traditional walled garden is an idyllic setting for a relaxing day's reading, or even the occasional croquet match; the garden also has a secret, and you'll have to speak to Tony and Di for details!

Breakfasts here are excellent, and for dinner (by arrangement), a five-course table d'hôte is available. In keeping with the country-house atmosphere, vegetables in the kitchen are taken from the hotel's own garden whenever possible. Private dining can also be arranged for up to 16 people, making the hotel an excellent choice for a corporate retreat.

Kegworth House is refreshingly simple to get to from all corners of the country, with access to the M1, M42 and A50 only two minutes away. And there is plenty to do in the surrounding area - the Derbyshire Dales, Nottingham, Leicester, Derby, Donington Park race circuit and Rutland Water are all nearby.

LOCATION
Exit 24 off the M1 for the A6 (Loughborough) to Kegworth. Take the first right to the junction with the high street and turn left; the hotel is 65 yards on the left.

42 High Street, Kegworth, Derby, Derbyshire DE74 2DA

T (UK) 0870 432 8669
T 01509 672575
F 01509 670645
kegworth@bestloved.com
www.kegworth.bestloved.com

OWNERS
Tony and Di Belcher

ROOM RATES
Single occupancy	£79
5 Doubles	£95
4 Executive Doubles	£140
1 Suite	£195
Includes full breakfast and VAT	

CREDIT CARDS
AMERICAN EXPRESS • DC • JCB • MC • VI

RATINGS & AWARDS
AA ♦♦♦♦♦
AA Premier Collection

FACILITIES
On site: Garden
1 meeting room/max 16 people
Nearby: Golf, walking, boating

RESTRICTIONS
Children by arrangement
No smoking throughout
Pets by arrangement

ATTRACTIONS
Nottingham, Alton Towers, Newstead Abbey, Donington Park Raceway, Rutland Water, Derbyshire Dales, Staunton Harold Reservoir

NEAREST
CITY:
Derby - 11 miles/15 mins
Nottingham - 15 miles/20 mins

AIRPORT:
Nottingham EMA - 3 miles/6 mins
Birmingham - 40 miles/50 mins

RAIL STATION:
Derby - 11 miles/15 mins
Loughborough - 6 miles/10 mins

AFFILIATIONS
Independent

RESERVATIONS
National rate in UK: 0870 432 8669
Quote Best Loved

ACCESS CODES
Not applicable

MIDSHIRES

LACE MARKET HOTEL

Townhouse

MIDSHIRES

29 - 31 High Pavement,
Nottingham,
Nottinghamshire NG1 1HE

T (UK) 0870 432 8677
T 0115 8523232
F 0115 8523223
lacemarket@bestloved.com
www.lacemarket.bestloved.com

GENERAL MANAGER
Mark Cox

ROOM RATES
6 Singles	£90
17 Doubles/Twins	£110
11 Kings	£135
5 Superior Doubles	£169
3 Studios	£225

Includes VAT

CREDIT CARDS
AMERICAN EXPRESS • MC • VI

RATINGS & AWARDS
AA ★★★★ ❀ 68%
AA Town House

FACILITIES
On site: Restaurant, bar
3 meeting rooms/max 60 people
Nearby: Complimentary use of
local health club

RESTRICTIONS
Limited facilities for disabled guests
No children in restaurant after 8 p.m.
Smoking in bars only
Pets by arrangement

ATTRACTIONS
Nottingham Castle,
National Watersports Centre,
shopping, Wollaton Hall,
Belvoir Castle, Southwell Minster

NEAREST
CITY:
Nottingham

AIRPORT:
Nottingham EMA - 10 miles/20 mins

RAIL STATION:
Nottingham - ½ mile/5 mins

AFFILIATIONS
Design Hotels
The European Connection

RESERVATIONS
National rate in UK: 0870 432 8677
Quote Best Loved

ACCESS CODES
AMADEUS DS NOTLAC
APOLLO/GALILEO DS 17730
SABRE/ABACUS DS 47815
WORLDSPAN DS 05887

New and old combine in a successful combination of radical chic

In spite of the name, there isn't a lace doily or antimacassar in sight at the Lace Market Hotel. The exterior may be mature Georgian elegance, but the interior is very much of today - radical chic and cool minimalist.

Looking past the Georgian façade with its stately sash windows and classical portico, the interior is a totally refreshing juxtaposition of original architraves and coving with the sleek modern lines of brushed steel, smooth polished wood and custom-designed furniture. The wonderful sense of space is counterbalanced by warming earth colours. Of course, all the bedrooms have every modern convenience, including trendy bathrooms with glass basins and large, self-indulgent baths.

The hotel reflects the ambience of the newly restored Lace Market area of Nottingham, which buzzes with lively restaurants, wine bars, clubs and boutiques happily mixing young and old in every dimension. This small townhouse hotel is right in the heart of this contemporary revival. Its bar and restaurant, Merchants, combines European influences with today's British cuisine for a thoroughly modern flavour. The restaurant has recently undergone an extensive renovation - oak-panelling, a walk-in wine cave and red leather banquettes create a stunning blend of old and new in one of the hippest venues in town.

LOCATION

Follow signs for the city centre; then, follow brown signs for the Lace Market, Galleries of Justice and St Mary's Church.

Village hotel

THE LAMB AT BURFORD

The perfect Cotswold combination - a fine heritage hotel, pub, and great food

If you have stowed away an idyllic vision of the perfect English country hotel, The Lamb at Burford might just be the place - its unbeatable Cotswold location is combined with such traditional delights as stone floors, log fires, cosy furnishings and a peaceful garden. All 15 bedrooms (with evening baby-listening service available) are beautifully furnished, with views of the hotel's courtyard or Burford's charming side streets. And perhaps it's spoiling a surprise, but you'll find homemade cookies waiting in your room when you arrive.

In the kitchen, newly-appointed head chef Adrian Jones brings along the experience of a widely-varied 20-year career, and as an unflagging devotion to the Cotswolds' local larder. His unmistakably English style is elegantly accented by 'rootsy' and 'earthy' influences, in the form of Bibury trout, Evesham asparagus and a whole host of other local delicacies. Guests are welcome to dine in the garden, or in the classic comfort of the bar (well-stocked with draught local ales and a great wine list); children are especially welcome, and dine for half price.

There's a wealth of nearby attractions, from Burford High Street - voted 'Best Antique Shopping Street in Britain' by BBC Homes and Antiques magazine - to Blenheim Palace, Chedworth Roman Villa, Bibury Trout Farm or Cotswold Farm Park.

LOCATION

Twenty miles west of Oxford at the A40/A361 crossroads. From Burford high street, take the first left into Sheep Street. The hotel is 400m along on the right.

Sheep Street, Burford,
Oxfordshire OX18 4LR

T (UK) 0870 432 8681
T 01993 823155
F 01993 822228
lamb@bestloved.com
www.lamb.bestloved.com

OWNERS
Bruno and Rachel Cappuccini

ROOM RATES
9 Doubles/Twins   £130 - £160
6 Superior doubles   £140 - £200
Includes full breakfast and VAT

CREDIT CARDS
MC • VI

RATINGS & AWARDS
AA ★★★ ✿✿ 74%

FACILITIES
On site: Garden, courtyard, al fresco dining, traditional walled garden
1 meeting room/max 20 people
Nearby: Golf, fishing, riding, shooting, walking

RESTRICTIONS
No facilities for disabled guests
No smoking in bedrooms

ATTRACTIONS
Oxford, Bath, Cotswold Wildlife Park, Roman town of Cirencester, Stratford-upon-Avon, Blenheim Palace, Warwick Castle

NEAREST
CITY:
Oxford - 19 miles/25 mins

AIRPORT:
Birmingham - 60 miles/1 hr 30 mins
Heathrow - 65 miles/1 hr 10 mins

RAIL STATION:
Kingham - 10 miles/15 mins
Cheltenham - 22 miles/35 mins

AFFILIATIONS
Independent

RESERVATIONS
National rate in UK: 0870 432 8681
Quote Best Loved

ACCESS CODES
Not applicable

MIDSHIRES

Once in a blue moon it is still possible to come across a country house that makes one want to jump for joy

CRAIG BROWN, SUNDAY TIMES

LANGAR HALL

Restaurant with rooms

Langar,
Nottinghamshire NG13 9HG

T (UK) 0870 432 8682
T 01949 860559
F 01949 861045
langar@bestloved.com
www.langar.bestloved.com

OWNER
Imogen Skirving

ROOM RATES
Single occupancy   £65 - £100
8 Doubles/Twins   £100 - £140
1 Four-poster   £185
1 Suite   £185
Includes full breakfast and VAT

CREDIT CARDS
AMERICAN EXPRESS • DC • MC • VI

RATINGS & AWARDS
ETC ★★★ Silver Award
AA ★★★ ✿✿ 73%

FACILITIES
On site: Garden, heli-pad, fishing, croquet, licensed for weddings, children's adventure play area
2 meeting rooms/max 45 people
Nearby: Golf, riding, fitness, fishing, shooting, parachuting/parascending/hang-gliding, motorsport

RESTRICTIONS
Limited facilities for disabled guests
Smoking in sitting rooms only
Pets by arrangement

ATTRACTIONS
Newark antique fairs, Trent Bridge cricket, Nottingham Forest football, Belvoir Castle, Chatsworth House, Southwell and Lincoln cathedrals, Sherwood Forest, Hardwick Hall, Belton House, motorsport centre

NEAREST
CITY:
Nottingham - 12 miles/20 mins

AIRPORT:
Nottingham EMA - 20 miles/30 mins

RAIL STATION:
Grantham/Bingham - 4 miles/15 mins

AFFILIATIONS
Independent

RESERVATIONS
National rate in UK: 0870 432 8682
Quote Best Loved

ACCESS CODES
Not applicable

MIDSHIRES

A house of uncommon charm in the beautiful Vale of Belvoir

Langar Hall was built in 1837 on the site of a great historic house, the home of Admiral Lord Howe. It stands in quiet seclusion overlooking lovely gardens beyond which sheep graze among ancient trees; below the croquet lawn lies a romantic network of medieval fishponds stocked with carp.

This charming hotel is the family home of Imogen Skirving, who combines the standards of good hotelkeeping with the hospitality of an informal country house where children are welcome. Most of the bedrooms enjoy lovely views, and every one is quiet, comfortable and well-equipped, particularly for guests who have business in Nottingham.

Downstairs, explore the study, a quiet room for reading and meetings; the white sitting room, perfect for afternoon tea and drinks before dinner; the Indian room, ideal for private parties and conferences; and the dining room. This elegant pillared hall is open every day for lunch and dinner and is a popular neighbourhood restaurant serving fresh seasonal food with an emphasis on game in winter and fish in summer. With all this in mind, Langar Hall is also particularly suited to exclusive house parties.

LOCATION
Off the A52 between Nottingham and Grantham; turn at Bingham. Or, between Newark and Leicester off the A46 through Cropwell Bishop; both routes are signposted.

> "Le Manoir is one of the most sumptuous country house hotels in Great Britain and its restaurant the best in the nation"
>
> MICHAEL BALTER, BON APPETIT

Country house   LE MANOIR AUX QUAT' SAISONS

Le Manoir aux Quat' Saisons ... everything as it should be

Nestled in secluded and beautiful grounds a few miles south of the historic university town of Oxford, Le Manoir aux Quat' Saisons is one of Europe's finest restaurants and a lovely country house hotel. Le Manoir is the inspired creation of chef Raymond Blanc, whose extraordinary cooking has received the highest tributes from all international guides to culinary excellence. Uniquely, the Times gave Blanc's cooking 10 out of 10 and rated it 'the best in Britain'.

The restaurant is the natural focus of this lovely 15th-century manor house which stands in landscaped gardens, its sweeping lawns set against a backdrop of fine trees. A feature of the estate is a carefully-tended vegetable garden which supplies the kitchen with the finest and freshest organic produce. The atmosphere throughout is one of understated elegance, and all 32 bedrooms and suites offer guests the highest standards of comfort and luxury. Every need is anticipated, and service is a way of life here, never intrusive but always present - in the words of the Daily Telegraph, 'It is as if the entire staff has been touched by spirits beyond the reach of sordid commerce'.

LOCATION

From London, exit 7 on the M40. Turn left onto the A329 (Wallingford). The hotel is signed after one mile.

Church Road, Great Milton, Oxford, Oxfordshire OX44 7PD

T (UK) 0870 432 8683
T 01844 278881
F 01844 278847
manoir@bestloved.com
www.manoir.bestloved.com

OWNER
Raymond Blanc

GENERAL MANAGER
Jonathan Orr-Ewing

ROOM RATES
2 Standard Doubles	£275 - £300
4 Deluxe Doubles	£345 - £395
13 Superior Doubles	£465 - £495
5 Junior Suites	£510 - £575
7 Suites	£670 - £895
1 2-Bedroom Suite	£1,250
Includes VAT	

CREDIT CARDS
AMERICAN EXPRESS • DC • JCB • MC • VI

RATINGS & AWARDS
RAC Gold Ribbon ★★★★
Dining Award 5
AA ★★★★ ⊛⊛⊛⊛⊛
AA Top 200 - 2004/2005
The Which? Guide Hotel of the Year 2004

FACILITIES
On site: Heli-pad, croquet, licensed for weddings, cookery school 1 meeting room/max 50 people
Nearby: Fishing, golf, clay pigeon shooting, riding

RESTRICTIONS
No smoking in restaurant
Pets by arrangement

ATTRACTIONS
The Cotswolds, Blenheim Palace, Windsor Castle, Waddesdon Manor, Oxford

NEAREST
CITY:
Oxford - 7 miles/15 mins

AIRPORT:
Heathrow - 40 miles/45 mins

RAIL STATION:
Oxford - 7 miles/15 mins

AFFILIATIONS
Relais & Châteaux

RESERVATIONS
National rate in UK: 0870 432 8683
Toll free in US: 800-845-4274
or 800-735-2478
Quote Best Loved

ACCESS CODES
APOLLO/GALILEO WB 14966
SABRE/ABACUS WB 11557
WORLDSPAN WB GB04

MIDSHIRES

A veritable haven of peace and tranquillity

ANTHONY DONALDSON, LONDON

LORDS OF THE MANOR
Country house

**Upper Slaughter,
Near Bourton-on-the-Water,
Gloucestershire GL54 2JD**

T (UK) 0870 432 8693
T 01451 820243
F 01451 820696
lords@bestloved.com
www.lords.bestloved.com

RESIDENT MANAGER
Nicholas Davies

ROOM RATES
2 Singles £100
16 Doubles/Twins £160 - £245
6 Old Rectory Rooms £145 - £310
3 Suites £265 - £310
Includes full breakfast, service and VAT

CREDIT CARDS
AMERICAN EXPRESS • DC • JCB • MC • VI

RATINGS & AWARDS
RAC Gold Ribbon ★★★ Dining Award 4
AA ★★★
AA Top 200 - 2004/2005

FACILITIES
On site: Garden, fishing, croquet,
licensed for weddings
1 meeting room/max 20 people
Nearby: Clay pigeon shooting,
archery, golf, riding, quad biking

RESTRICTIONS
Limited facilities for disabled guests
No children under 7 years in
restaurant for dinner
No smoking in restaurant

ATTRACTIONS
The Cotswolds, Blenheim Palace,
Oxford, Stratford-upon-Avon,
Sudeley Castle, Hidcote Gardens

NEAREST
CITY:
Oxford - 35 miles/40 mins

AIRPORT:
Heathrow - 80 miles/1 hr 45 mins
Birmingham - 45 miles/1 hr 15 mins

RAIL STATION:
Moreton-in-Marsh - 8 miles/20 mins

AFFILIATIONS
Celebrated Hotels Collection
Small Luxury Hotels
Cotswolds Finest Hotels

RESERVATIONS
National rate in UK: 0870 432 8693
Toll free in US: 800-322-2403
or 800-872-4564
Quote Best Loved

ACCESS CODES
AMADEUS LX BRSLOM
APOLLO/GALILEO LX 32333
SABRE/ABACUS LX 31994
WORLDSPAN LX GLOLM

Paradise found in the heart of the Cotswolds

The Lords of the Manor is a 17th-century country house hotel in the heart of the Cotswolds. Built in 1650, this former rectory stands in eight acres of secluded gardens and parkland in Upper Slaughter, one of the Cotswolds' prettiest and most unspoilt villages.

Comfortable surroundings, big roaring fires, beautifully tended, well-loved gardens and croquet on the lawn create an idyllic setting. The award-winning restaurant at the Lords of the Manor has a fine reputation for its locally-sourced cuisine, while the rambling cellar produces a wine list to complement even the most diverse palate. All the bedrooms are furnished with period pieces, giving each room an individual character.

For leisure activities, guests can enjoy a game of croquet or try their hands at coarse fishing on the lake. Riding, golf and game and clay pigeon shooting can be arranged locally. The Lords of the Manor is also ideally situated to explore many of the honey-stoned villages which have made the Cotswolds a notable area for a truly memorable stay.

LOCATION
2 miles off the A429 between Stow-on-the-Wold and Bourton-on-the-Water, signed to the Slaughters.

> "A symphony of comfort and a vacation for the senses! Lower Slaughter Manor is our family's little slice of heaven"
>
> RON F DOCKSAI, WEST VIRGINIA

Country house
LOWER SLAUGHTER MANOR

A grand old English country home where food is taken very seriously

Off the beaten track in the heart of the Cotswolds runs a tiny part of England that the rapacious path of progress seems to have left alone: the River Eye, drifting under small stone bridges and between honey-coloured houses. In this Elysian scene stands Lower Slaughter Manor, built in 1658 by Valentine Strong for the High Sheriff of Gloucestershire, in whose family it remained for the next 300 years.

Today, it's yours to explore. Lower Slaughter Manor is a true country house hotel with a wonderful feeling of spaciousness, style and dignity, where the experienced staff tend the needs of visitors in the good old-fashioned manner of a family home. The Manor is furnished with antiques and four-poster beds blending happily with elegant china, beautiful paintings and sumptuous soft furnishings. Every bedroom has its own personality, with homemade biscuits and English toffees to welcome you.

All this is a good enough reason to enjoy this home from home, but there is a much more compelling purpose to this grand old Manor: the food - above all, the food! The restaurant has delighted the critics, leaving them bereft of superlatives.

LOCATION

Exit from the A424 (Burford-Stow-on-the-Wold) traffic lights for the A429 (Cirencester). After a mile and a half turn right for The Slaughters; the hotel is on the right after two bends.

Lower Slaughter, Gloucestershire GL54 2HP

T (UK) 0870 432 8695
T 01451 820456
F 01451 822150
slaughter@bestloved.com
www.slaughter.bestloved.com

GENERAL MANAGER
Anne Tarver

ROOM RATES
Single occupancy £150 - £325
16 Doubles/Twins £175 - £325
2 Four-posters £325
3 Suites £325 - £375
Includes early morning tea, full breakfast and VAT

CREDIT CARDS
AMERICAN EXPRESS • DC • MC • VI

RATINGS & AWARDS
RAC Blue Ribbon ★★★ Dining Award 2
AA ★★★ ❀❀
AA Top 200 - 2004/2005
Recommended Hotel & Restaurant - Andrew Harper's Hideaway Report

FACILITIES
On site: Heli-pad, croquet, tennis
2 meeting rooms/max 40 people
Nearby: Golf, fishing, riding, clay pigeon shooting

RESTRICTIONS
No facilities for disabled guests
No children under 12 years (discretionary)
No smoking in the restaurant

ATTRACTIONS
The Cotswolds, Bath, Oxford, Stratford-upon-Avon, Blenheim Palace

NEAREST
CITY:
Cheltenham - 18 miles/30 mins

AIRPORT:
Bristol - 55 miles/1 hr
Heathrow - 80 miles/1 hr 45 mins

RAIL STATION:
Kingham - 4 miles/10 mins

AFFILIATIONS
von Essen Hotels
Celebrated Hotels Collection
Leading Small Hotels

RESERVATIONS
National rate in UK: 0870 432 8695
Toll free in US: 800-322-2403
Quote Best Loved

ACCESS CODES
AMADEUS YX OXFLOW
APOLLO/GALILEO YX 71739
SABRE/ABACUS YX 57491
WORLDSPAN YX OXFLO
PEGASUS YXOXFMAN

MIDSHIRES

Mallory Court is a place to which my thoughts when I am busy, bothered or harassed turn longingly back

WENDY ARNOLD, HISTORIC HOTELS OF ENGLAND

MALLORY COURT HOTEL

Country house

Harbury Lane, Bishops Tachbrook,
Leamington Spa,
Warwickshire CV33 9QB

T (UK) 0870 432 8699
T 01926 330214
F 01926 451714
mallory@bestloved.com
www.mallory.bestloved.com

GENERAL MANAGER
Andrew Grahame

ROOM RATES
Single occupancy   £135 - £270
18 Doubles/Twins   £185 - £320
11 Executive Doubles £155 - £165
Includes continental breakfast and VAT

CREDIT CARDS
AMERICAN EXPRESS • DC • MC • VI

RATINGS & AWARDS
RAC ★★★ Dining Award 3
AA ★★★ ❀❀❀
AA Top 200 - 2004/2005

FACILITIES
On site: Heli-pad, outdoor pool,
croquet, tennis
4 meeting rooms/max 200 people
Nearby: Golf, riding and fishing, spa,
clay pigeon shooting

RESTRICTIONS
No children under 9 years in restaurant
No smoking in restaurant
Pets by arrangement

ATTRACTIONS
Stratford-upon-Avon,
Cotswold villages, Warwick Castle,
National Exhibition Centre,
Royal Shakespeare Theatre,
Charlecote House, Coughton Court,
Royal Leamington Polo Club

NEAREST
CITY:
Birmingham - 30 miles/40 mins

AIRPORT:
Birmingham - 25 miles/30 mins

RAIL STATION:
Leamington Spa - 3 miles/5 mins

AFFILIATIONS
Relais & Châteaux

RESERVATIONS
National rate in UK: 0870 432 8699
Toll free in US: 800-322-2403
Quote Best Loved

ACCESS CODES
AMADEUS WBBHXMAL
APOLLO/GALILEO WB14949
SABRE/ABACUS WB11541
WORLDSPAN WBGB14

MIDSHIRES

The three essentials of country living: hospitality, comfort and superb cuisine

Mallory Court has long been regarded as one of the finest country houses in England, recreating the traditions of gracious hospitality with elegant décor and a cheerful, unobtrusive staff. The house itself is built of mellow stone, an outstanding example of period architecture. Everything inside is polished and shining, and fresh flowers abound.

The 18 bedrooms in the house are luxuriously decorated, each as sumptuous as the next, offering stunning views across the 10 acres of grounds, including water gardens, rose gardens, croquet lawns and orchards. Many of the gardens' vegetables, herbs and fruits are used in the kitchen, where head chef Simon Haigh and his team prepare award-winning contemporary French and British cuisine.

Situated in the heart of England, Mallory Court has a beautiful setting surrounded by stunning countryside between Stratford-upon-Avon and Warwick, with views from the house drifting over the grounds to the Warwickshire countryside. Surprisingly accessible - just 3 miles from the M40 - Mallory Court is a wonderful venue for high-level business meetings or exclusive use, particularly since the completion of the stunning new Knights Suite, which incorporates 11 executive bedrooms and provides a contemporary contrast to the classic elegance of the main house.

LOCATION

Off the M40; from the south, three miles from, junction 13. From the north, three miles from junction 14.

> "Full of ambience, full of charm, full of lovely food - full of regrets at leaving"
> MR & MRS B, ASHBY DE LA ZOUCH

Country house

THE MALT HOUSE

Feel at home at this cosy, pleasant Cotswold hideaway

This 16th-century building originally provided the malt to make the ale for the village of Broad Campden. About a hundred years ago the malting house and its neighbouring cottages were combined together, creating today's charming property. The general atmosphere at the Malt House is utterly relaxed. Downstairs are a number of beautifully appointed rooms, providing cosy corners where guests can curl up with one of the hotel's many books - the window seat and fireside are particularly perfect places for this inactivity.

The bedrooms, some with king-sized beds, are pretty and traditional in décor, and it is evident that a great deal of thought has gone into making each one of them completely distinctive. There are many considerate details, too, ranging from flowers from the garden to fragrant bath oils. Each room has a view of the garden, which is almost indescribably beautiful with its orchard, stream and summer house. When the weather permits, there are many quiet corners here, too!

Owner Judi Wilkes is a mine of information when it comes to the surrounding attractions of the Cotswolds, and she will even create itineraries for special interest groups. This is the kind of place you could happily recommend to anyone.

LOCATION

In the village of Broad Campden, off the B4081 one mile west of Chipping Campden.

**Broad Campden,
Gloucestershire GL55 6UU**

T (UK) 0870 432 8701
T 01386 840295
F 01386 841334
malt@bestloved.com
www.malt.bestloved.com

OWNER
Judi Wilkes

ROOM RATES
6 Doubles/Twins   £95 - £134
1 Suite   £145 - £165
Includes full breakfast and VAT

CREDIT CARDS
AMERICAN EXPRESS • MC • VI

RATINGS & AWARDS
AA ◆◆◆◆◆
AA Premier Collection

FACILITIES
On site: Garden, croquet
1 meeting room/max 25 people
Nearby: Golf, riding, fishing

RESTRICTIONS
No facilities for disabled guests
No smoking throughout
No pets
Closed 24 - 30 Dec.

ATTRACTIONS
Stratford-upon-Avon,
Cotswold villages,
Warwick Castle,
Chipping Campden,
Cheltenham Races,
Oxford, Bath,
antiques, gardens

NEAREST
CITY:
Oxford - 35 miles/1 hr 15 mins

AIRPORT:
Birmingham - 32 miles/1 hr

RAIL STATION:
Moreton-in-Marsh - 2 miles/15 mins

AFFILIATIONS
Preston's Global Hotels

RESERVATIONS
National rate in UK: 0870 432 8701
Toll free in the US: 800-544-9993
Quote Best Loved

ACCESS CODES
Not applicable

MIDSHIRES

An oasis of peace and perfection

THE MANOR HOUSE

Country house

Barsham Road, Great Snoring,
Fakenham, Norfolk NR21 0HP

T (UK) 0870 432 8702
T 01328 820597
F 01328 820048
manornorfolk@bestloved.com
www.manornorfolk.bestloved.com

OWNER
Rosamund M Scoles

ROOM RATES
Single occupancy   £85
6 Doubles/Twins   £110 - £130
2 Sheltons Cottages £140
Includes early morning tea, full
breakfast and VAT

CREDIT CARDS
AMERICAN EXPRESS • JCB • MC • VI

RATINGS & AWARDS
Independent

FACILITIES
On site: Garden, heli-pad,
licensed for weddings
2 meeting rooms/max 40 people
Nearby: Riding, fishing, watersports

RESTRICTIONS
Limited facilities for disabled guests
Children by arrangement
Smoking in drawing room only
No pets

ATTRACTIONS
Norfolk Heritage Coast,
Sandringham House, Holkham Hall,
Norwich, Cambridge,
National Trust properties

NEAREST
CITY:
Norwich - 22 miles/30 mins

AIRPORT:
Heathrow - 115 miles/3 hrs
Stansted - 90 miles/2 hrs 30 mins

RAIL STATION:
King's Lynn - 22 miles/40 mins

AFFILIATIONS
Independent

RESERVATIONS
National rate in UK: 0870 432 8702
Quote Best Loved

ACCESS CODES
Not applicable

An historic home cradled in the timeless serenity of rural Norfolk

The Manor House at Great Snoring - even the name has a Rip van Winkle charm redolent of cottage gardens and church bells, cricket on the village green and afternoon tea served in delicate porcelain with scones and lashings of homemade jam. A nostalgic vision, perhaps - but if this England still exists, there is no better place to find it than right here in the unspoilt countryside of north Norfolk, just inland from the Heritage Coast.

Tucked behind the local church, the Grade II-listed Manor House is an architectural gem dating from 1500. It is home to the Scoles family and has just six homely bedrooms, ensuring a truly relaxed and personal atmosphere that makes you feel like a private guest rather than a paying one. This is a real English country house, full of character and furnished with family antiques in that apparently effortless style that interior designers struggle to recreate.

The good news now is that the Manor is also available for exclusive use and really is the perfect place for a house party, a family get-together or a holiday with a group of friends. The house can sleep 12 people from £950 per night, providing outstanding value for money. Truly a Best Loved hotel in every sense!

LOCATION
Great Snoring is three miles northeast of Fakenham off the A148. The hotel is behind the church, signposted to Barsham from the village street.

MIDSHIRES

Townhouse

MEADOWCROFT HOTEL

Trumpington Road, Cambridge,
Cambridgeshire CB2 2EX

T (UK) 0870 432 8706
T 01223 346120
F 01223 346138
meadowcroft@bestloved.com
www.meadowcroft.bestloved.com

OWNERS
Alison & Roger Foster

ROOM RATES
Single occupancy   £100 - £140
15 Doubles/Twins   £120 - £160
2 Four Posters   £140 - £180
Includes breakfast and VAT

CREDIT CARDS
AMERICAN EXPRESS • MC • VI

RATINGS & AWARDS
Awards Pending

FACILITIES
On site: Garden, croquet
1 meeting room/max 120 people
Nearby: Fishing, golf, pony riding,
fitness centre, swimming pool

RESTRICTIONS
Limited facilities for disabled guests
No smoking throughout
Pets by arrangement
Closed 25 Dec. - 4 Jan.

ATTRACTIONS
Cambridge University,
Imperial War Museum,
Wimpole Hall,
Fitzwilliam Museum,
punting on the Cam

NEAREST
CITY:
London - 55 miles/50 mins

AIRPORT:
Stansted - 30 miles/30 mins

RAIL STATION:
London King's Cross - 60 miles/55 mins

AFFILIATIONS
Independent

RESERVATIONS
National rate in UK: 0870 432 8706
Quote Best Loved

ACCESS CODES
Not applicable

MIDSHIRES

A peaceful Victorian haven just outside of Cambridge

Located just a mile from Cambridge centre, Meadowcroft Hotel offers tranquil, comfortable service without the faintest hint of city bustle. This lovely Victorian house has been carefully renovated to preserve its design and history whilst making the updates necessary to bring the hotel firmly into the modern era. Twelve light and airy bedrooms look out over the hotel gardens and offer such options as four-poster beds and, in several, sofa beds to accommodate entire families. A full valet service is also provided.

After a hearty English breakfast provided by the hotel's kitchen (their Brackenhurst Restaurant is also available for weddings and functions), it's time to take in the sights - and there are plenty of them, from Cambridge's historic splendour to the village of Grantchester, where Lord Byron lived when he was a student.

Meadowcroft is not a traditional 'conference hotel', but can nonetheless provide a splendid setting for small meetings without that impersonal business-hotel feel. For all, there's well-proportioned room to relax, from the calming garden to the intimate bar (complete with original Victorian fireplace) and the spacious lounge with exquisite wood-panelled fireplace. All in all, a haven with a little bit of heaven for every taste!

LOCATION

Leave the M11 at junction 11. Follow the A1309 toward the city centre for approximately two miles. The hotel is on the right.

Map p. 446, grid E6

NEW INN AT COLN

Inn

MIDSHIRES

Coln St-Aldwyns,
Near Cirencester,
Gloucestershire GL7 5AN

T (UK) 0870 432 8716
T 01285 750651
F 01285 750657
newinn@bestloved.com
www.newinn.bestloved.com

OWNER
Angela Kimmett

ROOM RATES
Single occupancy   £90 - £104
9 Doubles/Twins   £120 - £155
4 Four-posters   £155
Includes full breakfast and VAT

CREDIT CARDS
AMERICAN EXPRESS • MC • VI

RATINGS & AWARDS
RAC ★★ Dining Award 3
AA ★★ ✿✿ 80%

FACILITIES
On site: Private functions available
Nearby: Golf, riding, fishing,
water skiing

RESTRICTIONS
No facilities for disabled guests
No children under 10 years in
restaurant
No smoking in bedrooms or
restaurant
Pets by arrangement

ATTRACTIONS
Oxford, Bath, Westonbirt Arboretum,
the Cotswolds, Hidcote Gardens,
Sudeley & Berkeley Castles,
Cheltenham, Stratford-upon-Avon

NEAREST
CITY:
Oxford - 30 miles/40 mins

AIRPORT:
Heathrow - 70 miles/1 hr 15 mins
Birmingham - 70 miles/1 hr 15 mins

RAIL STATION:
Swindon - 18 miles/30 mins

AFFILIATIONS
Cotswolds Finest Hotels

RESERVATIONS
National rate in UK: 0870 432 8716
Quote Best Loved

ACCESS CODES
Not applicable

Founded in the reign of Elizabeth I - honoured in the reign of Elizabeth II

The New Inn at Coln was built 400 years ago, after Queen Elizabeth I decreed there should be a coaching inn within a day's travel of every major centre of population for the comfort and security of her subjects. It is still a great place to stay today - Angela Kimmett and staff welcome guests, willingly providing any help needed to enjoy the Cotswolds.

Each bedroom is a private castle of comfort, richly adorned with floral prints and English chintz curtains. The renowned restaurant serves food with flair, triumphantly reviving Old English recipes once long forgotten. Real ales, fine malt whiskies and a wide range of wines are there to be savoured beneath the ancient beams in the bar.

Away from the inn's dovecote and ivy-covered stone walls lie some of England's finest attractions. Dreamy cottages and lazy streams are on every Cotswold trail, and Oxford's quadrangles, Bath's regal squares and crescents and Cheltenham's racecourse are all within a short drive.

LOCATION
From the A40 (Burford), take the B4425 toward Bibury; turn left shortly after Aldsworth.

> **The whole experience of having dinner in the restaurant was the perfect end to our honeymoon**
>
> MR & MRS SCHONHUT, QUESTION OF SERVICE

Village hotel

THE NOEL ARMS

An historic inn with thoroughly modern service and unbeatable dining

Pass beneath the sign at this utterly charming historic hotel and you tread the footsteps of King Charles II, who came here to recover from his defeat by Oliver Cromwell at the Battle of Worcester in 1651. It was a fine old hostelry then - fit for a king, after all! - and it still is, although with the progress of time this Cotswold gem has become an appealing mix of the old and the new.

The bedrooms are quaint and quintessentially English, but also feature all modern comforts. If you can, ask for a night in the hotel's beautiful four-poster room, with a magnificent 17th-century carved bed to provide sweet dreams. Enjoy an unbeatable menu in The Oriental Restaurant, with Chinese, Japanese, Malaysian and Thai influences provided by chef Peter Xu, as well as a varied selection of vegetarian options and European dishes. The Dover's Bar, named after the founder of the famous Cotswold Olympick Games, offers original beams, and open log fire and a warm pub atmosphere in which to enjoy a pint of local ale and a bite from the light menu.

With its peaceful location in the village of Chipping Campden, the Noel Arms is also ideal for tracing the Cotswold Way, a beautiful tour of the British countryside that is certain to inspire - whether your travels take you by foot, cycle or car! There are a wealth of historic houses within easy reach, too, as well as Stratford-upon-Avon, Oxford and Cheltenham.

LOCATION

Chipping Campden is signposted off the A44 Oxford-Evesham road, five miles from Broadway. The hotel is in the high street.

High Street, Chipping Campden,
Gloucestershire GL55 6AT

T (UK) 0870 432 8718
T 01386 840317
F 01386 841136
noelarms@bestloved.com
www.noelarms.bestloved.com

OWNERS
Christa and Ian Taylor

ROOM RATES
Single occupancy   £100
23 Doubles/Twins   £135 - £175
2 Four-posters   £180 - £200
Includes full breakfast and VAT

CREDIT CARDS
AMERICAN EXPRESS • MC • VI

RATINGS & AWARDS
ETC ★★★
AA ★★★ ✿ 69%

FACILITIES
On site: Licensed for weddings
2 meeting rooms/max 50 people
Nearby: Golf, fishing, riding, walking, cycling

RESTRICTIONS
No facilities for disabled guests
Pets by arrangement

ATTRACTIONS
Bourton-on-the-Water, Blenheim Palace, Hidcote Gardens, Kiftsgate Gardens, Warwick Castle, Stratford-upon-Avon, antiques hunting, walking

NEAREST
CITY:
Oxford - 33 miles/45 mins
Cheltenham - 30 miles/40 mins

AIRPORT:
Heathrow - 78 miles/1 hr 45 mins
Birmingham - 30 miles/30 mins

RAIL STATION:
Moreton-in-Marsh - 7 miles/10 mins

AFFILIATIONS
Classic British Hotels

RESERVATIONS
National rate in UK: 0870 432 8718
or 0845 070 7090
Quote Best Loved

ACCESS CODES
AMADEUS YX BHXNOE
APOLLO/GALILEO YX 15074
SABRE/ABACUS YX 5328
WORLDSPAN YX 40776
PEGASUS YX BHXNOE

MIDSHIRES

Sheer perfection ... faultless

NUTHURST GRANGE

Country house

Nuthurst Grange Lane,
Hockley Heath,
Warwickshire B94 5NL

T (UK) 0870 432 8721
T 01564 783972
F 01564 783919
nuthurst@bestloved.com
www.nuthurst.bestloved.com

OWNERS
David and Karen Randolph

ROOM RATES
Single occupancy   £139
13 Doubles/Twins   £165 - £185
1 Four-poster   £195
1 Suite   £195
Includes full breakfast and VAT

CREDIT CARDS
AMERICAN EXPRESS • DC • MC • VI

RATINGS & AWARDS
ETC ★★★ Gold Award
AA ★★★ ❀❀
AA Top 200 - 2004/2005

FACILITIES
On site: Garden, heli-pad, croquet,
licensed for weddings
3 meeting rooms/max 150 people
Nearby: Golf, riding, fishing, tennis,
gym, pool

RESTRICTIONS
Limited facilities for disabled guests
Smoking in one lounge only
Pets by arrangement

ATTRACTIONS
Stratford-upon-Avon, Warwick Castle,
Kenilworth Castle, the Cotswolds,
National Exhibition Centre

NEAREST
CITY:
Birmingham - 12 miles/25 mins

AIRPORT:
Birmingham - 7 miles/15 mins

RAIL STATION:
Birmingham Int'l - 7 miles/15 mins

AFFILIATIONS
Independent

RESERVATIONS
National rate in UK: 0870 432 8721
Quote Best Loved

ACCESS CODES
Not applicable

MIDSHIRES

Unashamed luxury in the very heart of England

A long tree-lined drive takes you to Nuthurst Grange, gently nestling in seven and a half acres of gardens and woodlands. The restaurant is the centrepiece of the hotel, providing an intimate and relaxing setting for luncheon or dinner. The head chef and his team have won many ratings and awards for their imaginative menus, which feature the freshest seasonal produce; complemented by a fine wine list, the cuisine embraces the best of modern and classical French and British cooking. The pre-meal canapés and the selection of bread, biscuits and petits fours are all homemade.

All 15 spacious bedrooms in the hotel are furnished and decorated in soft country-house style. Each has superb rural views through traditional leaded windows and private bathrooms with air-spa baths.

The seclusion of the hotel belies its easy accessibility. Just off the Stratford-upon-Avon to Birmingham road, the hotel is within 15 minutes of Birmingham International Airport and the heart of England's motorway network.

LOCATION

From the M42, exit 4; from the M40, exit 16. Located 1/2 mile south of Hockley Heath on the A3400; turn by the hotel signboard into Nuthurst Grange Lane.

> **For those in need of a little luxurious indulgence, this is exactly what the doctor of hedonism would order**
>
> ALISON DAVIDSON, BIRMINGHAM EVENING POST

Restaurant with rooms   OLD MILL HOTEL & FUSION CHINO

Mill Street, Shipston-on-Stour,
Warwickshire CV36 4AW

T (UK) 0870 432 8724
T 01608 666999
F 01608 666990
oldmillship@bestloved.com

OWNERS
Robert and Christine Lee

ROOM RATES
Single occupancy   £60
5 Doubles   £70 - £100
2 Family rooms   £100
Includes full English breakfast and VAT

CREDIT CARDS
MC • VI

RATINGS & AWARDS
Independent

FACILITIES
On site: Garden
Nearby: Riding, fishing, tennis,
swimming, boating, golf

RESTRICTIONS
Limited facilities for disabled guests
No pets

ATTRACTIONS
The Cotswolds , Stratford-upon-Avon,
Broughton Castle, Hidcote Gardens,
Charlecote Park, Snowshill Manor,
Warwick Castle

NEAREST
CITY:
Oxford - 28 miles/45 mins

AIRPORT:
Birmingham - 36 miles/45 mins
Heathrow - 74 miles/1 hr 30 mins

RAIL STATION:
Moreton-in-Marsh - 7 miles/10 mins
Stratford-upon-Avon - 10 miles/15 mins

AFFILIATIONS
Independent

RESERVATIONS
National rate in UK: 0870 432 8724
Quote Best Loved

ACCESS CODES
Not applicable

MIDSHIRES

Oriental fusion on a peaceful island at the edge of the Cotswolds

Twenty years after he invaded England in 1066, William the Conqueror ordered that every piece of land and building should be registered in what is now known as The Domesday Book. The Old Mill was one such entry and its association with France - albeit a very different one - continues today. The hotel is a converted flour mill, and all its rooms have been extensively refurbished and named after a specific French region; so the Burgundy Suite's exposed brick chimney breast and stripped wood floor work perfectly with the rich colour palette and original beams.

Owners Robert and Christine Lee have also brought with them a taste of the Far East - the new Fusion Chino Restaurant, which has great views out to the gardens and river, serves an exciting variety of Oriental cuisine with a hint of French, Spanish and Thai influences. Starters include pan-fried scallops with ginger, garlic, coriander and lime, and for a main dish, you might try sea bass in Szechuan sauce or sizzling fillet of beef Cantonese style. There are a number of vegetarian options, too.

The hotel has a peaceful location surrounded by beautiful gardens and the River Stour. Numerous attractions are close by, such as Warwick Castle, Cotswold villages and Stratford-upon-Avon.

LOCATION

10 miles south of Stratford-upon-Avon.
From the village centre, turn down Church Street,
which then becomes Mill Street.

> "My wife and I have spent some of our happiest times outside our own home at The Old Parsonage. We feel the Parsonage has been one of our real finds"
>
> JAMES NELSON, CUMBRIA

OLD PARSONAGE   Townhouse

1 Banbury Road,
Oxford, Oxfordshire OX2 6NN

T (UK) 0870 432 8725
T 01865 310210
F 01865 311262
oldparsoxon@bestloved.com
www.oldparsoxon.bestloved.com

OWNER
Jeremy Mogford

ROOM RATES
Single occupancy	£135
22 Doubles/Twins	£155
6 Suites	£200
Includes VAT	

CREDIT CARDS
AMERICAN EXPRESS • DC • JCB • MC • VI

RATINGS & AWARDS
ETC ★★★★
AA ★★★★ 70% Town House
Which? Hotel of the Year 2004

FACILITIES
On site: Garden, terrace and roof garden, broadband Internet, air conditioning, bikes, punts
Nearby: Golf, flying

RESTRICTIONS
Limited facilities for disabled guests
No smoking in bedrooms

ATTRACTIONS
Oxford University Colleges, Ashmolean Museum, Botanical Gardens, Sheldonian Theatre

NEAREST
CITY:
Oxford

AIRPORT:
Heathrow - 47 miles/1 hr

RAIL STATION:
Oxford - 2 miles/5 mins

AFFILIATIONS
Independent

RESERVATIONS
National rate in UK: 0870 432 8725
Quote Best Loved

ACCESS CODES
APOLLO/GALILEO YX 14857
SABRE/ABACUS YX 30442
WORLDSPAN YX PARSO

MIDSHIRES

Timeless serenity in the heart of the city

A haven of tranquillity, the Old Parsonage is a thoroughly grown-up establishment conveniently located a short walk from Oxford centre and less than an hour from London, lending the air of a countryside retreat despite its urban location. A real fire burns in the warm lobby, and traditional-meets-modern décor is immediately welcoming. Choose from 28 rooms situated over two floors around a herb and lavender roof garden; all rooms feature everything the modern-day traveller requires, including air conditioning and high-speed Internet.

The Parsonage Bar/Restaurant has the intimate appeal of a private members' club and is open from breakfast to 11 p.m. serving modern British classics. The chefs are local to the area and pride themselves on using solely local suppliers for their produce. Whether it's the simplicity of a good steak and chips, stunning seafood imported from Jersey or a lobster salad in summer, you'll be guaranteed great quality food and service.

From June to the end of September there is a nightly barbeque on the front terrace accompanied by live jazz on Fridays - and when you're ready for some exploring, travel round Oxford on the hotel's house bikes or punt and take a seasonal picnic prepared by the chefs.

LOCATION
Leave the northern ring road at the Banbury Road roundabout. Follow Banbury Road toward Oxford city centre. The hotel is on the right, next to St Giles church.

Country house — OLD VICARAGE HOTEL & RESTAURANT

A breathtakingly beautiful county just waiting to be discovered

The tiny conservation village of Worfield, nestling on the Welsh border in charming Shropshire countryside but just 15 minutes from the motorway, is home to a real gem in the Old Vicarage Hotel & Restaurant.

Originally an Edwardian vicarage, this historic hotel retains all the charm and elegance that characterise quintessential village life. Each of the bedrooms is named after a local hamlet, such as Claverly, Shipton, Chesterton and even Badger Dingle, where many of P G Wodehouse's famous Jeeves and Wooster stories were set. Furnishings are often antique, and all rooms have an individual character - particularly the luxury Allscot room, which has French windows opening onto its own private garden with views down to the River Worfe. With such tasteful historical décor, the hotel is also to be commended on its excellent disabled access, making it a treat for all.

Proprietors Sarah and David Blakstad have also added their personal touch to the restaurant, and the pair follow a philosophy that ensures a fine balance between formality and fun. Traditional dishes are prepared with locally-sourced produce to high culinary standards, ensuring a truly tasteful extension of your country village experience!

LOCATION

From Kidderminster, follow signs to Wolverhampton on the A454; three miles from Bridgnorth, turn left for Worfield. The hotel is one mile along on the right.

Worfield, Bridgnorth, Shropshire WV15 5JZ

T (UK) 0870 432 8727
T 01746 716497
F 01746 716552
oldvicshrop@bestloved.com
www.oldvicshrop.bestloved.com

OWNERS
David and Sarah Blakstad

ROOM RATES
Singles £75 - £110
8 Doubles/Twins £135 - £175
1 Family Room £155
1 Four-poster £175
4 Suites £175
Includes full breakfast, newspaper and VAT

CREDIT CARDS
AMERICAN EXPRESS • DC • MC • VI

RATINGS & AWARDS
ETC ★★★ Gold Award
AA ★★★ ❀❀❀
AA Top 200 - 2004/2005

FACILITIES
On site: Garden, croquet
3 meeting rooms/max 40 people
Nearby: Golf, fishing, riding

RESTRICTIONS
No smoking in bedrooms or dining rooms

ATTRACTIONS
Stratford-upon-Avon, the Cotswolds, Weston Park stately home, Ironbridge Gorge, Severn Valley Railway, Royal Worcester & Royal Doulton Potteries, Ludlow Castle

NEAREST
CITY:
Wolverhampton - 10 miles/30 mins

AIRPORT:
Birmingham - 45 miles/1 hr

RAIL STATION:
Wolverhampton - 10 miles/30 mins

AFFILIATIONS
Independent

RESERVATIONS
National rate in UK: 0870 432 8727
Toll free in US: 800-98-PRIDE
Quote Best Loved

ACCESS CODES
AMADEUS HK BHXOLD
APOLLO/GALILEO HT 20216
SABRE/ABACUS HK 33865
WORLDSPAN HK OLDVI

MIDSHIRES

THE PAINSWICK HOTEL & RESTAURANT   Country house

MIDSHIRES

Kemps Lane, Painswick,
Gloucestershire GL6 6YB

T (UK) 0870 432 8730
T 01452 812160
F 01452 814059
painswick@bestloved.com
www.painswick.bestloved.com

GENERAL MANAGER
Adela Kubas

ROOM RATES
2 Singles	£90
15 Doubles/Twins	£140 - £190
2 Four-posters	£215

Includes full breakfast,
newspaper and VAT

CREDIT CARDS
AMERICAN EXPRESS • MC • VI

RATINGS & AWARDS
ETC ★★★ Silver Award
RAC Blue Ribbon ★★★
Dining Award 4
AA ★★★❀❀ 77%

FACILITIES
On site: Garden, croquet,
licensed for weddings
3 meeting rooms/max 80 people
Nearby: Golf, riding, gliding,
hot-air ballooning,
clay pigeon shooting

RESTRICTIONS
No facilities for disabled guests
Smoking in bar only
Pets by arrangement

ATTRACTIONS
Sudeley Castle, Berkeley Castle,
Bath, Stratford-upon-Avon,
Painswick Rococo Gardens,
the Cotswolds

NEAREST
CITY:
Gloucester - 5 miles/10 mins
Cheltenham - 10 miles/20 mins

AIRPORT:
Bristol - 45 miles/1 hr
Heathrow - 90 miles/1 hr 45 mins

RAIL STATION:
Stroud - 3 miles/5 mins
Gloucester - 5 miles/10 mins

AFFILIATIONS
Preston's Global Hotels
Cotswolds Finest Hotels

RESERVATIONS
National rate in UK: 0870 432 8730
Toll free in US: 800-544-9993
Quote Best Loved

ACCESS CODES
Not applicable

'Sheer poetry', said His Majesty - a sentiment as true today as ever it was

In King Charles I's words, 'The valleys around Painswick are sheer poetry, in this Paradise'. This lovely village comprises medieval cottages lying cheek-by-jowl with the 17th- and 18th-century merchants' houses and has been accorded the title of the Queen of the Cotswolds. The village's former rectory, built in 1790 in the Palladian style, is today The Painswick Hotel.

The hotel has 19 elegant bedrooms, all with luxury toiletries, baskets of fresh fruit, mineral water, books, magazines and other amenities. The stunning fabrics, soft furnishings, antique furniture, period engravings and objets d'art all contribute to a lovely sense of well-being. In the pine-panelled dining room, simply delicious and tempting food is served with an emphasis on seafood, local game and Gloucestershire cheeses. The public rooms, all with distinct elegance and character, feature antique furniture and fine pictures punctuated by open fires; all express a quiet confidence reflecting the more leisured times in which they were built.

Painswick is a superb touring, sporting and cultural centre. All the pleasures of the Cotswolds, Regency Cheltenham and Bath, Gloucester and Stratford-upon-Avon are within an easy drive.

LOCATION

In the town centre behind the parish church. Exit 13 from the M5 or exit 15 from the M4; then, take the A419 to the A46 (north).

"Excellent - the best small hotel in the UK"

Contemporary hotel

THE PEACOCK HOTEL

149 Warwick Road, Kenilworth,
Warwickshire CV8 1HY

T (UK) 0870 432 8734
T 01926 851156
F 01926 864644
peacock@bestloved.com
www.peacock.bestloved.com

OWNERS
The Muthalagappan Family

GENERAL MANAGER
Karthik Kalaivanan

ROOM RATES
7 Singles	£55 - £100
7 Standard Doubles/Twins	£65 - £130
10 Executive Rooms	£75 - £140
4 Club Rooms	£110 - £160
1 Four-poster	£140

Includes full breakfast and VAT

CREDIT CARDS
AMERICAN EXPRESS • DC • JCB • MC • VI

RATINGS & AWARDS
ETC ★★★ Silver Award
RAC Blue Ribbon ★★★
Dining Award 2
AA ★★★ 76%
Pat Chapman - Best Restaurant Group
in the UK 2004/2005

FACILITIES
On site: Garden, licensed for weddings
3 meeting rooms/max 90 people
Nearby: Golf, leisure centre,
clay pigeon shooting, paintballing,
archery, quad biking, sailing

RESTRICTIONS
Limited facilities for disabled guests
No smoking in some bedrooms
No pets; guide dogs only

ATTRACTIONS
Kenilworth Castle, Coventry Cathedral,
Heritage Motor Centre, Warwick
Castle, Shakespeare's Birthplace, Anne
Hathaway's Cottage, National Sea Life
Centre, Cadbury World

NEAREST
CITY:
Coventry - 6 miles/10 mins
Birmingham - 15 miles/20 mins

AIRPORT:
Coventry - 8 miles/12 mins
Birmingham - 12 miles/18 mins

RAIL STATION:
Coventry - 6 miles/10 mins
Warwick Parkway - 6 miles/10 mins

AFFILIATIONS
Independent

RESERVATIONS
National rate in UK: 0870 432 8734
Quote Best Loved

ACCESS CODES
AMADEUS BW BHX828
APOLLO/GALILEO BW 61484
SABRE/ABACUS BW 54805
WORLDSPAN BW 83828

MIDSHIRES

A colourful showplace with a taste of the exotic

This intriguing hotel near centrally-placed Kenilworth offers guests a distinctive Eastern experience that is not to be missed! With 28 lavish, vibrant bedrooms, you'll be spoilt for choice; perhaps choose one of the club rooms, decorated with wooden floors, chandeliers and Persian rugs to create a colonial 1920s look. The adjoining bathrooms are equally luxurious, with finishing touches such as mosaic floors. All rooms also have a variety of modern facilities, including CD player and modem connection.

When it comes to culinary options, choices abound, too. The award-winning Coconut Lagoon Restaurant, offering a variety of Southern Indian dishes, has won two dining awards from the RAC and Best Restaurant Chain in the UK by Pat Chapman. Located just down the road is the hotel's other restaurant, Raffles, Britain's first colonial Malaysian restaurant. This is a popular and incredibly elegant setting for leisure travellers or conference delegates, accommodating groups of up to 90 people.

The Peacock Hotel sits beautifully in Shakespeare country, close to the NEC, within 20 minutes of Birmingham Airport and 10 minutes from Coventry and Warwick Castle. And with four conference rooms, it is a great venue for corporate travellers.

LOCATION
Take the A46/A452 (Kenilworth).
The hotel is on the right after St John's church.

Pretty, polished, professional, perfect

THE PEAR TREE AT PURTON

Country house

Church End, Purton,
Wiltshire SN5 4ED

T (UK) 0870 432 8735
T 01793 772100
F 01793 772369
peartree@bestloved.com
www.peartree.bestloved.com

OWNERS
Francis and Anne Young

ROOM RATES
Single occupancy   £115 - £155
10 Doubles/Twins   £115 - £135
7 Executive Doubles/Twins £135
2 Suites   £145 - £155
Includes full breakfast and VAT

CREDIT CARDS
AMERICAN EXPRESS • DC • JCB • MC • VI

RATINGS & AWARDS
RAC Blue Ribbon ★★★
Dining Award 3
AA ★★★ ❀❀ 78%

FACILITIES
On site: Garden, heli-pad, croquet,
licensed for weddings
4 meeting rooms/max 60 people
Nearby: Leisure centre, riding,
shooting, jet-skiing

RESTRICTIONS
Limited facilities for disabled guests
Closed 26-30 Dec.

ATTRACTIONS
Bowood House,
Steam GWR Rail Exhibition,
designer outlet village, Cirencester,
Cotswold Water Park, the Cotswolds

NEAREST
CITY:
Swindon - 5 miles/10 mins

AIRPORT:
Bristol - 30 miles/30 mins

RAIL STATION:
Swindon - 5 miles/10 mins

AFFILIATIONS
Pride of Britain

RESERVATIONS
National rate in UK: 0870 432 8735
Toll free in the US: 800-98-PRIDE
Quote Best Loved

ACCESS CODES
AMADEUS HK SWIPEA
APOLLO/GALILEO HT 14848
SABRE/ABACUS HK 30135
WORLDSPAN HK PEART

MIDSHIRES

A peaceful retreat in the lovely Vale of the White Horse

Not far from the source of the River Thames in the gently rolling landscape of north Wiltshire, The Pear Tree's rural surroundings belie its convenient location, just minutes from the M4, with easy access to Heathrow and four-star sightseeing attractions like Oxford and Bath. For those of a more mystical persuasion, the ancient Avebury Stone Circle and even Stonehenge are within striking distance, as are the white horses carved into the chalk hills of the Vale of the White Horse and Vale of Pewsey.

The Pear Tree occupies a handsome 16th-century former vicarage moved brick by brick in 1912 from its original position next to the unusual twin-towered church of St. Mary's 400 yards away. Each of the pretty and extremely comfortable rooms are named after famous local characters, from Anne Hyde, mother of Queen Mary and Queen Anne, to cricketer E H Budd. The conservatory restaurant is a key feature, with lovely views of the traditional English gardens scented with roses and fragrant stocks in summer. The hotel has a charmingly relaxed family-run air lent by hosts Francis and Anne Young, and the service is memorable for its genuine consideration and care toward guests.

LOCATION

Exit 16 from the M4 and follow signs to Purton. At Spar Grocers, turn right; the hotel is a quarter of a mile along on the left.

> **Neither of us have experienced such discreet and polite hospitality. For 'running such a beautiful ship' and for your friendliness, thank you very much**
>
> RICHARD WHITE, HIGH WYCOMBE

Country house

THE PLOUGH AT CLANFIELD

Deep-piled comfort and wonderful country food in a classic manor house

In Cirencester, a short drive from Clanfield, there is a marvellously intact Roman amphitheatre which is said to date from 1 BC. The structure is an admirable symbol of ancient Roman ingenuity - and if in a thousand years you stumbled upon the honey-coloured Cotswold manor house that is The Plough, you might be similarly struck with respect for Elizabethan architecture. This is a classic in every sense!

The Plough is very much the ideal of the country-house experience; voluminous sofas and oversized armchairs invite you to sink into comfort and pass an afternoon with a good book. Owners John and Rosemary Hodges have lovingly turned this graceful old house into a welcoming hostelry renowned throughout the region for fine food. In the evening, candlelit tables with proper napery beckon the guest to enjoy a wonderful repast. The bedrooms, in keeping with the rest of the house, have been tastefully and traditionally decorated and and include lovely little extras like decanters of sherry and plush bathrobes.

The Plough is the perfect base from which to explore Oxford, Bath, Stratford-upon-Avon and the pretty Cotswold villages.

LOCATION

Located on the edge of the village of Clanfield, at the junction of the A4095 and the B4020 between Witney and Faringdon.

Bourton Road, Clanfield,
Oxfordshire OX18 2RB

T (UK) 0870 432 8743
T 01367 810222
F 01367 810596
plough@bestloved.com
www.plough.bestloved.com

OWNERS
John and Rosemary Hodges

ROOM RATES
Single occupancy	£90
8 Doubles/Twins	£120
3 Four-posters	£130
1 Suite	£165

Includes continental or full breakfast and VAT

CREDIT CARDS
AMERICAN EXPRESS • MC • VI

RATINGS & AWARDS
AA ★★★ 69%

FACILITIES
On site: Garden
2 meeting rooms/max 40 people
Nearby: Golf, fishing, tennis, fitness centre, shooting, riding

RESTRICTIONS
No children under 12 years
Smoking in lounge bar only
No pets; guide dogs only
Closed Christmas

ATTRACTIONS
Blenheim Palace, Rousham House, Kelmscott Manor, Stonor Park, Oxford, Waterperry Gardens

NEAREST
CITY:
Oxford - 18 miles/25 mins

AIRPORT:
Heathrow - 65 miles/1 hr 30 mins

RAIL STATION:
Oxford - 18 miles/25 mins

AFFILIATIONS
Independent

RESERVATIONS
National rate in UK: 0870 432 8743
Quote Best Loved

ACCESS CODES
Not applicable

MIDSHIRES

THE RAVEN HOTEL & RESTAURANT

Inn

Barrow Street, Much Wenlock,
Shropshire TF13 6EN

T (UK) 0870 432 8752
T 01952 727251
F 01952 728416
ravenhotel@bestloved.com
www.ravenhotel.bestloved.com

OWNER
Kirk Heywood

ROOM RATES
Single occupancy	£65
10 Doubles/Twins	£95
2 Superior Doubles/Twins	£105
1 Four-poster	£105
1 Family Room	£115
1 Suite	£125
Includes full breakfast and VAT	

CREDIT CARDS
AMERICAN EXPRESS • DC • JCB • MC • VI

RATINGS & AWARDS
AA ★★★ ✿ 72%

FACILITIES
On site: Garden, health & beauty
1 meeting room/max 16 people
Nearby: Golf, tennis, fishing,
riding, swimming

RESTRICTIONS
No facilities for disabled guests
No smoking in restaurant
No pets
Closed Christmas

ATTRACTIONS
Ironbridge, Dudmaston Hall,
Coalport Pottery, Stokesay Castle,
Wenlock Priory,
Wroxeter Roman City,
Wenlock Edge, Attingham Park

NEAREST
CITY:
Telford - 10 miles/15 mins
Shrewsbury - 13 miles/20 mins

AIRPORT:
Birmingham - 53 miles/1 hr

RAIL STATION:
Shrewsbury - 13 miles/20 mins

AFFILIATIONS
Independent

RESERVATIONS
National rate in UK: 0870 432 8752
Quote Best Loved

ACCESS CODES
Not applicable

MIDSHIRES

Much praised in Much Wenlock - and only 10 minutes from Ironbridge

The modern Olympic Games owe much to a certain Dr Penny Brookes, who lived in Much Wenlock - he founded the Wenlock Olympian Society in 1850 and, years later, worked with Baron Coubertin to found the modern Olympic movement. In 1890, the Baron wrote: 'And of the Olympic Games ... it is not a Greek to whom one is indebted but rather to Dr W P Brookes'.

Since the games began, the Raven has been the haunt of spectators and competitors alike. Then, as now, the traditional welcome is as warm as a 500-year-old coaching inn can muster. The place has immense character. The flower-filled courtyard gives access to bedrooms which have been delightfully furnished and provided with every modern comfort. There are four-poster bedrooms and an imaginatively designed galleried suite that tastefully blends old and new.

Before you dine, have a look at the Olympian memorabilia on display in the public rooms - and then prepare yourself for a treat. Look at the menu, and you will agree with Paddy Burt of the Daily Telegraph: 'This is what I call serious food'. It's imaginative and delicious, with a good choice of something traditional, much higher up the culinary scale. All told, the Raven is without doubt an absolute winner!

LOCATION
10 miles from Telford, between Shrewsbury and Bridgnorth at the A4169/A458 junction.
Turn right at the end of the high street;
the hotel is 100 yards on the right.

> "I had the birthday of a lifetime. Your organisation and hospitality were second to none"
>
> ANNIE FURBANK, HUNTINGDON

Country house

RIVERSIDE HOUSE HOTEL

The height of hospitality in the splendour of the Peak District

It is no wonder the striking and magnificent moor-like landscapes of the Peak District were established as Britain's first national park. The interesting bit is that the Peak District doesn't have a single peak, the highest elevation being Kinder Scout, which nudges in at a mere 680 metres! But what this area lacks in height it makes up in mountains of hospitality: It is an area enormously popular with British travellers and only recently discovered by foreign visitors seeking a glimpse of 'real England'.

Here's an example: In a picturesque village by the River Wye is the aptly named Riverside House Hotel. This secluded and cosy ivy-clad Georgian house is the ideal spot from which to explore the Peaks and Dales of Derbyshire, Chatsworth and Dovedale.

Informality and friendliness are the order of the day at the Riverside. The pleasures of good customer care, tastefully designed bedrooms and the Riverside Room restaurant's modern English cuisine come together to create the perfect setting for a totally relaxing break. Whether for a special night out or as a touring base of the very best of Derbyshire, Riverside House Hotel delivers.

LOCATION

A mile and a half outside Bakewell on the A6 to Buxton. The entrance to the hotel is at the edge by the Sheepwash Bridge.

Fennel Street,
Ashford-in-the-Water, Bakewell,
Derbyshire DE45 1QF

T (UK) 0870 432 8754
T 01629 814275
F 01629 812873
riverside@bestloved.com
www.riverside.bestloved.com

GENERAL MANAGER
James Lamb

ROOM RATES
Single occupancy	£85 - £120
14 Doubles/Twins	£120 - £135
1 Four-poster	£135 - £155

Includes full breakfast and VAT

CREDIT CARDS
AMERICAN EXPRESS • DC • MC • VI

RATINGS & AWARDS
AA ★★★ ✿✿ 79%
AA Customer Care Hotel of the Year 2001
Karen Brown Recommended

FACILITIES
On site: Garden, croquet,
licensed for weddings
1 meeting room/max 30 people
Nearby: Golf, river fishing,
shooting, riding

RESTRICTIONS
Limited facilities for disabled guests
No children under 12 years
Smoking in bar area only
No pets; guide dogs only

ATTRACTIONS
Derbyshire Dales, Hardwick Hall,
Chatsworth House, Plague Village,
Haddon Hall, Blue John Mines

NEAREST
CITY:
Sheffield - 16 miles/30 mins

AIRPORT:
Manchester - 40 miles/1 hr

RAIL STATION:
Chesterfield - 12 miles/30 mins

AFFILIATIONS
Penelope Thornton Hotels Ltd

RESERVATIONS
National rate in UK: 0870 432 8754
Quote Best Loved

ACCESS CODES
Not applicable

MIDSHIRES

> "This had everything that makes an enjoyable break away - lovely rooms, warm welcome and amazing food and drink. Can't wait to come back"
>
> CHARLOTTE WEST, LONDON

THE ROYALIST HOTEL

Inn

Digbeth Street,
Stow-on-the-Wold,
Gloucestershire GL54 1BN

T (UK) 0870 432 8763
T 01451 830670
F 01451 870048
royalist@bestloved.com
www.royalist.bestloved.com

OWNERS
Peter and Amanda Rowan

GENERAL MANAGER
Tracey Davies

ROOM RATES
Single occupancy	£50 - £90
6 Doubles/Twins	£70 - £140
1 Four-poster	£110 - £160
1 Suite	£130 - £180

Includes continental breakfast and VAT

CREDIT CARDS
AMERICAN EXPRESS • DC • JCB • MC • VI

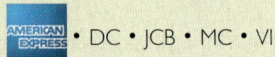

RATINGS & AWARDS
ETC ★★★ Silver Award
AA ★★★ 73%

FACILITIES
On site: Bar
1 meeting room/max 30 people
Nearby: Riding, fishing, quad biking,
clay pigeon shooting

RESTRICTIONS
No facilities for disabled guests
No children under 10 years
in restaurant
Smoking in bar only
No pets

ATTRACTIONS
Warwick Castle, the Cotswolds,
Oxford, Blenheim Palace,
Hidcote Gardens,
Stratford-upon-Avon

NEAREST
CITY:
Oxford - 35 miles/40 mins

AIRPORT:
Birmingham - 43 miles/1 hr 15 mins

RAIL STATION:
Kingham - 4 miles/10 mins

AFFILIATIONS
Cotswolds Finest Hotels

RESERVATIONS
National rate in UK: 0870 432 8763
Quote Best Loved

ACCESS CODES
Not applicable

A restaurant, a hotel and an inn: Three into one does go!

The Royalist is the oldest inn in England, dating back to 947 AD, when it was a hospice and almshouse owned by the Knights of St John. It is truly atmospheric, with antique beams, spooky marks to ward off witches and a Babylonian frieze dating from the Crusades.

While it would be hard to improve on this hospitable landmark, owners Peter and Amanda Rowan continue to raise the standards of comfort, food and service. Behind the mellow 17th-century Cotswold stone façade, there are eight individually-designed bedrooms. For something really unusual, check out the jewel-like Porch House Room, created out of the 1615 porch and glassed in on three sides.

For the fine dining experience, there is Restaurant 947AD, whilst for those seeking something more informal, take a stroll over the flagstones to The Eagle and Child, which offers a selection of real ales, sensibly-priced wines and an impressive range of dishes, qualifying it as one of the top 10 inns in the UK, according to The Independent. In all, the Royalist is a real find, so book now before word gets out!

LOCATION
At Stow-on-the-Wold, turn off the A429 for Chipping Norton. The hotel is 300 yards on the left, behind the green.

Country house

THE SHAVEN CROWN

A medieval hall with 600 years of history and a family welcome

The Shaven Crown is beautifully situated in the heart of the Cotswolds. Originally a 14th-century hospice to Bruern Abbey, the hotel is built of local honey-coloured stone around a central medieval courtyard garden and has the mellowed charm of 700 years of hospitality. The establishment is owned by Philip Mehrtens, who is actively engaged in its daily running.

The pride of the Shaven Crown Hotel, in addition to its original 14th-century gateway, is the medieval hall, now the residents' lounge. An intimate candlelit restaurant serves food fresh every day. The bar offers an imaginative array of bar meals beside the log fire for lunch and dinner seven days a week, and you may eat al fresco in the courtyard whenever you choose. All the bedrooms in this charming hotel have tea and coffee-making facilities, television and private bathrooms and are centrally heated throughout.

When it comes time to explore, keep in mind that the area is justly renowned for antique hunting. In addition, Cheltenham and the other towns and villages of the Cotswolds are within easy reach, as are Oxford, Stratford-upon-Avon and Cirencester. Blenheim Palace, birthplace of Sir Winston Churchill, is one of the many great stately homes in the district.

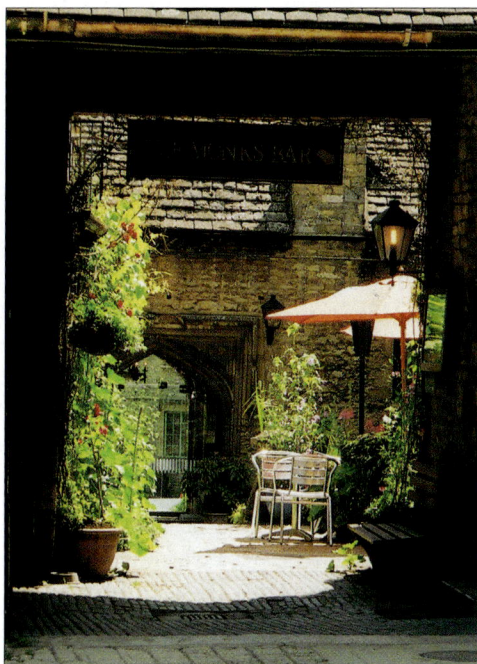

LOCATION

On the A361, four miles north of Burford and six miles south of Chipping Norton.

High Street,
Shipton-under-Wychwood,
Oxfordshire OX7 6BA

T (UK) 0870 432 8769
T 01993 830330
F 01993 832136
shaven@bestloved.com
www.shaven.bestloved.com

OWNER
Philip Mehrtens

ROOM RATES
Single occupancy   £65
8 Doubles/Twins   £85 - £120
1 Four-poster   £120
Includes full breakfast and VAT

CREDIT CARDS
AMERICAN EXPRESS • MC • VI

RATINGS & AWARDS
Independent

FACILITIES
On site: Garden, bowling green
1 meeting room/max 40 people
Nearby: Golf, fishing, riding

RESTRICTIONS
Limited facilities for disabled guests
Pets by arrangement
Smoking in some rooms and bar only

ATTRACTIONS
The Cotswolds, Blenheim Palace,
Burford, Bourton-on-the-Water,
Stow-on-the-Wold, Cheltenham

NEAREST
CITY:
Oxford - 26 miles/30 mins

AIRPORT:
Heathrow - 70 miles/1 hr 30 mins
Birmingham - 55 miles/1 hr 15 mins

RAIL STATION:
Charlbury - 6 miles/10 mins

AFFILIATIONS
Independent

RESERVATIONS
National rate in UK: 0870 432 8769
Quote Best Loved

ACCESS CODES
Not applicable

MIDSHIRES

STAPLEFORD PARK

Stately home

Stapleford Park,
Near Melton Mowbray,
Leicestershire LE14 2EF

T (UK) 0870 432 8776
T 01572 787522
F 01572 787651
stapleford@bestloved.com
www.stapleford.bestloved.com

GENERAL MANAGER
William Boulton-Smith

SALES MANAGER
Sarah Jane Wood

ROOM RATES
1 Single	£205
48 Doubles/Twins	£232 - £425
2 Suites	£595
Includes breakfast, newspaper and VAT

CREDIT CARDS
AMERICAN EXPRESS • DC • MC • VI

RATINGS & AWARDS
RAC Gold Ribbon ★★★★
Dining Award 4
AA ★★★★ ✿✿
AA Top 200 - 2004/2005

FACILITIES
On site: Garden, gym, snooker,
heli-pad, 18-hole golf course, tennis,
indoor pool, licensed for weddings,
archery, sauna, Jacuzzi, Clarins Spa,
falconry, petanque, boules,
mountain bikes, clay shooting,
off-road driving
8 meeting rooms/max 300 people
Nearby: Shooting, riding

RESTRICTIONS
Limited facilities for disabled guests
No smoking in bedrooms

ATTRACTIONS
Burghley House, Belvoir Castle,
Rutland Water, Chatsworth House,
Belton House, Stamford

NEAREST
CITY:
Leicester - 18 miles/35 mins
AIRPORT:
Nottingham EMA - 20 miles/45 mins
RAIL STATION:
Grantham - 15 miles/25 mins

AFFILIATIONS
Celebrated Hotels Collection

RESERVATIONS
National rate in UK: 0870 432 8776
Toll free in US: 800-322-2403
Quote Best Loved

ACCESS CODES
Not applicable

MIDSHIRES

An historic stately home with sumptuous treats for everyone

Stapleford is one of England's finest stately homes, with a pedigree stretching back to the 14th century. Set in 500 acres of woods, parkland and beautiful gardens, the house is a miraculously balanced and harmonious blend of architectural periods with an interior magnificently restored and furnished in spectacular style. Embellishments throughout this long and illustrious history have included outstanding works of art such as the glorious 17th-century Grinling Gibbons carvings in the dining room, inspired by the Spanish Riding School in Vienna.

Guests can relax in the lap of luxury, whether in the elegant drawing room, the comfortable saloon with its leather sofas or the heavenly bedrooms. The cosseting continues in the hotel's spa, with its 22m pool (complete with aquarium), Jacuzzi, steam room, solarium and Clarins beauty therapy rooms. Outside, the challenging 18-hole golf course designed by Donald Steel will enthral all comers, and the golf pavilion has stunning views over the 18th green. Guests can also enjoy six tennis courts. And for the more energetic, the Victorian stable block has been partially converted into a state-of-the-art gymnasium - a fabulous addition to this quintessential country house.

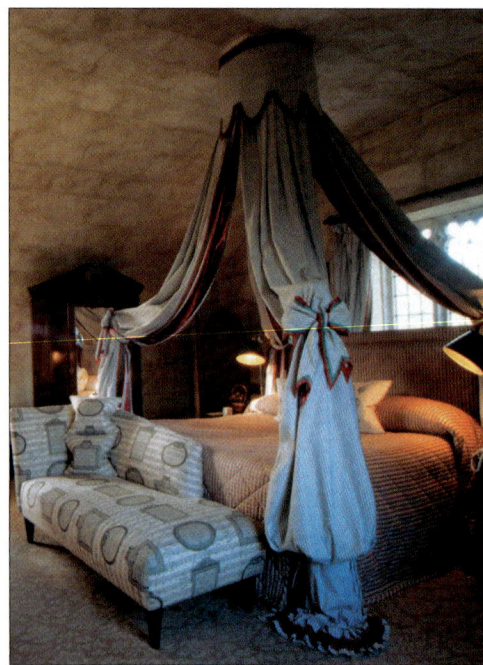

LOCATION
Situated four miles east of Melton Mowbray on the B676, toward Colsterworth and the A1.

Village hotel

STRETTON HALL

All Stretton, Church Stretton,
Shropshire SY6 6HG

T (UK) 0870 432 8781
T 01694 723224
F 01694 724365
strettonhall@bestloved.com
www.strettonhall.bestloved.com

OWNERS
The Baker Family

ROOM RATES
Single occupancy	£50
11 Doubles/Twins	£80 - £130
1 Four-poster	£130

Includes full breakfast and VAT

CREDIT CARDS
AMERICAN EXPRESS • DC • MC • VI

RATINGS & AWARDS
AA ★★★ ❀❀ 68%

FACILITIES
On site: Garden, licensed for weddings
3 meeting rooms/max 95 people
Nearby: Golf, riding, gliding

RESTRICTIONS
No facilities for disabled guests
Closed 26 - 30 Dec.

ATTRACTIONS
Stokesay, Ludlow and Chirk Castles,
Ironbridge Gorge and Museum,
Severn Valley Railway, Long Mynd,
Ludlow Racecourse, Attingham Park,
Acton Scott Historic Working Farm

NEAREST
CITY:
Shrewsbury - 13 miles/20 mins

AIRPORT:
Birmingham - 69 miles/1 hr 30 mins

RAIL STATION:
Church Stretton - 1 mile/5 mins
Shrewsbury - 13 miles/20 mins

AFFILIATIONS
Independent

RESERVATIONS
National rate in UK: 0870 432 8781
Quote Best Loved

ACCESS CODES
Not applicable

MIDSHIRES

A fresh and appealing country house hotel with a gourmet twist

At the heart of the quiet South Shropshire village of All Stretton, Stretton Hall may date from the Georgian era, but there is nothing dated about this relaxed and welcoming hotel. Many of the house's most impressive period features remain unchanged, from stone mullioned windows and imposing fireplaces to oak panelling and a beautiful staircase. In keeping with this spirit of opulence, these fine originals have been deftly combined with carefully chosen fabrics and essential modern-day comforts to create attractive and mercifully unfussy bedrooms and a charming dining room.

Stretton Hall's Lemon Tree Restaurant is gaining the sort of reputation that would be the envy of a far larger establishment. Here, the first-class seasonal menus are a paean to local produce with an occasional exotic or unusual twist, such as the mini rack of lamb with pomegranate jus. Children's meals are also available, and there is even toddler-friendly cutlery, as befits a hotel run by a young family!

This marvellously unspoilt corner of Britain offers fantastic walking country, with views of Long Mynd and the heights of Caer Caradoc visible from the hotel. There are castles at Ludlow and Stokesay, horse riding, working farms and much, much more to explore.

LOCATION
13 miles south of Shrewsbury, just off the A49.

Map p. 446, grid H5

> **The combination of oak beams, inglenook fireplace and medieval wall paintings in our bedroom made our stay particularly memorable - and the food was wonderful**
>
> MR P GREEN, GREAT YARMOUTH

THE SWAN

Village hotel

High Street, Lavenham,
Suffolk CO10 9QA

T (UK) 0870 432 8510
T 01787 247477
F 01787 248286
swanlavenham@bestloved.com
www.swanlavenham.bestloved.com

GENERAL MANAGER
John Hewitt

ROOM RATES
9 Singles   £90
25 Doubles/Twins   £140 - £200
11 Feature Rooms   £160
3 Suites   £200
3 Four-posters   £180
Includes breakfast and VAT

CREDIT CARDS
AMERICAN EXPRESS • DC • MC • VI

RATINGS & AWARDS
AA ★★★★ ✿✿ 73%

FACILITIES
On site: Garden
3 meeting rooms/max 20 people

RESTRICTIONS
Limited facilities for disabled guests
Children by arrangement
No smoking in bedrooms

ATTRACTIONS
Cambridge, Suffolk Heritage Coast,
Norwich, Constable Country,
Sutton Hoo, Newmarket

NEAREST
CITY:
Cambridge - 40 miles/55 mins

AIRPORT:
Stansted - 38 miles/55 mins
Heathrow - 102 miles/2 hrs

RAIL STATION:
Sudbury - 6 miles/10 mins
Colchester - 20 miles/40 mins

FERRY PORT:
Harwich - 32 miles/1 hr

AFFILIATIONS
Thorpeness & Aldeburgh Hotels

RESERVATIONS
National rate in UK: 0870 432 8510
Quote Best Loved

ACCESS CODES
Not applicable

An historic hotel bursting with charm and character

This beautiful hotel nestles in the heart of the medieval village of Lavenham, renowned for its splendid array of listed buildings. The hotel itself is brimming with charm and history, with its oak beams, panelled walls and luxurious modern furnishings, providing the perfect retreat for rest, relaxation and culture.

There is no shortage of dining options - The Swan's restaurants offer fresh menus daily, serving quality cuisine created by Master Chef Simon Reynolds who uses ingredients sourced from Suffolk and Norfolk suppliers. The main restaurant offers a wonderfully elegant setting for special occasions; the Garden Bar Restaurant has a bright and fresh atmosphere and the Old Bar offers a relaxed and cosy ambience. If you are looking for a meeting venue with a difference, The Swan is quite unique. Its three historic meeting rooms, The Wool Hall, Suffolk Room and McCullum Lounge, all offer excellent conference facilities, including a modern range of AV equipment.

There is so much to do in the surrounding area that guests are simply spoilt for choice! Newmarket, Cambridge, Hadleigh and Bury St. Edmunds are all nearby.

LOCATION
Take the A1141, off the A134 (Sudbury-Bury St Edmunds), directly into Lavenham; the hotel is on the high street.

Country house

SWYNFORD PADDOCKS

Six Mile Bottom, Newmarket, Suffolk CB8 0UE

T (UK) 0870 432 8785
T 01638 570234
F 01638 570283
swynford@bestloved.com
www.swynford.bestloved.com

GENERAL MANAGER
John Hewitt

ROOM RATES
Single occupancy   £110 - £140
13 Doubles/Twins   £135 - £165
2 Four-posters   £155 - £195
Includes full breakfast and VAT

CREDIT CARDS
AMERICAN EXPRESS • DC • MC • VI

RATINGS & AWARDS
ETC ★★★
RAC ★★★ Dining Award 1
AA ★★★ ❀ 74%

FACILITIES
On site: Garden, heli-pad, tennis, putting green
2 meeting rooms/max 230 people
Nearby: Golf, riding

RESTRICTIONS
No facilities for disabled guests
No smoking in restaurant
No pets in public areas

ATTRACTIONS
Newmarket Racecourse & Museum and National Stud,
Lavenham & Long Melford,
Duxford Imperial War Museum,
Ely Cathedral, Cambridge,
Ickworth House

NEAREST
CITY:
Cambridge - 12 miles/20 mins

AIRPORT:
Stansted - 20 miles/30 mins

RAIL STATION:
Cambridge - 12 miles/20 mins

FERRY PORT:
Harwich - 64 miles/50 mins

AFFILIATIONS
Independent

RESERVATIONS
National rate in UK: 0870 432 8785
Quote Best Loved

ACCESS CODES
Not applicable

MIDSHIRES

A classy thoroughbred handily placed for Cambridge and Newmarket

Swynford Paddocks' racing connection is not just confined to its name. There is a working stud farm within the 62-acre grounds, and the hotel's address at Six Mile Bottom refers to its excellent location six miles as the crow flies from Cambridge and Newmarket, the headquarters of British horseracing for more than 300 years.

An elegant country house surrounded by its namesake paddocks, Swynford also has a notorious past. In 1813, the Romantic poet Lord Byron conducted a passionate affair with his married half-sister Augusta Leigh, who lived at Swynford. Later - and perhaps more conventionally - the house was owned by Lord and Lady Halifax before it was sympathetically converted into a country hotel.

The hotel makes a great base for exploring East Anglia's diverse attractions: day trips to Cambridge, punting on the River Isis or a stroll along the 'Backs', as the riverbanks are known. For fans of the turf, the flat racing at Newmarket is a major draw and visits are easily made to the National Stud and National Horseracing Museum. The hotel can also arrange behind-the-scenes tours. Other popular trips include Ely Cathedral, the picturesque old wool towns of Lavenham and Long Melford, and the Imperial War Museum at Duxford.

LOCATION

From the M11, exit 9, take the A11 toward Newmarket. After 10 miles, exit for the A1304 (Newmarket). The hotel is three-quarters of a mile on the left.

THORNBURY CASTLE
Castle

Thornbury,
South Gloucestershire BS35 1HH
T (UK) 0870 432 8795
T 01454 281182
F 01454 416188
thornbury@bestloved.com
www.thornbury.bestloved.com

GENERAL MANAGER
Brian A Jarvis

ROOM RATES
2 Singles £80 - £110
8 Classic Doubles/Twins £130 - £190
11 Deluxe £220 - £290
3 Deluxe Suites £295 - £370
1 2-Bedroomed Gatehouse £295 - £370
Includes full breakfast, early morning tea, newspaper and VAT

CREDIT CARDS
AMERICAN EXPRESS • DC • MC • VI

RATINGS & AWARDS
RAC Gold Ribbon ★★★ Dining Award 3
AA ★★★ ⊛⊛
AA Top 200 - 2004/2005
'Super Star Hotel', Reed Travel Group, USA

FACILITIES
On site: Garden, heli-pad, croquet, licensed for weddings
4 meeting rooms/max 100 people
Nearby: Golf, tennis, shooting, horse riding, ballooning

RESTRICTIONS
Limited facilities for disabled guests
No smoking in restaurant
Pets by arrangement

ATTRACTIONS
Berkeley Castle, Chepstow Castle, the Cotswolds, Tintern Abbey, Bath, Bristol, Wye Valley

NEAREST
CITY:
Bristol - 15 miles/20 mins
Bath - 23 miles/45 mins
AIRPORT:
Bristol - 21 miles/35 mins
RAIL STATION:
Bristol Parkway - 12 miles/15 mins

AFFILIATIONS
von Essen Hotels
Celebrated Hotels Collection
Pride of Britain
Cotswolds Finest Hotels

RESERVATIONS
National rate in UK: 0870 432 8795
Toll free in US: 800-322-2403
or 800-98-PRIDE
Quote Best Loved

ACCESS CODES
AMADEUS HK BRSTHO
APOLLO/GALILEO HT 41651
SABRE/ABACUS HK 36355
WORLDSPAN HK THORN

MIDSHIRES

'The top hotel in Europe' - and a great deal more besides

The building of Thornbury Castle began in 1511 by Edward Stafford, third Duke of Buckingham, and ended in 1521 when he was beheaded by Henry VIII. Buckingham's vast estates, including Thornbury, were confiscated by the king, who stayed here with Anne Boleyn in 1535. Henry's daughter, Mary Tudor, lived here as a princess, and when she became Queen she returned the Castle to the descendants of the late duke - a more peaceful end to a rather hectic history!

Today, this Tudor castle-palace - rated the top hotel in Europe by Condé Nast Traveler magazine - stands serenely in 15 acres with distant views of the Severn Estuary and the hills of South Gloucestershire and Wales. Fine old panelling, tapestries and paintings enrich the interiors. There are 30 carefully restored bedchambers, most overlooking the vineyard or the oldest Tudor garden in England; many have luxurious four-poster beds and huge Tudor fireplaces.

The three intimate dining rooms have a gracious ambience to suit the superb cuisine.

Thornbury is an ideal base from which to discover the many historic sites, villages and towns located within an hour's drive of the castle, or cross the Severn Bridge into Wales and explore that beautiful country.

LOCATION
Exit 20 on the M4 or exit 16 on the M5; take the A38 north for five miles, then turn left to Thornbury, following the brown signs.

Village hotel

TITCHWELL MANOR HOTEL

Refreshing hospitality and inspired cuisine on the north Norfolk coast

Located on the North Norfolk coast, Titchwell Manor and its beautiful original walled garden were built more than 100 years ago. The house is now a family-run hotel that has been nurtured by owners Margaret and Ian Snaith. With Margaret and Ian at the helm, Titchwell has become a welcoming and refreshing retreat for business and leisure travellers - bedrooms here are fresh and light, and relaxing lounge areas are warmed with roaring log fires in the winter.

The kitchen is run by the Snaith's son Eric, who has created a seafood restaurant that is now a main feature of the hotel. Eric's trip to Australia and the Far East inspired the menu, which fuses international cuisine with local Norfolk produce. Dishes include monkfish wrapped in Serrano ham with slow-roasted leek and wild mushroom, red onion and pumpkin seed jam, or chargrilled fillet of Norfolk beef with fondant potato, horseradish shallot compote, cauliflower puree, jus & black pepper brandy snap!

Before dinner, there is plenty for guests to explore, with pretty Norfolk villages and coastal walks on the doorstep, plus an abundance of attractions such as Holkham Hall, Sandringham and the RSPB Bird Reserve nearby.

LOCATION

From King's Lynn, take the A149 toward Hunstanton. Continue past Hunstanton and Holme to the high street. The hotel is between Thornham and Brancaster, on the right.

Titchwell, Brancaster, King's Lynn, Norfolk PE31 8BB

T (UK) 0870 432 8801
T 01485 210221
F 01485 210104
titchwell@bestloved.com
www.titchwell.bestloved.com

OWNERS
Margaret and Ian Snaith

ROOM RATES
1 Single   £55 - £69
14 Doubles/Twins   £84 - £138
Includes full breakfast and VAT

CREDIT CARDS
AMERICAN EXPRESS • JCB • MC • VI

RATINGS & AWARDS
ETC ★★ Silver Award
AA ★★ ❀❀ 78%

FACILITIES
On site: Walled garden
Nearby: Golf, walks, beaches, tennis, fitness centre

RESTRICTIONS
Limited facilities for disabled guests
No smoking in restaurant or bedrooms
Pets by arrangement

ATTRACTIONS
North Norfolk Coast,
Burnham Market, Holkham Beach,
RSPB Bird Reserve,
Brancaster Harbour,
Championship golf courses,
Sandringham

NEAREST
CITY:
King's Lynn - 22 miles/35 mins

AIRPORT:
Norwich - 40 miles/1 hr
Stansted - 97 miles/2 hrs 10 mins

RAIL STATION:
King's Lynn - 22 miles/35 mins

AFFILIATIONS
Independent

RESERVATIONS
National rate in UK: 0870 432 8801
Quote Best Loved

ACCESS CODES
Not applicable

MIDSHIRES

> "We found your staff, facilities and overall atmosphere excellent, and will most certainly recommend The Unicorn"
>
> MR & MRS R W F MUNDY, QUESTION OF SERVICE

THE UNICORN HOTEL

Inn

Sheep Street,
Stow-on-the-Wold,
Gloucestershire GL54 1HQ

T (UK) 0870 432 8805
T 01451 830257
F 01451 831090
unicorn@bestloved.com
www.unicorn.bestloved.com

MANAGER
Nabil Lai

ROOM RATES
2 Singles	£60 - £65
13 Doubles/Twins	£78 - £105
4 Superior Rooms	£100 - £125
1 Four-poster	£135 - £138

Includes full breakfast and VAT

CREDIT CARDS
AMERICAN EXPRESS • DC • JCB • MC • VI

RATINGS & AWARDS
ETC ★★★
RAC ★★★ Dining Award 1
AA ★★★ 70%

FACILITIES
On site: Licensed for weddings
1 meeting room/max 50 people
Nearby: Golf, fishing, riding, tennis

RESTRICTIONS
Limited facilities for disabled guests
Pets by arrangement
Smoking in some bedrooms only

ATTRACTIONS
Bourton-on-the-Water,
Blenheim Palace, Warwick Castle,
Stratford-upon-Avon,
antiques hunting, walking,
Cheltenham Racecourse

NEAREST
CITY:
Oxford - 29 miles/40 mins
Cheltenham - 19 miles/20 mins

AIRPORT:
Heathrow - 75 miles/1 hr 30 mins
Birmingham - 40 miles/45 mins

RAIL STATION:
Moreton-in-Marsh - 5 miles/10 mins

AFFILIATIONS
Grand Heritage Hotels

RESERVATIONS
National rate in UK: 0870 432 8805
Toll free in US: 888-93-GRAND
Quote Best Loved

ACCESS CODES
AMADEUS UI GLOUNH
APOLLO/GALILEO UI 13389
SABRE/ABACUS UI 43640
WORLDSPAN UI 40752

The best of the Cotswolds with fine dining and a friendly atmosphere

The perfect blend of traditional charm and modern comfort, this 17th-century hotel has long been a meeting place as popular with local residents as with those touring the Cotswolds. The former coaching inn's honey-coloured stone exterior is in keeping with its pretty market town location; colourful window boxes and hanging baskets adorning the walls are a hint of the quaint, welcoming atmosphere to be found inside.

The interior exudes old-world charm, from the sitting room with blazing inglenook fireplace through to the bedrooms, where antique furniture contrasts with modern fabrics and ancient beams rest on colour-washed walls. Guests are invited to relax with a drink and a light meal in the bar, or dine in the Shepherd's restaurant, where traditional English cuisine is served in an elegant Georgian setting.

The busy market town of Stow-on-the-Wold is high up in the rolling Cotswold countryside and has been popular since Roman times. It is strewn with antique shops for which the town has become famous. Itself designated an area of Outstanding Natural Beauty, Stow is a central location close to many other celebrated Cotswold attractions: Bourton-on-the-Water, Bibury, Shipping Campden, Cheltenham and Stratford are all nearby.

LOCATION
In Sheep Street near the market square, in the centre of Stow-on-the-Wold; reach the town on the A429.

Country house

WASHBOURNE COURT HOTEL

Lower Slaughter,
Gloucestershire GL54 2HS

T (UK) 0870 432 8812
T 01451 822143
F 01451 821045
washbourne@bestloved.com
www.washbourne.bestloved.com

GENERAL MANAGER
Anne Hutchinson

ROOM RATES
Single occupancy	£100 - £120
14 Doubles/Twins	£120 - £170
10 Cottages	£200
4 Deluxe Rooms	£200
2 Two-bedroom Suites	£300

Includes full breakfast and VAT

CREDIT CARDS
AMERICAN EXPRESS • DC • MC • VI

RATINGS & AWARDS
RAC ★★★ Dining Award 2
AA ★★★ ⊗⊗ 75%

FACILITIES
On site: Garden, heli-pad, tennis
2 meeting rooms/max 80 people
Nearby: Golf, riding, quad biking,
clay pigeon shooting, ballooning

RESTRICTIONS
Limited facilities for disabled guests
No children under 12 years in dining room
No smoking in dining room
No pets

ATTRACTIONS
Blenheim Palace, Oxford,
Stratford-upon-Avon,
Old Roman Fosseway,
Bath, the Cotswolds

NEAREST
CITY:
Oxford - 25 miles/40 mins

AIRPORT:
Heathrow - 80 miles/1 hr 45 mins
Birmingham - 55 miles/45 mins

RAIL STATION:
Kingham - 5 miles/10 mins

AFFILIATIONS
Preston's Global Hotels
von Essen Hotels

RESERVATIONS
National rate in UK: 0870 432 8812
Toll free in US: 800-544-9993
Quote Best Loved

ACCESS CODES
AMADEUS YX BZZWAS
APOLLO/GALILEO YX 71334
SABRE/ABACUS YX 55825
WORLDSPAN YX BZZWA
PEGASUS YX OXFWAS

MIDSHIRES

A true gem right in the heart of the Cotswolds

Washbourne Court is a truly magnificent hotel: Partly housed in a 17th-century building with four acres of grounds, it nestles alongside the River Eye in the centre of Lower Slaughter, undoubtedly one of the most beautiful and unspoilt of all the Cotswold villages. Whatever the season, the building retains all the original charm and character that has been gently acquired over the last 400 years.

The bedrooms at Washbourne Court are comfortable, each with its own character and all very well appointed - some even have their own Jacuzzis. For choice, there are also cottage accommodations that help you to feel even more part of village life. The intimate riverside restaurant offers the finest of modern English cuisine with ambience and atmosphere to be savoured.

Lower Slaughter is famous for its outstanding scenic beauty, and is the perfect location for exploring the beautiful north Cotswolds and nearby villages. If you are in search of peace, tranquillity and the epitome of English country life, then Washbourne Court may just be your perfect choice.

LOCATION

Half a mile off the A429 between
Stow-on-the-Wold and Bourton-on-the-Water;
signed to The Slaughters.

" You have a great team who provided us with magnificent service during the evening "

PHILIP SIMS, HSBC BANK

WESTWOOD COUNTRY HOTEL — Country house

Hinksey Hill Top, Near Boars Hill,
Oxford OX1 5BG

T (UK) 0870 432 8814
T 01865 735408
F 01865 736536
westwood@bestloved.com
www.westwood.bestloved.com

OWNER
Anthony Healy

MANAGER
Jackie Sperlich

ROOM RATES
2 Singles £75
12 Doubles/Twins £99
2 Four-posters £130
3 Family Rooms £135
Includes full breakfast and VAT

CREDIT CARDS
AMERICAN EXPRESS • DC • MC • VI

RATINGS & AWARDS
ETC ★★★
AA ★★★ 66%

FACILITIES
On site: Garden, licensed for weddings,
woodlands, car park
4 meeting rooms/max 70 people
Nearby: Golf, archery, riding,
clay pigeon shooting, fishing, swimming

RESTRICTIONS
Pets by arrangement
Closed Christmas - New Year

ATTRACTIONS
Oxford Botanical Gardens,
Oxford University colleges, Stratford,
the Cotswolds, Blenheim Palace,
Waddesdon Manor

NEAREST
CITY:
Oxford - 2 miles/10 mins

AIRPORT:
Heathrow - 50 miles/1 hr

RAIL STATION:
Oxford - 2 miles/10 mins

AFFILIATIONS
Independent

RESERVATIONS
National rate in UK: 0870 432 8814
Quote Best Loved

ACCESS CODES
Not applicable

A beautiful woodland setting close to Oxford's dreaming spires

Just two miles from the heart of Oxford lies a 400-acre ancient woodland preserve offering sanctuary to numerous species of birds and wildlife. In the midst of this idyllic scenery, the Westwood basks in the quiet of the countryside, surrounded by its own lovely woodland gardens.

The house was built as an Edwardian private residence and has been thoughtfully extended and refurbished as a hotel. The comfortable bedrooms have been decorated with fabrics and papers by the Zoffany design house. Two of the rooms have four-poster beds, while others have a private terrace or balcony overlooking the grounds.

There is a warm welcome to be found in the Oaks Bar and fine cuisine in the Oaks Restaurant. Corporate clients can make use of four well-equipped conference rooms or enjoy a challenging round of golf at nearby Frilford Heath Golf Course - Anthony Healy is a member and can wholly recommend it! The hotel is a popular venue for weddings and parties, whether inside or out in the gardens. Westwood's gardens, after all, are a delight. Opened by renowned naturalist David Bellamy in 1995, they are a work in progress, and a small lake has been resurrected to include a romantic summer house where guests can barbecue in warm weather.

LOCATION
From the A34 Hinksey Hill interchange, take the exit signed Boars Hill. The road curves to the left; the hotel is on the right.

> " Tina and Dino are two of the most welcoming and hospitable hosts in the Cotswolds "
>
> DREW SMITH, EDITOR, TASTE MAGAZINE

Inn

THE WILD DUCK

**Drakes Island,
Ewen, Cirencester,
Gloucestershire GL7 6BY**

T (UK) 0870 432 8817
T 01285 770310
F 01285 770924
wilduck@bestloved.com
www.wilduck.bestloved.com

OWNER
Tina Mussell

ROOM RATES
Single occupancy	£70
8 Doubles	£95
2 Four-posters	£120
I Directors Double	£120
I Suite	£150

Includes continental breakfast and VAT

CREDIT CARDS
AMERICAN EXPRESS • MC • VI

RATINGS & AWARDS
RAC ★★ Dining Award 2
AA ★★ ✪ 68%

FACILITIES
Nearby: Sailing, jet skiing, golf, riding, fishing

RESTRICTIONS
Limited facilities for disabled guests
Pets by arrangement; £10 surcharge

ATTRACTIONS
Slimbridge Wild Fowl Sanctuary,
Badminton and Gatcombe
Horse Trials,
Bath, the Cotswolds,
Stratford-upon-Avon,
Cirencester Park Polo Club

NEAREST
CITY:
Bath - 25 miles/35 mins

AIRPORT:
Heathrow - 70 miles/1 hr 45 mins
Bristol - 40 miles/45 mins

RAIL STATION:
Kemble - 3 miles/3 mins

AFFILIATIONS
Independent

RESERVATIONS
National rate in UK: 0870 432 8817
Quote Best Loved

ACCESS CODES
Not applicable

MIDSHIRES

A quintessential local English inn of 15th-century character

The Wild Duck is a mellow Cotswold stone Elizabethan inn - a typical local English inn, warm and welcoming, rich in colours and hung with old oil portraits of English ancestors. Large open log fires burn in the bar and the oak-panelled residents' lounge in wintertime.

There are 11 bedrooms, two of which have four-poster beds and overlook the garden. The inn's garden is secluded, delightful and perfect for al fresco dining in the summer. The bar offers six real ales, and the wine list is extensive and innovative. The country-style dining room offers fresh seasonal food, including game in the winter and fresh fish delivered overnight from Brixham in Devon - this can include such exotic fare as parrotfish and tilapia!

Within a mile's journey, The Wild Duck is surrounded by the Cotswold Water Park, with 80 lakes providing fishing, swimming, sailing, water skiing and jet skiing. Polo at nearby Cirencester Park is a regular event, and every March Cheltenham holds the Gold Cup Race Meeting. Horse trials at Gatcombe Park and Badminton are also held annually - an excellent incentive for a visit.

LOCATION

Exit 17 from the M4 (Cirencester).
Before Cirencester, turn right at Kemble and follow the signs to Ewen.

WROXTON HOUSE HOTEL

Village hotel

MIDSHIRES

Wroxton St. Mary, Banbury,
Oxfordshire OX15 6QB

T (UK) 0870 432 8826
T 01295 730777
F 01295 730800
wroxtonhse@bestloved.com
www.wroxtonhse.bestloved.com

MANAGING DIRECTOR
Tristan McEwen

ROOM RATES
5 Singles	£95
24 Doubles	£100 - £125
2 Four-posters	£150
1 Suite	£150
Includes VAT	

CREDIT CARDS
AMERICAN EXPRESS • DC • MC • VI

RATINGS & AWARDS
AA ★★★ 69%

FACILITIES
On site: Heli-pad,
licensed for weddings
2 meeting rooms/max 100 people
Nearby: Golf, gliding and riding

RESTRICTIONS
Limited facilities for disabled guests
Smoking in some rooms only

ATTRACTIONS
Stratford-upon-Avon, Oxford,
Warwick Castle, Blenheim Palace,
Batsford Arboretum, Stanway House,
Snowshill Manor, antiques hunting

NEAREST
CITY:
Oxford - 30 miles/35 mins

AIRPORT:
Birmingham - 42 miles/40 mins

RAIL STATION:
Banbury - 3 miles/5 mins

AFFILIATIONS
Best Western

RESERVATIONS
National rate in UK: 0870 432 8826
Quote Best Loved

ACCESS CODES
AMADEUS BW BHX294
APOLLO/GALILEO BW 05965
SABRE/ABACUS BW 18418
WORLDSPAN BW 83294

A traditional Cotswold welcome midway between Oxford and Stratford

Handily placed for the M40, but with an atmosphere evoking the heart of the country, this lovingly restored village manor house and cottages have been recently redecorated and refurbished to make the best of an already good thing!

An ideal home for leisure or business travel - Wroxton House can cater for up to 100 meeting delegates - the hotel offers atmosphere evocative of a cosy home from home; original timbers are preserved throughout much of the hotel, and a warmly pleasing restaurant offers inglenooks, carved oak recesses and traditional touches as a backdrop to delicious English cooking.

The bedrooms echo this homely feel, offering beams and stone fireplaces in some, and all with comfortable, well-appointed amenities including satellite television, hair dryer, trouser press and excellent room service. A conservatory lounge welcomes on sunnier days as a pleasant place to relax with a chat or a book, and, of course, there's plenty to do outdoors. Wroxton village is a treat in itself, with mellow Cotswold stone cottages, thatched roofs and country lanes providing idyllic atmosphere. The hotel is midway between Stratford-upon-Avon and Oxford, and more than a dozen magnificent gardens and mansions - including Blenheim, Broughton and Upton - are within half an hour's drive. For racing fans, there's easy access to Silverstone, too.

LOCATION

Exit the M40, junction 11; then, follow the A422 toward Stratford for three miles.

PRESENT PERFECT

MAR HALL, NEAR GLASGOW (PAGE 64)

Give your friends or family memories they'll cherish for a lifetime ... a great meal or a stay at a Best Loved Hotel.

The **Best Loved Hotels Gift Voucher Package** includes

- The latest 456-page Best Loved Hotels - UK/Ireland full-colour directory, packed with enticing travel ideas
- £100 gift certificate valid for accommodation or dining
- One year's free membership in the Red Rosette Travel Club
- All beautifully gift-wrapped with your special message and sent to the address of your choice

Only £149.95, including VAT, postage and packing

Already have a copy of the book? Vouchers alone are available in values of £50, £100, £150 and up.

Or, give a perfect present in pocket size - the **Little Gold Book Gift Voucher Package** for just £129.95, including VAT, postage and packing. Includes a £100 voucher, a year's membership in the Red Rosette Travel Club, gift wrapping and a copy of the Best Loved Hotels Little Gold Book, packed with special offers at more than 350 great places to stay throughout the UK and Ireland.

LLANGOED HALL, BRECON, POWYS (PAGE 152)

COTTAGE HOTEL, BROCKENHURST (PAGE 304)

Call today for a gift that won't soon be forgotten!

WEST

AN ISLAND HOTEL
Hell Bay, Isles of Scilly

A TOWNHOUSE
The Royal Crescent Hotel, Bath

A SEASIDE HOTEL
Trevalsa Court Country House, Cornwall

REPRESENTING
the best of the
WEST

A COUNTRY HOUSE HOTEL
Bovey Castle, Devon

Best Loved Hotels offer the cream of the crop across Great Britain and Ireland - from stately palaces to welcoming inns - each the best of its kind within its locality and price range.

Whichever place you choose as your own place to stay, you'll find every hotel offers character, charm and the best delights and attractions of its region.

And each, in its own special way, is best-loved by someone who's been there.

A HARBOUR INN
The Lugger Hotel, Cornwall

A STATELY HOME
Ston Easton Park, Somerset

AN ISLAND HOTEL
Island Hotel, Isles of Scilly

A SEASIDE HOTEL
Hotel Riviera, Devon

AN IDEAL ESCAPE:
The West Country

FROM BATH'S SPLENDID HISTORY to a bit of seaside fun in Devon, the West Country offers something for every season, every age and every interest. Soak in the sun on a Blue Flag beach or soak up the legend of Tintagel Castle - the choices are nearly endless.

Day One

Bath is such a fascinating mix of history through the ages that it's worth an entire weekend, but the main sights are certainly a good pull for a day. Begin your journey in the order of history: start from a vantage point of at least 8,000 years BC, when resident Celts threw coins into the water as offerings to their god; fast-forward to Roman Bath, where the only hot springs in Britain offered a tremendous pull.

Learn a bit more about the city's ancient history at the **Building of Bath Museum**, where the main exhibition shows a fascinating-for-all-ages timeline of the city's development, including a 1:500 scale model for a true bird's-eye view.

Next, see the real thing in person: the Roman town, Aquae Sulis, and **the baths** themselves, including a wealth of exhibits and Roman artefacts. Although it's no longer possible to take a dip in the original Roman baths, ongoing work continues on the city's extensive **Thermae Bath Spa** - and by the time you read these words, you may just be able to book a visit and get a taste of Bath's centuries-old bathing experience.

Georgian Bath is another stunning creature, with clean, strong lines and an abundance of local stone - in fact, it's an architectural mandate that new structures contain some element of Bath stone in their construction. **The Royal Crescent** is an architectural gem worth admiring from at least a few angles (and you can stay there, too! See page 280).

With such a wealth of Palladian architecture, it may be best to strike out on foot (car travel can be a bit slow in the centre) and stretch your legs in time for a leisurely stop for tea.

Day Two

From pastoral Somerset to seaside adventure - **Devon** isn't far from Bath, but it's a world away in atmosphere. If the weather's fine, take advantage of some of Britain's most peaceful

Bath's architecture is glorious, with or without the balloons

A festive ferry ride in Brixham

coastal areas - walk along pebble beaches or a sandy shore, or simply enjoy the views across the Channel or the Atlantic. Devon was awarded 11 Blue Flags for its beaches in 2005, more than any county in England - and as long as the weather is fine, nearly any stretch of shore is worth a visit.

Better still, strike out into the water yourself. The easiest and most relaxed may be a spur-of-the-moment **ferry ride** - try the half-hour journey between Brixham and Torquay, and take a break before returning for a bite to eat and a stroll around the pretty

A glorious SUMMERTIME on the English Riviera

Princess Gardens, named for Princess Louise, one of Queen Victoria's children who visited the seaside town in 1890. Certainly a slice of the 'English Riviera'! History enthusiasts can take the ferry from Dartmouth to **Dartmouth Castle**, a 15th-century structure with some fascinating Victorian additions.

If the weather's not co-operating, there is, of course, plenty to do indoors. For families, there are the **Totnes Museum** and **Totnes Costume Museum** (though the latter is only open from the spring bank holiday through the end of September), perfect for exploring anything from Victoriana to the story of mathematician Charles Babbage, who lived in Totnes.

Legend and history - as well as coastal charm - await at Tintagel Castle

DAY THREE

Day Three

Finish up your visit with a few hours spent in Eden - a trip to **Cornwall** wouldn't be complete without seeing the **Eden Project**, and its magnificent domes shelter more than 100,000 plants in a simulation of climate conditions across the globe. No matter the weather outside, you'll catch a glimpse of summer in the world's largest greenhouse.

Inspiration for the Eden Project came from another major Cornish landmark, the **Lost Gardens of Heligan**, once-magnificent 19th-century gardens surrounding a 1603 house re-discovered in 1990 after years of neglect, then restored to grandeur. Definitely worth a look.

There's much more than plants to be seen in Cornwall, though, ranging from open-air theatre at the **Minack Theatre** to **Lanhydrock**, a grand country house set in 450 acres of woods and parkland. To catch a glimpse of the region's legend, try **Tintagel Castle**, the legendary birthplace of King Arthur - in addition to some truly magical views, the castle and surrounding area offer more than adequate fuel for the imagination.

Step into a rainforest for the afternoon at the Eden Project

ESCAPE FROM YOUR DESKTOP

If you can't wait to get away, or if you'd simply like to do a little investigating before you make your West Country holiday, browse the links below. Remember, too, that thousands of places to see and things to do wait for you at Best Loved's Web site, **www.bestlovedhotels.com**.

Building of Bath Museum & Royal Crescent
www.bath-preservation-trust.org.uk

Roman Baths
www.romanbaths.co.uk

Thermae Bath Spa
www.thermaebathspa.com

Devon beach guide
www.bbc.co.uk/devon/discovering/
information/beach_guide.shtml

Dartmouth Castle
www.english-heritage.org.uk

Totnes Museum
www.totnes.com/museum

Eden Project
www.edenproject.com

Lost Gardens of Heligan
www.heligan.com

Minack Theatre
www.minack.com

Lanhydrock
www.nationaltrust.org.uk

Tintagel Castle
www.english-heritage.org.uk

A TASTE OF THE BEST
The West Country

THE WEST'S seaside views and country vistas are perfect companions to good dining, whether your tastes run toward contemporary creativity or traditional delights. Either way, you're certain to find something here to take your fancy.

BATH PRIORY HOTEL ❀❀❀

This delicious escape on the edge of Bath is complete with intriguing Gothic touches, luxurious decor and four acres of award-winning gardens. Their celebrated restaurant overlooks the stunning gardens and serves the creations of Michelin-starred Chef Robert Clayton, whose cuisine - including delights such as sautéed escalope of salmon with rosemary scented crushed potatoes and lobster sauce - is influenced by Mediterranean and modern French cooking, and uses organic vegetables and herbs produced from their own garden. Private dining is available for up to 64 guests, making it an even more tempting choice - after all, who wouldn't want to have a party in such a delightful place?

HELL BAY ❀❀

With a beautifully dramatic setting on the secluded island of Bryher, Hell Bay is a luxurious and contemporary resort hotel serving traditional cuisine with a modern twist. As one would expect from such a locale, dishes are created from the freshest ingredients, including hand-picked seafood from local boats and fresh meat, fruit and vegetables delivered daily. One of our favourites on the Hell Bay menu is the delicious char-grilled rib eye steak with fondant potatoes, tomato salsa and Béarnaise sauce - whether dining al fresco, or in the hotel's elegant restaurant, you are guaranteed top-quality cuisine, not to mention fantastic views!

Award-winning cuisine in a sumptuous setting at the Bath Priory

Relaxed luxury at The Well House

MILL END HOTEL ❀❀❀

A traditionally English hotel where cream teas and home-made jam are enjoyed by roaring log fires, Mill End is a real country house experience and one that wouldn't be complete without a meal in their restaurant. Head Chef Wayne Pearson is a Master Chef of Great Britain, and works with his team to produce fine cuisine made with the very best ingredients – free range eggs, freshly-caught fish, organic vegetables and local cheeses. Diners are treated to dishes such as beetroot and goat cheese risotto, followed perhaps by the Mill End's delicious roast pheasant and puy lentil casserole with roasted root vegetables. There are some incredibly tempting desserts, too, so be sure to save room for pudding!

LEWTRENCHARD MANOR ❀❀❀

Modern English cooking is served in the elegant dining room at this Jacobean manor near Okehampton, making for an experience that is as much a feast for the eyes as for the palate. Food is carefully prepared with fresh seasonal ingredients, including an emphasis on Devon game in the winter. On their seasonal menus, for example, you might find such delights as, Lewtrenchard assiette of organic salmon followed by sautéed loin of new season lamb with glazed sweetbread, pea puree and confit onions with thyme-infused jus. Vegetables and herbs used in the kitchen are carefully chosen and picked from the hotel's own walled garden - just another reason why dining at Lewtrenchard is so memorable.

A TASTE OF THE REGION

Looking for even more to tempt your palate? There are a wealth of fantastic places to dine in the West Country, all within the covers of this book! Have a browse to whet your appetite, or jump to some of our own favourites:

ISLAND HOTEL ❀❀

Set by white sandy beaches, seafood is a particular speciality at this luxurious, modern hotel. Its Tresco setting is a perfect backdrop to such delightful dining!

HUNSTRETE HOUSE ❀❀

The award-winning dining room opens out to the courtyard at this friendly stately house near Bath, and al fresco dining is available in the summer - a delightful way to while away an evening.

BOVEY CASTLE

There is no end of luxury at this breathtaking stately home and estate, including fresh organic cuisine served in the fine-dining Palm Court and the less formal Club House restaurants. Ideal fuel for a round or two of golf on the hotel's own green!

HAYDON HOUSE

A hospitable Edwardian townhouse in Bath where imaginative cuisine is just as important for breakfast as it is for dinner. And be sure not to miss the homemade shortbread ...

THE WELL HOUSE ❀❀❀

Twice voted the Good Food Guide's 'County Restaurant of the Year', this Victorian country manor's dining room has beautiful views over the lawns and serves traditional local dishes cooked with a contemporary edge. Head Chef Glenn Gatland's daily changing menu makes great use of fresh Cornish ingredients, with sea bass and lobster featuring prominently on the menu. Other dishes include fillet of West Country beef with ratatouille, pesto and dauphinoise potatoes, or caramelised chicory tart with crisp fried goat cheese. A selection of Cornish cheeses is available, too, for true local flair, and to accompany it all an impressive wine list is carefully chosen by proprietor Nick Wainford.

Local treats at Hell Bay

LOCAL SHELLFISH
LOBSTER - LIVE OR COOKED
CRAB - WHOLE OR PICKED
—
PLEASE INQUIRE AT TOP OF PATH.

A carefully-chosen WINE LIST *completes a meal at The Well House*

The desserts at Hell Bay are a delightful temptation

Menu
THE WELL HOUSE

Seared scallops and Cornish crab risotto with thyme oil
Confit of duck with red onion marmalade and puy lentil jus

Guinea Fowl Supreme with pancetta and pimento and basil cassoulet
Pan-roasted monkfish with summer green vegetables, lemongrass & ginger sauce

Summer pudding with chilled mascarpone cheese and spiced tuile biscuits
Lavender panna cotta with vanilla beignets and white peach sorbet

ANDREWS ON THE WEIR

Restaurant with rooms

Porlock Weir, Porlock,
Near Minehead,
Somerset TA24 8PB

T (UK) 0870 432 8518
T 01643 863300
F 01643 863311
andrews@bestloved.com
www.andrews.bestloved.com

OWNERS
Andrew and Sarah Dixon
and Rodney Sens

ROOM RATES
4 Doubles/Twins   £75 - £95
1 Four-poster   £120
Includes full breakfast and VAT

CREDIT CARDS
DC • MC • VI

RATINGS & AWARDS
AA ❀❀❀ 76%

FACILITIES
On site: Garden, private dining room
Nearby: Golf, riding, fishing

RESTRICTIONS
No facilities for disabled guests
No children under 12 years
in the restaurant
Smoking in lounge only
Closed January and Mondays and
Tuesdays

ATTRACTIONS
Dunster Castle and Gardens,
Lorna Doone Valley, Devon coast,
RHS Rosemoor,
Exmoor and Tarr Steps,
Arlington Court

NEAREST
CITY:
Taunton - 30 miles/45 mins

AIRPORT:
Bristol - 70 miles/1 hr 30 mins
Exeter - 60 miles/1 hr 30 mins

RAIL STATION:
Taunton - 30 miles/45 mins

AFFILIATIONS
Independent

RESERVATIONS
National rate in UK: 0870 432 8518
Quote Best Loved

ACCESS CODES
Not applicable

WEST COUNTRY

An intriguing setting and an experience to exceed expectations

From the lovely town of Porlock, you take a winding road that comes to a seemingly abrupt end at the intriguing Porlock Weir. To the right is a high shingle beach and to the left, almost tucked into the hillside, is Andrews on the Weir.

This remarkable hotel is owned and run by husband-and-wife team Andrew and Sarah Dixon. Andrew, with his notable culinary pedigree, heads up the brigade in the kitchen, and Sarah manages the restaurant. They are assisted by a talented and dedicated team and are collectively on a mission to create the finest dining 'experience' in the region. Andrew's team spirit extends to his suppliers - who, it seems, have become good friends. He is assured of the best Devon beef and Exmoor lamb, and the local park ranger supplies him with the finest mushrooms and game.

The five bedrooms are great value and won't disappoint; all are traditional in style and delightfully furnished with antiques. Ask if the four-poster master bedroom is available. With so little space to tell of this hotel's treasures, it will have to suffice to say that something very exciting has been created in this unusual little place and those that visit will be glad of the tip-off!

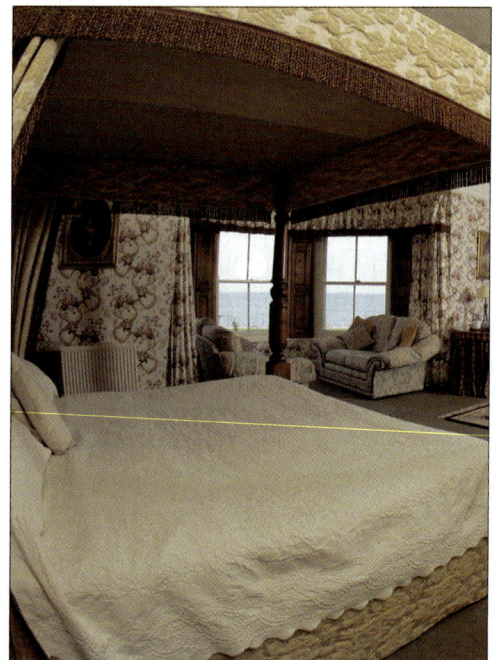

LOCATION
From Porlock, take B3225 to Porlock Weir. The hotel is at the end of the road on the left, opposite the car park.

> " A peep back into history - excellent! "
>
> ESTELLE AND LOUIS CLIGNON, LONDON

Inn

AT THE SIGN OF THE ANGEL

The quintessential English inn in a National Trust village

In the 15th century, a wool merchant built a house for his family in the Wiltshire village of Lacock; today, the oak-panelled lounge At The Sign of The Angel reflects the warmth of his family home. The beautiful old staircase looks down on a courtyard and gardens, and crackling log fires, squeaky floorboards and oak panels and beams add up to a quintessential English inn. Since 1953, the Levis family has run this remarkable hotel with enthusiasm and friendship.

The restaurant is renowned for traditional English cooking. Breakfasts feature the inn's own eggs, locally-cured bacon, homemade bread and Mrs Levis's marmalade. Lunch and dinner concentrate on traditional roasts, fish fresh from Cornwall and herbs, vegetables and asparagus from the kitchen garden. All the puddings are made on the premises.

Lacock is the archetypal English village, with winding streets, Gothic-arched grey-stone houses and half-timbered cottages. William Fox-Talbot, maker of the world's first photographic prints in 1833, lived here, and his house is now a world-famous museum of photography. The Roman city of Bath, as well as Stonehenge and Avebury, are within 40 minutes' drive, as are historic houses in Wiltshire, Somerset and Gloucestershire and the cathedral cities of Salisbury and Wells.

LOCATION

From the M4, exit 17, take the A350 towards Chippenham and follow signs into Lacock. The hotel is in Church Street.

6 Church Street, Lacock, Chippenham, Wiltshire SN15 2LB

T (UK) 0870 432 8522
T 01249 730230
F 01249 730527
atthesign@bestloved.com
www.atthesign.bestloved.com

OWNERS
George and Lorna Hardy

ROOM RATES
Single occupancy £77 - £89
7 Doubles/Twins £110 - £135
3 Superior rooms £136 - £150
Includes full breakfast and VAT

CREDIT CARDS
AMERICAN EXPRESS • DC • JCB • MC • VI

RATINGS & AWARDS
AA ◆◆◆◆◆
AA Premier Collection

FACILITIES
On site: Garden
2 meeting rooms/max 18 people
Nearby: Golf, riding

RESTRICTIONS
Limited facilities for disabled guests
No smoking in bedrooms
Pets by arrangement
Closed 23 - 31 Dec.

ATTRACTIONS
Lacock Abbey and village, Bath, Stonehenge, Avebury, Corsham Hall, Fox-Talbot Museum of Photography, Bradford-on-Avon

NEAREST
CITY:
Bath - 15 miles/30 mins

AIRPORT:
Heathrow - 90 miles/2 hrs

RAIL STATION:
Chippenham - 4 miles/15 mins

AFFILIATIONS
Independent

RESERVATIONS
National rate in UK: 0870 432 8522
Quote Best Loved

ACCESS CODES
Not applicable

WEST COUNTRY

BARRINGTON HOUSE

Country house

Mount Boone, Dartmouth,
Devon TQ6 9HZ

T (UK) 0870 432 8527
T 01803 835545
F 01803 835545
barrington@bestloved.com
www.barrington.bestloved.com

OWNERS
John and Christine Smither

ROOM RATES
4 Doubles/Twins   £90 - £115
Includes breakfast and VAT

CREDIT CARDS
AMERICAN EXPRESS • MC • VI

RATINGS & AWARDS
ETC ◆◆◆◆◆ Silver Award
AA ◆◆◆◆◆
AA Premier Collection

FACILITIES
On site: Garden, garden, parking
1 meeting room/max 30 people
Nearby: Golf, walks, riding, leisure
centre, health & beauty

RESTRICTIONS
No facilities for disabled guests
No children under 8 years
No smoking throughout
No pets

ATTRACTIONS
Dartmouth, Salcombe Estuary,
Dartmoor,
Blackpool Sands and Slapton Sands,
Plymouth, The Eden Project,
National Trust properties,
boat trips to Totnes

NEAREST
CITY:
Dartmouth

AIRPORT:
Exeter - 36 miles/1 hr
Plymouth - 38 miles/1 hr 10 mins

RAIL STATION:
Totnes - 13 miles/35 mins
Paignton - 9 miles/30 mins

AFFILIATIONS
Independent

RESERVATIONS
National rate in UK: 0870 432 8527
Quote Best Loved

ACCESS CODES
Not applicable

WEST COUNTRY

Restful hospitality frames fantastic views at this seaside escape

A blissfully quiet coastal retreat, Barrington House is an elegant Edwardian gem offering accommodation that is at once both pleasantly relaxed and eminently civilised. This beautifully-furnished house, home of owners John and Christine Smither, offers four en-suite double rooms, as well as a self-catering penthouse apartment to sleep six. Either way, you're assured of peaceful, restful rooms and fantastic views down the Dart and 10 miles out to sea.

It just might, however, be a sin to miss the food - the 'Barrington buffet' is a memorable Scandinavian-style feast, with smoked salmon, scrambled eggs, cheeses and cold cuts, plus plenty of fruit! For dinner, book a meal from Barrington's chef, Valerie Mould, whose prior work heading her own seafood restaurant in Salcombe shows in her menu's enticing treatment of locally-produced fish.

When you're ready to do some exploring, there's certainly more than enough to keep you busy, from an eye-opening day at the Eden Project to a wealth of National Trust properties and seaside delights. For sporting types, the nearby Dartmouth Golf and Country Club offers guests at Barrington House an alluring discount - whether it's on a round of golf or a few laps round the pool at the club's leisure and beauty centre.

LOCATION
Exit the A384 from the A38 to reach Dartmouth, joining the A3122; once in town, turn right into Townstal Road, then left down Mount Boone. The hotel is third on the left.

"Some places on earth can't be beaten - you've created one of those places"

JOHN & ANN WRIGHT, CAMBRIDGE

Village hotel

BATH LODGE HOTEL

Norton St Philip, Bath,
Somerset BA2 7NH

T (UK) 0870 432 8529
T 01225 723040
F 01225 723737
bathlodge@bestloved.com
www.bathlodge.bestloved.com

OWNERS
Richard and Susan Warren

ROOM RATES
1 Single   £45 - £85
3 Doubles/Twins   £85 - £115
3 Four Posters   £100 - £120
Includes full breakfast and VAT

CREDIT CARDS
AMERICAN EXPRESS • MC • VI

RATINGS & AWARDS
AA ◆◆◆◆◆
AA Premier Collection

FACILITIES
On site: Garden
Nearby: Golf, riding, shooting,
clay pigeon shooting, fishing

RESTRICTIONS
No facilities for disabled guests
No children under 10 years
No smoking throughout
No pets

ATTRACTIONS
Bath Spa, Roman Baths,
American Museum, Stonehenge,
Longleat, Stourhead, Wells,
Glastonbury

NEAREST
CITY:
Bath - 7 miles/15 mins

AIRPORT:
Heathrow - 100 miles/2 hrs
Bristol - 29 miles/45 mins

RAIL STATION:
Bath - 7 miles/15 mins

AFFILIATIONS
Independent

RESERVATIONS
National rate in UK: 0870 432 8529
Quote Best Loved

ACCESS CODES
Not applicable

WEST COUNTRY

Castle comforts amidst the romance of an ancient deer forest

Originally called Castle Lodge, the Bath Lodge Hotel has all the appearance of a pocket-sized medieval castle, from its impressive stone structure, portcullis and heraldic shields right up to the battlements and towers above. In reality, the Lodge was built between 1806 and 1813 as the principal of six gate lodges to the Farleigh estate.

The building boasts the original oak beams, natural masonry, log-burning fireplace and mullioned windows. All the rooms are beautifully decorated and furnished to a high standard, with elegant antique furniture happily co-existing with contemporary comforts and facilities. The original lodge rooms benefit from four-poster or brass bedsteads, showers in the turrets and balconies. Outside, a bubbling stream cascades through the garden clandestinely merging into the ancient deer forest where kings and barons once hunted - all very romantic!

Situated only seven miles outside Bath, the hotel is also ideally located for visiting the heritage sites of Stonehenge, Longleat, Stourhead and Wells, with its magnificent cathedral, as well as many other area attractions. That's why Bath Lodge likes to set its guests up for the day with an excellent breakfast. In the evening, the romantic and relaxed atmosphere provides the perfect end to the day.

LOCATION

From Bath, take the A36 Warminster Road. The hotel is approximately seven miles along on the left.

THE BATH PRIORY HOTEL & RESTAURANT — City hotel

Weston Road, Bath,
Somerset BA1 2XT

T (UK) 0870 432 8530
T 01225 331922
F 01225 448276
priorybath@bestloved.com
www.priorybath.bestloved.com

GENERAL MANAGER
Sue Williams

ROOM RATES
7 Superior Doubles £245
11 Deluxe Doubles £300
9 Superior Deluxe Doubles £360
4 Suites £425
Includes full breakfast and VAT

CREDIT CARDS
AMERICAN EXPRESS • DC • MC • VI

RATINGS & AWARDS
RAC Gold Ribbon ★★★★
Dining Award 4
AA ★★★★ ✿✿
AA Top 200 - 2004/2005

FACILITIES
On site: Garden, gym, croquet,
outdoor pool, indoor pool,
fitness centre,
beauty treatment rooms
3 meeting rooms/max 64 people
Nearby: Golf, ballooning,
boating, riding

RESTRICTIONS
Limited facilities for disabled guests
No children under 8 years in restaurant
for dinner, high tea provided
Smoking in drawing room only
No pets; guide dogs only

ATTRACTIONS
Roman Baths, Royal Crescent,
pump rooms, Bath Abbey,
Museum of Costume,
Royal Victoria Park, Lacock,
Castle Combe, Longleat,
Stourhead Gardens

NEAREST
CITY:
Bath - 1 mile/5 mins

AIRPORT:
Heathrow - 90 miles/1 hr 30 mins
Bristol - 15 miles/25 mins

RAIL STATION:
Bath Spa - 1 mile/5 mins

AFFILIATIONS
Celebrated Hotels Collection
Small Luxury Hotels
Grand Hotels of the World

RESERVATIONS
National rate in UK: 0870 432 8530
Toll free in US: 800-322-2403
or 800-525-4800
Quote Best Loved

ACCESS CODES
AMADEUS LX BRSTPH
APOLLO/GALILEO LX 87851
SABRE/ABACUS LX 41891
WORLDSPAN LX BRSPH

WEST COUNTRY

Utter sumptuousness in the Roman city of Bath

Set in four acres of award-winning landscaped gardens on the edge of the city, the Bath Priory Hotel was built in 1835 as a private residence and remains one of the finest examples of the Gothic architecture of its time. Now beautifully converted, it offers visitors comfort, peace and privacy as well as luxurious health spa facilities.

In the restaurant, overlooking the stunning gardens, guests can enjoy modern French and Mediterranean cuisine from Michelin-starred chef Robert Clayton under the direction of Restaurant Manager Vito Scaduto.

The Priory offers 27 sumptuous bedrooms and four luxurious suites, all of which are equipped with an ISDN line, voice mail, modem points, remote-control TV with satellite channels, marble bathrooms, antique furniture, and a wealth of objets d'art. Guests are free to use the health club, which features a fully equipped gymnasium, heated indoor and outdoor swimming pools, spa, steam room and solarium. In addition, theatres, museums, antique shops and the Roman baths are all within a pleasant walk. All this, combined with elegant surroundings and a friendly and attentive team of staff ensure that guests enjoy an utterly relaxing stay at The Bath Priory.

LOCATION
From the A46 to Bath, follow signs to Bristol (A4) until Victoria Park. Turn right at Park Lane and left at Weston Road. The hotel is 300 yards on the left.

Map p. 448, grid D4

249

Country house

BOVEY CASTLE

Moretonhampstead,
Devon TQ13 8RD

T (UK) 0870 432 8502
T 01647 445000
F 01647 445020
bovey@bestloved.com
www.bovey.bestloved.com

CLUB DIRECTOR
Henrietta Fergusson

GENERAL MANAGER
Ian Solkin

An unparalleled experience in the heart of Dartmoor National Park

A glorious West Country escape, Bovey Castle is one of those rare places that can truly offer something for every taste, all in a breathtakingly regal setting. A member of Peter de Savary's high-profile collection of golf and lifestyle clubs (other branches include the Abaco Club in The Bahamas and the Cherokee Plantation in South Carolina) this refreshing country estate is a newly-restored jewel in the group's crown.

Set in 368 square miles within Dartmoor National Park, Bovey Castle is a beautifully self-contained retreat from the everyday. The glorious reception rooms, bedrooms and suites are graced with wonderful views over the grounds. Rooms are individually-designed, with fresh flowers and twice-daily service. Dining is a delight too, with fresh organic produce served in the fine dining Palm Court and the less formal Club House.

Further indulgence can be found in the hotel's new holistic spa, complete with saunas, steam rooms, hydrotherapy, gymnasium and a stunning indoor pool housed in the orangery. There is a wealth of activity on and around the castle's grounds, whether on the internationally renowned J F Abercromby-designed golf course - described by PGA professional Richard Lewis as 'the most fulfilling game of golf I have ever enjoyed' - or boating, walking, shooting, riding or simply a delightfully relaxed picnic.

ROOM RATES
Single occupancy   £135 - £1,125
18 Mews Rooms   £180 - £245
13 Garden View Rooms   £220 - £290
22 Valley View Rooms   £245 - £345
6 State Rooms   £450 - £650
1 Gate Lodge   £950
4 Suites   £550 - £1,500
             Excludes VAT

CREDIT CARDS
AMERICAN EXPRESS • DC • MC • VI

RATINGS & AWARDS
Awards Pending

FACILITIES
On site: Garden, gym, snooker, heli-pad, fishing, croquet, riding, golf, tennis, cricket, indoor pool, health & beauty, licensed for weddings, falconry, shooting, badminton, biking, children's activities
3 meeting rooms/max 120
Nearby: balloon flights, expedition tours, helicopter flights, off-road driving, sailing

RESTRICTIONS
Smoking in some rooms only
Pets by arrangement

ATTRACTIONS
Exeter, Dartmoor, Plymouth, Dartmouth, Salcombe, Eden Project, antiques hunting

NEAREST
CITY:
Exeter - 12 miles/20 mins
Bristol - 100 miles/1 hr 15 mins

AIRPORT:
Exeter - 20 miles/20 mins
Bristol - 100 miles/1 hr 15 mins

RAIL STATION:
Exeter - 20 miles/20 mins

AFFILIATIONS
Celebrated Hotels Collection
Great Hotels of the World

RESERVATIONS
National rate in UK: 0870 432 8502
Toll free in US: 800-322-2403
Quote Best Loved

ACCESS CODES
AMADEUS GW EXT032
APOLLO/GALILEO GW 65076
SABRE/ABACUS GW 35708
WORLDSPAN GW 5032

LOCATION

Exit the M5 (Exeter) at junction 31 for the A30 (Okehampton); then, exit for the B3212 (Moretonhampstead). The hotel is a mile and a half after Moretonhampstead, on the left.

WEST COUNTRY

BROWNS HOTEL

Townhouse

80 West Street, Tavistock,
Devon PL19 8AQ

T (UK) 0870 432 8546
T 01822 618686
F 01822 618646
brownswb@bestloved.com
www.brownswb.bestloved.com

OWNERS
Peter Brown and Martin Ball

ROOM RATES
6 Singles	£65
12 Doubles/Twins	£90 - £140
1 Four-poster	£150
1 Family Room	£140

Includes full breakfast and VAT

CREDIT CARDS
AMERICAN EXPRESS • MC • VI

RATINGS & AWARDS
ETC ★★★★ Town House
RAC ★★★★ Dining Award 2

FACILITIES
On site: Gym, courtyard
Nearby: Golf, riding, fishing, swimming pool, bowls

RESTRICTIONS
Limited facilities for disabled guests
Smoking only in designated areas
Pets by arrangement

ATTRACTIONS
Eden Project,
Dartmoor National Park,
Rosemoor RHS Garden,
National Marine Aquarium,
Padstow, St Mawes

NEAREST
CITY:
Plymouth - 16 miles/25 mins

AIRPORT:
Plymouth - 12 miles/20 mins
Exeter - 47 miles/1 hr

RAIL STATION:
Plymouth - 16 miles/25 mins

AFFILIATIONS
Independent

RESERVATIONS
National rate in UK: 0870 432 8546
Quote Best Loved

ACCESS CODES
Not applicable

WEST COUNTRY

Chic youth meets tradition in a four-star townhouse

The historic West Country town of Tavistock was the birthplace of one of England's most intrepid explorers, Sir Francis Drake, and back in Victorian times it was renowned as the world's major copper-producing area. Today, it is a bustling market town and home to Browns, a converted 17th-century coaching inn situated right in the town centre and close to Dartmoor National Park.

Inside, you will find an interesting blend of trendy and traditional; the state-of-the-art gym is pure 21st-century and is highly acclaimed. The hotel also has its own well, believed to date as far back as Roman times. It's positioned under a glass panel in the conservatory; still and sparkling water is drawn from it, bottled on the premises and provided free to guests in their rooms. The brasserie menu includes regional produce and organic and GM-free foods as available and is a highly regarded local destination for the ubiquitous English Sunday roast.

Tourist attractions in the vicinity include the hugely popular Eden Project, the National Marine Aquarium and various National Trust properties. Just 20 minutes from Plymouth Airport and 16 miles from the city itself, the hotel is the ideal base from which to explore the beaches, coves and dramatic landscapes of both Cornwall and Devon.

LOCATION
From the town square, follow the road up the hill; the hotel is on the right.

> "Perfection is a very hard commodity to find and should be cherished. Thank you at Budock for coming so close"
>
> THE ST JOHN FAMILY, STRATFORD-UPON-AVON

Resort

BUDOCK VEAN - THE HOTEL ON THE RIVER

Indulgent living and superb sport facilities in a beautiful location

Budock Vean is an elegant, unspoilt retreat on the banks of the Helford River, a designated Area of Outstanding Natural Beauty. Located beside Britain's most dramatic coastline, it is ideal for a range of country pursuits, including fishing, shooting, golf, tennis, walking, riding and sailing - and the climate is so mild that the golf course plays well for the whole year. A spectacular indoor heated pool opens out onto the terrace in summer or, in winter, has its own log fire.

There is a feeling of privacy and exclusivity within the 65 acres of gardens and parkland. Many bedrooms have open views across the hotel's golf course and gardens; for that extra bit of privacy, old-world cottages in the grounds can also be rented.

Seafood is a speciality of the award-winning restaurant, with local Helford oysters and mussels a specialty. Less formal meals are served in the Country Club Room, whose large picture windows overlook the estate.

Cornwall has a unique identity rich in ancient heritage, rites and customs. With breathtaking coastal scenery, picturesque fishing villages and country footpaths, the area has stunning woodland walks beside the estuary. The superb gardens of Glendurgan and Trebah are a short stroll away.

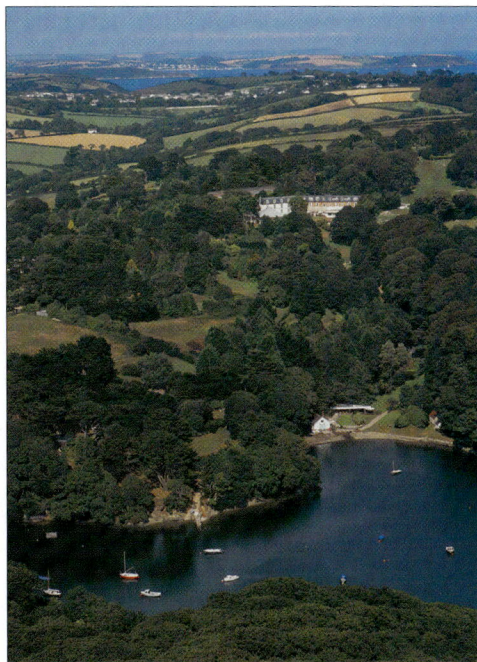

LOCATION

From the A39 Truro to Falmouth road, follow the brown signs to Trebah Gardens and continue for half a mile to Budock Vean.

Near Helford Passage, Mawnan Smith, Falmouth, Cornwall TR11 5LG

T (UK) 0870 432 8548
T 01326 252100
F 01326 250892
budock@bestloved.com
www.budock.bestloved.com

OWNERS
The Barlow Family

RATES PER PERSON
7 Singles	£68 - £112
48 Doubles/Twins	£68 - £112
1 Four-poster	£81 - £112
1 Suite	£116 - £147

Includes full breakfast, dinner, service and VAT

CREDIT CARDS
DC • MC • VI

RATINGS & AWARDS
ETC ★★★★ Silver Award Hotel
RAC Blue Ribbon ★★★★
Dining Award 2
AA ★★★★ ❀ 73%
South West Tourism
Large Hotel of the Year 2003
Cornwall Tourist Board
Hotel of the Year 2002 and 2003

FACILITIES
On site: Garden, snooker, heli-pad, golf, tennis, indoor pool, health & beauty, licensed for weddings, motor boat, private foreshore 2 meeting rooms/max 50 people
Nearby: Water skiing, yachting, riding, walks, fishing

RESTRICTIONS
Limited facilities for disabled guests
No children under 7 years in restaurant, high tea provided
No smoking in bedrooms
Pets by arrangement
Closed 2 - 21 Jan.

ATTRACTIONS
Lost Gardens of Heligan, Tate Gallery, Trebah Gardens, The Seal Sanctuary, St Michael's Mount, Minack Open Air Theatre, Eden Project, National Maritime Museum

NEAREST
CITY:
Truro - 15 miles/20 mins

AIRPORT:
Newquay - 30 miles/45 mins

RAIL STATION:
Falmouth - 6 miles/10 mins

FERRY PORT:
Falmouth - 6 miles/10 mins

AFFILIATIONS
Grand Heritage Hotels

RESERVATIONS
National rate in UK: 0870 432 8548
Toll free in UK: 0800 833 927
Toll free in US: 888-93-GRAND
Quote Best Loved

ACCESS CODES
Not applicable

WEST COUNTRY

"Everything at the Castle was perfection: the courtesy and attention of all the staff, the accommodation and, not to be forgotten, the food"

DR AND MRS P MINC, CANADA

THE CASTLE AT TAUNTON

Castle

Castle Green, Taunton,
Somerset TA1 1NF

T (UK) 0870 432 8556
T 01823 272671
F 01823 336066
castle@bestloved.com
www.castle.bestloved.com

OWNERS
The Chapman Family

DIRECTOR & GENERAL MANAGER
Kevin McCarthy

ROOM RATES
12 Singles   £110
27 Doubles/Twins   £180
5 Suites   £255
Includes full breakfast

CREDIT CARDS
AMERICAN EXPRESS • DC • MC • VI

RATINGS & AWARDS
RAC Gold Ribbon ★★★
Dining Award 4
AA ★★★ ❀❀
AA Top 200 - 2004/2005
Tatler Best Restaurant Out of London
Award 2002

FACILITIES
On site: Garden
4 meeting rooms/max 120 people
Nearby: Golf, leisure centre,
health & beauty, pony trekking

RESTRICTIONS
Limited facilities for disabled guests
Smoking in lounge only
No pets in public areas

ATTRACTIONS
Bath, Exmoor & the Quantocks,
Longleat Safari Park, Blackdown Hills,
Forde Abbey, Wells Cathedral,
National Trust properties & gardens

NEAREST
CITY:
Bristol - 50 miles/1 hr

AIRPORT:
Bristol - 40 miles/45 mins
Exeter - 35 miles/40 mins

RAIL STATION:
Taunton - 1 mile/5 mins

AFFILIATIONS
Independent

RESERVATIONS
National rate in UK: 0870 432 8556
Quote Best Loved

ACCESS CODES
AMADEUS NT BRSCAS
APOLLO/GALILEO NT 29738
SABRE/ABACUS NT 54280
WORLDSPAN NT TAUN

Twelve centuries of fascinating history and West Country hospitality

The Castle Hotel, once a Norman fortress, is steeped in the drama and romance of English history. In 1685, the Duke of Monmouth's officers were heard 'roistering at the Castle Inn' before they were defeated by the forces of King James II. Today, the Castle lives at peace with its turbulent past, but preserves an atmosphere of ancient tradition.

The Chapman family have been running the hotel for 54 years, and in that time it has acquired a worldwide reputation for the warmth of its hospitality. Furthermore, their first-class cuisine and excellent wine cellar are both widely acclaimed.

Located in the heart of England's beautiful West Country, the Castle Hotel is the ideal base for exploring a region rich in history. This is the land of King Arthur, King Alfred, Lorna Doone's Exmoor, the monastic foundations of Glastonbury and Wells, Roman and Regency Bath, Longleat House and the majestic gardens of Stourhead and Hestercombe. All this and much more can be discovered within easy driving distance of Taunton.

LOCATION
Exit at junction 25 of the M5 and follow signs for Taunton town centre. Once there, follow signs for the Castle Hotel.

City hotel

THE COUNTY HOTEL

18/19 Pulteney Road, Bath,
Somerset BA2 4EZ

T (UK) 0870 432 8577
T 01225 425003
F 01225 466493
county@bestloved.com
www.county.bestloved.com

OWNERS
Maureen and Charles Kent
and Sandra Masson

MANAGER
James Kent

ROOM RATES
2 Singles	£75 - £85
17 Doubles/Twins	£100 - £140
2 Superior Doubles/Twins	£160 - £185
1 Four-poster	£165 - £190

Includes full breakfast and VAT

CREDIT CARDS

AMERICAN EXPRESS • DC • JCB • MC • VI

RATINGS & AWARDS
ETC ♦♦♦♦♦ Gold Award
RAC ♦♦♦♦♦
RAC Little Gem, Sparkling Diamond
and Warm Welcome Awards
AA ♦♦♦♦♦
AA Premier Collection

FACILITIES
On site: Car park, bar
1 meeting room/max 20 people
Nearby: Golf, tennis, spa

RESTRICTIONS
No facilities for disabled guests
No children under 12 years
Smoking in bar only
No pets
Closed 22 Dec. - 5 Jan.

ATTRACTIONS
Roman Baths, the Pump Rooms,
Bath Abbey, Museum of Costume,
Castle Combe, Longleat Safari Park,
Thermae Spa

NEAREST
CITY:
Bath - 1 mile/5 mins

AIRPORT:
Heathrow - 90 miles/1 hr 30 mins

RAIL STATION:
Bath Spa - 1 mile/5 mins

AFFILIATIONS
Independent

RESERVATIONS
National rate in UK: 0870 432 8577
Quote Best Loved

ACCESS CODES
Not applicable

WEST COUNTRY

Put your feet up in front of one of the best skylines in Britain

'Perfect.' 'Fabulous hotel, fabulous time.' 'Nothing too much trouble. Excellent'. With hundreds of similar comments in the visitors' book, it's not surprising that The County Hotel has been showered with the highest awards.

The city of Bath is a must-see for everyone, but with so many attractions, it is easy to get 'museumed out' and desperate for somewhere friendly and relaxing to recover. Luckily, The County Hotel - within easy walking distance of the town centre - offers just that.

Relax and nestle into a sumptuous atmosphere, with classical furnishings and generous drapes around the large sash windows and beds. Each luxurious bedroom - equipped with every facility - reflects a different mood, while the gracious public rooms include the Jane Austen reading room and a popular bar, the only place in the hotel where smoking is permitted. The hotel's celebrated Bath breakfast is served in the elegant breakfast room and conservatory, both of which revel in the uninterrupted view over the county cricket ground and Bath's rugby pitch towards the Abbey and River Avon - a real bonus for a hotel in the heart of a city, as is the ample parking.

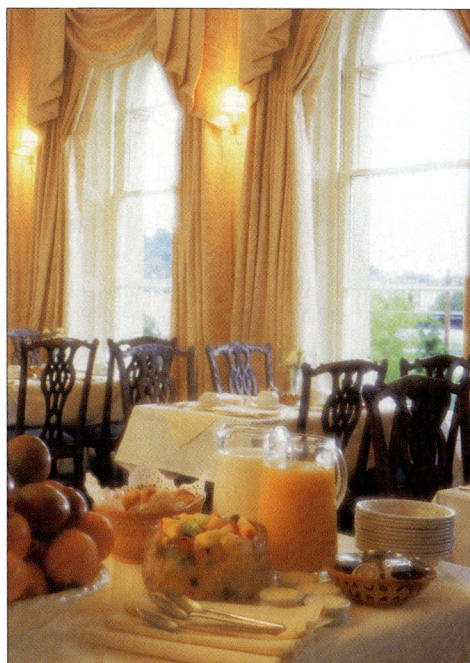

LOCATION

Upon entering Bath, follow signs for the Holbourne Museum. After the museum, go straight over the roundabout, following signs to Bristol/Exeter. The hotel is on the right.

COURT BARN

Country house

Clawton, Holsworthy,
Devon EX22 6PS

T (UK) 0870 432 8578
T 01409 271219
F 01409 271309
courtbarn@bestloved.com
www.courtbarn.bestloved.com

OWNERS
Robert and Susan Wood

ROOM RATES
Single occupancy   £45 - £60
6 Doubles/Twins   £70 - £80
1 Four-poster   £80 - £90
1 Small Suite   £110
Includes full breakfast and VAT

CREDIT CARDS
AMERICAN EXPRESS • DC • JCB • MC • VI

RATINGS & AWARDS
ETC ★★
AA ★★ 73%
Taste of the West
Various national wine honours

FACILITIES
On site: Garden, croquet, tennis,
badminton, 9-hole pitch & putt
2 meeting rooms/max 40 people
Nearby: Golf, riding, fishing, sailing,
archery, clay shooting, indoor pool,
leisure centre, water sports, cycle trails

RESTRICTIONS
Limited facilities for disabled guests
Smoking in bar and TV room only
Pets by arrangement

ATTRACTIONS
Boscastle, Clovelly, Tintagel,
Docton Mill, Hartland Abbey,
Route 3 Cycle Trail, Exmoor,
Eden Project, Tate Gallery,
Rosemoor RHS Garden, Dartmoor,
Bodmin Moor

NEAREST
CITY:
Exeter - 35 miles/50 mins

AIRPORT:
Heathrow - 240 miles/4 hrs

RAIL STATION:
Exeter - 35 miles/50 mins

AFFILIATIONS
Independent

RESERVATIONS
National rate in UK: 0870 432 8578
Quote Best Loved

ACCESS CODES
Not applicable

WEST COUNTRY

Crackling log fires, good food and wine in a romantic Devon hideaway

Built as the 'Sanctuary' around the 16th century, the present house at Court Barn was partly rebuilt in 1853, including its own chapel. It is a small but delightful country house set in parklike grounds with an aura of peace amidst glorious Devon countryside.

The hotel itself also has great charm. Attractive and individually furnished en suite-bedrooms, most with bath and shower, offer a wide range of facilities. Cracking log fires and a cosy, well-stocked bar create a warm, relaxed atmosphere in which to unwind. For duller days, there is a well-appointed library and the promise of board games, bridge and perhaps an indulgent cream tea.

Hoteliers Robert and Susan Wood are justifiably proud of their reputation for hospitality and good food. A selection of 350 wines accompany the mouthwatering four-course dinner, created from fresh local produce with a daily-changing menu. The breakfast room looks over the croquet lawns, and the restaurant, candlelit in the evenings and decorated with antiques, fresh flowers and crisp linen, has views of the garden. You will find good old-fashioned values of service and hospitality at Court Barn, the perfect base from which to discover this delightful part of unexplored Devon and Cornwall.

LOCATION
Two and a half miles south of Holsworthy off the A388, turn towards North Tamerton for half a mile. The hotel is next to Clawton Church.

> "Beautiful house, very warm and welcoming - can't wait to come back"
> THE BOWMAN FAMILY, MARTHA'S VINEYARD, MASSACHUSETTS USA

Townhouse

DORIAN HOUSE

I Upper Oldfield Park,
Bath, Somerset BA2 3JX

T (UK) 0870 432 8599
T 01225 426336
F 01225 444699
dorian@bestloved.com
www.dorian.bestloved.com

OWNERS
Tim and Kathryn Hugh

ROOM RATES
Single occupancy	£60 - £78
8 Doubles	£60 - £140
Includes breakfast and VAT	

CREDIT CARDS
AMERICAN EXPRESS • JCB • MC • VI

RATINGS & AWARDS
ETC ◆◆◆◆◆
RAC ◆◆◆◆◆
RAC Warm Welcome,
Sparkling Diamond Awards
AA ◆◆◆◆◆
AA Premier Collection

FACILITIES
On site: Garden
Nearby: Golf, riding, health & beauty

RESTRICTIONS
Limited facilities for disabled guests
No smoking throughout
No pets

ATTRACTIONS
Roman baths and pump rooms,
Royal Crescent, Thermae Bath Spa,
Bath Abbey, Longleat, Stonehenge,
the Cotswolds, Museum of Costume

NEAREST
CITY:
Bath

AIRPORT:
Heathrow - 110 miles/1 hr 30 mins

RAIL STATION:
Bath Spa - 1 mile/5 mins

AFFILIATIONS
Independent

RESERVATIONS
National rate in UK: 0870 432 8599
Quote Best Loved

ACCESS CODES
Not applicable

WEST COUNTRY

A truly harmonious experience in historic Bath

This beautifully proportioned Victorian stone house is an intimate, calming stay just slightly off the beaten path in fascinating Bath. Hoteliers Tim and Kathryn Hugh have transformed this period home into a restful hideaway, inspired both by the elegant brilliance of their surroundings and by their shared musical background (Tim is principal cellist with the London Symphony Orchestra, and guests can sample his recordings in the breakfast music library).

Eight roomy bedrooms, several with four-poster beds, offer a splendid vantage point for exploring the town's Roman history, with views extending out over the Royal Crescent or the house's own well-manicured gardens. Choose any of the rooms - given names inspired by musicians and composers like Jacqueline du Pre, George Gershwin and Edward Elgar - and enjoy the simple, blissful luxuries of crisp cotton sheets, personable décor and a particularly tasty morning meal.

When you're ready to venture outdoors after a relaxing morning in, there is, of course, no shortage of area attractions; Bath offers something for any interest imaginable, and Dorian House's proximity to Stonehenge, the Cotswolds and other prominent areas of interest make it a prime location for which to base either a short break or a full tour of the region.

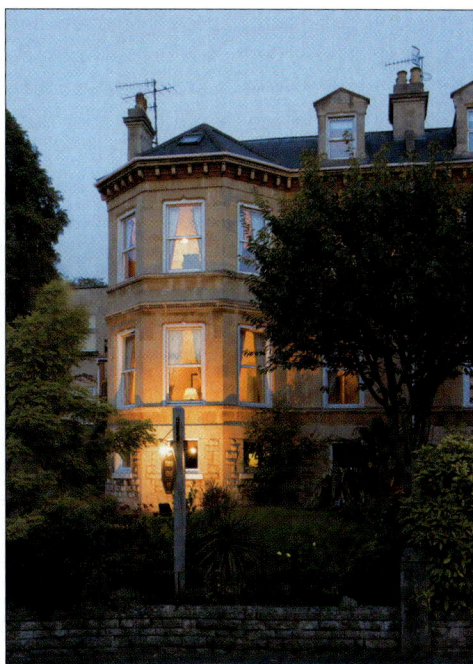

LOCATION
From the A36, join the A367, signposted Shepton Mallet. Upper Oldfield Park is first on the right, and the hotel is the third building on the left.

THE FOWEY HOTEL

Riverside hotel

The Esplanade, Fowey, Cornwall
PL23 IHX

T (UK) 0870 432 8618
T 01726 832551
F 01726 832125
fowey@bestloved.com
www.fowey.bestloved.com

OWNERS
Ann and Keith Richardson

GENERAL MANAGER
Andrea Callis

RATES PER PERSON
Single occupancy	£90 - £160
32 Doubles/Twins	£67 - £109
4 Four-posters	£119
I Suite	£129

Includes full breakfast, dinner and VAT

CREDIT CARDS
AMERICAN EXPRESS • DC • MC • VI

RATINGS & AWARDS
ETC ★★★ Silver Award
AA ★★★ ❀❀ 73%
Investors in People

FACILITIES
On site: Garden, fishing
I meeting room/max 70 people
Nearby: Golf, sailing

RESTRICTIONS
Limited facilities for disabled guests
Children by arrangement
No smoking in dining room or
bedrooms
Pets by arrangement

ATTRACTIONS
Lanhydrock House & Gardens,
Eden Project, Lost Gardens of Heligan,
Carlyon Bay, Truro, Pencarrow House
and Gardens, art galleries

NEAREST
CITY:
Truro - 25 miles/40 mins

AIRPORT:
Exeter - 85 miles/1 hr 45 mins
Bristol - 130 miles/2 hrs 30 mins

RAIL STATION:
Par - 4 miles/10 mins

AFFILIATIONS
Best Western
Richardson Hotels

RESERVATIONS
National rate in UK: 0870 432 8618
Toll free in UK: 0800 243 708
Toll free in US: 800-528-1234
Quote Best Loved

ACCESS CODES
Not applicable

WEST COUNTRY

A Victorian grand hotel on the banks of the River Fowey

Those Victorian hoteliers certainly appreciated a fine location when they saw one! It would be hard to beat the Fowey's spectacular position dominating the hillside above the busy river estuary, with views across the water to the fishing village of Polruan. Fowey itself is charming, its narrow lanes winding down to the water and the jetty where passenger ferries depart for the short crossing to Polruan. The hotel makes a perfect base for visiting Cornwall's most exciting attraction, the giant greenhouses of the Eden Project - they're just a 15-minute drive away. Another day trip treat for gardeners is the Lost Gardens of Heligan, near Mevagissey.

The Fowey Hotel was built on a grand scale in 1882, and owners Ann and Keith Richardson have done a terrific job in recreating the handsome Victorian interior using period colour schemes and furnishings. To reach the upper floors, where many of the rooms boast river views, guests can summon the Old Lady, a splendid original Victorian lift. The hotel restaurant enjoys a fine reputation, and there are comfortable lounges for relaxing. On a summer's afternoon, the Victorian Tea Garden is just the place for a Cornish tea on the water's edge.

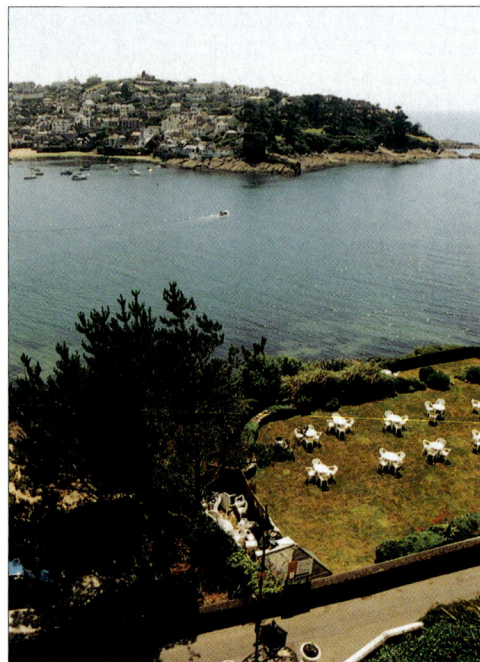

LOCATION
From the M5, take the A30 to Bodmin, then the B3269 Lostwithiel (A390) to Fowey. The hotel is on the right, on the esplanade.

"A haven of peace and tranquillity

PREVIOUS GUEST

Country house

GABRIEL COURT HOTEL

Five centuries of heritage and a sunny disposition

For nearly 500 years, this fascinating hotel was the home of the Churchward family, the Squires of Stoke Gabriel. In 1928 the house was converted into a hotel, and since then has earned an excellent reputation for hospitality and comfort. This charming property is a wonderful base for exploring bountiful nearby attractions - Dartmoor, the Heritage Coast, National Trust properties, Totnes and Dartmouth, to name but a few. Even closer to home, Gabriel Court's terraced Elizabethan garden - complete with clipped yew arches, box hedges and magnolia trees - is nearly three acres of delight within high surrounding walls.

The food at the hotel's comfortable Churchward Bar & Restaurant is vibrant and imaginative, with fruit and vegetables in season from the kitchen garden, salmon and sea trout from the Dart, venison and game from Devon estates and poultry and eggs from neighbouring farms. The restaurant's motto, 'to dine well is to dine leisurely', is reflected by the cosy lounge bar, which boasts a wide range of malt whisky and an extensive wine list with a superb selection of half bottles.

Add in the hotel's sunny disposition - its south-facing vistas enjoy the light all year round - and the welcome is even warmer as Susie Letchford and Douglas Nicol welcome you to Gabriel Court.

LOCATION

Leave the A38 at Buckfastleigh; take the A384 to Totnes, then the A385 toward Paignton. Turn right toward the village at Parker's Arms.

Stoke Gabriel, Near Totnes,
Devon TQ9 6SF

T (UK) 0870 432 8620
T 01803 782206
F 01803 782333
gabriel@bestloved.com
www.gabriel.bestloved.com

OWNERS
Susie Letchford and Douglas Nicol

ROOM RATES
Single occupancy   £73
14 Doubles/Twins   £98 - £125
1 Family Suite   £161 - £197
Includes full breakfast and VAT

CREDIT CARDS
AMERICAN EXPRESS • MC • VI

RATINGS & AWARDS
RAC ★★★
AA ★★★ 73%

FACILITIES
On site: Garden, tennis, heated outdoor pool
1 meeting room/max 20 people
Nearby: Golf, riding, walking, fishing

RESTRICTIONS
Limited facilities for disabled guests
No children under 7 years in restaurant, high tea provided
Smoking in Churchward Bar only

ATTRACTIONS
Dartmoor National Park, Totnes, River Dart, Dartmouth Castle, Coleton Fishacre, South Devon coastline

NEAREST
CITY:
Plymouth - 28 miles/40 mins

AIRPORT:
Exeter - 28 miles/40 mins
Heathrow - 190 miles/3 hrs 45 mins

RAIL STATION:
Totnes - 4 miles/15 mins

AFFILIATIONS
Independent

RESERVATIONS
National rate in UK: 0870 432 8620
Quote Best Loved

ACCESS CODES
Not applicable

WEST COUNTRY

> "As usual, everything, especially the cuisine, was superb - outshone only by Kilby hospitality"
>
> JOYCE & BOB HINZE, USA

THE GARRACK HOTEL

Seaside hotel

Burthallan Lane, St Ives, Cornwall TR26 3AA

T (UK) 0870 432 8621
T 01736 796199
F 01736 798955
garrack@bestloved.com
www.garrack.bestloved.com

OWNERS
The Kilby Family
(Frances, Michael, Stephen)

ROOM RATES
1 Single   £66 - £68
16 Doubles/Twins   £110 - £160
1 Four-poster   £156 - £160
Includes full breakfast and VAT

CREDIT CARDS
AMERICAN EXPRESS • DC • MC • VI

RATINGS & AWARDS
ETC ★★★ Silver Award
RAC ★★★ Dining Award 3

FACILITIES
On site: Garden, gym, indoor pool, spa, solarium, gym, licensed coffee shop, special facilities for the disabled
1 meeting room/max 30 people
Nearby: Golf, riding, fishing

RESTRICTIONS
No smoking in restaurant or leisure centre
Pets by arrangement

ATTRACTIONS
St Ives Tate Gallery, Newlyn, Land's End, Eden Project, St Michael's Mount, Cornish coastal path

NEAREST
CITY:
Truro - 25 miles/45 mins

AIRPORT:
Exeter - 110 miles/2 hrs 15 mins
Heathrow - 300 miles/6 hrs

RAIL STATION:
St Ives - 1 mile/3 mins

AFFILIATIONS
Relais du Silence

RESERVATIONS
National rate in UK: 0870 432 8621
Quote Best Loved

ACCESS CODES
Not applicable

The connoisseur's choice for visiting Cornwall and southwest England

Cornwall is unique both for its history and its scenery: It is a land of contrasts, from its rugged coastline, precipitous cliffs and often angry seas to lazy wooded creeks, small fishing harbours and sandy coves.

Originally a private house known in the Cornish language as Chy-an-Garrack - which translates into English as The House on the Rock - the Garrack was the home of Lady Ebury prior to becoming a hotel in 1947. Since then, the Kilby family has made many changes; new bedrooms have been added as well as a small leisure centre, with a swimming pool, sauna and solarium.

The hotel is a secluded, vine-covered granite building, standing in two acres of gardens high above Porthmeor Beach with fabulous views of St Ives Bay and the coastal landscape beyond. Of the 18 bedrooms, some have four-poster beds; others have personal spa baths. The Garrack's restaurant is proud of its reputation for good culinary standards and for an extensive wine list.

The hotel is dedicated to providing comfort in tranquil and beautiful surroundings, accompanied by good food, good service and good company - here, the customers' interests are paramount. As a base for visiting the many area attractions, including the renowned Tate Gallery, St Ives and the Garrack have no equal.

LOCATION

From the A30, take the second exit to St Ives; then take the B3311, then join the B3306, towards St Ives. Take the third left after the petrol station; after 400 yards, the hotel is signposted.

Country house

GLAZEBROOK HOUSE HOTEL

Glazebrook, South Brent,
Devon TQ10 9JE

T (UK) 0870 432 8625
T 01364 73322
F 01364 72350
glazebrook@bestloved.com
www.glazebrook.bestloved.com

OWNERS
Alan & Maggie Davey

ROOM RATES
3 Singles   £50 - £55
4 Doubles/Twins   £75 - £85
3 Four-posters   £105 - £145
Includes full breakfast and VAT

CREDIT CARDS
JCB • MC • VI

RATINGS & AWARDS
AA ★★ ❀ 73%
South Hams District Council -
Silver Award for Green Tourism
Dartmoor Charter for
Sustainable Tourism

FACILITIES
On site: Garden
2 meeting rooms/max 100 people
Nearby: Golf, fishing, tennis, fitness,
riding, shooting, walking

RESTRICTIONS
No facilities for disabled guests
Children by arrangement
No smoking throughout
No pets; guide dogs only

ATTRACTIONS
Saltram House, Eden Project,
River Dart Country Park,
Buckfast Abbey, Dartmouth Castle,
Dartmoor National Park, walking,
South Hams Coast

NEAREST
CITY:
Plymouth - 12 miles/15 mins

AIRPORT:
Heathrow - 190 miles/3 hrs 30 mins
Exeter - 20 miles/30 mins

RAIL STATION:
Totnes - 6 miles/10 mins

AFFILIATIONS
Independent

RESERVATIONS
National rate in UK: 0870 432 8625
Quote Best Loved

ACCESS CODES
Not applicable

WEST COUNTRY

Tradition, comfort and conviviality in the heart of South Devon

Glazebrook House Hotel, an elegant mid-Victorian country house surrounded by picturesque mature gardens and woodland, nestles on the southern slopes of Dartmoor National Park.

The hotel's bedrooms, including four-poster suites, are all beautifully furnished and enjoy lovely countryside and garden views. The restaurant provides first-class cuisine in a perfect, stylish setting for a romantic dinner or small party. All of the dishes are prepared with the freshest local ingredients under the watchful eye of chef David Merriman. The cellar stocks a wide range of fine wines, ensuring there is something to suit every palate. After dinner, guests will find it easy to relax in the friendly atmosphere of the comfortable lounge bar.

Glazebrook is the ideal venue for exploring South Devon's beautiful scenery, with its miles of unspoilt coastline and the magnificent Dartmoor National Park. National Trust properties including Castle Drogo, Saltram House, Coleton Fishacres, Greenways and Buckland Abbey are all on the doorstep. The gardens at Overbecks, The Garden House, and Lukesland are also nearby, and the Lost Gardens of Heligan and the Eden Project are within an hour's drive.

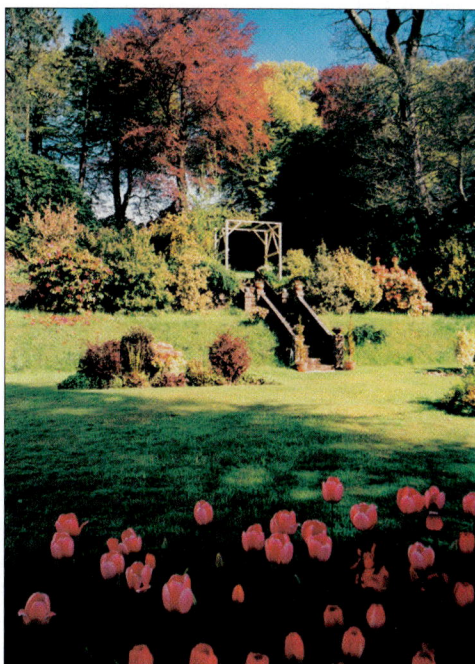

LOCATION

From Exeter, take the A38 to the South Brent/Avonwick turnoff. Follow the hotel signs to South Brent and take the second right after the London Inn.

HAYDON HOUSE

City hotel

9 Bloomfield Park, Bath,
Somerset BA2 2BY

T (UK) 0870 432 8640
T 01225 444919
F 01225 427351
haydon@bestloved.com
www.haydon.bestloved.com

OWNERS
Gordon and Magdalene Ashman-Marr

ROOM RATES
Single occupancy   £50 - £75
3 Doubles/Twins   £80 - £120
1 Four-poster   £90 - £125
1 Suite   £90 - £125
Includes full breakfast and VAT

CREDIT CARDS
AMERICAN EXPRESS • JCB • MC • VI

RATINGS & AWARDS
ETC ♦♦♦♦♦ Silver Award
AA ♦♦♦♦♦
AA Premier Collection

FACILITIES
On site: Garden, sun terrace
Nearby: Golf, riding, health club

RESTRICTIONS
No facilities for disabled guests
Children by arrangement
No smoking throughout
No pets

ATTRACTIONS
Bath, Wells Cathedral, Glastonbury,
Cotswolds, Avebury, Salisbury,
Stonehenge

NEAREST
CITY:
Bath

AIRPORT:
Heathrow - 90 miles/1 hr 30 mins
Bristol - 15 miles/30 mins

RAIL STATION:
Bath Spa - 1 mile/5 mins

AFFILIATIONS
Independent

RESERVATIONS
National rate in UK: 0870 432 8640
Quote Best Loved

ACCESS CODES
Not applicable

WEST COUNTRY

Jane Austen wrote about the secrets of Bath ... here's another

Bath needs little introduction as one of the loveliest cities in the world, with so much more to enjoy than simply taking the waters as in Roman times or the wider range of secret pleasures available in Jane Austen's day. Nowadays, it holds one more secret, a secret you should know - Haydon House. It looks like any other Edwardian house typical of the residential streets of Bath. Inside, however, an oasis of tranquillity and elegance awaits you and high standards of hospitality prevail - as reflected in the hotel's host of awards, including a Michelin accolade.

The reception rooms are tastefully furnished with antiques, whilst the five guest bedrooms are decorated to a very high standard. All rooms have private facilities, televisions and direct-dial telephones and a generous hospitality tray offering complimentary homemade shortbread and a decanter of sherry. Innovative breakfasts are stylishly served and there is a lovely garden in which to relax.

The hosts' aim at Haydon is to make your stay - however short or long - truly happy and memorable by providing a secluded retreat from which you can readily enjoy all the pleasures of Georgian Bath, yet escape the tourist bustle.

LOCATION
Half a mile south of the city centre on the A367; fork right off Wellsway, then turn at the second right.

> **Absolutely stunning, fantastic views ... could stay here forever!**
>
> ROSE, SHARON, LEAH AND JASMINE, CORNWALL

Island hotel

HELL BAY

Contemporary luxury on the last piece of England

The evocatively named Hell Bay occupies a most dramatic setting on one of the Scillies' most beautiful and secluded islands. Over the last several years, the hotel, which is owned by the famous Dorrien-Smith family of Tresco, has been rebuilt and rebranded to create an exceptionally stylish and contemporary island retreat.

The interiors have a distinctive east-coast air about them and make a striking first impression. A nautical chalky blue colour scheme pervades throughout, large windows introduce lots of natural light and the furnishings are classically modern. Fantastic canvases of blue and white by neighbouring artist Richard Pearce add to the sense of brightness, completing an overall atmosphere that's relaxed and unstuffy. All the suites, each named after a local gig (pilot boat), are straight out of the pages of the best interior design magazines. All have private sitting rooms and luxury bathrooms; some have balconies or patios, and there are two-bedroom suites suitable for families. Looking to ask for a room by name? The Emperor and the Boathouse Suites are spectacular.

A complete destination unto itself, the hotel also boasts a pool, fitness suite, sauna and spa, a children's play area and par-3 golf. Pay no attention to the name - this place is pure heaven!

LOCATION

On the island of Bryher, one of the Isles of Scilly.

Bryher, Isles of Scilly,
Cornwall TR23 0PR

T (UK) 0870 432 8641
T 01720 422947
F 01720 423004
hellbay@bestloved.com
www.hellbay.bestloved.com

OWNER
Robert Dorrien-Smith

GENERAL MANAGER
Euan Rodger

RATES PER PERSON
20 Standard Suites   £110 - £150
4 Superior Suites   £130 - £200
Includes full breakfast, dinner and VAT

CREDIT CARDS
MC • VI

RATINGS & AWARDS
ETC ★★★ Silver Award
RAC Gold Ribbon ★★★ Dining Award 3
AA ★★★ ✿✿ 80%

FACILITIES
On site: Outdoor pool, croquet, sauna, spa bath, fitness suite, games room, children's play area, boules, par-3 golf
1 meeting room/max 20 people
Nearby: Heli-pad

RESTRICTIONS
Limited facilities for disabled guests
No smoking in bedrooms
Closed January - February

ATTRACTIONS
Tresco Abbey Gardens, island and wildlife boat trips, Bishop Rock Lighthouse, beaches and walks, gig races, Richard Pearce Art Gallery

NEAREST
CITY:
Penzance - 40 miles/2 hrs 30 mins (ferry) or 20 mins (helicopter)

AIRPORT:
Heathrow - 320 miles/4 hrs
Direct flights to St Mary's available from Southampton, Bristol, Exeter, Newquay and Land's End

RAIL STATION:
Penzance - 40 miles/2 hrs 30 mins (ferry) or 20 mins (helicopter)

FERRY PORT:
St Mary's (passenger ship from Penzance)

AFFILIATIONS
Independent

RESERVATIONS
National rate in UK: 0870 432 8641
Quote Best Loved

ACCESS CODES
Not applicable

WEST COUNTRY

"We came for peace and tranquillity and found it in abundance"
DAVID & SARAH BOULAY, IPSWICH

HOLNE CHASE HOTEL | Country house

Ashburton, Devon TQ13 7NS

T (UK) 0870 432 8645
T 01364 631471
F 01364 631453
holnechase@bestloved.com
www.holnechase.bestloved.com

OWNERS
Sebastian and Philippa Hughes

ROOM RATES
Single occupancy £115 - £125
9 Doubles/Twins £145 - £165
1 Four-poster £195
7 Suites £205 - £235
Includes full breakfast and VAT

CREDIT CARDS
DC • MC • VI

RATINGS & AWARDS
AA ★★★ ❀❀ 74%
AA Pet Friendly Hotel of the Year 2004

FACILITIES
On site: Garden, heli-pad, fishing, licensed for weddings, beauty treatments, dog grooming parlour, stables, self-catering cottage for six 2 meeting rooms/max 80 people
Nearby: Riding, golf, shooting

RESTRICTIONS
Limited facilities for disabled guests
No children under 12 years in restaurant for dinner
No smoking in restaurant
No pets in public rooms

ATTRACTIONS
Dartmoor National Park, Buckfast Abbey, Darlington Hall, Totnes, Plymouth, Dartmouth Castle

NEAREST
CITY:
Exeter/Plymouth - 22 miles/30 mins
AIRPORT:
Exeter - 22 miles/30 mins
Bristol - 90 miles/1 hr 45 mins
RAIL STATION:
Newton Abbot - 10 miles/20 mins

AFFILIATIONS
The European Connection

RESERVATIONS
National rate in UK: 0870 432 8645
Quote Best Loved

ACCESS CODES
Not applicable

WEST COUNTRY

A peculiarly secluded and romantic situation

Remarkably, the above description from White's Directory of Devon of 1850 still rings true today. Holne Chase nestles in a woodland clearing overlooking a pocket of sloping lawns within the Dartmoor National Park. Its origins lie back in the 11th century, when the abbots of Buckfast Abbey kept a hunting lodge here, and the present Victorian era country house is very much a sporting retreat as well as a restorative escape from everyday stresses and strains.

Sebastian and Philippa Hughes run the hotel like a private home with the loyal assistance of Batty the Bassett hound, who maintains her own Web site and is particularly keen to welcome animal lovers and canine visitors to her patch. The five handsomely converted Stable Suites are ideally suited to sporting visitors keen to fish, ride, shoot, or hike on the moors, and all the rooms in the main hotel have been recently refurbished with pretty English fabrics mirroring fresh flowers from the garden. There is also a self-catering cottage, which sleeps six, set in the walled garden.

Holne Chase's walled garden also provides fruit and vegetables for the kitchen, and the chef's enthusiasm for good food made with top quality local ingredients embraces seafood from Brixham and Looe, and seasonal game dishes.

LOCATION
From M5, join the A38 towards Plymouth. Take the second turning for Ashburton at Pear Tree Cross, following signs for Dartmeet. The hotel entrance is on the right, 300 metres after Holne Bridge.

> **"** We have had a wonderful time - thank you. Best vegetarian meal ever **"**
>
> J AND H DAWES, SURREY

Country house

HOMEWOOD PARK

Charm and unassuming luxury just minutes from Bath

Homewood Park is a relaxing escape from the everyday, yet just minutes away from bustling Bath. In the summer, award-winning gardens beckon you outdoors, and log fires provide atmosphere during the winter months. Inside are 19 individually-decorated bedrooms and suites, each with their own special charm - and most enjoy views of the gardens and grounds.

Dining is not to be missed, with an acclaimed restaurant offering modern English cuisine ranging from pan-fried sea bass with crushed potatoes, hazelnuts and a fennel and cardamom mousse to a decadent pudding of flaming sambuca soufflé with almond-milk ice cream and tarragon biscotti. As with the rest of the hotel, the service is thoughtful without being too formal - and, of course, both group dining and meetings can easily be accommodated, whether you are planning a business meeting or wedding.

There is much to do in the surrounding area, from Bath's many notable sights to a wealth of stately homes and gardens. And if you can't bear to leave the comfort of your room, the hotel can arrange a visit by their aromatherapist to put the finishing touch on a thoroughly relaxing stay.

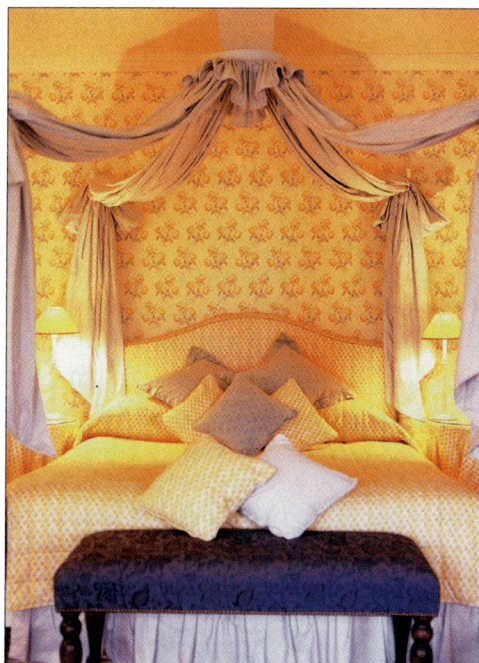

LOCATION

From the M4, exit junction 18 for the A46 (Bath); in Bath, exit for the A36 (Warminster/Salisbury). The hotel is signposted after five miles.

Hinton Charterhouse, Bath, Somerset BA3 6BB

T (UK) 0870 432 8646
T 01225 723731
F 01225 723820
homewood@bestloved.com
www.homewood.bestloved.com

GENERAL MANAGER
Janine Black

ROOM RATES
Single occupancy	£125
7 Standard	£155
7 Superior	£195
3 Junior Suites	£230
2 Suites	£275

Includes breakfast, early morning tea, newspaper and VAT

CREDIT CARDS
AMERICAN EXPRESS • DC • MC • VI

RATINGS & AWARDS
AA ★★★ ✿✿ 73%

FACILITIES
On site: Garden, heli-pad, outdoor pool, croquet, tennis, licensed for weddings
3 meeting rooms/max 40 people
Nearby: Walking, health & beauty, clay shooting, quad biking, archery, go-karting, 4x4 driving

RESTRICTIONS
Smoking in some rooms only
No pets; guide dogs only

ATTRACTIONS
Bath, Stourhead, Longleat, Glastonbury, Castle Combe, Stonehenge, Wells

NEAREST
CITY:
Bath - 5 miles/7 mins

AIRPORT:
Bristol - 20 miles/40 mins

RAIL STATION:
Freshford - 2 miles/5 mins
Bath - 5 miles/7 mins

AFFILIATIONS
von Essen Hotels
Small Luxury Hotels
Pride of Britain

RESERVATIONS
National rate in UK: 0870 432 8646
Toll free in US: 800-98-PRIDE
or 800-525-4800
Quote Best Loved

ACCESS CODES
AMADEUS LX BRSHWP
APOLLO/GALILEO LX 58479
SABRE/ABACUS LX 13167
WORLDSPAN LX BRSHP

WEST COUNTRY

THE HORN OF PLENTY

Country house

Gulworthy, Tavistock,
Devon PL19 8JD

T (UK) 0870 432 8647
T 01822 832528
F 01822 832528
hornofplenty@bestloved.com
www.hornofplenty.bestloved.com

OWNERS
Peter Gorton and Paul Roston

ROOM RATES
Single occupancy   £110 - £220
5 Doubles/Twins   £120 - £150
3 Deluxe Doubles   £150 - £195
2 Superior Doubles   £230
Includes full breakfast and VAT

CREDIT CARDS
AMERICAN EXPRESS • MC • VI

RATINGS & AWARDS
AA ★★★ ✿✿✿ 77%

FACILITIES
On site: Garden
1 meeting room/max 35 people
Nearby: Golf, riding, fishing,
sailing, canoeing

RESTRICTIONS
Smoking in drawing room only
Pets by arrangement
Closed 24 - 27 Dec.

ATTRACTIONS
Dartmoor National Park,
Eden Project, Lost Gardens of Heligan,
Buckland Abbey,
RHS Rosemoor Gardens,
Devon coastline, sailing, walking

NEAREST
CITY:
Plymouth - 22 miles/35 mins

AIRPORT:
Plymouth - 17 miles/30 mins

RAIL STATION:
Plymouth - 22 miles/35 mins

AFFILIATIONS
Independent

RESERVATIONS
National rate in UK: 0870 432 8647
Quote Best Loved

ACCESS CODES
Not applicable

WEST COUNTRY

A cornucopia overflowing with good food and charm in an English country garden

If you were designing a doll's house, the Horn of Plenty could be your model, with its perfect proportions, wisteria-covered porch, sweeping lawns and manicured flower beds. Sitting neatly between the rugged areas of Bodmin Moor and Dartmoor, this quintessentially English country house is set in lush countryside between the rivers Tamar and Tay, both famous for trout and salmon fishing. Within easy reach of sailing in Plymouth and the famous surfing beaches of the north coast, this really is a gem of a hotel.

The Horn of Plenty has five acres of spectacular gardens and untamed orchards in which to wander, with secret arbours and constant changes of vista. The bedrooms in the Coach House have balconies overlooking the fragrant, sunny walled garden. Indeed, the scent of fresh flowers fills the house, whether the elegant drawing room with its welcoming log fire or the luxuriously furnished bedrooms.

Originally started as a restaurant with rooms, the focus at the Horn of Plenty has always been on the food. The cuisine in the elegant restaurant is among the best in Devon, with international recognition for its outstanding quality - so eating will be high on your list of things to do!

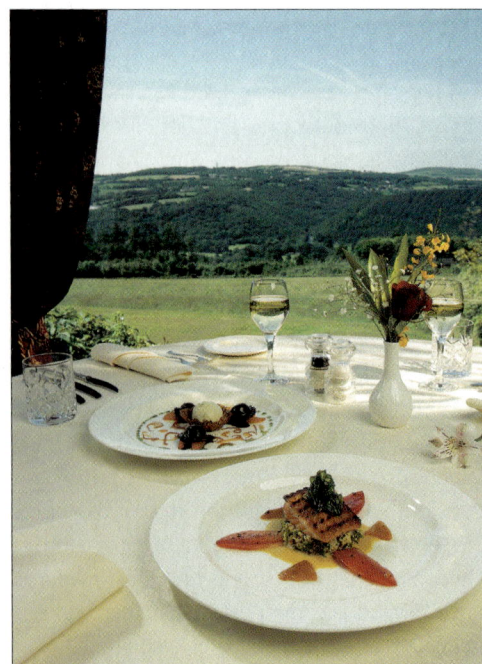

LOCATION

Exit 31 from the M5, then onto the A30 (Okehampton). After 27 miles, turn left for the A386 (Tavistock), then the A390. After three miles, turn right at Gulworthy Cross; follow signs to the hotel.

Seaside hotel

HOTEL RIVIERA

Elegance and Regency charm in an 18th-century seaside resort

Is there any finer place in Devon to sit and watch the world go by than the terrace at the Hotel Riviera, located on Sidmouth's famous Georgian esplanade? With the beach a stone's throw across the broad promenade, this is the perfect place to drink coffee, take tea or sip a sundowner. Welcome to one of the few hotels in Britain with the coveted Courtesy and Care award from the Automobile Association - little wonder, then, that Peter Wharton's Hotel Riviera, with its fine Regency façade, bow-fronted windows, handsome public rooms and beautifully appointed en-suite bedrooms - many with sea views - is arguably one of the most comfortable and certainly the most welcoming in this ancient and beautiful southwest corner of England.

Perfectly located in Sidmouth, which lover of architecture and England's Poet Laureate Sir John Betjeman called his favourite holiday place, the Riviera enjoys superb cuisine prepared by English- and French-trained chefs, a fine cellar and elegant dining in a handsome salon overlooking Lyme Bay. Close by are gardens, coastal walks, golf, bowling, croquet, putting, tennis, fishing, sailing and riding; the cathedral city of Exeter is also nearby, and lush countryside and stunning coastline to explore all around.

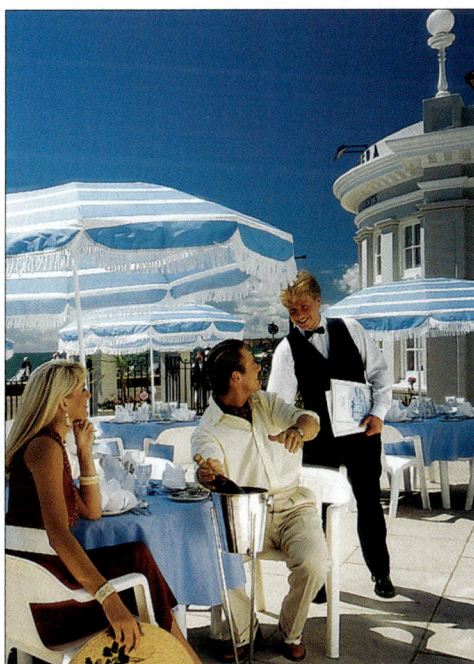

LOCATION

Sidmouth is 13 miles from the M5, exit 30 (follow the A3052).

The Esplanade, Sidmouth,
Devon EX10 8AY

T (UK) 0870 432 8656
T 01395 515201
F 01395 577775
riviera@bestloved.com
www.riviera.bestloved.com

OWNER
Peter S Wharton

RATES PER PERSON
7 Singles   £109 - £143
18 Doubles/Twins   £98 - £132
2 Suites   £142 - £152
Includes full breakfast, 7-course
table d'hôte dinner and VAT

CREDIT CARDS
AMERICAN EXPRESS • DC • MC • VI

RATINGS & AWARDS
ETC ★★★★ Gold Award
RAC Blue Ribbon ★★★★ Dining Award 3
AA ★★★★ ✿✿ 74%

FACILITIES
On site: Patio
1 meeting room/max 90 people
Nearby: Golf, riding, fishing, tennis,
croquet, game shooting

RESTRICTIONS
Limited facilities for disabled guests
No smoking in restaurant
and some rooms
Pets by arrangement

ATTRACTIONS
Killerton House, Exeter Cathedral,
Bicton Park and Gardens,
Dartmoor and Exmoor

NEAREST
CITY:
Exeter - 13 miles/30 mins
London - 165 miles/3 hrs 30 mins

AIRPORT:
Heathrow - 153 miles/3 hrs 30 mins
Exeter - 10 miles/30 mins

RAIL STATION:
Exeter - 13 miles/30 mins

AFFILIATIONS
Independent

RESERVATIONS
National rate in UK: 0870 432 8656
Quote Best Loved

ACCESS CODES
Not applicable

WEST COUNTRY

"One of the most completely satisfying evenings we have enjoyed for some time. An impeccable example of the marriage of kitchen, cellar, service and setting"

N H BAGOT, BRISTOL

HUNSTRETE HOUSE

Country house

Hunstrete, Chelwood,
Near Bath, Somerset BS39 4NS

T (UK) 0870 432 8507
T 01761 490490
F 01761 490732
hunstrete@bestloved.com
www.hunstrete.bestloved.com

MANAGING DIRECTOR
R H Gillis

ROOM RATES
Single occupancy £135 - £145
16 Doubles/Twins £170 - £205
5 Four-posters £170 - £275
4 Suites £265 - £275
Includes full breakfast and VAT

CREDIT CARDS
AMERICAN EXPRESS • DC • MC • VI

RATINGS & AWARDS
AA ★★★ ◎◎ 79% Country House

FACILITIES
On site: Garden, heli-pad, croquet, tennis, heated outdoor pool, licensed for weddings
3 meeting rooms/max 80 people
Nearby: Golf, fishing, riding, paintballing, orienteering

RESTRICTIONS
Limited facilities for disabled guests
Smoking in library only
Pets by arrangement
Closed 4 -13 Jan.

ATTRACTIONS
Bath, Wells Cathedral, Longleat, Glastonbury, Stonehenge, Avebury

NEAREST
CITY:
Bath - 7 miles/15 mins

AIRPORT:
Heathrow - 90 miles/2 hrs
Bristol - 11 miles/30 mins

RAIL STATION:
Bath - 8 miles/15 mins

AFFILIATIONS
Celebrated Hotels Collection

RESERVATIONS
National rate in UK: 0870 432 8507
Toll free in US: 800-322-2403
Quote Best Loved

ACCESS CODES
AMADEUS UZ BRSHUN
APOLLO/GALILEO UZ 22206
SABRE/ABACUS UZ 49148
WORLDSPAN UZ 40925

A lovely stately house, gardens and top dining near Roman Bath

The 'Houndstreet' estate has a colourful history dating back to 963 AD. The diarist John Evelyn referred to 'Old Sir Francis (Popham), he lived like a hog at Hownstret in Somerset, with a moderate pittance'. Rest assured guests will find some welcome changes!

Hunstrete House was a private home from the mid 18th century and became a hotel in 1978. Since then, it has established itself as a first-rate restaurant and a splendid country house hotel - although they play the hotel bit down: One is encouraged to treat the place as your own.

Some invitation! The drawing room and library are splendidly furnished with antiques, original paintings and collections of fine porcelain. The house looks out onto two acres of formal gardens and beyond to the 71-acre park, with sweeping lawns, intimate bowers, woodland walks and a walled garden of astonishing botanic variety. The dining room opens into the flower-filled courtyard, where al fresco dining makes the best of summer. The 25 princely bedrooms are an exhibition of romantic design, fairytale settings for very special occasions - and all, of course, is made even better by the friendly, efficient staff.

Once you have experienced the Hunstrete magic, it will be calling you back. Count on it!

LOCATION

From the M4, exit 18, take the A46 to Bath. Leave Bath on the A4 to Bristol and take the A39 to Wells and Weston. Hunstrete is five miles on the right.

> " As always, the food was superb. The staff are always so friendly and courteous, and the rooms so attractive and spotlessly clean "
>
> SARAH FLOOD, BATH

Inn

THE IDLE ROCKS HOTEL

A spectacular Cornish dream brought to life

A small idyllic harbour, narrow lanes of fishermen's cottages and green fields sloping to the sea - this is the view from the Idle Rocks, where genuine, personal service and elegantly appointed rooms provide a level of comfort that encourages guests to relax as soon as they arrive. Far from old-fashioned, the hotel is has entered a new era with a brasserie-style restaurant alongside a fine-dining restaurant featuring tiers that make the most of the fantastic views and a dining terrace open during the al fresco season. Their six premier rooms also encapsulate this updated style, and are spacious and luxurious, with large bathrooms, walk-in showers, balconettes and great views.

The food is superb. Breakfast can be traditional with a touch of imagination or simply light continental. Dinner is prepared with attention and flair from locally-grown Cornish produce, including early-season fruit and vegetables, fresh sea fish and the best quality meats and poultry.

The Idle Rocks is on the Roseland Peninsula, famously picturesque with lovely beaches, breathtaking cliffs, coastal walks, historic castles, pretty villages and a huge range of outdoor activities to enjoy.

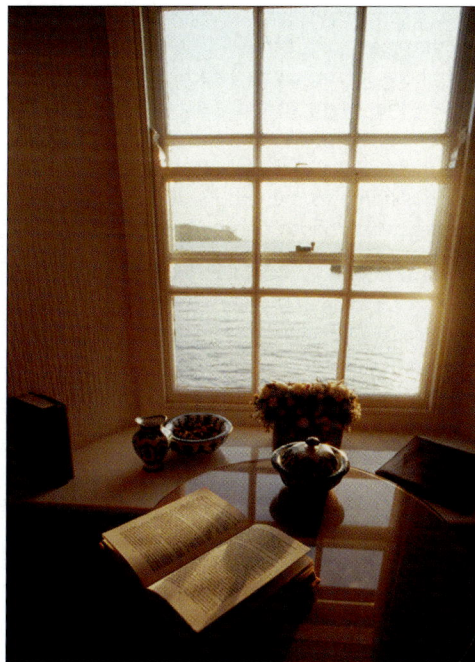

LOCATION

Take the M5 to the A30 (Truro), the B3275 to Probus and the A3078 to St Mawes. Idle Rocks is the first hotel on the left.

Harbourside, St Mawes,
Cornwall TR2 5AN

T (UK) 0870 432 8659
T 01326 270771
F 01326 270062
idlerocks@bestloved.com
www.idlerocks.bestloved.com

OWNERS
Keith and Ann Richardson

GENERAL MANAGER
Amanda Griffiths

RATES PER PERSON
2 Singles	£64
20 Doubles/Twins	£64 - £109
4 Four-posters	£79 - £109
1 Suite	£99 - £129
6 Premier Rooms	£99 - £149

Includes full breakfast, dinner and VAT

CREDIT CARDS
AMERICAN EXPRESS • MC • VI

RATINGS & AWARDS
AA ★★★ ◎◎ 77%
AA Romantic Hotel

FACILITIES
On site: Sea-view terrace
Nearby: Tennis, fishing, riding, yachting

RESTRICTIONS
Limited facilities for disabled guests
No children under 10 years
in dining room after 7 p.m.
No smoking in dining room
Pets by arrangement

ATTRACTIONS
The Eden Project, Trelissick Gardens,
Heligan Gardens, St Mawes Castle,
Lanhydrock House, Trebah Gardens,
St Michael's Mount,
National Maritime Museum

NEAREST
CITY:
Truro - 20 miles/40 mins

AIRPORT:
Bristol - 190 miles/3 hrs 30 mins

RAIL STATION:
Truro - 22 miles/45 mins

AFFILIATIONS
Richardson Hotels

RESERVATIONS
National rate in UK: 0870 432 8659
Toll free in UK: 0800 243 020
Quote Best Loved

ACCESS CODES
Not applicable

WEST COUNTRY

THE ISLAND HOTEL

Resort

Tresco, Isles of Scilly,
Cornwall TR24 0PU

T (UK) 0870 432 8665
T 01720 422883
F 01720 423008
island@bestloved.com
www.island.bestloved.com

OWNER
Robert Dorrien Smith

GENERAL MANAGER
Jame Le Friec

RATES PER PERSON
5 Singles	£117 - £157
40 Doubles/Twins	£128 - £208
3 Suites	£164 - £283

Includes full breakfast, dinner and VAT

CREDIT CARDS
MC • VI

RATINGS & AWARDS
ETC ★★★ Gold Award
RAC Gold Ribbon ★★★ Dining Award 3
AA ★★★ ⊛⊛
AA Top 200 - 2004/2005

FACILITIES
On site: Garden, heli-pad, outdoor
pool, croquet, tennis, games room,
cycle hire, boutique-style hotel shop
2 meeting rooms/max 50 people
Nearby: Golf, riding

RESTRICTIONS
Smoking in Terrace Bar only
No pets
Closed 1 Nov. - 28 Feb.

ATTRACTIONS
Lectures & slide shows,
Tresco Abbey gardens, sailing school,
island boat trips,
Bishop Rock Lighthouse,
wildlife tours, beaches and walks

NEAREST
CITY:
Penzance - 40 miles/2 hrs 30 mins (ferry)
or 20 mins (helicopter)

AIRPORT:
Heathrow - 320 miles/2 hrs
Direct flights to St Mary's available
from Southampton, Bristol, Exeter,
Newquay and Land's End

RAIL STATION:
Penzance - 40 miles/2 hrs 30 mins (ferry)
or 20 mins (helicopter)

FERRY PORT:
St Mary's (passenger ship from Penzance)

AFFILIATIONS
Independent

RESERVATIONS
National rate in UK: 0870 432 8665
Quote Best Loved

ACCESS CODES
Not applicable

WEST COUNTRY

A South Sea island paradise off the coast of Cornwall

It is sometimes hard to imagine that 28 miles off the coast of Cornwall is a tiny archipelago with pure white sandy beaches, shallow clear waters and, owing to the warming effects of the gulfstream, flower-filled fields and hedgerows. The most exotic of the islands has to be Tresco, which is home to the famous subtropical Abbey Gardens that flourish despite the Atlantic gales.

This uncommon place was settled by Augustus Smith more than 160 years ago and is still owned and managed by his descendants. The current Dorrien-Smith family have created a first-class English resort hotel which caters well for everyone from young families to more mature guests. Discreetly set in a small bay, the hotel is spacious, airy and bright and the open plan bar-cum-conservatory forms the heart of the property.

The bedrooms are all very comfortably furnished, with the views stealing the show. The restaurant provides a large part of the evening's entertainment, with seafood being a particular speciality.

Whilst there are no cars and no crime on the island, there is a pool, tennis courts, bicycles and even a sailing school. The hotel prides itself on offering 'less of a holiday, more of an experience' - and we would agree!

LOCATION
On the isle of Tresco, one of the Isles of Scilly.

Country house

LEWTRENCHARD MANOR

Lewdown, Near Okehampton,
Devon EX20 4PN

T (UK) 0870 432 8685
T 01566 783222
F 01566 783332
lewtrenchard@bestloved.com
www.lewtrenchard.bestloved.com

GENERAL MANAGER
Sarah Harvey

ROOM RATES
2 Doubles	£135
3 Superior Twins	£185
4 Kings/Twins	£185
1 Disabled King/Twin	£150
3 Four-posters	£185
2 Suites	£200
1 Family Room	£200
1 Bridal Tower House	£220
Includes full breakfast and VAT	

CREDIT CARDS
AMERICAN EXPRESS • DC • MC • VI

RATINGS & AWARDS
RAC Blue Ribbon ★★★ Dining Award 3
AA ★★★ ❀❀
AA Top 200 - 2004/2005

FACILITIES
On site: Garden, heli-pad, fishing,
croquet, licensed for weddings
2 meeting rooms/max 100 people
Nearby: Riding, fishing, golf

RESTRICTIONS
Children under 8 years by arrangement
No smoking in dining rooms
No pets in public rooms

ATTRACTIONS
Dartmoor National Park,
Eden Project, Cotehele House,
Buckland Abbey,
RHS Rosemoor Gardens,
Devon & Cornwall coast,
Lydford Gorge,
Lost Gardens of Heligan

NEAREST
CITY:
Exeter/Plymouth - 30 miles/45 mins

AIRPORT:
Exeter/Plymouth - 30 miles/45 mins
Heathrow - 195 miles/3 hrs 30 mins

RAIL STATION:
Exeter/Plymouth - 30 miles/45 mins

AFFILIATIONS
von Essen Hotels
Pride of Britain

RESERVATIONS
National rate in UK: 0870 432 8685
Toll free in US: 800-98-PRIDE
Quote Best Loved

ACCESS CODES
AMADEUS HK EXTLEW
APOLLO/GALILEO HT 41201
SABRE/ABACUS HK 34815
WORLDSPAN HK LEWTR

WEST COUNTRY

Grandeur and good living in a splendid Jacobean manor

Built by the Monk family on the site of an earlier house, this Jacobean manor was embellished by the Victorian hymn writer Sabine Baring Gould, including granite mullion windows with 19th-century stained glass and high ceilings with decorative plasterwork set off by rich oak panelling. Bedrooms at this lovely house-turned-hotel, some with four-poster beds, are tastefully decorated, and the views are of formal and informal gardens. The grand oak staircase descends from the long gallery to an imposing entrance hall that gleams with brass, and there are log fires and fresh flowers everywhere; in the dining room, with its crisp white linen, you can enjoy classic English cooking with modern interpretations.

The hotel offers trout fishing, clay pigeon shooting and croquet in the grounds, and there are riding, golf and tennis facilities nearby. Guests can be met at both Exeter and Plymouth stations and airports.

Lewtrenchard Manor is well placed for The Eden Project and the Lost Gardens of Heligan, as well as National Trust properties, Dartmoor and the Devon or Cornish coasts.

LOCATION

Take the A30 (Okehampton - Bodmin) from Exeter. After 25 miles, exit for Tavistock/Plymouth. Follow signs to Lewdown and then Lewtrenchard. The hotel is signposted.

"This is quite the most enjoyable stay that I've had in a hotel, and I've travelled and stayed worldwide!"

L M DEUCHAR, WILTSHIRE

THE LUGGER HOTEL

Contemporary hotel

Portloe, Near Truro,
Cornwall TR2 5RD

T (UK) 0870 432 8696
T 01872 501322
F 01872 501691
lugger@bestloved.com
www.lugger.bestloved.com

OWNERS
Sheryl and Richard Young

RATES PER PERSON
21 Doubles/Twins   £90 - £155
Includes full breakfast, dinner and VAT

CREDIT CARDS
AMERICAN EXPRESS • DC • JCB • MC • VI

RATINGS & AWARDS
RAC Blue Ribbon ★★★ Dining Award 2
AA ★★★ ⊛ 74%

FACILITIES
On site: Terrace
Nearby: Riding, tennis, bowls, cliff walks

RESTRICTIONS
No facilities for disabled guests
No children under 12 years
No smoking in dining room or bedrooms
No pets; guide dogs only

ATTRACTIONS
St Just in Roseland,
St Mawes Castle,
Lands' End,
Penzance,
Pendennis Castle,
Trelissick Gardens,
Eden Project

NEAREST
CITY:
Truro - 12 miles/25 mins

AIRPORT:
Newquay - 20 miles/35 mins
Heathrow - 220 miles/5 hrs

RAIL STATION:
Truro - 12 miles/25 mins

AFFILIATIONS
Preston's Global Hotels
The European Connection

RESERVATIONS
National rate in UK: 0870 432 8696
Toll free in US: 800-544-9993
Quote Best Loved

ACCESS CODES
Not applicable

Simplistic perfection, seaside heritage and all the romance imaginable

The Lugger is an original 17th-century smugglers' inn protected from the often-wild Atlantic by its setting in a perfectly protected Cornish harbour. Evocative of scenes from Du Maurier's 'Jamaica Inn' and Stevenson's 'Treasure Island', there's no doubt that it's one of the most romantic hotels ever.

Richard and Sheryl Young have brought this historic inn into the new era of hotel, where the essence of the historical property is maintained, but enhanced by an interior that's luxurious, spacious, stylish and offers all the up-to-the-minute facilities expected by today's sophisticated guest. In keeping with the current Cornish 'revolution', The Lugger's classical cuisine makes the very best of regional produce, particularly the excellent local seafood.

For those interested in area traditions, lobster and crab potting are still a part of Portloe life, and for further adventure at sea, the hotel is also close to St Mawes and the stunning beaches at Pendower and Carne. There are endless other attractions on the Roseland peninsula as well as, of course, the nearby Eden Project and Lost Gardens of Heligan. With so much to offer, The Lugger is place that's hard to do justice to in so few words, but one that could be everyone's favourite.

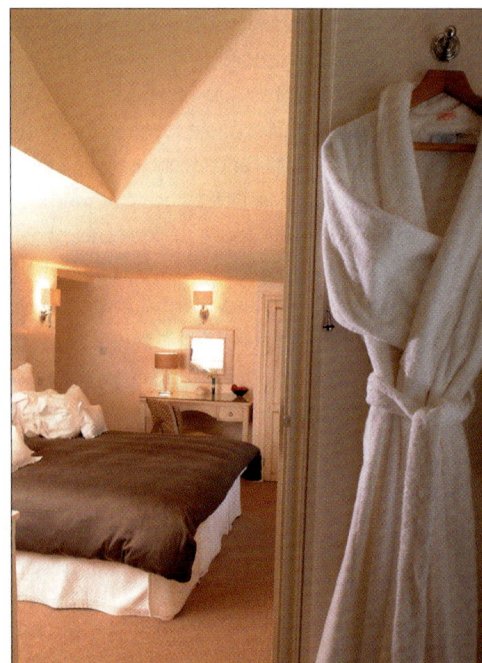

LOCATION
Turn off the A390 St Austell to Truro road onto the B3287 to Tregony. Then, take the A3078 (St Mawes); after 2 miles, fork left for Veryan and Portloe, turning left at the T-junction for Portloe.

Inn

THE LUTTRELL ARMS

32-36 High Street, Dunster,
Somerset TA24 6SG

T (UK) 0870 432 8697
T 01643 821555
F 01643 821567
luttrell@bestloved.com
www.luttrell.bestloved.com

OWNER
Paul Toogood

RATES PER PERSON
Single occupancy	£85 - £105
23 Doubles/Twins	£63 - £73
5 Four-posters	£85

Includes full breakfast, dinner and VAT

CREDIT CARDS
AMERICAN EXPRESS • MC • VI

RATINGS & AWARDS
AA ★★★ ❀ 71%

FACILITIES
On site: Garden, deer park
1 meeting room/max 35 people
Nearby: Golf, riding, walking, safaris

RESTRICTIONS
Limited facilities for disabled guests
No smoking in bedrooms or restaurant

ATTRACTIONS
Dunster Castle and Mill, Exmoor
National Park,
Rosemoor RHS Garden,
Hestercombe Gardens,
West Somerset Steam Railway,
Knighthayes Court

NEAREST
CITY:
Bristol - 66 miles/1 hr 30 mins
Exeter - 44 miles/1 hr 15 mins

AIRPORT:
Bristol - 50 miles/1 hr 30 mins

RAIL STATION:
Taunton - 23 miles/30 mins

AFFILIATIONS
Independent

RESERVATIONS
National rate in UK: 0870 432 8697
Quote Best Loved

ACCESS CODES
Not applicable

WEST COUNTRY

This sleepy inn was once favoured by the medieval Abbots of Cleeve

The pretty village of Dunster lies at the foot of a wooded hill topped with a dramatic flourish by the outline of Dunster Castle. This site has been fortified since Norman times, and a water mill on the River Avill merits a mention in the Doomsday Survey of 1086. Yet Dunster remains one of North Somerset's best kept secrets - despite its fabulous position within the Exmoor National Park, a short drive from the Bristol Channel.

Located on Dunster's one and only street, the hotel can trace its origins back to the 15th century. Stylish and comfortable, it's a perfect spot to relax and unwind; five of the bedrooms are furnished with massive four-poster beds, and in several rooms, impressively high ceilings are supported on handsome antique oak beams. Downstairs, the Luttrell Restaurant offers creative modern British cuisine. Cumin-seared scallops, fillet of beef with salt-roasted potatoes and a Somerset apple soufflé are just a few of the menu highlights. For a more informal meal or a quiet drink, the bar is a traditional English pub serving meals on the garden terrace in summer.

LOCATION
From the A39, turn south toward Tiverton on the A396. This is the Steep, which becomes Dunster high street; the hotel is on the left.

THE METROPOLE

Townhouse

Station Road, Padstow,
Cornwall PL28 8DB

T (UK) 0870 432 8709
T 01841 532486
F 01841 532867
metropole@bestloved.com
www.metropole.bestloved.com

OWNER
Keith Richardson

GENERAL MANAGER
Andrew Jenkins

RATES PER PERSON
Single occupancy	£69 - £87
41 Doubles/Twins	£69 - £93
3 Four-posters	£89 - £105
6 Mini Suites	£84 - £99

Includes full breakfast, dinner and VAT

CREDIT CARDS
AMERICAN EXPRESS • MC • VI

RATINGS & AWARDS
AA ❀ ★★★ 70%

FACILITIES
On site: Garden, heated outdoor
pool (July and August only)
1 meeting room/max 25 people
Nearby: Sea fishing, golf, riding, cycle
hire, boat trips, surfing

RESTRICTIONS
Limited facilities for disabled guests
Smoking in bar and some rooms only

ATTRACTIONS
The Eden Project, Prideaux Place,
Maritime Museum,
National Lobster Hatchery,
Bodmin Town Museum,
Pencarrow Mansion and Gardens,
Lanhydrock Gardens

NEAREST
CITY:
Newquay - 13 miles/25 mins
Truro - 25 miles/40 minutes

AIRPORT:
Newquay - 9 miles/20 mins

RAIL STATION:
Bodmin - 20 miles/30 mins

AFFILIATIONS
Best Western
Richardson Hotels

RESERVATIONS
National rate in UK: 0870 432 8709
Toll free in UK: 0800-197-0198
Quote Best Loved

ACCESS CODES
Not applicable

WEST COUNTRY

Drink in the views at one of Padstow's best gourmet seafood restaurants

There is no doubt that The Metropole boasts the finest views in - or, rather, over! - Padstow. Set on a hill high above the picturesque old fishing port, the views stretch across the working harbour to the Camel Estuary and its entertaining bustle of river traffic - a lively seascape of day trip cruisers, private yachts and local ferries pootling across to the popular resort of Rock.

A Victorian grande dame, The Metropole offers a traditional setting with modern amenities. For something a little bit special, there are four-poster rooms, or 'settle' for the view in one of the spacious feature rooms. The restaurant serves a varied menu with inspiration drawn from around the world and, of course, a selection of fresh fish dishes. For a relaxing drink or informal meal, the Met Café Bar basks in the views from the front of the house.

In and around Padstow there is plenty to see and do, from shopping in the historic town centre to surfing or cycling the Camel Trail (bike hire can be arranged by the hotel). Further afield, the stunning Eden Project boasts luxuriant rainforests housed in the world's largest conservatories.

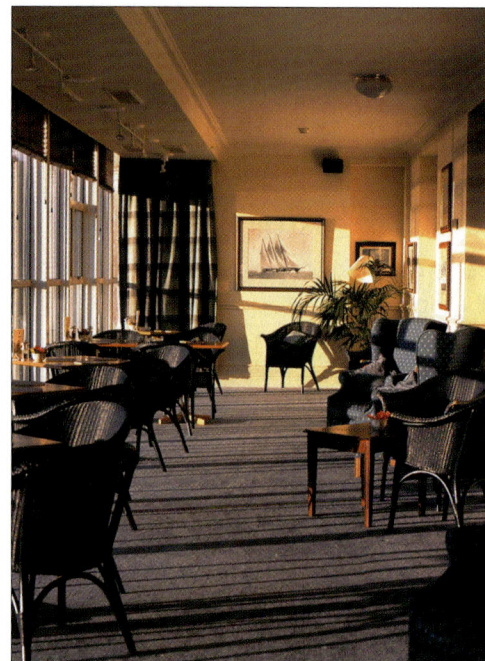

LOCATION
From the A389 near Wadebridge, follow the B3890 into town and around Padstow docks. The hotel overlooks the docks.

Country house

MILL END HOTEL

Chagford, Devon TQ13 8JN

T (UK) 0870 432 8711
T 01647 432282
F 01647 433106
millend@bestloved.com
www.millend.bestloved.com

OWNER
Keith Green

ROOM RATES
13 Doubles/Twins   £100 - £140
1 Suite   £160 - £200
Includes full breakfast and VAT

CREDIT CARDS
JCB • MC • VI

RATINGS & AWARDS
AA ★★★ ⊛⊛ 76%

FACILITIES
On site: Garden, fishing, croquet
3 meeting rooms/max 40 people
Nearby: Golf, riding, fishing

RESTRICTIONS
Limited facilities for disabled guests
Smoking in bar and small lounge only
Closed 1-20 Jan.

ATTRACTIONS
Drogo Castle, Dartmoor National
Park, Rosemoor RHS Gardens,
Teign Gorge, Exeter Cathedral

NEAREST
CITY:
Exeter - 20 miles/35 mins

AIRPORT:
Exeter - 25 miles/50 mins

RAIL STATION:
Exeter - 20 miles/35 mins

AFFILIATIONS
Independent

RESERVATIONS
National rate in UK: 0870 432 8711

Quote Best Loved

ACCESS CODES
Not applicable

WEST COUNTRY

Mill End is quintessentially English - and proud of it

Think cream teas and cricket, chintz and homemade jam, log fires in winter and the lazy buzz of bumblebees in summer and you will have conjured up an image of an almost-forgotten Britain that we are happy to report is alive and well at Mill End. The term 'country house hotel' does not do justice to this delectable time capsule housed in an 18th-century former flour mill on the River Teign. The experience is far more cosy and personal, rather like staying with a favourite branch of the family.

Mill End has been a hotel since 1929 and has preserved all manner of nooks and crannies where guests can hole up with a good book and relax. Upstairs bedrooms have lovely views, while downstairs rooms enjoy private stone-flagged patios. The award-winning fine cuisine in the restaurant is augmented by an impressive cheese board laden with local specialities, and regular guests rave about the dangerously tempting desserts.

There are plenty of ways to work off the calories - hiking in Dartmoor National Park, local walks, pony trekking and golf are easily arranged, and Mill End also offers private salmon and trout fishing. Local attractions include the pretty village of Chagford and Castle Drogo, a Sir Edwin Lutyens-designed National Trust property. The north and south Devon coasts are also within striking distance.

LOCATION

Located on the A382 just off the A30 Exeter to Okehampton road, at Whiddon Down. Be sure not turn into Chagford village from the A382!

> **There is no greater luxury than to feel at home**
>
> CHRIS MARKIEWICZ, BARNET

THE MOUNT SOMERSET

Country house

Henlade, Taunton,
Somerset TA3 5NB

T (UK) 0870 432 8715
T 01823 442500
F 01823 442900
somerset@bestloved.com
www.somerset.bestloved.com

GENERAL MANAGER
Barbara Loadwick

ROOM RATES
Single occupancy   £95
7 Doubles/Twins   £135
3 Suites   £185
1 Four-poster Suites   £200
Includes morning tea/coffee,
newspaper and VAT

CREDIT CARDS
AMERICAN EXPRESS • DC • JCB • MC • VI

RATINGS & AWARDS
RAC ★★★ Dining Award 3
AA ★★★ ⊛⊛ 73%

FACILITIES
On site: Garden, heli-pad, croquet
3 meeting rooms/max 60 people
Nearby: Riding, fishing, tennis, golf

RESTRICTIONS
Limited facilities for disabled guests
No smoking in restaurant
Pets by arrangement

ATTRACTIONS
Somerset County Cricket Ground,
Cheddar Gorge, Bath,
Wells Cathedral,
Exmoor and Dartmoor,
Stonehenge, Taunton Racecourse

NEAREST
CITY:
Taunton - 2 miles/10 mins
Exeter - 30 miles/30 mins

AIRPORT:
Bristol - 40 miles/45 mins
Heathrow - 120 miles/2 hrs

RAIL STATION:
Taunton - 4 miles/10 mins

AFFILIATIONS
von Essen Hotels
Preston's Global Hotels

RESERVATIONS
National rate in UK: 0870 432 8715
Toll free in US: 800-544-9993
Quote Best Loved

ACCESS CODES
AMADEUS YX EXTMOU
APOLLO/GALILEO YX 71026
SABRE/ABACUS YX 54971
WORLDSPAN YX QQXMS
PEGASUS YX QQXMOU

WEST COUNTRY

Arrive at this magnificent place as a guest - leave as a friend

High on the slopes of the Blackdown Hills stands The Mount Somerset. This magnificent find was built in 1805 by an Italian architect; today, much of its original plasterwork has been preserved to blend with the décor, antiques and lavish furnishings, giving a feeling of maturity and, elegance. It is much more a home than a hotel, and every encouragement is given to make you feel at ease.

Both the dining room and the garden room, with its French doors opening onto a sunny terrace, create the perfect setting for a grand repast. Inspired dishes make the most of local produce as well as delicacies from home and abroad, and a well-chosen wine list completes a truly delightful experience. There are 11 luxuriously furnished bedrooms and suites rich in colour-co-ordinated fabrics and carpeting, including the Barrington Suite, which, with its elaborately carved and decorated queen-sized bed, is palatial both in size and décor! The luxurious bathrooms, most with double whirlpool spa baths and twin hand basins set in marble, are a perfect complement to the bedrooms.

The local area is rich in places to visit and things to do: sport, wildlife, natural phenomena, museums, churches and stately homes are only a few of the many attractions that await your visit.

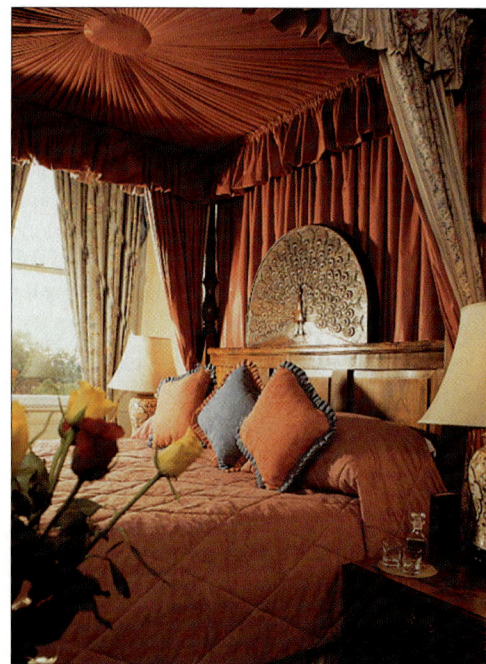

LOCATION
From the M5, exit 25 for the A358 (Chard). After Henlade, turn right toward Stoke St Mary, then left at the T-junction; the hotel's drive is 100 yards on the right.

> **Wonderful - like staying with new friends for the weekend**
>
> L & C PERKINS, NEAR HITCHIN

Country house

THE OLD RECTORY

Cricket Malherbie, Ilminster,
Somerset TA19 0PW

T (UK) 0870 432 8726
T 01460 54364
F 01460 57374
malherbieoldrec@bestloved.com
www.malherbieoldrec.bestloved.com

OWNERS
Michael and Patricia Fry-Foley

ROOM RATES
Single occupancy   £55 - £65
5 Doubles/Twins   £85 - £95
Includes full breakfast and VAT

CREDIT CARDS
JCB • MC • VI

RATINGS & AWARDS
RAC ◆◆◆◆◆ Dining Award 1
RAC Sparkling Diamond,
Warm Welcome Awards
AA ◆◆◆◆◆
AA Premier Collection
Which? Guide to Good Hotels -
Country Knockout 2003
Taste of the West - South West
Bed & Breakfast of the Year 2003

FACILITIES
On site: Garden
Nearby: Golf, riding, freshwater fishing

RESTRICTIONS
No facilities for disabled guests
No children under 16 years
No smoking throughout
No pets; guide dogs only

ATTRACTIONS
Montague House,
Ford Abbey Garden,
East Lambrook Manor,
Tintinhull Hall Garden, Bath,
Stonehenge, Barrington Court

NEAREST
CITY:
Taunton - 13 miles/25 mins

AIRPORT:
Bristol - 44 miles/1 hr
Exeter - 30 miles/40 mins

RAIL STATION:
Crewkerne - 9 miles/15 mins

AFFILIATIONS
Independent

RESERVATIONS
National rate in UK: 0870 432 8726
Quote Best Loved

ACCESS CODES
Not applicable

WEST COUNTRY

Wake to birdsong with breakfast at this heavenly country retreat

It would be hard to imagine a more perfect setting for a quiet weekend or romantic tryst than this lovely old stone rectory nestled in the depths of the Somerset countryside. Even the directions sound enticing, as you wend your way down leafy lanes to the conservation hamlet of Cricket Malherbie (a name conjured straight out of a 1930s whodunit!) and look out for the turn past the church. Crunching up the gravel driveway, you may find your fingers crossed in the hope that your bedroom features one of those pretty Strawberry Hill Gothic windows piercing the thatched roof.

Michael and Patricia Fry-Foley are passionate about their beautiful home. They have preserved its historic character, Tudor oak beams and the flagged hall while adding an appealing blend of antique furnishings and modern paintings by local artists. The bedrooms are blessed with huge beds and views over the gardens to the farmland beyond.

Downstairs, breakfast is taken in the dining room, and the evening meal is served dinner-party style around the dining table laid with silver, linen and fine bone china. The home cooking is delicious, and ingredients are sourced locally where possible - in all, a remarkable find!

LOCATION
From its junction with A303, take the A358 south toward Chard. After Donyatt, follow signs to Ilminster; turn right for Cricket Malherbie. The hotel is on the left, 200 yards past the church.

THE PORT GAVERNE HOTEL

Seaside hotel

Port Gaverne, Near Port Isaac,
Cornwall PL29 3SQ

T (UK) 0870 432 8745
T 01208 880244
F 01208 880151
portgav@bestloved.com
www.portgav.bestloved.com

OWNERS
Graham and Annabelle Sylvester

RATES PER PERSON
14 Doubles/Twins/Family   £40 - £50
Includes breakfast and VAT

CREDIT CARDS
MC • VI

RATINGS & AWARDS
AA ★★ 68%

FACILITIES
On site: Sea access

RESTRICTIONS
No facilities for disabled guests
Smoking in some lounge areas only
Closed early January - mid-February

ATTRACTIONS
Eden Project, Land's End,
Lanhydrock House,
Pencarrow Mansion and Gardens,
National Shire Horse Centre,
Fistral Beach

NEAREST
CITY:
Truro - 30 miles/45 mins

AIRPORT:
Newquay - 23 miles/40 mins

RAIL STATION:
Bodmin Parkway - 18 miles/35 mins
Truro - 30 miles/45 mins

FERRY PORT:
Plymouth - 55 miles/1 hr 30 mins

AFFILIATIONS
Independent

RESERVATIONS
National rate in UK: 0870 432 8745
Quote Best Loved

ACCESS CODES
Not applicable

WEST COUNTRY

A comfortable welcome in blissfully secluded North Cornwall

Port Gaverne, a quiet cove next to the ancient fishing village of Port Isaac, is a splendid hideaway tucked into the Cornish coast. The sea is at your door, with a small beach waiting for your footsteps, and further afield is the length of the North Cornwall Heritage Coast, home to breathtaking walks and memorable views.

The Port Gaverne Hotel, run by owners Graham and Annabelle Sylvester, is a suitably charming restored inn that was once a stopover for the crews of slate vessels back in the days when Port Gaverne was a thriving trading port! Well-decorated bedrooms with all modern amenities await, as does delicious food in-house - in fact, with the coastal sunsets urging you to linger just a bit longer, there may well be no reason to leave this place.

However, there's much to do in the area, with riding, tennis, or boating awaiting, as well as, of course, all those remarkable walks. Cornwall has more golf courses per resident than anywhere else in the United Kingdom - not surprising due to its beautiful setting and mild climate! Explore a number of favoured courses within a short distance from Port Gaverne, from classic dune-strewn links to spectacular cliff-top holes.

LOCATION
From the A39, take the B3267 toward Port Isaac, then the local road for Port Gaverne. The hotel is signposted.

> "Perhaps the finest English hotel I've had the pleasure of visiting"
>
> SCOTT BURGESS, WEST LONDON

Country house

PRINCE HALL HOTEL

The joy of the great outdoors, combined with conviviality and good food

Once a former stable and hunting lodge of the Duke of Cornwall (aka The Prince of Wales), Prince Hall - hence the name - is today an elegantly and attractively furnished country house hotel. A perennial favourite of those seeking a few days' rest and relaxation in magnificent Dartmoor, Prince Hall combines peace and quiet with fresh air, stunning scenery, comfort, good food and unfussy hospitality.

You will find no nicer nor more easy-going hosts than owners John and Anne Grove. Their desire for everyone to relax is evident in the friendly atmosphere, in which their commitment and caring approach play an important part.

If you enjoy outdoor activities, look no further - once you deposit your car you need not think about it until you leave! From walking and fishing to shooting, riding and mountain biking, Dartmoor is the perfect setting for working up a hearty appetite. Fortunately, the creative menus reflect a clear passion for Dartmoor and West Country produce. An ample wine list rounds out what is, no doubt, a truly memorable off-the-beaten-track experience.

LOCATION

From the M5, take the A38 towards Plymouth, then the B3357 towards Princetown. The hotel is 10 miles along on the left a mile before Two Bridges junction.

Near Two Bridges,
Dartmoor, Devon PL20 6SA

T (UK) 0870 432 8747
T 01822 890403
F 01822 890676
princehall@bestloved.com
www.princehall.bestloved.com

OWNERS
John and Anne Grove

RATES PER PERSON
1 Single	£85
6 Doubles/Twins	£84 - £115
2 Four-posters	£84 - £100

Includes full breakfast, dinner, service and VAT

CREDIT CARDS
AMERICAN EXPRESS • DC • MC • VI

RATINGS & AWARDS
ETC ★★ Silver Award
AA ★★ ⊛
AA Top 200 - 2004/2005

FACILITIES
On site: Garden, fishing, clay pigeon shooting, fly fishing
1 meeting room/max 20 people
Nearby: Golf, fishing, shooting, riding, walking trails

RESTRICTIONS
No facilities for disabled guests
No children under 10 years
Smoking in bar only
Closed mid-December - early February

ATTRACTIONS
Dartmoor,
Merrivale Prehistoric Settlement,
Buckland Abbey,
Cotehele House, Castle Drogo,
Lanhydrock Gardens, Eden Project

NEAREST
CITY:
Plymouth - 21 miles/30 mins

AIRPORT:
Plymouth - 21 miles/30 mins

RAIL STATION:
Plymouth - 21 miles/30 mins

AFFILIATIONS
Independent

RESERVATIONS
National rate in UK: 0870 432 8747
Quote Best Loved

ACCESS CODES
Not applicable

WEST COUNTRY

"Our stay at the Queensberry ranks as our most memorable hotel stay in England"

HEATHER CAMERON, NEW YORK

QUEENSBERRY HOTEL

Townhouse

Russel Street, Bath,
Somerset BA1 2QF

T (UK) 0870 432 8751
T 01225 447928
F 01225 446065
queensberry@bestloved.com
www.queensberry.bestloved.com

OWNERS
Laurence & Helen Beere

ROOM RATES
16 Doubles   £100 - £145
10 Deluxe Doubles   £120 - £195
3 Suites   £155 - £285
Includes VAT

CREDIT CARDS
AMERICAN EXPRESS • MC • VI

RATINGS & AWARDS
RAC Gold Ribbon ★★★ Dining Award 3
AA ★★★ ✪✪
AA Top 200 - 2004/2005

FACILITIES
On site: Courtyard garden
1 meeting room/max 40 people
Nearby: Golf, riding, leisure centre

RESTRICTIONS
Limited facilities for disabled guests
No pets; guide dogs only

ATTRACTIONS
Bath Abbey, Roman Baths,
Stonehenge, Wells, Longleat,
Stourhead Gardens,
Museum of Costume

NEAREST
CITY:
Bath

AIRPORT:
Heathrow - 90 miles/1 hr 45 mins
Bristol - 15 miles/30 mins

RAIL STATION:
Bath Spa - 1 mile/5 mins

AFFILIATIONS
Preston's Global Hotels

RESERVATIONS
National rate in UK: 0870 432 8751
Toll free in US: 800-544-9993
Quote Best Loved

ACCESS CODES
AMADEUS YX 53025
APOLLO/GALILEO YX 59863
SABRE/ABACUS YX BRSQUE
WORLDSPAN YX QUEEN

WEST COUNTRY

An architecturally acclaimed Georgian house in the Roman city of Bath

The Queensberry - luxurious, decorative and intimate - is just a few minutes' walk from the Roman baths, but itself is in the heart of Georgian Bath. Built by John Wood of Royal Crescent fame for the Marquis of Queensberry in 1772, the house retains its splendid period plasterwork and fireplaces. There is a delightful courtyard garden, drawing room and cocktail bar, but the focal point of the hotel is The Olive Tree Restaurant, which proprietor Laurence Beere describes as a 'contemporary restaurant' - informal and modestly priced with English cooking that combines excellent local produce with the robust flavours of the Mediterranean.

The Queensberry could not be better placed for visiting the highlights of Bath; the Roman Baths, Theatre Royal, Assembly Rooms and Royal Crescent are all close by. A meander downhill takes you past the antiques markets and the best shops outside of London and on to Bath Abbey, where the famous spa waters await your toes.

LOCATION
Exit 18 on the M4 for the A46 to Bath. Turn right at the T-junction, right at the mini-roundabout, a sharp right at Lansdown Road and the second left into Bennet Street; Russel Street is the first right.

Country house   ROSE-IN-VALE COUNTRY HOUSE HOTEL

An aptly-named country hideaway amidst rose gardens in a quiet Cornish valley

Deep in the heart of the Cornish countryside, a pretty lane winds through the hedgerows to Rose-in-Vale. This delectable Georgian country house enjoys an idyllic setting in an 11-acre valley of pasture, woodlands and gardens just outside Mithian, one of Cornwall's oldest villages.

Here, Chris and Veronica Thomas and their exceptionally friendly and helpful staff (many of whom have been here for years) make it a priority to go that extra mile for their guests. Everyone is made to feel especially welcome, from families keen to explore the North Cornwall coast and garden enthusiasts heading for the Eden Project to couples in search of a quiet romantic break.

Rose-in-Vale has a special charm in all seasons. In summer, the heated pool is a fabulous sun trap surrounded by lawns and flowerbeds. There's croquet, badminton and lovely walks. Winter's chills are kept at bay by log fires and maybe a steam in the sauna.

The finest local seasonal produce dictates the menu in the Valley Restaurant, where specialities include fresh Cornish seafood treats such as crab and lobster. Vegetarian and special diets are also easily catered for – and the Cornish cream teas come highly recommended!

LOCATION
Take the A30 through Cornwall and turn right onto the B3277, signed St. Agnes. Pick up Rose-in-Vale directions within 500 yards.

Mithian, St Agnes,
Cornwall TR5 0QD

T (UK) 0870 432 8756
T 01872 552202
F 01872 552700
roseinvale@bestloved.com
www.roseinvale.bestloved.com

OWNERS
Chris and Veronica Thomas

ROOM RATES
2 Singles	£68
13 Doubles/Twins	£120 - £160
3 Four-posters	£160 - £180
Includes full breakfast and VAT	

CREDIT CARDS
MC • VI

RATINGS & AWARDS
RAC ★★★ Dining Award 2
AA ★★★ 72%

FACILITIES
On site: Garden, outdoor pool, croquet, licensed for weddings, sauna, table tennis
2 meeting rooms/max 75 people
Nearby: Golf, riding, gliding, fishing, surfing, windsurfing, diving

RESTRICTIONS
Limited facilities for disabled guests
No children in restaurant after 7 p.m.
No smoking in bedrooms
No pets in public areas
Closed January and February

ATTRACTIONS
The Eden Project,
The Lost Gardens of Heligan,
National Trust properties,
art galleries, coastal walks

NEAREST
CITY:
Truro - 8 miles/15 mins

AIRPORT:
Exeter - 90 miles/2 hrs

RAIL STATION:
Truro - 8 miles/15 mins

AFFILIATIONS
Independent

RESERVATIONS
National rate in UK: 0870 432 8756
Quote Best Loved

ACCESS CODES
Not applicable

WEST COUNTRY

THE ROYAL CRESCENT HOTEL

Townhouse

16 The Royal Crescent,
Bath, Somerset BA1 2LS

T (UK) 0870 432 8759
T 01225 823333
F 01225 339401
royalcrescent@bestloved.com
www.royalcrescent.bestloved.com

GENERAL MANAGER
Sharon Love

ROOM RATES
16 Classic Doubles/Twins £190 - £260
15 Deluxe Doubles/Twins £265 - £360
6 Classic Suites   £365 - £500
5 Deluxe Suites   £500 - £670
5 Master Suites   £570 - £820
Includes breakfast and VAT

CREDIT CARDS
AMERICAN EXPRESS • DC • JCB • MC • VI

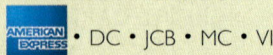

RATINGS & AWARDS
RAC Blue Ribbon ★★★★★
Dining Award 4
AA ★★★★★ ✿✿ 72%

FACILITIES
On site: Garden, gym, croquet,
indoor pool, health & beauty,
licensed for weddings
1 meeting room/max 40 people
Nearby: Golf, tennis, riding,
hot-air ballooning, heli-pad

RESTRICTIONS
Limited facilities for disabled guests
No smoking in restaurant
Pets by arrangement

ATTRACTIONS
Roman Baths, Museum of Costume,
the Royal Crescent,
Holborne Museum of Art,
Bath Theatre Royal

NEAREST
CITY:
Bath
Bristol - 12 miles/25 mins

AIRPORT:
Heathrow - 100 miles/1 hr 30 mins
Bristol - 18 miles/35 mins

RAIL STATION:
Bath Spa - ½ mile/10 mins

AFFILIATIONS
von Essen Hotels
Celebrated Hotels Collection

RESERVATIONS
National rate in UK: 0870 432 8759
Toll free in US: 800-322-2403
Quote Best Loved

ACCESS CODES
AMADEUS YX QQXROY
APOLLO/GALILEO YX 84077
SABRE/ABACUS YX 31079
WORLDSPAN YX RCRES
PEGASUS YX QQXROY

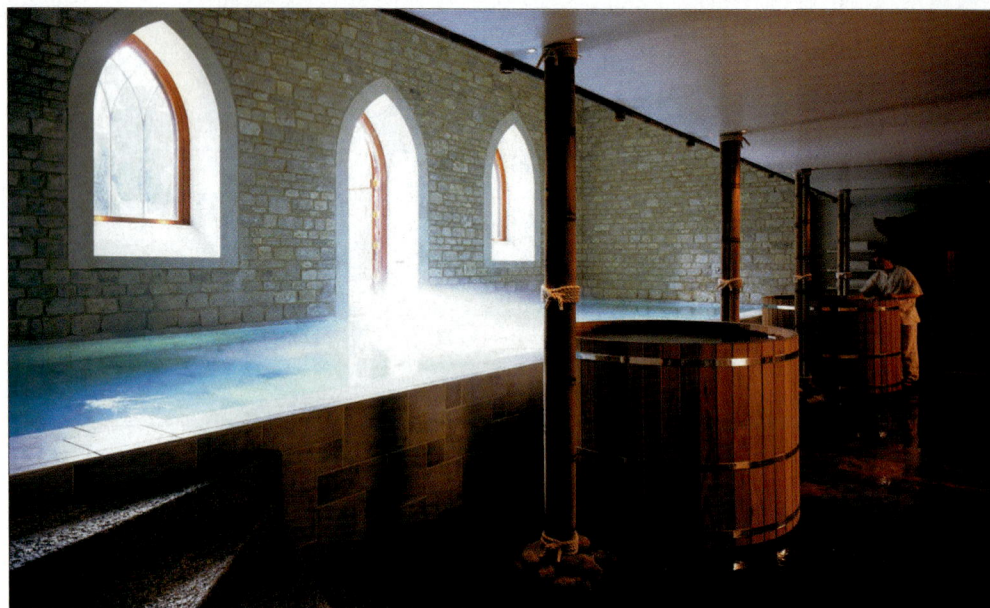

WEST COUNTRY

A fine luxury hotel from which to take the waters

Discreetly situated in the centre of the famous Royal Crescent, this luxurious hotel embodies the Georgian elegance of Bath. Restored in 1998 to a glorious standard, it retains a traditional grace, with an original 18th-century staircase and chequered entrance hall, not to mention a grand art collection - and all this is within strolling distance of Bath's major attractions!

Undoubtedly the most famous of Bath's attractions are the Roman baths and the most exciting new development, the Thermae Bath Spa. The new spa provides an exciting environment in which to bathe in the hot springs as the Romans once did, renowned as a natural way to heal and bring well-being. The Bath House at The Royal Crescent Hotel was created in 1998 with the famous Roman baths in mind; today's developments, however, also include a wealth of more modern therapies and treatments, all in a traditional Roman bathing experience.

Many of The Royal Crescent's sumptuous bedrooms have a fine, authentic appearance down to the smallest detail, and with some with custom-made beds and large deep baths, comfort is clearly a priority, too! Another great place to unwind is Pimpernel's restaurant, which serves contemporary British food in a relaxed atmosphere overlooking the hotel's beautiful walled gardens.

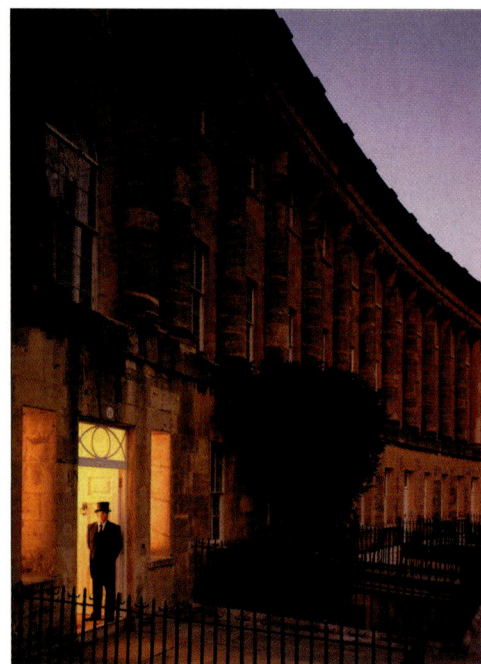

LOCATION
Situated in the centre of the Royal Crescent, just 10 minutes' walk from the centre of Bath.

> " A stately home with elegance, yet a most comfortable country house "
>
> J TAYLOR, CRICKET ST THOMAS

Stately home

STON EASTON PARK

A Palladian mansion grand in style and effervescent in spirit

One of Britain's most glorious Palladian mansions, Ston Easton Park epitomises the very essence of the aristocratic English country house, set in grounds created by the 18th-century landscape supremo Humphry Repton.

Ston Easton is at once ineffably elegant and stately, yet surprisingly human in scale. A private home until recently, many of its furnishings, paintings and objets d'art have been amassed over the years and are intrinsic to the overall effect. Opulent stucco decorations and trompe l'oeil murals are highlights of the magnificent Saloon, and Regency mahogany furnishings can be found in the library and yellow dining room. The bedrooms are delicate and pretty, with fine antique beds and garden views. For guests wanting utter privacy, the 17th-century Gardener's Cottage is an idyllic retreat on the wooded banks of the River Norr.

Ston Easton's atmosphere mirrors the grand yet human feel of the house. On the one hand, impeccably trained staff squeeze the lemon and stir the sugar into your tea in the manner of old-school butlers. On the other, the General Manager and Sorrel and Sweep the friendly spaniels materialise as if by magic to greet guests as they pull into the drive, adding that elusive personal touch that gives Ston Easton such a special sense of ease.

LOCATION

Exit the M4 onto the M32 (Bristol), then the A37 (Wells/Shepton). The hotel is on the left and is well-signed. Pilots, note heli-pad grid reference OS 183 ST 624 540 N51 16.9 W002 32.5.

Ston Easton, Near Bath, Somerset BA3 4DF

T (UK) 0870 432 8779
T 01761 241631
F 01761 241377
stoneaston@bestloved.com
www.stoneaston.bestloved.com

GENERAL MANAGER
Andrew Chantrell

ROOM RATES
6 Classic Doubles/Twins £150 - £195
4 Superior Rooms £210 - £265
5 Deluxe Rooms £295 - £330
7 State Rooms £335 - £395
1 Gardener's Cottage £695 - £815
Includes full English breakfast, early morning tea, newspaper and VAT

CREDIT CARDS
AMERICAN EXPRESS • DC • MC • VI

RATINGS & AWARDS
RAC Gold Ribbon ★★★★ Dining Award 3
AA ★★★★ ❀❀
AA Top 200 - 2004/2005

FACILITIES
On site: Garden, heli-pad, fishing, croquet, tennis, licensed for weddings, ballooning, laser shooting, hunting, off-road driving, falconry, billiards 8 meeting rooms/max 120 people
Nearby: Clay pigeon shooting, riding, golf

RESTRICTIONS
No facilities for disabled guests
No smoking in restaurant
Pets by arrangement

ATTRACTIONS
Bath, Longleat House, Glastonbury, Wells Cathedral, American Museum, Stourhead Gardens, Cheddar Gorge, Wookey Hole Caves, Lacock Abbey

NEAREST
CITY:
Bath - 11 miles/25 mins

AIRPORT:
Bristol - 12 miles/20 mins

RAIL STATION:
Bath Spa - 11 miles/25 mins
Castle Cary - 4 miles/10 mins

AFFILIATIONS
von Essen Hotels
Celebrated Hotels Collection
Pride of Britain
Grand Heritage Hotels

RESERVATIONS
National rate in UK: 0870 432 8779
Toll free in US: 800-322-2403
or 800-98-PRIDE or 800-93-GRAND
Quote Best Loved

ACCESS CODES
AMADEUS YX BRSEAS
APOLLO/GALILEO YX 66849
SABRE/ABACUS YX 42700
WORLDSPAN YX BRSSE
PEGASUS YX EASTON

WEST COUNTRY

> **The food was excellent, neither 'gourmet' nor home-cooking, with menus suited for a long stay - different every night**
>
> THE GOOD HOTEL GUIDE

TALLAND BAY HOTEL

Seaside hotel

Talland-by-Looe,
Cornwall PL13 2JB

T (UK) 0870 432 8789
T 01503 272667
F 01503 272940
tallandbay@bestloved.com
www.tallandbay.bestloved.com

OWNERS
George and Mary Granville

GENERAL MANAGER
Maureen Le Page

ROOM RATES
2 Singles	£50 - £90
17 Doubles/Twins	£100 - £180
1 Four-poster	£140 - £180

Includes full breakfast and VAT

CREDIT CARDS
MC • VI

RATINGS & AWARDS
AA ★★★ ✿✿ 76%

FACILITIES
On site: Garden, outdoor pool, croquet, putting green
Nearby: Golf, riding, sailing, boating, sea fishing, tennis

RESTRICTIONS
No facilities for disabled guests
No smoking in restaurant or bedrooms
Pets by arrangement

ATTRACTIONS
The Eden Project, Bodmin Moor, St Catherine's Castle, Fowey, St Michael's Mount, Lanhydrock Gardens, Lost Gardens of Heligan

NEAREST
CITY:
Plymouth - 25 miles/30 mins

AIRPORT:
Plymouth - 25 miles/30 mins
Newquay - 32 miles/50 mins

RAIL STATION:
Liskeard - 10 miles/15 mins

AFFILIATIONS
Independent

RESERVATIONS
National rate in UK: 0870 432 8789
Quote Best Loved

ACCESS CODES
Not applicable

WEST COUNTRY

A rare example of a fine country house hotel by the sea

Hidden down a typically Cornish lane leading to the sea, Talland Bay Hotel just gets better and better. Owners George and Mary Granville - who, incidentally, are wonderful hosts - have taken this stylishly converted old manor to new heights. This is best illustrated by the dining room's crisp white linen, fresh flowers, Villeroy & Bosch china, Reidel wine glasses and high-quality, well-presented food. Cornwall's bracing sea air is bound to build up an appetite, and menus display a healthy bias in favour of fresh Looe crab and lobster, Cornish lamb and West Country cheeses.

The hotel is nestled in two acres of glorious gardens and enjoys splendid views of the twin headlands flanking its namesake bay. Comfort and quiet are two key components in Talland Bay's unpretentious and relaxing atmosphere. The library and sitting room open onto a pool terrace, where palm trees add a distinctly Mediterranean air in summer. The bright and airy bedrooms are decorated with carefully selected furnishings, and many have sea views. As for the bathrooms, well, you'll want to take them home with you!

Local explorations range from coastal walks to visits to the famous Lost Gardens of Heligan and the spectacular Eden Project. Sporting types can try their hand at golf, riding, sailing, and sea fishing.

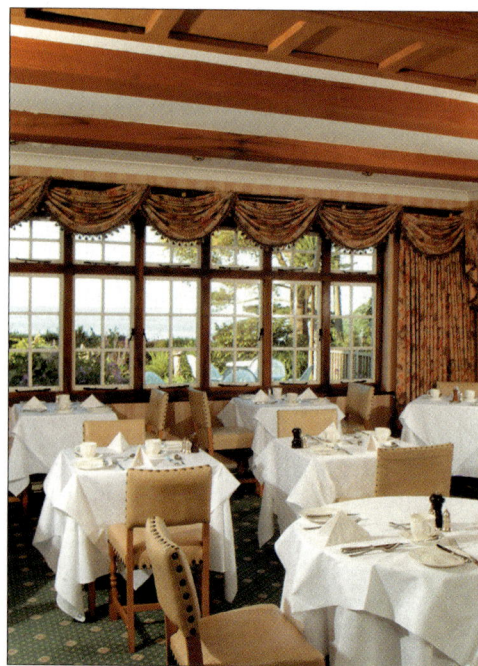

LOCATION
From Plymouth, take the A38 south, then the B3251 to Looe. Head toward Polperro for two miles and turn left at the crossroads.

> "Completely relaxed, wholly pampered and now totally addicted"
>
> GEORGE TURNER III, WASHINGTON USA

Seaside hotel

TIDES REACH HOTEL

South Sands, Salcombe,
Devon TQ8 8LJ

T (UK) 0870 432 8798
T 01548 843466
F 01548 843954
tidesreach@bestloved.com
www.tidesreach.bestloved.com

OWNER
John Edwards

RATES PER PERSON
2 Singles   £71 - £120
28 Doubles/Twins   £60 - £140
2 Suites   £75 - £125
3 Family Suites   £65 - £150
Includes full breakfast, dinner and VAT

CREDIT CARDS
AMERICAN EXPRESS • DC • MC • VI

RATINGS & AWARDS
ETC ★★★ Gold Award
RAC Blue Ribbon ★★★ Dining Award 2
AA ★★★ ❀ 77%

FACILITIES
On site: Garden, indoor pool,
health & beauty, squash, snooker,
fitness centre, sauna,
windsurfing, sailing
Nearby: Golf, riding, beaches

RESTRICTIONS
Limited facilities for disabled guests
No children under 8 years
No smoking in restaurant, two
lounges and some bedrooms
Closed 1 Dec. - 10 Feb.

ATTRACTIONS
National Maritime Aquarium,
Dartmoor, Dartmouth
and Totnes castles, Plymouth,
Overbeck Museum,
South Devon coast

NEAREST
CITY:
Plymouth - 24 miles/40 mins

AIRPORT:
Heathrow - 220 miles/4 hrs 30 mins
Plymouth - 24 miles/40 mins

RAIL STATION:
Totnes - 20 miles/30 mins

AFFILIATIONS
Independent

RESERVATIONS
National rate in UK: 0870 432 8798
Quote Best Loved

ACCESS CODES
Not applicable

WEST COUNTRY

An ideal holiday location for total seaside relaxation

Elegant and luxuriously appointed, the Tides Reach Hotel has been under the personal supervision of the Edwards family for more than 30 years. They have built up an enviable reputation for cuisine and standards of service complementing the hotel's situation, which must be one of the most naturally beautiful in the British Isles.

Set in a commanding position facing south in the tree-fringed sandy cove of South Sands, Tides Reach is the ideal location for a short break or relaxing holiday. The hotel stands just inside the mouth of the outstandingly scenic Salcombe Estuary.

At Tides Reach, one of the most important ingredients is the service. Highly trained staff carefully chosen for their caring and courteous service are dedicated to making your stay a pleasant and memorable one. In the Garden Room Restaurant, the connoisseur of fine food and wine will find great satisfaction; fresh fish and carefully-selected local produce are expertly prepared to uphold the hotel's international reputation.

LOCATION

Leave the A38 at Totnes, then follow the A381 to Kingsbridge and then to Salcombe as signposted.

TREVALSA COURT COUNTRY HOUSE   Seaside hotel

School Hill, Mevagissey,
St Austell, Cornwall PL26 6TH

T (UK) 0870 432 8803
T 01726 842468
F 01726 844482
trevalsa@bestloved.com
www.trevalsa.bestloved.com

OWNER
Klaus Wagner

GENERAL MANAGER
Matthew Mainka

ROOM RATES
2 Singles   £49 - £98
10 Doubles/Twins   £78 - £138
2 Suites   £110 - £170
Includes breakfast and VAT

CREDIT CARDS
AMERICAN EXPRESS • MC • VI

RATINGS & AWARDS
Independent

FACILITIES
On site: Garden, terrace
Nearby: Golf, riding, sailing, fishing

RESTRICTIONS
No facilities for disabled guests
No children under 12 years
Smoking in bar only
No pets
Closed December-January

ATTRACTIONS
Eden Project, Lost Gardens of Heligan,
Lanhydrock Gardens, Tate Gallery,
Falmouth Maritime Museum,
Daphne du Maurier's House

NEAREST
CITY:
Truro - 20 miles/30 mins

AIRPORT:
Bristol - 150 miles/3 hrs
Newquay - 15 miles/30 mins

RAIL STATION:
Truro - 20 miles/30 mins

AFFILIATIONS
Independent

RESERVATIONS
National rate in UK: 0870 432 8803
Quote Best Loved

ACCESS CODES
Not applicable

WEST COUNTRY

Magnificently positioned on the Cornish coast with sea views stretching for miles

Set in south-facing gardens above the sloping sands of Polstreath Beach, Trevalsa Court commands spectacular views over Mevagissey Bay and beyond. This lovely house dates from the 1930s, and it is full of character and several unusual additions such as the 19th-century oak panelling in the hall brought from Yorkshire and the handsome oak beams in the dining room which once supported the decks of a 16th-century Cornish sailing ship.

Resident owner Klaus Wagner and manager Matthew Mainka found Trevalsa in 1999, and it has been a labour of love to restore the property and revive its casual but elegant country house feel. The décor is an eclectic blend of traditional and modern styles with the emphasis on comfort and relaxation and there is a sense of fun and informality, which draws guests into the ethos of the hotel.

If you need to work up an appetite for dinner it is as easy as taking a dip in the sea at the bottom of the garden or strolling down to Mevagissey's bustling harbour a few minutes away. Slightly further afield, the Cornish Cycle Way leads to the fabulous Lost Gardens of Heligan in just 20 minutes.

LOCATION
From St Austell, take the B3273 to Mevagissey. The hotel is on the left, 1/2 mile before the village itself.

"After leaving you, we went on to stay at another hotel. We paid twice as much and didn't enjoy it half as much. You are the best innkeeper in the UK"

Country house

THE WELL HOUSE

St Keyne, Liskeard,
Cornwall PL14 4RN

T (UK) 0870 432 8813
T 01579 342001
F 01579 343891
wellhouse@bestloved.com
www.wellhouse.bestloved.com

OWNERS
Nick Wainford & Ione Nurdin

MANAGER
Mark Watts

ROOM RATES
Single occupancy   £75 - £95
9 Doubles/Twins   £115 - £195
Includes full breakfast and VAT

CREDIT CARDS
JCB • MC • VI

RATINGS & AWARDS
AA ★★ ✿✿
AA Top 200 - 2004/2005
The Good Hotel Guide Cesar Award 2004

FACILITIES
On site: Garden, outdoor pool,
croquet, tennis
1 meeting room/max 60 people
Nearby: Golf, riding, fishing

RESTRICTIONS
No facilities for disabled guests
No children under 8 years in the
restaurant, high tea provided
No smoking in restaurant
Pets by arrangement

ATTRACTIONS
The Eden Project,
Heligan and 70 other gardens,
Restormel Castle, Land's End,
Cothele, St Michael's Mount, fishing
villages of Looe, Polperro and Fowey

NEAREST
CITY:
Plymouth -16 miles/25 mins

AIRPORT:
Heathrow - 220 miles/3 hrs 30 mins
Plymouth - 16 miles/25 mins

RAIL STATION:
Liskeard - 3 miles/5 mins

FERRY PORT:
Plymouth - 18 miles/35 mins

AFFILIATIONS
Independent

RESERVATIONS
National rate in UK: 0870 432 8813
Quote Best Loved

ACCESS CODES
Not applicable

WEST COUNTRY

Discover Cornwall from this delightfully secluded manor

An intimate nine-bedroomed Victorian country manor, The Well House is tucked away down a country lane deep in Cornwall's Looe Valley just beyond the River Tamar. Its facade, wrapped in rambling wisteria and jasmine trailers, is just one of a continuous series of delights that include top-quality service, modern luxury and impeccable standards of comfort.

The dining room at The Well House, with its magnificent bay windows and sun terrace overlooking the lawns, has a contemporary style echoed in the cooking, though the traditions of the area are clearly in evidence. Cornish fish soup and freshly caught sea bass, turbot or lobster, along with wild boar, partridge and local English cheeses, are all features of the daily-changing menu at this internationally acclaimed and Michelin-honoured restaurant.

The hotel is set in four acres of gardens with an all-weather tennis court, swimming pool and croquet lawn - all in a spectacular setting. Excellent fishing, riding and golf can be found nearby, and the coastline offers matchless scenery and walking territory.

LOCATION

From Liskeard, take the B3254 to St Keyne, three miles south of Liskeard. Take the left fork by the church; the hotel is half a mile from there.

A friendly service and relaxing atmosphere. The gardens are peaceful and the food is superb

AA INSPECTOR

WIDBROOK GRANGE

Country house

Widbrook, Bradford-on-Avon, Near Bath, Wiltshire BA15 1UH

T (UK) 0870 432 8828
T 01225 864750
F 01225 862890
widbrook@bestloved.com
www.widbrook.bestloved.com

OWNERS
Peter and Jane Wragg

ROOM RATES
1 Single	£65 - £105
11 Doubles/Twins	£90 - £110
6 Four-posters	£125
3 Family Rooms	£140 - £170

Includes full breakfast and VAT

CREDIT CARDS
AMERICAN EXPRESS • DC • MC • VI

RATINGS & AWARDS
ETC ◆◆◆◆◆ Guesthouse
RAC ◆◆◆◆◆ Dining Award 2
RAC Warm Welcome,
Little Gem Awards
AA ◆◆◆◆◆ ❀
AA Premier Collection

FACILITIES
On site: Garden, gym, indoor pool,
licensed for weddings
3 meeting rooms/max 50 people
Nearby: Golf, horse riding,
cycle and boat hire

RESTRICTIONS
No pets; guide dogs only
Closed 24 - 30 Dec.

ATTRACTIONS
Bath, narrow boat hire on the
Kennet & Avon, Bradford Saxon
Church and Tithe Barn,
Longleat House & Safari Park,
Stonehenge, Wells, Salisbury

NEAREST
CITY:
Bath - 8 miles/17 mins

AIRPORT:
Heathrow - 90 miles/2 hrs
Bristol - 27 miles/50 mins

RAIL STATION:
Bath Spa - 8 miles/17 mins
Bradford-on-Avon - 1 mile/5 mins

AFFILIATIONS
Independent

RESERVATIONS
National rate in UK: 0870 432 8828
Quote Best Loved

ACCESS CODES
Not applicable

A homely base for exploring historic Bath and the surrounding countryside

Widbrook Grange, home of resident owners Jane and Peter Wragg, is an elegant 250 year-old Georgian country house located in 11 acres of peaceful grounds. The house is surrounded by rolling Wiltshire countryside, yet is only 17 minutes from the city of Bath.

Cosy lounges and a log fire burning on cold winter nights create an atmosphere of warmth and informality. Service is attentive, yet unobtrusive, and for this, Widbrook has been named RAC 'Little Gem' for the last six years. Spacious and tastefully decorated bedrooms in the main house, courtyard and gardens include romantic four-posters, family rooms and facilities for disabled guests. A welcoming retreat for families and business travellers alike, Widbrook offers the chance to relax by the heated indoor pool and dine in the award-winning Medlar Tree Restaurant, which has earned an AA rosette for its fine British regional cuisine created using fresh home-grown produce and complemented by an interesting selection of wines.

Walks from the hotel lead to the Kennet and Avon canal with its picturesque narrow boats, then on to the Saxon Tithe Barn and Church in the medieval town of Bradford-on-Avon. Longleat, Stonehenge and Lacock Abbey are all within easy driving distance and for the more energetic, golf, riding and boat and cycle hire can be arranged.

LOCATION
On the A363 Bradford-upon-Avon to Trowbridge Road, one mile from Bradford-upon-Avon centre and two miles from Trowbridge.

> "Warmest of welcomes, sweetest of suites, finest of foods and the cleverest of chefs - what a delightful retreat for our Cornish adventure"
>
> SILVIA AND PIER STARRS, LONDON

Country house

WISTERIA LODGE

Boscundle, Tregrehan,
St Austell, Cornwall PL25 3RJ

T (UK) 0870 432 8819
T 01726 810800
wisteria@bestloved.com
www.wisteria.bestloved.com

OWNERS
Sally and James Wilkins

ROOM RATES
2 Doubles	£90 - £115
3 Suites	£125 - £190
4 Premier Suites (in March 05)	£190
1 Apartment (in March 05)	£250

Includes full breakfast and VAT

CREDIT CARDS
AMERICAN EXPRESS • MC • VI

RATINGS & AWARDS
ETC ◆◆◆◆◆ Silver Award
AA ◆◆◆◆◆
AA Premier Collection
AA Dinner Award
Cornish Tourist Board Highly Commended
Daily Mirror Hotel of the Week

FACILITIES
On site: Garden, hot tub, spa treatments
1 meeting room/max 15 people
Nearby: Golf, beaches, swimming

RESTRICTIONS
Limited facilities for disabled guests
No children under 12 years
No smoking throughout
No pets; guide dogs only
Closed three weeks in January

ATTRACTIONS
Eden Project,
Lost Gardens of Heligan,
Padstow, Fowey,
National Maritime Museum,
Tate Gallery

NEAREST
CITY:
Truro - 17 miles/25 mins

AIRPORT:
Newquay - 15 miles/30 mins

RAIL STATION:
St Austell - 3 miles/5 mins

AFFILIATIONS
Independent

RESERVATIONS
National rate in UK: 0870 432 8819
Quote Best Loved

ACCESS CODES
Not applicable

WEST COUNTRY

Comfort and indulgence close to the best of Cornwall's attractions

This elegant small hotel is owned by James and Sally Wilkins, who are dedicated to ensuring that their guests feel relaxed and pampered!

Situated on the edge of St Austell, guests at Wisteria are in a wonderful location for visiting many of Cornwall's most popular attractions, with the Eden Project only a five-minute drive away and the Lost Gardens of Heligan just a 10-minute journey. The National Maritime Museum and the renowned Tate Gallery are also nearby.

The cuisine at Wisteria Lodge is as tempting as the accommodation, with a gourmet dinner menu that includes a selection of freshly-caught fish and a variety of locally-sourced meat and produce. The accommodation at Wisteria is elegant and chic, and includes four premier suites with lounges and whirlpool baths.

James and Sally are also putting the finishing touches on new apartments to be opened in the spring. Accommodating two to six people, they're perfect for small groups and meetings. A daily maid will attend the apartments, which can be rented for three or more nights and have a great position overlooking the sea.

LOCATION

Off the A390 one mile west of St Blazey and two miles east of St Austell. Turn left before the roundabout (Tregrehan), then left for Boscundle Close. The hotel is just before Boscundle Manor.

> ❝ Five-star welcome, food, beds and service. Thank you very much! ❞
>
> TONY AND PAT BARRON, EAST YORKSHIRE

WOODLANDS COUNTRY HOUSE HOTEL Country house

Hill Lane, Brent Knoll,
Somerset TA9 4DF

T (UK) 0870 432 8821
T 01278 760232
F 01278 769090
woodlands@bestloved.com
www.woodlands.bestloved.com

OWNERS
Colin and Angie Lapage

ROOM RATES
Single occupancy	£69 - £95
4 Superior Doubles	£99
2 King Doubles/Twins	£120
2 Suite/Four-posters	£135
1 Family Suite	£155

Includes full breakfast and VAT

CREDIT CARDS
AMERICAN EXPRESS • MC • VI

RATINGS & AWARDS
AA ★★ 72%

FACILITIES
On site: Garden, outdoor pool,
licensed for weddings, teambuilding
2 meeting rooms/max 40 people
Nearby: Golf, riding, fishing, tennis,
shooting, fitness

RESTRICTIONS
No facilities for disabled guests
No children under 10 years in restaurant
Smoking in bar only
No pets; guide dogs only

ATTRACTIONS
Cheddar Gorge, Wookey Hole Caves,
Wells Cathedral,
Glastonbury Abbey & Tor,
Bath, Quantock Hills

NEAREST
CITY:
Bristol - 33 miles/40 mins

AIRPORT:
Bristol - 16 miles/25 mins

RAIL STATION:
Highbridge - 3 miles/10 mins

AFFILIATIONS
Independent

RESERVATIONS
National rate in UK: 0870 432 8821
Quote Best Loved

ACCESS CODES
Not applicable

WEST COUNTRY

Relax and unwind in the peaceful shadow of history

This mellow country house hotel nestles at the foot of Brent Knoll in an extraordinarily peaceful corner of West Somerset. This is the land of Arthurian legend; Glastonbury, mythical burial site of King Arthur and final resting place of the Holy Grail, is nearby, as is the cathedral city of Wells.

Owners of Woodlands, Colin and Angie Lapage, are the epitome of the perfect hosts - nothing, it seems, is ever too much trouble, and you do get the feeling that you are more of a family friend than a guest.

Enjoy an aperitif in the cosy bar and on cooler days a crackling log fire will create a warm, relaxed atmosphere in which to unwind. The very comfortable bedrooms are individually decorated and furnished, and there are many thoughtful touches. The views through the sash windows unfold way into the distance.

The restaurant has built up an enthusiastic local following - always a good sign - and imaginative, creative and well-prepared dishes are served in the charming Victorian dining room.

With the M5 just five minutes away, Woodlands is ideally located for exploring the delights of Somerset, and really is perfect for that rare escape, whether for business or pleasure!

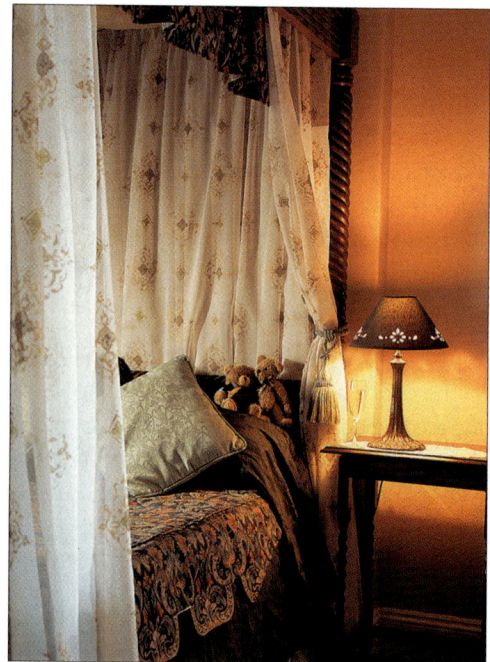

LOCATION
Exit the M5 at junction 22 and take the A38 north for half a mile. Turn left following the signs to Brent Knoll.

Of all the hotels and restaurants I supply, this is one of my favourites; delicious food, professional and friendly service

IAN BULLIS, PROPRIETOR, CELTIC FISH & GAME, CORNWALL

Country house

WOOLVERTON HOUSE

The quintessential English country house within easy reach of Bath

Woolverton House was originally built as a rectory in the early 19th century and still retains a slightly ecclesiastical air, with its steeply pitched roofs and Gothic style mullioned windows. Mature trees cast patches of shade across the sunny lawns and carefully tended gardens, and there are marvellous views stretching out across the old glebe lands to the rolling Somerset and Wiltshire landscape.

Woolverton's interior is just as it should be, furnished with antiques and warmed by log fires in winter. It's no trouble to rustle up a chess set if guests fancy a game, and there is an airy and inviting conservatory with deep sofas and armchairs. In summer, a cool Pimms can be delivered to a quiet corner of the garden or the croquet lawn, as well as the tennis court. Chef Proprietor Ric House shares responsibility for the restaurant with chef Peter Holmes, and the varied menu makes full use of the finest fresh local ingredients. Upstairs, each of the 12 bedrooms is both charming and extremely comfortable.

This is a great base for exploring nearby Bath and England's smallest city, Wells. Garden buffs should make tracks for the horticultural glories of Stourhead House near Warminster.

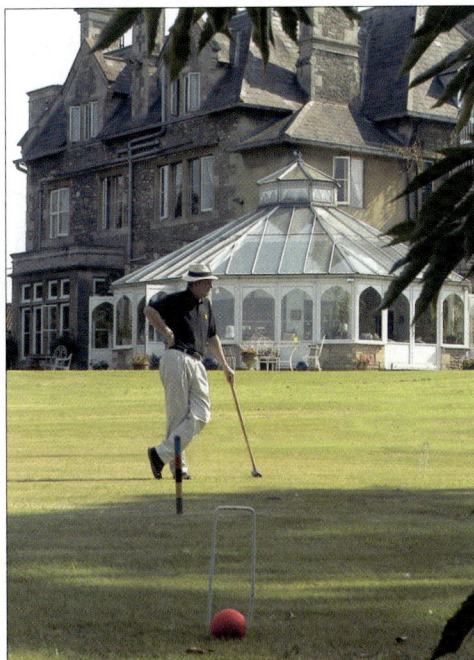

LOCATION

Take the A36 Warminster road to the village of Woolverton, located eight miles south of Bath.

Woolverton, Bath,
Somerset BA2 7QS

T (UK) 0870 432 8824
T 01373 830415
F 01373 831243
woolverton@bestloved.com
www.woolverton.bestloved.com

OWNERS
Richard and Gina House

ROOM RATES
Single occupancy   £65
13 Doubles/Twins   £85 - £113
2 Suites   £119 - £148
Includes full breakfast and VAT

CREDIT CARDS
MC • VI

RATINGS & AWARDS
Independent

FACILITIES
On site: Garden, croquet, tennis, putting green
1 meeting room/max 80 people
Nearby: Golf, riding, walking, swimming

RESTRICTIONS
Children by arrangement
Smoking in conservatory and drawing room only
No pets

ATTRACTIONS
City of Bath, Longleat House, Holborne Museum of Art, Stonehenge, Stourhead Gardens, Wells Cathedral, Salisbury Cathedral, Thermae Bath Spa

NEAREST
CITY:
Bath - 8 miles/12 mins

AIRPORT:
Bristol - 30 miles/50 mins

RAIL STATION:
Bath - 8 miles/12 mins
Westbury - 6 miles/10 mins

AFFILIATIONS
Independent

RESERVATIONS
National rate in UK: 0870 432 8824
Quote Best Loved

ACCESS CODES
Not applicable

WEST COUNTRY

SOUTH

AN ISLAND HOTEL
Chateau Valeuse, Jersey

A CASTLE
Amberley Castle, West Sussex

A TOWNHOUSE
Hotel du Vin & Bistro, Brighton

REPRESENTING
the best of the
SOUTH

A STATELY HOME
Cliveden House, Berkshire

Best Loved Hotels offer the cream of the crop across Great Britain and Ireland - from stately palaces to welcoming inns - each the best of its kind within its locality and price range.

Whichever place you choose as your own place to stay, you'll find every hotel offers character, charm and the best delights and attractions of its region.

And each, in its own special way, is best-loved by someone who's been there.

A COTTAGE INN
Thatched Cottage Hotel, Hampshire

A SEASIDE HOTEL
Priory Bay Hotel, Isle of Wight

AN ISLAND HOTEL
Old Government House Hotel, Guernsey

A SPA HOTEL
Hartwell House, Buckinghamshire

AN IDEAL ESCAPE:
The South

A REGION OF CONTRASTS from pastoral vistas in the Home Counties to the mossy clearings of the New Forest and seaside glamour in Brighton, the South has a little something for everyone - and it's best to sample some of it all.

Day One

Though London may be the pulse of the South, its heart and history are certainly spread throughout the region. Spend a bit of time north of the City in the village of **Woburn**, where a magnificent stately home awaits in the form of **Woburn Abbey**, a lovely local-stone building on 3,000 acres of elegant grounds. Families will particularly enjoy the nearby **Woburn Safari Park**, complete with wolves, bears and big cats. Nearby, too, are **Stowe Landscape Gardens**, a pleasant escape from the everyday on a surprisingly grand scale.

Another delight for families is the **Roald Dahl Children's Gallery**, in Aylesbury; children (of all ages!) will enjoy a guided tour of Dahl's books, complete with, of course, a giant peach.

The Roman town of Verulamium - today, the heart of **St Albans** - is also certainly worth a visit. Founded soon after the Roman invasion, the town's later incarnation as St Albans marked it as both a religious centre and a flourishing trading town for London travellers on their way to points farther north. Visit the **cathedral** to take in the layers of history in the town; here, it's literally written on the walls just how much things have changed over the centuries. To hear a bit more about St Albans' story, there's the **Verulamium Museum**, too, where some lovely Roman mosaics draw the eye.

A bit of song at St Albans Cathedral

Wildlife at Woburn

Day Two

A drive is certainly in order if you want to get the most out of your visit; it's well worth taking a day out to see some sights from the comfort of your car - and a great excuse for packing a picnic lunch! A wealth of destinations await, and it's up to you to take your pick. **Windsor Castle** is a firm favourite, especially if you're visiting from abroad; however, with stunning interiors and more than 900 years of history as a working castle, there's something to interest all. If you can, visit between September and March, when George IV's private apartments are open to the public.

Don't let the fact that you can't get up close and personal with the stones deter you - **Stonehenge** is awe-inspiring from any distance, and well worth the visit if you've never seen the ancient monument in the sheer grandeur of its full scale.

Or, if you're in a more rural frame of mind, the **New Forest** beckons, full of sheltered paths, green-carpeted walks and even the occasional pony amongst the 145 miles of woodland. Take some time to stroll, and if you have the chance,

Stonehenge is AWE-INSPIRING from any distance

enjoy dinner at the **Thatched Cottage Hotel** in Brockenhurst (see page 335), where locally-sourced dining is not to be missed! Automotive enthusiasts can take heart, too, with the **National Motor Museum** in Beaulieu, home to Damon Hill's F1 world championship car and other treats.

Windsor Castle is breathtaking, no matter the time of year

Day Three

End your holiday with a little seaside fun in **Brighton**. Whether you're visiting on your own, or with children, there's a world to see and do, from the architecturally striking **Royal Pavilion** (its onion domes and Regency gardens mask a brilliantly decadent collection of chinoiserie) to simply lying out on the **pebble beach** for a while and soaking in some sun - after all, that's what gave this once sleepy fishing village its reputation during the 18th-century trend for sea bathing. Shoppers can lose themselves in the **Lanes**, where narrow cobbled alleyways are home to a range of eclectic shops and a busker or two.

If you're feeling ambitious, make your seaside journey complete by a boat trip out to the **Isle of Wight**. Sixty miles of coastline await, as well as a grand glimpse of nature at **Ventnor Botanic Gardens** and **Carisbrooke Castle**, the medieval castle where King Charles I stayed as a prisoner in 1647-8.

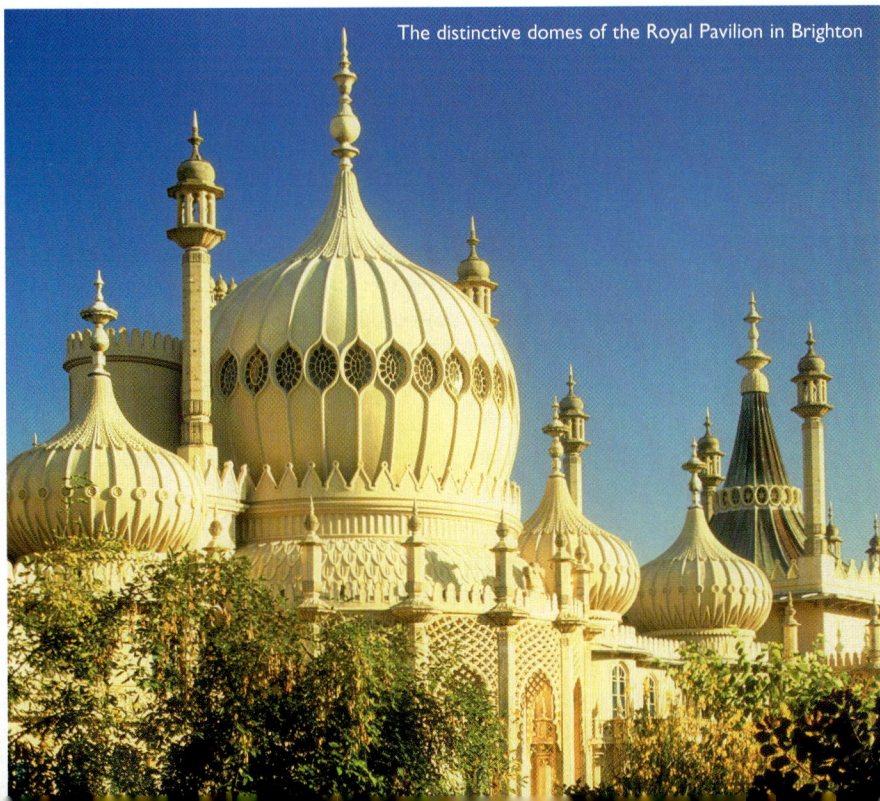

The distinctive domes of the Royal Pavilion in Brighton

ESCAPE FROM YOUR DESKTOP

If you can't wait to get away, or if you'd simply like to do a little investigating before you make your holiday in the South, browse the links below. Remember, too, that thousands of places to see and things to do await at Best Loved's Web site, **www.bestlovedhotels.com**.

Woburn Abbey and Safari Park
www.woburnabbey.co.uk

Stowe Landscape Gardens
www.nationaltrust.org.uk

Roald Dahl Children's Gallery
www.buckscc.gov.uk/museum

Verulamium Museum
www.stalbansmuseums.org.uk

Windsor Castle
www.windsor.gov.uk/attractions/castle.htm

New Forest visitors guide
www.hants.gov.uk/newforest

National Motor Museum
www.beaulieu.co.uk

Brighton visitors guide
tourism.brighton.co.uk

Royal Pavilion
www.royalpavilion.org.uk

Ventnor Botanic Garden
www.botanic.co.uk

Carisbrooke Castle
www.carisbrookecastlemuseum.org.uk

A TASTE OF THE BEST

The South

ATMOSPHERE IS KEY in the South, whether it means dining in a castle or a riverside retreat. Either way, a world of delights await you, from top-quality local ingredients all the way to the perfect dessert. Cheers!

AMBERLEY CASTLE ✿✿

This luxurious 12th-century castle serves fine cuisine with a modern flair in a choice of spectacular settings. The elegant Queen's Room – the main dining room - has a barrel-vaulted ceiling; the Great Room, with polished oak floors and suits of armour providing an atmospheric historic touch, is perfect for groups of up to 48 people, and the more intimate King Charles Room, with a capacity of up to 12 diners, has dark panelled walls and a striking fireplace, making an ideal place to hold a small get-together or intimate celebration. In all, fascinating settings in which to enjoy their award-winning cuisine!

HINTLESHAM HALL ✿✿✿

There are three dining rooms at this fine Elizabethan manor, including The Salon, which offers an extensive à la carte menu with vegetarian options. Head Chef Alan Ford is dedicated to using the very best ingredients to produce his top-quality, healthy fare - and it certainly shows on the plate. Fish is prominent on the menu, with mouth-watering options such as grilled fillet of swordfish with a delightful mint, cucumber and coriander cous cous. Fresh herbs are grown in Hintlesham Hall's stunning herb garden - lending even more of a personal touch to your dining experience - and an award-winning wine list complements their cuisine.

MAISON TALBOOTH ✿✿

This charming Victorian country house in the heart of Constable country lies just across the river from its sister restaurant, Le Talbooth. Notable for its diverse menu, Le Talbooth offers treats

Amberley Castle is a beautifully historic backdrop for fine dining

such as fricassee of monkfish and lobster with broad beans, herbs, tomato vermouth sauce and basmati rice, or roast breast of Telmara duck with green peppercorns and glazed apples. The restaurant is interesting for art lovers too, as the building can also be seen in John Constable's famous painting of the Dedham Vale, now hanging in the National Gallery of Scotland.

ST MICHAEL'S MANOR ✿✿

Close to the centre of the ancient Roman city of St Albans, this lovely lakeside hotel's Terrace Room restaurant features a striking Victorian conservatory in which diners can enjoy seasonal, modern British cuisine such as seared skate wing and courgette spaghetti in a light curry sauce, followed by a wholly irresistible dessert of poached fresh pineapple in red pepper with vanilla ice cream and chocolate tuile. For an after-dinner treat, a fine selection of malt whisky is also available in the hotel's atmospheric Garden Bar.

THE VINEYARD AT STOCKCROSS ✿✿✿✿

This stylish restaurant with suites is home to an internationally renowned Michelin-starred restaurant, making the best of an already good thing! The Vineyard's elegant restaurant has been carefully designed with stylish European furnishings, down to specially-chosen glassware, cutlery and china. Peerless modern

Hintlesham Hall features extensive dining options in a glorious setting

Riverside dining at Le Talbooth

British fare, including such dishes as roast saddle and braised shoulder of lamb with parsley puree and lemon and caper jus, is meticulously created and accompanied by an impressive wine list. There are several menus available, including the two- or three-course Market Menu lunch or dinner, the Vegetarian Menu and the Tasting Menu, all mouth-watering and all highly recommended - especially if you stay for coffee and truffles! A full fixed-price a la carte menu is also available.

Hintlesham Hall's HERB GARDEN *adds a flavourful touch*

A TASTE OF THE REGION

Looking for even more to tempt your palate? There are a wealth of fantastic places to dine in the South, all within the covers of this book! Have a browse to whet your appetite, or jump to some of our own favourites:

PRIORY BAY HOTEL ⊛⊛

A diverse menu is available at this seaside hotel on the Isle of Wight, as well as al fresco dining in the summer – perfect for enjoying the stunning sea views.

ESSEBORNE MANOR ⊛⊛

A country house set in farmland close to Stonehenge, this peacefully luxurious house offers an elegant dining room and celebrated cellar.

LANGSHOTT MANOR ⊛⊛

This stylish manor house with award-winning gardens offers a tempting menu of classical treats accompanied by a great wine list.

THE THREE LIONS ⊛⊛⊛

Owner/Chef Mike Womersley has worked in Michelin-starred restaurants in Britain and France, and now heads the kitchen at The Three Lions. Mike uses organic and locally-produced ingredients in his fare, which is accompanied by a 180-bin wine list.

Menu

ST MICHAEL'S MANOR

Hot smoked saddle of hare with a haricot blanc and chorizo cassoulet

Sweet Chanterelle melon with pink grapefruit sorbet and frosted fruits

Honey glazed duck supreme, red cabbage marmalade and a port reduction

Steamed fillet of turbot with baby leeks and asparagus with a saffron nage

Elderflower crème brulee with a lemon peel shortbread
Traditional Bakewell tart with Cornish clotted cream

ALEXANDER HOUSE HOTEL

Country house

Turners Hill,
West Sussex RH10 4QD

T (UK) 0870 432 8501
T 01342 714914
F 01342 717328
alexander@bestloved.com
www.alexander.bestloved.com

GENERAL MANAGER
Mark E Chambers

ROOM RATES
1 Single		£125
10 Doubles		£155 - £210
4 Feature Doubles		£260
3 Four-posters		£295 - £370
	Includes VAT	

CREDIT CARDS
AMERICAN EXPRESS • DC • MC • VI

RATINGS & AWARDS
RAC Gold Ribbon ★★★
Dining Award 4
AA ★★★ ❀❀
AA Top 200 - 2004/2005

FACILITIES
On site: Garden, croquet, tennis,
licensed for weddings
4 meeting rooms/max 80 people
Nearby: Golf, fishing, rifle shooting,
archery, team building activities, riding

RESTRICTIONS
No facilities for disabled guests
No children under 7 years
in the restaurant
Smoking in bar and library only
No pets

ATTRACTIONS
Hever Castle, Chartwell House,
Glyndebourne, Wakehurst Place,
Brighton

NEAREST
CITY:
Brighton - 24 miles/35 mins

AIRPORT:
Gatwick - 9 miles/15 mins

RAIL STATION:
East Grinstead - 4 miles/10 mins
Gatwick - 9 miles/15 mins

AFFILIATIONS
Celebrated Hotels Collection
Small Luxury Hotels
Utopia Group

RESERVATIONS
National rate in UK: 0870 432 8501
Toll free in US: 800-322-2403
or 800-525-4800
Quote Best Loved

ACCESS CODES
AMADEUS LX LGWALE
APOLLO/GALILEO LX 64741
SABRE/ABACUS LX 20136
WORLDSPAN LX ALEXT

SOUTH & ISLANDS

Comfort and dedicated service in Shelley's historic home

The Alexander House estate has a recorded history dating back to 1332. Some of England's most important families have made it their home, including Percy Bysshe Shelley, the famous Romantic poet, and William Campbell, Governor of the Bank of England.

Today, Alexander House is an exclusive country house hotel set in 175 acres of private parkland. With 18 bedrooms and a wealth of public rooms and meeting rooms, it successfully combines tradition with all the modern comforts and amenities. From the moment guests arrive, the dedicated staff attend to their every wish.

A superb daily choice of menus is served in the dining room, and the chef has established a fine reputation for particularly delicious classic English and French cuisine. Menus emphasise fresh natural foods, carefully prepared and artistically presented.

The hotel has a range of amenities for the outdoor-minded, including croquet and tennis. The area is also rich in places of interest, from the opera at Glyndebourne and racing at Lingfield to National Trust properties at Wakehurst Place and Chartwell, former home of Sir Winston Churchill.

LOCATION
Exit 10 off the M23 for East Grinstead. At the second roundabout, follow signs for Turners Hill (B2028). At Turners Hill, turn left (B2110) for East Grinstead. The hotel is 1 ½ miles on the left.

Amberley Castle - the friendliest castle in the world

MRS R SIMPSON

Castle

AMBERLEY CASTLE

Amberley, Arundel,
West Sussex BN18 9LT

T (UK) 0870 432 8517
T 01798 831992
F 01798 831998
amberley@bestloved.com
www.amberley.bestloved.com

OWNERS
Joy and Martin Cummings

GENERAL MANAGER
Clive and Tanith Cummings

ROOM RATES
6 Doubles/Twins	£155 - £210
7 Four-posters	£210 - £335
6 Suites	£275 - £375
Includes VAT	

CREDIT CARDS
AMERICAN EXPRESS • DC • MC • VI

RATINGS & AWARDS
AA ★★★ ✿✿
AA Top 200 - 2004/2005

FACILITIES
On site: Garden, heli-pad, croquet,
tennis, licensed for weddings,
en-suite Jacuzzis,
professional-class putting course
2 meeting rooms/max 48 people
Nearby: Golf, riding, shooting, fishing

RESTRICTIONS
No facilities for disabled guests
No children under 12 years
Smoking in lounges only
No pets

ATTRACTIONS
Arundel Castle, Petworth,
Brighton Royal Pavilion,
Amberley Chalk Pits Museum,
Goodwood House,
Chichester, Parham House

NEAREST
CITY:
London - 55 miles/1 hr 15 mins
AIRPORT:
Gatwick - 30 miles/45 mins
RAIL STATION:
Amberley - 1 mile/5 mins

AFFILIATIONS
Relais & Châteaux

RESERVATIONS
National rate in UK: 0870 432 8517
Toll free in US: 800-735-2478
Quote Best Loved

ACCESS CODES
AMADEUS WB LONB28
APOLLO/GALILEO WB 66247
SABRE/ABACUS WB 26404
WORLDSPAN WB GB28

Peace and serenity within the towering walls of a 900-year-old castle

Amberley Castle, which recently celebrated its 900th anniversary, stands in a serene landscape of undulating downland and hauntingly beautiful water meadows. Built originally by Bishop Luffa of Chichester as a country retreat, the magnificent building has extended hospitality to Henry VIII, Elizabeth I and Charles II.

Lovingly restored by resident owners Joy and Martin Cummings, Amberley Castle was transformed into England's only medieval castle hotel in 1988. With its 19 bedrooms, each with Jacuzzi bathroom, this magnificent castle offers superb luxury and every convenience while retaining all its authentic grandeur.

The 12th-century Queen's Room, with its barrel-vaulted ceiling and 17th-century mural, and the elegant Great Room offer splendid settings for award-winning cuisine based on a modern-day interpretation of English culinary heritage.

Just 60 miles from London and convenient for air and channel ferry ports, Amberley Castle lies beside one of the prettiest Sussex downland villages amidst a host of historic landmarks such as Arundel Castle and Petworth House. Shopping and theatre await in Brighton and Chichester, horse racing at Glorious Goodwood, polo at Cowdray Park and much more.

LOCATION
Amberley Castle is on the B2139, off the A29 between Storrington and Bury.

SOUTH & ISLANDS

> "I couldn't have thought of any better 'home' to spend the last few weeks on my business project. Very friendly staff, a definite 10 out of 10. Thank you!"
>
> MR JOOST BOS, SIDCUP, KENT

BEECH HOUSE HOTEL

Townhouse

60 Bath Road, Reading,
Berkshire RG30 2AY

T (UK) 0870 432 8533
T 0118 959 1901
F 0118 958 3200
beech@bestloved.com
www.beech.bestloved.com

OWNER
Michael Bissell

ROOM RATES
4 Singles	£65 - £85
7 Doubles	£75 - £95
4 Super Kings	£90 - £120

Includes full breakfast and VAT

CREDIT CARDS
AMERICAN EXPRESS • DC • MC • VI

RATINGS & AWARDS
Independent

FACILITIES
On site: Garden
1 meeting room/max 14 people
Nearby: Walking, riding, leisure centres

RESTRICTIONS
No smoking throughout
Closed Christmas week

ATTRACTIONS
Forbury Gardens, Windsor Castle, Horse racing at Ascot, Newbury and Windsor racecourses, Henley Royal Regatta, Reading Abbey, Wellington Country Park and Bucklebury Farm Park, London, Oxford, Bath

NEAREST
CITY:
Reading

AIRPORT:
Heathrow - 30 miles/45 mins

RAIL STATION:
Reading West - 1 mile/5 mins

AFFILIATIONS
Independent

RESERVATIONS
National rate in UK: 0870 432 8533
Quote Best Loved

ACCESS CODES
Not applicable

SOUTH & ISLANDS

This comfortable Victorian home is ideally located for business or pleasure

Whether you're visiting Reading for business or leisure, Beech House Hotel might just be your perfect choice. Recently renovated, this charming and relaxing late Victorian house - once a family home - boasts 15 individual rooms, all en-suite and all quite inviting.

Well-situated for the Thames Valley, London and all the business links and touring pleasures of both, Beech House Hotel is an ideal base for travelling, offering a central but peaceful location near the centre of Reading as well as a wealth of bus and train links. Full English breakfast is served in the hotel, and Reading's variety of restaurants assures that you'll be pleasantly catered for in the evenings, too.

But any description of Beech House Hotel would not be complete with a mention of its sunny, welcoming atmosphere and the warm personality of the staff. Whether your day's activities include business meetings, a tour of the region, a day in London or an afternoon's walk, you'll receive a welcome that will immediately make you feel at home.

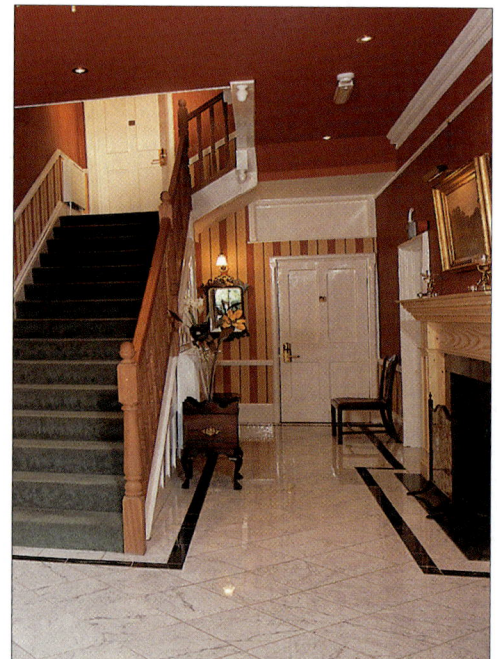

LOCATION
Take the M4 and at Junction 12 follow the A4 Bath Road to Reading. The hotel is situated just before Southcote Road, on the left.

" Warm, friendly, totally relaxing. What more can I say?

PHILLIP NESS **"**

299

Map p. 450, grid C3

Country house

BISHOPSTROW HOUSE

An inviting house in the country, complete with luxury spa

There's a great deal to say about Bishopstrow House, as it's a place that manages to be all things to all people - and does them all exceptionally well!

This is the kind of hotel where you'll find welly boots and walking sticks by the front door. The public rooms, including the drawing room, bar and library, are comfortable and welcoming, with antique furnishings and open log fires. The bedrooms are the epitome of English country house elegance, and some of the suites have extravagant bathrooms - a must for anyone taking a romantic getaway.

For leisure visitors, Bishopstrow House couldn't be more perfect. The grounds are a paradise, with a rotunda temple, pretty summer house and peaceful riverbank. The Mulberry Restaurant offers superb locally-influenced cooking, and to cap it all The Ragdale Spa offers everything from a wonderful pool to all manner of pampering treatments, including a world-class hair salon. From a corporate perspective, the hotel has two well-appointed rooms ideal for private functions or meetings.

All this doesn't leave much room to say that being situated between Bath and Salisbury opens up all sorts of sightseeing opportunities. To make the most of your visit, plan to stay an extra day.

LOCATION
Exit the A36 for the B3414;
the hotel is one mile south of Warminster.

Warminster,
Wiltshire BA12 9HH

T (UK) 0870 432 8536
T 01985 212312
F 01985 216769
bishopstrow@bestloved.com
www.bishopstrow.bestloved.com

GENERAL MANAGER
Mark Dicks

ROOM RATES
19 Doubles/Twins   £160
9 Deluxe Doubles   £245
4 Suites   £330
Includes full breakfast and VAT

CREDIT CARDS
AMERICAN EXPRESS • DC • JCB • MC • VI

RATINGS & AWARDS
AA ★★★★ ⊛⊛ 74%

FACILITIES
On site: Garden, gym, heli-pad, fishing, croquet, tennis, licensed for weddings, indoor & outdoor pool, spa, hair & beauty salon 3 meeting rooms/max 120 people
Nearby: Golf, riding

RESTRICTIONS
None

ATTRACTIONS
Salisbury Cathedral, Bath, Stonehenge & Old Sarum, Avebury, Longleat, Stourhead, Sherbourne Castle

NEAREST
CITY:
Salisbury - 20 miles/30 mins

AIRPORT:
Bristol - 34 miles/1 hr
Heathrow - 88 miles/1 hr 45 mins

RAIL STATION:
Westbury - 4 miles/10 mins

AFFILIATIONS
von Essen Hotels

RESERVATIONS
National rate in UK: 0870 432 8536
Quote Best Loved

ACCESS CODES
AMADEUS YX BRSBIS
APOLLO/GALILEO YX 04509
SABRE/ABACUS YX 22223
WORLDSPAN YX BRSBH

SOUTH & ISLANDS

BEST LOVED HOTELS

> **Every single member of staff is an absolute credit to you ... Every meal in the restaurant was of the highest quality**
>
> SUSAN CHISHAM, FAREHAM, HAMPSHIRE

CAREYS MANOR HOTEL & SPA

Country house

Brockenhurst,
Hampshire SO42 7RH

T (UK) 0870 432 8503
T 01590 623551
F 01590 622799
careys@bestloved.com
www.careys.bestloved.com

GENERAL MANAGER
Christopher Biggin

ROOM RATES
71 Doubles/Twins   £158
5 Four-posters   £190
1 Suite   £210
Includes full breakfast and VAT

CREDIT CARDS
AMERICAN EXPRESS • DC • MC • VI

RATINGS & AWARDS
AA ★★★ ❀❀ 73%

FACILITIES
On site: Gardens, indoor pool,
licensed for weddings, Jacuzzi, sauna,
steam room, fitness suite,
Oriental spa, hydrotherapy pool,
relaxation areas, 17 treatment rooms
9 meeting rooms/max 140 people
Nearby: Riding, shooting, golf, sailing

RESTRICTIONS
Limited facilities for disabled guests
No children under 7 years in
restaurant
No children in spa and health club
Smoking in some bedrooms only
No pets; guide dogs only

ATTRACTIONS
New Forest, Beaulieu Motor Museum,
Isle of Wight,
Salisbury & Winchester cathedrals,
Exbury Gardens, Wilton House,
Lymington and the coast

NEAREST
CITY:
Southampton - 13 miles/25 mins

AIRPORT:
Southampton - 15 miles/30 mins
Heathrow - 80 miles/1 hr 30 mins

RAIL STATION:
Brockenhurst - ¼ mile/5 mins

AFFILIATIONS
Independent

RESERVATIONS
National rate in UK: 0870 432 8503
Quote Best Loved

ACCESS CODES
Not applicable

SOUTH & ISLANDS

Everything you'll ever need for your New Forest stay

Situated on the edge of the mellow village of Brockenhurst in the heart of the New Forest, the red-brick Victorian façade of Careys Manor offers an unpretentious welcome to this wonderfully comfortable spa hotel.

Many of the bedrooms are in the Garden Wing and offer private terraces or balconies overlooking the grounds. Guests are welcome at the hotel's well-equipped health club, which centres on the magnificent ozone pool and also offers a sauna, steam room, Jacuzzi and gym. Guests can upgrade their stay and enjoy the use of the SenSpa, where the facilities are almost endless - 17 treatment rooms, a tepidarium, mud room, foot spas, water beds and an ice room, to mention but a few.

If you can tear yourself away from Careys' numerous temptations, the New Forest is on the doorstep and activities range from mountain biking to sailing and pony trekking. A whole host of easy side trips include the National Motor Museum at Beaulieu, Romsey Abbey, Winchester and the picturesque waterfront village of Bucklers Hard.

Careys appeals equally to the business and leisure traveller, combining all the ingredients for a relaxing break with excellent facilities for meetings and corporate retreats. In addition, the hotel can arrange a variety of tailor-made teambuilding activities.

LOCATION

Exit the M27 at junction 1, signed for the New Forest. Take the A337 to Brockenhurst; the hotel is the first on the left after a '30 mph' speed-limit sign.

Townhouse

CHASE LODGE

This stylish and affordable small family-run hotel is a capital idea

Looking for the perfect small hotel that provides a convenient base for exploring London, but without the bustle and the expense of more centrally-located accommodation? A hotel that can deliver plenty of character, attractive rooms at appealing rates, individual service and a little something extra? Here's a great idea for visitors to the capital who value a spot of insider knowledge.

Chase Lodge, which dates from the 1870s, is situated in the heart of Hampton Wick, a 500-year-old village on the Thames, 30 minutes by train from central London, eight miles from Heathrow airport and just minutes from excellent shopping in Kingston and Henry VIII's Hampton Court Palace. Nigel and Denise Stafford-Haworth run their charming bed-and-breakfast hotel with a combination of professional dedication and personal pride, ensuring that every guest feels welcome and relaxed from the moment they arrive. There are just 11 bedrooms, each individually and handsomely finished with an eclectic blend of bold fabrics, antiques and 21st-century extras, including Internet access - and some even have steam rooms or Jacuzzis! For dining, the hotel's Wickers Restaurant is a popular spot with locals and residents alike.

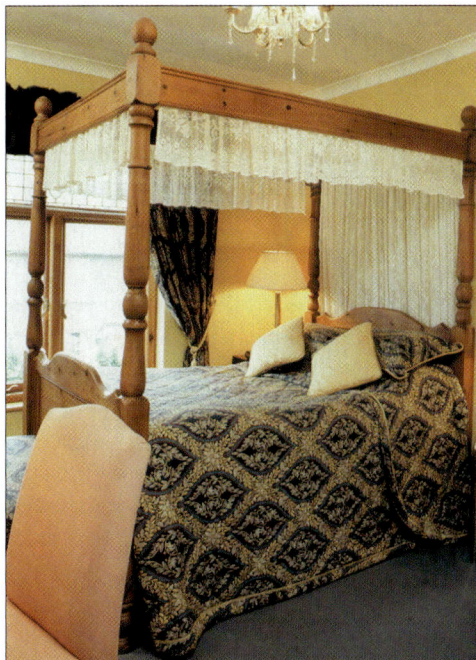

LOCATION

Hampton Wick is easily reached from the A310 and the A308; Park Road is just off Teddington Road, the A310.

10 Park Road, Hampton Wick, Kingston-upon-Thames, Surrey KT1 4AS

T (UK) 0870 432 8563
T 020 8943 1862
F 020 8943 9363
chaselodge@bestloved.com
www.chaselodge.bestloved.com

OWNERS
Nigel and Denise Stafford-Haworth

ROOM RATES
1 Single	£55 - £65
1 Twin	£71 - £98
9 Doubles	£71 - £185

Includes full breakfast and VAT

CREDIT CARDS
AMERICAN EXPRESS • DC • JCB • MC • VI

RATINGS & AWARDS
AA ◆◆◆◆

FACILITIES
On site: Courtyard
2 meeting rooms/ max 120 people
Nearby: Golf, tennis, horse riding, swimming, squash, boating

RESTRICTIONS
No facilities for disabled guests

ATTRACTIONS
Twickenham, Hampton Court Palace, Kew Gardens, Marble Hill House, Osterley House, River Thames, Wisley

NEAREST
CITY:
London - 20 miles/20 mins
Kingston upon Thames - 3 miles/5 mins

AIRPORT:
Heathrow - 7 miles/15 mins

RAIL STATION:
Hampton Wick - 500 yards/5 mins

AFFILIATIONS
Independent

RESERVATIONS
National rate in UK: 0870 432 8563
Quote Best Loved

ACCESS CODES
Not applicable

SOUTH & ISLANDS

CHATEAU VALEUSE

Island hotel

St Brelade's Bay,
Jersey JE3 8EE

T (UK) 0870 432 8564
T 01534 746281
F 01534 747110
valeuse@bestloved.com
www.valeuse.bestloved.com

OWNERS
Tom and Mary Jordan

ROOM RATES
4 Singles	£39 - £64
29 Doubles/Twins	£77 - £128
1 Family room	£107 - £170

Includes full breakfast (VAT exempt)

CREDIT CARDS
MC • VI

RATINGS & AWARDS
Jersey Tourism 3 Suns
RAC ★★★ Dining Award 1

FACILITIES
On site: Garden, outdoor pool,
putting green
Nearby: Golf, riding

RESTRICTIONS
No facilities for disabled guests
No children under 5 years
No smoking in restaurant
No pets
Closed mid-October - Easter

ATTRACTIONS
Elizabeth Castle and Hermitage,
Maritime Museum,
Island Fortress and Occupation
Museum, War Tunnels,
La Corbiere Lighthouse,
Gerald Durrell Wildlife Trust,
Eric Young Orchid Trust

NEAREST
CITY:
St Helier - 5 miles/15 mins

AIRPORT:
Jersey - 2 miles/10 mins

FERRY PORT:
St Helier - 5 miles/15 mins

AFFILIATIONS
Independent

RESERVATIONS
National rate in UK: 0870 432 8564
Quote Best Loved

ACCESS CODES
Not applicable

A traditional, family-run island hotel with service that's sure to please

This privately-owned, traditional seaside hotel is a treat with two particularly great things to recommend it: First, its location in St Brelade's Bay, which is regarded by many locals as the finest bay on the island. Second - but by no means in second place - is the homely and easy atmosphere created by the genuine charm and warmth of owners Tom and Mary Jordan.

The Jordans, it seems, pride themselves on being a little 'old-fashioned'. This really means that they still do things properly around here, resulting in a quality of service and standards that far exceeds their three-star status. Dinner, for instance, is served on lovely china, and the reasonably priced menu is full of classical choices. On Sundays, there's a real roast, and best of all, they have a dessert trolley groaning under the weight of what Mary describes as lots of fabulously fattening things!

The atmosphere is utterly charming, too; the hotel has its own beautiful award-winning gardens, the climate here is warm and sunny and, if you can bear to leave the poolside, Mary and Tom will give you plenty ideas of places to visit to make the most of your stay on the island.

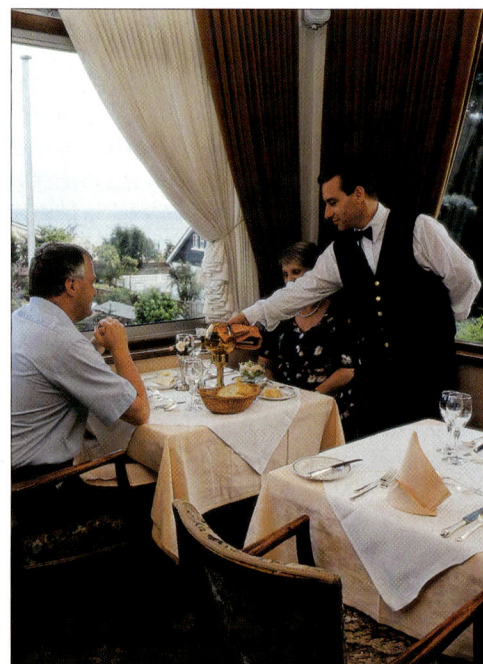

LOCATION
Situated in St Brelade's Bay in the southwest corner of Jersey.

SOUTH & ISLANDS

"Despite the sophistication, one feels at home. The staff are exceptional; without their warmth and care, it would not be the great hotel it is"

LADY NAPLEY

Stately home

CLIVEDEN HOUSE

Taplow, Berkshire SL6 0JF

T (UK) 0870 432 8565
T 01628 668561
F 01628 661837
cliveden@bestloved.com
www.cliveden.bestloved.com

Britain's only five-star stately home is truly an experience to be remembered

This grand country house has long been recognised as one of the world's finest and most luxurious residences. A Royal favourite throughout the centuries, Cliveden was once the country seat of the Astors, during which time it became the centre of a great social scene, particularly among the political and literary circles of the day.

An Italianate mansion built in 1666, this architectural treasure is surrounded by an extensive private estate, with expansive views across the Thames Valley. Everything about Cliveden is opulent and grand with lavish excess. The décor is magnificent, and fine art adorns the walls; members of staff are dressed in traditional period clothes and all guests are greeted by footmen upon arrival.

Retaining its traditional flair for entertaining, Cliveden is the perfect place for a special occasion. Guests can choose from the Terrace Dining Room, with its stunning views down the Parterre, or Waldo's, for dishes of real flair. For those travelling with a party, Spring Cottage, accommodating up to six with a private garden, is ideal. The Cliveden Spa offers a huge range of first-class treatments, and for the more active, there are tennis and squash courts on site. Surprisingly enough, all this is just 20 minutes from Heathrow and with a direct train route to London Paddington.

LOCATION

The main gates are opposite The Feathers in Taplow between junction 7 of the M4 and junction 2 of the M40.

GENERAL MANAGER
Tim Pettifer

ROOM RATES
5 Standard Doubles	£225 - £335
5 Classic Doubles/Twins	£295 - £390
13 Deluxe Doubles/Twins	£395 - £505
9 Suites	£480 - £605
6 Deluxe Suites	£595 - £950

Includes full breakfast and VAT

CREDIT CARDS
AMERICAN EXPRESS • DC • JCB • MC • VI

RATINGS & AWARDS
RAC Gold Ribbon ★★★★★
Dining Award 4
AA ★★★★★ ⊛⊛⊛
AA Top 200 - 2004/2005
Recommended Hotel & Restaurant,
Andrew Harper's Hideaway Report

FACILITIES
On site: Garden, gym, outdoor pool, indoor pool, croquet, tennis, heli-pad, health & beauty, licensed for weddings, squash, three vintage launches
2 meeting rooms/max 100 people
Nearby: Golf, shooting, riding

RESTRICTIONS
No smoking in bedrooms

ATTRACTIONS
Windsor Castle, Royal Ascot, Henley-on-Thames, Newbury and Windsor racecourses, Thames River cruises, Blenheim Palace

NEAREST
CITY:
London - 20 miles/45 mins

AIRPORT:
Heathrow - 15 miles/16 mins

RAIL STATION:
Slough - 6 miles/25 mins
Burnham - 2 miles/4 mins

AFFILIATIONS
von Essen Hotels
Celebrated Hotels Collection
Grand Heritage Hotels

RESERVATIONS
National rate in UK: 0870 432 8565
Toll free in US: 800-322-2403
or 888-93-GRAND
Quote Best Loved

ACCESS CODES
AMADEUS YX LHRCLV
APOLLO/GALILEO YX 89547
SABRE/ABACUS YX 24479
WORLDSPAN YX DNCLI
PEGASUS YX LHRCLI

SOUTH & ISLANDS

THE COTTAGE HOTEL

Village hotel

Sway Road, Brockenhurst,
Hampshire SO42 7SH

T (UK) 0870 432 8573
T 01590 622296
F 01590 623014
cottagehotel@bestloved.com
www.cottagehotel.bestloved.com

OWNERS
Christina Simons and David Mascord

ROOM RATES
Single occupancy	£50 - £95
3 Doubles	£65 - £115
2 Deluxe doubles	£90 - £140

Includes full breakfast and VAT

CREDIT CARDS
MC • VI

RATINGS & AWARDS
AA ◆◆◆◆

FACILITIES
On site: Garden
1 meeting room/max 14 people
Nearby: Golf, riding, cycling, walking,
leisure centre, sailing

RESTRICTIONS
Limited facilities for disabled guests
No children under 10 years
No smoking throughout
Dogs in ground floor bedroom only
Closed Christmas week

ATTRACTIONS
New Forest, National Motor Museum,
Winchester, Exbury Gardens,
Lymington market, Isle of Wight,
Hampshire coast

NEAREST
CITY:
Southampton - 13 miles/30 mins

AIRPORT:
Heathrow - 80 miles/2 hrs

RAIL STATION:
Brockenhurst - 1/4 mile/5 mins

AFFILIATIONS
Independent

RESERVATIONS
National rate in UK: 0870 432 8573
Quote Best Loved

ACCESS CODES
Not applicable

SOUTH & ISLANDS

A blissful escape just 90 minutes from London

The Cottage Hotel really was a cottage as far back as 1650 - or rather, two forester's cottages set in the pretty village of Brockenhurst. Today, it's your own home from home, with six charming en-suite bedrooms, a cosy beamed bar with warming open fires in the winter and a comfortable, inviting breakfast room. Individually-decorated bedrooms give a feeling that this place really is one-of-a-kind. Each room is complete with minibar, television and video (ask to borrow a film from the Cottage's library if you're tempted by a night in!), books and magazines, hair dryers and tea and coffee facilities. Breakfast at the hotel's own Gillies Restaurant is delightful, and guests are more than welcome at the nearby Thatched Cottage Restaurant, a famed local haunt where chef Martin Matysik can cater for larger groups.

As if that weren't enough of an enticement, there is, of course, the entire New Forest at your feet. Brockenhurst is one of the few villages where animals are allowed to roam freely, and as a result you just may have a visit from a pony or donkey! Your own steed is also welcome, with stabling subject to availability, and dogs are welcome in the ground-floor Verderer's Rest room. In autumn and winter, the Cottage and the Thatched Cottage host three-night breaks introducing visitors to some of the New Forest's lesser-known sights - call for details.

LOCATION
Exit junction 1 off the M27 for the A337 (Lymington). In Lyndhurst, turn right into Gosport Lane for the A337 (Lymington/Brockenhurst). The hotel is in Brockenhurst on Sway Road (the B3055).

"Having had tea at the Mandarin in Hong Kong, Singapore Slings at Raffles in Singapore and tea at the Ritz, none of them come close to Donnington Valley Hotel"

H S, NEWBURY

Country house | DONNINGTON VALLEY HOTEL

Old Oxford Road, Donnington,
Newbury, Berkshire RG14 3AG

T (UK) 0870 432 8598
T 01635 551199
F 01635 551123
donnington@bestloved.com
www.donnington.bestloved.com

MANAGING DIRECTOR
Andrew McKenzie

GENERAL MANAGER
Ben Danielsen

ROOM RATES
Single occupancy   £158
53 Doubles/Twins   £195
5 Suites   £230
Includes VAT

CREDIT CARDS
AMERICAN EXPRESS • DC • MC • VI

RATINGS & AWARDS
ETC ★★★★ Silver Award
RAC ★★★★ Dining Award 2
AA ★★★★ ❀❀ 72%

FACILITIES
On site: Garden, heli-pad,
licensed for weddings,
18-hole golf course
9 meeting rooms/max 140 people
Nearby: Fishing, tennis, shooting, riding

RESTRICTIONS
No pets; guide dogs only

ATTRACTIONS
Oxford, Bath, London,
Highclere Castle,
Newbury Racecourse

NEAREST
CITY:
Oxford - 25 miles/30 mins

AIRPORT:
Heathrow - 50 miles/50 mins

RAIL STATION:
Newbury - 2 miles/5 mins

AFFILIATIONS
Classic British Hotels

RESERVATIONS
National rate in UK: 0870 432 8598
Toll free in US: 800-856-5813
Quote Best Loved

ACCESS CODES
AMADEUS UI EWYDON
APOLLO/GALILEO UI 25903
SABRE/ABACUS UI 30972
WORLDSPAN UI 42936

A sporting hotel set in Royal Berkshire with historic cities in every direction

Located in the beautiful countryside of Royal Berkshire, Donnington Valley Hotel blends charm and elegance with the luxury and personal service expected from a privately-owned hotel. In addition to boasting its own 18-hole par-71 golf course, the hotel is a 40-minute drive from England's top championship courses of Sunningdale and Wentworth. Inside, uncompromising quality extends to each of the 58 guest rooms and suites, which all enjoy peaceful views and ensure total comfort.

The Wine Press Restaurant offers an intimate yet informal atmosphere where guests can enjoy superb cuisine complemented by wines from an excellent cellar, whilst the uniquely-designed 'Greens' restaurant is the perfect setting for exclusive private parties and gourmet dinners.

A host of activities are available on the estate, offering any combination of golfing, clay pigeon shooting or a day at Newbury Races. Being at the crossroads of England, you have the perfect touring base for visits to the historic cities of Oxford, Windsor and Bath, and still are only an hour's drive from central London. Personal service and attention to detail will ensure a warm welcome and a memorable stay.

LOCATION

Exit 13 on the M4 south for the A34 (Newbury); leave at the first exit, signed Donnington Castle. Turn right, then left; the hotel is one mile on the right.

SOUTH & ISLANDS

THE EASTBURY HOTEL

Townhouse

Long Street, Sherborne,
Dorset DT9 3BY

T (UK) 0870 432 8604
T 01935 813131
F 01935 817296
eastbury@bestloved.com
www.eastbury.bestloved.com

OWNERS
Paul and Nicola King

ROOM RATES
6 Singles	£50 - £70
7 Doubles	£90 - £110
1 Family Room	£90 - £175
1 Four-poster	£100 - £135
6 Executive Rooms	£100 - £135
1 Honeymoon Suite	£100 - £160
1 Two-bedroom Flat	£400 weekly

Includes full breakfast and VAT

CREDIT CARDS
AMERICAN EXPRESS • MC • VI

RATINGS & AWARDS
ETC ★★★ Silver Award
AA ★★★ ⍟⍟ 73%

FACILITIES
On site: Garden, croquet
4 meeting rooms/max 120 people
Nearby: Golf, riding,
fitness and leisure centre

RESTRICTIONS
Limited facilities for disabled guests
No pets; guide dogs only

ATTRACTIONS
Sherborne Abbey and Castles,
Stourhead Gardens, Montacute House,
Corfe Castle, Portland Bill,
Jurassic Coast, Lulworth Cove,
Hardy's Cottage

NEAREST
CITY:
Yeovil - 5 miles/10 mins

AIRPORT:
Bristol - 42 miles/1 hr 15 mins

RAIL STATION:
Sherborne - ¼ mile/5 mins

AFFILIATIONS
Independent

RESERVATIONS
National rate in UK: 0870 432 8604
Quote Best Loved

ACCESS CODES
Not applicable

A Georgian residence surrounded by medieval history in a peerless Dorset setting

Sherborne is the ancient capital of Dorset and is known for its medieval architecture and famous Abbey. It is also a town that can boast not one but two castles: The Old Castle was leased to Sir Walter Raleigh in 1592 by Elizabeth I, but after an unsatisfactory attempt to modernise he went and built his own more 'up-to-date' version instead!

In the middle of all this history is The Eastbury, which was once a private Georgian residence. In keeping with the period, the house is spacious and bright. Bedrooms are scrupulously clean, very comfortable and thoughtfully furnished, and some overlook the very English walled garden. The restaurant is housed within a lovely conservatory, and in summer guests can also eat outside on the terrace if they wish. The style of cooking is decidedly English, and the region provides an abundance of high-quality produce. It's always a good sign when a restaurant is popular with the locals - and The Eastbury certainly seems to be that.

In Sherborne itself there is much to see, making The Eastbury even more tempting - but there is also an inexhaustible list of places to visit in the surrounding area, which should not be overlooked.

LOCATION
In Sherborne, follow the A30 (Shaftesbury). After the fire station, take the first right into North Road; turn left at the end into Long Street. The hotel is on the right.

> "Your charm was only exceeded by the hospitality
>
> KATHRYN & FRANCIS WILLIAMS

Country house

EASTWELL MANOR

Eastwell Park, Boughton Lees,
Ashford, Kent TN25 4HR

T (UK) 0870 432 8605
T 01233 213 000
F 01233 213 017
eastwell@bestloved.com
www.eastwell.bestloved.com

CHIEF EXECUTIVE
Neil Beech

ROOM RATES
Single occupancy	£190 - £365
18 Doubles/Twins	£220 - £310
5 Suites	£285 - £395
19 Mews Cottages	£220 - £310

Includes newspaper,
full breakfast and VAT

CREDIT CARDS
AMERICAN EXPRESS • DC • JCB • MC • VI

RATINGS & AWARDS
ETC ★★★★ Gold Award
RAC Blue Ribbon ★★★★
Dining Award 4
AA ★★★★ ✿✿
AA Top 200 - 2004/2005

FACILITIES
On site: Garden, gym, heli-pad,
croquet, tennis,
licensed for weddings,
Pavilion Club & Spa,
Brasserie, marquee
7 meeting rooms/max 120 people
Nearby: Golf, fishing, riding

RESTRICTIONS
No smoking in restaurant
Pets by arrangement

ATTRACTIONS
Leeds Castle, Canterbury Cathedral,
Sissinghurst Gardens, Hever Castle,
Dover Castle, Great Dixter

NEAREST
CITY:
Canterbury - 10 miles/20 mins

AIRPORT:
Gatwick - 70 miles/1 hr 20 mins

RAIL STATION:
Ashford - 4 miles/10 mins

FERRY PORT:
Folkestone/Dover - 20 miles/30 mins

AFFILIATIONS
Celebrated Hotels Collection
Pride of Britain

RESERVATIONS
National rate in UK: 0870 432 8605
Toll free in the US: 800-322-2403
or 800-98-PRIDE
Quote Best Loved

ACCESS CODES
AMADEUS HK QDHEAS
APOLLO/GALILEO HK 53902
SABRE/ABACUS HK 39704
WORLDSPAN HK 42949

SOUTH & ISLANDS

The Garden of England
with Paris and Brussels a day trip away

Gloriously positioned in the tranquil Kent countryside, Eastwell Manor lies on 62 acres of picturesque gardens and grounds set in the midst of a 3,000-acre estate. Queen Victoria and King Edward VII were frequent visitors to the manor a century ago; today it is an independent, family-owned hotel offering an appealing combination of exceptional service, fine cuisine and luxurious surroundings.

There are 23 sumptuous guest rooms in the main house and a further 39 in one-, two- or three-bedroom mews cottages converted from the original Victorian stables. The hotel's superb facilities include The Pavilion Leisure Spa, one of the finest in England, complete with a 20-metre pool, large hydrotherapy pool, steam room, sauna and Jacuzzi. The state-of-the-art gymnasium contains the very latest equipment, while Dreams is dedicated to an extensive range of beauty and therapy treatments for men and women.

Eastwell is ideally situated for visiting historic Canterbury, Leeds Castle and other attractions in the aptly named Garden of England. Fast trains from Ashford station can also whisk you to Paris or Brussels for the day and home in time for dinner in the traditional Manor Restaurant or the informal Brasserie.

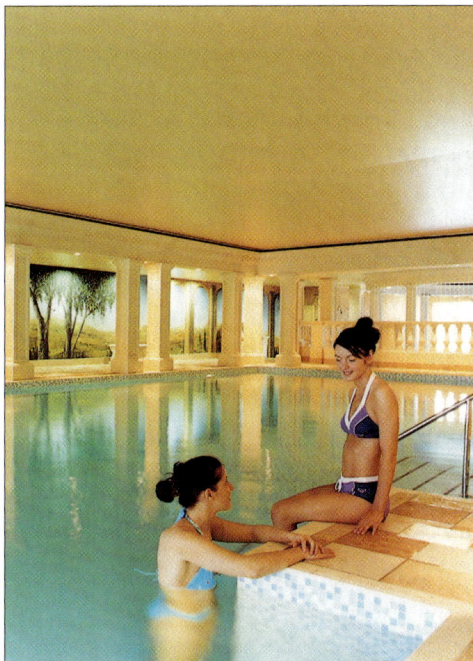

LOCATION

Exit 9 from the M20 at Ashford; turn left at the roundabout into Trinity Road. At the traffic lights, turn left into Faversham Road; the hotel's entrance is on the left.

ESSEBORNE MANOR

Country house

Hurstbourne Tarrant, Andover, Hampshire SP11 0ER

T (UK) 0870 432 8610
T 01264 736444
F 01264 736725
esseborne@bestloved.com
www.esseborne.bestloved.com

OWNERS
Ian and Lucilla Hamilton

GENERAL MANAGER
Mark Hamilton

ROOM RATES
Single occupancy   £95 - £105
15 Doubles/Twins   £100 - £180
Includes full breakfast and VAT

CREDIT CARDS
AMERICAN EXPRESS • DC • MC • VI

RATINGS & AWARDS
AA ★★★ ✿✿ 73%

FACILITIES
On site: Garden, heli-pad, croquet, tennis, licensed for weddings 2 meeting rooms/max 40 people
Nearby: Golf, riding, fitness centre

RESTRICTIONS
Limited facilities for disabled guests
No smoking in restaurant
No pets in public areas

ATTRACTIONS
Stonehenge, Highclere Castle, Broadlands, Windsor, Salisbury Cathedral, Winchester Cathedral

NEAREST
CITY:
Andover - 6 miles/15 mins

AIRPORT:
Heathrow - 55 miles/1 hr

RAIL STATION:
Andover - 6 miles/15 mins

AFFILIATIONS
Independent

RESERVATIONS
National rate in UK: 0870 432 8610
Quote Best Loved

ACCESS CODES
Not applicable

SOUTH & ISLANDS

Close to Stonehenge in the heart of southern England

Esseborne Manor, set in rich farmland high on the north Wessex Downs, is an ideal location for exploring the South, with Highclere Castle, mystical Stonehenge, Avebury and the Iron Age Danebury Rings - as well as famous gardens and the great cathedral cities of Salisbury and Winchester - close by. London and the historic towns of Bath and Oxford are within an hour and a half's drive. Altogether, it's one of the finest places to discover a slice of Britain's heritage that goes back over almost 4,000 years!

Privately owned, the hotel, described as 'invitingly snug', has 15 individually-designed bedrooms with comfortable sitting rooms that complement the elegant dining room, itself reflecting the importance placed by the owners on their cuisine and celebrated cellar.

The gardens are for enjoying and lazing, and traffic-free walks abound. The more energetic may in summer play croquet on the finely-manicured lawns, try some tennis year-round on the all-weather court or golf on a nearby course.

In short, Esseborne Manor is an ideal centre for staying and touring where every comfort is provided by hospitable hosts and caring staff.

LOCATION

Exit 13 off the M4 (Newbury) for the A34 south, then the A343 (Highclere); turn right for Andover. The hotel is 1 ½ miles north of Hurstbourne Tarrant on the A343, or take the M3/A303 to Andover.

> "Wonderful hotel ... unpretentious, warm and friendly"

BARRY D JONES, SINGAPORE

Map p. 450, grid F4
309

Country house

FLACKLEY ASH HOTEL

Peasmarsh, Rye,
East Sussex TN31 6YH

T (UK) 0870 432 8613
T 01797 230651
F 01797 230510
flackley@bestloved.com
www.flackley.bestloved.com

MANAGING DIRECTOR
Joseph Betteridge

ROOM RATES
Single occupancy   £87 - £112
38 Doubles/Twins   £132 - £156
3 Four-posters   £156
4 Suites   £172 - £182
Includes full breakfast and VAT

CREDIT CARDS
AMERICAN EXPRESS • DC • MC • VI

RATINGS & AWARDS
RAC ★★★
AA ★★★ 77%

FACILITIES
On site: Garden, gym, heli-pad, croquet, indoor pool, health & beauty, licensed for weddings, putting green, sauna, spa, steam room
2 meeting rooms/max 100 people
Nearby: Riding, cycle hire, golf

RESTRICTIONS
Limited facilities for disabled guests
Pets by arrangement

ATTRACTIONS
Cinque Port of Rye,
Bodiam & Sissinghurst castles,
Kent & East Sussex Steam Railway,
Canterbury Cathedral,
Tenterden Steam Train

NEAREST
CITY:
London - 60 miles/2 hrs

AIRPORT:
Heathrow - 86 miles/1 hr 45 mins
Gatwick - 40 miles/1 hr 45 mins

RAIL STATION:
Rye - 4 miles/10 mins

AFFILIATIONS
Best Western

RESERVATIONS
National rate in UK: 0870 432 8613
Toll free in US: 800-528-1234
Quote Best Loved

ACCESS CODES
AMADEUS BW VLW138
APOLLO/GALILEO BW 13106
SABRE/ABACUS BW 11492

SOUTH & ISLANDS

This Georgian country house near Rye is the perfect place to relax

Deep in the Sussex countryside nestles the pretty village of Peasmarsh - and the delightful Flackley Ash Hotel. A far cry from the hustle and bustle of modern city life, this Georgian country house is the ideal place to enjoy a relaxing holiday.

The fine traditions of comfort and service are maintained to a high standard by owners, The Betteridge Family. Their aim, through a warm and friendly welcome is to let you feel as though you have been invited into their home. The bedrooms are furnished in the style of a traditional country home and have all the modern facilities. In the lounge you can read the morning paper, meet other guests or relax with coffee after a dinner in the candlelit restaurant.

In such a place, it is easy to drift back in time, and you can wander the cobbled streets of medieval Rye, with its potteries, antique shops, taverns and tea shops. Discover the enchantingly beautiful Bodiam Castle and Bateman's, as well as the house where Kipling lived - or follow in the footsteps of William the Conqueror to the fields where the first 'Battle of Britain' was fought and the abbey that was built to mark his victory.

Back at the hotel, you can relax with croquet or putting in the pretty gardens or head to the indoor swimming pool and leisure centre, with gym, saunas, whirlpool spa, steam room and beauty rooms.

LOCATION
From the M25, exit 5 (signposted A21 Hastings), turn left onto the A268 at the Flimwell lights. Proceed through Hawkhurst and Northiam to Peasmarsh.

FRENCH HORN HOTEL

Country house

**Sonning on Thames,
Berkshire RG4 6TN**

T (UK) 0870 432 8619
T 0118 9692204
F 0118 9442210
frenchhorn@bestloved.com
www.frenchhorn.bestloved.com

OWNERS
The Emmanuel Family

ROOM RATES
Single occupancy	£110 - £175
16 Doubles	£140 - £175
5 Luxury Suites	£175 - £205

Includes full breakfast and VAT

CREDIT CARDS
AMERICAN EXPRESS • DC • MC • VI

RATINGS & AWARDS
AA ★★★ ✸✸ 78%

FACILITIES
On site: Garden, heli-pad, fishing
1 meeting room/max 24 people
Nearby: Golf, riding, health centre

RESTRICTIONS
No pets

ATTRACTIONS
Blenheim Palace, Windsor Castle,
Mapledurham House,
Stratfield Saye House,
Ascot Racecourse, Windsor,
Newbury, Legoland

NEAREST
CITY:
London - 36 miles/1 hr
Reading - 3 miles/5 mins

AIRPORT:
Heathrow - 20 miles/45 mins

RAIL STATION:
Reading - 4 miles/15 mins

AFFILIATIONS
Pride of Britain

RESERVATIONS
National rate in UK: 0870 432 8619
Toll free in US: 800-98-PRIDE
Quote Best Loved

ACCESS CODES
AMADEUS HK XREFRE
APOLLO/GALILEO HT 59569
SABRE/ABACUS HK 10413
WORLDSPAN HK FRENC

SOUTH & ISLANDS

Peace and plenty
on the banks of the River Thames

At the foot of the Chilterns beside the tranquil River Thames is a very special English country house - The French Horn at Sonning. For over 150 years, the hotel has provided a riverside retreat from the cares of the world. Today it offers comfortable rooms and outstanding cooking in the most beautiful of settings.

By day, the sunny restaurant is the perfect rendezvous for an enjoyable lunch. At night, the graceful weeping willows fringing the Thames are romantically floodlit. The cuisine is a traditional mixture of French and English cooking using the freshest ingredients, many local, and the French Horn's wine list is amongst the finest in Europe, including many rare and unusual bottles. In the old panelled bar, ducks roast on a spit before an open fire. Upstairs, the beautifully decorated suites and rooms look out over landscaped grounds. The French Horn has five luxury suites and 16 well-appointed suites and double rooms, each with a television, alarm radio and direct-dial telephone.

The Emmanuels continue the tradition of family ownership at the French Horn, ensuring that their standard of excellence is maintained throughout this stunning setting.

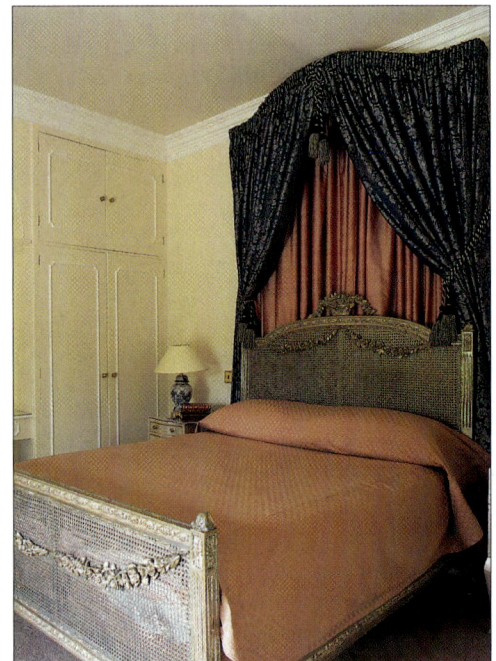

LOCATION
Sonning is just off the A4, five miles east of Reading.

> "Beautiful views, quality room, wonderful service"
>
> NANCY JACOBS, RHODE ISLAND USA

Townhouse

GRASMERE HOUSE

A pleasant, personalised home that's perfect for exploring historic Britain

Originally built in 1896 as a private house, this pretty hotel with superb views is just the right size for offering a wealth of amenities without being impersonally big - Grasmere House can cater for business meetings of up to 145, but is also a welcoming venue for weddings, family holidays or even a weekend escape. All rooms are en suite and offer broadband and telephone connections and satellite television. Four rooms feature sumptuous four-poster beds; for families, there is a three-bedroom apartment with separate lounge, and some of the hotel's twin rooms cater for triple or quadruple family accommodation.

When it comes to dining, Grasmere offers their lovely conservatory restaurant, the Bistro on the River. As with the entire hotel, the views are splendid, and offer an excellent accompaniment to the dining experience: the menu (which is often influenced by the best-quality offerings on the local market!) is a tasty mix of classic English cuisine and a world of eclectic global influences.

Of course, there's far more than just good food and a good night's sleep to be had in Salisbury and surrounding environs - some of England's best attractions are within an afternoon's journey, from Stonehenge and stately homes to the beautiful Salisbury Cathedral, just a short walk - or a glance! - from your doorstep.

LOCATION

On the south side of Salisbury, on the A3094 Harnham Road next to Harnham Parish Church and near Salisbury Cathedral.

---

70 Harnham Road, Salisbury, Wiltshire SP2 8JN

T (UK) 0870 432 8634
T 01722 338388
F 01722 333710
grasmere@bestloved.com
www.grasmere.bestloved.com

PROPRIETOR
Dale Naug

MANAGER
Babs Heiden

ROOM RATES
Single occupancy   £90 - £105
18 Superior rooms   £115 - £136
13 Deluxe rooms   £140
4 Four-posters   £155 - £165
Includes full breakfast, service and VAT

CREDIT CARDS
AMERICAN EXPRESS • JCB • MC • VI

RATINGS & AWARDS
AA ★★★ 67%
Best View in Britain -
Country Life Magazine

FACILITIES
On site: Garden, heli-pad,
licensed for weddings
7 meeting rooms/max 160 people
Nearby: Horse riding, fishing, golf

RESTRICTIONS
Smoking in bar and lounge only
Pets by arrangement

ATTRACTIONS
Stonehenge, Salisbury Cathedral,
Wilton House, Broadlands, Longleat,
Avebury, New Forest

NEAREST
CITY:
Salisbury

AIRPORT:
Heathrow - 85 miles/1 hr 30 mins

RAIL STATION:
Salisbury - 3 miles/5 mins

AFFILIATIONS
Independent

RESERVATIONS
National rate in UK: 0870 432 8634
Quote Best Loved

ACCESS CODES
AMADEUS NT XSRGRA
APOLLO/GALILEO NT 66317
SABRE/ABACUS NT 63337
WORLDSPAN NT XHGH

SOUTH & ISLANDS

Altogether delightful. Very comfortable accommodation, an excellent dinner and a superb spa. We shall return yet again

HARTWELL HOUSE HOTEL, RESTAURANT & SPA   Country house

Oxford Road, Near Aylesbury,
Buckinghamshire HP17 8NL

T (UK) 0870 432 8639
T 01296 747444
F 01296 747450
hartwell@bestloved.com
www.hartwell.bestloved.com

DIRECTOR AND GENERAL MANAGER
Jonathan Thompson

ROOM RATES
7 Singles	£155 - £205
16 Doubles/Twins	£260
5 Four-posters	£360 - £450
18 Suites	£360 - £700

Includes early morning tea, continental breakfast, service and VAT

CREDIT CARDS
AMERICAN EXPRESS • MC • VI

RATINGS & AWARDS
RAC Gold Ribbon ★★★★
Dining Award 4
AA ★★★★ ⊕⊕⊕
AA Top 200 - 2004/2005

FACILITIES
On site: Garden, heli-pad, fishing, croquet, tennis, indoor pool, health & beauty, parkland
4 meeting rooms/max 100 people
Nearby: Golf, riding

RESTRICTIONS
No children under 8 years
No smoking in dining room or drawing rooms
Pets by arrangement

ATTRACTIONS
Waddesdon Manor, Blenheim Palace, Woburn Abbey, Stowe Landscape Gardens, Chiltern Hills, Oxford

NEAREST
CITY:
Oxford - 21 miles/30 mins
AIRPORT:
Heathrow - 35 miles/45 mins
RAIL STATION:
Aylesbury - 2 miles/5 mins

AFFILIATIONS
Celebrated Hotels Collection
Pride of Britain
Historic House Hotels Ltd

RESERVATIONS
National rate in UK: 0870 432 8639
Toll free in US: 800-322-2403
or 800-735-2478 or 800-98-PRIDE
Quote Best Loved

ACCESS CODES
AMADEUS YX LHRBO5
APOLLO/GALILEO YX 15217
SABRE/ABACUS YX 32002
WORLDSPAN YX GB05

SOUTH & ISLANDS

'Why wouldst thou leave calm Hartwell's green abode?' pondered Lord Byron

Why indeed, though the subject of Byron's musings, Louis XVIII of France, had more reason than most: He was returning home to claim the throne of France after a five-year sojourn at Hartwell. Set in 90 acres of landscaped parkland in the Vale of Aylesbury, Hartwell's long and distinguished history stretches back to the Domesday Book, though the present house dates from the early 17th century, when it was built for ancestors of General Robert E Lee. This is a stately home hotel in the classical mould, with large, historic public rooms filled with fine antiques and oil paintings and an ornate rococo-style morning room boasting a superb carved plaster ceiling.

There are 30 rooms and suites in the main house (several named after the members of the Bourbon family who once occupied them), while the converted stable block, Hartwell Court, houses a further 16 rooms. Guests are free to explore the grounds and seek out the various 18th-century pavilions and monuments. And when it's time to relax, the Hartwell Spa has a large swimming pool, steam room, saunas and a gym as well as beauty salons offering a range of treatments.

LOCATION
At the M40, junction 7, follow signs to Aylesbury; in Aylesbury, take the A418 toward Oxford. Hartwell House is two miles on the right.

> " Surely one of the finest in England in all respects "

DIANA NORONHA

Country house

HINTLESHAM HALL

Hintlesham, Ipswich,
Suffolk IP8 3NS

T (UK) 0870 432 8642
T 01473 652334
F 01473 652463
hintlesham@bestloved.com
www.hintlesham.bestloved.com

OWNER
Dee Ludlow

ROOM RATES
Single occupancy   £98 - £125
27 Doubles/Twins   £110 - £235
2 Four-posters   £165 - £325
4 Suites   £225 - £375
Includes continental breakfast and VAT

CREDIT CARDS
AMERICAN EXPRESS • DC • MC • VI

RATINGS & AWARDS
ETC ★★★★ Gold Award
RAC Gold Ribbon ★★★★
Dining Award 4
AA ★★★★ ✿✿
AA Top 200 - 2004/2005

FACILITIES
On site: Garden, heli-pad,
outdoor pool, croquet, golf,
tennis, health & beauty,
licensed for weddings, gym, sauna
6 meeting rooms/max 120 people
Nearby: Riding, fishing

RESTRICTIONS
Limited facilities for disabled guests
No children under 12 years in restaurant
No smoking in restaurant
Pets by arrangement

ATTRACTIONS
Cambridge, Suffolk Heritage Coast,
Norwich, Constable Country,
Sutton Hoo

NEAREST
CITY:
Ipswich - 5 miles/10 mins

AIRPORT:
Heathrow - 85 miles/2 hrs
Stansted - 50 miles/1 hr

RAIL STATION:
Ipswich - 5 miles/10 mins

FERRY PORT:
Harwich - 34 miles/40 mins

AFFILIATIONS
Small Luxury Hotels

RESERVATIONS
National rate in UK: 0870 432 8642
Toll free in US: 800-525-4800
Quote Best Loved

ACCESS CODES
AMADEUS LX IPWHHH
APOLLO/GALILEO LX 21652
SABRE/ABACUS LX 31110
WORLDSPAN LX IPWHH

A great house with an international reputation for excellence

More than 15 monarchs have been on the throne of England since Hintlesham Hall was built in the mid-1400s, and for much of that time the lord of the manor has been in residence.

Today, as a Grade 1 listed Elizabethan manor, the Hall is surrounded by 175 acres of inspiring Suffolk countryside. Leisure facilities are impressive, and include an array of treatments at the Health and Fitness Club, plus the associated par-72 championship golf course whose clubhouse is the winner of an architectural award. The hotel can be booked exclusively for house parties and weddings, and three of the magnificent rooms are licensed for civil ceremonies.

Dining is as required: There are three private rooms, climaxing in the elegant grandeur of the Salon, which can seat up to 90. The restaurant has extensive à la carte and set menus with vegetarian options. Fish is well-represented, as you would expect in this neck of the woods, and seasonal delicacies include pheasant, grouse, crayfish, crab and truffles. Even better, there is an extensive, award-winning wine list, and the added allure of fresh herbs cut from the hotel's renowned herb garden.

LOCATION
Take the A12 toward Ipswich centre; at the A12/A14 roundabout, turn left for the A1071 (Hadleigh). Follow road three miles into Hintlesham; entrance to the hotel is past the church on the right.

SOUTH & ISLANDS

HOTEL DU VIN & BISTRO

Townhouse

Ship Street, Brighton,
East Sussex BN1 2AD

T (UK) 0870 432 8651
T 01273 718588
F 01273 718599
duvinbright@bestloved.com
www.duvinbright.bestloved.com

GENERAL MANAGER
Lora Strizic

ROOM RATES
34 Doubles/Twins   £125 - £160
3 Suites   £230 - £355
Includes VAT

CREDIT CARDS
AMERICAN EXPRESS • DC • MC • VI

RATINGS & AWARDS
AA ★★★★⊛ 71%

FACILITIES
On site: Courtyard
2 meeting rooms/max 48 people
Nearby: Golf, leisure centre,
tennis, beach

RESTRICTIONS
Limited facilities for disabled guests
Smoking in bar and on terrace only
No pets; guide dogs only

ATTRACTIONS
Bodium Castle,
Herstmonceux Castle,
The Bluebell Railway,
Wilderness Wood,
Eastbourne, Hastings

NEAREST
CITY:
Brighton

AIRPORT:
Gatwick - 29 miles/35 mins
Heathrow - 70 miles/1 hr 15 mins

RAIL STATION:
Brighton - 1 ½ miles/3 mins

AFFILIATIONS
Preston's Global Hotels
Hotel du Vin Ltd
The European Connection

RESERVATIONS
National rate in UK: 0870 432 8651
Toll free in US: 800-544-9993
Quote Best Loved

ACCESS CODES
Not applicable

A touch of decadence
in Britain's trendiest city

Strictly speaking, Hotel du Vin Brighton is part of a chain - but what a chain! Each of the hotels in the du Vin group has been carefully chosen with an eye for the beautiful, the eccentric and the stunning. Among the group are a tobacco warehouse and a Victorian eye hospital, but this quirky building can happily compete with these. Once inside the massive Gothic-revival hall with its soaring cathedral-like ceiling, heavily carved staircase and bizarre gargoyles, you would never guess you were only 50 yards from Brighton's trendy seafront.

Brighton bustles with a Bohemian and flamboyantly sexy air - its trademark for many years - and the Brighton Pavilion and the narrow streets of The Lanes with their maze of antique, bric-a-brac and jewellery shops are popular with artists and celebrities.

Into this melee has come a haven of luxury with good food, good wine and that certain something extra - and entering fully into the spirit of Brighton, the Loft Suite offers a 'party' shower room and an eight-foot bed, while three other suites have a pair of side-by-side baths with sea views - perfect for that 'dirty weekend'!

LOCATION
In the heart of Brighton just off the Kings Road.

Country house

HOWARD'S HOUSE

A truly tasteful experience in every sense of the word

Teffont Evias is stunningly pretty and has hardly changed in 300 years - it's a real trip back in time and a quintessential pastoral setting. Howard's House itself sits in two acres of meandering Wiltshire country garden and croquet lawn, and ancient box hedges and secret corners add to the romance.

The House was built in 1623 and extended and renovated in 1837 following a previous owner's trip to Switzerland, the inspiration for the steeply pitched Swiss-style roof. On a more modern note, owner Noële Thompson has redecorated and added her own tasteful touches; the result is a relaxed yet confident air of style and comfort that carries right through to the kitchen.

Chef Nick Wentworth produces a menu yielding a treasure trove of delights. This place is all about good food, utter charm and comfort - in fact, if you can't relax here, you can't relax anywhere.

Howard's House is also a lovely, peaceful base from which to explore the many fascinating sights in the vicinity, including the Cathedral at Salisbury, Old Sarum and Stonehenge.

LOCATION

Take the A36 (Warminster) from Salisbury; at Wilton, fork left onto the A30 and at Barford St. Martin, fork right onto the B3089. The turning for Teffont Evias is on the left just before Teffont Magna.

Teffont Evias, Near Salisbury,
Wiltshire SP3 5RJ

T (UK) 0870 432 8658
T 01722 716392
F 01722 716820
howardshse@bestloved.com
www.howardshse.bestloved.com

OWNER
Noële Thompson

ROOM RATES
Single occupancy	£95
7 Doubles/Twins	£145
1 Four-poster	£165
1 Family Room	£175
Includes full breakfast and VAT	

CREDIT CARDS
AMERICAN EXPRESS • MC • VI

RATINGS & AWARDS
Independent

FACILITIES
On site: Garden, croquet
1 meeting room/max 36 people
Nearby: Golf, swimming, riding

RESTRICTIONS
Limited facilities for disabled guests
No smoking in restaurant

ATTRACTIONS
Salisbury town and Cathedral,
Stonehenge, Old Sarum, Bath,
Stourhead Gardens,
Longleat House and Safari Park

NEAREST
CITY:
Salisbury - 10 miles/20 mins

AIRPORT:
Heathrow - 84 miles/1 hr 45 mins

RAIL STATION:
Salisbury - 10 miles/20 mins

AFFILIATIONS
Independent

RESERVATIONS
National rate in UK: 0870 432 8658
Quote Best Loved

ACCESS CODES
Not applicable

SOUTH & ISLANDS

THE INN ON THE GREEN

Restaurant with rooms

The Old Cricket Common,
Cookham Dean,
Berkshire SL6 9NZ

T (UK) 0870 432 8663
T 01628 482638
F 01628 487474
inngreen@bestloved.com
www.inngreen.bestloved.com

OWNERS
Mark Fuller and Garry Hollihead

ROOM RATES
4 Doubles   £130
4 Superior Doubles £160 - £180
1 Four-poster   £195
Includes full breakfast and VAT

CREDIT CARDS
AMERICAN EXPRESS • MC • VI

RATINGS & AWARDS
AA ✿✿ Restaurant with Rooms

FACILITIES
On site: Garden, Jacuzzi, gazebos,
licensed for weddings
3 meeting rooms/max 120 people
Nearby: Fishing, boat trips, golf

RESTRICTIONS
Limited facilities for disabled guests
No pets; guide dogs only

ATTRACTIONS
Windsor Castle, Royal Ascot,
Henley-on-Thames,
Newbury and Windsor racecourses,
Eton, Thorpe Park

NEAREST
CITY:
London - 30 miles/45 mins

AIRPORT:
Heathrow - 18 miles/25 mins

RAIL STATION:
Maidenhead - 3 miles/5 mins

AFFILIATIONS
The Embassy Group

RESERVATIONS
National rate in UK: 0870 432 8663
Quote Best Loved

ACCESS CODES
Not applicable

SOUTH & ISLANDS

A luxurious hideaway with food as good as the scenery

This picturesque hotel surrounded by National Trust countryside has been completely refurbished to create a sumptuous Restaurant with Rooms with five-star service. Lavish furnishings such as wooden beams, red velvet sofas and enormous armchairs create an utterly relaxed atmosphere, whilst the nine bedrooms provide all modern amenities including Sky television and CD and DVD players.

Renowned chef Gary Hollihead creates first-class cuisine with a modern European influence, and an impressive wine list complements the menu. The three distinctive dining rooms make dinner a real experience - the Lamp Room is modern with original brick work and is lit by a central chandelier. The Stublie Room is reminiscent of Swiss log cabins and the conservatory offers a fresh and bright atmosphere, leading out onto the courtyard.

The Inn on the Green makes a refreshing venue for meetings and conferences and with its choice of dining rooms and Mediterranean courtyard is an idyllic setting for weddings too. The Inn can even be hired for exclusive use, with a professional team of staff on-hand to give advice on themes, entertainment and catering. Located just 45 minutes from central London and 20 minutes from Windsor, the Inn on the Green provides a peaceful and convenient retreat from the city.

LOCATION
From the M4, exit junction 8/9 toward Marlow; once in Cookham Dean, turn right onto the Common by the war memorial.

Country house

LANGSHOTT MANOR

Astonishing antiquity, style and seclusion right next door to Gatwick

Cocooned by the centuries and a three-acre award-winning garden complete with moat is Langshott Manor. As if by some historical sleight of hand, it stands just eight minutes' drive from Gatwick airport - but once within its embrace, the strident sounds of today ebb in diminuendo; only far, far away might you catch the occasional reminder of our age.

The illusion of time in reverse continues inside the house. Two cottages dating from the 1500s were joined by Victorian owners, who then added a bell tower and a mews. The eccentricities of the building give great character to the rooms, which the décor has exploited to great effect! The picturesque bedrooms, despite their great age, have a fresh individuality given greater charm by posies of flowers in every nook and cranny. Concessions are made, however, to the modern world, so the facilities are luxuriously right up to the minute! The dining room will tempt you with an array of classic delights and an enticing wine list that is a wonderful compliment to the chef's gastronomic inspirations.

All in all, Langshott Manor is an enchanted place, so near and yet so far from London, Brighton and the Southeast.

LOCATION
From the A23 in Horley, take Ladbroke Road to Langshott. The hotel is located three quarters of a mile on.

Horley, Near Gatwick,
Surrey RH6 9LN

T (UK) 0870 432 8508
T 01293 786680
F 01293 783905
langshott@bestloved.com
www.langshott.bestloved.com

OWNERS
Peter and Deborah Hinchcliffe

GENERAL MANAGER
Simon M Steele

ROOM RATES
Single occupancy	£165 - £270
16 Doubles/Twins	£185 - £260
5 Four-posters	£250 - £260
1 Suite	£275 - £290

Includes full breakfast, newspaper, service, transfer to the airport and VAT

CREDIT CARDS
AMERICAN EXPRESS • DC • MC • VI

RATINGS & AWARDS
RAC Gold Ribbon ★★★Dining Award 3
AA ★★★ ✿✿
AA Top 200 - 2004/2005

FACILITIES
On site: Garden, croquet, licensed for weddings
3 meeting rooms/max 60 people
Nearby: Golf, fishing, fitness centre, shooting, riding

RESTRICTIONS
Limited facilities for disabled guests
Pets by arrangement
Smoking in Morning Room only

ATTRACTIONS
Windsor, Brighton, Chartwell House, Glyndebourne, RHS Wisley, London

NEAREST
CITY:
London - 28 miles/30 mins

AIRPORT:
Gatwick - 3 miles/8 mins

RAIL STATION:
Horley - ½ mile/5 mins

AFFILIATIONS
Celebrated Hotels Collection
Small Luxury Hotels
Utopia Group

RESERVATIONS
National rate in UK: 0870 432 8508
Toll free in US: 800-322-2403
or 800-525-4800
Quote Best Loved

ACCESS CODES
AMADEUS LX LGW249
APOLLO/GALILEO LX 92710
SABRE/ABACUS LX 42115
WORLDSPAN LX 11674

SOUTH & ISLANDS

> **There** is no one person to single out when it comes to saying thank you. We had six-star service and courtesy from start to finish
>
> JAMES RIGBY, BOURNEMOUTH

THE LORD BUTE

Seaside hotel

179-185 Lymington Road,
Highcliffe, Dorset BH23 4JS

T (UK) 0870 432 8692
T 01425 278884
F 01425 279258
lordbute@bestloved.com
www.lordbute.bestloved.com

OWNERS
Simon Box and Gary Payne

HOTEL MANAGER
Andrea Amey

ROOM RATES
Single occupancy	£75 - £85
4 Standard Doubles	£95
6 Superior Doubles	£105
1 Coach House Suite	£120
1 Lord Bute Suite	£140 - £180

Includes continental breakfast
and VAT

CREDIT CARDS
AMERICAN EXPRESS • JCB • MC • VI

RATINGS & AWARDS
Independent

FACILITIES
On site:
1 meeting room/max 25 people
Nearby: Beaches, swimming,
horse riding

RESTRICTIONS
Limited facilities for disabled guests
Smoking in bar only
Pets by arrangement

ATTRACTIONS
New Forest, Christchurch,
Lymington Marina,
Bournemouth Beach,
Beaulieu Motor Museum,
Abbey House, Isle of Wight,
Lyndhurst

NEAREST
CITY:
Southampton - 25 miles/45 mins

AIRPORT:
Bournemouth - 8 miles/20 mins
Southampton - 20 miles/40 mins

RAIL STATION:
New Milton - 4 miles/10 mins
Christchurch - 4 miles/10 mins

FERRY PORT:
Poole - 15 miles/35 mins
Southampton - 10 miles/25 mins

AFFILIATIONS
Independent

RESERVATIONS
National rate in UK: 0870 432 8692
Quote Best Loved

ACCESS CODES
Not applicable

This delectable cliffside retreat offers a taste of the good life

Lord Bute, Prime Minister to George III from 1762-1763, escaped from his mercifully short reign in London to the breathtaking high cliffs of Christchurch Bay, where he was so taken by the area that he commissioned architect Robert Adam to build him a house - 'High Cliff', which was completed in 1770.

The original building failed to weather the cliffside conditions, but its descendent Highcliffe Castle remains and today, the original gatehouses to Highcliffe Castle are the entrance lodges to a remarkable purpose-built hotel and restaurant. Inside, you'll find 12 rooms and the remarkable Lord Bute Suite. And when you're ready for a bite to eat, there's a bounty to pick from, including what the proprietors call a 'traditional Sunday luncheon' - but an ordinary lunch this is not! On the menu is a selection from the chef's repertoire of soups, a rosemary and garlic roasted leg of lamb with redcurrant sauce and a stunning selection of homemade desserts, to name a few. Alternately, the Coach House Suite can be self-catering, if you so desire.

And when you've had your fill and are ready for a jaunt outdoors, the Lord Bute's convenient location near the beach and Bournemouth offers world-class shopping, entertainment and a taste of the beach life. Golfing, sailing and short trips to the Isle of Wight can also be arranged.

LOCATION

Follow signs towards Bournemouth along the A35. At the Somerford Roundabout, take the A337 exit signposted Lymington. Follow the A337 to Highcliffe Road.

Country house

MAISON TALBOOTH

Fine art and great cooking in beautiful Constable country

A Victorian country house blessed with a superb position overlooking the Stour river valley and the medieval church of Stratford St Mary, Maison Talbooth is the hotel arm of the renowned Le Talbooth restaurant, which lies just a short distance along the riverbank. The hotel is a charmer, with 10 spacious and appealing bedrooms decorated with a real eye for colour and thoughtful touches that emphasise the Milsom family's dedication to guests' comfort. A courtesy car is on hand to whisk guests between the hotel and restaurant at lunch and dinner; breakfast and light meals are available at the hotel.

Le Talbooth itself occupies a delightful 16th-century timber-frame house with a riverside terrace that is transformed into a glorious outdoor dining room in summer. A gourmet pilgrimage of note, Le Talbooth's other claim to fame is that the building is featured in John Constable's famous painting of Dedham Vale. Do make time to explore around Dedham and Flatford and admire the scenery that inspired England's greatest landscape painter. There is another artistic connection at Sudbury, where the great portraitist Gainsborough's family home can be visited - and it's conveniently close to the old wool towns and antiques centres of Lavenham and Long Melford.

LOCATION

Follow A12 to Ipswich, bypassing Colchester. Exit for Stratford St Mary; turn right at the bottom of the hill to Dedham. The hotel is after the bridge 300 yards on.

Dedham, Colchester,
Essex CO7 6HN

T (UK) 0870 432 8698
T 01206 322367
F 01206 322752
talbooth@bestloved.com
www.talbooth.bestloved.com

OWNERS
Gerald and Paul Milsom

ROOM RATES
Single occupancy   £120 - £160
5 Doubles/Twins   £160 - £180
5 Suites   £200 - £220
Includes continental breakfast and VAT

CREDIT CARDS
AMERICAN EXPRESS • DC • MC • VI

RATINGS & AWARDS
RAC Blue Ribbon ★★★ Dining Award 3
AA ★★★ ⊛⊛
AA Top 200 - 2004/2005

FACILITIES
On site: Garden, heli-pad, croquet,
licensed for weddings, garden chess
1 meeting room/max 150 people
Nearby: Golf, river fishing,
shooting, riding

RESTRICTIONS
Limited facilities for disabled guests
No pets; guide dogs only

ATTRACTIONS
Constable Country,
Flatford and Willy Lott's cottages,
Lavenham, Colchester Castle,
Cambridge, Beth Chatto's Gardens

NEAREST
CITY:
Colchester - 6 miles/10 mins

AIRPORT:
Heathrow - 90 miles/1 hr 30 mins
Stansted - 45 miles/50 mins

RAIL STATION:
Colchester - 10 miles/15 mins

AFFILIATIONS
Celebrated Hotels Collection
Pride of Britain

RESERVATIONS
National rate in UK: 0870 432 8698
Toll free in US: 800-322-2403
or 800-98-PRIDE
Quote Best Loved

ACCESS CODES
AMADEUS HK STNMAI
APOLLO/GALILEO HT 41203
SABRE/ABACUS HK 34711
WORLDSPAN HK MAISO

SOUTH & ISLANDS

THE MANSION HOUSE HOTEL
Townhouse

Thames Street, Poole,
Dorset BH15 1JN

T (UK) 0870 432 8703
T 01202 685666
F 01202 665709
mansionpoole@bestloved.com
www.mansionpoole.bestloved.com

OWNERS
Jackie and Gerry Godden

ROOM RATES
9 Singles	£75 - £95
21 Doubles/Twins	£130 - £140
2 Four-posters	£145

Includes full breakfast, early morning tea, newspaper and VAT

CREDIT CARDS
AMERICAN EXPRESS • DC • JCB • MC • VI

RATINGS & AWARDS
RAC ★★★ Dining Award 3
AA ★★★ ⊛⊛
AA Top 200 - 2004/2005

FACILITIES
On site: Licensed for weddings, restaurant, Bistro
3 meeting rooms/max 40 people
Nearby: Golf, fishing, sailing, yachting, fitness centre, shooting, riding

RESTRICTIONS
No facilities for disabled guests
No smoking in restaurant and some bedrooms
No pets; guide dogs only

ATTRACTIONS
Poole Old Town, Corfe Castle, Hurst Castle, Hardy Country, The New Forest, Abbotsbury Abbey, Dorset villages, Blue Flag beaches

NEAREST
CITY:
Poole

AIRPORT:
Heathrow - 100 miles/2 hrs 15 mins

RAIL STATION:
Poole - 1 mile/5 mins

FERRY PORT:
Poole - ½ mile/3 mins

AFFILIATIONS
Best Western

RESERVATIONS
National rate in UK: 0870 432 8703
Toll free in US: 800-528-1234
Quote Best Loved

ACCESS CODES
AMADEUS BW BOH382
APOLLO/GALILEO BW 58155
SABRE/ABACUS BW 14103
WORLDSPAN BW 83382

SOUTH & ISLANDS

A stylish Georgian townhouse with a highly-rated dining experience

Set down a quiet cul-de-sac a few minutes stroll from the quayside, the Mansion House was Poole's original mayoral house, dating back to the 1780s. This charming corner of Old Poole is redolent with the town's distinguished maritime history, and the house itself was built for a leading merchant family whose fortunes were founded on the Newfoundland cod trade (and an unusual memento of their New World connections is the 'cod fillet' fireplace in the Benjamin Lester suite!).

This privately owned hotel has been sympathetically restored and furnished with period antiques whilst providing every modern luxury for today's discerning guest. Each of the 32 bedrooms is individually designed, from those with subtle themes of Indian summer, Versailles or English rose to those named after famous Georgian or Victorian characters. Guests can dine in the informal surroundings of the Bistro or enjoy the ambience of the cherrywood-panelled restaurant, where chef Gerry Godden's outstanding modern British menu might feature signature dishes such as Dorset mussels with Thai spices, roast wood pigeon and a creatively-prepared catch of the day.

Poole is a renowned yachting centre and excellent base for exploring Thomas Hardy country and the New Forest. Golf, sailing and water sport are easily arranged.

LOCATION
Once in Poole, follow the signs to Channel Ferry. Take the inside lane at Poole Bridge and turn left into Poole Quay, then first left after 200 yards into Thames Street; the hotel is on the left.

Country house

THE MONTAGU ARMS HOTEL

Palace Lane, Beaulieu,
Hampshire SO42 7ZL

T (UK) 0870 432 8509
T 01590 612324
F 01590 612188
montaguarms@bestloved.com
www.montaguarms.bestloved.com

MANAGER
Everton Farmer

ROOM RATES
1 Single	£100
13 Doubles/Twins	£160 - £170
6 Junior Suites	£190
3 Suites	£210

Includes breakfast and VAT

CREDIT CARDS
AMERICAN EXPRESS • DC • MC • VI

RATINGS & AWARDS
AA ★★★ ✿✿
AA Courtesy & Care Award
AA Top 200 - 2004/2005

FACILITIES
On site: Garden, croquet,
licensed for weddings
3 meeting rooms/max 50 people
Nearby: Complimentary use of
leisure club, shooting, fishing, riding

RESTRICTIONS
No facilities for disabled guests
No children under 7 years in the
Terrace Restaurant

ATTRACTIONS
National Motor Museum,
Isle of Wight, Stonehenge,
Bucklers Hard, Exbury Gardens

NEAREST
CITY:
Southampton - 10 miles/15 mins

AIRPORT:
Heathrow - 80 miles/2 hrs

RAIL STATION:
Brockenhurst - 5 miles/10 mins

AFFILIATIONS
Independent

RESERVATIONS
National rate in UK: 0870 432 8509
Quote Best Loved

ACCESS CODES
Not applicable

SOUTH & ISLANDS

Atmosphere, character and a great location in the New Forest

The picturesque village of Beaulieu nestles quietly in the depths of the New Forest, yet it would be hard to find a more convenient touring base for exploring central southern England. Adventurous visitors can strike out for Dorchester and Thomas Hardy country to the west, head north to ancient Stonehenge and the cathedral cities of Salisbury and Winchester or travel east to Portsmouth's Royal Naval Dockyard, home to Lord Nelson's flagship Victory and the salvaged Tudor battleship Mary Rose. Closer to home are the glorious Exbury Gardens and Lymington's steep cobbled streets, Saturday market and ferries to the Isle of Wight. The National Motor Museum at the Montagu family estate is right on the doorstep.

The Montagu Arms can trace its origins back to the 17th century, and has retained many atmospheric period features from panelled walls to beamed ceilings. The luxurious bedrooms are a delight, charmingly decorated in traditional English fabrics, and several of the spacious suites have four-poster beds. Guests can dine in the cosy atmosphere of Monty's bar and brasserie, or enjoy the elegant Terrace Restaurant with views over a splendid terraced garden. Alternatively, take advantage of the private dining rooms for business and special occasions.

LOCATION

From the M3, take the M27 (Bournemouth); exit junction 2 for the A326 (Beaulieu).
Take the B3054 to Beaulieu;
the hotel is on the left as you enter the village.

> *We could not have wished for a better day; from the food to the service, there was not one part of our day that we and our guests did not enjoy!*
>
> DOUG AND JILL BOSWELL

NEW PARK MANOR

Country house

Lyndhurst Road, Brockenhurst,
Hampshire SO42 7QH

T (UK) 0870 432 8717
T 01590 623467
F 01590 622268
newparkmanor@bestloved.com
www.newparkmanor.bestloved.com

GENERAL MANAGER
Hervé Goulet

ROOM RATES
9 Classic Doubles   £120
4 Manor Rooms   £160
8 Forest Rooms   £190
3 Suites   £210
Includes full breakfast and VAT

CREDIT CARDS
AMERICAN EXPRESS • DC • MC • VI

RATINGS & AWARDS
RAC ★★★ Dining Award 3
AA ★★★ ⊛⊛ 73%

FACILITIES
On site: Garden, heli-pad,
outdoor pool, croquet,
licensed for weddings,
equestrian centre,
spa (opening May 2005)
5 meeting rooms/max 80 people
Nearby: Golf, fishing

RESTRICTIONS
Limited facilities for disabled guests
No smoking in restaurant

ATTRACTIONS
New Forest, Exbury Gardens,
Beaulieu Motor Museum,
Highcliffe Castle, Stonehenge,
Broadlands at Romsey, Isle of Wight

NEAREST
CITY:
Southampton - 10 miles/20 mins

AIRPORT:
Heathrow - 80 miles/1 hr 30 mins
Southampton - 14 miles/50 mins

RAIL STATION:
Brockenhurst - 1 ½ miles/5 mins

AFFILIATIONS
von Essen Hotels
Preston's Global Hotels

RESERVATIONS
National rate in UK: 0870 432 8717
Toll free in the US: 800-544-9993
Quote Best Loved

ACCESS CODES
AMADEUS YX SOUNEW
APOLLO/GALILEO YX 71694
SABRE/ABACUS YX 54956
WORLDSPAN YX SOUNP
PEGASUS YX SOUNEW

SOUTH & ISLANDS

Once King Charles II's favourite hunting lodge - today a matchless hideaway

New Park Manor has the most magical setting deep within the New Forest, an area that was once the royal hunting ground of William the Conqueror. The Forest fringes the hotel grounds on all sides, bringing with it not only the squirrels and fallow deer but a certain hush, an insulation from the outside world - yet this splendid location is little over an hour's drive from London.

In the main house at New Park Manor, the bedrooms are traditional in style, with classic fabrics and furnishings; some rooms have period features and four-poster beds. In the recently-refurbished Forest Wing, the rooms are stunning; highly stylised and indulgent, they offer some of the most fabulous beds you've ever slept in. The bathrooms are complete with LCD TVs, and the hotel's good-humoured brochure invites you to 'lie back in the bubbles and enjoy a good old weepy movie'.

The Forest Wing's transformation also extends to the restaurant, Stags, which serves modern rustic English cuisine with an emphasis on local specialities.

The Forest can be explored on a hired bike or on horseback, arranged through the hotel's own equestrian centre - and if the Forest lets you out of its grip, the area offers endless ideas for local outings!

LOCATION
From the M27, follow the A337 six miles south past Lyndhurst. Turn right at the sign for New Park Manor; the hotel is half a mile into the forest.

> **"** A lovely atmosphere and very friendly, helpful staff. Nothing was too much trouble. We will be back! **"**
>
> ROBERT & JOAN, BEXHILL

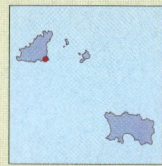

Island hotel   OLD GOVERNMENT HOUSE HOTEL & SPA

This gracious former governors' residence is an island institution

Old Government House (or OGH, as it is affectionately known) occupies a prime position at the centre of Guernsey's capital, St Peter Port. Within easy walking distance of the business and finance districts, fine restaurants and shopping, it also boasts spectacular views over the harbour and neighbouring Channel Islands of Sark and Herm.

The hotel has been welcoming visitors to Guernsey since 1858, and has recently undergone a £2.5 million renovation programme emerging as an elegant and superbly comfortable address equally appealing to business and leisure travellers. The wings of the hotel form a courtyard around the attractive pool area, which is a popular spot for al fresco dining in warm weather, while the restaurant's fine-dining menus feature the best local and continental produce accompanied by a comprehensive wine list. For a relaxed drink there's a choice of bars, including the historic Governor's Bar and Restaurant.

For daytime relaxation, the hotel spa has a gym, sauna, solarium and a range of pampering beauty treatments. Further afield, Guernsey is there to explore in all its quiet charm, as are the sister islands and historic French port of St Malo a ferry ride away, plus sport from golf to windsurfing.

LOCATION
Off St Julian's Avenue in the town centre.

Ann's Place, St Peter Port, Guernsey GY1 4AZ

T (UK) 0870 432 8722
T 01481 724921
F 01481 724429
oldgov@bestloved.com
www.oldgov.bestloved.com

GENERAL MANAGER
Simon Courtenay-Warren

ROOM RATES
13 Singles   £105 - £125
15 Queen-sized Doubles £140 - £150
32 King-sized doubles/twins £140 - £215
8 Suites   £160 - £285
Includes breakfast (VAT exempt)

CREDIT CARDS
AMERICAN EXPRESS • DC • MC • VI

RATINGS & AWARDS
GTB ★★★★ Gold Award
RAC ★★★★ Dining Award 1
AA ★★★★ ⊛ 72%
AA Accessible Hotel
of the Year UK 2002/2003

FACILITIES
On site: Gym, outdoor pool, health & beauty, sauna, steam room, whirlpools, aerobics studio
5 meeting rooms/max 275 people
Nearby: Leisure centre

RESTRICTIONS
No pets; guide dogs only

ATTRACTIONS
Maison Victor Hugo, Sausmarez Manor, Castle Cornet, Guernsey Tapestry, Concert Hall, islands of Herm, Sark and Jersey

NEAREST
TOWN:
St Peter Port

AIRPORT:
Guernsey - 4 miles /20 mins

FERRY PORT:
St Peter Port - 1 ¼ mile/10 mins

AFFILIATIONS
Independent

RESERVATIONS
National rate in UK: 0870 432 8722
Quote Best Loved

ACCESS CODES
AMADEUS 1A GC1OLD
APOLLO/GALILEO UA 93772
SABRE/ABACUS UI 23420
WORLDSPAN IP 40200

SOUTH & ISLANDS

You have managed to find the perfect mix of great service, marvellous accommodation and magnificent dining

SARAH LOMAS, COLCHESTER

THE PIER AT HARWICH

Seaside hotel

The Quay, Harwich,
Essex CO12 3HH

T (UK) 0870 432 8741
T 01255 241212
F 01255 551922
pier@bestloved.com
www.pier.bestloved.com

OWNERS
Gerald and Paul Milsom

CHEF/ DIRECTOR
Chris Oakley

ROOM RATES
Single occupancy   £70 - £100
13 Doubles/Twins   £95 - £115
1 Suite   £170
Includes continental breakfast and VAT

CREDIT CARDS
AMERICAN EXPRESS • DC • MC • VI

RATINGS & AWARDS
RAC ★★★ Dining Award 2
AA ★★★ ✿✿ 74%

FACILITIES
On site: Licensed for weddings
1 meeting room/max 100 people
Nearby: Pool, golf, tennis, boating,
fishing, sailing

RESTRICTIONS
Limited facilities for disabled guests
No smoking in bedrooms
No pets; guide dogs only

ATTRACTIONS
Harwich Maritime and Lifeboat
museums, Kentwell Hall & Lavenham,
Beth Chatto's Gardens,
Colchester Castle,
Flatford Mill and Constable Country

NEAREST
CITY:
Harwich

AIRPORT:
Stansted - 60 miles/50 mins

RAIL STATION:
Harwich - 1/2 mile/2 mins

FERRY PORT:
Harwich International - 1 mile/3 mins

AFFILIATIONS
Preston's Global Hotels
The Great Inns of Britain

RESERVATIONS
National rate in UK: 0870 432 8741
Toll free in US: 800-544-9993
Quote Best Loved

ACCESS CODES
Not applicable

SOUTH & ISLANDS

Quayside seafood restaurants tempt you from rooms with harbour views

The Harbourside Restaurant and its more casual little sister, The Ha-Penny Bistro, sit right on Old Harwich Quay. Over the years, this remarkable pair have established an enviable reputation for the quality and variety of their seafood menus - which will come as no surprise to foodies when they realise that the owners are the Milsom family of Le Talbooth fame (a watchword for fine dining in East Anglia).

Located adjacent to the restaurants, one of The Pier's chief charms is its harbour views, which are constantly enlivened by the coming and going of yachtsmen and traditional fishing boats. The 14 bedrooms breathe a distinctly nautical chic of their own; the imaginative use of seashells and rope, weatherboarding and natural fibre floor coverings augmented by marine paintings and photographs lends a wonderfully briny air, and there are numerous creative touches to amuse and entertain throughout the hotel.

The Pier makes a welcome overnight stop en route to the Continent, or take advantage of the hotel's great-value sailing weekends. There are also short break offers in conjunction with Colchester hotel Maison Talbooth.

LOCATION
Take the A120 to Harwich and continue straight until the road on the quayside of Old Harwich. The hotel is on the right opposite the lifeboat station.

> ❝ The perfect country house hotel by the sea. Fabulous gardens, food and beach ❞
> PREVIOUS GUEST

Seaside hotel

PRIORY BAY HOTEL

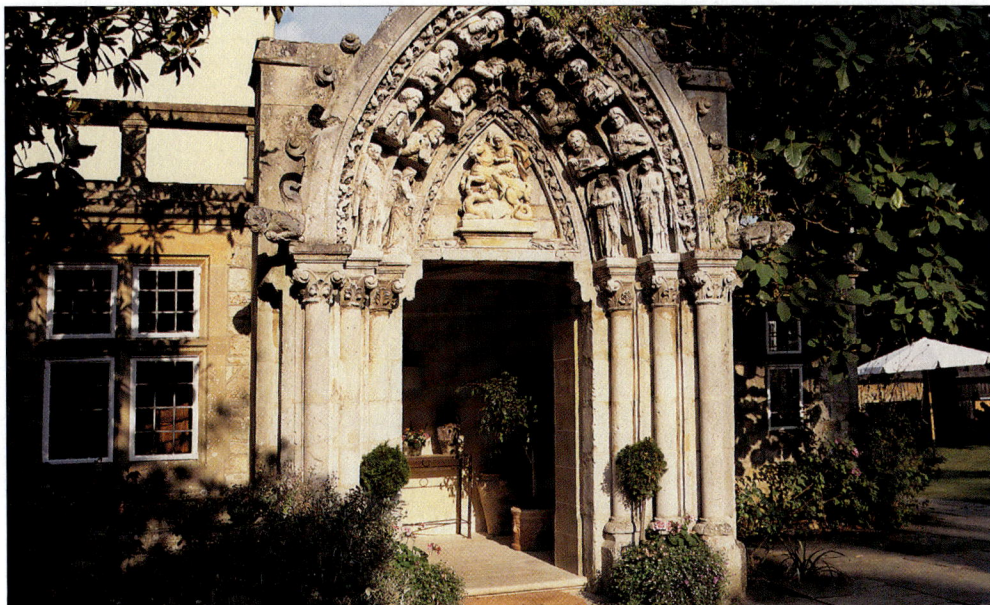

Cluniac monks, Tudor farmers and Georgian gentry all shaped Priory Bay

The quiet sandy strand of Priory Bay lies between the seaside towns of Bembridge and Seaview on the north coast of the Isle of Wight. Set above the beach, this gorgeous site is named for a Cluniac priory established by French monks soon after the Norman Conquest. The surrounding estate has been tended for almost a thousand years, and the present house probably originated as a Tudor farmhouse later extended and improved until it came to resemble the engaging medley of beautiful buildings, sloping lawns and terraced gardens of Priory Bay Hotel.

Just over two and a half hours from London - including a relaxing ferry crossing - this is no run-of-the-mill country house hotel, as guests will discover from the minute they enter the stunning medieval carved portico brought from France and reconstructed stone by stone! The public rooms have been stylishly restored and furnished with antiques, while the guestrooms run the gamut from classic Regency to cool Shaker style in the main building and purpose-built cottages in the grounds.

An excellent menu offers plenty of choice, including al fresco dining in fine weather. The summer-season seafood restaurant, The Priory Oyster (open July-August) is set in the woods above the beach and is a wholly tempting excursion.

LOCATION

From Ryde, take the B330, then the B3340 toward Seaview; go through Nettlestone but do not turn for Seaview. Watch for the hotel's signs half a mile on.

Priory Drive, Seaview,
Isle of Wight PO34 5BU

T (UK) 0870 432 8748
T 01983 613146
F 01983 616539
priorybay@bestloved.com
www.priorybay.bestloved.com

OWNERS
Andrew and James Palmer

ROOM RATES
Single occupancy	£69 - £195
9 Doubles/Twins	£108 - £198
7 Deluxe Doubles/Twins	£140 - £258
2 Family Rooms	£108 - £300

Includes full breakfast and VAT

CREDIT CARDS
AMERICAN EXPRESS • MC • VI

RATINGS & AWARDS
AA ★★★ ❀❀ 77%

FACILITIES
On site: Garden, heli-pad, outdoor pool, croquet, golf, tennis, licensed for weddings, private beach, seafront cafe, moorings
2 meeting rooms/max 90 people
Nearby: Golf, riding, sailing

RESTRICTIONS
No facilities for disabled guests
No pets

ATTRACTIONS
Cowes Marina, Osborne House, The Needles, Sandown Zoo, Carisbrooke Castle, Island Steam Railway

NEAREST
CITY:
Portsmouth - 7 miles/35 mins

AIRPORT:
Southampton - 28 miles/40 mins

RAIL STATION:
Portsmouth - 7 miles/35 mins

AFFILIATIONS
Independent

RESERVATIONS
National rate in UK: 0870 432 8748
Quote Best Loved

ACCESS CODES
Not applicable

SOUTH & ISLANDS

The Priory is the sort of hotel I'd recommend other hoteliers to stay in

PADDY BURT, DAILY TELEGRAPH

PRIORY HOTEL

Country house

Church Green, Wareham,
Dorset BH20 4ND

T (UK) 0870 432 8749
T 01929 551666
F 01929 554519
prioryware@bestloved.com
www.prioryware.bestloved.com

GENERAL MANAGER
Jeremy Merchant

ROOM RATES
2 Singles   £110
12 Doubles/Twins   £140 - £210
2 Four-posters   £245
2 Suites   £295
Includes full breakfast, early morning
tea or coffee, newspaper and VAT

CREDIT CARDS
DC • JCB • MC • VI

RATINGS & AWARDS
ETC ★★★ Gold Award
RAC Gold Ribbon ★★★
Dining Award 3

FACILITIES
On site: Garden, croquet
1 meeting room/max 20 people
Nearby: Fishing, sailing, riding, cycling, golf

RESTRICTIONS
No facilities for disabled guests
No children under 8 years
No smoking in restaurants
No pets; guide dogs only

ATTRACTIONS
Corfe Castle, Purbeck, Lulworth Cove,
Kingston Lacey, Poole Harbour,
Hardy Country, Blue Flag beaches

NEAREST
CITY:
Poole - 15 miles/20 mins
Bournemouth - 25 miles/ 35 mins

AIRPORT:
Heathrow - 100 miles/2 hours

RAIL STATION:
Wareham - 1 mile/5 mins

AFFILIATIONS
Independent

RESERVATIONS
National rate in UK: 0870 432 8749
Quote Best Loved

ACCESS CODES
Not applicable

Steeped in history and an idyllic sanctuary for the world-weary

Dating from the early 16th century, the one-time Lady St Mary Priory has offered sanctuary for hundreds of years. Far from the hustle and bustle of city life, The Priory stands in four acres of immaculate gardens on the banks of the River Frome surrounded by idyllic Dorset countryside.

Rooted in history as well as peaceful scenery, The Priory has undergone a sympathetic conversion to a charming yet unpretentious hotel. Each bedroom is distinctively styled, with family antiques lending character; many rooms have commanding views of the Purbeck Hills. A 16th-century clay barn nearby has been transformed into the Boathouse, adding four spacious luxury suites at the river's edge. There are also moorings for guests arriving by boat. Tastefully furnished, the drawing room, residents' lounge and intimate bar together create a convivial atmosphere. The Garden Room is open for breakfast and lunch, while dinner is served in the Abbots Cellar Restaurant.

Dating back to the 9th century, the market town of Wareham has more than 200 listed buildings and is an ideal excursion for the curious. Corfe Castle, Lulworth Cove, Poole and Swanage are all close by.

LOCATION
Wareham is on the A351 to the west of Bournemouth and Poole; the hotel is on the River Frome just off the quay.

Spa hotel

ROWHILL GRANGE HOTEL & SPA

Wilmington, Dartford,
Kent DA2 7QH

T (UK) 0870 432 8758
T 01322 615136
F 01322 615137
rowhill@bestloved.com
www.rowhill.bestloved.com

GENERAL MANAGER
Jonathan Owen

ROOM RATES
Single occupancy   £155 - £270
29 Doubles/Twins   £180 - £330
5 Four-posters   £155 - £330
4 Suites   £190 - £330
Includes VAT

CREDIT CARDS
AMERICAN EXPRESS • DC • MC • VI

RATINGS & AWARDS
RAC Blue Ribbon ★★★★
Dining Award 3
AA ★★★★ ◎◎ 77%

FACILITIES
On site: Garden, croquet, indoor pool, Japanese therapy pool, health & beauty, hair salon, gym, aerobics studio, licensed for weddings
7 meeting rooms/max 200 people
Nearby: Golf

RESTRICTIONS
Limited facilities for disabled guests
No children under 16 years in restaurant
No smoking in bedrooms
No pets; guide dogs only

ATTRACTIONS
Brands Hatch Race Circuit, Eltham Place, London, Leeds & Hever castles, Rochester, Canterbury, Lingfield Racecourse

NEAREST
CITY:
London - 20 miles/50 mins

AIRPORT:
Heathrow - 60 miles/1 hr
Stansted - 40 miles/45 mins

RAIL STATION:
Swanley - 1 ½ miles/5 mins

AFFILIATIONS
VIP International

RESERVATIONS
National rate in UK: 0870 432 8758
Quote Best Loved

ACCESS CODES
AMADEUS IA LGW001
APOLLO/GALILEO UA 52487
SABRE/ABACUS AA 44679
WORLDSPAN TW 0312

A remarkable spa hotel that's the ultimate location for business or pleasure

The Mail on Sunday rated Rowhill Grange's Utopia Spa as one of the top 50 in the world. With 19 treatment rooms, Japanese showers, underwater massage beds and a Jacuzzi, guests are invited to completely indulge themselves - reflexology, Indian head massages and a therapy pool are just a few of the treats on offer. A wonderful range of customised spa breaks and gift vouchers are available and are an excellent way to treat someone.

The spa's sense of relaxation extends to the accommodation, too. All rooms are tastefully and lavishly furnished with solid wood furniture and designer fabrics. Many have four-posters or sleigh beds, and all have luxury Egyptian linen. Dining options include an à la carte restaurant with conservatory dining, a more casual brasserie or private dining rooms.

Set within nine acres of mature woodland including a walled Victorian garden, Rowhill is an ideal venue for a wedding. The Clockhouse Suite, with its own courtyard area, accommodates up to 150 guests. In addition, the hotel's corporate facilities are popular with many large companies, partly due to its surprisingly convenient location for the M25, M20, London and Brands Hatch. In short, Rowhill Grange is perfect for meetings, wedding or a getaway - and all only 20 miles from London!

LOCATION
From the M25, exit junction 3 for the B2173 (Swanley). At Swanley, take the B258 (Hextable) through four small roundabouts. The hotel is a mile and a half after the last roundabout, on the left.

SOUTH & ISLANDS

Map p. 450, grid F4

RYE LODGE

Townhouse

Hilders Cliff, Rye,
East Sussex TN31 7LD

T (UK) 0870 432 8764
T 01797 223838
F 01797 223585
rye@bestloved.com
www.rye.bestloved.com

OWNERS
The de Courcy Family

ROOM RATES
18 Doubles/Twins £190
Includes full breakfast and VAT

CREDIT CARDS
AMERICAN EXPRESS • DC • MC • VI

RATINGS & AWARDS
ETC ★★★ Silver Award Hotel
RAC ★★★ Dining Award 1
AA ★★★ 72%

FACILITIES
On site: Indoor pool, health & beauty, sauna, spa bath, steam cabinet, private car park
Nearby: Golf, fishing, sailing

RESTRICTIONS
Limited facilities for disabled guests
No smoking in restaurant

ATTRACTIONS
Leeds Castle, Rye Town, Canterbury Cathedral, Battle Abbey & Battlefield, Sissinghurst Gardens, Martello Gardens, Bodiam Castle, Hever Castle, nature reserves

NEAREST
CITY:
Canterbury - 35 miles/50 mins
Ashford - 10 miles/20 mins

AIRPORT:
Gatwick - 50 miles/1 hr 15 mins

RAIL STATION:
Rye - ¼ mile/5 mins

AFFILIATIONS
Grand Heritage Hotels

RESERVATIONS
National rate in UK: 0870 432 8764
Toll free in US: 888-93-GRAND
Quote Best Loved

ACCESS CODES
Not applicable

SOUTH & ISLANDS

Elegance, restful charm and a rare attention to detail in historic Rye

The English Channel once lapped at the very toes of Rye, an ancient hilltop town and Cinque Port that now lies on the sheltered Rother Estuary surrounded by the wetlands of Romney Marsh. Before the sea receded, the only access to the citadel was through the medieval Landgate, which still stands not a stone's throw from Rye Lodge.

The hotel occupies a wonderful position on East Cliff, with panoramic views down to the harbour, where the Rye fishing fleet gathers. A few steps away are the bustling high street, Rye Castle and picturesque cobbled streets of quaint Tudor and Elizabethan buildings festooned with flower-filled window boxes and hanging baskets.

Rye Lodge is a labour of love for the de Courcy family and their small, dedicated staff. Relaxation and attention to detail are two key elements in the hotel's ethos - guests can relax, and the service is second to none. There are 18 attractive bedrooms, a friendly bar and a scenic terrace for sunny days. In the elegant marble-floored Terrace Restaurant, guests can enjoy local specialities such as Rye Bay plaice and Romney Marsh lamb, and the extensive wine list features wines from around the world, with 'R' de Ruinart setting the standard as the house champagne!

LOCATION
Exit 10 off the M20 for the A2070 (Lydd); at the Brooklands roundabout, take the A259 to Rye town centre. The hotel is 100 yards on the right after the Landgate arch.

> **"The experience was unusual in that courtesy, kindness and efficiency were of the highest order"**
>
> ELEANOR SANDERSON, LONDON

Inn

SHELLEYS

The High Street, Lewes,
Sussex BN7 1XS

T (UK) 0870 432 8771
T 01273 472361
F 01273 483152
shelleys@bestloved.com
www.shelleys.bestloved.com

OWNERS
Peter and Sylvie Pattenden

GENERAL MANAGER
Graeme Coles

ROOM RATES
1 Single	£95 - £120
5 Standard Doubles/Twins	£130 - £160
10 Superior Doubles/Twins	£150 - £185
1 Deluxe Double/Twin	£200 - £250
1 Superior Suite	£200 - £250
1 Four-poster	£220 - £270

Includes VAT

CREDIT CARDS
AMERICAN EXPRESS • DC • JCB • MC • VI

RATINGS & AWARDS
ETC ★★★ Silver Award
RAC White Ribbon ★★★
Dining Award 2
AA ★★★ ❀❀ 75%

FACILITIES
On site: Garden, licensed for weddings
3 meeting rooms/max 60 people
Nearby: Golf, riding

RESTRICTIONS
Limited facilities for disabled guests

ATTRACTIONS
Charleston Farm House,
Virginia Woolf's House, Brighton,
Glyndebourne, Beachy Head,
Goodwood Races, South Downs,
coastline at the Seven Sisters

NEAREST
CITY:
Brighton - 7 miles/20 mins

AIRPORT:
Gatwick - 30 miles/40 mins

RAIL STATION:
Lewes - 1 mile/5 mins

AFFILIATIONS
Independent

RESERVATIONS
National rate in UK: 0870 432 8771
Quote Best Loved

ACCESS CODES
Not applicable

An historic coaching inn in a lovely Sussex setting

Built as an inn in 1526, this Grade II listed building is a famous local landmark. Converted to a manor house by the Earl of Dorset in 1590, today's hotel took its name from its next occupants, the Shelley family, parents of poet Percy Bysshe Shelley. The manor eventually became a hotel in 1932.

Today, after extensive refurbishment, the hotel gleams with historical grandeur, including a lovely drawing room, and elegant banqueting room for 50 overlooking the delightful private garden. The deluxe guest rooms are a delight as well, from the luxurious Earl of Dorset suite to the spacious Pelham Room, with a four-poster bed overlooking the gardens. And then there's the dining - under the direction of Head Chef Matthew Budden, the hotel offers a range of tempting traditional choices as well as lighter, more contemporary dining.

Shelleys' conveniently-placed location makes it exceedingly popular with guests visiting the Glyndebourne Opera Season, as well as enjoying a reputation as one of the closest country house hotels to Brighton (eight miles) and a good central point for circular South Downs walkers. Just 40 minutes from Gatwick airport, Lewes is easily accessible by motorway. Better still, Shelleys offers exciting short break packages throughout the year, with special bed and breakfast rates from £55 to £90 per person per night, minimum two nights.

LOCATION

From London, take the M23/A23 toward Brighton, then the ring road link to the A27. Follow for four miles to Lewes; the hotel is on the left before the town centre.

SOUTH & ISLANDS

SIR CHRISTOPHER WREN'S HOUSE — City hotel

Thames Street, Windsor,
Berkshire SL4 1PX

T (UK) 0870 432 8772
T 01753 861354
F 01753 860172
wren@bestloved.com
www.wren.bestloved.com

GENERAL MANAGER
Christian Devaux

ROOM RATES
11 Singles	£75 - £160
30 Doubles/Twins	£85 - £213
21 Executive Doubles/Twins	£95 - £239
7 Suites	£200 - £292

Includes service and VAT

CREDIT CARDS
AMERICAN EXPRESS • DC • JCB • MC • VI

RATINGS & AWARDS
AA ★★★★ ❀❀ 69%

FACILITIES
On site: Licensed for weddings, Wren's Club Health and Beauty Centre, Martini Bar & Restaurant, riverside terrace
8 meeting rooms/max 90 people
Nearby: Golf, riding, fishing, tennis, water skiing

RESTRICTIONS
Limited facilities for disabled guests
No pets; guide dogs only
Smoking in some rooms only

ATTRACTIONS
Windsor Castle, Eton, Legoland, Thorpe Park, Henley on Thames, Royal Ascot Races, London, Thames River cruises

NEAREST
CITY:
London - 25 miles/40 mins

AIRPORT:
Heathrow - 7 miles/20 mins

RAIL STATION:
Windsor Central - 1/2 mile/5 mins

AFFILIATIONS
Wren's Hotels
Preston's Global Hotels
Grand Heritage Hotels

RESERVATIONS
National rate in UK: 0870 432 8772
Toll free in US: 800-544-9993
or 888-93-GRAND
Quote Best Loved

ACCESS CODES
AMADEUS UI LHR300
APOLLO/GALILEO UI 95105
SABRE/ABACUS UI 43762
WORLDSPAN UI 40753

SOUTH & ISLANDS

Architect-designed - and what an architect for this memorable place!

Once the family home of the world-famous British architect Sir Christopher Wren, this 17th-century gem holds a unique place in English heritage. Today, it's a world-class hotel with many original features still proudly visible, among them a fine alabaster fireplace in the drawing room.

All 90 bedrooms at Sir Christopher Wren's House are fully equipped with modern amenities, including interactive televisions offering games, music, films and Internet access. The house is fascinating to explore, too; elegant public rooms lead to a light, leafy conservatory and out on to the terrace. The conservatory is also an extension of the hotel's restaurant, where meals are prepared freshly and imaginatively for both meals and private functions alike.

Just a stone's throw away is a towpath along an attractive stretch of the River Thames, and the regal skyline of Windsor Castle towers above. Guests are never short of things to do here - beauty treatments and workouts are available at the hotel's state-of-the-art health and beauty centre. The antiques centres of Eton lie just across the bridge, and within a short drive are Henley on Thames, Legoland, Royal Ascot races and Thorpe Park. So is London, with the 51 churches that Wren built after the 1666 Great Fire, and Oxford, with the architect's fabulous Sheldonian Theatre.

LOCATION
In the heart of Windsor, 40 minutes from London. The hotel is close to the M4 (exit 6) and within easy reach of the M40, M3 and M25.

Country house

ST MICHAEL'S MANOR

Village charm and hidden lakeside gardens in historic St Albans

Nestled in the shadow of Verulamium, ancient Roman heart of St Albans, and the imposing abbey and cathedral named for the Roman soldier who became Britain's first Christian martyr in 209 AD, the gentle curve of Fishpool Street winds through the picturesque heritage district of St Michael's Village. Here, St Michael's Manor fronts five acres of gardens arranged around a peaceful lake and shaded by mature trees.

The original manor was built on medieval foundations for the Gape family circa 1512, and the site of the family's tannery business was discovered at the bottom of the lake during the drought of 1976. The manor has been harmoniously altered and extended over the centuries, but remains rich in character and architectural detail whilst offering an enviable degree of comfort and service. The bedrooms have been thoughtfully supplied with games, books and magazines; many rooms feature fine antiques, and some have views over the garden. The Garden Bar offers one of the finest selections of malt whiskys outside Scotland, while the notable Terrace Room restaurant features creative modern British cuisine accompanied by an extensive wine list - tempting dishes include blackened lamb loin with a red lentil and haricot vert compote, cumin-crusted loin of tuna with white flageolet beans and artichoke and, for dessert, a hot chocolate fondant with Chantilly cream and blood orange sauce.

LOCATION

By road, take the M1/M25 or M4/M40 motorways. By train, located 20 minutes from London's Kings Cross and a short taxi ride from St Albans station.

St Michael's Village,
Fishpool Street, St Albans,
Hertfordshire AL3 4RY

T (UK) 0870 432 8773
T 01727 864444
F 01727 848909
stmichaels@bestloved.com
www.stmichaels.bestloved.com

OWNERS
The Newling Ward Family

ROOM RATES
1 Singles £145
10 Standard Doubles/Twins £145 - £180
6 Executive Doubles/Twins £155 - £190
4 Superior Doubles £180 - £250
1 Four-poster £230 - £310
Includes full breakfast and VAT

CREDIT CARDS
AMERICAN EXPRESS • DC • MC • VI

RATINGS & AWARDS
ETC ★★★ Silver Award
RAC Blue Ribbon ★★★
Dining Award 3
AA ★★★ ✹✹ 82%

FACILITIES
On site: Garden, fishing, croquet, licensed for weddings
3 meeting rooms/max 90 people
Nearby: Golf, fitness, tennis, riding, water skiing, yachting

RESTRICTIONS
Limited facilities for disabled guests
No smoking in restaurant
No pets

ATTRACTIONS
St Albans Abbey, Knebworth House, Roman Museum, Hatfield House, RAF Museum, Whipsnade Zoo

NEAREST
CITY:
St Albans - ¼ mile/10 mins

AIRPORT:
Heathrow - 25 miles/45 mins
Luton - 10 miles/15 mins

RAIL STATION:
St Albans City - 2 miles/10 mins

AFFILIATIONS
Preston's Global Hotels

RESERVATIONS
National rate in UK: 0870 432 8773
Toll free in US: 800-544-9993
Quote Best Loved

ACCESS CODES
Not applicable

SOUTH & ISLANDS

"The service was seamless, professional and full of enthusiasm"

OLYMPIC GAMES 2012 COMMITTEE

STANHILL COURT HOTEL

Country house

Stanhill Road, Charlwood,
Horley, Surrey RH6 0EP

T (UK) 0870 432 8775
T 01293 862166
F 01293 862773
stanhill@bestloved.com
www.stanhill.bestloved.com

GENERAL MANAGER
Eamonn Canavan

ROOM RATES
Single occupancy	£110
8 Doubles/Twins	£125
3 Four Posters	£150
4 Deluxe Four-posters	£165

Includes full breakfast and VAT

CREDIT CARDS
AMERICAN EXPRESS • DC • MC • VI

RATINGS & AWARDS
RAC White Ribbon ★★★
Dining Award 3
AA ★★★ ☺ 75%
AA Romantic Hotel

FACILITIES
On site: Garden
6 meeting rooms/max 200 people

RESTRICTIONS
Limited facilities for disabled guests
No smoking throughout
No pets; guide dogs only

ATTRACTIONS
Windsor, Brighton, London,
Chartwell House, Glyndebourne,
Hickstead, antique fairs, gardens

NEAREST
CITY:
London - 28 miles/40 mins

AIRPORT:
Gatwick - 5 miles/10 mins

RAIL STATION:
Gatwick - 5 miles/10 mins
Horley - 4 miles/6 mins

AFFILIATIONS
Independent

RESERVATIONS
National rate in UK: 0870 432 8775
Toll free in UK: 0800 594 3619
Quote Best Loved

ACCESS CODES
Not applicable

This beautifully-decorated Victorian home is a perfect romantic getaway

This secluded Victorian country house set in 35 acres of gardens and woodland makes for a romantic setting. Once inside, décor includes wood panelling and stained glass windows, and many of the rooms have four-poster beds. This is a place where guests matter, a place that is often described by visitors as 'unique' or 'unforgettable'.

The restaurant is lavishly decorated with wood panelling, large windows draped with bright curtains, and elegant paintings and furnishings. The menu offers a variety of international cuisine from pan-fried organic salmon with fresh free-range egg tagliatelle, velute of asparagus, gratin potatoes and Dublin bay prawns to vegetarian options, like claret-braised red onion and caprini goat's cheese tart tatin with aged balsamic vinegar and wild Chinese honey - all accompanied by an extensive and impressive wine list.

Despite its private surroundings, Stanhill Court lies just a few minutes from Horley railway station and Gatwick airport (but not beneath the flight path), making it an incredibly accessible getaway ideal for leisure travellers and fantastic for corporate meetings. What's more, those looking for something a little different and full of character can hire Stanhill Court for exclusive use - with such romantic charm, the hotel is perfect for weddings.

LOCATION
From Gatwick airport, take the A23 (Redhill) from the north terminal roundabout. At next roundabout, exit for Charlwood; turn right onto Norwood Hill road after village and watch for hotel signs.

Country house

TAPLOW HOUSE & RESTAURANT

A stately welcome and princely comfort not an hour from London

American readers might be amused to know that 22 years before the Pilgrims landed on Plymouth Rock in 1620, the Taplow House estate was given by King James I to the first Governor of Virginia. Its splendid six acres include a tree said to have been planted by Queen Elizabeth I, as well as Europe's tallest tulip tree. The park is virtually unchanged since it was originally landscaped.

The mansion stands out of earshot, but within 15 minutes, of Heathrow airport, providing a fitting welcome and a convenient home-from-home for our newly-arrived New World cousins. It is a fine example of Georgian classicism, with Doric columns, high decorative ceilings, chandeliers and chiselled brass balusters - and the period design is subtly combined with contemporary amenities and creature comforts.

This is no ordinary hotel. All the 32 luxury bedrooms could happily feature in a mega-budget period drama, and to be seated in the dining room, enjoying award-winning cuisine, is quite the stately occasion. Memories are made of this! As you stroll like a lord through your very own estate, it is hard to believe you are so close to the capital - within an hour of London's West End, and so near Windsor, Oxford, Henley and other royal beauty spots along the Thames Valley.

LOCATION

From the M4, exit 7 (Maidenhead); after two and a half miles, pass under the large railway arch and turn right at the traffic lights into Berryhill. The hotel is 200 yards on the right.

Berry Hill, Taplow,
Buckinghamshire SL6 0DA

T (UK) 0870 432 8791
T 01628 670056
F 01628 773625
taplow@bestloved.com
www.taplow.bestloved.com

GENERAL MANAGER
Mathew Griffin

ROOM RATES
4 Singles	£70 - £134
23 Doubles/Twins	£85 - £175
4 Junior Suites	£85 - £175
1 Suite	£85 - £230

Includes full breakfast and VAT

CREDIT CARDS
AMERICAN EXPRESS • DC • MC • VI

RATINGS & AWARDS
AA ★★★ 70%

FACILITIES
On site: Garden, croquet, licensed for weddings
7 meeting rooms/max 100 people
Nearby: Golf, river cruises, cycling, walking, riding, swimming, tennis, squash, gym

RESTRICTIONS
Limited facilities for disabled guests
No smoking in restaurant and some bedrooms
No pets; guide dogs only

ATTRACTIONS
Windsor Castle, Legoland, Royal Ascot, Henley-on-Thames, Thorpe Park, Windsor Races, boating on the Thames, Cliveden National Trust properties, Kew Gardens

NEAREST
CITY:
London - 20 miles/35 mins

AIRPORT:
Heathrow - 10 miles/15 mins

RAIL STATION:
Maidenhead - 3 miles/2 mins

AFFILIATIONS
Wren's Hotels
Preston's Global Hotels
Grand Heritage Hotels

RESERVATIONS
National rate in UK: 0870 432 8791
Toll free in US: 800-544-9993
or 888-93-GRAND
Quote Best Loved

ACCESS CODES
AMADEUS UI LHR100
APOLLO/GALILEO UI 94922
SABRE/ABACUS UI 19742
WORLDSPAN UI 40754

SOUTH & ISLANDS

> As the sun floods through the French windows, the toughest choice will be whether to go for the Continental or the full English breakfast
>
> TIME OUT LONDON

THAMESMEAD HOUSE HOTEL — Townhouse

Remenham Lane,
Henley-on-Thames,
Oxfordshire RG9 2LR

T (UK) 0870 432 8793
T 01491 574745
F 01491 579944
thamesmead@bestloved.com
www.thamesmead.bestloved.com

OWNER
Patricia Thorburn-Muirhead

ASSISTANT MANAGER
Stuart Davies

ROOM RATES
Single occupancy   £110 - £130
4 Doubles   £130
1 Twin/Superking   £145
Includes full breakfast and VAT

CREDIT CARDS
AMERICAN EXPRESS • JCB • MC • VI

RATINGS & AWARDS
ETC ◆◆◆◆◆ Silver Award
RAC ◆◆◆◆◆
RAC Warm Welcome,
Sparkling Diamond Awards
AA ◆◆◆◆◆
AA Premier Collection
UK Small Hotel Winner 2002 -
Successful Housekeeping Magazine

FACILITIES
On site: 1 meeting room/max 12 people
Nearby: Golf, gym, walks, fishing

RESTRICTIONS
Limited facilities for disabled guests
No children under 10 years
Smoking on porch only
No pets
Closed Christmas week

ATTRACTIONS
Stonor Park, Hambleden,
Grey's Court, The Bohun Gallery,
Luxters, Henley Exhibition Centre,
Blenheim Palace, Oxford

NEAREST
CITY:
Reading - 10 miles/15 mins

AIRPORT:
Heathrow - 30 miles/40 mins

RAIL STATION:
Reading - 10 miles/15 mins
Twyford - 12 miles/15 mins

AFFILIATIONS
Independent

RESERVATIONS
National rate in UK: 0870 432 8793
Quote Best Loved

ACCESS CODES
Not applicable

Chic, relaxed and just minutes from Henley-on-Thames

Graced with an unbeatable location and a divinely relaxed atmosphere, this charming townhouse complete with views overlooking the cricket green is just three minutes' walk from the centre of Henley-on-Thames. Inside Thamesmead House Hotel, you'll find courtesy and charm as alluring as the surroundings; staff are friendly and genuine, and the décor is stylish but subtle, inspired by the relaxing clean lines of Scandinavian design and mixed with a sprinkling of period features. In fact, 'simple yet luxurious' may well be this charming hotel's maxim - and a great success at that! Natural fabrics lend an air of calm, while luxurious linens invite a blissful morning in bed.

If you're tempted out in time, an excellent full English breakfast awaits; if you're heading out for the afternoon, sandwiches are made to order, or you might treat yourself to a picnic lunch. After all, there's much to do in Henley-on-Thames and the surrounding area. Henley Bridge, the end of the famed Regatta Course, is a short walk from the hotel. Good walking is in abundance, as are galleries, shops and, a bit further afield, Blenheim Palace, Oxford and Hambleden, a treat for anyone who has seen its brick-and-flint facades in Hollywood films!

LOCATION
From the M4, exit for the A404 (Henley/Marlow), then the A4130 (Henley); turn right at the Little Angel pub before Henley Bridge.

335

Map p. 450, grid D4

Inn — THATCHED COTTAGE HOTEL

16 Brookley Road, Brockenhurst,
Hampshire SO42 7RR

T (UK) 0870 432 8794
T 01590 623090
F 01590 623479
thatchedcottage@bestloved.com
www.thatchedcottage.bestloved.com

OWNERS
The Matysik Family

ROOM RATES
4 Doubles	£90 - £140
1 Four-poster	£140 - £160
1 Suite	£160 - £175

Includes full breakfast and VAT

CREDIT CARDS
AMERICAN EXPRESS • MC • VI

RATINGS & AWARDS
AA ◆◆◆◆◆ ❀❀
AA Premier Collection

FACILITIES
On site: Garden
1 meeting room/max 30 people
Nearby: Golf, fishing, yachting, riding,
mountain biking

RESTRICTIONS
No facilities for disabled guests
No children under 12 years
Smoking in lounge only
Pets by arrangement

ATTRACTIONS
New Forest, Beaulieu Motor Museum,
Exbury Gardens, Isle of Wight,
Winchester, Salisbury, Lymington

NEAREST
CITY:
Southampton - 12 miles/20 mins

AIRPORT:
Heathrow - 76 miles/1 hr 30 mins

RAIL STATION:
Brockenhurst - ½ mile/5 mins

AFFILIATIONS
Independent

RESERVATIONS
National rate in UK: 0870 432 8794
Quote Best Loved

ACCESS CODES
Not applicable

A peaceful, quaint cottage for the happy few

The Matysik family has over a century's worth of knowledge and experience in the hotel industry, and this heritage is reflected in the careful transformation that has gone into turning this enchanting cottage into a boutique hotel.

Set in one of the prettiest villages in the heart of the New Forest, the hotel's modernisation for the comfort of guests has not detracted from its original country charm. The individually-decorates double bedrooms have a unique old-world warmth, each room featuring either a four-poster bed, open-hearth gas fire place or even a Turkish steam shower.

Breakfast includes six different cooked meals to choose from, and is served as late as 11 a.m so that guests can lie in that little bit longer! Later on, why not enjoy lunch or an award-winning afternoon cream tea in the peaceful garden? The cosy beamed lounge is the ideal place for an aperitif before entering the dining room, where the menus offer delights from the New Forest such as wild mushrooms and venison. All ingredients are freshly prepared in the open-to-view kitchen starring the 'chefs-on-show', where the cuisine, is presented with flair and imagination. These culinary delights have been much acclaimed by the British and international press.

LOCATION
Take exit 1 from the M27 and drive south on the A337 to Brockenhurst. Turn right onto Brookley Road just before the level crossing.

SOUTH & ISLANDS

BEST LOVED HOTELS

"This is a professional and relaxed operation - not an easy combination to achieve, but it's lovely for the punter"

PADDY BURT, THE DAILY TELEGRAPH

THE THREE LIONS

Restaurant with rooms

Stuckton, Fordingbridge,
Hampshire SP6 2HF

T (UK) 0870 432 8797
T 01425 652489
F 01425 656 144
threelions@bestloved.com
www.threelions.bestloved.com

OWNERS
Mike and Jane Womersley

ROOM RATES
Single occupancy   £65 - £75
3 Doubles/Twins   £75 - £95
2 Garden suites   £90 - £115
Includes continental breakfast and VAT

CREDIT CARDS
AMERICAN EXPRESS • MC • VI

RATINGS & AWARDS
ETC ♦♦♦♦♦ Gold Award
AA ♦♦♦♦♦ ✿✿✿
AA Premier Collection
Which? Hotel Newcomer of the Year
2002

FACILITIES
On site: Garden, licensed for
weddings, Jacuzzi/hot tub, sauna
1 meeting room/max 35 people
Nearby: Golf, river and sea fishing,
water skiing, yachting, tennis,
fitness centre, hunting and shooting,
riding, cycling

RESTRICTIONS
Limited facilities for disabled guests
Smoking in bar only
Pets by arrangement
Closed mid-January - mid-February

ATTRACTIONS
Salisbury Cathedral,
Stonehenge & Avebury,
Beaulieu Motor Museum,
Brockenhurst & Burley,
the New Forest, Exbury Gardens,
Broadlands, Poltons Park

NEAREST
CITY:
Salisbury - 14 miles/20 mins

AIRPORT:
Heathrow - 83 miles/1 hr 30 mins
Bournemouth - 16 miles/25 mins

RAIL STATION:
Salisbury - 16 miles/20 mins

AFFILIATIONS
Independent

RESERVATIONS
National rate in UK: 0870 432 8797
Quote Best Loved

ACCESS CODES
Not applicable

Cooking from the heart on the edge of the New Forest

Built in 1863 as a farmhouse in the hamlet of Stuckton on the edge of the New Forest, the Three Lions is now a destination of note for dining enthusiasts. It is personally owned and run by Mike and Jayne, who live on the premises; Mike learnt his craft over ten years in two- and three-star Michelin restaurants in France and Britain, and his personal style of cuisine is based on the best local produce available, most of it organically grown. The 180-bin wine list is compiled from personally tasted and selected wines from all over the world.

The rooms are very comfortable and quiet, and a spacious conservatory is connected to the accommodation and overlooks manicured gardens. Guests can also find a little peace in the Catalina whirlpool spa and Jacuzzi or the hotel's sauna, which are open year-round. With such relaxing facilities, the Three Lions is a place where you can come and go as you please without the formality of a hotel.

The Three Lions is ideally situated for exploring the New Forest, and the inviting sandy beaches of the South Coast or Studland's nature reserve are half an hour away. A little further afield are Salisbury, Poole, Rockbourne, Winchester and many picturesque Dorset villages, all of which you can visit in a day and still be back for dinner.

LOCATION
Half a mile east of Fordingbridge on the A338 or B3078. From the Q8 garage, follow the brown signs marked 'Three Lions'.

"You really do have a 'gem' in The Vineyard

RAYMOND BLANC

Country house   THE VINEYARD AT STOCKCROSS

Sublime food and wine in an elegantly-appointed environment

The Vineyard at Stockcross was opened in 1998 by Sir Peter Michael, founder of Classic FM radio. This restaurant with suites is a showcase for the finest Californian wines, including those from his renowned Peter Michael Winery; Director of wine Edoardo Amadi has created a Burke's Peerage of wines in a wide, innovative wine list. The Michelin-starred restaurant, under the direction of chef John Campbell, offers modern British cuisine.

The Vineyard at Stockcross was built in the 19th century as the country retreat of the lords of the manor of Stanford Dingley. On a more modern note, the purpose-built restaurant matches the original warm Bath stone, featuring full-length windows set between contemporary pillars. Suites and rooms provide an elegant, spacious and well-appointed environment and have been designed in French provincial style with both authentic French and contemporary furniture - and all of this is blissfully complemented by a notable collection of paintings and sculptures.

Fine dining and peaceful accommodation aren't the only benefits of this delightful place to stay. The Vineyard Spa is a paragon of luxury and tranquillity in which to relax or exercise - altogether an indulgence for all the senses!

LOCATION

Exit 13 on the M4 for the A34 (Newbury). At the first roundabout, exit for Hungerford (A4); at the second exit, head for Stockcross. The hotel is on the right.

Stockcross, Newbury, Berkshire RG20 8JU

T (UK) 0870 432 8807
T 01635 528770
F 01635 528398
vineyard@bestloved.com
www.vineyard.bestloved.com

OWNER
Sir Peter Michael

MANAGING DIRECTOR
Andrew McKenzie

ROOM RATES
6 Singles   £198
10 Doubles/Twins   £283
31 Suites   £350 - £487
2 Four-posters   £740
   Includes breakfast and VAT

CREDIT CARDS
AMERICAN EXPRESS • DC • MC • VI

RATINGS & AWARDS
ETC ★★★★★ Gold Award
RAC Gold Ribbon ★★★★★
Dining Award 4
AA ★★★★★ ❀❀❀❀
AA Top 200 - 2004/2005
AA Wine Award
Caterer and Hotelkeeper -
Independent Hotel of the Year 2003

FACILITIES
On site: Garden, gym, indoor pool, health & beauty, sauna, spa bath, steam room, licensed for weddings 4 meeting rooms/max 140 people
Nearby: Golf, fishing, tennis, shooting, riding

RESTRICTIONS
Limited facilities for disabled guests
No smoking in bedrooms
No pets; guide dogs only

ATTRACTIONS
Oxford, the Cotswolds, Bath, Newbury Racecourse, Highclere Castle, Windsor Castle

NEAREST
CITY:
Oxford - 29 miles/30 mins

AIRPORT:
Heathrow - 50 miles/1 hr

RAIL STATION:
Newbury - 2 miles/15 mins

AFFILIATIONS
Celebrated Hotels Collection
Relais & Châteaux

RESERVATIONS
National rate in UK: 0870 432 8807
Toll free in UK: 0800 VINEYARD
Toll free in US: 800-322-2403
or 800-735-2478
Quote Best Loved

ACCESS CODES
AMADEUS WB EWYB27
APOLLO/GALILEO WB 53771
SABRE/ABACUS WB 30971
WORLDSPAN WB GB27

SOUTH & ISLANDS

A peaceful haven in a hectic world

VISCOUNT RICHARD GIRLING, BATTERSEA

WALLETT'S COURT

Country house

Westcliffe, St Margaret's-At-Cliffe,
Dover, Kent CT15 6EW

T (UK) 0870 432 8809
T 01304 852424
F 01304 853430
walletts@bestloved.com
www.walletts.bestloved.com

OWNERS
Christopher and Leonora Oakley

GENERAL MANAGER
Gavin Oakley

ROOM RATES
Single occupancy   £99 - £119
12 Doubles/Twins   £119
2 Four-posters   £159
2 Suites   £159
        Includes VAT

CREDIT CARDS
AMERICAN EXPRESS • DC • JCB • MC • VI

RATINGS & AWARDS
ETC ★★★ Silver Award
RAC White Ribbon ★★★
        Dining Award 3
AA ★★★ ⊛⊛ 75%

FACILITIES
On site: Garden, gym, heli-pad,
croquet, tennis, indoor pool,
health & beauty, sauna, steam room,
Jacuzzi, golf practice area
3 meeting rooms/max 80 people
Nearby: Golf, fishing, shooting,
yachting, windsurfing, surfing

RESTRICTIONS
Limited facilities for disabled guests
No pets
Closed 24 - 27 Dec.

ATTRACTIONS
Canterbury Cathedral, Dover Castle,
Leeds Castle, Tenterden,
Sissinghurst Gardens, Eurostar to Paris

NEAREST
CITY:
Canterbury - 15 miles/20 mins

AIRPORT:
Gatwick - 60 miles/1 hr

RAIL STATION:
Dover Priory - 3 miles/10 mins

FERRY PORT:
Dover - 3 miles/10 mins

AFFILIATIONS
Independent

RESERVATIONS
National rate in UK: 0870 432 8809
Quote Best Loved

ACCESS CODES
Not applicable

SOUTH & ISLANDS

A glorious retreat near Canterbury in the heart of White Cliffs country

Wallett's Court is owned and run by the Oakley family, who first discovered the building, near derelict, on a summer's day in 1975. It was listed as the Manor of Westcliffe in the Domesday Book, and its history embraces such luminaries as Bishop Odo of Bayeux, Queen Eleanor of Castille, historian Edward Gibbon, Admiral Lord Aylmer and Prime Minister William Pitt.

Today, Wallet's Court it is a family home and country house hotel with 16 large, comfortable bedrooms. The style is homely; you can settle in the old leather sofa by a blazing fire, hear the grandfather clock ticking or relax in the conservatory.

The indoor pool, sauna, steam and fitness rooms, as well as the luxurious health spa housed within a Kentish barn, add an attractive dimension to the hotel - as, indeed, does its location. close to Canterbury and on the doorstep of the Continent with the ever-expanding Cruise Terminal only four miles away.

The surrounding area is designated as being of Outstanding Natural Beauty. A mile away is St Margaret's Bay, and on a clear day you can see France. History enthusiasts can visit Leeds Castle, Canterbury Cathedral and the secret wartime tunnels of Dover Castle.

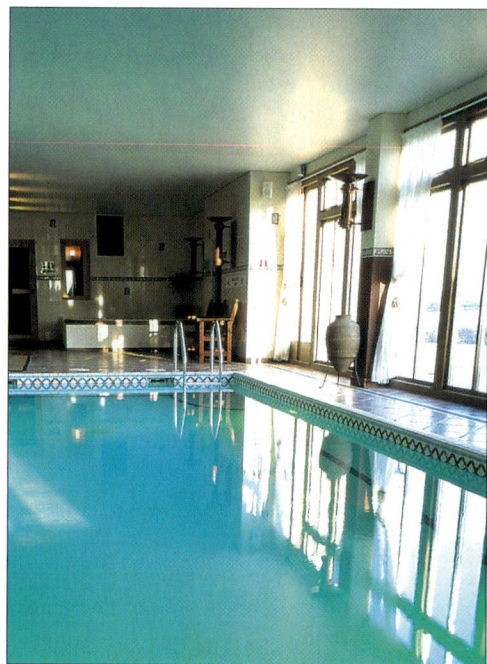

LOCATION

From the M2/A2 or M20/A20, exit for the A258 (Deal). After Swingate Inn, turn right to Westcliffe, St Margaret's; the hotel is one mile along on the right.

THE PERFECT COMPANION

LONDON

AN ITALIAN SHOWPLACE
Baglioni Hotel London, Kensington

A SELF-CONTAINED VILLAGE
Dolphin Square Hotel, Westminster

LUXURIOUS APARTMENTS
Beaufort House Apartments, Knightsbridge

REPRESENTING *the best of* LONDON

A SLOANE SQUARE TOWNHOUSE
Draycott Hotel, Chelsea

Best Loved Hotels offer the cream of the crop across Great Britain and Ireland - from stately palaces to welcoming inns - each the best of its kind within its locality and price range.

Whichever place you choose as your own place to stay, you'll find every hotel offers character, charm and the best delights and attractions of its region.

And each, in its own special way, is best-loved by someone who's been there.

A LITTLE VENICE GEM
The Colonnade Town House, Little Venice

A SHOPPER'S FAVOURITE
The Leonard, near Oxford Street

A DISCREET LUXURY TOWNHOUSE
Parkes, Knightsbridge

A HOME IN THE FINANCIAL DISTRICT
Threadneedles, Threadneedle Street

AN IDEAL ESCAPE:
London

A WEEKEND REALLY ISN'T ENOUGH to explore all that London has to offer: top-class shopping, incomparable theatre and entertainment and cultural activities to interest all tastes and all ages. Make the most of your London break by sampling a bit of all three.

Day One

If you're a newcomer to the City, you may want to consider a guided tour of London to get in all the major sights - but if you're up for the adventure, nothing beats dodging the beaten path and seeing the famous sights at your own leisure, whether on foot, by taxi or from the top deck of a red bus.

If you've got youngsters in tow, or you're simply curious yourself, an afternoon tour of the **BBC Television Centre** offers an interesting behind-the-scenes look at what goes on behind the camera. Planning in advance can also net you tickets to the **taping of your own favourite television or radio show** - check the BBC's Web site (see right) to see what's on offer during your visit.

If live theatre or music is more to your liking, there are virtually unlimited possibilities to choose from - but nothing beats the experience of taking in a **West End show** in one of the area's more than 40 classic picture-frame theatres. Arrive early enough for dinner (but be sure to book in advance or you may be disappointed!) and allow a bit of time to take in the atmosphere; you won't regret it.

Day Two

You've been inspired by television and theatre - now it's time for some serious retail therapy. And with something on offer for all tastes and all budgets, it's best to sample some of everything!

First on the list are the famous **Harrods and Harvey Nichols**, as well as their **Knightsbridge** friends in between. Harrods, the grande dame of London shopping, is a must if only to visit the food halls, which haven't lost a bit of their Victorian splendour.

Saville Row and Jermyn Street are, of course, legendary, and the legend still lives on, from handmade Jermyn Street shirts (Turnbull & Asser are Prince Charles' choice) and Saville Row suits to brilliant leather goods and Floris, London's first parfumerie.

The glittering lights of West End theatres

Browsing in Portobello Market

London's markets are an experience worth having, and **Portobello Road** is the classic example. Take your time and walk the length of the market, from the jewellery, silver and antiques at the top to the clothing and more traditional market stalls at the end - and drink in some **Notting Hill** atmosphere at the same time. Film buffs may also want to try **Borough Market** (seen in Bridget Jones' Diary and Richard III), complete with classic Victorian architecture. Better still, pick up the ingredients while you're there for a prime picnic in nearby **Greenwich Park**.

Drink in some ATMOSPHERE *at a London market*

End your day with a 'flight' on the **London Eye**, which hasn't dimmed at all since its unveiling as one of London's millennium attractions. If you're lucky enough to arrive just before sunset (a 'flight' takes roughly 45 minutes) you'll be treated to a view to remember.

Trafalgar Square beckons before a visit to the National Gallery

Day Three

Make a leisurely end to your weekend by chilling out with some culture at a few choice London museums and galleries. Kensington's museum district alone could provide a weekend's interest, particularly if you're bringing along the kids, but with a little bit of walking - and a long pause for lunch! - it's certainly worth making the rounds.

Begin at South Kensington tube for a stop at the **Victoria & Albert Museum**, where all sorts of fascinating design artefacts await, from beautifully reconstructed period rooms and fascinating fashion retrospectives to silver ranging from cutlery to swords. The **Natural History and Science museums** are just opposite, and even if you don't have hours of time to spend inside, both are worth a brief look round - especially as both (as with many larger London museums and galleries) offer free admission. The dinosaurs alone are worth a visit, though be prepared for queues! The young at heart will also find delight in **Pollock's Toy Museum**, a fun stop along the way between Tottenham Court Road and Goodge Street, and the **Museum of Childhood** at Bethnal Green.

Art is everywhere in London, whether your tastes run from modern sparkle to pre-Raphaelite splendour, and a visit to London's galleries could eat up an entire weekend. If you're short of time, two of our favourites are the **Tate Modern** - the building, a converted power station on the South Bank, is itself nearly a work of art, and their changing roster of exhibitions never fails to challenge and delight - and the **National Portrait Gallery** (right next door to the **National Gallery**); with faces from kings to queens to rock stars, you'll never look at a famous face in quite the same way.

Classic menswear at Turnbull & Asser

A TASTE OF THE BEST

London

WITH SO MUCH to see and do in the capital, you're bound to work up an appetite - and there is truly something for all tastes in London, whether you're craving modern British fare or something a bit more exotic. Have a look, and be inspired.

THE CAPITAL ✿✿✿✿

This opulent townhouse serves first-class cuisine in a refreshingly elegant setting. As the only London restaurant within a hotel to have earned two Michelin stars, the Capital boasts Head Chef Eric Chavot, whose creative flair has been highly acclaimed by critics. His imaginative dishes - such as pan-fried langoustines and slow cooked pork belly with sweet spice, followed by pot-roasted lobster with tagliatelle pasta and saffron dressing - are accompanied by wine list that in itself makes good reading, including Levin vintages from the owner's own vineyard. Desserts are truly irresistible – the iced coffee parfait with hot chocolate fondant is recommended with the Australian Yalumba Antique Tawny wine, or try the confit apple with spiced bread and crème brulee with the 1983 Sauternes, Chateau La Tour Blanche, Bordeaux. A degustation menu for both fare and wine is also available if you just can't resist a little taste of everything.

Capital indulgence in the form of Eric Chavot's inspired cuisine

DOLPHIN SQUARE HOTEL ✿✿

Dolphin Square's exciting Allium Restaurant serves an inspired range contemporary European cuisine created by Chef Patron Anton Edelmann. The restaurant has just celebrated an acclaimed first year, and seems to be continuing from strength to strength! Tempting dishes on the menu include seared bream with crushed potatoes, tomato and herbs, as well as mouth-watering desserts such as a very tasty hazelnut parfait with passion fruit coulis. If you're planning a longer stay in the Square, there is also the less formal Brasserie, where innovative fare is accompanied by a great cellar.

Anton Edelmann of Dolphin Square

THE GORING ✿✿

This esteemed London residence's highly acclaimed restaurant serves excellent English fare with a continental twist, and the wine list is said to be one of the best in London. Their excellent seasonally-changing menu might include during your visit such dishes as carpaccio of Balmoral venison with beetroot, Beenleigh blue cheese and a black pepper cream, or poached fillet of smoked haddock with a poached egg and horseradish sauce. Private dining is also available in their elegant drawing room if you're looking to plan your next get-together.

THE MONTCALM ✿✿

Just two minutes from Marble Arch and Oxford Street, this delightful Georgian townhouse is home to the elegant Crescent Restaurant, a light and airy atmosphere in which to enjoy inspired modern British cuisine. With a belief that food should be all about taste rather than complex presentation, the Crescent concentrates on simple, flavoursome cuisine and the results are simply superb. Begin with a starter of grilled salmon with scallop on a bed of braised fennel with saffron sauce, followed by pan-fried calves liver and kidneys with garlic mashed potatoes and mustard sauce. And for a different touch, why not try their delightful, healthy Japanese breakfast, also served in the Crescent Restaurant? Private dining rooms are also available.

THREADNEEDLES

Located in the heart of London's financial district, Threadneedles' Bonds Restaurant and Bar is a chic and refreshing environment in which to enjoy imaginative modern French cuisine created by Executive Chef Barry Tonks. His vast experience in London restaurants has earned him a Michelin star, and with such delights on Bonds' menu as roast wild duck with confit cabbage and sour cherries, followed by warm Tuscan chocolate fondant with almond milk emulsion, it's no wonder that since starting at Bonds, Barry has received plenty of rave reviews!

Threadneedles' dining has received RAVE REVIEWS *in the financial district*

A TASTE OF THE REGION

Looking for even more to tempt your palate? There are a wealth of fantastic places to dine in London, all within the covers of this book! Have a browse to whet your appetite, or jump to some of our own favourites:

BAGLIONI HOTEL LONDON

The Brunello Restaurant at this deliciously stylish Italian retreat offers a taste of Italy that can't be matched, including a wine list of some 400 bins! A perfect complement to a sparkling city gem with a notable day spa.

COLONNADE TOWN HOUSE

This Little Venice gem's new tapas restaurant is a delightfully atmospheric hideout for the evening - and better still, when your night's over, the Colonnade's understated luxury awaits.

FLEMINGS MAYFAIR

A delicious breakfast buffet is matched by traditional elegance in this Mayfair hotel's fine restaurant. Wind down after a hectic day with their table d'hôte menu - and perhaps be renewed for a night on the town!

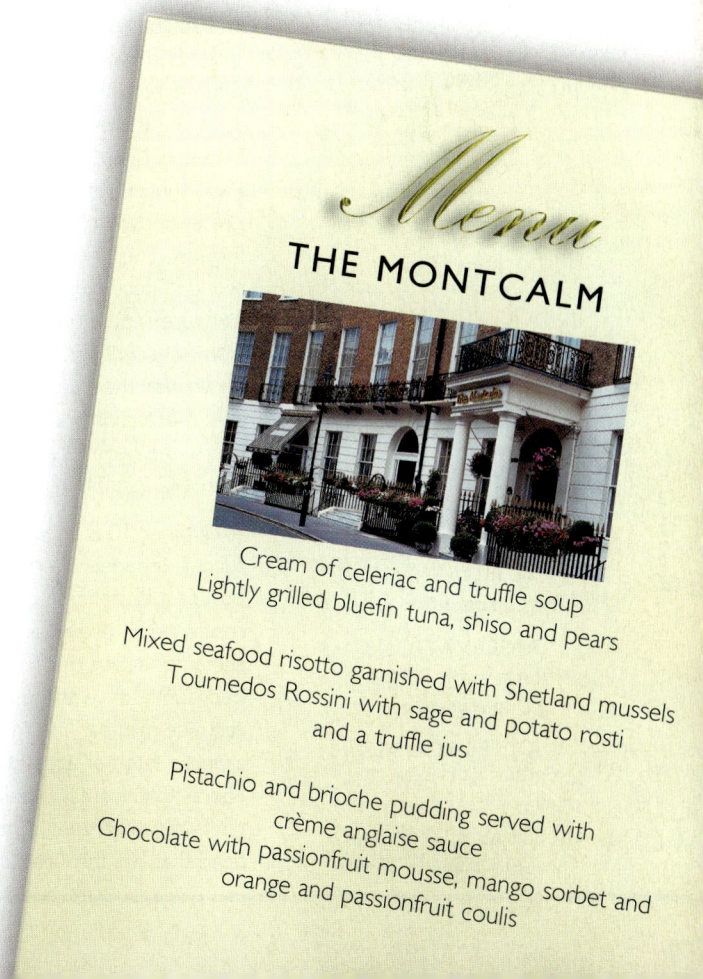

Menu

THE MONTCALM

Cream of celeriac and truffle soup
Lightly grilled bluefin tuna, shiso and pears

Mixed seafood risotto garnished with Shetland mussels
Tournedos Rossini with sage and potato rosti and a truffle jus

Pistachio and brioche pudding served with crème anglaise sauce
Chocolate with passionfruit mousse, mango sorbet and orange and passionfruit coulis

10 MANCHESTER STREET

Townhouse

10 Manchester Street,
London W1U 4DG

T (UK) 0870 432 8513
T 020 7486 6669
F 020 7224 0348
10manchester@bestloved.com
www.10manchester.bestloved.com

GENERAL MANAGER
Neville Isaac

ROOM RATES
Single occupancy   £120
37 Doubles/Twins   £150
9 Suites   £195
Includes continental breakfast and VAT

CREDIT CARDS
AMERICAN EXPRESS • MC • VI

RATINGS & AWARDS
ETC ♦♦♦♦

FACILITIES
Nearby: Health club

RESTRICTIONS
No facilities for disabled guests
No pets

ATTRACTIONS
Wallace Collection,
Madame Tussauds,
London Planetarium,
Theatreland, Bond Street,
Oxford Street

NEAREST
CITY:
London

AIRPORT:
Heathrow - 15 miles/50 mins
Gatwick - 30 miles/1 hr 15 mins

RAIL STATION:
Paddington - ½ mile/10 mins
Baker Street Underground

AFFILIATIONS
The European Connection

RESERVATIONS
National rate in UK: 0870 432 8513
Quote Best Loved

ACCESS CODES
AMADEUS UI LONTEN
APOLLO/GALILEO UI 31791
SABRE/ABACUS UI 21060
WORLDSPAN UI 13400

LONDON

Location, location, location! The best of London on your doorstep

Manchester Street is in the heart of London's West End, with everything the 'big smoke' has to offer right on its doorstep. Tourist attractions such as Madame Tussauds and the London Planetarium are a short walk away, as is Regent's Park, the emerald jewel in the capital's crown. Lesser-known places of interest in the vicinity include The Wallace Collection, one of the world's finest exhibitions of 18th-century French furniture. You won't need to catch a cab home from Oxford Street, unless you're too laden down with the many bargains on offer - although the more upmarket shopper will no doubt prefer the luxury fashion houses of Bond Street and St Christopher's Place.

Number 10 is a 'boutique townhouse', and as such, is the ideal alternative to a hotel. Purpose-built as a hostelrie in 1919, this elegant red-brick residence provides stylish, high-quality accommodation that includes nine suites and 37 bedrooms, all with satellite television and the requisite mini-bar and trouser press. There is also a public Internet access terminal and a lift to all floors. Continental breakfast is included in the tariff, and there are a good number of special deals that run throughout the year.

LOCATION
Five minutes' walk from Baker Street Underground station.

> " The entire staff was gracious, and the facilities were impeccable "
>
> KIM & MARK RILEY, ENGLEWOOD, NEW JERSEY USA

Townhouse

THE ACADEMY TOWN HOUSE

Top marks and top value in the bookish quarter of central London

Mention Bloomsbury, and the mind conjures up names like Virginia Woolf, Lytton Strachey and J M Keynes - English writers, aesthetes and philosophers whose contributions to 20th-century culture are widely acknowledged today. The presence of the British Museum lends the area the hush of a library, but the bright lights of Covent Garden and the West End are within a few minutes' walk.

The Academy, The Bloomsbury Town House, occupies five Georgian terraced houses in the heart of this secluded yet accessible corner of London. At the rear, there are private gardens where guests can take tea or drinks in summer and a conservatory for cooler days. There is a choice of cosy lounges and an informal basement restaurant. Luxurious bedrooms benefit from gleaming bathrooms, pure linen bedsheets, carefully-chosen ornaments and in-room Internet access. Each room is completely different, so regular guests develop particular favourites.

The Academy also has one very special trick up its sleeve: it can devote one whole house, with eight guest bedrooms and exclusive use of a garden and the library, for a private party. It is the only hotel in London to offer this unique feature, perfect for a corporate 'do' or a wedding party.

LOCATION

In Bloomsbury, on Gower Street equidistant from Tottenham Court Road and Goodge Street Underground stations.

21 Gower Street,
London WC1E 6HG

T (UK) 0870 432 8515
T 020 7631 4115
F 020 7636 3442
academy@bestloved.com
www.academy.bestloved.com

GENERAL MANAGER
Yolanda Garcia Morris

ROOM RATES
12 Singles   £160 - £168
26 Doubles/Twins   £187 - £222
11 Studio Suites   £252 - £265
Includes full breakfast, service and VAT

CREDIT CARDS
AMERICAN EXPRESS • DC • JCB • MC • VI

RATINGS & AWARDS
Independent

FACILITIES
On site: Courtyard gardens
1 meeting room/max 14 people
Nearby: Leisure centre

RESTRICTIONS
Limited facilities for disabled guests
Smoking in designated areas only
No pets

ATTRACTIONS
British Museum, Theatreland,
Covent Garden, National Gallery,
Bloomsbury squares

NEAREST
CITY:
London

AIRPORT:
Heathrow - 15 miles/45 mins
Gatwick - 40 miles/1 hr

RAIL STATION:
Euston - ½ mile/5 mins
Goodge Street Underground

AFFILIATIONS
Preston's Global Hotels
Summit Hotels & Resorts
The Eton Group

RESERVATIONS
National rate in UK: 0870 432 8515
Toll free in US: 800-544-9993
or 800-457-4000
Quote Best Loved

ACCESS CODES
AMADEUS XL LONACA
APOLLO/GALILEO XL 62068
SABRE/ABACUS XL 20496
WORLDSPAN XL 41062

LONDON

> **The Baglioni is the perfect illustration of Italian style, with its unique décor and great food**
>
> JACQUETTA WHEELER, MODEL

BAGLIONI HOTEL LONDON

City hotel

60 Hyde Park Gate,
Kensington,
London SW7 5BB

T (UK) 0870 432 8524
T 020 7368 5700
F 020 7368 5701
baglioni@bestloved.com
www.baglioni.bestloved.com

GENERAL MANAGER
Luca Virgilio

ROOM RATES
10 Superior Rooms	£300
6 Deluxe Rooms	£325
17 Junior Suites	£500
28 Superior Suites	£800
2 Executive Suites	£1,500
2 Presidential Suites	£1,900

Excludes VAT

CREDIT CARDS
AMERICAN EXPRESS • DC • JCB • MC • VI

RATINGS & AWARDS
Awards Pending

FACILITIES
On site: Gym, health & beauty,
licensed for weddings
1 meeting room/max 80 people
Nearby: tennis, golf, riding

RESTRICTIONS
Limited facilities for disabled guests
Smoking in some rooms only
No pets; guide dogs only

ATTRACTIONS
Kensington Palace and Gardens,
Hyde Park, Knightsbridge shopping,
Victoria & Albert Museum,
Natural History Museum,
Science Museum, Royal Albert Hall

NEAREST
CITY:
London

AIRPORT:
London City - 10 miles/30 mins
Heathrow - 15 miles/40 mins

RAIL STATION:
Victoria - 1 ½ miles/5 mins
South Kensington Underground

AFFILIATIONS
Baglioni Group

RESERVATIONS
National rate in UK: 0870 432 8524
Quote Best Loved

ACCESS CODES
AMADEUS GW LON017
APOLLO/GALILEO GW 3551
SABRE/ABACUS GW 3551
WORLDSPAN GW 64335

LONDON

A taste of Italian elegance at the pulse of London

The Baglioni Hotel's motto - 'uno stile di vita' - can be applied to every aspect of this extraordinarily stylish luxury hotel in the heart of Kensington; in fact, there is nothing about the Baglioni that does not breathe decadence and a certain stylish flair! From the tasteful yet sophisticated individually-designed bedrooms (contemporary, yet warm and inviting, down to the views of Kensington Palace and gardens) to the buzzing atmosphere in Sixty, a members-only retreat open to hotel residents and a select guest list.

The Baglioni's Brunello Restaurant offers contemporary Italian cuisine with ingredients brought in fresh from Italy to offer a truly authentic feel. A wine list of some 400 vintages makes the dining experience an even more memorable one - and, if you can't bear to leave your room, there is an Illy coffee machine, along with fresh flowers (changed daily), in each. For further pampering, the hotel's Caroli Health Club is an inspired day spa featuring products sourced from Italian organic farms.

As for area attractions, the best of London awaits within a few paces, whether you're seeking top-class shopping in Knightsbridge, cultural attractions in Kensington's museum district or any number of the City's offerings.

LOCATION
In the heart of Kensington at Hyde Park Gate.

City hotel

BASIL STREET HOTEL

Basil Street, Knightsbridge,
London SW3 1AH

T (UK) 0870 432 8528
T 020 7581 3311
F 020 7581 3693
basil@bestloved.com
www.basil.bestloved.com

GENERAL MANAGER
Charles Lagares

ROOM RATES

34 Singles	£117
49 Doubles/Twins	£168
5 Family Rooms	£233
Excludes VAT	

CREDIT CARDS
AMERICAN EXPRESS • JCB • MC • VI

RATINGS & AWARDS
RAC ★★★
AA ★★★ 73%

FACILITIES
On site: Restaurant, business centre,
The Parrot Club (for women)
3 meeting rooms/max 200 people

RESTRICTIONS
Limited facilities for disabled guests
No pets in public rooms

ATTRACTIONS
Harrods, Victoria & Albert Museum,
Royal Academy of Art,
Houses of Parliament, Theatreland,
Bond Street, Tower of London,
Buckingham Palace

NEAREST
CITY:
London

AIRPORT:
Heathrow - 18 miles/45 mins
Gatwick - 30 miles/1 hr 15 mins

RAIL STATION:
Victoria - 1 1/4 miles/15 mins
Knightsbridge Underground

AFFILIATIONS
Preston's Global Hotels
Grand Heritage Hotels

RESERVATIONS
National rate in UK: 0870 432 8528
Toll free in US: 800-544-9993
or 800-448-8355 or 888-93-GRAND
Quote Best Loved

ACCESS CODES
AMADEUS UI LONBAS
APOLLO/GALILEO UI 18513
SABRE/ABACUS UI 264
WORLDSPAN UI 3896

A peaceful home from home in the bustle of the City

The Basil is an island of hospitality in an increasingly brusque, modern life, and that is why their guests come back again and again. Many of this lovely hotel's returning guests have said that The Basil is just like coming home. Tradition is respected, nothing is contrived and there is warmth and friendliness in the air. The interior is full of English and Oriental antiques, and at every turn there is something to delight the eye.

Each of the 88 comfortable bedrooms is different in shape and décor, and regular visitors are given their favourites whenever possible. Fully-furnished rooms are also available for private parties; in short, The Basil is large enough to contain all the amenities expected in a cosmopolitan hotel, yet not too large to become impersonal.

General Manager Charles Lagares and his colleagues carry on the traditions that have become synonymous with The Basil. They will do their utmost to ensure that your visit is an enjoyable one. Few world-class hotels in a city centre are so perfectly situated for both business and pleasure.

LOCATION

In Knightsbridge a few steps away from Harrods, Harvey Nichols and Knightsbridge Underground station.

LONDON

Map p. 452, grid E6

THE BEAUFORT

Townhouse

33 Beaufort Gardens,
Knightsbridge,
London SW3 1PP

T (UK) 0870 432 8531
T 020 7584 5252
F 020 7589 2834
beaufort@bestloved.com
www.beaufort.bestloved.com

OWNER
Ahmed Jajbhay

GENERAL MANAGER
Anna Bambrook

ROOM RATES
3 Singles	£182
10 Doubles	£229
9 Deluxe Doubles/Twins	£306
7 Junior Suites	£364

Includes afternoon tea, all drinks (including champagne) and VAT; breakfast £10 surcharge

CREDIT CARDS
AMERICAN EXPRESS • DC • JCB • MC • VI

RATINGS & AWARDS
AA ★★★★
AA Town House
Courvoisier's Book of the Best
Zagat - Highest Rated Hotel in
London for Service (26/30)

FACILITIES
1 meeting room/max 6 people
Nearby: Health club & pool, riding

RESTRICTIONS
No facilities for disabled guests
No pets

ATTRACTIONS
Harrods, Victoria & Albert Museum,
Buckingham Palace, Theatreland,
Royal Academy of Art

NEAREST
CITY:
London

AIRPORT:
Heathrow - 14 miles/45 mins
Gatwick - 30 miles/1 hr 15 mins

RAIL STATION:
Victoria - 1 mile/5 mins
Knightsbridge Underground

AFFILIATIONS
Independent

RESERVATIONS
National rate in UK: 0870 432 8531
Toll free fax in US: 800-548-7764
Quote Best Loved

ACCESS CODES
AMADEUS UI LONBEA
APOLLO/GALILEO UI 16376
SABRE/ABACUS UI 31342
WORLDSPAN UI 42508

LONDON

Great value, service and much more await you in elegant Knightsbridge

Step back to a time when customer service really mattered at The Beaufort, a perfectly-formed gem of 29 bedrooms (large enough for business, small enough for privacy) where the staff goes that extra mile to ensure guests have a truly memorable stay. This lovely townhouse exudes the calm and charm of an English country house, but at a fashionable London address!

Home to the world's largest collection of English watercolours, paintings are lovingly displayed throughout the hotel, complemented by soft, calm colours, elegant maple furniture and an understated sense of comfort and luxury. Rooms boast air conditioning, CD players and radios, state-of-the-art television with free Internet, e-mail and movies, a hospitality tray and fresh flowers and magazines, plus twice-daily maid service. Almost as large as the bedrooms, the beautiful marble bathrooms have power showers, splendid baths and, of course, plenty of fluffy towels.

Complimentary offerings for guests to enjoy include drinks from the Sitting Room bar and a truly scrumptious cream tea with homemade scones and clotted cream. In short, everything is designed to make guests feel as relaxed and spoilt as possible - reflected in the extraordinary worldwide reputation of this small hotel, its imaginative owners and personable staff.

LOCATION
Quietly situated in the heart of Knightsbridge.

Apartments — BEAUFORT HOUSE APARTMENTS

Fully-serviced traditional apartments just around the corner from Harrods

Situated in Beaufort Gardens, a quiet, tree-lined Regency cul-de-sac in the heart of Knightsbridge and 250 yards from Harrods, Beaufort House is an exclusive establishment comprising 21 self-contained, fully serviced luxury apartments. All the comforts of a first-class hotel are combined with privacy, discretion and the relaxed atmosphere of home.

Accommodation ranges in size from intimate one-bedroomed to spacious four-bedroomed apartments. Each apartment has been decorated in a traditional style to a standard that is rigorously maintained; all have telephones with voice mail, personal safes, satellite television, CD players, videos, DVD players and high-speed Internet access. A number of the apartments also feature private balconies or patios - a definite luxury in the centre of London! All the kitchens are fully equipped with everything guests will need for their stay, together with a daily maid service. Full laundry and dry-cleaning services are also available.

For your extra security, a concierge is on duty 24 hours a day, from whom taxis, theatre tickets, restaurant reservations and other services are available. Complimentary membership to Aquilla's Health Club is also offered to all guests for the duration of their stay.

LOCATION
Beaufort Gardens is 250 yards from Harrods off Brompton Road.

---

45 Beaufort Gardens,
Knightsbridge, London SW3 1PN

T (UK) 0870 432 8532
T 020 7584 2600
F 020 7584 6532
beauforthouse@bestloved.com
www.beauforthouse.bestloved.com

GENERAL MANAGER
Bettina Hoff

ROOM RATES
9 One-Bedroom Apts   £241 - £364
2 Two-Bedroom Apts   £423 - £523
9 Three-Bedroom Apts £535 - £705
1 Four-Bedroom Apt   £705 - £799
Includes daily maid service,
24-hour concierge and VAT

CREDIT CARDS
AMERICAN EXPRESS • DC • MC • VI

RATINGS & AWARDS
ETC ★★★★★ Serviced Apartments

FACILITIES
On site: Laundry facility
Nearby: Health & fitness club

RESTRICTIONS
No facilities for disabled guests
No pets

ATTRACTIONS
Hyde Park, Harrods,
Buckingham Palace,
West End theatre,
Science Museum,
Apsley House

NEAREST
CITY:
London

AIRPORT:
Heathrow - 15 miles/45 mins
Gatwick - 30 miles/1 hr 15 mins

RAIL STATION:
Victoria - 1 mile/5 mins
Knightsbridge Underground

AFFILIATIONS
Celebrated Hotels Collection

RESERVATIONS
National rate in UK: 0870 432 8532
Toll free in US: 800-322-2403
Quote Best Loved

ACCESS CODES
Not applicable

LONDON

> A faultlessly assured, elegant, thoughtful, poignant, intelligent, top-of-the-range, exceedingly rare handmade dinner
>
> A A GILL, RESTAURANT CRITIC

THE CAPITAL

City hotel

Basil Street, Knightsbridge,
London SW3 1AT

T (UK) 0870 432 8554
T 020 7589 5171
F 020 7225 0011
capital@bestloved.com
www.capital.bestloved.com

OWNER
David Levin

GENERAL MANAGER
Henrik Muehle

ROOM RATES
12 Singles	£223
22 Doubles/Twins	£288
6 Deluxe Doubles	£370
8 Junior Suites	£441
Includes VAT	

CREDIT CARDS
AMERICAN EXPRESS • DC • JCB • MC • VI

RATINGS & AWARDS
RAC Blue Ribbon ★★★★
Dining Award 5
AA ★★★★★ ✿✿✿ Town House
AA Top 200 - 2004/2005
LTB Hotel of the Year 2003
Restaurateurs Restaurant Awards -
Hotel Restaurant of the Year 2004

FACILITIES
On site: 2 meeting rooms/max 35 people
Nearby: Health club

RESTRICTIONS
Limited facilities for disabled guests
Pets by arrangement

ATTRACTIONS
Buckingham Palace,
Royal Academy of Art,
Victoria & Albert Museum,
Harrods, Harvey Nichols,
Sloane Street, Theatreland

NEAREST
CITY:
London

AIRPORT:
Heathrow - 18 miles/45 mins
London City - 10 miles/35 minutes

RAIL STATION:
Victoria - ¼ mile/15 mins
Knightsbridge Underground

AFFILIATIONS
Celebrated Hotels Collection
Small Luxury Hotels
Great Hotels of the World

RESERVATIONS
National rate in UK: 0870 432 8554
Toll free in the US: 800-322-2403
or 800-525-4800
Quote Best Loved

ACCESS CODES
AMADEUS LX LON800
APOLLO/GALILEO LX 01074
SABRE/ABACUS LX 45738
WORLDSPAN LX 00800

LONDON

Matured excellence in an exceptionally-decorated central London setting

'It takes a long time to bring excellence to maturity', so the maxim goes - but this cannot be true of The Capital. In just 33 years David Levin and family have achieved absolute perfection in this elegantly traditional 'grand' hotel that more closely resembles a fine private residence.

Here at The Capital everything is exceptional. The interiors are the work of some of Britain's most prominent designers; the antique furnishings have been hand-selected by the Levin family themselves, and their private art collection adorns the walls; all a testament to the attention to detail and personal service that has become standard. The bedrooms boast Egyptian cotton sheets, handmade mattresses and luxurious, spacious marble bathrooms.

The restaurant at The Capital, recently re-designed with a suave yet understated look inspired by the 1940s, is widely celebrated in its own right. As the possessor of two Michelin stars, no further description of the hotel's food is required; however, an interesting inclusion on the wine list is the Levin Wine, from the family's own vineyard in the Loire.

Finally, the hotel's location is superb for accessing the best of London, and Head Concierge Clive Smith will ensure that you do. Whether you're planning on residing or dining, book well in advance.

LOCATION
20 yards from Harrods and Knightsbridge Underground.

Townhouse — THE COLONNADE TOWN HOUSE

2 Warrington Crescent,
London W9 1ER

T (UK) 0870 432 8567
T 020 7286 1052
F 020 7286 1057
colonnade@bestloved.com
www.colonnade.bestloved.com

GENERAL MANAGER
Katherine Moore

ROOM RATES
6 Singles	£148
10 Doubles	£173
18 Deluxe Doubles/Twins	£210
8 Suites	£270 - £289

Includes service and VAT

CREDIT CARDS
AMERICAN EXPRESS • DC • JCB • MC • VI

RATINGS & AWARDS
ETC ★★★★ Silver Award
London Tourist Board Hotel of
the Year 2003

FACILITIES
On site: Terrace
Nearby: Golf, tennis, riding, squash

RESTRICTIONS
Limited facilities for disabled guests
Pets by arrangement

ATTRACTIONS
Little Venice, Regents Park,
Camden Market,
Lords Cricket Ground,
Portobello Road, London Zoo,
Madame Tussauds

NEAREST
CITY:
London

AIRPORT:
Heathrow - 15 miles/25 mins

RAIL STATION:
Paddington - 1 mile/5 mins
Warwick Avenue Underground

AFFILIATIONS
Celebrated Hotels Collection
Summit Hotels & Resorts
The Eton Group

RESERVATIONS
National rate in UK: 0870 432 8567
Toll free in US: 800-322-2403
or 800-457-4000
Quote Best Loved

ACCESS CODES
AMADEUS XL LONMCO
APOLLO/GALILEO XL 82381
SABRE/ABACUS XL 41050
WORLDSPAN XL 40747

LONDON

Indulgent luxury in leafy Little Venice - relaxed, convenient and a good value

Contrary to expectations, five-star luxury does not have to be contained to the likes of Mayfair - and The Colonnade, The Little Venice Town House, is the exception that proves the rule. It stands amongst the leafy gardens of Little Venice within easy reach of Piccadilly and Heathrow airport (25 minutes), yet it competes room-for-room on equal terms with the highest standards you will find anywhere in central London.

The Colonnade is the result of a conversion of an elegant Victorian mansion frequented by Sigmund Freud and noted as the birthplace of Alan Turing, breaker of the Enigma Code in World War II. The furnishings are lavish, the fabrics sumptuous and the objets d'art genuinely antique. There are only 43 bedrooms - some with four-poster beds and even a private terrace - and all of them have the latest e-facilities.

Underneath The Colonnade lies the e bar, a modern cocktail lounge serving authentic Spanish tapas. A series of unique 'Signature Cocktails' has been created especially for the bar, and patrons are invited to relax on comfortable sofas whilst dining and drinking.

LOCATION

50 yards from Warwick Avenue Underground station with direct trains to central London. Five minutes from Paddington and the Heathrow Express; 12 minutes from Oxford Circus.

THE CRANLEY ON BINA GARDENS | Townhouse

10-12 Bina Gardens,
South Kensington,
London SW5 0LA

T (UK) 0870 432 8580
T 020 7373 0123
F 020 7373 9497
cranley@bestloved.com
www.cranley.bestloved.com

FRONT OFFICE MANAGER
Lory Caprioli

ROOM RATES
4 Singles	£182
26 Doubles/Twins	£212 - £223
8 Four-posters	£259
1 Penthouse Suite	£355

Includes afternoon tea, champagne, service and VAT

CREDIT CARDS
AMERICAN EXPRESS • DC • JCB • MC • VI

RATINGS & AWARDS
AA ★★★★ 72% Town House

FACILITIES
On site: Air conditioning, honesty bar, patio, room service, broadband
Nearby: Use of local health club, pool

RESTRICTIONS
No facilities for disabled guests
No pets

ATTRACTIONS
Harrods, museums of South Kensington, King's Road, London Eye, Royal Albert Hall, Buckingham Palace, Kensington Gardens, Westminster, House of Commons, Earl's Court Exhibition & Conference Centre

NEAREST
CITY:
London

AIRPORT:
Heathrow - 15 miles/40 mins

RAIL STATION:
Victoria - 3 miles/15 mins
Gloucester Road Underground

AFFILIATIONS
Argyll Townhouse Hotels
Grand Heritage Hotels

RESERVATIONS
National rate in UK: 0870 432 8580
Toll free in US: 800-98-GRAND
or 888-989-1768
Quote Best Loved

ACCESS CODES
AMADEUS UI LONCRA
APOLLO/GALILEO UI 61263
SABRE/ABACUS UI 32652
WORLDSPAN UI 21563

LONDON

Your relaxed, luxurious home in Royal Kensington and Chelsea

Most first-time visitors do a double take and recheck the address when they arrive outside The Cranley. It looks so quiet, so private, blending seamlessly into one of London's smartest residential neighbourhoods. However, closer inspection reveals the discreet gold plaque confirming that these three elegant mansion houses are indeed a hotel.

Another captivating first impression is created by the bold Prussian blue lounge, where the reception arrangements are confined to an unobtrusive desk next to the honour bar. Already, you feel at home, and tempted to sink gratefully into the depths of a comfy sofa after your journey. Relieved of luggage by enthusiastic staff (who, miraculously, know your name already), you'll be offered a complimentary glass of sherry or whisky, or the opportunity to relax in your room first. The bedrooms are furnished in soft gold, beige and cream tones; some luxurious suites boast four-posters and seating/breakfasting areas in bay windows. Rooms are also equipped with custom-built desks, modem connections, broadband, voicemail and DVD players. A short step beyond The Cranley's front door, several excellent restaurants serve lunch and dinner, and the celebrated Victoria & Albert, Science and Natural History museums vie with world-class shopping for your attention.

LOCATION

Four minutes' walk south of Gloucester Road Underground station, just north of Old Brompton Road.

Map p. 452, grid D4

> "Your hotel was a real find for us, and we look forward to making The Darlington our regular home away from home"
>
> PHIL LEWIS, DALLAS, TEXAS USA

Townhouse

THE DARLINGTON HYDE PARK

Just 20 minutes from Heathrow - and earning top marks for value

The fastest way to and from London Heathrow these days is the high-speed, high-tech, non-stop Heathrow Express, linking the airport with Paddington Station in 15 minutes, every 15 minutes. The distance from Paddington to The Darlington is so close, you ll earn a derisory quip from a cabbie if you stop him; it's not five minutes on foot.

The other notable feature about The Darlington is that it is one of a new breed of places to stay in London: clean and comfortable, simple without being stark, and provisioned with all the facilities you need as a business or leisure traveller. It is centrally located, but in a quieter part of town, living up to the highest standards of hotelkeeping but without the frills. Result: great value!

The Conservatory Restaurant serves a freshly cooked traditional breakfast, or you can help yourself to a continental buffet. For lunch and dinner, there are many excellent places on the doorstep with a cosmopolitan choice of cuisine. If you are more ambitious, the glitter of the West End and the world's highest concentration of theatres, concert halls and galleries is about 20 minutes away by cab. With all this in its favour, The Darlington may well appeal beyond the budget-conscious traveller - its convenience and comfort factors get top marks!

LOCATION

Five minutes' walk from both Paddington (Heathrow Express terminal) and Lancaster Gate Underground station, next to Hyde Park.

111-117 Sussex Gardens, London W2 2RU

T (UK) 0870 432 8593
T 020 7460 8800
F 020 7460 8828
darlington@bestloved.com
www.darlington.bestloved.com

OWNER
Yulaine Kvello

ROOM RATES

5 Singles	£95 - £150
27 Doubles/Twins	£140 - £150
6 Suites	£150 - £160
2 Family Rooms	£145 - £155

Includes breakfast and VAT

CREDIT CARDS

AMERICAN EXPRESS • DC • MC • VI

RATINGS & AWARDS
RAC ◆◆◆◆ Sparkling Diamond

FACILITIES
On site: Self-service guest laundry
Nearby: Tennis, fitness

RESTRICTIONS
No facilities for disabled guests
No smoking throughout
No pets; guide dogs only

ATTRACTIONS
Hyde Park, Knightsbridge, Theatreland, Oxford Street, Windsor Castle, Hampton Court

NEAREST
CITY:
London

AIRPORT:
Heathrow - 15 miles/45 mins
Gatwick - 30 miles/1 hr 30 mins

RAIL STATION:
Paddington - ¼ mile/5 mins
Paddington Underground

AFFILIATIONS
Preston's Global Hotels

RESERVATIONS
National rate in UK: 0870 432 8593
Toll free in US: 800-544-9993
Quote Best Loved

ACCESS CODES
Not applicable

LONDON

DOLPHIN SQUARE HOTEL

City hotel

Dolphin Square, Westminster,
London, SW1V 3LX

T (UK) 0870 432 8597
T 020 7798 8890
F 020 7798 8896
dolphin@bestloved.com
www.dolphin.bestloved.com

HOTEL MANAGER
Clare Stewart

ROOM RATES
30 Studios   £185 - £235
89 One-Bedroom Suites   £205 - £450
26 Two-Bedroom Suites   £290 - £450
3 Three-Bedroom Suites   £450
Includes newspapers, service and VAT

CREDIT CARDS
AMERICAN EXPRESS • DC • JCB • MC • VI

RATINGS & AWARDS
ETC ★★★★ Silver Award Hotel
AA ★★★★ ❀❀ 72%

FACILITIES
On site: Garden, tennis, indoor pool,
gym, squash, shops, bureau de change,
business centre, fine-dining restaurant,
sauna, steam room
3 meeting rooms/max 200 people
Nearby: Golf, riding

RESTRICTIONS
Limited facilities for disabled guests
No pets; guide dogs only

ATTRACTIONS
Houses of Parliament,
Westminster, Tate Britain,
West End theatres, Knightsbridge,
Buckingham Palace, London Eye

NEAREST
CITY:
London

AIRPORT:
Heathrow - 15 miles/30 mins
Gatwick - 30 miles/40 mins
London City - 8 miles/30 mins

RAIL STATION:
Victoria - ½ mile/10 mins
Pimlico Underground

AFFILIATIONS
Utell International
Preston's Global Hotels

RESERVATIONS
National rate in UK: 0870 432 8597
Toll free in UK: 0800 616 607
Toll free in US: 800-544-9993
or 800-44-UTELL
Quote Best Loved

ACCESS CODES
AMADEUS UI LONDSH
APOLLO/GALILEO UI 96713
SABRE/ABACUS UI 32611
WORLDSPAN UI 40411

LONDON

A unique property by the Thames with its own shops, bar and restaurants

Despite its prominent position on the Embankment, Dolphin Square maintains a remarkably low profile - a fact much appreciated by residents and visitors, many of whom are well-known public figures. The building is, in effect, a self-contained village, with its own small shopping area, health spa and 3 1/2-acre flowering garden that surprises everyone who discovers it.

Located on the north side of the Square, the hotel offers apartment-style accommodation in studios and one-, two- and three-bedroom suites, all of which are complemented by mini kitchens, bathrooms and living areas suitable for anyone from a single person to a whole family and ideal for short or long lets. Guests can also enjoy the facilities at Zest! Health and Fitness Spa, which includes an extensively equipped gymnasium, 18-metre swimming pool, aerobics classes and tennis courts. There are pampering treatments, too: facials, massage, reflexology and aromatherapy, to name but a few.

The hotel's renowned restaurant, Allium, offers the best of French and British cuisine under the direction of renowned chef Anton Edelmann. Alternatively, guests can dine in the less formal surroundings of the Brasserie. For drinks and a relaxing meeting place, look no further than the nautically-themed Clipper Bar.

LOCATION

Central London, beside the Thames and off Grosvenor Road.

> "Most hotels only give you a sense you're on your way to somewhere else. This one gives you the impression that this is where you're meant to be"
>
> PREVIOUS GUEST

Townhouse

DRAYCOTT HOTEL

Luxury and privacy, met with an unbeatable London location

This gracious retreat from bustling London defies cliche, as it really does feel like someone's welcoming home - and a rather grand one at that! Fascinating paintings, fine porcelain and well-worn books adorn the interior, especially the lounge, the heart of the hotel, which is scented by white lilies and hand-picked sweet peas. French windows open out onto a peaceful private garden.

This level of charm and detail spills out throughout the hotel. All 35 bedrooms (your name appears on the door rather than a number) are generously sized, and while left to settle in, you are elegantly welcomed with a well-stocked honesty bar, a crackling fire in the winter and jellybeans and books by the bedside. But don't be fooled by the traditional décor – rooms are supplied with modern electronic entertainment, too, and the hotel is equipped throughout for the modern business traveller, including wi-fi connection and a pleasantly discreet boardroom for 12 or even, if you wish, the ability to book exclusive use of one of the Draycott's three redbrick Edwardian townhouses.

Each visitor's every whim is anticipated and fully met by the Draycott's concierge service - and with such a wealth of attractions nearby, from London's best shopping to the glamour of the theatre, you'll never be short for something to put a sparkle in your eye.

LOCATION

Just off Sloane Square in Chelsea and a few minutes' walk to Sloane Square Underground station.

26 Cadogan Gardens,
Chelsea,
London SW3 2RP

T (UK) 0870 432 8601
T 020 7730 6466
F 020 7730 0236
draycott@bestloved.com
www.draycott.bestloved.com

GENERAL MANAGER
John Hanna

ROOM RATES
6 Singles	£120
4 Doubles	£160 - £195
14 Deluxe Doubles	£220 - £255
11 Suites	£320 - £640
Excludes VAT	

CREDIT CARDS
AMERICAN EXPRESS • DC • MC • VI

RATINGS & AWARDS
RAC ★★★★★
AA ★★★★★ 65% Town House

FACILITIES
On site: Garden, breakfast room, private dining
1 meeting room/max 25 people
Nearby: Gym, health & beauty

RESTRICTIONS
No facilities for disabled guests
No smoking in bedrooms

ATTRACTIONS
Harrods, Buckingham Palace, Sloane Street, Theatre Lane, Victoria & Albert Museum, Hyde Park, Chelsea Flower Show, Kings Road

NEAREST
CITY:
London

AIRPORT:
Heathrow - 15 miles/35 mins
Gatwick - 30 miles/1 hr 15 mins

RAIL STATION:
Victoria - ¾ mile/15 mins
Sloane Square Underground

AFFILIATIONS
Celebrated Hotels Collection

RESERVATIONS
National rate in UK: 0870 432 8601
Toll free in US: 800-322-2403
or 800-747-4942
Quote Best Loved

ACCESS CODES
AMADEUS YX LONCLI
APOLLO/GALILEO YX 85436
SABRE/ABACUS YX 31114
WORLDSPAN YX DNCTH

LONDON

"The total ambience of the hotel is delightful, and the staff really caring and sensitive to the needs of the guests"

JOHN C GROOME, HULL

FLEMINGS MAYFAIR

City hotel

7 - 12 Half Moon Street,
London W1J 7BH

T (UK) 0870 432 8614
T 020 7499 2964
F 020 7499 1817
flemings@bestloved.com
www.flemings.bestloved.com

GENERAL MANAGER
Simon Scarborough

ROOM RATES
28 Singles	£198 - £220
74 Doubles/Twins	£234
13 Executive Rooms	£264
4 Junior Suites	£323
10 Apartments	£446 - £646
Includes VAT	

CREDIT CARDS
AMERICAN EXPRESS • DC • JCB • MC • VI

RATINGS & AWARDS
Independent

FACILITIES
On site: Restaurant, Bodeca Bar
3 meeting rooms/max 55 people
Nearby: Tennis, riding, golf, gym

RESTRICTIONS
Limited facilities for disabled guests
Smoking in some bedrooms only
No pets; guide dogs only

ATTRACTIONS
Buckingham Palace, Bond Street,
Regents Street, Piccadilly Circus,
Trafalgar Square, Hyde Park

NEAREST
CITY:
London

AIRPORT:
Heathrow - 15 miles/45 mins
Gatwick - 30 miles/1 hr 15 mins

RAIL STATION:
Victoria - 2 miles/15 mins
Green Park Underground

AFFILIATIONS
Grand Heritage Hotels

RESERVATIONS
National rate in UK: 0870 432 8614
Toll free in US: 888-93-GRAND
or 800-348-4685 or 800-44-UTELL
Quote Best Loved

ACCESS CODES
AMADEUS UI LONFLE
APOLLO/GALILEO UI 5265
SABRE/ABACUS UI 13258
WORLDSPAN UI 0393

LONDON

A high-quality hotel offering the best of London on your doorstep

The elegance of the Georgian age, together with the best of English hospitality, can be found in the heart of London's exclusive Mayfair, where Flemings Hotel has been welcoming guests since the early 1900s. Its location is superb - only a couple of minutes' walk from Green Park Underground station and within easy reach of all the West End's attractions, yet in a quiet street tucked away from the bustle of Piccadilly.

The opulent lounge is a pleasant place for afternoon tea, and the magnificent restaurant offers a menu of traditional British and Continental cuisine. There are 119 bedrooms, as well as 10 luxury self-contained apartments, all dressed to a five-star standard. Flemings has full 24-hour room service, and the experience of the concierge team is there to help you make the most of your visit.

London really does belong to you when you stay at Flemings. Buckingham Palace, Regent Street, Bond Street, Piccadilly Circus, the West End's Theatreland, the Royal Academy of Arts and Trafalgar Square are all within easy walking distance.

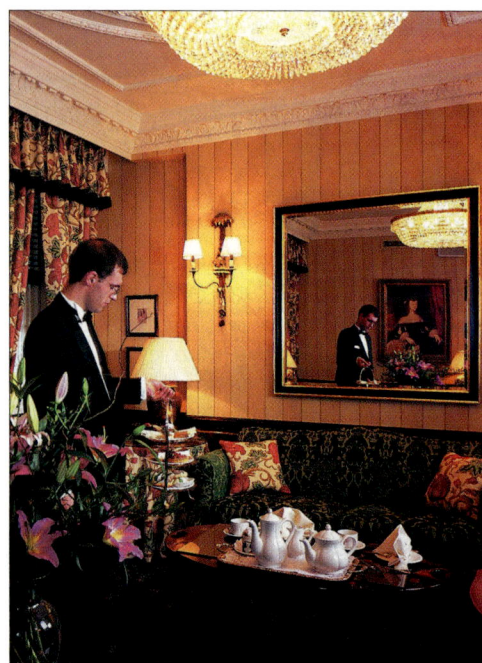

LOCATION

Turn right out of the Piccadilly (north) exit at Green Park Underground station and walk two minutes down Piccadilly past Bolton Street and toward Hyde Park Corner.

> **"** From the moment I checked in I knew I was going to be pampered. Radiating charm and tranquillity, it resembles a country hotel in the midst of a bustling city **"**
>
> CHRISTOPHER PLUMMER

City hotel

THE GORING

A prestigious privately-owned London residence

Chairman George Goring is proud to operate one of London's most prestigious hotels, which has been in his family since 1910.

The 67 bedrooms and seven suites are designed to cater for guests' every need. Beds are made with goose-down pillows and fine Egyptian cotton sheets, and the marble bathrooms are wholly indulgent. Each room has air conditioning and is fitted with modern conveniences, including televisions, broadband Internet and voice mail. Fresh flowers provide that final thoughtful touch.

The Garden Bar overlooks the 'secret garden' and is a lovely setting for afternoon tea. In the evenings it comes alive with the warmth of atmosphere, making it one of the most delightful meeting places in London. The Dining Room is renowned for its excellent English food with a few Continental touches. The wine list is regarded among the best in the Capital, and the hotel is unusual among its peers as it continues in laying down some of the finest wines for the future enjoyment of guests.

The Goring is located in a quiet haven adjacent to Buckingham Palace, the Queen's Gallery and the Royal Mews. It is also close to principal shopping areas and the West End, making it an ideal stay no matter the reason.

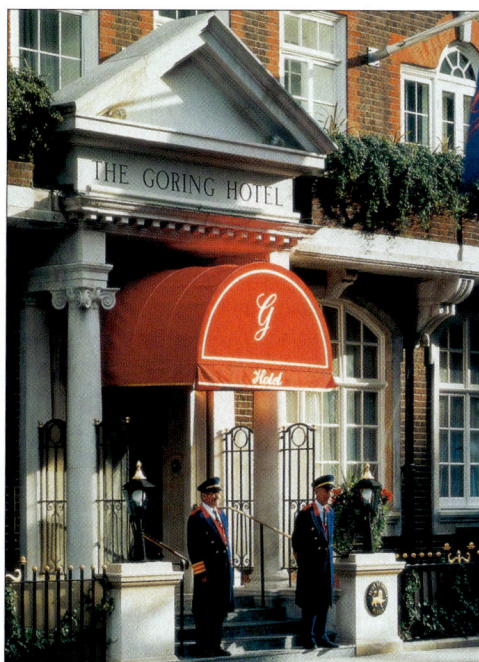

LOCATION

Beeston Place is a small, quiet street between Grosvenor Gardens and Buckingham Palace, close to Victoria rail and Underground stations.

Beeston Place,
London SW1W 0JW

T (UK) 0870 432 8629
T 020 7396 9000
F 020 7834 4393
goring@bestloved.com
www.goring.bestloved.com

OWNER
George Goring

MANAGING DIRECTOR
William Cowpe

ROOM RATES
20 Singles	£212 - £247
31 Doubles/Twins	£259 - £335
16 Deluxe Doubles	£318 - £412
7 Suites	£347 - £529

Includes service and VAT

CREDIT CARDS
AMERICAN EXPRESS • DC • MC • VI

RATINGS & AWARDS
ETC ★★★★★ Hotel
RAC Blue Ribbon ★★★★★
Dining Award 3
AA ★★★★★ ❀❀
AA Top 200 - 2004/2005

FACILITIES
On site: Garden, licensed for weddings
4 meeting rooms/max 100 people
Nearby: Golf, riding,
free use of local health club

RESTRICTIONS
Limited facilities for disabled guests
No pets; guide dogs only

ATTRACTIONS
Buckingham Palace, royal parks,
West End, Houses of Parliament

NEAREST
CITY:
London

AIRPORT:
Heathrow - 16 miles/45 mins

RAIL STATION:
Victoria - 100 yards/2 mins
Victoria Underground

AFFILIATIONS
Celebrated Hotels Collection
Pride of Britain

RESERVATIONS
National rate in UK: 0870 432 8629
Toll free in US: 800-322-2403
or 800-98-PRIDE or 800-225-4255
Quote Best Loved

ACCESS CODES
AMADEUS HK LONGOR
APOLLO/GALILEO HT 14860
SABRE/ABACUS HK 30136
WORLDSPAN HK GORIN

LONDON

GRIM'S DYKE HOTEL

Country house

Old Redding, Harrow Weald,
London HA3 6SH

T (UK) 0870 432 8638
T 020 8385 3100
F 020 8954 4560
grimsdyke@bestloved.com
www.grimsdyke.bestloved.com

DIRECTOR
Paul Follows

ROOM RATES
Single occupancy   £125
35 Doubles/Twins   £152
9 Suites   £170 - £325
Includes full breakfast and VAT

CREDIT CARDS
AMERICAN EXPRESS • DC • MC • VI

RATINGS & AWARDS
ETC ★★★ Silver Award Hotel
RAC ★★★ Dining Award 2
AA ★★★ ❀ 68%

FACILITIES
On site: Garden, croquet,
licensed for weddings
4 meeting rooms/max 90 people
Nearby: Golf

RESTRICTIONS
Pets by arrangement

ATTRACTIONS
London's West End, London Eye,
Windsor Castle,
RNRS Gardens of the Rose,
Kew Gardens, Kenwood House

NEAREST
CITY:
London - 14 miles/35 mins

AIRPORT:
Heathrow - 16 miles/30 mins

RAIL STATION:
Watford Junction - 4 miles/10 mins
Stanmore Underground - 2 miles/5 mins

AFFILIATIONS
Grand Heritage Hotels

RESERVATIONS
National rate in UK: 0870 432 8638
Toll free in US: 888-93-GRAND
Quote Best Loved

ACCESS CODES
AMADEUS UI LONGDH
APOLLO/GALILEO UI 84448
SABRE/ABACUS UI 38999
WORLDSPAN UI 40704

LONDON

A country setting with a theatrical twist close to Central London

The original Grim's Dyke is an ancient earthwork set in Harrow Weald, north of London. The name was adopted by Victorian painter Frederick Goodall for his country home, designed by architect Norman Shaw and constructed parallel to the earthwork between 1870 and 1872. Later, the house was home to librettist W S Gilbert, the wordsmith of Gilbert and Sullivan fame.

Shaw's design was a splendid Tudoresque affair adorned with gables and tall chimney stacks, mullioned windows and half-timbering. The Grade II-listed house sits in 40 acres of lovely grounds with lawns, shrubberies ablaze with rhododendrons and azaleas in spring and quiet woodlands crisscrossed by paths. The immaculate interior has retained its ornate ceilings and cornices as well as several magnificent fireplaces. One of these, in Cornish alabaster, graces the Music Room, which was used in Gilbert's time to stage operas and is now the scene of monthly evenings of costumed operetta with dinner. The recently refurbished Gilberts restaurant serves modern English food and has a significant local following. At weekends, diners can enjoy the sound of the piano in the background, and in summer, guests can eat out on the terrace overlooking the lawn. All this is conveniently near to tube and train connections and the West End 35 minutes away.

LOCATION
Exit the M25, junction 23, for the A1 south (London). Follow the A411 (Watford/Elstree), then the A411 (Bushey) and the A409 (Harrow/Harrow Weald). Turn right into Old Redding.

For more than 10 years, Knightsbridge Green has been my 'home' in London ... it is a very nice place to come back to

MR PETER YEO

City hotel   KNIGHTSBRIDGE GREEN HOTEL

A rare personal touch
in the bustling heart of the city

Knightsbridge Green is a small hotel with a big difference: with Harrods just across the street and Hyde Park virtually on your doorstep, it is hard to believe that these days, a family-owned establishment could exist in such a wonderfully central position. And yet here it is, combining the comforts and pleasures of the larger consortia hotels with the personality and friendliness you can only find in a privately-owned business.

Knightsbridge Green is an elegant, well-kept mixture of eclectic furnishings and top quality fittings and fixtures; double glazing keeps the peace in one of London's busiest areas, and air conditioning in all the bedrooms and suites allows you to find your own comfort level. The rooms are exceptionally large - a single at the Knightsbridge Green is the size of many a double anywhere else!

The area is blessed with a great range of cafés, restaurants, pubs, wine bars and bistros offering all kinds of cuisine, so a restaurant in the hotel is superfluous - although a hearty breakfast will be served in your room, if you wish. An excellent concierge service means that when you want help in booking a restaurant, theatre tickets, limousine or hire car, all you have to do is ask.

LOCATION
In Knightsbridge, adjacent to Hyde Park.

159 Knightsbridge, London SW1X 7PD

T (UK) 0870 432 8673
T 020 7584 6274
F 020 7225 1635
knightsbridge@bestloved.com
www.knightsbridge.bestloved.com

OWNERS
The Marler Family

MANAGER
Paul Fizia

ROOM RATES
7 Singles   £90 - £110
9 Doubles/Twins   £115 - £145
12 Suites   £140 - £170
Includes service and VAT

CREDIT CARDS
AMERICAN EXPRESS • DC • MC • VI

RATINGS & AWARDS
ETC ♦♦♦♦ Silver Award
B&B Award Scheme
Commended Past Winner of BTA
London Certificate of Distinction

FACILITIES
Nearby: Riding

RESTRICTIONS
Limited facilities for disabled guests
No smoking throughout
No pets

ATTRACTIONS
Harrods, Harvey Nichols,
Kensington Palace,
Victoria & Albert Museum,
Natural History Museum,
West End theatre

NEAREST
CITY:
London

AIRPORT:
Heathrow - 15 miles/45 mins
Gatwick - 30 miles/1 hr 15 mins

RAIL STATION:
Victoria - ½ mile/10 mins
Knightsbridge Underground

AFFILIATIONS
Preston's Global Hotels

RESERVATIONS
National rate in UK: 0870 432 8673
Toll free in US: 800-544-9993
Quote Best Loved

ACCESS CODES
AMADEUS VE LON47A
APOLLO/GALILEO VE 43430
SABRE/ABACUS VE 16315
WORLDSPAN VE 22660

LONDON

THE LEONARD

Townhouse

15 Seymour Street,
Marble Arch,
London W1H 7JW

T (UK) 0870 432 8684
T 020 7935 2010
F 020 7935 6700
leonard@bestloved.com
www.leonard.bestloved.com

MANAGING DIRECTOR
Paul Sehgal

ROOM RATES
Single occupancy   £235
23 Doubles/Twins   £259
21 Suites   £329 - £588
Includes VAT

CREDIT CARDS
AMERICAN EXPRESS • DC • JCB • MC • VI

RATINGS & AWARDS
ETC ★★★★ Silver Award
ETC Town House

FACILITIES
On site: Gym, roof terrace
4 meeting rooms/max 40 people
Nearby: Riding

RESTRICTIONS
No pets

ATTRACTIONS
Buckingham Palace, Hyde Park,
Bond Street,
Victoria & Albert Museum,
Wallace Collection

NEAREST
CITY:
London

AIRPORT:
Heathrow - 15 miles/45 mins
Gatwick - 30 miles/1 hr 15 mins

RAIL STATION:
Paddington - 1 mile/5 mins
Marble Arch Underground

AFFILIATIONS
Celebrated Hotels Collection
The European Connection
Small Hotel Company

RESERVATIONS
National rate in UK: 0870 432 8684
Toll free in US: 800-322-2403
Quote Best Loved

ACCESS CODES
AMADEUS KH LON434
APOLLO/GALILEO KH 85121
SABRE/ABACUS KH 25558
WORLDSPAN KH 08434

LONDON

A discreet luxury townhouse address near Oxford Street shopping

Since its opening in 1996, The Leonard has gained a reputation for being a very discreet luxury residence and has become a regular bolthole for many high-profile guests, especially those from the worlds of business and entertainment.

Created out of four 18th-century townhouses, The Leonard is exquisitely decorated and furnished throughout, retaining a wonderful air of understated Georgian elegance. There are 21 suites and 23 bedrooms in total, all of which have lavish interiors and marble bathrooms. The Grand Suites on the first floor are very spacious indeed, and all the larger suites come with either a fully-equipped kitchen or butler's pantry. Each room has air conditioning and all the other modern facilities you would expect, including hi-fi music, video and modem access.

The café bar serves a fine breakfast as well as light meals throughout the day. They really have overlooked nothing, and provide 24-hour room service, full secretarial support services, a compact exercise room and a beautiful roof terrace. The service, as you would expect of an exclusive residence, is outstanding. And the final plus point - the shops of Oxford Street and Bond Street are just around the corner!

LOCATION

Situated on the south side of Seymour Street just west of Portman Square. Car parking is available in Bryanston Street.

City hotel

THE MONTCALM HOTEL

A discreet residence just two minutes from Marble Arch and Oxford Street

Tucked away in a quiet, tree-lined crescent behind Marble Arch and the bustling Oxford Street shopping district, The Montcalm makes an exceptional base for the discerning traveller in one of the greatest cities in the world.

The hotel was named after an 18th-century general, the Marquis de Montcalm, who was renowned for his dignity and style. These two qualities are admirably reflected in the surroundings and atmosphere of this London outpost of the highly regarded Nikko Hotel group. Behind the discreet Georgian façade, comfortable traditional bedrooms and duplex suites feature modern conveniences from modem access and voice mail to satellite and CNN television channels. The spacious lobby is an ideal meeting point for friends and business colleagues, or there is the wood-panelled bar, where afternoon tea is served and an open fire provides a cosy focus in winter.

The Montcalm's elegant Crescent Restaurant has a light and airy feel, with tall windows and an Arcadian mural of a formal English garden stretching off into the distant countryside. Typical offerings of the restaurant's modern British cuisine include tournedos of Scottish beef with woodland mushrooms and a delice of salmon on spinach and wild rice with a caviar and vodka butter. Private dining rooms are also available.

LOCATION

Two minutes' walk from Marble Arch and Oxford Street.

Great Cumberland Place,
London W1H 7TW

T (UK) 0870 432 8714
T 020 7402 4288
F 020 7724 9180
montcalm@bestloved.com
www.montcalm.bestloved.com

GENERAL MANAGER
Gernod Dünwald

ROOM RATES
43 Singles	£180 - £260
63 Doubles/Twins	£180 - £290
14 Suites	£370 - £705
Includes VAT	

CREDIT CARDS
AMERICAN EXPRESS • DC • JCB • MC • VI

RATINGS & AWARDS
AA ★★★★ ✿✿ 78%

FACILITIES
On site: High-speed Internet, voicemail, photocopier and printer, chauffeur service, secretarial services, bicycles 3 meeting rooms/max 100 people
Nearby: Jogging, riding, swimming

RESTRICTIONS
Limited facilities for disabled guests
Pets by arrangement
Smoking in designated rooms only

ATTRACTIONS
Buckingham Palace,
Wellington Museum,
The Wallace Collection,
Madame Tussauds,
shopping on Oxford Street
and Bond Street

NEAREST
CITY:
London

AIRPORT:
Heathrow - 15 miles/50 mins
Gatwick - 30 miles/1 hr 15 mins

RAIL STATION:
Paddington - ½ mile/10 mins
Marble Arch Underground

AFFILIATIONS
Celebrated Hotels Collection
Nikko Hotels International

RESERVATIONS
National rate in UK: 0870 432 8714
Toll free in US: 800-322-2403
or 800-645-5687
Quote Best Loved

ACCESS CODES
AMADEUS NK LON001
APOLLO/GALILEO NK 26211
SABRE/ABACUS NK 14527
WORLDSPAN NK 14527

LONDON

PARKES

Townhouse

41 Beaufort Gardens,
Knightsbridge,
London SW3 1PW

T (UK) 0870 432 8732
T 020 7581 9944
F 020 7581 1999
parkes@bestloved.com
www.parkes.bestloved.com

GENERAL MANAGER
Susan Burns

ASSISTANT GENERAL MANAGER
Beverley Luff

ROOM RATES
4 Single	£195
2 Doubles	£240
9 Deluxe Doubles	£290
4 Junior Suites	£325
8 One-bedroom Suites	£325
6 Superior One-bedroom Suites	£415

Excludes VAT

CREDIT CARDS
AMERICAN EXPRESS • DC • JCB • MC • VI

RATINGS & AWARDS
RAC ★★★★
AA ★★★★ 71%

FACILITIES
On site:
2 meeting rooms/max 50 people
Nearby: Health clubs

RESTRICTIONS
No facilities for disabled guests
No pets

ATTRACTIONS
London Eye, Harrods,
Victoria & Albert Museum,
Natural History Museum,
Buckingham Palace,
Theatreland, Royal Albert Hall,
Hyde Park, Tate Modern

NEAREST
CITY:
London

AIRPORT:
Heathrow - 15 mile/45 mins
Gatwick - 30 miles/1 hr 15 mins

RAIL STATION:
Victoria - 1 mile/5 mins
Knightsbridge Underground

AFFILIATIONS
Ensemble
Celebrated Hotels Collection

RESERVATIONS
National rate in UK: 0870 432 8732
Toll free in US: 800-306-5054
or 800-322-2403
Toll free in Sweden 020 795 101
Quote Best Loved

ACCESS CODES
AMADEUS UI LONPAR
APOLLO/GALILEO UI 84251
SABRE/ABACUS UI 33912
WORLDSPAN UI 27029

LONDON

Relax in luxury
with London's best on your doorstep

Parkes Hotel's location alone, on a tree-lined cul-de-sac in the midst of Knightsbridge's finest shops and restaurants, would be enough to tempt you to stay at this charming townhouse - when you add in a friendly staff, luxurious rooms and peerless amenities it's clearly a winner. Formed from three 1860s townhouses, the hotel sparkles after a recent renovation, mixing timeless luxury with modern technology.

This really is a hotel with a difference. Each extravagantly spacious room offers wi-fi access, multi-line phone with voice mail, individual climate control, digital satellite TV with DVD and a minibar stocked with a wealth of goodies. In the decadent marble bathrooms you'll find underfloor heating, amazing showers, mist-free mirrors, Molton Brown toiletries and fluffy white robes. An excellent concierge service is available to look after your needs and there is a chauffeur service for easy access to and from London's airports.

Situated just steps away from Harrods and a few minutes' walk from Harvey Nichols and the fabulous shops on Sloane Street, Parkes is an ideal base for exploring such London landmarks as Kensington Palace, Hyde Park, the new Princess Diana memorial fountain and a wealth of museums and galleries. Dining in the area is not to be missed, though you won't want to skip the hotel's own delicious breakfast, with your morning meal prepared to order by the resident chef!

LOCATION
Located in the heart of Knightsbridge 100 metres from Harrods and three minutes from South Kensington Underground.

Map p. 452, grid D4

> Exuding contemporary style and elegance and brimming with fine Georgian and Victorian antiques "
>
> JONTY HEARNDEN

Townhouse

THE ROYAL PARK HOTEL

This stunning newcomer offers a splendid City stay

Far from being just another London hotel, this addition to the City's roster of places to stay is really an exceptional experience. Once you step inside, it's apparent what a gem this newly-opened property is - inside the elegant shell of a 19th-century townhouse, all the needs of today's business or leisure traveller are at your fingertips, with a whole complement of modern amenities sharing space with elegant, traditional style. It's utterly relaxing, too, with soothing décor that's a magnificent blend of classic and eclectic, down to the marble bathrooms perfect for a long soak at the end of an eventful day.

Hyde Park is just a glance from your doorstep, and you're a mere 15 minutes from Heathrow airport on the speedy, quiet Heathrow Express and around the corner from Paddington station. When it comes to attractions, nearly everything you might desire is within minutes: the Royal Park is 10 minutes from every major shopping destination, including Oxford Street, Bond Street and Knightsbridge, and close enough to West End theatres to make it to your favourite show in a heartbeat.

Better still, with so much to offer, the Royal Park is really a fantastic example of value for money - all the better for further City adventures!

LOCATION

A few steps from Lancaster Gate Underground station and a brief walk up Westbourne Terrace from Hyde Park.

3 Westbourne Terrace,
Lancaster Gate, Hyde Park,
London W2 3UL

T (UK) 0870 432 8761
T 020 7479 6600
F 020 7479 6601
royalpark@bestloved.com
www.royalpark.bestloved.com

MANAGER
Angela Stoppani

ROOM RATES
2 Singles	£100 - £165
15 Doubles	£125 - £200
18 Executive Doubles/Twins	£135 - £210
2 Four-posters	£165 - £240
8 Four-poster/twin Suites	£200 - £280
3 Deluxe Four-poster Suites	£220 - £315

Includes welcome drink, afternoon tea, champagne and canapés, breakfast and VAT

CREDIT CARDS
AMERICAN EXPRESS • DC • JCB • MC • VI

RATINGS & AWARDS
AA ★★★★ 76%

FACILITIES
On site: Turn-down service, residential bar, garden, concierge, 24-hour room service, broadband
1 meeting room/max10 people
Nearby: Swimming pool, gardens, tennis, riding

RESTRICTIONS
No facilities for disabled guests
No pets; guide dogs only

ATTRACTIONS
Kensington Palace & Gardens, The Wallace Collection, Madame Tussauds, Oxford Street, Hyde Park, Buckingham Palace, Mayfair, Bond Street

NEAREST
CITY:
London

AIRPORT:
Heathrow - 15 miles/15 mins

RAIL STATION:
Paddington - 500 yards/5 mins
Lancaster Gate Underground

AFFILIATIONS
Celebrated Hotels Collection
Grand Heritage Hotels

RESERVATIONS
National rate in UK: 0870 432 8761
Toll free in US: 888-989-1768
or 800-322-2403 or 888-93-GRAND
Quote Best Loved

ACCESS CODES
AMADEUS UI LONRPK
APOLLO/GALILEO UI 64336
SABRE/ABACUS UI 62143
WORLDSPAN UI 43220

LONDON

The Stafford is ideal if you want to be in the middle of everything and have privacy too. Top-notch staff ensure that you have a pleasing stay

CONDÉ NAST TRAVELER

THE STAFFORD
City hotel

16-18 St James's Place,
London SW1A 1NJ

T (UK) 0870 432 8774
T 020 7493 0111
F 020 7493 7121
stafford@bestloved.com
www.stafford.bestloved.com

EXECUTIVE DIRECTOR
Terry Holmes

ROOM RATES
11 Single occupancy	£230
30 Doubles	£250 - £305
29 Deluxe Doubles	£335 - £425
13 Suites	£405 - £495
The Guv'nor's Suite	£835

CREDIT CARDS
AMERICAN EXPRESS • DC • MC • VI

RATINGS & AWARDS
RAC Gold Ribbon ★★★★
Dining Award 2
AA ★★★★ ⊛⊛
AA Top 200 - 2004/2005
Harper's Hideaway Report 2003 -
Best Hotel in London
Leaders Magazine -
Top Ten Hotels in the World

FACILITIES
On site: Licensed for weddings
4 meeting rooms/max 75 people
Nearby: Complimentary fitness club
membership

RESTRICTIONS
Limited facilities for disabled guests
No pets; guide dogs only

ATTRACTIONS
Buckingham Palace,
St Paul's Cathedral, National Gallery,
Trafalgar Square, London Eye,
Hyde Park, West End theatre

NEAREST
CITY:
London

AIRPORT:
Heathrow - 15 miles/45 mins

RAIL STATION:
Victoria - ¾ mile/10 mins
Green Park Underground

AFFILIATIONS
Celebrated Hotels Collection
Small Luxury Hotels
Pride of Britain

RESERVATIONS
National rate in UK: 0870 432 8774
Toll free in US: 800-544-9993
or 800-525-4800 or 800-98-PRIDE
Quote Best Loved

ACCESS CODES
AMADEUS LX LONSTA
APOLLO/GALILEO LX 8207
SABRE/ABACUS LX 7192
WORLDSPAN LX LONTS

LONDON

A superlative experience in the centre of London's best

Nestled in the heart of London - just 39 steps away from Green Park - The Stafford offers a quintessential London experience. This 18th-century townhouse was originally the home of Lord and Lady Lyttleton and took its current form as an exquisite city hotel in 1912. During World War II, The Stafford served a brief stint as a club for American and Canadian soldiers stationed overseas - today, it's a fabulous place to make your own home.

Sink yourself into the rooms' luxurious individually-decorated furnishings, or venture out-of-doors for a walk amongst Piccadilly Circus, the National Gallery, Trafalgar Square, Buckingham Palace or any number of famous London landmarks - it's your choice, and here, you're spoilt for it. Shoppers will feel right at home, with all the famous haunts nearby, and if you're looking for something a bit more strenuous, there's always your personal invitation to Champneys Piccadilly health club.

Once your hunger for attractions is satiated, feed your appetite at The Stafford's award-winning kitchen, led by executive chef David Smith. Explore the selections from the wine list, where contemporary wines and rare vintages share space in the hotel's stunning 350-year-old cellars.

LOCATION
In the heart of Mayfair a few minutes' walk from Green Park Underground.

City hotel

THREADNEEDLES

5 Threadneedle Street,
London EC2R 8AY

T (UK) 0870 432 8796
T 020 7657 8080
F 020 7657 8100
threadneedles@bestloved.com
www.threadneedles.bestloved.com

GENERAL MANAGER
Jo dos Santos

ROOM RATES
19 Luxury		£175 - £265
27 Standard Doubles		£175 - £310
11 Executive Kings		£175 - £345
4 Studio Suites		£200 - £395
	Includes VAT	

CREDIT CARDS
AMERICAN EXPRESS • DC • JCB • MC • VI

RATINGS & AWARDS
Awards Pending

FACILITIES
On site: Health & beauty,
access to nearby leisure centre
3 meeting rooms/max 50 people

RESTRICTIONS
No pets

ATTRACTIONS
St Paul's Cathedral,
The Tower of London, London Bridge,
St Mary-le-Bow Church,
Millennium Bridge,
Shakespeare's Globe Theatre,
Tate Modern

NEAREST
CITY:
London

AIRPORT:
Heathrow - 25 miles/1 hr

RAIL STATION:
Liverpool Street - 1/4 mile/2 mins
Bank Underground

AFFILIATIONS
The European Connection
Summit Hotels & Resorts
The Eton Group

RESERVATIONS
National rate in UK: 0870 432 8796
Quote Best Loved

ACCESS CODES
AMADEUS XL LONTNN
APOLLO/GALILEO XL 39163
SABRE/ABACUS XL 60812
WORLDSPAN XL LONTN

LONDON

Style and sophistication you can bank on

At the heart of the City in London's historic financial district, the Old Lady of Threadneedle Street has been presiding over the nation's fortunes for hundreds of years. More respectfully known as the Bank of England, she has a new neighbour a short walk down one of the City's oldest thoroughfares said to be named for the emblem of the Needlemakers' Company back in the 14th century. In a former incarnation Threadneedles was also a bank, and a very grand one at that. Today, it shines as a recently-refurbished luxury hotel, offering understated elegance in the form of 70 well-appointed contemporary rooms and suites, a bright and energising fitness club and an exciting restaurant and bar.

The style here can best be described as city chic with all the trimmings: Egyptian cotton and duck down Frette duvets grace the beds, while limestone bathrooms welcome you for a calming bath at the end of a long day. Guests arriving for leisure can take their pick from the West End's bright lights, innumerable museums and galleries or shopping. For the business-minded, there are three state-of-the-art meeting rooms with a full menu of audiovisual resources. And where menus are concerned, Bonds Restaurant and Bar certainly won't disappoint.

LOCATION
A few steps away from Bank Underground in the centre of London's financial district.

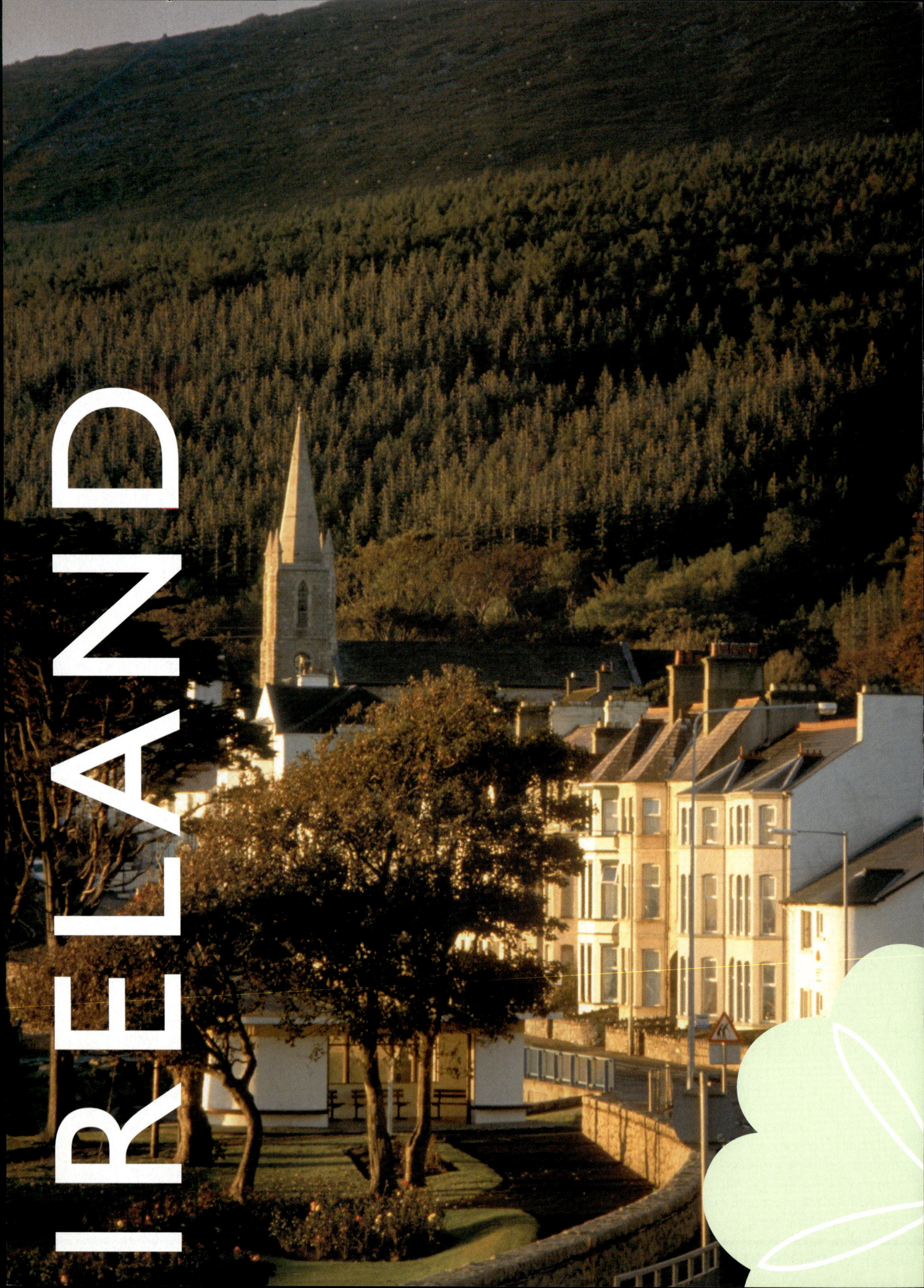

IRELAND

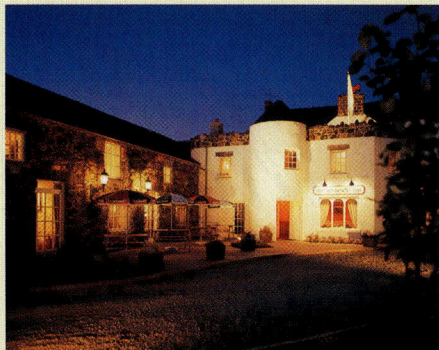

A WELCOMING INN
Bushmills Inn Hotel, Co Antrim

A RESORT
Portmarnock Hotel and Golf Links, Co Dublin

A STATELY HOME
Culloden Estate and Spa, Co Down

REPRESENTING
the best of
IRELAND

A CITY HOTEL
Fitzwilliam Hotel, Dublin

Best Loved Hotels offer the cream of the crop across Great Britain and Ireland - from stately palaces to welcoming inns - each the best of its kind within its locality and price range.

Whichever place you choose as your own place to stay, you'll find every hotel offers character, charm and the best delights and attractions of its region.

And each, in its own special way, is best-loved by someone who's been there.

A CASTLE
Ashford Castle, Co Mayo

A COUNTRY HOUSE IN THE CITY
Hayfield Manor, Cork

A RESTAURANT WITH ROOMS
King Sitric, Co Dublin

A CONTEMPORARY HOTEL
Maryborough House Hotel , Cork

AN IDEAL ESCAPE:
Ireland

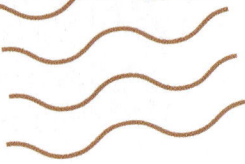

MUCH TOO MUCH for just a weekend, Ireland promises history, mystery, legend and culture, with activities and events to attract all tastes. But if you've only got a few days, a whirlwind trip round this splendid island is still certain to delight.

Day One

Thoughts of notable sights in Northern Ireland usually begin with the **Giant's Causeway**, and for good reason. Some 60 million years old, the unique rock formations along this stunning stretch of the Irish coast are immediately both intriguing and awe-inspiring. Windswept Atlantic coast, craggy cliffs and grassy dunes - not to mention excellent golfing! - mark the region's allure.

Stop on your way back down for some R&R in **Bushmills**, home to the world's oldest whisky distillery. Operating since 1608 and still a connoisseur's favourite, the **Old Bushmills Distillery** is an interesting tour - just be sure to check the available times on the day of your visit.

Of course, **Belfast** is worth a weekend on its own, but if you're just travelling through, be sure to stop for a bit of shopping in **Donegall Square** and a drink in one of the city's Victorian pubs. The **Ulster Museum** offers exhibits from art to archaeology to natural history, and it's located on the grounds of the city's **Botanic Gardens**, perfect for an afternoon browse. Climb up **Cave Hill**, too, before you go, and take in a marvellous view of the city.

Day Two

Whether you're a confirmed urbanite or a devout countryside rambler, **Dublin** is a city you'll look back upon with fond memories. Begin your tour of the capital in **Temple Bar** - known as 'Dublin's Left Bank', the area offers a wealth of bohemian flavour in clubs, galleries and lively pubs, while Georgian architecture in the city's south side lends an elegance to Dublin's leafy squares and the pleasantly civilised **St Stephen's Green**. If you see no other museum, be sure to stop and visit the famed library at nearby **Trinity College**, where among other

Angling awaits near Cork

treasures, you can see the ornately-scribed Book of Kells. However, if you've got the chance, the **Dublin Writers' Museum** is also a great find for the literary-minded.

Of course, if you're seeking to sample some local flavour of a different sort, there's the **Guinness Storehouse** - though you can't tour the actual Guinness brewery, this attraction is a good substitute, with six floors of exhibitions and a stylish pub to boot.

Day Three

Finish your cross-country trek in the southern cities of **Waterford** and **Cork**. The city known worldwide for its famed crystal is also a pleasant stop for a walking tour, offered by Waterford's tourist authority. Be sure, though, to allow enough time for a stroll if you do stop for a tour of the **Waterford factory** - it's the sort of attraction that can take an entire afternoon, not including shopping for just the right souvenir!

Cork is also a fabulous city for shoppers, with a bountiful retail

Cork's plentiful is a real treat

Flavourful heritage in Bushmills

The striking rock formations at the Giant's Causeway will intrigue and delight

district running along **St Patrick's Street** in the centre of the city. For a more offbeat experience, detour slightly for **Oliver Plunkett Street**, where smaller, more personal shops offer an alternative to the high-street experience.

For foodies, there's the **English Market**, where butchers, cheesemakers and bakers offer incredibly tempting wares - arrive early enough and you just might see area chefs picking up their ingredients for the day's dinner menu. It's a great excuse for a picnic, but be sure to save some room for supper! In the meantime, take in a little culture; the **Triskel Arts Centre** is another must-see, an appealing mix of art, literature, education and a wealth of performance. If you can bear to leave the city, **fishing** galore gives angling enthusiasts a perfect excuse to get out on the water. Also nearby is the famous **Blarney Castle** - though we can't be entirely sure if the legend of the famous Blarney stone holds true, a visit is still a memorable experience.

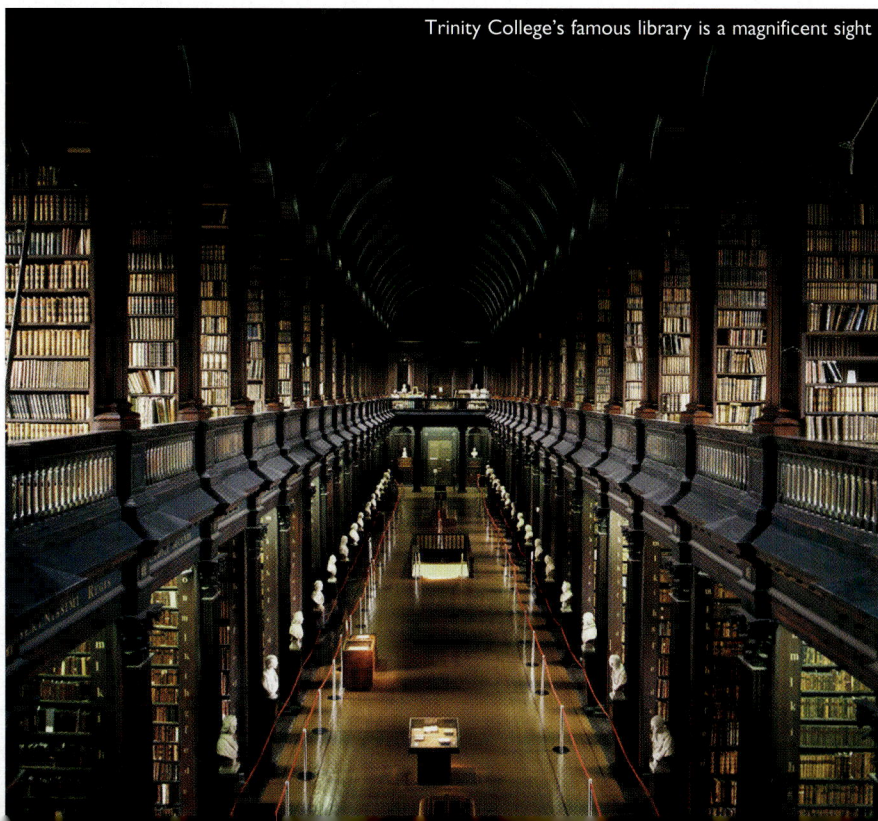

Trinity College's famous library is a magnificent sight

A TASTE OF THE BEST
Ireland

TAKE SOME TIME out from seeing Ireland's magnificent sights to enjoy deliciously creative cuisine at one - or a few! - of Best Loved's Irish favourites. From stunningly fresh fish to devilishly tempting desserts, there are memories to be made at the table.

FITZWILLIAM HOTEL ✿✿

This contemporary Dublin hotel's stylishly elegant restaurant, Thornton's, is run by Kevin Thornton and has two Michelin stars for its cuisine. The entire menu is a treat, but we'd recommend roast loin and terrine of rabbit with mushroom risotto, parmesan tuile and hazelnut sauce, and for a main course, delectable options include roast magret of goose glazed with honey and pistachio confit, red cabbage and morel sauce. With such an enticing menu, it's not surprising that it's referred to by some as Dublin's finest restaurant - why not see for yourself?

KING SITRIC

Aidan and Joan MacManus' famed fish restaurant relies on trusty local suppliers to provide organically grown vegetables, plus fresh lobster and crab from Balscadden Bay and other great quality seafood - most of their fish is from the shores of their own town of Howth. Starters such as lobster salad are followed by delicious dishes like strips of monkfish tossed with a julienne of vegetables, topped with hollandaise sauce and glazed under the grill. Their cuisine is complemented by an award-winning wine list to make the experience just that little bit more memorable. Take a look at their special value menu, too!

LACKEN HOUSE

One of the most talked-about restaurants in Ireland, Lacken House's à la carte menu features a wealth of tasty local produce, including the house specialty, a divine roast crispy duckling. Or try the five-course table d'hôte dinner, which might feature such dishes as roast sirloin of Irish Aberdeen Angus beef, Café de Paris butter, Pont Neuf potatoes and broad beans. For dessert, you really are spoilt for choice – one favourite is the homemade cheddar cheese tart with light apple and sultana sponge, or Lacken crème brulée for a taste of luxury.

Friendly atmosphere at King Sitric

Don't forget dessert at the Mustard Seed

MUSTARD SEED AT ECHO LODGE

Restaurateur Daniel Mullane bought Echo Lodge as the perfect country hotel in which to house his Mustard Seed Restaurant. Dishes here are created from produce from the best of Ireland's organic farms and cheesemakers, plus herbs and vegetables picked from the hotel's impressive kitchen garden. Head Chef Toni Schwartz prepares the seasonally changing four-course table d'hôte menu, which features a wealth of creative dishes such as loin of venison with buttered greens, spiced pear, vanilla and lime mash and port wine reduction, or pan-seared Irish beef with a red onion marmalade, ratatouille and a roast garlic jus. If that isn't enough of an endorsement on its own, Mustard Seed was also voted 'Best Country House Hotel and Restaurant in Munster' by Food and Wine Magazine.

PARK HOTEL KENMARE ✿✿✿

This sumptuous Victorian country hotel overlooking Kenmare Bay has a highly-acclaimed restaurant where Head Chef Joe Ryan offers a diverse range of dishes on his seasonal menus. With an emphasis on local fish, beef, duck, pork and lamb (as well as some notable vegetarian options), the menu includes home-smoked duck breast and duck leg rillette with crispy wild mushroom won ton, caramelised orange segments and ruby port reduction – and

Memorable terrace dining at Park Hotel Kenmare

that's just for starters! Tempting main dishes include roast monkfish on the bone with risotto of Castletownbere crabmeat and sweetcorn and grilled baby fennel and clam vinaigrette. To complete your experience at Park Hotel Kenmare, the dining room has fantastic views of the gardens out to Kenmare Bay, so al fresco dining in the summer months is highly recommended.

PERRYVILLE

There is no end of first-class restaurants near this Georgian residence situated in Kinsale - said to be the gourmet capital of Ireland. But make sure you make time during your stay for a taste of Perryville's notable breakfasts! Their tempting buffet includes cereals, fresh fruits, local farmhouse cheeses, honey and free range eggs - a perfect start to a day of sporting delights or a visit to nearby Cork.

A TASTE OF THE REGION

Looking for even more to tempt your palate? There are a wealth of fantastic places to dine in Ireland, all within the covers of this book! Have a browse to whet your appetite, or jump to some of our own favourites:

AGHADOE HEIGHTS HOTEL ✿✿✿

A splendid location in the Lakes of Killarney National Park – and their Fredrick's Restaurant is among the top 10 in Ireland.

MERRION HOTEL ✿✿✿✿

This five-star Georgian hotel in Dublin leaves you spoilt for choice between their Restaurant Patrick Guildbaud and the less formal Cellar Restaurant.

SEA VIEW HOUSE HOTEL ✿✿

This country hotel surrounded by mountains, lakes and coastline has a fine reputation for 'country house cooking'.

Dine al fresco with FANTASTIC VIEWS *over Kenmare Bay*

Menu
MUSTARD SEED AT ECHO LODGE

Poached oysters in their shell on a potato salad with a horseradish mayonnaise

Spaghetti of wild mushrooms, onion veloute, cherry tomato and white truffle oil

Carrot, apple and ginger soup
Blackcurrant and vodka sorbet

Pan-fried fillet of halibut with glaze salsify, curly kale an a sun-dried tomato veloute

Baked Irish salmon with a fondue of leeks, roast chorizo and a wholegrain mustard cream

Petits fours

Aberdeen is frequently filled with regular customers, which is probably the best recommendation you can make

JOHN & SALLY MCKENNA, BRIDGESTONE 100 BEST PLACES TO STAY IN IRELAND 2004

ABERDEEN LODGE

Townhouse

53 Park Avenue, off Ailesbury Rd,
Ballsbridge, Dublin 4
Republic of Ireland

T +353 (0)1 283 8155
F +353 (0)1 283 7877
aberdeenlodge@bestloved.com
www.aberdeenlodge.bestloved.com

OWNER
Pat Halpin

ROOM RATES
3 Singles   €106 - €139
10 Doubles/Twins €139 - €189
2 Four-posters   €169 - €229
2 Suites   €190 - €299
      Includes full breakfast,
      newspaper and VAT

CREDIT CARDS
• DC • JCB • MC • VI

RATINGS & AWARDS
ITB ★★★★
RAC ◆◆◆◆◆
RAC Warm Welcome,
Sparkling Diamond Awards
AA ◆◆◆◆◆
AA Premier Collection
Galtee Breakfast Award

FACILITIES
On site: Garden, wireless Internet,
car park
2 meeting rooms/max 30 people
Nearby: Golf, riding, fitness centre,
tennis, shooting, fishing, water skiing

RESTRICTIONS
Limited facilities for disabled guests
No pets

ATTRACTIONS
Trinity College, National Art Gallery,
Christchurch, Gardens of Wicklow,
New Grange, Powerscourt Gardens,
Druids Glen Golf Course

NEAREST
CITY:
Dublin

AIRPORT:
Dublin - 6 miles/20 mins

RAIL STATION:
Sydney Parade - 1/4 mile/5 mins

FERRY PORT:
Dun Laoghaire - 1/2 mile/10 mins

AFFILIATIONS
Utell International
Preston's Global Hotels
Relais du Silence
Luxe Worldwide Hotels
JDB Collection

RESERVATIONS
Toll free in US: 800-617-3178
Toll free in UK: 0800 0964 748
Quote Best Loved

ACCESS CODES
AMADEUS UI DUBABE
APOLLO/GALILEO UI 1400
SABRE/ABACUS UI 35428
WORLDSPAN UI 19689

IRELAND

A peaceful, private address in Dublin's fashionable Embassy District

Nestled in the heart of Ballsbridge, Dublin's leafy embassy belt, is Aberdeen Lodge, selected as one of Ireland's 100 best places to stay 2004 by the Bridgestone Guide. This exclusive south-city-centre property is just minutes from Dublin's fashionable shopping, theatre, restaurants and attractions (and, to make your stay that much more pleasant, a private hotel chauffeur service is available), providing all the comforts of a first-class hotel combined with privacy, luxury and a relaxed, welcoming atmosphere.

Aberdeen Lodge, a converted Edwardian house, is an affordable, well-located option for any visitor, providing high standards of comfort and service within the generous proportions of its rooms. Each en-suite bedroom lists a multichannel television, direct-dial telephone, trouser press and hairdryer amongst its facilities. Additionally, the elegant suites include whirlpool spas and fine period furniture.

The hotel is owned and run by the Halpin family who, as well-established hoteliers, know the needs of their guests and how to indulge them. This particularly applies to the dining room, where you can enjoy excellent food and wine in a lovely setting overlooking the garden. In short, Aberdeen Lodge can match most of the qualities of Dublin's city-centre hotels, but adds to their merits greater seclusion and excellent value.

LOCATION

From the city centre, take Merrion Road toward the Sydney Parade DART station and then the first left into Park Avenue.

> " Magic place, magic people, magic peace
>
> JOE O'CONNOR, ATLANTA, GEORGIA USA

Map p. 454, grid B9

Country house

AGHADOE HEIGHTS HOTEL

The luck of the Irish grants you hospitality and good food in 'this little bit of heaven'

Images of Ireland are often of quaint crofts, rough-walled tracks, limpid lakes and mist-swirled mountains - perhaps even enhanced by a dancing leprechaun. Well, the lakes and mountains are certainly there when you visit Aghadoe Heights, in its enviable location right in the Lakes of Killarney National Park, but the hotel will prevent any bouts of whimsy by bringing you straight into the 21st century. The contemporary design, with its large upstairs lounge, picture windows and balconies, does justice to the outstanding surroundings. The well-equipped suites and rooms are spacious and comfortably furnished with a mix of contemporary styles and carefully-selected antiques. The swimming pool, fitness and spa facilities are top-class, while the internationally applauded Fredrick's Restaurant is among the top 10 in Ireland.

What is really admirable about Aghadoe is the warmth and professionalism of the service - plenty of genuine Irish hospitality from staff who have dedicated many years to the well-being of guests, bringing delightful touches such as tea served by white-gloved waiters. With superb salmon and trout fishing and several championship golf courses nearby, what more could anyone want?

LOCATION

From the centre of Killarney, head toward the N22 Tralee Road. Where the road forks with the N22, veer right and follow signs for the hotel.

Lakes of Killarney,
Killarney, Co Kerry
Republic of Ireland

T +353 (0)64 31766
F +353 (0)64 31345
aghadoe@bestloved.com
www.aghadoe.bestloved.com

GENERAL MANAGERS
Pat and Marie Chawke

ROOM RATES
Single occupancy	€200 - €350
47 Doubles/Twins	€200 - €450
24 Studio Suites	€330 - €650
1 Suite	€600 - €700
1 Penthouse	€950 - €1,500

Includes full breakfast and VAT

CREDIT CARDS
AMERICAN EXPRESS • DC • MC • VI

RATINGS & AWARDS
ITB ★★★★★
RAC Gold Ribbon ★★★★
RAC Dining Award 3
AA ★★★★ ❀❀
AA Top 200 - 2004/2005
AA Irish Hotel of the Year 2001/2002

FACILITIES
On site: Garden, gym, fishing, tennis, indoor pool, hair salon, wellness spa
2 meeting rooms/max 120 people
Nearby: Golf, beach, walking

RESTRICTIONS
Limited facilities for disabled guests
No smoking throughout
Pets by arrangement
Closed 29 Dec. - 27 Jan.

ATTRACTIONS
Ring of Kerry, Muckross House & Gardens, Killarney National Park, Gap of Dunloe, Torc Waterfall, Ballybunion, Waterville & Tralee golf courses

NEAREST
CITY:
Cork - 60 miles/1 hr 30 mins

AIRPORT:
Cork - 60 miles/1 hr 30 mins

RAIL STATION:
Killarney - 3 miles/5 mins

AFFILIATIONS
Preferred Hotels & Resorts

RESERVATIONS
Toll free in US: 800-323-7500
Quote Best Loved

ACCESS CODES
AMADEUS PH KIRAGH
APOLLO/GALILEO PH 36489
SABRE/ABACUS PH 21798
WORLDSPAN PH AGHD

IRELAND

They are surrounded by the finest fish in the sea

AHERNES

Restaurant with rooms

163 North Main St,
Youghal, Co Cork
Republic of Ireland

T +353 (0)24 92424
F +353 (0)24 93633
ahernes@bestloved.com
www.ahernes.bestloved.com

OWNERS
The Fitzgibbon Family

ROOM RATES
Single occupancy €115 - €120
13 Doubles/Twins €160 - €200
Includes full breakfast and VAT

CREDIT CARDS
AMERICAN EXPRESS • DC • MC • VI

RATINGS & AWARDS
ITB ★★★★ Guest House
RAC ◆◆◆◆◆ Dining Award 2
RAC Warm Welcome, Sparkling
Diamond, Little Gem Awards
AA ® Restaurant with Rooms
AA Romantic Hotel

FACILITIES
On site: 1 meeting room/max 50 people
Nearby: Golf, fishing, riding,
hill walking

RESTRICTIONS
Limited facilities for disabled guests
No smoking throughout
No pets; guide dogs only

ATTRACTIONS
Fota Island Golf Course,
Jameson Heritage Centre,
Waterford Crystal, Blarney Castle,
Cobh Heritage Centre,
National Hunt Racing

NEAREST
CITY:
Cork - 30 miles/45 mins
AIRPORT:
Cork - 30 miles/45 mins
RAIL STATION:
Cork - 30 miles/45 mins

AFFILIATIONS
Ireland's Blue Book
Preston's Global Hotels

RESERVATIONS
Toll free in US: 800-544-9993
or 800-323-5463
Quote Best Loved

ACCESS CODES
Not applicable

IRELAND

Luxury rooms with a seafood view - an attraction for all palates

Ahernes is in the heart of the picturesque Youghal (pronounced 'Yawl'), the old historic walled port at the mouth of the River Blackwater. It is a family pub transformed by the Fitzgibbons (third-generation) into a renowned restaurant specialising in the freshest local seafood: Lobster, crab, sole, salmon, monkfish, mussels and clams all feature on tempting menus that change daily.

The 13 luxurious bedrooms, generous in size, have been tastefully decorated and furnished, combining modern features (six-foot bed, hair dryer, television, direct-dial telephone and trouser press) with carefully-chosen antiques that blend perfectly together.

East Cork is a primary tourist area on the splendid south coast of Ireland. Ancient historic buildings include the still-used 12th-century Collegiate Church, the unique Clock Tower and Ireland's first post-Norman university, founded in 1464. Close to Ahernes are an 18-hole golf course, deep sea and river angling, riding, two Blue Flag beaches and superb walks through beautiful countryside. From the moment you are first greeted by the family, you will find Ahernes is a marvellous place to relax and enjoy yourself.

LOCATION
On Youghal's main street.

> **The days at Ard na Sidhe are the highlight of our visit in Ireland**
>
> HANS JÜRGEN LINSCHIND

Country house

ARD NA SIDHE

Mystical history set in an award-winning garden

Ard na Sidhe translates as 'the Hill of the Fairies'. This 18-bedroom mansion hotel on the edge of Caragh Lake has the modern facilities, high cuisine and service you would expect from Killarney Hotels, one of Ireland's leading leisure groups - yet it also has a mystic history that reaches deep into the country's distant and magical past.

Lady Gordon, a lady of titled Irish lineage, built the house in 1913. The building is long, low and gabled, with casement windows set in stone mullions, 'and never', said Lady Gordon, 'looked new'. The ghost of her ancestor, Bess Stokes, is said to haunt the grounds, but it was 'The Hill of the Fairies' long before Bess.

The house fits harmoniously into superbly romantic scenery beside Ireland's highest mountain, McGillicuddy's Reeks. All around is magnificently beautiful countryside for fishing, cycling and boating on the lakes, and several of the country's finest golf courses are within an easy and delightful drive away - or take a stroll in the hotel's own award-winning garden. At the Ard na Sidhe, you're within easy reach of the full range of leisure and historical touring attractions that have made Killarney one of the best-loved places in the world - and there is an extra special something in the unique and mystical history of The Hill of the Fairies.

LOCATION

Right at the edge of beautiful Caragh Lake at Killarney.

**Caragh Lake,
Killorglin, Co Kerry
Republic of Ireland**

T +353 (0)66 9769105
F +353 (0)66 9769282
ardnasidhe@bestloved.com
www.ardnasidhe.bestloved.com

RESIDENT MANAGER
Adrian O'Sullivan

ROOM RATES
Single occupancy   €215 - €309
11 Doubles/Twins   €215 - €260
7 Superior Doubles/Twins €260 - €309
Includes full breakfast, service and VAT

CREDIT CARDS
AMERICAN EXPRESS • DC • MC • VI

RATINGS & AWARDS
ITB ★★★★ Hotel
National Garden Competition Winner

FACILITIES
On site: Garden, fishing, boating
Nearby: Golf, horse riding

RESTRICTIONS
No facilities for disabled guests
No children
No smoking throughout
No pets
Closed 1 Oct. - 30 April

ATTRACTIONS
Ring of Kerry, Caragh Lake,
Killarney National Park,
Dingle Peninsula, Ballybunion,
Waterville and Tralee golf courses

NEAREST
CITY:
Cork - 67 miles/2 hrs 15 mins

AIRPORT:
Shannon - 95 miles/2 hrs 15 mins
Cork - 95 miles/2 hrs 15 mins

RAIL STATION:
Killarney - 17 miles/40 mins

AFFILIATIONS
Killarney Hotels Ltd
Preston's Global Hotels

RESERVATIONS
Toll free in US: 800-544-9993
or 800-537-8483
Quote Best Loved

ACCESS CODES
Not applicable

IRELAND

One hundred percent relaxation in a beautiful house with great food and outstanding service

PAULA AND C J SMITH, BELFAST

ARDTARA COUNTRY HOUSE

Country house

8 Gorteade Road, Upperlands,
Co Londonderry BT46 5SA
Northern Ireland

T (UK) 0870 432 8521
T 028 7964 4490
F 028 7964 5080
ardtara@bestloved.com
www.ardtara.bestloved.com

PROPRIETOR
Alistair Hanna

GENERAL MANAGER
Mary Breslin

RATES PER PERSON
Single occupancy   £95
8 Doubles   £75
Includes full breakfast and VAT

CREDIT CARDS
AMERICAN EXPRESS • MC • VI

RATINGS & AWARDS
NITB ★★★★ Guest House
AA ★★ ❀❀ 79%
Fodor's Choice

FACILITIES
On site: Garden, tennis,
available for ministerial weddings
1 meeting room/max 50 people
Nearby: Golf, fishing, hiking, walking

RESTRICTIONS
Limited facilities for disabled guests
No smoking in restaurant
or bedrooms
No pets; guide dogs only
Closed Christmas and Boxing Day

ATTRACTIONS
Giant's Causeway, Dunluce Castle,
Old Bushmills Distillery,
Royal Portrush Golf Club, Bushmills
Steam Railway, Sperrin Mountains

NEAREST
CITY:
Belfast - 35 miles/50 mins
Londonderry - 30 miles/40 mins

AIRPORT:
Belfast - 30 miles/40 mins

RAIL STATION:
Ballymoney - 7 miles/15 mins

FERRY PORT:
Belfast - 35 miles/50 mins

AFFILIATIONS
Ireland's Blue Book

RESERVATIONS
National rate in UK: 0870 432 8521
Toll-free in US: 800-628-4893
Quote Best Loved

ACCESS CODES
Not applicable

Fine food and Victorian elegance in a golfer's paradise

This Victorian estate house snuggled into the South Londonderry village of Upperlands is the best of old and new, a captivating historical stay with modern amenities and timeless service. Originally the family home of linen magnate Harry Jackson Clark, the house still bears his influence in the form of some of the treasures he brought back from his travels to the New World. The service, too, belongs to a bygone era - Ardtara's warm, friendly staff are always happy to make your stay more comfortable, whether it's arranging a tee time or making suggestions for a day's drive.

However, you might just choose to stay in - the hotel's eight bedrooms are all quite tempting, offering roaring fires and views over the hotel's eight acres of grounds. It's just as grand, too, in Ardtara's comfortable lounges and dining room, where chef Martin Nelson offers his own brand of 'country house cooking' - think delicacies like cannelloni of crab and Dublin Bay prawns with fennel broth.

Working up an appetite is certainly no problem , either, with an all-weather tennis court and, of course, some of the world's best golfing at nearby Royal Portrush. Anglers can have an afternoon on the River Bann, and if you're just up for a walk, there's much to be enjoyed along the splendid, rugged Londonderry coast.

LOCATION
Gorteade Road is a left turn from the B75 (accessible from Belfast via the M2, then A6 and A29), just past the turning for Upperlands.

IRELAND

"I just wish that I had the eloquence of diction or the brilliance of metaphor to adequately describe this fine castle"

MR J O'NEIL, TEXAS USA

Castle

ASHFORD CASTLE

Cong, Co Mayo
Republic of Ireland

T +353 (0)94 9546003
F +353 (0)94 9546260
ashford@bestloved.com
www.ashford.bestloved.com

GENERAL MANAGER
Niall Rochford

ROOM RATES
40 Standard Doubles/Twins €225 - €457
32 Deluxe Doubles/Twins €345 - €546
5 State Rooms €599 - €792
6 Suites €725 - €1,095
Includes service and VAT

CREDIT CARDS
AMERICAN EXPRESS • DC • MC • VI

RATINGS & AWARDS
ITB ★★★★★ Hotel

FACILITIES
On site: Garden, gym, heli-pad, fishing, riding, golf, tennis, health & beauty, archery, snooker, clay pigeon shooting, gym, falconry
1 meeting room/max 110 people

RESTRICTIONS
Limited facilities for disabled guests
No smoking throughout
No pets

ATTRACTIONS
Westport, Clifden, Connemara National Park, Kylemore Abbey, Galway, Ceidhe Fields

NEAREST
CITY:
Galway - 35 miles/45 mins

AIRPORT:
Shannon - 90 miles/1 hr 30 mins

RAIL STATION:
Galway - 35 miles/45 mins

AFFILIATIONS
Leading Small Hotels

RESERVATIONS
Toll free in US: 800-346-7007
Quote Best Loved

ACCESS CODES
Not applicable

A stately home, sporting complex and the best of the west of Ireland

Until 1939, Ashford Castle was part of an estate owned by the Guinness family and the residence of Lord Ardilaun. It was later transformed into a luxury hotel and its lavish furnishings, the rich panelling of the Great Hall, the objets d'art and masterpiece paintings came into the domain of those guests fortunate enough to stay there. The lordly bedrooms are sumptuously furnished to the highest standards and most overlook the lough or the river.

The estate provides an almost inexhaustible array of sporting pleasures: a nine-hole golf course, indoor equestrian centre, clay pigeon shooting, archery, fishing, a fully equipped gymnasium, a health centre and some of the most magnificent walks in Ireland, as well as the country's only school of falconry.

Everything about Ashford Castle reflects its aristocratic antecedents: the comfort, the service and, not least, the food. This area of Ireland is famous for the quality of its produce, especially the seafood, which comes from the cleanest waters in Europe. You have a choice between traditional and French cuisine dining in either the George V or The Connaught restaurants. An evening drink in the Dungeon Bar is accompanied by a resident pianist and harpist.

LOCATION

From Galway, take the N84 north (Headford), then the R334 to the R346 (Cong). At Cross, turn left at the church and drive through the castle gates.

IRELAND

ASHLEE LODGE

Contemporary hotel

**Tower, Blarney, Co Cork
Republic of Ireland**

T +353 (0)21 4385346
F +353 (0)21 4385726
ashlee@bestloved.com
www.ashlee.bestloved.com

OWNERS
John and Anne O'Leary

ROOM RATES
Single occupancy   €100 - €160
6 Executive Doubles/Twins €140 - €155
2 Mini Suites   €160 - €175
2 Master Suites   €170 - €200
Includes full breakfast and VAT

CREDIT CARDS
AMERICAN EXPRESS • DC • MC • VI

RATINGS & AWARDS
ITB ★★★★ Guest House
RAC ◆◆◆◆◆
RAC Warm Welcome, Sparkling
Diamond, Little Gem Awards
AA ◆◆◆◆◆
AA Premier Collection
Irish Accommodation Services Institute
National Award Winner 2004

FACILITIES
On site: Garden, sauna,
Canadian hot tub
Nearby: Golf, fishing, riding,
leisure centre

RESTRICTIONS
No smoking throughout
Pets by arrangement

ATTRACTIONS
Blarney Castle, Blarney Woollen Mills,
Cork City Gaol, English Market,
Cobh - Queenstown Story,
Jameson Heritage Centre

NEAREST
CITY:
Cork - 9 miles/15 mins

AIRPORT:
Cork - 11 miles/20 mins

RAIL STATION:
Cork - 9 miles/15 mins

AFFILIATIONS
Independent

RESERVATIONS
Direct with hotel
Quote Best Loved

ACCESS CODES
AMADEUS YX ORKASH
APOLLO/GALILEO YX 71484
SABRE/ABACUS YX 56318
WORLDSPAN YX ORKAL
PEGASUS YX ORKASH

IRELAND

Your luxurious retreat a stone's throw from Blarney Castle and Cork

John and Anne O'Leary are justifiably proud of Ashlee Lodge. Every detail was carefully considered so visitors from all over the world would instantly feel cocooned by the best of Irish hospitality.

Only 10 minutes from Cork, Ashlee Lodge is near many of Ireland's greatest sights and immersed in a golfer's paradise. To reflect this, the 10 spacious bedrooms are named after famous local golf courses. Each light, airy room is exceptionally well-equipped with a king-size bed, independent heating, wide-screen television, modem access and a luxurious bathroom. The two master suites and the two garden suites also have whirlpool baths, and for all a Canadian hot tub and sauna await in an attractive rooftop garden.

Breakfast is the only meal served at the hotel, in order to tempt you to the many pubs and restaurants within a few minutes' walk. But what a breakfast! Taken in the greenery-filled Conservatory, there is a superb cold buffet plus a choice of 10 hot dishes influenced by local produce. Although visitors may end up kissing the Blarney Stone at the nearby castle, no one is exaggerating when Ashlee Lodge is described as a place that puts you first.

LOCATION
On the R617 Blarney-Killarney road
a mile outside of Blarney.

> "Thank you all for the excellent hospitality and warm welcome"
>
> MÁIRTÍN Ó FATHAIGH, UNIVERSITY COLLEGE, CORK

City hotel

ATHENAEUM HOUSE HOTEL

A state-of-the-art lifestyle overlooking Ireland's second city

A splendid 18th-century house reborn as a chic, smart boutique hotel, Athenaeum House Hotel is perched on the banks of the River Suir with views overlooking both Waterford City and the hotel's 10 acres of parkland - an ideal mix of city life and peaceful pleasures. Featuring 25 en-suite bedrooms and four magnificent suites, this riverside treat is an easy choice; business travellers can take advantage of the hotel's three meeting rooms, while holiday visitors can enjoy the relaxing grounds or explore Waterford's history, beauty and shopping. For both, there are the luxuries of individually-decorated bedrooms, flat-screen televisions and hi-fi equipment, in-room voicemail and ISDN access. Each bedroom is named after a distinguished writer, artist, musician or inventor - and with any luck, you'll find your own personal favourite, whether it's the John Lennon or the James Joyce.

Dining at Athenaeum House is a treat, too, with ZAKS Restaurant offering an eclectic blend of Irish and continental cuisine with views over Waterford harbour. On Friday and Saturday evenings, the experience is accompanied by the music of the house's resident pianist - a relaxing opportunity to sit back and enjoy selections such as freshly caught cod topped with avocado, salmon and a hollandaise glaze. All, of course, are accompanied by a vibrant selection of wines specially chosen by the staff. Cheers!

LOCATION

In Waterford city centre, just off Abbey Road on the north bank of the River Suir.

Christendom, Ferrybank,
Waterford, Co Waterford
Republic of Ireland

T +353 (0)51 833 999
F +353 (0)51 833 977
athenaeum@bestloved.com
www.athenaeum.bestloved.com

OWNERS
Stan and Mailo Power

ROOM RATES
Single occupancy	€110 - €150
25 Doubles/Twins	€110 - €170
4 Suites	€220 - €250

Includes VAT and service

CREDIT CARDS
AMERICAN EXPRESS • MC • VI

RATINGS & AWARDS
AA ★★★ 72%

FACILITIES
On site: Garden, licensed for weddings
3 meeting rooms/max 150 people
Nearby: Golf, fishing, horse riding

RESTRICTIONS
Limited facilities for disabled guests
Smoking on terrace only
No pets; guide dogs only

ATTRACTIONS
Waterford Crystal showrooms,
Reginalds Tower Museum,
Waterford Treasures Museum,
Christchurch Cathedral,
Waterford walking tours

NEAREST
CITY:
Waterford

AIRPORT:
Waterford - 7 miles/20 mins
Cork - 80 miles/2 hrs

RAIL STATION:
Waterford - 1 mile/5 mins

AFFILIATIONS
Independent

RESERVATIONS
Direct with hotel
Quote Best Loved

ACCESS CODES
Not applicable

IRELAND

I have travelled the globe for 30 years. This house equals most and tops the rest. It's a credit to you

MR SHANKS, DUBLIN, IRELAND

BALLYGARRY HOUSE

Country house

Killarney Road, Tralee, Co Kerry
Republic of Ireland

T +353 (0)66 7123322
F +353 (0)66 7127630
ballygarry@bestloved.com
www.ballygarry.bestloved.com

OWNER/MANAGER
Padraig McGillicuddy

ROOM RATES
Single occupancy	€120
7 Doubles/Twins	€150
32 Superior Doubles/Twins	€190
7 Junior Suites	€250
Includes full breakfast and VAT	

CREDIT CARDS
AMERICAN EXPRESS • MC • VI

RATINGS & AWARDS
ITB ★★★★ Hotel
RAC ★★★★ Blue Ribbon
AA ★★★★ 70%

FACILITIES
On site: Garden, heli-pad
1 meeting room/max 400
Nearby: Golf, fishing, riding, clay pigeon shooting

RESTRICTIONS
No smoking throughout
No pets
Closed 24 - 27 Dec. & 3 - 21 Jan.

ATTRACTIONS
Dingle Peninsula, Ring of Kerry, Killarney National Park, Muckross House, Jeanie Johnston Emigrant Ship, Blennerville Windmill

NEAREST
CITY:
Tralee

AIRPORT:
Shannon - 82 miles/2 hrs
Kerry - 5 miles/10 mins

RAIL STATION:
Tralee - 1 mile/5 mins

AFFILIATIONS
Independent

RESERVATIONS
Toll free in UK: 0800 894 351
Toll free in US: 800-537-8483
Quote Best Loved

ACCESS CODES
AMADEUS LM KIR030
APOLLO/GALILEO LM 52861
SABRE/ABACUS LM 8228
WORLDSPAN LM 09030

A wonderful welcome and the drama of Ireland's breathtaking Atlantic coast

For 50 years, the family-run Ballygarry House has invited all who stay there to make themselves at home. This traditional warm welcome is authentic to this southwestern corner of Ireland, also home to some of the country's premier championship and links golf courses, including Tralee, Ballybunion and Mahoney's Point. This hospitality is also echoed in the décor: well-chosen antiques, blazing open fires and freshly-cut flowers all contribute to the cordial environment, and the surrounding grounds are equally enticing.

Ballygarry is really all about style and imagination. The staff are quite simply the backbone of the hotel, and nothing is too much trouble for them! The bedrooms are spacious and individually designed, and fluffy towels and bathrobes adorn elegant bathrooms. In the split-level dining room, culinary delights include chargrilled black Angus beef on a bed of chive mash or seared pepper-crusted yellowfin tuna on a warm spinach salad.

Set in six acres of mature gardens at the foot of the Kerry Mountains, the local countryside also offers a variety of lake, woodland and sea with a plethora of fascinating walks and trails in the vicinity. A host of outdoor activities can also be arranged.

LOCATION
One mile from Tralee on the Killarney road.

IRELAND

> "Significant parts of my life are spent in four- and five-star hotels. The atmosphere and presentation of the Bayview matches the best of them"
>
> PETER MAXWELL, HAMPSHIRE

Seaside hotel

BAYVIEW HOTEL

Superb food and marvellous views of a spectacular coastline

Bayview Hotel at Ballycotton overlooks a small, unspoilt fishing harbour, and every bedroom has a view over miles of spectacular coastline. Combining modern luxury with the charm and warmth of bygone days, the style at Bayview is informal and friendly; the dinners are superb, based on fresh local ingredients to provide dishes with the right balance of flavour, texture and presentation - truly delightful! The hotel's original garden offers invigorating air and a peek into the work of a traditional fishing harbour.

The hotel is excellently placed for sea angling, especially for warm-water fish such as shark and conger, and for birdwatching, coastal walking and swimming. Six golf courses, links and woodland, are within 30 minutes' drive.

Ballycotton is a traditional fishing village dating back to 1250. It is ideally located for exploring the many treasures of East Cork and the wider environs of counties Cork and Waterford. Close at hand are Fota Wildlife Park, the Jameson Whiskey Heritage Centre, Queenstown Harbour with its Titanic connections and the Queenstown Story at Cobh, where many Irish emigrants set sail for America from the mid-19th century to the 1950s.

LOCATION

At Castlemartyr on the N25, turn onto the R632 toward Garryvoe. From Garryvoe, follow signs for Shanagarry and Ballycotton.

Ballycotton, Co Cork
Republic of Ireland

T +353 (0)21 4646746
F +353 (0)21 4646075
bayview@bestloved.com
www.bayview.bestloved.com

OWNER
John O'Brien

GENERAL MANAGER
Stephen Belton

ROOM RATES
Single occupancy   €111 - €129
33 Doubles/Twins   €158 - €194
2 Suites   €218 - €254
Includes full breakfast and VAT

CREDIT CARDS
AMERICAN EXPRESS • DC • MC • VI

RATINGS & AWARDS
ITB ★★★★ Hotel
RAC ★★★ Dining Award 2
AA ★★★ ❀❀ 77%

FACILITIES
On site: Garden, fishing, sea fishing
2 meeting rooms/max 40 people
Nearby: Golf, fishing, tennis, riding

RESTRICTIONS
Limited facilities for disabled guests
No children under 5 years in restaurant, high tea provided
No smoking in public areas
No pets
Closed 1 Nov. - 1 March

ATTRACTIONS
Cobb Heritage Centre,
Youghal Cathedral, Titanic Trail,
Fota Wildlife Park,
Jameson Heritage Centre, Fota House,
Ballymaloc Cookery School

NEAREST
CITY:
Midleton - 12 miles/30 mins

AIRPORT:
Cork - 23 miles/45 mins

RAIL STATION:
Cork - 23 miles/45 mins

AFFILIATIONS
Manor House Hotels of Ireland

RESERVATIONS
Toll free in US/Canada: 800-44-UTELL
Quote Best Loved

ACCESS CODES
AMADEUS UI ORKBAY
APOLLO/GALILEO UI 91672
SABRE/ABACUS UI 27287
WORLDSPAN UI 40022

IRELAND

BROWNES

Townhouse

22 St Stephen's Green, Dublin 2
Republic of Ireland

T +353 (0)1 638 3939
F +353 (0)1 638 3900
brownes@bestloved.com
www.brownes.bestloved.com

GENERAL MANAGER
Sonia Santana

ROOM RATES
Single occupancy   €175 - €190
7 Doubles/Twins   €220 - €250
1 Suite   €375
Includes VAT

CREDIT CARDS
AMERICAN EXPRESS • MC • VI

RATINGS & AWARDS
ITB ★★★★ Guest House
AA ◆◆◆◆◆
AA Premier Collection

FACILITIES
On site: Private dining
1 meeting room/max 33 people
Nearby: Golf, tennis, fitness,
water skiing, fishing, riding, shooting

RESTRICTIONS
Limited facilities for disabled guests
No smoking throughout
No pets

ATTRACTIONS
St Stephen's Green, Trinity College,
National Museum,
Grafton Street, Temple Bar,
Powerscourt House & Gardens,
National Art Gallery,
Guinness Hopstore

NEAREST
CITY:
Dublin

AIRPORT:
Dublin - 15 miles/30 mins

RAIL STATION:
Heuston - 6 miles/15 mins

AFFILIATIONS
Celebrated Hotels Collection

RESERVATIONS
Toll free in US: 800-322-2403
Quote Best Loved

ACCESS CODES
Not applicable

The talk of Dublin stylishly set in the city's remarkable cultural centre

Sophisticated but relaxed - this is the atmosphere that pervades this Georgian townhouse whose tall windows overlook St Stephen's Green, the spacious and prestigious park right in the heart of Dublin. Close by are the buildings of Trinity College and the National Museum, Grafton Street's fashionable shopping district, many of the city's most popular pubs and all the gathering places of trendy Temple Bar.

Brownes is a city centre guest house, but with the intimacy and warmth of a country home. The 12 bedrooms and suites are equipped with all the facilities a business guest requires (including ISDN and a direct fax line), but each is individually designed and traditionally decorated and furnished with comfort and luxury in mind.

Brownes Brasserie is a gracious split-level dining room whose plush deep-red seating is set off by the crisp white table linen. Known by locals for its sumptuous cuisine, the Brasserie is, like the townhouse, stylish in a traditional manner with a contemporary, relaxed ambience. It prides itself on being the perfect setting for a casual meal with friends, a lunch with business colleagues, or a romantic dinner a deux. There is also a suite for small private meetings and a private dining room with views of St Stephen's Green. Full of life, Brownes is a place to see and be seen!

LOCATION
From the airport, follow signs to the city centre
and then St Stephen's Green. Brownes is
on the north side.

IRELAND

> "It's one of those places where you hope it rains all day so you have an excuse to snuggle indoors"
>
> IAN CRUIKSHANK, JOURNALIST, CANADA

Inn

BUSHMILLS INN HOTEL

At the world's oldest distillery, between the Giant's Causeway and Royal Portrush

The Giant's Causeway Coast is considered some of the most spectacular coastline in Europe - wide, sandy beaches washed by Atlantic rollers, neat fishing harbours nestling between craggy cliffs and grassy dunes supporting a wealth of wildlife. The area is a golfer's paradise, with eight courses (including Royal Portrush) within easy driving range; for anglers, the River Bush is within casting distance of the hotel gardens.

The welcoming glow of their four turf fires is just one of many features that give this historic inn its unique and intriguing character. The oak-beamed loft is the gateway to the Mill House and 22 spacious, cottage-style bedrooms, each with private sitting room area, on the banks of the River Bush. The original 10 coaching inn bedrooms are smaller and overlook the village. There is a secret room - if you can find it! - and in the bar, still lit by gaslight, you can treat yourself to a glass of 25-year-old Bushmills malt whiskey from the hotel's private cask before anticipating the pleasures of the Taste of Ulster Restaurant. Within the restaurant's whitewashed walls and intimate snugs you can enjoy excellent, freshly prepared dishes and expertly chosen wines.

The inn epitomises the true spirit of Ulster hospitality, and is regularly featured by television presenters and travel writers from all over the world.

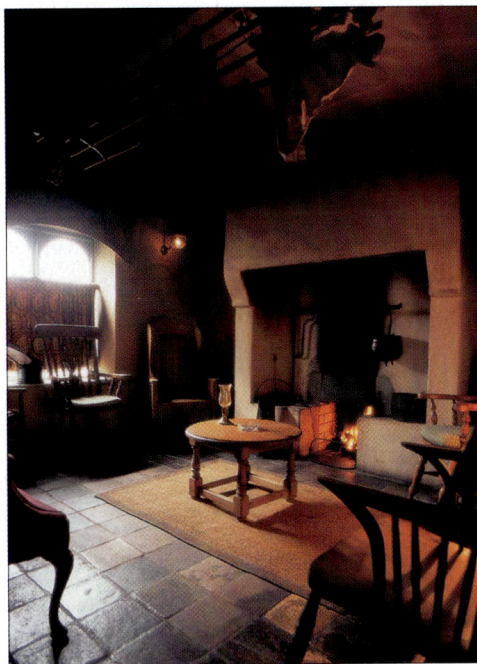

LOCATION

On the A2 Antrim coast road, in the village of Bushmills as you cross the River Bush - follow the Giant's Causeway signs.

9 Dunluce Road, Bushmills,
Co Antrim BT57 8QG
Northern Ireland

T (UK) 0870 432 8551
T 028 2073 3000
F 028 2073 2048
bushmills@bestloved.com
www.bushmills.bestloved.com

MANAGERS
Alan Dunlop and Stella Minogue

ROOM RATES
4 Singles   £68 - £78
28 Doubles/Twins   £98 - £248
Includes full breakfast and VAT

CREDIT CARDS
MC • VI

RATINGS & AWARDS
NITB ★★★ Hotel
NITB Accessibility Category 1
Taste of Ulster
Irish Golf Tour Operators Association -
Ireland's Golf Hotel of the Year 2003

FACILITIES
On site: Garden, heli-pad, fishing
3 meeting rooms/max 40 people
Nearby: Golf, riding, fishing

RESTRICTIONS
Limited facilities for disabled guests
No smoking in bedrooms or restaurant
No pets; guide dogs only

ATTRACTIONS
Giant's Causeway, Dunluce Castle,
Old Bushmills Distillery,
Carrick-a-Rede rope bridge,
Royal Portrush Golf Club,
Bushmills Steam Railway

NEAREST
CITY:
Belfast - 60 miles/1 hr

AIRPORT:
Belfast - 48 miles/1 hr
City of Derry - 35 miles/55 mins

RAIL STATION:
Coleraine - 9 miles/15 mins

AFFILIATIONS
Ireland's Blue Book
Preston's Global Hotels
Northern Ireland's Best Kept Secrets

RESERVATIONS
National rate in UK: 0870 432 8551
Toll free in US: 800-323-5463
or 800-544-9993
Quote Best Loved

ACCESS CODES
Not applicable

IRELAND

BUTLERS TOWN HOUSE

Townhouse

44 Lansdowne Road,
Ballsbridge, Dublin 4
Republic of Ireland

T +353 (0)1 667 4022
F +353 (0)1 667 3960
butlers@bestloved.com
www.butlers.bestloved.com

GENERAL MANAGER
Adrian Harkins

ROOM RATES
Single occupancy   €140
16 Doubles/Twins   €190
4 Deluxe Doubles   €215
Includes buffet breakfast, 24-hour
complimentary tea and coffee,
service and VAT

CREDIT CARDS

AMERICAN EXPRESS • DC • MC • VI

RATINGS & AWARDS
ITB ★★★★ Guest House

FACILITIES
On site: Garden
1 meeting room/max 22 people
Nearby: Golf, tennis, fitness,
riding, sea fishing

RESTRICTIONS
Limited facilities for disabled guests
No smoking throughout
No pets
Closed 23 Dec. - 3 Jan.

ATTRACTIONS
Trinity College, National Museum,
St Stephen's Green, National Gallery,
Christchurch, Grafton Street,
Royal Dublin Society

NEAREST
CITY:
Dublin

AIRPORT:
Dublin - 8 miles/25 mins

RAIL STATION:
Heuston - 3 miles/15 mins

FERRY PORT:
Dun Laoghaire - 2 miles/10 mins

AFFILIATIONS
Manor House Hotels of Ireland
The Charming Hotels

RESERVATIONS
Toll free in US: 800-44-UTELL
Quote Best Loved

ACCESS CODES
AMADEUS UI DUBBUT
APOLLO/GALILEO UI 82012
SABRE/ABACUS UI 3779
WORLDSPAN UI 26133

IRELAND

A haven of calm in the heart of cosmopolitan Dublin

Located on a quiet, leafy avenue in the Victorian quarter of Ballsbridge, the red brick façade of Butlers Town House is pierced by one of the city's characteristic painted doors. Behind this particular one, you will find peaceful and stylish surroundings and the service that regular visitors to Butlers value so highly.

This elegant townhouse has retained many of its original features imaginatively interwoven with 21st-century conveniences, from air conditioning and modem points in the bedrooms to a computer for guests' use in the reception area. The ambience is intimate, even clubby, with a degree of personalised service that belongs to a more leisured age, and the skilled staff appear positively telepathic in their ability to anticipate your needs.

The gourmet Irish breakfast is designed to set up the most demanding appetite for the day. Menu choices include traditional favourites such as black and white puddings and scrambled eggs with Irish cheddar and tomatoes, as well as more exotic fare ranging from poached eggs with salmon and hollandaise sauce to French toast with maple syrup. There is also a light room-service menu and a plethora of excellent restaurants nearby.

LOCATION

From the M1, follow the signs for East Link Toll Bridge. Drive to the top of Bath Avenue and turn left; Butlers is 100 yards on the right.

> We wanted something peaceful and elegant within walking distance to Killarney town. The mountain and lake views were a bonus. The Cahernane exceeded all our expectations
>
> JAKKI AND VICTOR MONTICA, TORONTO

Country house

CAHERNANE HOUSE HOTEL

Step into history at this beautiful escape from the everyday

As you approach Cahernane House, the final quarter mile of your journey is through a tunnel of peaceful, lush greenery - a perfect prelude to a place that's more a retreat from everyday life than an ordinary hotel.

Formerly the residence of the Earls of Pembroke, this splendidly-appointed house dates from 1877; after a meticulous renovation, period features are elegantly accented in 38 individually-furnished bedrooms and grand public areas, adding up to true 19th-century flavour. Many rooms also feature Jacuzzi baths or private balconies for an even more satisfying sense of escape. A tastefully-designed extension offers a touch of the modern that's expertly blended with the house's past. Award-winning meals are the order of the day in the gracious dining room, and a charming cellar bar rounds off the indoor attractions. Well, not quite - there's also the highly impressive wine cellar that serves as the bar's backdrop, listing hundreds of well-judged wines.

Outside, there is golf (Killarney's beautiful Championship courses are world-famous), the charms of Killarney town and (need we even mention it?) the limitless attractions of Killarney National Park - an area of Outstanding National Beauty and yours to explore.

LOCATION

From Killarney town centre, follow road to Kenmare and Muckross House for half a mile. The hotel's entrance is on the right.

Muckross Road,
Killarney, Co Kerry
Republic of Ireland

T +353 (0)64 31895
F +353 (0)64 34340
cahernane@bestloved.com
www.cahernane.bestloved.com

MANAGING DIRECTOR
Sara Browne

ROOM RATES
12 Standard Rooms €225 - €264
24 Superior Rooms €245 - €299
2 Suites   €290 - €380
Includes full breakfast and VAT

CREDIT CARDS
AMERICAN EXPRESS • DC • JCB • MC • VI

RATINGS & AWARDS
ITB ★★★★ Hotel
RAC ★★★★ Dining Award 2

FACILITIES
On site: Garden, croquet, tennis
1 meeting room/max 25 people
Nearby: Pool, golf, fishing,
health & beauty, riding, walks

RESTRICTIONS
Limited facilities for disabled guests
No smoking in public areas
No pets; guide dogs only
Closed mid-December - mid-February

ATTRACTIONS
Killarney National Park,
Ring of Kerry Drive,
Muckross House and Gardens,
Gap of Dunloe Experience,
hill walking, river fishing, shopping

NEAREST
CITY:
Cork- 55 miles/1 hr
Limerick - 70 miles/1 hr 30 mins

AIRPORT:
Cork - 55 miles/1 hr
Shannon - 85 miles/2 hrs 30 mins

RAIL STATION:
Killarney - 1/2 mile/5 mins

FERRY PORT:
Cork - 70 miles/1 hr 30 mins

AFFILIATIONS
Manor House Hotels of Ireland

RESERVATIONS
Direct with hotel
Quote Best Loved

ACCESS CODES
AMADEUS UZ KIRCAH
APOLLO/GALILEO UZ 91734
SABRE/ABACUS UZ 28759
WORLDSPAN UZ 40041

IRELAND

CARAGH LODGE

Country house

Caragh Lake, Co Kerry
Republic of Ireland

T +353 (0)66 9769115
F +353 (0)66 9769316
caragh@bestloved.com
www.caragh.bestloved.com

OWNER
Mary Gaunt

ROOM RATES
1 Single   €140
13 Doubles/Twins   €195 - €250
1 Suite   €350
Includes full breakfast, service and VAT

CREDIT CARDS
AMERICAN EXPRESS • DC • MC • VI

RATINGS & AWARDS
ITB ★★★★ Guest House
RAC Gold Ribbon ★★ Dining Award 3
Karen Brown Recommended
Gilbeys Hotel and Catering Award

FACILITIES
On site: Garden, fishing
1 meeting room/max 15 people
Nearby: Golf, riding, beaches

RESTRICTIONS
No facilities for disabled guests
No children under 12 years
No smoking throughout
No pets
Closed late October - late April

ATTRACTIONS
Ring of Kerry, Dingle Peninsula,
Killarney, Skelligs Rock

NEAREST
CITY:
Cork - 70 miles/2 hrs

AIRPORT:
Shannon/Cork - 70 miles/2 hrs
Kerry Airport - 16 miles/30 mins

RAIL STATION:
Killarney - 14 miles/30 mins

AFFILIATIONS
Ireland's Blue Book
Preston's Global Hotels

RESERVATIONS
Toll free in US: 800-544-9993
or 800-323-5463
Quote Best Loved

ACCESS CODES
Not applicable

IRELAND

A gracious house a stone's throw from the spectacular Ring of Kerry

Less than one mile from the spectacular Ring of Kerry and four miles from the golden beaches of Dingle Bay, Caragh Lodge sits on the shore of Caragh Lake looking toward the breathtaking slopes of the McGillycuddy Reeks, Ireland's highest mountains.

The rooms are sumptuously decorated with period furnishings and antiques, and the converted garden rooms offer spectacular views over stunning displays of magnolias, rhododendrons, azaleas, camellias and rare shrubs. Exquisite furnishings and welcoming log fires in the main house's lounges provide the perfect place to end the day. Overlooking the lake, the dining room features local treats such as freshly-caught wild salmon, succulent Kerry lamb, garden-grown vegetables and home-baked breads, all personally prepared by Mary Gaunt.

Golfers will find Caragh Lodge the perfect base. With eight courses nearby, tee-off times can be easily arranged prior to your stay. Salmon and brown trout fishing are on the doorstep, and two boats are available for guests. Ghillies or any necessary permits for fishing in the two local rivers can easily be arranged.

LOCATION

From the N70 (Killorglin to Glenbeigh), take the road signposted for Caragh Lodge.
Turn left at the lake; the hotel is on the right.

Stately home   CASTLE DURROW COUNTRY HOUSE

**Durrow, Co Laois
Republic of Ireland**

T +353 (0)502 36555
F +353 (0)502 36559
durrow@bestloved.com
www.durrow.bestloved.com

OWNERS
Peter and Shelly Stokes

RATES PER PERSON
Single occupancy   €130 - €190
6 Standard Doubles   €90
6 Deluxe Doubles/Twins   €110
10 Master Rooms   €130
1 Suite   €150
4 Deluxe Family Rooms   POA
Includes full breakfast and VAT

CREDIT CARDS
AMERICAN EXPRESS • MC • VI

RATINGS & AWARDS
Awards Pending

FACILITIES
On site: Extensive gardens with tours, heli-pad, tennis, parkland walks, equestrian centre, pony trekking, snooker room, children's playroom, computer room
3 meeting rooms/max 200 people
Nearby: Golf, fishing, polo club, hunting, shooting

RESTRICTIONS
Limited facilities for disabled guests
No smoking throughout
Pets by arrangement
Closed 24 Dec. - 17 Jan.

ATTRACTIONS
Kilkenny Medieval City and Castle, Rock of Cashel, Holycross Abbey, Irish National Stud and Japanese Gardens, Mount Juliet Golf Course, Kildare Golf & Country Club, three nearby parkland golf courses, Curragh Racecourse, Punchestown Racecourse, Dunmore Caves

NEAREST
CITY:
Kilkenny - 16 miles/25 mins

AIRPORT:
Dublin - 70 miles/1 hr 30 mins

RAIL STATION:
Portlaoise - 15 miles/20 mins

AFFILIATIONS
Ireland's Blue Book

RESERVATIONS
Toll free in US: 800-323-5463
Quote Best Loved

ACCESS CODES
Not applicable

Feel like lord and lady of the manor with a taste of 18th-century high life

Sweeping up the Castle Durrow's drive, guests are transported to the elegant world of this 18th-century mansion looking out over the River Erkina and 30 acres of rolling countryside and manicured gardens. Inside, true to its origins, the high-ceilinged, colonnaded reception rooms are furnished with beautiful antiques cleverly complemented by outstanding modern classics.

Glitteringly polished oak floors gleam with light from the tall, elegantly draped windows and sparkling chandeliers. Each of the 26 bedrooms is individual, from the huge 'mistress' rooms with four-poster beds, antiques and sumptuous drapes to the contemporary deluxe rooms with their king-size sleighbeds and classic Colonial furnishings. The top-floor rooms are idiosyncratic, with beamed, sloping ceilings and antique Oriental furnishings in the fashion of the 18th century. Everywhere, the incredible attention to detail is apparent.

The restaurant, with its classical Georgian décor, serves inspired international and regional favourites using the fresh produce for which Ireland is famed. Only 90 minutes from Dublin - and with up-to-date facilities for meetings and unlimited nearby attractions and activities nearby - Castle Durrow is ideal for conferences or weddings.

LOCATION
From Dublin, take the N7 to Portlaoise and then the N8 (Cork). Once in the village of Durrow, the hotel is on the right.

IRELAND

CULLODEN ESTATE AND SPA

Stately home

Bangor Road, Holywood,
Co Down BT18 0EX
Northern Ireland

T (UK) 0870 432 8588
T 028 9042 1066
F 028 9042 6777
culloden@bestloved.com
www.culloden.bestloved.com

GENERAL MANAGER
Kenneth Sharp

ROOM RATES
Single occupancy   £95 - £180
69 Doubles/Twins   £135 - £220
16 Suites   £300 - £600
Includes VAT and full use of spa

CREDIT CARDS
AMERICAN EXPRESS • DC • MC • VI

RATINGS & AWARDS
NITB ★★★★★ Hotel
RAC Blue Ribbon ★★★★★
RAC Dining Award 3

FACILITIES
On site: Heli-pad, croquet,
indoor pool, health & beauty,
licensed for weddings
12 meeting rooms/max 1200 people
Nearby: Golf, fishing, yachting, riding

RESTRICTIONS
No smoking in restaurant
No pets; guide dogs only

ATTRACTIONS
Carrickfergus Castle,
Lough Neagh,
Ulster Folk & Transport Museum,
Tyrone Crystal Factory,
Bushmills Distillery

NEAREST
CITY:
Belfast - 5 miles/15 mins

AIRPORT:
Belfast City - 2 miles/6 mins
Belfast International - 20 miles/40 mins

RAIL STATION:
Cultra - ¼ mile/2 mins
Belfast Central - 6 miles/10 mins

AFFILIATIONS
Celebrated Hotels Collection
Small Luxury Hotels
Hastings Hotels

RESERVATIONS
National rate in UK: 0870 432 8588
Toll free in UK: 00800 525 48000
Toll free in US: 800-322-2403
Quote Best Loved

ACCESS CODES
AMADEUS LX BFSCUL
APOLLO/GALILEO LX 77774
SABRE/ABACUS LX 7652
WORLDSPAN LX BFSCH

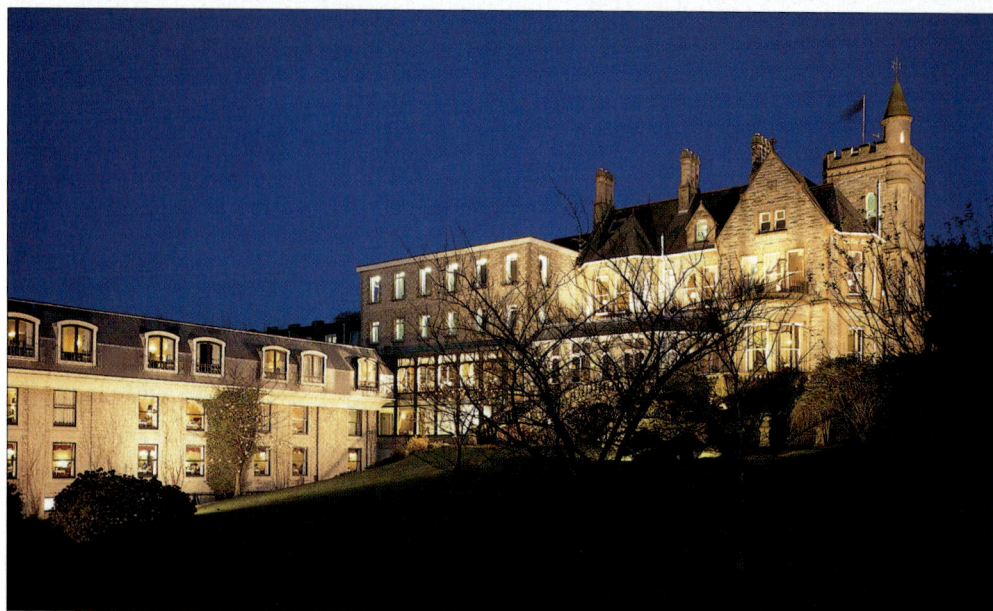

IRELAND

Built for a bishop ... fit for a king!

Of all the palaces in Ireland - and there are many! - few compare with this former Bishops of Down residence at Holywood, just east of Belfast. It is a grand sight standing in its own park on the slopes of Belfast Lough. Inside, too, the Culloden Hotel is magnificent: glowing antiques, original works of art, Louis XV chandeliers and sumptuous fabrics. Oversized rooms offer big picture windows looking over the grounds' panoramic views, and if you're seeking an even more opulent experience, the four suites in the Tower Rooms are in a class of their own.

But for all of Culloden's stylish hauteur, you will find the service friendly and attentive with a will to please - something at which the Irish excel. The Mitre Restaurant, like everything else in this hotel, is stylish and worthy of its accolades. For something lighter, but just as tempting, try the Cultra Inn. The Elysium Spa has been attractively designed and given every facility to indulge mind and body. Golfers will be delighted to know that the hotel will arrange tee-off times at the local golf course - the Royal Belfast, no less! Belfast city centre is a new mecca for shopping, dining, theatre and a variety of entertainment, and is only ten minutes' drive from Culloden. This is one of those hotels you would go to for its own sake, not just because business or pleasure takes you to the area.

LOCATION

From Belfast centre, follow signs for City Airport/Bangor. Pass both the airport and the village of Holywood; the hotel is 300 yards farther on.

"My expectations were huge - my experience was out of this world

ROBERTO DE BURCA, CORAL GABLES, FLORIDA USA

Castle

DROMOLAND CASTLE

Supreme comfort in this castle on an historic estate

In the 16th century, the Dromoland Estate became the seat of the O'Brien clan, descendants of 'Brian Boru', High King of Ireland. Today the castle is one of Europe's top luxury hotels, blending period pieces with modern comfort. Its gallery has one of Ireland's largest collections of portraits, most notably Lucius O'Brien painted by the Swedish artist Michael Dahl. The 17th Baron Inchiquin gave musical recitals in the drawing room where guests now take tea or coffee, and his study has become the Library Bar.

The 410-acre estate is supremely beautiful, with many private facilities for guests. Fine trout await in the lake, and the Castle has its own 18-hole Championship golf course and clubhouse with brassiere restaurant and health and beauty spa. Fishing, shooting, horse riding, jogging trails and tennis are also all on the estate.

The splendid dining room gives panoramic views of the lake and golf course. David McCann, head chef of international repute, presents house specialities including lamb with foie gras and steamed fillets of turbot in fennel. There is an outstanding list of wines from the cellar, which guests are welcome to visit. In short, your home will be your castle when you make Dromoland Castle your home.

LOCATION

Eight miles north of Shannon airport.

Newmarket-on-Fergus,
Co Clare
Republic of Ireland

T +353 (0)61 368144
F +353 (0)61 363355
dromoland@bestloved.com
www.dromoland.bestloved.com

GENERAL MANAGER
Mark Nolan

ROOM RATES
Single occupancy	€225 - €417
29 Doubles	€225 - €417
26 Deluxe Rooms	€345 - €509
18 East Wing Rooms	€390 - €546
13 Executive Deluxe Rooms	€424 - €573
8 Staterooms	€470 - €828
6 Suites	€594 - €1,288

Includes VAT

CREDIT CARDS
AMERICAN EXPRESS • DC • MC • VI

RATINGS & AWARDS
ITB ★★★★★ Silver Award Hotel
AA ★★★★★ ⊛ ⊛
AA Top 200 - 2004/2005
Travel & Leisure Magazine
'Top 50 in Europe'

FACILITIES
On site: Garden, gym, snooker, heli-pad, fishing, riding, golf, indoor pool, health & beauty, snooker, gym, sauna
6 meeting rooms/max 450 people

RESTRICTIONS
Limited facilities for disabled guests
No smoking throughout
No pets

ATTRACTIONS
Cliffs of Moher, The Burren, Bunratty Castle, King John's Castle, Craggaunowen Project, Aran Islands, Hunt Museum, Ballybunion, Doonbeg & Lahinch golf courses

NEAREST
CITY:
Limerick - 17 miles/25mins

AIRPORT:
Shannon - 8 miles/15 mins

RAIL STATION:
Limerick - 18 miles/30 mins

AFFILIATIONS
Preferred Hotels & Resorts

RESERVATIONS
Toll free in US: 800-346-7007
Quote Best Loved

ACCESS CODES
Not applicable

IRELAND

Thank you for the *fáilte*

DUNBRODY COUNTRY HOUSE HOTEL Country house

Arthurstown,
Near Waterford, Co Wexford
Republic of Ireland

T +353 (0)51 389 600
F +353 (0)51 389 601
dunbrody@bestloved.com
www.dunbrody.bestloved.com

OWNERS
Kevin and Catherine Dundon

ROOM RATES
Single occupancy   €120 - €325
15 Doubles/Twins   €220 - €325
7 Suites   €320 - €420
Includes full breakfast and VAT

CREDIT CARDS
AMERICAN EXPRESS • DC • MC • VI

RATINGS & AWARDS
ITB ★★★★ Hotel
RAC Gold Ribbon ★★★
Dining Award 3
Bushmills Restaurant of the Year 2004
Andrew Harper's Grand Award 2002

FACILITIES
On site: Garden, croquet, clay pigeon
shooting, cookery school, spa
3 meeting rooms/max 110 people
Nearby: Golf, fishing, polocrosse

RESTRICTIONS
Children by arrangement
No smoking throughout
Limited facilities for disabled guests
No pets; guide dogs only
Closed 20 - 27 Dec.

ATTRACTIONS
Waterford Crystal, Tintern Abbey,
Hook Peninsula and Lighthouse,
JFK Arboretum, beaches, shark fishing

NEAREST
CITY:
Waterford - 10 miles/15 mins

AIRPORT:
Dublin - 100 miles/2 hrs

RAIL STATION:
Waterford - 10 miles/15 mins

FERRY PORT:
Rosslare - 40 miles/45 mins

AFFILIATIONS
Ireland's Blue Book
Celebrated Hotels Collection
Small Luxury Hotels

RESERVATIONS
Toll free in US: 800-322-2403
or 800-323-5463
or 800-525-4800
Quote Best Loved

ACCESS CODES
AMADEUS LX DUBDCH
APOLLO/GALILEO LX 30267
SABRE/ABACUS LX 55137
WORLDSPAN LX DUBDH

IRELAND

All the attributes of a fine country house with a restaurant to grace any great city

Epicures amongst you who reckon they can tell the difference between a restaurant in a country hotel and its modish city counterpart may have to adjust their mindsets. Dunbrody House is your archetypal country house, with spacious bedrooms, a 20-acre woodland and manicured garden settings - but there the cliché ends.

Dunbrody's restaurant has the gastronomic authority you will find in any European capital and a discerning, well-travelled, appreciative clientele to prove it. In the restaurant, gone is that ghastly hush; this place buzzes with enthusiasm - as true of the diners as of the cheerful young staff who attend them. Now offering a delightful cookery school with two- and four-day residential courses, Dunbrody will become more and more of a destination for food lovers. For all, the new Molton Brown Spa is sure to be popular among anyone in need of total relaxation and pampering.

The front of house is managed by Catherine Dundon, whose marketing background blends perfectly with Kevin's creative talents. They must be very happy with their achievement; their welcome says it all! The final garnish on this unexpected pleasure is the hotel's gorgeous location on Ireland's Sunshine Coast on a long promontory in historic and luscious County Wexford.

LOCATION
From Wexford, take the R733 to Duncannon and Arthurstown. Dunbrody is on the left coming into Arthurstown.

Country house

DUNLOE CASTLE

Killarney, Co Kerry
Republic of Ireland

T +353 (0)64 44111
F +353 (0)64 44583
dunloe@bestloved.com
www.dunloe.bestloved.com

MANAGER
Hillary O'Mara

ROOM RATES
74 Doubles/Twins	€228
19 Superior Doubles/Twins	€298
9 Executive Superiors	€340
1 Suite	€575

Includes service and VAT

CREDIT CARDS
AMERICAN EXPRESS • DC • MC • VI

RATINGS & AWARDS
ITB ★★★★★ Hotel

FACILITIES
On site: Garden, riding, tennis,
indoor pool, steam room, sauna
6 meeting rooms/max 250 people
Nearby: Golf

RESTRICTIONS
Limited facilities for disabled guests
No smoking throughout
No pets
Closed 30 Oct. - 1 May

ATTRACTIONS
Gap of Dunloe, Dunloe Castle,
Ring of Kerry, Dingle Peninsula,
Killarney National Park,
numerous golf courses

NEAREST
CITY:
Cork - 57 miles/1 hr 15 mins

AIRPORT:
Cork - 60 miles/1 hr 15 mins
Shannon - 90 miles/2 hrs

RAIL STATION:
Killarney - 7 miles/20 mins

AFFILIATIONS
Killarney Hotels Ltd

RESERVATIONS
Toll free in US: 800-537-8483
Quote Best Loved

ACCESS CODES
Not applicable

Peace and birdsong in an historic Killarney setting

Dunloe Castle is pure magic: this five-star hotel is in the midst of a fascinating landscape, and the Emerald Isle's magic is reflected in the hotel's own park, an award-winning botanic collection of international renown (it's no surprise, then, that the hotel is a member of the Historic Houses and Gardens Association). An unbelievable assortment of flowers and plants flourish here, Haflinger horses graze nearby and the park looks out to the famous Gap of Dunloe and the beauties of unspoilt nature.

Dunloe Castle's furnishings are elegant and comfortable. The décor is stylish with a wealth of exquisite details, and the 103 rooms and mini-suites have each been designed to include world-class deluxe appointments.

You can enjoy the best of international and Irish cuisine amongst the most beautiful of natural settings in the gourmet restaurant. A magnificent list of wines is there to complement your meal, and you can have a Guinness, an Irish whiskey or anything else you fancy in the cocktail bar. The countless opportunities for leisure activities within easy reach include no fewer than 10 golf courses.

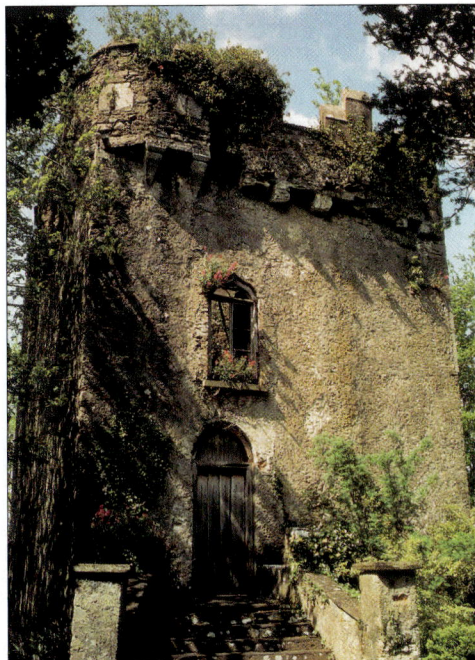

LOCATION
From Killarney, take the N72 (Killorglin). After four and a half miles, turn left toward Gap of Dunloe; the hotel is then signposted.

IRELAND

FITZWILLIAM HOTEL

City hotel

St Stephens Green, Dublin
Republic of Ireland

T +353 (0)1 478 7000
F +353 (0)1 478 7878
fitzwilliam@bestloved.com
www.fitzwilliam.bestloved.com

GENERAL MANAGER
John Kavanagh

ROOM RATES
105 Executive Rooms €310 - €350
25 Superior Rooms €360 - €400
10 Deluxe Rooms   €410 - €450
Includes service and VAT

CREDIT CARDS
AMERICAN EXPRESS • DC • JCB • MC • VI

RATINGS & AWARDS
AA ★★★★ ⊛⊛ 78%

FACILITIES
On site: Gym, health & beauty, salon
3 meeting rooms/max 100

RESTRICTIONS
Limited facilities for disabled guests
Smoking in some rooms only
No pets; guide dogs only

ATTRACTIONS
Trinity College, Dublin Castle,
Guinness Storehouse,
St Stephen's Green, Grafton Street,
Temple Bar, National Museum,
Christchurch

NEAREST
CITY:
Dublin

AIRPORT:
Dublin - 10 miles/30 mins

RAIL STATION:
Heuston - 2 miles/15 mins

AFFILIATIONS
Summit Hotels & Resorts

RESERVATIONS
Toll-free in US: 800-457-4000
Quote Best Loved

ACCESS CODES
AMADEUS XL DUBFIT
APOLLO/GALILEO XL 92803
SABRE/ABACUS XL 42294
WORLDSPAN XL 40081

IRELAND

Luxurious chic
in the heart of Dublin

From the moment you step into the Fitzwilliam Hotel, you'll notice a certain buzz - from its well-placed location in Dublin's most popular shopping district, this high-energy charmer is certain to rejuvenate you, whether you're visiting for business or pleasure. Designed by Sir Terence Conran, the Fitzwilliam offers a thoroughly contemporary experience that's stylish, yet relaxing, from the warmth of the staff to award-winning dining and a full menu of exciting experiences on the doorstep. To one side, there's St Stephen's Green, calm and tranquil; to the other, there's Grafton Street, shopping mecca and just steps away from cultural, historical and leisure attractions.

For dining, however, you might just want to stay in: the Fitzwilliam offers Thornton's, chef Kevin Thornton's two-Michelin-starred contemporary restaurant, Citron, a European-style cafe, and cocktails worth stopping for in The Inn on the Green.

Further adding to the atmosphere is the hotel's Free Spirit hair and beauty salon, offering a wealth of treatments from soothing facials to manicures and hairstyling for that special event; an excellent gym, for those with an active streak; and complementary car parking for all residents. For the business-minded, three state-of-the-art conference rooms await, as well as unlimited free broadband access in all rooms.

LOCATION

On St Stephen's Green in the centre of Dublin, paces away from Grafton Street.

"Wonderful hotel, warm people, beautiful setting"
JEAN KENNEDY SMITH, US AMBASSADOR TO IRELAND, DUBLIN

Country house

GLENLO ABBEY HOTEL

Bushypark, Galway, Co Galway
Republic of Ireland

T +353 (0)91 526666
F +353 (0)91 527800
glenlo@bestloved.com
www.glenlo.bestloved.com

OWNER
John Bourke

ROOM RATES
Single occupancy   €149 - €254
43 Doubles/Twins   €199 - €314
3 Suites   €410 - €780
Includes VAT

CREDIT CARDS
AMERICAN EXPRESS • DC • MC • VI

RATINGS & AWARDS
ITB ★★★★★
RAC Blue Ribbon ★★★★
Dining Award 3
AA ★★★★ ✿ 77%

The Orient Express awaits you at Galway's most luxurious hotel

Built in 1740, Glenlo Abbey was the ancestral home of the Ffrench family, one of the 14 tribes that ruled Galway for five centuries. Set on 138 acres on the shores of Lough Corrib, the estate has a nine-hole golf course, driving range, fishing rights and opportunities for boating.

Owners Peggy and John Bourke spent many years painstakingly restoring the property into a luxury hotel, but one with a difference: Three centuries of antiques furnish the house, recent works by local artists hang on its walls and the skilled plasterwork and handwoven carpets are by local craftsmen. The overall effect is comfortably grand and very stylish without being overbearing.

But what gives the hotel its novelty is the Pullman Restaurant, housed in two of the original carriages from the Orient Express. Indeed, one of the carriages 'starred' in Murder on the Orient Express and long before that carried many a celebrity, including Sir Winston Churchill. The restaurant's menu is themed on some of the famous train's destinations: Paris, St Petersburg, Istanbul ... A more local destination, just three miles away, is the medieval city of Galway, which offers infinite pleasures, not least the pubs, boutiques, and heritage shops, as well as excellent theatre and concerts.

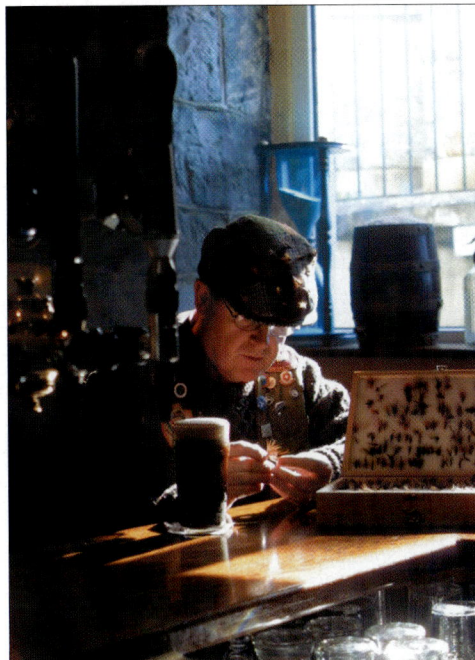

FACILITIES
On site: Garden, heli-pad, fishing, golf, driving range, putting green, boating, clay pigeon shooting, business centre 9 meeting rooms/max 220 people
Nearby: Yachting, tennis, fitness centre, shooting, riding, water sport

RESTRICTIONS
Limited facilities for disabled guests
No smoking throughout
No pets; guide dogs only

ATTRACTIONS
Lough Corrib, Aran Islands, The Burren, Cliffs of Moher, Connemara, Galway City

NEAREST
CITY:
Galway - 2 ½ miles/10 mins

AIRPORT:
Shannon - 56 miles/1 hr 30 mins

RAIL STATION:
Galway - 2 miles/10 mins

AFFILIATIONS
Celebrated Hotels Collection
Small Luxury Hotels

RESERVATIONS
Toll free in US: 800-322-2403
or 800-525-4800
Toll free in UK: 00800-4536-5666
Quote Best Loved

ACCESS CODES
AMADEUS LX GWYGAH
APOLLO/GALILEO LX 58443
SABRE/ABACUS LX 13705
WORLDSPAN LX GWYGA

LOCATION
The hotel is located on the N59 two and a half miles from Galway.

IRELAND

GLIN CASTLE

Castle

Glin, Co Limerick
Republic of Ireland

T +353 (0)68 34173
F +353 (0)68 34364
glin@bestloved.com
www.glin.bestloved.com

OWNERS
Desmond FitzGerald, Knight of Glin
and Madam FitzGerald

GENERAL MANAGER
Bob Duff

ROOM RATES
Single occupancy   €280 - €440
4 Standard Doubles/Twins €280
7 Superior Doubles/Twins €360
4 Deluxe Rooms   €440
Includes full breakfast and VAT

CREDIT CARDS
AMERICAN EXPRESS • DC • MC • VI

RATINGS & AWARDS
Independent

FACILITIES
On site: Garden, croquet, tennis
1 meeting room/max 20 people
Nearby: Golf, riding, yachting

RESTRICTIONS
No facilities for disabled guests
No children under 10 years
No smoking throughout
Pets by arrangement
Closed 30 Nov. - 1 March

ATTRACTIONS
Cliffs of Moher, The Burren,
Ring of Kerry, Dingle Peninsula,
Birr Castle and Demesne,
Adare and Limerick, Bunratty,
Ballybunion,
Tralee and Doonbeg golf courses

NEAREST
CITY:
Limerick - 32 miles/45 mins

AIRPORT:
Shannon - 45 miles/1 hr

RAIL STATION:
Limerick - 32 miles/45 mins

FERRY PORT:
Cork - 70 miles/2 hrs

AFFILIATIONS
Ireland's Blue Book
Celebrated Hotels Collection

RESERVATIONS
Toll Free in US: 800-322-2403
or 800-323-5463
Quote Best Loved

ACCESS CODES
AMADEUS SNN 599
APOLLO/GALILEO SNN 22779
SABRE/ABACUS SNN 49606
WORLDSPAN SNN 05599

IRELAND

Art and architecture meet at this regal historic home

The 29th Knight of Glin and Madam FitzGerald welcome guests to their award-winning castle in supreme style. The present Glin Castle succeeds the medieval ruin in the village of Glin, and was built in the late 18th century with entertaining in mind. The building is steeped in Ireland's history and its architectural pleasures: The entrance hall has a screen of Corinthian pillars, a superb neoclassical plaster ceiling and a unique collection of Irish mahogany furniture. Family portraits and Irish pictures line the walls. The details are incredible - the library bookcase has a secret door, and the hall a rare flying staircase.

The drawing room is a superb setting for coffee and conversation. It has an Adam period ceiling, a beautiful Bossi chimneypiece and six long windows looking out to the croquet lawn. Upstairs are sets of bedrooms, bathrooms and dressing rooms with wall-to-wall carpets, chaises longues and comfortable chintz-covered beds.

The cooking is good Irish country-house style, using vegetables from the walled garden and fresh local fish, poultry and meats. The castle garden grows its own flowers and fruit, and raises bees for honey and hens for free-range eggs. The staff take great care to welcome visitors and make sure they enjoy their visit to this unique historic home.

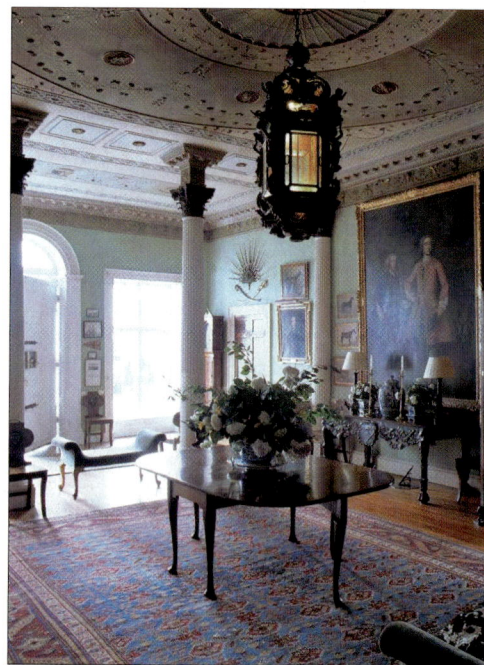

LOCATION
Off the N69, 32 miles to the west of Limerick.

> "Like The Burren itself, Gregans Castle is one of the quiet treasures of Ireland. Superb management is matched only by the warmth of their welcome"
>
> GIBBONS & KAY RUARK, PENNSYLVANIA USA

Country house

GREGANS CASTLE

Ballyvaughan, Co Clare
Republic of Ireland

T +353 (0)65 707 7005
F +353 (0)65 707 7111
gregans@bestloved.com
www.gregans.bestloved.com

OWNERS
The Haden Family

ROOM RATES
Single occupancy   €120 - €270
14 Doubles/Twins   €170 - €290
4 Suites   €210 - €400
Includes full breakfast and VAT

CREDIT CARDS
AMERICAN EXPRESS • MC • VI

RATINGS & AWARDS
ITB ★★★★ Hotel
RAC Blue Ribbon ★★★
Dining Award 2
AA ★★★ ⊗⊗
AA Top 200 - 2004/2005

FACILITIES
On site: Garden, croquet, walking trail
1 meeting room/max 25 people
Nearby: Golf, riding, fishing

RESTRICTIONS
Limited facilities for disabled guests
No smoking throughout
No pets; kennels available
Closed 25 Oct. - 23 March

ATTRACTIONS
The Burren, Cliffs of Moher,
Galway Bay, Aran Islands,
Lahinch Golf Club, guided walking tours

NEAREST
CITY:
Galway - 33 miles/45 mins

AIRPORT:
Shannon - 36 miles/1 hr

RAIL STATION:
Gort - 22 miles/25 mins

AFFILIATIONS
Ireland's Blue Book
Preston's Global Hotels

RESERVATIONS
Toll free in US: 800-544-9993
or 800-323-5463
Quote Best Loved

ACCESS CODES
AMADEUS LM SNNGRG
APOLLO/GALILEO LM 5417
SABRE/ABACUS LM 27478

IRELAND

Excellence through family ownership for 29 years

Gregans Castle is a welcome surprise in a remote part of the west of Ireland. Nestling at the foot of Corkscrew Hill with majestic views of bare limestone mountains and Galway Bay, this country house offers warmth, welcome and every possible comfort.

Gregans Castle was built as a private house more than 150 years ago for the Martyn family to replace their home in the old castle nearby. Today, it is one of the most comfortable hostelries on the west coast of Ireland, and is owned and managed by the Haden family. The rooms are splendidly relaxing, and dinner is an essential - and award-winning! - part of the day, with a special emphasis placed on local produce.

Only an hour's scenic drive from Shannon airport, Gregans' magnificent locale is called The Burren and is known worldwide for wildflowers and distinctive scenery. A rich legacy of ancient monuments tells the story of inhabitants as far back as 5,000 years. The seascapes are dramatic: the Atlantic Ocean, Galway Bay, the famous Cliffs of Moher, two golden beaches and several small local fishing harbours of character.

LOCATION

On the N67 on the west coast of Ireland, three and a half miles south of the village of Ballyvaughan in County Clare.

HALPIN'S HOTEL

Townhouse

Erin Street, Kilkee, Co Clare
Republic of Ireland

T +353 (0)65 9056032
F +353 (0)65 905 6317
halpins@bestloved.com
www.halpins.bestloved.com

OWNER
Pat Halpin

MANAGER
Ann Keane

ROOM RATES
2 Singles   €69 - €99
8 Doubles/Twins   €89 - €139
2 Executive Rooms €99 - €169
Includes full breakfast,
newspaper and VAT

CREDIT CARDS
AMERICAN EXPRESS • DC • JCB • MC • VI

RATINGS & AWARDS
ITB ★★★ Hotel
RAC ◆◆◆◆ Dining Award 1
RAC Sparkling Diamond,
Warm Welcome Awards

FACILITIES
On site: Garden
1 meeting room/max 40 people
Nearby: Golf, riding, leisure centre,
tennis, fishing, water skiing

RESTRICTIONS
Limited facilities for disabled guests
No smoking throughout
No pets; guide dogs only
Closed 15 Nov. - 15 March

ATTRACTIONS
Cliffs of Moher, The Burren,
Bunratty Castle, Aran Islands,
Lakes of Killarney,
Lahinch and Ballybunion golf courses,
Doonbeg Golf Course

NEAREST
CITY:
Ennis - 30 miles/30 mins

AIRPORT:
Shannon - 40 miles/50 mins

RAIL STATION:
Kilkee - ¼ mile/5 mins

AFFILIATIONS
Utell International
Preston's Global Hotels
Elegant Small Hotels

RESERVATIONS
Toll free in US: 800-617-3178
Toll free in UK: 0800 0964 748
Quote Best Loved

ACCESS CODES
AMADEUS UI SNNHAL
APOLLO/GALILEO UI 1437
SABRE/ABACUS UI 36170
WORLDSPAN UI 19690

IRELAND

Welcoming and friendly, the place to find the true taste of Ireland

Located in the centre of the picturesque Victorian resort village of Kilkee, which stands in a horseshoe bay midway between the cliffs of Moher and the Ring of Kerry, Halpin's Hotel is a delight. The scenic cliff walks around the town are fantastic, and golfers can play the local Kilkee golf course one day and the next head off to play the Greg Norman-designed Doonbeg Golf Links, Lahinch, Ballybunion or numerous other courses - perfect for a week's golfing holiday!

This small townhouse has been owned and run by the Halpin family for 20 years and has earned a reputation for its excellent standards and welcoming atmosphere. Modestly priced and as unpretentious as the town it stands in, its looks belie its true character. The bedrooms are comfortable and offer every modern facility. The hotel bar, with its open hearth fire and flagstone floor, is the perfect place to relax at the end of the day and chat with the locals.

Its close proximity to Shannon airport and Killimer car ferry ensures that Halpin's Hotel is an excellent base for touring the west and southwest coasts. Area attractions include scenic drives, heritage sites, cliffs, beaches and caves – and all kinds of sport, ensuring that Halpin's is surely a place to discover the true taste of Ireland.

LOCATION

50 minutes from Shannon airport on the N67, in the centre of Kilkee.

> " Hayfield Manor is one of the most charming hotels we have ever stayed in "
>
> EDSEL B FORD II, FORD MOTOR COMPANY

Country house

HAYFIELD MANOR

A charming luxury manor with a true Irish welcome

Hayfield Manor offers the best of both worlds in several respects: It is Cork's award-winning five-star hotel, offering every modern comfort, as well as a country house standing among the old parkland trees of a two-acre mature garden with a well-concealed private car park. Better still, it's within a mile of Cork's city centre.

At Hayfield Manor, the staff are friendly and attentive - staying and dining are a delight. The grandeur and style of the Manor Room restaurant combine with superb cuisine to create a magnificent gourmet experience. The spacious guest rooms are matched by luxurious marble bathrooms with oversized claw-footed baths and fluffy terry bathrobes. From your room, you have direct access to the spa (where even the pool has views across the formal garden!) where you can enjoy a well-being massage, the steam room or simply a relaxing soak in the outdoor Jacuzzi.

Cork has much to commend it as a touring centre, and Hayfield Manor is well-placed for all of it: the Cobh Heritage Centre, Midleton Distillery, and nearby Killarney, the Ring of Kerry, Kinsale, Blarney Castle and Waterford, famous for its crystal.

LOCATION
Take the N22 (Killarney) west from Cork city centre. Turn left at University Gates, off Western Rd; at the top, turn right, then left - the hotel is at the end of the avenue.

Perrott Avenue, College Road,
Cork, Co Cork
Republic of Ireland

T +353 (0)21 4845900
F +353 (0)21 4316839
hayfield@bestloved.com
www.hayfield.bestloved.com

OWNERS
Margaret and Joseph Scally

GENERAL MANAGER
Margaret Naughton

ROOM RATES
Single occupancy   €215 - €280
73 Doubles/Twins   €300 - €365
15 Suites   €420 - €990
Includes full breakfast, service and VAT

CREDIT CARDS
AMERICAN EXPRESS • DC • MC • VI

RATINGS & AWARDS
ITB ★★★★★ Hotel
RAC Gold Ribbon ★★★★
Dining Award 3
AA ★★★★ ⊛⊛
AA Top 200 - 2004/2005
AA Hotel of the Year 2003/2004

FACILITIES
On site: Garden, gym, indoor pool, health & beauty, steam room, Jacuzzi
4 meeting rooms/max 150 people
Nearby: Riding, golf, tennis, fishing, water skiing

RESTRICTIONS
Smoking in some bedrooms only
No pets; guide dogs only

ATTRACTIONS
Midleton Distillery, Kinsale, Waterford Crystal,
Ring of Kerry, Killarney,
Blarney Castle, Cobh Heritage Centre

NEAREST
CITY:
Cork - 1 mile/5 mins

AIRPORT:
Cork - 6 miles/20 mins

RAIL STATION:
Cork (Kent) - 2 miles/15 mins

AFFILIATIONS
Celebrated Hotels Collection
Small Luxury Hotels

RESERVATIONS
Toll free in US: 800-322-2403
or 800-525-4800
Quote Best Loved

ACCESS CODES
AMADEUS LX ORKHMR
APOLLO/GALILEO LX 78441
SABRE/ABACUS LX 31327
WORLDSPAN LX ORKHM

IRELAND

HUNTER'S HOTEL

Inn

Newrath Bridge,
Rathnew, Co Wicklow
Republic of Ireland

T +353 (0)404 40106
F +353 (0)404 40338
hunters@bestloved.com
www.hunters.bestloved.com

OWNERS
The Gelletlie Family

ROOM RATES
2 Singles   €95 - €115
14 Doubles/Twins   €178 - €216
Includes full breakfast and VAT

CREDIT CARDS
AMERICAN EXPRESS • MC • VI

RATINGS & AWARDS
ITB ★★★ Silver Award Hotel
AA ★★★ ⊛ 67%

FACILITIES
On site: Garden
1 meeting room/max 40 people
Nearby: Golf, riding, fishing, walking

RESTRICTIONS
No smoking throughout
No pets
Closed Christmas

ATTRACTIONS
Mount Usher Gardens,
Powerscourt Gardens and Waterfall,
Glendalough, Russborough House

NEAREST
CITY:
Dublin - 28 miles/45 mins

AIRPORT:
Dublin - 40 miles/1 hr 15 mins

RAIL STATION:
Wicklow - 3 miles/5 mins

AFFILIATIONS
Ireland's Blue Book

RESERVATIONS
Toll free in US: 800-323-5463
Quote Best Loved

ACCESS CODES
Not applicable

IRELAND

Good food and old-world charm - a family tradition of five generations

Hunter's Hotel, one of Ireland's oldest coaching inns, has been established for over 270 years - since the days of post horses and carriages! Run by the same family for five generations, the hotel has today built up a strong tradition based upon good food, comfortable surroundings and old-world charm. Set in one of Ireland's most beautiful counties, Hunter's stands in gardens bordering the River Vartry. All the rooms retain the character of bygone days, with antique furniture, open fires, fresh flowers and polished brass in show. Most of the 16 attractive bedrooms overlook the gardens.

Sea angling, riding, hunting, tennis, swimming and hiking are all in the immediate locality. There are 18 golf courses within 30 minutes' drive, including Druids Glen and The European Club. The beautiful Wicklow countryside, known as the Garden of Ireland, lies at your doorstep. Lovely sandy beaches, breathtaking mountain scenery, quiet glens and well-known beauty spots - including Mount Usher Gardens, Powerscourt, Russborough House, Avondale House, Glendalough, the Devil's Glen and Roundwood - are all within easy reach. Whether you're looking for a country base from which to visit Dublin, a peaceful rural holiday or a pleasant overnight stop after the ferry, Hunter's Hotel is the ideal location.

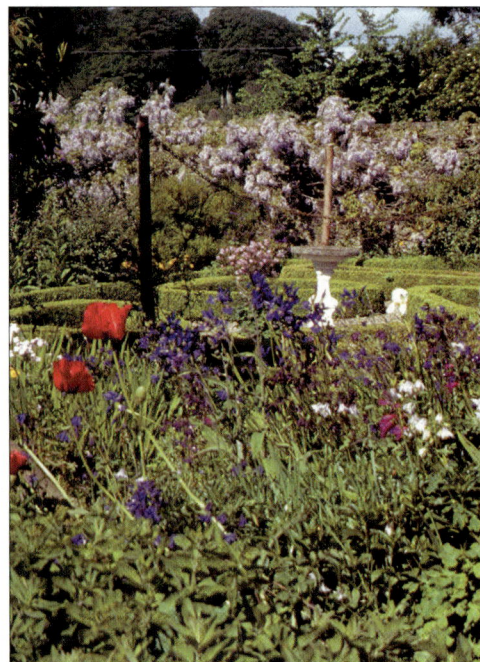

LOCATION
Take the N11 toward Rathnew. Turn left just before the village on the Dublin side.

City hotel
KILKENNY HIBERNIAN HOTEL

Bank on a comfortable stay in Ireland's Marble City

Large tracts of County Kilkenny in the southeast of Ireland are formed of a limestone rock that turns black when polished, and much of the historic city of Kilkenny is built with this characteristic local stone - hence the moniker Marble City.

Marble is no stranger to the handsome face of Kilkenny Hibernian Hotel. This gracious old Victorian bank, located in the shadow of Kilkenny Castle, has been sympathetically transformed and substantially extended into a welcoming boutique hotel with a grand lobby area and many original features such as the marble fireplaces in the bedrooms - survivors from an even earlier incarnation as a private residence.

The hotel's 46 comfortable bedrooms feature generous king-size beds, sleek bathrooms and Irish fabrics in soft, warm tones with floral touches. Guests can relax over a drink, morning savouries or afternoon tea and the daily newspapers in the traditional Hibernian Bar, or sample the more lively ambience of Morrissons Bar. Jacobs Cottage restaurant, one of the region's leading eateries, offers an eclectic menu of Irish and international cuisine. If you need to work off a surfeit of pudding, guests also enjoy membership of a health and leisure centre with a pool, gym, sauna and steam room close to the hotel.

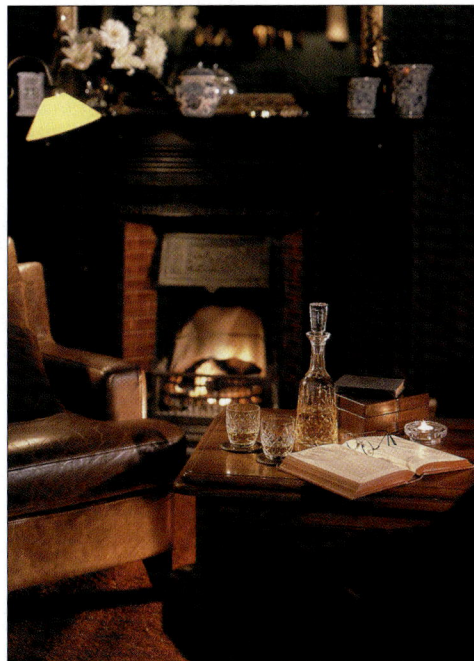

LOCATION
From the N10, exit the Waterford Road roundabout for the city centre. Turn left at the end of Patrick Street onto Ormonde Street; the hotel is on the immediate left.

1 Ormonde Street,
Kilkenny, Co Kilkenny
Republic of Ireland

T +353 (0)56 7771888
F +353 (0)56 7771877
ckhibernian@bestloved.com
www.ckhibernian.bestloved.com

OWNERS
Gerry Byrne and David Lawlor

ROOM RATES
40 Doubles/Twins   €120 - €200
3 Junior Suites   €220 - €250
3 Penthouse Suites   €250 - €300
Includes full breakfast, service and VAT

CREDIT CARDS
AMERICAN EXPRESS • DC • MC • VI

RATINGS & AWARDS
The Black & White Hotel Bar of the
Year Award 2004 - Regional Winner
Only The Best Hotels
'Best Boutique Hotel in Ireland' 2003

FACILITIES
On site: 1 meeting room/max 40 people
Nearby: Golf, riding, tennis, fishing,
leisure centre

RESTRICTIONS
Limited facilities for disabled guests
Smoking in some bedrooms only
No pets
Closed 24 - 25 Dec.

ATTRACTIONS
Kilkenny Castle, Waterford Crystal,
Rock of Cashel, Smithicks Brewery,
Craft Trail, walking tours,
Saint Canices Cathedral,
Dunmore Caves

NEAREST
CITY:
Waterford - 30 miles/40 mins
Dublin - 80 miles/1 hr 45 mins

AIRPORT:
Dublin - 85 miles/2 hrs

RAIL STATION:
Kilkenny - 1 mile/5 mins

AFFILIATIONS
Preston's Global Hotels
Only The Best Hotels

RESERVATIONS
Toll free in US: 800-544-9993
Quote Best Loved

ACCESS CODES
Not applicable

IRELAND

> **"The wonderful service, the great accommodation, your fantastic dining room and staff make the Royal a truly first-class establishment"**
>
> MRS DESMOND, LONDON

KILLARNEY ROYAL HOTEL   Townhouse

College Street,
Killarney, Co Kerry
Republic of Ireland

T +353 (0)64 31853
F +353 (0)64 34001
killarney@bestloved.com
www.killarney.bestloved.com

OWNERS
Joe and Margaret Scally

ROOM RATES
Single occupancy   €140 - €200
24 Doubles/Twins   €225 - €320
5 Junior Suites   €320 - €380
Includes full breakfast and VAT

CREDIT CARDS
AMERICAN EXPRESS • DC • MC • VI

RATINGS & AWARDS
RAC ★★★★ Dining Award 2
AA ★★★ 66%

FACILITIES
On site: 1 meeting room/max 50 people
Nearby: Golf, tennis, leisure centre,
fishing, riding, leisure centre

RESTRICTIONS
No smoking throughout
Closed 23 - 26 Dec.

ATTRACTIONS
Ring of Kerry, Dingle Peninsula,
Gap of Dunloe, Lakes of Killarney,
Muckross House & Gardens,
Torc Waterfall

NEAREST
CITY:
Cork - 55 miles/1 hr 15 mins

AIRPORT:
Kerry Airport - 9 miles/15 mins

RAIL STATION:
Killarney

AFFILIATIONS
Preston's Global Hotels

RESERVATIONS
Toll free in US: 800-544-9993
Quote Best Loved

ACCESS CODES
AMADEUS LM KIR170
APOLLO/GALILEO LM 38135
SABRE/ABACUS LM 60601
WORLDSPAN LM 08170

IRELAND

Right royal hospitality and good food in Ireland's romantic southwest

Visitors to Killarney have a spectacular touring base for all of Ireland's southwest, from the legendary Ring of Kerry to the scenic Dingle Peninsula or 21-mile-long Bantry Bay; from the 25,000 acres of Killarney National Park and the town's two championship courses to the excellent local brown trout; from Victorian Muckross House and Gardens to Kate Kearney's Cottage. But even with all those at the doorstep, many visitors have said the highlight of their trip was their stay at the Killarney Royal!

Originally known as the Munster Arms, the hotel was built in 1900 and purchased in 1961 by Marie and Marcus Treacy, who transformed it from what was then the Criterion to the new Royal Hotel. In 1976, the Treacys' daughter Margaret and her husband, Joe Scally, inherited the hotel.

Today, the Killarney Royal is an exclusive four-star boutique-style treat; after a major refurbishment in 1998, including air conditioning, individually-styled decorating and sensitive renovations completely in keeping with period style, the hotel is a grand success. After three generations of ownership, the Scallys see excellence as the main ingredient for this reputation, an aim seen in their staff's genuine desire to please.

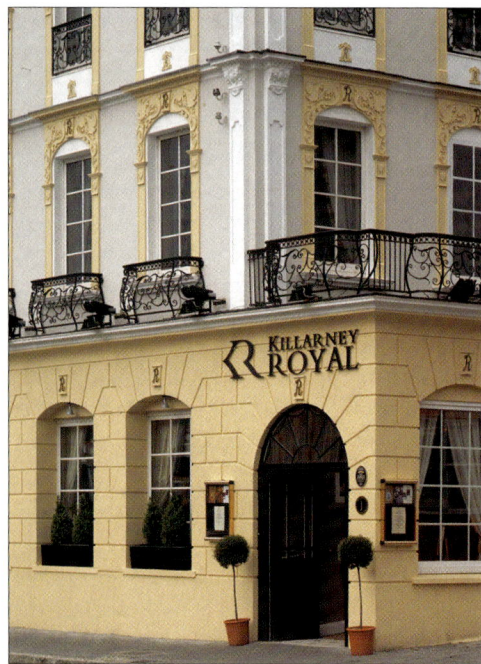

LOCATION
In the centre of Killarney,
on College Street off the N22.

Restaurant with rooms

KING SITRIC

East Pier, Howth, Co Dublin
Republic of Ireland

T +353 (0)1 832 5235
F +353 (0)1 839 2442
sitric@bestloved.com
www.sitric.bestloved.com

OWNERS/CHEF PROPRIETOR
Joan and Aidan MacManus

ROOM RATES
Single occupancy   €100 - €135
8 Doubles/Twins   €138 - €200
Includes breakfast and VAT

CREDIT CARDS
AMERICAN EXPRESS • MC • VI

RATINGS & AWARDS
ITB ★★★★ Guest House
Karen Brown Recommended
Gilbeys Gold Medal for
Catering Excellence

FACILITIES
On site: Private dining room
Nearby: Golf, boating, beaches,
water sport, walking

RESTRICTIONS
No facilities for disabled guests
No smoking throughout
No pets

ATTRACTIONS
Port of Howth and Yacht Marina,
National Transport Museum,
Howth Head, Malahide Castle,
Newbridge House Donabate,
Dublin City

NEAREST
CITY:
Dublin - 9 miles/25 mins

AIRPORT:
Dublin - 6 miles/20 mins

RAIL STATION:
Howth - ⅓ mile/2 mins

AFFILIATIONS
Ireland's Blue Book

RESERVATIONS
Toll free in US: 800-323-5463
Quote Best Loved

ACCESS CODES
Not applicable

Rooms with a view at County Dublin's best-known fish restaurant

A deft flick of the wrist could launch a fish from Dublin Bay into a waiting pan in Aidan MacManus' kitchen. As it is, the ocean's finest tends to travel the 400 yards from Howth Pier in a rather more sedate fashion, since only the pick of the morning's catch passes muster in this renowned fish restaurant.

Aidan and Joan MacManus first opened their restaurant business more than 30 years ago and have since nurtured a network of trusty suppliers who can rustle up everything from locally-caught lobster and crab to organically-grown vegetables. To complement the menu, there is a well-stocked wine cellar, and guests can enjoy a pre-dinner drink while choosing from the award-winning wine list.

In 2000, Aidan and Joan completed a major refurbishment of the old harbour master's house. The new look is light and bright, with a subtle nautical theme, a first-floor restaurant offering splendid bay views and eight charming sea-facing guest rooms.

Howth is just 25 minutes from central Dublin by DART rail link and a great base for golfers and sailors. Horse riding can be arranged, and walkers can hike the unspoilt cliff path and trails around Howth Head.

LOCATION

At the end of the M50, take the N32 toward Malahide, signed for Baldoyle and Howth. The hotel is across the harbour front, at the end of the road on the right.

IRELAND

> "Our first visit to Westport has been brilliant, largely due to our choice of accommodation, which has been splendid in every respect"
>
> ANNETTE, MARTIN & CLAIRE MURPHY, BELFAST

KNOCKRANNY HOUSE HOTEL — Country house

Westport, Co Mayo
Republic of Ireland

T +353 (0)98 28600
F +353 (0)98 28611
knockranny@bestloved.com
www.knockranny.bestloved.com

OWNERS
Adrian and Geraldine Noonan

ROOM RATES
Single occupancy	€170
42 Doubles/Twins	€250
9 Deluxe Doubles/Twins	€290
3 Four-posters	€320

Includes full breakfast and VAT

CREDIT CARDS
AMERICAN EXPRESS • MC • VI

RATINGS & AWARDS
ITB ★★★★ Hotel
RAC ★★★★ Dining Award 2

FACILITIES
On site: Garden, heli-pad, health spa & leisure facilities to open in Spring 2005
4 meeting rooms/max 700 people
Nearby: Golf, riding, fishing, tennis, complimentary leisure facilities

RESTRICTIONS
Smoking in third-floor rooms only
No pets; guide dogs only
Closed 22 - 27 Dec.

ATTRACTIONS
Croagh Patrick Mountain, Westport House, Clew Bay, Clare Island, Ceide Fields, Kylemore Abbey, Connemara National Park, Blue Flag beaches

NEAREST
CITY:
Galway - 55 miles/1 hr

AIRPORT:
Shannon - 125 miles/1 hr 45 mins
Knock - 45 miles/50 mins

RAIL STATION:
Westport - ½ mile/5 mins

AFFILIATIONS
Manor House Hotels of Ireland

RESERVATIONS
Direct with hotel
Quote Best Loved

ACCESS CODES
AMADEUS LW GWYKNO
APOLLO/GALILEO LM 21893
SABRE/ABACUS LM 17342
WORLDSPAN LM KNOCI

IRELAND

Irish hospitality and an island for every day of the year in Clew Bay

Locals claim there is an island for every day of the year anchored in the broad and peaceful embrace of Clew Bay. On the shore, the seaside town of Westport - often described as the cultural capital of Mayo - is a marvellous touring base for County Mayo and neighbouring County Galway.

One of the great charms of Knockranny House is its enviable position with views over the bay and Croagh Patrick, Ireland's famous pilgrimage mountain. Knockranny is a Victorian-style hotel successfully combining period looks with modern comforts and a very friendly and efficient staff headed by welcoming hosts Adrian and Geraldine. From the moment you walk in, a sense of spaciousness and brightness extends throughout. The dining room enjoys yet more wonderful views, and dinner is accompanied by a classical pianist. The hotel's team of award-winning chefs concentrates on presenting the very best of Irish cuisine with an international flavour; their menus feature a multitude of dishes, many using local fish and fresh herbs from their own garden.

With three meeting rooms, Knockranny offers excellent conference facilities for up to 500 delegates. And for both leisure and business travellers, their spa is an unbeatable treat!

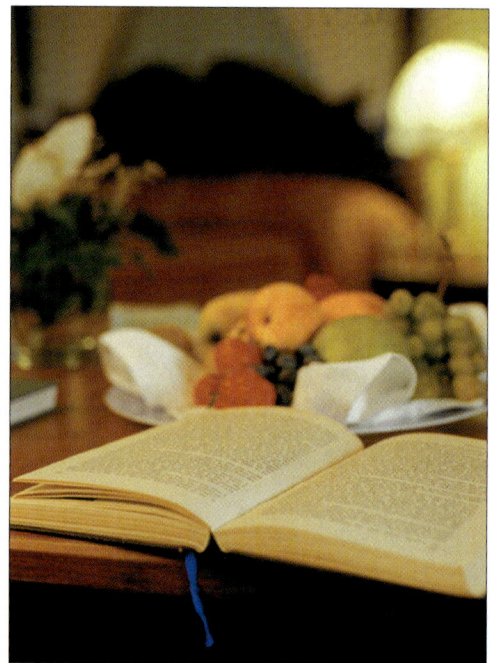

LOCATION
Take the N5/N60 from Castlebar; the hotel is on the left before entering Westport.

> "Couldn't have found a fault if we tried! The food was superb and the service was excellent ... staff couldn't have been more helpful"
>
> LEONIE WOODCOCK

Map p. 454, grid F8

City hotel

LACKEN HOUSE

So welcoming and friendly - but just five minutes from Kilkenny centre

This stylish but eminently welcoming hotel located just five minutes' walk from the centre of Kilkenny has the added advantage of one of the most talked-about restaurants in Ireland!

Lacken House, a lovely Victorian home originally built as a dower house in 1847 for the Lord Viscount Mortmorency, is today owned and managed by the husband-and-wife team of Trevor Toner and Jackie Kennedy. For business needs, the hotel offers their Kells Conference Room, and the restaurant is a superb venue for wedding parties. The 11 comfortable bedrooms are a perfect backdrop to any Ireland adventure; some feature added luxuries like whirlpool baths and all are a glorious place to wake up before heading to the dining room for breakfast!

The food at Lacken House is something that's certainly not to be missed. The award-winning dining is an ideal complement to a day in Kilkenny, with a splendid five-course table d'hôte dinner featuring delights like wild nettle and fish soup, oven-baked South African ostrich fillet with sweet potato puree, pineapple salsa and wasabi crème fraiche, and, for dessert, a luxurious pineapple sorbet with white truffle foam and apple and rosemary sauce.

LOCATION

On Dublin Road in the centre of Kilkenny, just beyond the station.

Dublin Road,
Kilkenny, Co Kilkenny
Republic of Ireland

T +353 (0)56 776 1085
F +353 (0)56 776 2435
lacken@bestloved.com
www.lacken.bestloved.com

OWNERS
Trevor Toner and Jackie Kennedy

ROOM RATES
Single occupancy   €99 - €175
10 Doubles/Twins   €130 - €180
2 Junior Suites   €150 - €250
1 Family Suite   €200 - €350
Includes breakfast and VAT

CREDIT CARDS
AMERICAN EXPRESS • MC • VI

RATINGS & AWARDS
ITB ★★★ Guest House
Georgina Campbell's Jameson Guide
Highly Recommended
Les Routiers
Best Irish Guest House with Restaurant
Bord Bia Féile Bia Food Award 2005

FACILITIES
On site: Garden, licensed for weddings
1 meeting room/max 27 people
Nearby: Tennis, fishing, golf,
pitch & putt, riding, health & beauty

RESTRICTIONS
No facilities for disabled guests
No smoking throughout
No pets; guide dogs only
Closed 24 - 26 December

ATTRACTIONS
Kilkenny Castle,
Kilkenny Craft Pottery Trail,
Jerpoint Abbey, Dunmore Caves,
Rock of Cashel,
Waterford Crystal Visitor Centre,
Woodstock Gardens

NEAREST
CITY:
Kilkenny

AIRPORT:
Dublin - 85 miles/2 hrs
Cork - 120 miles/2 hrs 30 mins

RAIL STATION:
Kilkenny - 500 metres/5 mins

FERRY PORT:
Rosslare - 35 miles/45 mins

AFFILIATIONS
Les Routiers

RESERVATIONS
Direct with hotel
Quote Best Loved

ACCESS CODES
Not applicable

IRELAND

Map p. 454, grid G7

LONGFIELD'S

City hotel

9-10 Fitzwilliam Street Lower,
Dublin 2
Republic of Ireland

T +353 (0)1 676 1367
F +353 (0)1 676 1542
longfield@bestloved.com
www.longfield.bestloved.com

GENERAL MANAGER
Alan Sillett

ROOM RATES
2 Singles   €120 - €150
22 Doubles/Twins   €180 - €215
2 Four-posters   €205 - €255
Includes full breakfast and VAT

CREDIT CARDS
AMERICAN EXPRESS • DC • MC • VI

RATINGS & AWARDS
ITB ★★★ Hotel
RAC ★★★ Dining Award 2
AA ★★★ 67%

FACILITIES
On site: 'No 10' Restaurant
1 meeting room/max 22 people
Nearby: Tennis, fishing,
fitness, riding, golf

RESTRICTIONS
Limited facilities for disabled guests
No smoking throughout
No pets; guide dogs only

ATTRACTIONS
Trinity College, National Library,
St Stephen's Green,
National Art Gallery, Grafton Street,
Christchurch Cathedral

NEAREST
CITY:
Dublin

AIRPORT:
Dublin - 7 miles/30 mins

RAIL STATION:
Dublin - ½ mile/5 mins

FERRY PORT:
Dun Laoghaire - 4 miles/20 mins

AFFILIATIONS
Manor House Hotels of Ireland

RESERVATIONS
Toll free in US: 800-44-UTELL
Quote Best Loved

ACCESS CODES
AMADEUS UI DUBLON
APOLLO/GALILEO UI 91673
SABRE/ABACUS UI 33792
WORLDSPAN UI 40025

IRELAND

A home in the centre of Dublin you could almost call your own

'During this morning walk in Dublin, I continued to believe that no matter where I looked I would find traces of the faces, the laughter and the voices which gave birth to this city and whose buildings and streets had a way of making you feel they belonged to you'. This is how Irish-American novelist J P Donleavy described one of Europe's smallest cities and, arguably, its most endearing and entertaining.

Within walking distance of the principal attractions of Dublin is Longfield's, gracing one of the many elegant Georgian terraces for which this part of the city is famous. If you were not staying there, you might be tempted by No 10, the below-stairs restaurant, whose intimate ambience, excellent cuisine and splendid cellar entice and satisfy its business and residential guests.

If you find the the restaurant to your liking, you will surely fall for the other pleasures of this erstwhile home of Lord Longfield. The high-ceilinged rooms have all the refinements of which his lordship would have thoroughly approved - and many he could never have dreamed of, introduced as some have been in an ongoing major refurbishment of the property. Indeed, as the charming staff put you at your ease, you may reflect, like Donleavy, that this haven in some way belongs to you.

LOCATION
Ten minutes from Grafton Street
and Dublin city centre.

> **Addiction is the word that springs to mind. Had a fabulous weekend. Thanks a million again. See you next time**
> COLMAN FINLAY & CLAIRE BOLAN, IRELAND

Country house

LOUGH INAGH LODGE HOTEL

A beautiful place for hill-walking, sporting pursuits and seeing Connemara

Lough Inagh Lodge is set on the shores of Lough Inagh, one of Connemara's most beautiful lakes. Sturdily built in the 1880s, this charming lodge hotel combines the comforts and pleasures of a modern hotel with its own old-world charm. The original lodge record books make fascinating reading for fishermen, and everyone can enjoy Ireland's finest panoramic views with morning coffee or afternoon tea in the sitting room.

Each bedroom has a separate dressing room and fabulous vistas over the lake and the Twelve Bens mountains. Open log fires in the library and the oak-panelled bar symbolise the warmth of Inagh hospitality; on the table, seafood and wild game dishes are specialities of the house and are complemented by an excellent wine list.

Amidst the most spectacular scenery in Ireland, visitors can fish, shoot, pony trek, cycle, play golf or simply relax. Outdoor action is unlimited, including game fishing on Lough Inagh, sea fishing within 10 miles, driven woodcock shooting, riding and golf. Irish craftware is available in the many shops at nearby Recess, Kylemore and Clifden. The lodge is the ideal base for a tour of Connemara, and is surrounded by noted beauty spots, including Connemara National Park and Kylemore Abbey.

LOCATION

Take the N59 (Clifden) just past Recess; turn right onto the R344 (Letterfrack). The hotel is five miles from this junction.

Recess, Connemara,
Co Galway
Republic of Ireland

T +353 (0)95 34706
F +353 (0)95 34708
loughinagh@bestloved.com
www.loughinagh.bestloved.com

OWNER
Maire O'Connor

ROOM RATES
Single occupancy €111 - €129
12 Doubles/Twins €178 - €213
Includes full breakfast and VAT

CREDIT CARDS
AMERICAN EXPRESS • DC • MC • VI

RATINGS & AWARDS
ITB ★★★★ Hotel
RAC ★★★ Dining Award 1
AA ★★★ ✿✿ 77%
AA Romantic Hotel

FACILITIES
On site: Garden, heli-pad, fishing, shooting, walking, cycle hire
1 meeting room/max 24 people
Nearby: Golf, sea fishing, riding, scuba diving

RESTRICTIONS
Limited facilities for disabled guests
Smoking in some bedrooms only
Closed mid-Dec. - mid-March

ATTRACTIONS
Connemara National Park,
Twelve Bens Mountain Range,
Kylemore Abbey,
Letterfrack Furniture College,
The Victoria Walled Garden,
local craft shops

NEAREST
CITY:
Galway - 42 miles/1 hr

AIRPORT:
Shannon - 99 miles/2 hrs 30 mins
Knock - 75 miles/2 hrs 30 mins

RAIL STATION:
Knock - 75 miles/2 hrs 30 mins

AFFILIATIONS
Manor House Hotels of Ireland
Great Fishing Houses of Ireland

RESERVATIONS
Direct with hotel
Quote Best Loved

ACCESS CODES
Not applicable

IRELAND

MARKREE CASTLE

Castle

Collooney, Co Sligo
Republic of Ireland

T +353 (0)71 9167800
F +353 (0)71 9167840
markree@bestloved.com
www.markree.bestloved.com

OWNERS
Charles and Mary Cooper

ROOM RATES
Single occupancy	€111 - €122
18 Doubles/Twins	€191 - €214
12 Triples	€232 - €257

Includes full breakfast and VAT

CREDIT CARDS
AMERICAN EXPRESS • DC • MC • VI

RATINGS & AWARDS
Bewley's Best Coffee Award
Bridgestone Top 100 Best Hotels

FACILITIES
On site: Garden, fishing, riding
Nearby: Golf, fishing

RESTRICTIONS
Limited facilities for disabled guests
No smoking throughout
No pets; guide dogs only
Closed 24 - 26 Dec.

ATTRACTIONS
Yeats country, Lough Gill,
Carrowmore megalithic remains,
Parke's Castle

NEAREST
CITY:
Galway - 80 miles/2 hrs

AIRPORT:
Dublin/Shannon - 125 miles/3 hrs
Knock - 40 miles/30 mins

RAIL STATION:
Collooney - 1½ miles/5 mins

AFFILIATIONS
Independent

RESERVATIONS
Direct with hotel
Quote Best Loved

ACCESS CODES
Not applicable

IRELAND

The Coopers have lived here for 350 years - the welcome is as warm as ever

Home of the Cooper family for more than 350 years, Markree Castle is now run as a small family hotel by Charles and Mary Cooper, the 10th generation of the family to live at Markree.

Set in a large estate with lovely gardens, the original house has been altered many times over the years, with the primary addition added in 1802 by the architect Francis Johnston. The enormous oak staircase is overlooked by a stained-glass window depicting 20 generations of the Cooper family tree, and the Louis Philippe-style plasterwork in the dining room makes it one of Ireland's most spectacular rooms.

Charles Cooper worked in hotels in many other countries before returning to Markree in 1989. Since then, much has been restored, creating a family hotel of distinctive character. The bedrooms all have private bathrooms, telephones and efficient heating, yet great care has been taken to retain the character of the old building and the family atmosphere rather than the formal, impersonal atmosphere of more luxurious hotels. The restaurant has also become well known for carefully-prepared meals of a high standard.

LOCATION
Eight miles south of Sligo just off the N4/N17 junction.

Contemporary hotel   MARYBOROUGH HOUSE HOTEL

A warm welcome and attention to detail that stands out from the crowd

It is a rare hotel that successfully combines top-flight corporate and leisure facilities with the individual personal touch that makes a stay memorable. The Maryborough is just such a rarity, and the hotel's beautiful parkland setting just ten minutes from Cork's international airport and city centre is an additional plus whether you are visiting Cork for business or pleasure.

The Georgian mansion at the centre of the property offers an air of timeless elegance complemented by antique furnishings, fresh flowers and an impressive spiral stairwell rising to five lovely suites with exposed beams and open fireplaces. The main accommodation is in thoughtfully-equipped executive rooms situated in an attractively designed extension, where verandas and balconies maximise the views over the centuries old gardens and woodland.

Zings Restaurant offers chic, contemporary décor, award-winning service and a relaxing ambience where diners can enjoy a broad-ranging menu of modern and traditional European-influenced dishes. If the delicious desserts prove too tempting, the Maryborough Club is the perfect place to get back in shape. Alongside a 21-station gym, 18-metre swimming pool, steam room and sauna, spa, beauty and relaxation therapies are also available.

LOCATION

10 mins from Cork city centre. Follow signs for Douglas until you reach Maryborough Hill; the hotel is on the left.

Maryborough Hill, Douglas, Cork, Co Cork
Republic of Ireland

T +353 (0)21 436 5555
F +353 (0)21 436 5662
maryboro@bestloved.com
www.maryboro.bestloved.com

GENERAL MANAGER
Justin McCarthy

ROOM RATES
Single occupancy	€145 - €260
74 Executive Doubles/Twins	€190 - €260
5 Suites	€280 - €550

Includes full breakfast and VAT

CREDIT CARDS
AMERICAN EXPRESS • DC • MC • VI

RATINGS & AWARDS
ITB ★★★★
AA ★★★★ ❀ 71%
Ireland's Best
Excellence in Tourism Award

FACILITIES
On site: Garden, gym, indoor pool, health & beauty, sauna, steam room, Jacuzzi
11 meeting rooms/max 600 people
Nearby: Golf, riding

RESTRICTIONS
Limited facilities for disabled guests
No children under 10 years in the restaurant after 7 p.m.
Smoking in bedrooms only
No pets; guide dogs only
Closed 24 - 26 Dec.

ATTRACTIONS
Cobh Heritage Centre, Blarney Castle, Midleton Distillery, Bantry Bay, Ring of Kerry, Kinsale, Fota Island Golf Course

NEAREST
CITY:
Cork - 5 miles/10mins

AIRPORT:
Cork - 5 miles/15mins

RAIL STATION:
Cork - 5 miles/10 mins

AFFILIATIONS
Special Hotels of the World

RESERVATIONS
Toll free in UK: 08705 300 200
Toll free in US: 800-448-8355
Quote Best Loved

ACCESS CODES
AMADEUS UK ORKMHH
APOLLO/GALILEO UK 90975
SABRE/ABACUS UK 14371
WORLDSPAN UK 27585

IRELAND

MERRION HALL

Townhouse

54 Merrion Road, Ballsbridge,
Dublin 4
Republic of Ireland

T +353 (0)1 668 1426
F +353 (0)1 283 7877
merrionhall@bestloved.com
www.merrionhall.bestloved.com

OWNER
Pat Halpin

ROOM RATES
Single occupancy	€106 - €139
8 Doubles/Twins	€139 - €189
12 Deluxe Spa Rooms	€169 - €249
4 Garden Suites	€239 - €319

Includes full breakfast and VAT

CREDIT CARDS
AMERICAN EXPRESS • DC • JCB • MC • VI

RATINGS & AWARDS
ITB ★★★★
RAC ◆◆◆◆◆
RAC Warm Welcome,
Sparkling Diamond Awards
AA ◆◆◆◆◆
Galtee Breakfast Award

FACILITIES
On site: Garden, car park
3 meeting rooms/max 80 people
Nearby: Leisure club, golf,
riding, fishing

RESTRICTIONS
Limited facilities for disabled guests
No pets; guide dogs only

ATTRACTIONS
Trinity College, National Art Gallery,
Christchurch, Gardens of Wicklow,
New Grange, Powerscourt Gardens

NEAREST
CITY:
Dublin

AIRPORT:
Dublin - 6 miles/20 mins

RAIL STATION:
Sydney Parade - ¼ mile/5 mins

FERRY PORT:
Dun Laoghaire - ½ mile/10 mins

AFFILIATIONS
Utell International
Preston's Global Hotels
Grand Heritage Hotels
Luxe Worldwide Hotels

RESERVATIONS
Toll free in US: 800-617-3178
Toll free in UK: 0800 0964 748
Quote Best Loved

ACCESS CODES
AMADEUS UK DUBMHH
APOLLO/GALILEO UK 25226
SABRE/ABACUS UK 50151
WORLDSPAN UK 41063

Secluded, comfortable and a great value close to downtown Dublin

This exclusive Edwardian townhouse - commended by a wealth of travel guides and featured in Bridgestone's 100 Best Places to Stay in Ireland - is located just minutes from downtown Dublin, opposite the Royal Dublin Society Convention Centre and next to the Four Seasons hotel and the US and British embassies.

For such a central location, the bedrooms at Merrion Hall are generously spacious, and are thoughtfully well-equipped for the modern traveller, including complimentary wireless Internet access. The four-poster and executive suites also have air conditioning and whirlpool spas. In keeping with Dublin's rich literary history, the Merrion has a well-stocked library with a wide selection of classic and contemporary literature, including plenty of Irish titles. In addition to the library, a drawing room also provides a quiet corner for afternoon tea or a nightcap.

One notable feature of Merrion Hall is an award-winning Irish breakfast, which can be enjoyed overlooking mature secluded gardens. There are also numerous restaurants within a short stroll of the hotel, leaving guests utterly spoilt for choice! In summary, the art of good housekeeping is evident in every detail at Merrion Hall, as in its recently restored sister property, Blakes Townhouse.

LOCATION

From the city centre, take Merrion Road; the hotel is on the left opposite the RDS Convention Centre.

"It is rare to find such an *esprit de corps* and positive helpful attitude throughout the entire staff"

K G NELSON, PITTSTON, PENNSYLVANIA USA

City hotel

MERRION HOTEL

Dublin's most gracious Georgian hotel with five-star modern facilities

Four Georgian houses were sensitively restored and two magnificent 18th-century formal landscaped gardens combined to create The Merrion, Dublin's most gracious hotel. This oasis of tranquillity is ideally situated close to exclusive Grafton Street and even closer to the leafy walks and shady lawns of Merrion Square.

The 142 rooms and suites are designed to recall the elegance of the Georgian era and achieve five-star standards of luxury. Each has individually controllable air conditioning, an in-room safe, broadband Internet connection and 24-hour valet and room service. The splendid salons are in authentic period style, and contemporary Irish art from the country's finest collection is on display. When it comes to dining, Restaurant Patrick Guilbaud presents a renowned gastronomic menu in classical style, while The Cellar Restaurant offers superb Irish cuisine in a more relaxed environment. The Cellar Bar is graced by the vaulted ceilings of the original Georgian wine cellars.

Located in the heart of Dublin, The Merrion is directly opposite Government Buildings, and Trinity College, the Natural History Museum and National Gallery are among its nearest neighbours. Yet such is the peace in the gardens that the only sounds are the songs of the birds.

LOCATION

In the heart of Dublin.

Upper Merrion St, Dublin 2
Republic of Ireland

T +353 (0)1 603 0600
F +353 (0)1 603 0700
merrion@bestloved.com
www.merrion.bestloved.com

GENERAL MANAGER
Peter MacCann

ROOM RATES
43 Singles   €350 - €450
79 Doubles/Twins   €370 - €470
20 Suites   €650 - €2,200
Includes VAT

CREDIT CARDS
AMERICAN EXPRESS • DC • MC • VI

RATINGS & AWARDS
ITB ★★★★★ Hotel
RAC Gold Ribbon ★★★★★
Dining Award 5
AA ★★★★★ ✿✿✿
AA Top 200 - 2004/2005
The American Academy of Hospitality
Science Five Star Diamond Award 2002
Top Irish Hotel, Zagat Survey 2001

FACILITIES
On site: Garden, gym, indoor pool, health & beauty, steam room
6 meeting rooms/max 100 people
Nearby: Golf, riding, fishing, tennis

RESTRICTIONS
No smoking throughout
No pets; guide dogs only

ATTRACTIONS
Trinity College, National Art Gallery, Grafton Street, National Concert Hall, Christchurch Cathedral, Powerscourt House and Gardens

NEAREST
CITY:
Dublin

AIRPORT:
Dublin - 8 miles/40 mins

RAIL STATION:
Heuston - 2 miles/15 mins

AFFILIATIONS
Celebrated Hotels Collection
Leading Hotels of the World
The European Connection

RESERVATIONS
Toll free in US: 800-223-6800
or 800-322-2403
Toll free in UK: 0800 181123
Quote Best Loved

ACCESS CODES
AMADEUS LW DUB430
APOLLO/GALILEO LW 93859
SABRE/ABACUS LW 8715
WORLDSPAN LW 8430

IRELAND

I came here and thought it would be just another guesthouse. Few times in my life have I been this wrong!

ROBERT BJARK, USA

MOY HOUSE

Lahinch, Co Clare
Republic of Ireland

T +353 (0)65 708 2800
F +353 (0)65 708 2500
moyhouse@bestloved.com
www.moyhouse.bestloved.com

GENERAL MANAGER
Bernadette Merry

ROOM RATES
3 Singles   €127 - €159
6 Doubles/Twins   €200 - €239
Includes full breakfast and VAT

CREDIT CARDS
AMERICAN EXPRESS • JCB • MC • VI

RATINGS & AWARDS
ITB ★★★★ Guest House
AA ◆◆◆◆◆
AA Premier Collection
Georgina Campbell -
Country House of the Year 2003

FACILITIES
On site: Garden
Nearby: Golf, beach, cycling,
swimming pool, sauna & Jacuzzi

RESTRICTIONS
No facilities for disabled guests
Not suitable for children
No smoking throughout
No pets

ATTRACTIONS
Cliffs of Moher, Bunratty Castle,
King John's Castle, Aran Islands,
Doonbeg and Lahinch golf courses,
Hunt Museum

NEAREST
CITY:
Limerick - 42 miles/1 hr

AIRPORT:
Shannon - 35 miles/50 mins

RAIL STATION:
Ennis - 20 miles/30 mins

AFFILIATIONS
Ireland's Blue Book

RESERVATIONS
Toll free in US: 800-323-5463
Quote Best Loved

ACCESS CODES
Not applicable

IRELAND

The romantic Atlantic awaits at this idyllic retreat on Lahinch Bay

Moy House was originally built for Sir Augustine Fitzgerald in the mid-18th century and occupies a superb position overlooking Lahinch Bay on the County Clare coast. This country house is set in 15 acres of gardens and grounds with mature woodlands and a picturesque river, beyond which sweeps a sandy Atlantic beach renowned for surfing and sunbathing in the warmer months and breathtaking seascapes year-round.

Moy House itself is a wonderfully stylish and appealing country retreat deftly blending traditional character and antiques with the best of contemporary design and comfort. The spacious and delightful bedrooms benefit from wonderful views, and the kitchen, where breakfast and dinner are prepared, is open for guests to use at their leisure.

Fortified by a hearty breakfast, there are any number of sightseeing and sporting activities to choose from. Lahinch is synonymous with golf, offering both the famous Castle Golf Course and the Greg Norman-designed links course at Doonberg. Golfers, walkers, cyclists (there are two house bikes) and sea bathers can depart from the front door. Further afield, things to see include the Cliffs of Moher, the Burren and the Ailwee Caves.

LOCATION
Situated on the coast road
one mile south of Lahinch.

Country house   MUSTARD SEED AT ECHO LODGE

Ballingarry, Co Limerick
Republic of Ireland

T +353 (0)69 68508
F +353 (0)69 68511
mustard@bestloved.com
www.mustard.bestloved.com

OWNER
Daniel Mullane

ROOM RATES
Single occupancy   €110 - €190
13 Doubles/Twins   €180 - €300
1 Four-poster   €300
2 Suites   €300
Includes full breakfast and VAT

CREDIT CARDS
AMERICAN EXPRESS • MC • VI

RATINGS & AWARDS
ITB ★★★★ Hotel
Bridgestone 100 Best Places
to Stay in Ireland
Gilbeys Gold Medal Award
for Catering Excellence in Ireland
Bushmills Best Restaurant Outside of
Dublin Award 2002/2003
Food & Wine Magazine Best Country
House Hotel in Munster

FACILITIES
On site: Garden, health & beauty,
sauna, massage room, exercise room
1 meeting room/max 20 people
Nearby: Golf, riding, fishing

RESTRICTIONS
Children by arrangement
No smoking throughout
Pets by arrangement
Closed 23 - 26 Dec.

ATTRACTIONS
Glin Castle & Gardens,
Islandmore Gardens, Ring of Kerry,
Adare's antique shops,
Clonshire Equestrian Centre,
Cliffs of Moher, The Burren

NEAREST
CITY:
Limerick - 20 miles/35 mins

AIRPORT:
Shannon - 33 miles/1 hr

RAIL STATION:
Limerick - 20 miles/45 mins

AFFILIATIONS
Ireland's Blue Book
Preston's Global Hotels

RESERVATIONS
Toll free in US/Canada: 800-544-9993
or 800-323-5463
Quote Best Loved

ACCESS CODES
Not applicable

Share your Irish country home with one of the nation's most respected restaurants

Daniel Mullane's Mustard Seed Restaurant in Adare village is one of Ireland's most respected eateries. In 1995, the restaurateur bought Echo Lodge, a fine Victorian country house built in 1884 in the tranquil village of Ballingarry, near Adare. Into it he has put his restaurant and his love for the space and elegance of a bygone age, plus a wealth of today's comforts and amenities. Guests are welcomed for dinner with an overnight stay in one of the 16 bedrooms, all beautifully decorated and furnished. There are seven acres of lawns, pleasure grounds and, above all, peace; inside, the library has an unusual and excellent book collection.

The restaurant is memorable. Great care is taken to source ingredients from the best of Ireland's organic farms and cheesemakers, and the herbs are grown in the garden. The menu is made up of the delightful flavour of the very best of Irish cuisine, both traditional and modern, and is complemented by a serious wine list.

Peaceful countryside with opportunities for delightful walks is all around, and the air is enchanting. For those with an interest in sport, cycling, five golf courses, angling and horse riding are within the locality.

LOCATION
From the top of Adare, take the N21 for a quarter of a mile. Turn left at the first junction, toward Ballingarry; after eight miles, the hotel is signed in the village.

IRELAND

“Set fair to become the outstanding hotel in Ireland”

TRAVEL & LEISURE MAGAZINE

PARK HOTEL KENMARE

Country house

Kenmare, Co Kerry
Republic of Ireland

T +353 (0)64 41200
F +353 (0)64 41402
kenmare@bestloved.com
www.kenmare.bestloved.com

OWNER
Francis Brennan

GENERAL MANAGER
John Brennan

RATES PER PERSON
4 Singles   €149 - €191
36 Doubles/Twins €116 - €207
9 Suites   €241 - €297
Room only; includes VAT,
excludes 15% service charge

CREDIT CARDS
AMERICAN EXPRESS • DC • MC • VI

RATINGS & AWARDS
ITB ★★★★★ Hotel
RAC Gold Ribbon ★★★★
Dining Award 4
AA ★★★★ ❀❀
AA Top 200 - 2004/2005
Courvoisier's Book of the Best
Past winner, Andrew Harper's
Hideaway Report Hotel of the Year

FACILITIES
On site: Garden, heli-pad, croquet,
golf, tennis, health & beauty, fitness,
spa, golf adjacent
2 meeting rooms/max 30 people
Nearby: Fishing, cycling, riding

RESTRICTIONS
No children in restaurant after 6 p.m.
No smoking throughout
No pets in hotel, kennels available
Closed 4 Jan. - 5 Feb.

ATTRACTIONS
Ring of Kerry, Lakes of Killarney,
world-renowned gardens

NEAREST
CITY:
Cork - 60 miles/1 hr 30 mins

AIRPORT:
Cork - 60 miles/1 hr 30 mins

RAIL STATION:
Killarney - 20 miles/45 mins

FERRY PORT:
Cork - 60 miles/1 hr 30 mins

AFFILIATIONS
Ireland's Blue Book
Celebrated Hotels Collection
Small Luxury Hotels

RESERVATIONS
Toll free in US: 800-322-2403
or 800-323-5463
Quote Best Loved

ACCESS CODES
AMADEUS LX KIRPHK
APOLLO/GALILEO LX 32328
SABRE/ABACUS LX 30947
WORLDSPAN LX KIRPH

IRELAND

A truly luxurious destination for body, mind and soul

This luxurious hotel overlooking Kenmare Bay was built in 1897 by the Great Southern and Western Railway Company to provide accommodation for passengers travelling to Parknasilla, 17 miles away.

Today, owner Francis Brennan and his team have successfully maintained a standard of superior comfort for guests - they have doubled the size of the bedrooms and added balconies to some rooms, allowing wonderful views of the river. They have also created a world-class spa, SÁMAS, which translated from Gaelic signifies 'indulgence of the senses'. The spa, located in a wooded knoll overlooking the water, includes a heat experience room, shower temple, ice fountain, outdoor vitality pool, beauty suite and gym. Separate male and female facilities are available, or for romantic getaways, why not book a deluxe treatment suite with a double treatment area and private garden with pool.

The hotel is also well noted for its highly acclaimed restaurant, and Kenmare itself - recently designated Ireland's Tidiest Town - is home to many restaurants and quaint pubs. Numerous outdoor activities include Championship links golf courses in addition to the adjacent Kenmare course. Horseback riding, sea angling, mountain walks and coastal drives are all nearby.

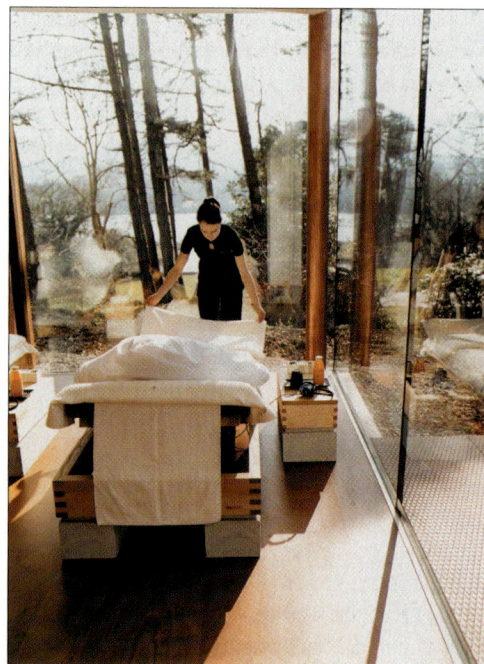

LOCATION

In southwest Ireland off the N70 from Killarney on the Ring of Kerry.

Townhouse

PERRYVILLE

Pretty town, pretty hotel and pretty good breakfast, too!

Nestled above its rocky harbour since medieval times, Kinsale has witnessed invasions by the Spanish, the French and the English, resulting in two strong forts nearby. Now, the invaders are tourists, tempted to visit Ireland's gourmet capital with its annual food festival and top-class restaurants - and, we think, Perryville House.

This Georgian building, with its ornate front door and fine wrought-iron balcony, was evidently created for a wealthy merchant or sea captain. In prime position overlooking the busy marina, the hotel is one of the prettiest houses in a pretty town, with twisting streets festooned with hanging baskets. Laura Corcoran has taken Perryville House to heart and recreated a classic interior with Irish antiques, four-poster beds and blazing turf fires. The generously proportioned bedrooms boast equally sumptuous bathrooms, crisp cotton bed linen and fresh flowers grown in Laura's own garden. With so many restaurants nearby, only breakfast is offered - but one irresistible to any food lover!

In easy reach of Cork, there are excellent coastal walks, as well as sailing, riding, fishing and golfing - plenty of opportunity to work up an appetite for those gourmet meals!

LOCATION

In the centre of Kinsale, overlooking the marina.

Kinsale, Co Cork
Republic of Ireland

T +353 (0)21 477 2731
F +353 (0)21 4772298
perryville@bestloved.com
www.perryville.bestloved.com

OWNERS
Andrew and Laura Corcoran

GENERAL MANAGER
Barry McDermott

ROOM RATES
Single occupancy	€200
13 Doubles/Twins	€200
4 Superior Doubles	€255
3 Deluxe Doubles	€300
6 Superior Deluxe Doubles	€380

Includes continental breakfast and VAT

CREDIT CARDS
MC • VI

RATINGS & AWARDS
ITB ★★★★ Guest House
RAC ◆◆◆◆◆
RAC Sparkling Diamond

FACILITIES
On site: Garden
Nearby: Golf, sailing, fishing, riding, cycling

RESTRICTIONS
No facilities for disabled guests
No children under 13 years
No smoking throughout
No pets
Closed 1 Nov. - 6 April

ATTRACTIONS
Charles Fort, Desmond Castle, West Cork Scenic Drive, Cobh Heritage Centre, Fota Wildlife Park, The Titanic Trail, Fota Island Golf Course, Old Head of Kinsale Golf Links

NEAREST
CITY:
Cork - 18 miles/30 mins

AIRPORT:
Cork - 15 miles/25 mins

RAIL STATION:
Cork - 18 miles/30 mins

AFFILIATIONS
Manor House Hotels of Ireland
Celebrated Hotels Collection

RESERVATIONS
Toll free in US: 800-322-2403
Quote Best Loved

ACCESS CODES
Not applicable

IRELAND

The friendly Irish welcome, the traditional love of golf and the beauty of the place leave you with just one regret - that the visit was not for longer.

JOHN PRINCE, MANCHESTER EVENING NEWS

PORTMARNOCK HOTEL AND GOLF LINKS Resort

Strand Road, Portmarnock,
Co Dublin
Republic of Ireland

T +353 (0)1 846 0611
F +353 (0)1 846 2442
portmarnock@bestloved.com
www.portmarnock.bestloved.com

GENERAL MANAGER
Shane Cookman

ROOM RATES
Single occupancy   €220 - €320
98 Doubles/Twins   €295 - €367
Includes full breakfast and VAT

CREDIT CARDS
AMERICAN EXPRESS • DC • JCB • MC • VI

RATINGS & AWARDS
ITB ★★★★ Hotel
AA ★★★★ ⊗⊗
AA Top 200 - 2004/2005

FACILITIES
On site: Garden, gym, golf,
health & beauty, sauna
6 meeting rooms/max 350 people
Nearby: riding, sailing, fishing

RESTRICTIONS
Limited facilities for disabled guests
No smoking throughout
No pets; guide dogs only

ATTRACTIONS
Dublin, Malahide Castle,
Talbot Botanical Gardens,
Fry Model Railway,
Newbridge House & Farm,
Lusk Heritage Centre, New Grange

NEAREST
CITY:
Dublin - 15 miles/25 mins

AIRPORT:
Dublin - 9 miles/15 mins

RAIL STATION:
Portmarnock - 1 mile/5 mins

AFFILIATIONS
Summit Hotels & Resorts

RESERVATIONS
Toll free in US: 800-457-4000
Quote Best Loved

ACCESS CODES
Not applicable

IRELAND

Sea views with Dublin on the doorstep for golfers and non-golfers alike

The Jameson family of Irish whiskey fame built Portmarnock, though it was known as St. Marnock's House back in 1864. In the 1880s, expert yachtsman Willy Jameson entertained the Prince of Wales (later Edward VII) here. He gave the prince a yacht named Britannia, but turned down a knighthood on the grounds that 'the name Jameson was known world-wide by those who drank anyway'. A golf course was laid out on the seashore in 1894, and the old Portmarnock Golf Club hosted several classic events before Bernard Langer's magnificent Championship course was opened in 1996. It makes optimum use of the challenging links terrain and is the only PGA European Tour course in Ireland.

Each of the hotel's 98 bedrooms has a view of the golf course or the sea, and guests can choose between comfortable modern executive suites, deluxe rooms and bedrooms in the original house furnished with historic four-poster beds. There is a choice of restaurants too, with the more formal Osborne Restaurant, named for the artist who painted several well known views from the house, and the casual Links Restaurant. Portmarnock is just 15 miles from Dublin and convenient for the airport.

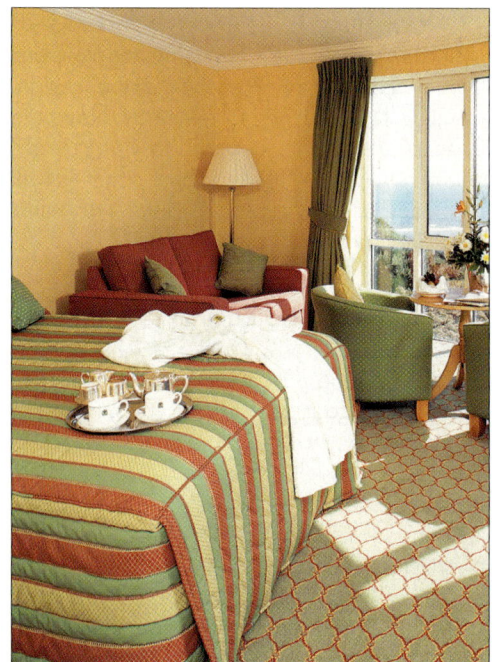

LOCATION
From Dublin airport, take N1 (Drogheda).
At Malahide roundabout, take the third exit.
At R106 (Malahide) Junction with R107, turn left.
Hotel is approximately 4 miles on the left.

> **My bedroom overlooked rolling lawns and ancient oaks. The bed was the size of a croquet lawn**
>
> ALAN BESTIC, SUNDAY TELEGRAPH

Country house

RATHSALLAGH HOUSE

The most stylish and entertaining 19th hole you'll ever find!

Take 530 acres of gorgeous Irish parkland at the foot of the Wicklow Mountains, convert some ivy-covered Queen Anne stables into a country house and surround it with an 18-hole Championship golf course and you have everything for a superb holiday - whether or not you play golf!

Rathsallagh House is the home of Joe and Kay O'Flynn, and their welcome is as big as the countryside around them. The house has a happy and relaxed atmosphere reflected in the genial warmth of the log and turf fires blazing away in the reception rooms. Upstairs, bedrooms are luxuriously appointed with views of the park.

The food is country-house cooking at its best, with a light modern influence from head chef John Kostiuk: game in season, fresh fish from the Wexford coast and breakfasts to drool over - after all, Rathsallagh has won the National Breakfast Awards four times! All this is a tribute to Kay's imagination and mastery of the culinary arts.

The Championship golf course has a fantastic setting and was designed by former world amateur champion Peter McEvoy and leading Irish professional Christie O'Connor. Other facilities include a tennis court, billiard room and spa room.

LOCATION

From Dublin airport, exit the M50 for the Naas bypass (M7) south; then, exit for the M9 southbound (Carlow). After eight miles, turn left for Rathsallagh.

Dunlavin, Co Wicklow
Republic of Ireland

T +353 (0)45 403112
F +353 (0)45 403343
rathsallagh@bestloved.com
www.rathsallagh.bestloved.com

OWNERS
The O'Flynn Family

ROOM RATES
Single occupancy   €175 - €260
26 Doubles/Twins   €260 - €300
1 Four-poster   €300
2 Suites   €300
Includes full breakfast and VAT

CREDIT CARDS
AMERICAN EXPRESS • DC • JCB • MC • VI

RATINGS & AWARDS
ITB ★★★★ Guest House
AA ◆◆◆◆◆
AA Premier Collection
Four National Breakfast Awards
Irish Country House
Restaurant of the Year 2002

FACILITIES
On site: Garden, snooker, heli-pad, croquet, golf, tennis, snooker, clay pigeon shooting, archery, sauna, steam room, Jacuzzi
5 meeting rooms/max 75 people
Nearby: Fishing, riding

RESTRICTIONS
Limited facilities for disabled guests
No children under 12 years
No smoking throughout
Pets by arrangement

ATTRACTIONS
Russborough House, National Stud, Curragh Racecourse, Glendalough, Punchestown Racecourse

NEAREST
CITY:
Dublin - 35 miles/1 hr

AIRPORT:
Dublin - 45 miles/1 hr 30 mins

RAIL STATION:
Kildare - 15 miles/30 mins

AFFILIATIONS
Ireland's Blue Book
Small Luxury Hotels

RESERVATIONS
Toll free in US: 800-323-5463,
800-544-9993 or 800-525-4800
Quote Best Loved

ACCESS CODES
AMADEUS LX DUBRHG
APOLLO/GALILEO LX 52732
SABRE/ABACUS LX 45779
WORLDSPAN LX DUBRH

IRELAND

Map p. 454, grid C6

It is indeed a rare luxury today to experience such a warm, friendly and family atmosphere that you both so naturally provide at Ross Lake House

PADDY AND CLODAGH DONOVAN, DUBLIN

ROSS LAKE HOUSE HOTEL
Country house

Rosscahill,
Oughterard, Co Galway
Republic of Ireland

T +353 (0)91 550109
F +353 (0)91 550184
rosslake@bestloved.com
www.rosslake.bestloved.com

OWNERS
Henry and Elaine Reid

ROOM RATES
Single occupancy   €105 - €130
7 Doubles/Twins   €150 - €170
3 Suites   €260 - €300
3 Superior Rooms   €170 - €200
Includes full breakfast and VAT

CREDIT CARDS
AMERICAN EXPRESS • DC • MC • VI

RATINGS & AWARDS
ITB ★★★ Hotel

FACILITIES
On site: Garden, tennis
1 meeting room/max 150 people
Nearby: Golf, fishing, riding

RESTRICTIONS
Limited facilities for disabled guests
No smoking throughout
No pets in public rooms
Closed 1 Nov. - 15 March

ATTRACTIONS
Aughnanure Castle,
Connemara National Park,
Cliffs of Moher, Kylemore Abbey,
Aran Islands, The Burren

NEAREST
CITY:
Galway - 14 miles/30 mins

AIRPORT:
Shannon - 65 miles/2 hrs

RAIL STATION:
Galway - 14 miles/30 mins

AFFILIATIONS
Preston's Global Hotels
The Green Book of Ireland

RESERVATIONS
Toll free in US: 800-544-9993
or 800-888-1199
Toll free in UK: 0800 371425
Quote Best Loved

ACCESS CODES
AMADEUS LE GWY279
APOLLO/GALILEO LE 26193
SABRE/ABACUS LE 42799
WORLDSPAN LE 42799

IRELAND

A wonderful old house at the gateway to Connemara

Ross Lake is a wonderful country house whose former glory has been revived by owners Henry and Elaine Reid. This 19th-century mansion was once an estate house of the landed gentry, who prized it for its serenity; today, it is has three suites and 10 comfortable, well-appointed double bedrooms.

From the moment you arrive, Henry and Elaine will make you feel at home. The intimate bar is ideal for a drink before dinner. A high-quality Irish menu is delightfully prepared and presented featuring a tempting variety of fresh produce from the nearby Connemara hills, streams and lakes - as well as fish straight from the Atlantic!

Ross Lake House has its own magnificent gardens. For the sport-minded, hard court tennis is on site, Oughterard golf course is two miles away and Lough Corrib and local lakes are famous for game and coarse fishing. The surrounding countryside is rich in superb mountain walks and climbs. Nearby attractions include Aughnanure Castle, Kylemore Abbey, Connemara National Park, the Aran Islands, the Cliffs of Moher and the Burren.

LOCATION
Fourteen miles from Galway on the N59, the main Galway-Clifden road. Turn left after the village of Rosscahill.

> "Thank you for such a lovely stay. Sea View House was utterly charming. It's just my kind of place - elegant but not pretentious"
>
> BILL SERTL, TRAVEL EDITOR, SAVEUR GARDEN DESIGN, NEW YORK USA

Country house

SEA VIEW HOUSE HOTEL

Ballylickey, Bantry, Co Cork
Republic of Ireland

T +353 (0)27 50462
F +353 (0)27 51555
seaview@bestloved.com
www.seaview.bestloved.com

OWNER
Kathleen O'Sullivan

ROOM RATES
Single occupancy	€70 - €100
21 Doubles/Twins	€140 - €175
2 Suites	€175 - €190

Includes newspaper, full breakfast and VAT

CREDIT CARDS
AMERICAN EXPRESS • DC • MC • VI

RATINGS & AWARDS
ITB ★★★★ Hotel
ITB Award for Excellence
RAC ★★★
AA ★★★ ⊛⊛
AA Top 200 - 2004/2005
Gilbeys Gold Medal Award
for Catering Excellence in Ireland

FACILITIES
On site: Garden
1 meeting room/max 20 people
Nearby: Golf, fishing, tennis, riding

RESTRICTIONS
No smoking throughout
No pets in public rooms
Closed mid-Nov. - mid-March

ATTRACTIONS
Gougane Barra, Killarney, Bantry House, Armada Centre, Garnish Island, Peninsula Barra

NEAREST
CITY:
Cork - 56 miles/1 hr 30 mins

AIRPORT:
Cork - 56 miles/1 hr 30 mins
Shannon - 120 miles/3 hrs

RAIL STATION:
Cork - 56 miles/1 hr 30 mins

AFFILIATIONS
Celebrated Hotels Collection
Manor House Hotels of Ireland

RESERVATIONS
Toll free in US: 800-322-2403
Quote Best Loved

ACCESS CODES
Not applicable

A resplendent, secluded haven amongst the delights of Ireland

This exceptional hotel combines the perfect location with food that is worth going out of your way for! This is possibly one of the most romantic areas in the world, all mountains, lakes and a coastline praised in songs that have passed down the generations across the world. Seashore and landscapes provide neverending pleasure, from golfing to walking, pony trekking and fishing. Culturally, it is a rich seam of gold that spans prehistory, the Celts, the dawn of Christendom and modern history. Relics and remains are preserved for all to see. Whatever your interest, there is nowhere more beautiful in which to enjoy it.

Sea View House nestles comfortably into this idyllic picture, an elegant haven that stands aloof from worldly pressures and basks in a well-earned reputation for good food. 'It's really a country house with country house cooking', says Kathleen O'Sullivan, who owns and runs the hotel. She has a nose for good wine, so it stands to reason the cellar is also a veritable treasure trove!

She also has an eye for beauty, and her splendid collection of antiques is displayed throughout the house and in the charming, well-appointed bedrooms - it is, after all, her home. What makes it so special is that so many of her guests have been encouraged to call it theirs, too!

LOCATION
Seventy yards off the N71 Bantry - Glengarriff road close to Ballylickey Bridge.

IRELAND

ST CLERANS

Country house

Craughwell, Co Galway
Republic of Ireland

T +353 (0)91 846555
F +353 (0)91 846752
stclerans@bestloved.com
www.stclerans.bestloved.com

OWNER
Merv Griffin

ROOM RATES
Single occupancy   €355 - €495
12 Doubles/Twins   €355 - €495
Includes full breakfast and VAT

CREDIT CARDS
AMERICAN EXPRESS • MC • VI

RATINGS & AWARDS
ITB ★★★★ Guest House
AA ◆◆◆◆◆

FACILITIES
On site: Heli-pad, croquet,
country walks, massage & beauty
treatments by arrangement
1 meeting room/max 25 people
Nearby: Golf, riding, fishing,
hunting/shooting, clay pigeon shooting

RESTRICTIONS
No children under 12 years in restaurant
No pets; guide dogs only

ATTRACTIONS
Historical sites,
Cliffs of Moher and
The Burren in County Clare,
Connemara National Park,
Kylemore Abbey,
the Aran Islands

NEAREST
CITY:
Galway - 20 miles/45 mins

AIRPORT:
Shannon - 60 miles/1 hr 30 mins
Galway - 20 miles/45 mins

RAIL STATION:
Athenry - 10 miles/15 mins

AFFILIATIONS
Celebrated Hotels Collection

RESERVATIONS
Toll free in US: 800-322-2403
or 800-323-5463
Quote Best Loved

ACCESS CODES
Not applicable

This splendid historical manor house is the choice of Hollywood's best

Celebrated US film director John Huston once owned this delightful manor house and described it as one of the most beautiful houses in all of Ireland. As someone with an eye for the picturesque, he was undoubtedly drawn to the dramatic setting, unique character and magical atmosphere of this classic country house.

Today restored to its original splendour, the house is decorated in an exquisite and elegant manner and boasts 12 deluxe guest rooms that blend tradition, luxury and bold contemporary colours to create high style and great individuality. It is the perfect setting for exclusive meetings or small weddings. The richly furnished library with its dark volumes, open chess board and games makes the perfect setting to imagine some great mystery or romance enfolding within the hotel's tranquil setting. The sumptuous dining room that once played host to princes and the cream of Hollywood celebrities has now become renowned for its outstanding cuisine created by Japanese chef Hishashi Kumagi.

The hotel is surrounded by the most breathtaking countryside - and once inside, the warmth of the interior is matched in full by the warmth of the welcome and the home-from-home friendliness of the hotel's staff.

LOCATION

Follow the N6 from Loughrea toward Galway.
Turn right one mile outside Loughrea (signposted Athenry). Drive three and a half miles, then turn left for the hotel, which is signposted.

City hotel

TEN SQUARE

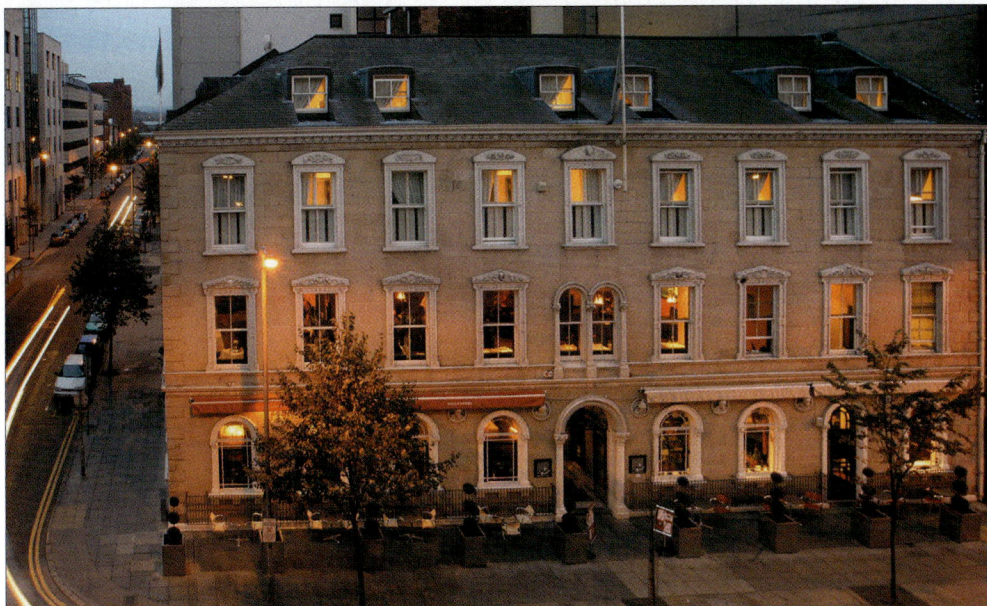

Elegant on the outside, opulent on the inside - and a remarkable stay

China's legendary Pudong district is world-renowned for its sumptuous five-star hotels. The first of its kind in Ireland, the unique, exquisite Ten Square makes it possible to experience the same refined Oriental opulence.

One of the most innovative and stylish hotels in Belfast, the 23 bedrooms are a luxury showpiece of Asian splendour, with warm, rich cream carpets as a base for low-level dark timber beds with Frette linens, opal glass-inset shutters and elegant freestanding wardrobes - all adding up to a chic interior that's promoted a new aesthetic for hospitality amongst cosmopolitan residents and city-hopping visitors.

The newly-reopened Porcelain Restaurant offers an exclusive, intimate fine-dining experience, with a fusion of European flavours creating a heady blend of sights, smells and tastes complemented by an award-winning wine list and highly contemporary, yet relaxed surroundings. For something more sociable, why not try the ultra-trendy new Grill Room & Bar? With its distinct Colonial theme of rich wooden furniture coupled with soft leather seating, this is the perfect setting for a casual drink or a bite to eat.

LOCATION
Located in Donegall Square across from City Hall.

10 Donegall Square South,
Belfast BT1 5JD
Northern Ireland

T (UK) 0870 432 8792
T 028 9024 1001
F 028 9024 3210
tensq@bestloved.com
www.tensq.bestloved.com

OWNERS
Nicholas and Paul Hill

GENERAL MANAGER
Kevin Smyth

ROOM RATES
20 Superior Double/Twins	£160
2 Deluxe Doubles/Twins	£200
1 Mini Suite	£240

Includes full breakfast and VAT

CREDIT CARDS
AMERICAN EXPRESS • MC • VI

RATINGS & AWARDS
NITB ★★★★ Hotel

FACILITIES
On site: 1 meeting room/max 250 people

RESTRICTIONS
No pets; guide dogs only

ATTRACTIONS
The Odyssey, Belfast Zoo, Waterfront Hall, Saint Patrick Centre, Ulster American Folk Park, Causeway Coast and Glens

NEAREST
CITY:
Belfast

AIRPORT:
Belfast International - 18 miles/25 mins
Belfast City - 5 miles/10 mins

RAIL STATION:
Belfast - ½ mile/5 mins

AFFILIATIONS
Independent

RESERVATIONS
National rate in UK: 0870 432 8792
Quote Best Loved

ACCESS CODES
APOLLO/GALILEO YX 61318
SABRE/ABACUS YX 57620
WORLDSPAN YX TENSQ

IRELAND

> *In a world of hotels where the anodyne and the anonymous are the norm, Tinakilly House is a beacon to restore hope to the traveller's heart*
>
> 1996 BON APPETIT SPECIAL COLLECTOR'S EDITION

TINAKILLY HOUSE

Country house

Wicklow (Rathnew),
Co Wicklow
Republic of Ireland

T +353 (0)404 69274
F +353 (0)404 67806
tinakilly@bestloved.com
www.tinakilly.bestloved.com

OWNERS
Raymond and Josephine Power

ROOM RATES
Single occupancy	€167 - €388
12 Doubles/Twins	€212 - €262
10 Four-posters	€264 - €332
23 Junior Suites	€264 - €332
5 Captain Suites	€352 - €444
1 Admirals State Room	€494 - €654

Includes full breakfast and VAT

CREDIT CARDS
AMERICAN EXPRESS • DC • MC • VI

RATINGS & AWARDS
ITB ★★★★ Hotel
RAC Blue Ribbon ★★★ Dining Award 3
AA ★★★★ ❀ 69%

FACILITIES
On site: Garden, heli-pad,
croquet, tennis
3 meeting rooms/max 65 people
Nearby: Golf, riding, hiking

RESTRICTIONS
Limited facilities for disabled guests
No smoking throughout
No pets; guide dogs only
Closed 24-25 December

ATTRACTIONS
Glendalough, Mount Usher,
Powerscourt Gardens & Waterfall,
Dublin City, Trinity College

NEAREST
CITY:
Dublin - 29 miles/45 mins

AIRPORT:
Dublin - 35 miles/1 hr 30 mins

RAIL STATION:
Wicklow - 2 miles/5 mins

FERRY PORT:
Dun Laoghaire - 20 miles/40 mins

AFFILIATIONS
Ireland's Blue Book
Celebrated Hotels Collection
Small Luxury Hotels

RESERVATIONS
Toll free in US: 800-322-2403
or 800-323-5463
Quote Best Loved

ACCESS CODES
AMADEUS LX DUBTCH
APOLLO/GALILEO LX 67443
SABRE/ABACUS LX 30077
WORLDSPAN LX DUBTC

Splendid fresh food in richly elegant Victorian surroundings

Truly a romantic secret hideaway, this gracious Victorian Italianate manor just south of Dublin stands on seven acres of gardens that sweep down to the Irish Sea. Built for Captain Halpin, who laid the world's telegraph cables, the ornate interiors of Tinakilly House are rich in period furnishings, oil paintings and seafaring memorabilia. Tinakilly is now the home of the Power family, who together with their friendly staff bid you a warm welcome.

Each of the 51 bedrooms is a perfect blend of Victorian splendour and modern comfort. The Captain Suites and Four-poster Junior Suites enjoy breathtaking sea and garden views. At the table, chef Ross Quinn uses fresh local produce, including fish and Wicklow lamb flavoured with herbs from Tinakilly's own gardens. Ross' creations are also complemented by an award-winning wine cellar. Brown bread is baked daily, which is especially delicious with the locally-smoked Irish salmon.

A host of nearby visitor attractions include the Wicklow Mountains and the 6th-century monastic city of Glendalough. Excellent local golf courses include the links European Club and parkland Druid's Glen, home of the 1996-1999 Irish Open.

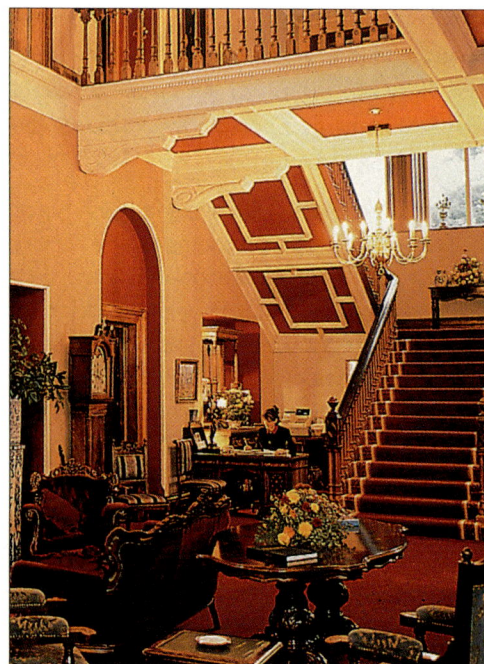

LOCATION

From Dublin, follow the N11/M11 to Rathnew and then the R570 toward Wicklow. The hotel's entrance is on the left 450 yards outside Rathnew.

> "I came tired and left relaxed. One of the best hotels in the world"
> MICHAEL & IRENE DOWD, NEW YORK USA

Castle — WATERFORD CASTLE HOTEL & GOLF CLUB

The Island, Ballinakill,
Waterford, Co Waterford
Republic of Ireland

T +353 (0)51 878203
F +353 (0)51 879316
waterford@bestloved.com
www.waterford.bestloved.com

GENERAL MANAGER
Gillian Butler

ROOM RATES
1 Single	€162 - €240
13 Doubles/Twins	€195 - €445
4 Deluxe four-poster Suites	€375 - €560
1 Presidential Suite	€460 - €635

Includes VAT

CREDIT CARDS
AMERICAN EXPRESS • DC • MC • VI

RATINGS & AWARDS
AA ★★★★ ❀❀
AA Top 200 - 2004/2005

FACILITIES
On site: Garden, heli-pad, golf, tennis,
18 hole golf course,
clay pigeon shooting,
archery and team building events,
driving range, scenic walks
2 meeting rooms/max 22 people
Nearby: Fishing, riding,
free use of local fitness centre

RESTRICTIONS
Limited facilities for disabled guests
No smoking throughout
No pets; guide dogs only
Closed Christmas

ATTRACTIONS
Waterford Crystal showrooms,
Waterford walking tours,
Reginalds Tower Museum,
Christchurch Cathedral,
The Waterford Show,
Waterford Treasures Museum

NEAREST
CITY:
Waterford - 3 miles/10 mins
AIRPORT:
Dublin - 109 miles/3 hrs
RAIL STATION:
Waterford - 3 miles/10 mins
FERRY PORT:
Rosslare 50 miles/1 hr

AFFILIATIONS
Celebrated Hotels Collection

RESERVATIONS
Toll free in US: 800-322-2403
Quote Best Loved

ACCESS CODES
Not applicable

Take the ferry to a secluded island with luxury hotel and golf course

Waterford Castle, former home of the Fitzgerald family, dates back to the 15th century; today, to stay here is to pass into another world of legend and folklore, starting with the car ferry across from reality to this enchanted island. From there, the drive leads to the greystone castle, as proud and romantic as your imagination will allow. This gracious hotel, filled with antiques, is redolent of an elegant past; the carved granite archway leads into the grand entrance hall, dominated by a cavernous fireplace. Bedrooms are bright and airy, with stunning views of the surrounding island estate.

This fairytale illusion is continued at dinner: With the menu as your guidebook, crested plates bear culinary delights and confections dreamed up by the castle's gifted chefs. The food is divine, as bewitching as the castle itself.

Completing the picture is the spectacular 18-hole Championship golf course, laid out over 200 acres of beautiful and mature parkland. First-class leisure facilities are just two minutes drive from the car ferry, and such outdoor activities as riding and fishing are also available.

LOCATION
From the N9, cross the bridge and stay by the River Suir. At the Tower Hotel, turn left for Dunmore Road and take the fourth turn on the left; follow the ferry signs.

IRELAND

WINEPORT LODGE

Contemporary hotel

Glasson, Athlone,
Co Westmeath
Republic of Ireland

T +353 (0)90 64 39010
F +353 (0)90 64 85471
wineport@bestloved.com
www.wineport.bestloved.com

OWNERS
Ray Byrne and Jane English

MANAGER
Norma Wilson

ROOM RATES
Single occupancy   €150 - €295
10 Doubles/Twins   €200 - €295
Includes full breakfast and VAT

CREDIT CARDS
AMERICAN EXPRESS • DC • MC • VI

RATINGS & AWARDS
AA ✿ Restaurant with Rooms
Jameson Guide Hideaway
of the Year Award 2003

FACILITIES
On site: Massage treatments
2 meeting rooms/max 150 people
Nearby: Golf, riding, leisure centre

RESTRICTIONS
Limited facilities for disabled guests
No smoking throughout
No pets

ATTRACTIONS
Clonmacnoise,
Birr Castle,
Strokestown Park House

NEAREST
CITY:
Galway - 57 miles/1 hr 15 mins

AIRPORT:
Dublin - 79 miles/1 hr 45 mins

RAIL STATION:
Athlone - 4 miles/10 mins

AFFILIATIONS
Ireland's Blue Book

RESERVATIONS
Toll free in US: 800-323-5463
Quote Best Loved

ACCESS CODES
Not applicable

IRELAND

A perfectly set gem in the centre of the Emerald Isle

Wineport Lodge is blissfully located on the edge of Ireland's peaceful Inland Waterways. Housed in an impressively modern cedar-clad structure, it is the perfect place to dine and stay, either for business or pleasure, in an easily accessible destination.

Stunning lake views are afforded from every room, and the west-facing balconies ensure sunset is something really special to be savoured. Extra-large bathrooms with underfloor heating are a sensual addition, and all rooms feature specially-commissioned walnut furniture by leading designer Robert English. Each guest bedroom is linked exclusively with a wine theme, making Wineport Lodge a must-see for the wine lover - the same goes for the centrepiece of the Lodge, the light-filled double-height Taittinger Champagne Lounge, perfect for relaxing in any time of day. In the newly restyled restaurant, Eurotoques Chef Feargal O'Donnell's delicious food is matched by genuinely friendly and expert service.

Glasson Golf Club is just a short boat trip away from their jetty, and a stroll around the lake begins outside their door. After all that, a resident masseuse is available to soothe your stresses away. If you're looking for the ideal hideaway to escape to, then Wineport Lodge is the right place to drop in and revive your jaded soul.

LOCATION

From Athlone, take the N55 Longford road. After three miles, fork left at the Dog & Duck. The hotel is one mile further on the left.

THE PERFECT ACCESSORY

ANGEL AND ROYAL HOTEL, LINCOLNSHIRE (PAGE 171)

THAMESMEAD HOUSE HOTEL, HENLEY-ON-THAMES (PAGE 334)

Keep tabs on all the latest news at Best Loved Hotels! Join our exclusive **Red Rosette Travel Club** for the most up-to-date information on offers, events and updates at Best Loved's member hotels. Your membership includes

- £60 in travel vouchers for selected Best Loved Hotels, valid for stays or meals

- Exclusive Red Rosette Club e-newsletter

- Special offers and invitations from selected hotels and our Red Rosette Club affiliates and sponsors

- Membership card and welcome kit

Your annual membership in Best Loved's **Red Rosette Travel Club** is a great value at **just £9.95!**

ARDTARA COUNTRY HOUSE, CO LONDONDERRY (PAGE 378)

Call today to receive members-only benefits!

ORDERS/INFO: 0870 432 8700 (UK) OR +44 208 962 9555   E-MAIL ORDERS@BESTLOVED.COM

OR USE THE FREEPOST ORDER/INFORMATION FORM LOCATED IN THE BACK OF THIS BOOK

A-Z INDEX OF HOTELS

◆ Children welcome; please contact hotels directly for any applicable restrictions.

A-Z INDEX OF HOTELS

◆ Children welcome; please contact hotels directly for any applicable restrictions.

REGIONAL INDEX

● Double room: up to £95 per night ● Double room: £96 - £145 per night ● Double room: £146 - £195 per night ● Double room: more than £196 per night

REGIONAL INDEX

● Double room: up to £95 per night   ● Double room: £96 - £145 per night   ● Double room: £146 - £195 per night   ● Double room: more than £196 per night

REGIONAL INDEX

HOTEL	PRICE	MAP	PG
SHROPSHIRE			
Old Vicarage Hotel & Restaurant	●	D4	217
Raven Hotel & Restaurant	●	C4	222
Stretton Hall	●	C4	227
SOUTH GLOUCESTERSHIRE			
Thornbury Castle	●	C6	230
STAFFORDSHIRE			
Brookhouse	●	E4	175
SUFFOLK			
Swan	●	H5	228
Swynford Paddocks	●	G5	229
WARWICKSHIRE			
Mallory Court Hotel	●	E5	208
Nuthurst Grange	●	D5	214
Old Mill Hotel	●	E5	215
Peacock Hotel	●	E5	219
WILTSHIRE			
Pear Tree at Purton	●	C3	220
WORCESTERSHIRE			
Brockencote Hall	●	D5	174
Colwall Park Hotel	●	D5	181
Cottage in the Wood	●	D5	184
Dormy House	●	D5	189
Elms	●	D5	190
Grafton Manor	●	D5	194

WEST COUNTRY

HOTEL	PRICE	MAP	PG
CORNWALL			
Budock Vean	●	B5	251
Fowey Hotel	●	C5	256
Garrack Hotel	●	B5	258
Hell Bay	●	B6	261
Idle Rocks Hotel	●	B5	267
Island Hotel	●	B6	268
Lugger Hotel	●	C5	270
Metropole	●	C4	272
Port Gaverne Hotel	●	C4	276
Rose-In-Vale Country House Hotel	●	B5	279
Talland Bay Hotel	●	C5	282
Trevalsa Court Country House	●	C5	284
Well House	●	C5	285
Wisteria Lodge	●	C5	287

HOTEL	PRICE	MAP	PG
DEVON			
Barrington House	●	E5	246
Bovey Castle	●	D4	249
Browns Hotel	●	D4	250
Court Barn	●	C4	254
Gabriel Court Hotel	●	D5	257
Glazebrook House Hotel	●	D4	259
Holne Chase Hotel	●	D4	262
Horn of Plenty	●	D4	264
Hotel Riviera	●	E4	265
Lewtrenchard Manor	●	D4	269
Mill End Hotel	●	D4	273
Prince Hall Hotel	●	D4	277
Tides Reach Hotel	●	D5	283
SOMERSET			
Andrews on the Weir	●	E3	244
Bath Lodge Hotel	●	F3	247
Bath Priory Hotel & Restaurant	●	F2	248
Castle at Taunton	●	E3	252
County Hotel	●	F2	253
Dorian House	●	F2	255
Haydon House	●	F2	260
Homewood Park	●	F2	263
Hunstrete House	●	F2	266
Luttrell Arms	●	E3	271
Mount Somerset	●	E3	274
Old Rectory	●	F3	275
Queensberry Hotel	●	F2	278
Royal Crescent Hotel	●	F2	280
Ston Easton Park	●	F3	281
Woodlands Country House Hotel	●	E3	288
Woolverton House	●	F2	289
WILTSHIRE			
At The Sign Of The Angel	●	G2	245
Widbrook Grange	●	G2	286

SOUTH/ISLANDS

HOTEL	PRICE	MAP	PG
BERKSHIRE			
Beech House Hotel	●	D3	298
Cliveden House	●	E3	303
Donnington Valley Hotel	●	D3	305
French Horn Hotel	●	D3	310
Inn on the Green	●	E3	316
Sir Christopher Wren's House	●	E3	330
Vineyard At Stockcross	●	D3	337

HOTEL	PRICE	MAP	PG
BUCKINGHAMSHIRE			
Hartwell House	●	D2	312
Taplow House & Restaurant	●	E3	333
DORSET			
Eastbury Hotel	●	F3	306
Lord Bute	●	C4	318
Mansion House Hotel	●	C4	320
Priory Hotel	●	C4	326
EAST SUSSEX			
Flackley Ash Hotel	●	F4	309
Hotel du Vin & Bistro	●	E4	314
Rye Lodge	●	F4	328
ESSEX			
Maison Talbooth	●	F2	319
Pier at Harwich	●	G2	324
GUERNSEY			
Old Government House	●	inset	323
HAMPSHIRE			
Careys Manor Hotel & Spa	●	D4	300
Cottage Hotel	●	D4	304
Esseborne Manor	●	D3	308
Montagu Arms Hotel	●	D4	321
New Park Manor	●	D4	322
Thatched Cottage Hotel	●	D4	335
Three Lions	●	C4	336
HERTFORDSHIRE			
St Michael's Manor	●	E2	331
ISLE OF WIGHT			
Priory Bay Hotel	●	D4	325
JERSEY			
Chateau Valeuse	●	inset	302
KENT			
Eastwell Manor	●	F3	307
Rowhill Grange Hotel & Spa	●	F3	327
Wallett's Court	●	G3	338
OXFORDSHIRE			
Thamesmead House Hotel	●	D3	334

● Double room: up to £95 per night   ● Double room: £96 - £145 per night   ● Double room: £146 - £195 per night   ● Double room: more than £196 per night

● Double room: up to €156 per night ● Double room: €157 - €238 per night ● Double room: €239 - €320 per night ● Double room: more than €321 per night

ON-SITE FACILITIES

SWIMMING POOL

SCOTLAND
Cally Palace Hotel	24
Dunain Park Hotel	38
Isle of Eriska	56
Mar Hall	64
Royal Marine Hotel	73
Scotsman	75

NORTH
Armathwaite Hall Hotel	88
Devonshire	95
Feversham Arms	97
Lindeth Howe Country House	108
Middlethorpe Hall and Spa	112
Pheasant Hotel	117
Sefton Hotel	123
Swan Hotel	125
Underscar Manor	128
Wordsworth Hotel	133

WALES
Bodysgallen Hall and Spa	144
Castell Deudraeth	145
Empire	147
Penally Abbey	157

MIDSHIRES
Calcot Manor	177
Charingworth Manor	178
Mallory Court Hotel	208
Stapleford Park	226

WEST COUNTRY
Bath Priory Hotel & Restaurant	248
Bovey Castle	249
Budock Vean - The Hotel on the River	251
Gabriel Court Hotel	257
Garrack Hotel	258
Hell Bay	261
Homewood Park	263
Hunstrete House	266
Island Hotel	268
Rose-In-Vale Country House Hotel	279
Royal Crescent Hotel	280
Talland Bay Hotel	282
Tides Reach Hotel	283
Well House	285
Widbrook Grange	286
Woodlands Country House Hotel	288

SOUTH
Bishopstrow House	299
Careys Manor Hotel & Spa	300
Chateau Valeuse	302
Cliveden House	303
Eastwell Manor	307
Flackley Ash Hotel	309
Hartwell House Hotel, Restaurant & Spa	312
Hintlesham Hall	313
New Park Manor	322
Old Government House Hotel & Spa	323
Priory Bay Hotel	325
Rowhill Grange Hotel & Spa	327
Rye Lodge	328
Vineyard At Stockcross	337
Wallett's Court	338

LONDON
Dolphin Square Hotel	356

IRELAND
Aghadoe Heights Hotel	375
Culloden Estate and Spa	390
Dromoland Castle	391
Dunloe Castle	393
Hayfield Manor	399
Maryborough House Hotel	409
Merrion Hotel	411

HEALTH & BEAUTY

SCOTLAND
Dalhousie Castle & Spa	36
Isle of Eriska	56
Mar Hall	64
Scotsman	75

NORTH
Devonshire	95
Holbeck Ghyll Hotel & Spa	104
Middlethorpe Hall and Spa	112
Seaham Hall Hotel & Serenity Spa	122
Sefton Hotel	123
Swinton Park	126
Underscar Manor	128

WALES
Bodysgallen Hall and Spa	144
Castell Deudraeth	145
Empire	147

MIDSHIRES
Calcot Manor	177
Fawsley Hall	191
Raven Hotel & Restaurant	222

WEST COUNTRY
Bath Priory Hotel & Restaurant	248
Bovey Castle	249
Budock Vean - The Hotel on the River	251
Royal Crescent Hotel	280
Tides Reach Hotel	283

SOUTH
Bishopstrow House	299
Careys Manor Hotel & Spa	300
Cliveden House	303
Eastwell Manor	307
Flackley Ash Hotel	309

(continued)
Hartwell House Hotel, Restaurant & Spa	312
Hintlesham Hall	313
New Park Manor	322
Old Government House Hotel & Spa	323
Rowhill Grange Hotel & Spa	327
Rye Lodge	328
Vineyard At Stockcross	337
Wallett's Court	338

LONDON
Baglioni Hotel London	348
Threadneedles	367

IRELAND
Ashford Castle	379
Culloden Estate and Spa	390
Dromoland Castle	391
Fitzwilliam Hotel	394
Hayfield Manor	399
Maryborough House Hotel	409
Merrion Hotel	411
Mustard Seed At Echo Lodge	413
Park Hotel Kenmare	414
Portmarnock Hotel and Golf Links	416

GYM

SCOTLAND
Isle of Eriska	56
Mar Hall	64
One Devonshire Gardens	68
Royal Marine Hotel	73
Scotsman	75

NORTH
Devonshire	95
Eleven Didsbury Park	96
Feversham Arms	97
Judges Country House Hotel	106
Wordsworth Hotel	133

MIDSHIRES
Calcot Manor	177
Charingworth Manor	178
Dormy House	189
Stapleford Park	226

WEST COUNTRY
Bath Priory Hotel & Restaurant	248
Bovey Castle	249
Browns Hotel	250
Garrack Hotel	258
Royal Crescent Hotel	280
Widbrook Grange	286

SOUTH
Bishopstrow House	299
Cliveden House	303
Eastwell Manor	307
Flackley Ash Hotel	309
Old Government House Hotel & Spa	323
Rowhill Grange Hotel & Spa	327
Vineyard At Stockcross	337
Wallett's Court	338

ON-SITE FACILITIES

LONDON
Baglioni Hotel London	348
Leonard	362

IRELAND
Aghadoe Heights Hotel	375
Ashford Castle	379
Dromoland Castle	391
Fitzwilliam Hotel	394
Hayfield Manor	399
Maryborough House Hotel	409
Merrion Hotel	411
Portmarnock Hotel and Golf Links	416

TENNIS

SCOTLAND
Cally Palace Hotel	24
Craigellachie Hotel of Speyside	30
Cringletie House	31
Culloden House	34
Glenapp Castle	46
Greywalls	49
Isle of Eriska	56
Mar Hall	64

NORTH
Armathwaite Hall Hotel	88
Crewe Hall	92
Devonshire	95
Feversham Arms	97
Holbeck Ghyll Hotel & Spa	104

WALES
Bodysgallen Hall and Spa	144
Lake Country House	150
Lake Vyrnwy Hotel	151
Llangoed Hall	152

MIDSHIRES
Brockencote Hall	174
Calcot Manor	177
Charingworth Manor	178
Congham Hall	182
Elms	190
Fawsley Hall	191
Lower Slaughter Manor	207
Mallory Court Hotel	208
Stapleford Park	226
Swynford Paddocks	229
Washbourne Court Hotel	233

WEST COUNTRY
Bovey Castle	249
Budock Vean - The Hotel on the River	251
Court Barn	254
Gabriel Court Hotel	257
Hunstrete House	266
Island Hotel	268
Ston Easton Park	281

Well House	285
Woolverton House	289

SOUTH
Alexander House Hotel	296
Amberley Castle	297
Bishopstrow House	299
Cliveden House	303
Eastwell Manor	307
Esseborne Manor	308
Hartwell House Hotel, Restaurant & Spa	312
Hintlesham Hall	313
Priory Bay Hotel	325
Wallett's Court	338

LONDON
Dolphin Square Hotel	356

IRELAND
Aghadoe Heights Hotel	375
Ardtara Country House	378
Ashford Castle	379
Cahernane House Hotel	387
Castle Durrow Country House	389
Dunloe Castle	393
Glin Castle	396
Park Hotel Kenmare	414
Rathsallagh House	417
Ross Lake House Hotel	418
Tinakilly House	422
Waterford Castle Hotel & Golf Club	423

FISHING

SCOTLAND
Ballathie House Hotel	18
Bunchrew House Hotel	23
Cally Palace Hotel	24
Cavens Country House Hotel	26
Corriegour Lodge Hotel	28
Cromlix House	32
Flodigarry Country House Hotel	42
Four Seasons Hotel	43
Glenmoriston Arms Hotel	48
Hotel Eilean Iarmain	50
Inverlochy Castle	54
Isle of Eriska	56
Kilcamb Lodge	57
Kinloch Lodge	58
Melfort Pier & Harbour	65
Roman Camp Country House	72
Taychreggan	78
Tigh an Eilean	79

NORTH
Armathwaite Hall Hotel	88
Dale Head Hall	94
Devonshire	95
Linthwaite House	109

Swan Hotel	125
Swinton Park	126
Wordsworth Hotel	133

WALES
Lake Country House	150
Lake Vyrnwy Hotel	151
Llangoed Hall	152
Palé Hall Country House	155
Penmaenuchaf Hall	159

MIDSHIRES
Brockencote Hall	174
Langar Hall	204
Lords of the Manor	206

WEST COUNTRY
Bovey Castle	249
Fowey Hotel	256
Holne Chase Hotel	262
Lewtrenchard Manor	269
Mill End Hotel	273
Prince Hall Hotel	277
Ston Easton Park	281

SOUTH
Bishopstrow House	299
French Horn Hotel	310
Hartwell House Hotel, Restaurant & Spa	312
St Michael's Manor	331

IRELAND
Aghadoe Heights Hotel	375
Ard na Sidhe	377
Ashford Castle	379
Bayview Hotel	383
Bushmills Inn Hotel	385
Dromoland Castle	391
Glenlo Abbey Hotel	395
Lough Inagh Lodge Hotel	407
Markree Castle	408

RIDING

NORTH
Feversham Arms	97
Swinton Park	126

WEST COUNTRY
Bovey Castle	249

SOUTH
New Park Manor	322

IRELAND
Ashford Castle	379
Dromoland Castle	391
Dunloe Castle	393
Markree Castle	408

MEETING & RECEPTION FACILITIES

UP TO 25 GUESTS

SCOTLAND

HOTEL	ROOMS	GUESTS	PG
Airds Hotel	1	12	16
Edinburgh Residence	1	12	40
Enterkine Country House	1	24	41
Glenmorangie Highland Home	1	12	47
Glenmoriston Arms Hotel	1	24	48
Howard	2	18	51
Kilcamb Lodge	1	22	57
Ladyburn	1	20	62
Melfort Pier & Harbour	1	12	65
Peat Inn	1	12	69

NORTH

HOTEL	ROOMS	GUESTS	PG
Crosby Lodge	2	14	93
Eleven Didsbury Park	2	20	96
Green Bough Hotel	1	24	102
Hob Green Hotel, Restaurant & Gardens	1	12	103
Quebecs	3	6	118
Samling	1	18	121
Waren House Hotel	1	20	130
White Swan	1	20	131

WALES

HOTEL	ROOMS	GUESTS	PG
Hotel Maes-y-Neuadd	1	16	148
Penally Abbey	1	20	157

MIDSHIRES

HOTEL	ROOMS	GUESTS	PG
Brockencote Hall	2	20	174
Brookhouse	1	20	175
Cottage in the Wood	1	14	184
Dannah Farm	1	15	187
Dial House Hotel	1	20	188
Hotel on the Park	1	18	200
Kegworth House Hotel	1	16	201
Lamb at Burford	1	20	203
Lords of the Manor	1	20	206
Raven Hotel & Restaurant	1	16	222
Swan	3	20	228

WEST COUNTRY

HOTEL	ROOMS	GUESTS	PG
At The Sign Of The Angel	2	18	245
County Hotel	1	20	253
Gabriel Court Hotel	1	20	257
Hell Bay	1	20	261
Prince Hall Hotel	1	20	277
Wisteria Lodge	1	15	287

SOUTH

HOTEL	ROOMS	GUESTS	PG
Beech House Hotel	1	14	298
Cottage Hotel	1	14	304
French Horn Hotel	1	24	310
Priory Hotel	1	20	326
Thamesmead House Hotel	1	12	334

LONDON

HOTEL	ROOMS	GUESTS	PG
Academy Town House	1	14	347
Beaufort	1	6	350
Royal Park Hotel	1	10	365

IRELAND

HOTEL	ROOMS	GUESTS	PG
Butlers Town House	1	22	386
Caragh Lodge	1	15	388
Glin Castle	1	20	396
Longfield's	1	22	406
Lough Inagh Lodge Hotel	1	24	407
Mustard Seed At Echo Lodge	1	20	413
Sea View House Hotel	1	20	419
Waterford Castle Hotel	2	22	423

25 - 50 GUESTS

SCOTLAND

HOTEL	ROOMS	GUESTS	PG
Archiestown Hotel	1	25	17
Cally Palace Hotel	1	30	24
Castleton House Hotel	3	40	25
Channings	2	35	27
Cromlix House	3	50	32
Darroch Learg	1	40	37
Flodigarry Country House Hotel	1	40	42
Glasshouse	3	36	45
Glenapp Castle	3	34	46
Greywalls	1	50	49
Hotel Eilean Iarmain	2	50	50
Inverlochy Castle	1	25	54
Isle of Barra Hotel	1	50	55
Isle of Eriska	3	40	56
Knockinaam Lodge	1	40	60
One Devonshire Gardens	3	50	68
Taychreggan	2	30	78

NORTH

HOTEL	ROOMS	GUESTS	PG
Blue Lion	2	50	89
Broxton Hall	1	45	91
Feversham Arms	1	30	97
General Tarleton Inn	1	40	98
L'Enclume	1	25	107
Lindeth Howe Country House	2	30	108
Lovelady Shield	2	45	110
Miller Howe Hotel	2	40	113
Rothay Manor	1	34	120
Studley Hotel	1	50	124
Traddock	1	30	127
Yorke Arms	2	25	134

WALES

HOTEL	ROOMS	GUESTS	PG
Castell Deudraeth	1	30	145
Castle Hotel	2	30	146
Empire	1	30	147
Inn at the Elm Tree	2	40	149
Palé Hall Country House	2	40	155
Penbontbren Farm	1	40	158
Penmaenuchaf Hall	2	50	159

MIDSHIRES

HOTEL	ROOMS	GUESTS	PG
Beeches Hotel	1	40	172
Blenheim House Hotel	2	40	173
Cockliffe Country House Hotel	1	50	180
Congham Hall	1	50	182
Crown at Blockley	1	50	186
Elms	3	50	190
Feathers	2	50	192
Greenway	2	40	196
Langar Hall	2	45	204
Le Manoir Aux Quat' Saisons	1	50	205
Lower Slaughter Manor	2	40	207
Malt House	1	25	209
Manor House	2	40	210
Noel Arms	2	50	213
Old Vicarage Hotel & Restaurant	3	40	217
Plough At Clanfield	2	40	221
Riverside House Hotel	1	30	223
Royalist Hotel	1	30	224
Shaven Crown	1	40	225
Unicorn Hotel	1	50	232

WEST COUNTRY

HOTEL	ROOMS	GUESTS	PG
Barrington House	1	30	246
Budock Vean	2	50	251
Court Barn	2	40	254
Garrack Hotel	1	30	258
Horn of Plenty	1	35	264
Island Hotel	2	50	268
Luttrell Arms	1	35	271
Metropole	1	25	272
Mill End Hotel	3	40	273
Queensberry Hotel	1	40	278
Royal Crescent Hotel	1	40	280
Widbrook Grange	3	50	286
Woodlands Country House Hotel	2	40	288

SOUTH

HOTEL	ROOMS	GUESTS	PG
Amberley Castle	2	48	297
Esseborne Manor	2	40	308
Hotel du Vin & Bistro	2	48	314
Howard's House	1	40	315
Lord Bute	1	25	318
Mansion House Hotel	3	40	320
Montagu Arms Hotel	3	50	321
Thatched Cottage Hotel	1	30	335
Three Lions	1	35	336

LONDON

HOTEL	ROOMS	GUESTS	PG
Capital	2	35	352
Draycott Hotel	1	25	357
Leonard	4	40	362
Parkes	2	50	364
Threadneedles	3	50	367

IRELAND

HOTEL	ROOMS	GUESTS	PG
Aberdeen Lodge	2	30	374
Ahernes	1	50	376
Ardtara Country House	1	50	378
Bayview Hotel	2	40	383
Brownes	1	33	384
Bushmills Inn Hotel	3	40	385
Cahernane House Hotel	1	25	387
Gregans Castle	1	25	397
Halpin's Hotel	1	40	398
Hunter's Hotel	1	40	400
Kilkenny Hibernian Hotel	1	40	401
Killarney Royal Hotel	1	50	402
Lacken House	1	27	405
Park Hotel Kenmare	2	30	414
St Clerans	1	25	420

51 - 75 GUESTS

SCOTLAND

HOTEL	ROOMS	GUESTS	PG
Ballathie House Hotel	3	60	18
Bonham	1	70	21
Craigellachie Hotel of Speyside	3	70	30
Dunalastair Hotel	3	70	39
Inn At Lathones	1	60	53
Knockomie Hotel	2	70	61
Royal Marine Hotel	2	70	73

MEETING & RECEPTION FACILITIES

HOTEL	ROOMS	GUESTS	PG
NORTH			
Holbeck Ghyll Hotel & Spa	2	65	104
Linthwaite House	3	60	109
Middlethorpe Hall and Spa	2	60	112
WALES			
Bell at Skenfrith	1	60	143
Bodysgallen Hall and Spa	3	60	144
Llangoed Hall	3	70	152
MIDSHIRES			
Angel and Royal Hotel	3	65	171
Charingworth Manor	3	60	178
Country Cottage Hotel	4	60	185
Fosse Manor	1	60	193
Hotel des Clos	1	60	198
Lace Market Hotel	3	60	202
Pear Tree at Purton	4	60	220
Westwood Country Hotel	4	70	234
WEST			
Bath Priory Hotel & Restaurant	3	64	248
Fowey Hotel	1	70	256
Mount Somerset	3	60	274
Rose-In-Vale Country House Hotel	2	75	279
Well House	1	60	285
Langshott Manor	3	60	317
Shelleys	3	60	329
LONDON			
Flemings Mayfair	3	55	358
Stafford			
IRELAND			
	4	75	366
Rathsallagh House	5	75	417
Tinakilly House	3	65	422

76 - 100 GUESTS

HOTEL	ROOMS	GUESTS	PG
SCOTLAND			
Boat Hotel	2	80	20
Bunchrew House Hotel	3	100	23
Cavens Country House Hotel	1	100	26
Coul House Hotel	3	80	29
Cringletie House	4	80	31
Culloden House	3	100	34
Melvin House Hotel	4	100	66
Roman Camp Country House	2	100	72
Woodside Hotel	2	100	80
NORTH			
Armathwaite Hall Hotel	4	80	88
Grange Hotel	2	100	100
Grants Hotel	5	80	101
Monk Fryston Hall	3	80	114
Northcote Manor	1	100	115
Nunsmere Hall	4	100	116
Red Lion Hotel & Restaurant	2	80	119
Sefton Hotel	3	80	123
WALES			
Bae Abermaw	1	100	142
MIDSHIRES			
Calcot Manor	2	100	177
Cotswold House Hotel	3	80	183
Hoste Arms	3	80	197
Hotel Felix	4	100	199

HOTEL	ROOMS	GUESTS	PG
Painswick Hotel & Restaurant	3	80	218
Peacock Hotel	3	90	219
Stretton Hall	3	95	227
Thornbury Castle	4	100	230
Washbourne Court Hotel	2	80	233
Wroxton House Hotel	2	100	236
WEST COUNTRY			
Holne Chase Hotel	2	80	262
Hotel Riviera	1	90	265
Hunstrete House	3	80	266
Lewtrenchard Manor	2	100	269
Woolverton House	1	80	289
SOUTH			
Alexander House Hotel	4	80	296
Cliveden House	2	100	303
Flackley Ash Hotel	2	100	309
Hartwell House	4	100	312
New Park Manor	5	80	322
Pier at Harwich	1	100	324
Priory Bay Hotel	2	90	325
Sir Christopher Wren's House	8	90	330
St Michael's Manor	3	90	331
Wallett's Court	3	80	338
LONDON			
Baglioni Hotel London	1	80	348
Goring	4	100	359
Grim's Dyke Hotel	4	90	360
Montcalm Hotel	3	100	363
IRELAND			
Fitzwilliam Hotel	3	100	394
Merrion Hall	3	80	410
Merrion Hotel	6	100	411

101 - 150 GUESTS

HOTEL	ROOMS	GUESTS	PG
SCOTLAND			
Banchory Lodge	2	130	19
Dalhousie Castle & Spa	5	120	36
Four Seasons Hotel	3	140	43
Garvock House Hotel	4	150	44
NORTH			
Devonshire	4	120	95
Horton Grange	3	150	105
Matfen Hall	8	150	111
Seaham Hall Hotel & Serenity Spa	4	120	122
Swan Hotel	3	150	125
Swinton Park	5	150	126
Wordsworth Hotel	3	120	133
WALES			
Lake Country House	3	150	150
Lake Vyrnwy Hotel	3	130	151
MIDSHIRES			
Colwall Park Hotel	4	150	181
Grapevine Hotel	2	120	195
Meadowcroft Hotel	1	120	211
Nuthurst Grange	3	150	214
WEST COUNTRY			
Bovey Castle	3	120	249
Castle at Taunton	4	120	252
Glazebrook House Hotel	2	100	259
Ston Easton Park	8	120	281

HOTEL	ROOMS	GUESTS	PG
SOUTH			
Bishopstrow House	3	120	299
Careys Manor Hotel & Spa	9	140	300
Chase Lodge	2	120	301
Donnington Valley Hotel	9	140	305
Eastbury Hotel	4	120	306
Eastwell Manor	7	120	307
Hintlesham Hall	6	120	313
Inn on the Green	3	120	316
Maison Talbooth	1	150	319
Taplow House & Restaurant	7	100	333
Vineyard At Stockcross	4	140	337
IRELAND			
Aghadoe Heights Hotel	2	120	375
Ashford Castle	1	110	379
Athenaeum House Hotel	3	150	381
Dunbrody Country House Hotel	3	110	392
Hayfield Manor	4	150	399
Ross Lake House Hotel	1	150	418
Wineport Lodge	2	150	424

MORE THAN 150 GUESTS

HOTEL	ROOMS	GUESTS	PG
SCOTLAND			
Mar Hall	7	250	64
Old Manor Hotel	3	180	67
Prestonfield	6	1,000	71
Scotsman	7	250	75
Stonefield Castle Hotel	4	200	76
NORTH			
Crewe Hall	17	350	92
Judges Country House Hotel	7	600	106
Vermont Hotel	7	250	129
Willington Hall	4	180	132
WALES			
Llansantffraed Court Hotel	3	200	153
Wolfscastle Country Hotel	2	180	162
MIDSHIRES			
Chase Hotel	5	400	179
Dormy House	5	170	189
Fawsley Hall	6	200	191
Grafton Manor	2	180	194
Mallory Court Hotel	4	200	208
Stapleford Park	8	300	226
Swynford Paddocks	2	230	229
SOUTH			
Grasmere House	7	160	311
Old Government House	5	275	323
Rowhill Grange Hotel & Spa	7	200	327
Stanhill Court Hotel	6	200	332
Basil Street Hotel	3	200	349
Dolphin Square Hotel	3	200	356
IRELAND			
Ballygarry House	1	400	382
Castle Durrow Country House	3	200	389
Culloden Estate and Spa	12	1200	390
Dromoland Castle	6	450	391
Dunloe Castle	6	250	393
Glenlo Abbey Hotel	9	220	395
Knockranny House Hotel	4	700	404
Maryborough House Hotel	11	600	409
Portmarnock Hotel & Golf Links	6	350	416
Ten Square	1	250	421

GOLF GUIDE

ON-SITE GOLF COURSES

Ashford Castle	379
Bovey Castle	249
Budock Vean	251
Cally Palace Hotel	24
Donnington Valley Hotel	305
Dromoland Castle	391
Glenlo Abbey Hotel	395
Hintlesham Hall	313
Isle of Eriska	56
Lake Country House	150
Mar Hall	64
Matfen Hall	111
Portmarnock Hotel and Golf Links	416
Prestonfield	71
Rathsallagh House	417
Royal Marine Hotel	73
Stapleford Park	226
Swinton Park	126
Waterford Castle	423

SCOTLAND

HOTEL	COURSE	MILES	PG
Airds Hotel	Dragons Tooth	9	16
Archiestown Hotel	Rothes	5	17
Ballathie House Hotel	Blairgowrie	5	18
Banchory Lodge	Banchory	1	19
Boat Hotel	Boat of Garten	Adj.	20
Bonham	Dalmahoy	9	21
Bridge Hotel & Tackle Shop	Brora	12	22
Bunchrew House Hotel	Inverness	4	23
Castleton House Hotel	Aylth	5	25
Cavens Country House	Southerness	2	26
Channings	Silverknowes	1	27
Corriegour Lodge Hotel	Fort Augustus	17	28
Coul House Hotel	Strathpeffer Spa	3	29
Craigellachie Hotel	Dufftown	5	30
Cringletie House	Peebles	2	31
Cromlix House	Dunblane	5	32
Culdearn House	Grantown-on-Spey	1	33
Culloden House	Inverness	3	34
Culzean Castle	Turnberry	4	35
Dalhousie Castle & Spa	Broomieknowe	1	36
Darroch Learg	Ballater	½	37
Dunain Park Hotel	Torvean	1	38
Dunalastair Hotel	Taymouth Castle	14	39
Edinburgh Residence	Dalmahoy	9	40
Enterkine Country House	Royal Troon	5	41
Flodigarry Country House	Sconser	20	42
Four Seasons Hotel	St Fillans	1	43
Garvock House Hotel	Pitreavie	2	44
Glasshouse	Murrayfield	4	45
Glenapp Castle	Stranraer	20	46
Glenmorangie Highland Home	Royal Dornoch	15	47
Glenmoriston Arms Hotel	Fort Augustus	7	48
Greywalls	Muirfield	Adj.	49
Hotel Eilean Iarmain	Sconser	22	50
Howard	Dalmahoy	9	51
Inn at Ardgour	Dragon's Tooth	5	52
Inn At Lathones	St Andrews Old	5	53
Inverlochy Castle	Fort William	1	54
Isle of Barra Hotel	Isle of Barra	3	55
Kilcamb Lodge	Resapol	6	57
Kinloch Lodge	Sconser	20	58
Knight Residence	Braid Hills	3	59
Knockinaam Lodge	Dunsky	3	60
Knockomie Hotel	Forres	1	61
Ladyburn	Brunston Castle	3	62
Lodge - Daviot Mains	Inverness	5	63
Melfort Pier & Harbour	Oban	18	65
Melvin House Hotel	Murrayfield	2	66
Old Manor Hotel	Lundin Links	¼	67
One Devonshire Gardens	Dougalston	7	68
Peat Inn	St Andrews	6	69
Plockton Hotel	Loch Carron	30	70
Roman Camp Country House	Callander	⅓	72
Royal Scotsman	Edinburgh	4	74
Scotsman	Prestonfield	1 ½	75
Stonefield Castle Hotel	Tarbert	1 ½	76
Summer Isles	Ullapool	25	77
Taychreggan	Oban	20	78
Tigh an Eilean	Lochcarron	12	79
Woodside Hotel	Aberdour	1/4	80

NORTH

HOTEL	COURSE	MILES	PG
Armathwaite Hall Hotel	Cockermouth	2	88
Blue Lion	Masham	5	89
Borrowdale Gates	Keswick	8	90
Broxton Hall	Carden Park	2	91
Crewe Hall	Western	2	92
Crosby Lodge	Eden	1	93
Dale Head Hall	Keswick	5	94
Devonshire	Ilkley	6	95
Eleven Didsbury Park	Didsbury	¼	96
Feversham Arms	Kirbymoorside	6	97
General Tarleton Inn	Knaresborough	1	98
Gilpin Lodge Hotel	Windermere	¼	99
Grange Hotel	Forest of Galtres	4	100
Grants Hotel	Oakdale	½	101
Green Bough Hotel	Vicars Cross	2	102
Hob Green Hotel, Restaurant and Gardens	Oakdale	7	103
Holbeck Ghyll Hotel & Spa	Windermere	5	104
Horton Grange	Morpeth	5	105
Judges Country House	Eaglescliffe	5	106
L'Enclume	Grange-over-Sands	3 ½	107
Lindeth Howe	Windemere	1	108
Linthwaite House	Windermere	½	109
Lovelady Shield	Alston Moor	2	110
Middlethorpe Hall and Spa	Fulford	2	112
Miller Howe Hotel	Windermere	3	113
Monk Fryston Hall	Scarthingwell	4	114
Northcote Manor	Wilpshire	10	115
Nunsmere Hall	Delamere	3	116
Pheasant Hotel	Kirkbymoorside	5	117
Quebecs	Leeds	2	118
Red Lion	Skipton	8	119
Rothay Manor	Windermere	6	120
Samling	Windermere	4	121
Seaham Hall	Durham City	10	122
Sefton Hotel	Mount Murray	6	123
Studley Hotel	Oakdale	1	124
Swan Hotel	Ulverston	8	125
Traddock	Settle	3 ½	127
Underscar Manor	Keswick	4	128
Vermont Hotel	Gosforth	7	129
Waren House Hotel	Bamburgh Castle	2	130
White Swan	Kirbymoorside	7	131
Willington Hall	Pryors Hayes	2	132
Wordsworth Hotel	Windermere	15	133
Yorke Arms	Masham	12	134

WALES

HOTEL	COURSE	MILES	PG
Bae Abermaw	Royal St David's	8	142
Bell at Skenfrith	Rolls of Monmouth	6	143
Bodysgallen Hall and Spa	Conwy	2	144
Castell Deudraeth	Porthmadog	5	145
Castle Hotel	Conwy	2	146
Empire	Maesdu	1	147
Hotel Maes-y-Neuadd	Royal St David's	3	148
Inn at the Elm Tree	Newport	7	149
Lake Vyrnwy Hotel	Oswestry	24	151
Llangoed Hall	Builth Wells	12	152
Llansantffraed Court Hotel	Celtic Manor	8	153
Osborne House	Maesdu	1 ½	154
Palé Hall Country House	Bala Lake	4	155
Parva Farmhouse Hotel	St Pierre	5	156
Penally Abbey	Tenby	2	157
Penbontbren Farm	Cardigan	9	158
Penmaenuchaf Hall	Royal St David's	19	159
Sychnant Pass House	Conwy	1 ½	160
Tan-y-Foel Country House	Betws-y-Coed	2	161
Wolfscastle Country Hotel	Haverfordwest	7	162

MIDSHIRES

HOTEL	COURSE	MILES	PG
Abbey Hotel	Barnham Broom	8	170
Angel and Royal Hotel	Belton Woods	4	171
Beeches Hotel	Royal Norwich	5	172
Blenheim House Hotel	Mickelover	3	173
Brockencote Hall	Blackwell	3	174
Brookhouse	Craythorne	1	175
Burford House	Burford	1	176
Calcot Manor	Cotswold Edge	3	177
Charingworth Manor	Broadway	6	178
Chase Hotel	Ross on Wye	2	179
Cockliffe Country House Hotel	Ramsdale	3	180
Colwall Park Hotel	Royal Worcester	3	181
Congham Hall	Middleton	5	182
Cotswold House Hotel	Broadway	4	183
Cottage in the Wood	Worcestershire	1	184
Country Cottage Hotel	Ruddington Grange	2	185
Crown at Blockley	Broadway	3	186
Dannah Farm	Kedleston	4	187
Dial House Hotel	Naunton Downs	3	188
Dormy House	Broadway	Adj.	189
Elms	Sapey	5	190
Fawsley Hall	Farthingstone	5	191
Feathers	Chipping Norton	12	192
Fosse Manor	Naunton Downs	5	193
Grafton Manor	Bromsgrove	3	194
Grapevine Hotel	Naunton Downs	5	195
Greenway	Cotswolds Hills	6	196
Hoste Arms	Royal W. Norfolk	3	197
Hotel des Clos	Ruddington Grange	1	198
Hotel Felix	Moat house	2	199
Hotel on the Park	Lilley Brook	3	200
Kegworth House Hotel	Allestree	16	201
Lace Market Hotel	Cotgrave	7	202
Lamb at Burford	Burford	1	203
Langar Hall	Cotgrave Place	5	204
Le Manoir Aux Quat' Saisons	Oxfordshire	6	205
Lords of the Manor	Naunton Downs	5	206

Many Best Loved hotels have partner offers with nearby golf clubs. Contact the hotels directly for details.

HOTEL	COURSE	MILES	PG
Lower Slaughter Manor	Naunton Downs	4	207
Mallory Court Hotel	Whitnash	1	208
Malt House	Broadway	5	209
Manor House	Royal W. Norfolk	17	210
Meadowcroft Hotel	Cambridge Lakes	Adj.	211
New Inn At Coln	Cirencester	9	212
Noel Arms	Broadway	3	213
Nuthurst Grange	Henley in Arden	2	214
Old Mill Hotel	Brailes	5	215
Old Parsonage	Studley Wood	6	216
Old Vicarage	Worfield	1 1/2	217
Painswick Hotel	Painswick	1/2	218
Peacock Hotel	Warwickshire	3	219
Pear Tree at Purton	Bowood	8	220
Plough At Clanfield	Carswell	7	221
Raven Hotel & Restaurant	Shrewsbury	10	222
Riverside House Hotel	Matlock	6	223
Royalist Hotel	Naunton Downs	6	224
Shaven Crown	Wychwood	3	225
Stretton Hall	Church Stretton	3/4	227
Swan	Hintlesham	12	228
Swynford Paddocks	Gog Magog	12	229
Thornbury Castle	Thornbury	1 1/2	230
Titchwell Manor Hotel	Royal W. Norfolk	1 1/2	231
Unicorn Hotel	Naunton Downs	5	232
Washbourne Court Hotel	Naunton Downs	2	233
Westwood Country Hotel	Frilford Heath	5	234
Wild Duck	Oaksey Park	5	235
Wroxton House Hotel	Rye Hill	7	236

WEST COUNTRY

Andrews on the Weir	Minehead	12	244
At The Sign Of The Angel	Bowood	3	245
Barrington House	Dartmouth	6	246
Bath Lodge Hotel	Orchardleigh	5	247
Bath Priory	The Approach	1/2	248
Browns Hotel	Tavistock	1	250
Castle at Taunton	Taunton Vale	4	252
County Hotel	Lansdown	2	253
Court Barn	Holsworthy	2 1/2	254
Dorian House	Entry Hill	2	255
Fowey Hotel	Carlyon Bay	5	256
Gabriel Court Hotel	Churston	3	257
Garrack Hotel	West Cornwall	5	258
Glazebrook House Hotel	Wrangaton	2	259
Haydon House	Bath	3	260
Hell Bay	St Mary's	1	261
Holne Chase Hotel	Hele Park	8	262
Homewood Park	Cumberwell Park	5	263
Horn of Plenty	Tavistock	4	264
Hotel Riviera	Woodbury Park	5	265
Hunstrete House	Farrington	10	266
Idle Rocks Hotel	Killiow	12	267
Island Hotel	St Mary's	3	268
Lewtrenchard Manor	Hurdwick	6	269
Lugger Hotel	St Austell	9	270
Luttrell Arms	Minehead	2	271
Metropole	Trevose	4	272
Mill End Hotel	Manor House	5	273
Mount Somerset	Taunton Vale	1 1/2	274
Old Rectory	Windwhistle	2	275
Port Gaverne Hotel	St Enodoc	5	276
Prince Hall Hotel	Yelverton	10	277
Queensberry Hotel	Sham Castle	1/2	278

HOTEL	COURSE	MILES	PG
Rose-In-Vale Country House	Perranporth Links	3	279
Royal Crescent Hotel	Bath	2	280
Ston Easton Park	Farrington	Adj.	281
Talland Bay Hotel	Looe	4	282
Tides Reach Hotel	Bigbury	10	283
Trevalsa Court	Carlagh Bay	4	284
Well House	Looe	4	285
Widbrook Grange	Cumberwell	2	286
Wisteria Lodge	Carlyon Bay	1/2	287
Woodlands Country House	Burnham & Berrow	3	288
Woolverton House	Orchard Leigh	5	289

SOUTH

Alexander House Hotel	Royal Ashdown	7	296
Amberley Castle	West Sussex	5	297
Beech House Hotel	Calcot Park	2	298
Bishopstrow House	West Wiltshire	1	299
Careys Manor Hotel & Spa	Brockenhurst Manor	2	300
Chase Lodge	Home Park	1/2	301
Chateau Valeuse	La Moye	2	302
Cliveden House	The Lambourne	2	303
Cottage Hotel	Brockenhurst Manor	1	304
Eastbury Hotel	Sherborne	1	306
Eastwell Manor	Chart Hills	14	307
Esseborne Manor	Hampshire	8	308
Flackley Ash Hotel	Tenterden	10	309
French Horn Hotel	Sonning	1	310
Grasmere House	South Wilts	3	311
Hartwell House	Aylesbury Park	2	312
Hotel du Vin & Bistro	Brighton & Hove	1/2	314
Howard's House	South Wiltshire	10	315
Inn on the Green	Winter Hill	1	316
Langshott Manor	Effingham Park	5	317
Lord Bute	Iford	6	318
Maison Talbooth	Hintlesham Hall	10	319
Mansion House Hotel	Parkstone	3	320
Montagu Arms Hotel	Brockenhurst	5	321
New Park Manor	Brockenhurst Manor	3	322
Old Government House	Royal Guernsey	4	323
Pier at Harwich	Harwich Dovercourt	3	324
Priory Bay Hotel	Ryde	3	325
Priory Hotel	Dorset	4	326
Rowhill Grange	London	6	327
Rye Lodge	Rye	3	328
Shelleys	Cooden Beach	20	329
Sir Christopher Wren's House	Datchet	2	330
St Michael's Manor	Batchwood	1	331
Stanhill Court Hotel	Ifield	5	332
Taplow House	Maidenhead	2	333
Thamesmead House Hotel	Badgemore	2	334
Thatched Cottage Hotel	Brockenhurst	1	335
Three Lions	Brook	10	336
Vineyard At Stockcross	Donnington Valley	3	337
Wallett's Court	Royal St Georges	10	338

LONDON

10 Manchester Street	Hendon	10	346
Academy Town House	Old Thorns	46	347
Baglioni Hotel London	Stoke Poges	20	348
Basil Street Hotel	Richmond	6	349
Beaufort	Stoke Poges	20	350
Beaufort House Apartments	Richmond	10	351
Capital	Liphook	45	352

HOTEL	COURSE	MILES	PG
Colonnade Town House	Stoke Poges	20	353
Cranley on Bina Gardens	Richmond	10	354
Darlington Hyde Park	Stoke Park	25	355
Dolphin Square Hotel	Richmond	10	356
Draycott Hotel	Wentworth	20	357
Flemings Mayfair	Bushey Hall	18	358
Goring	Royal Mid Surrey	5	359
Grim's Dyke Hotel	Grim's Dyke	Adj.	360
Knightsbridge Green Hotel	Richmond	8	361
Leonard	Wentworth	10	362
Montcalm Hotel	Buckinghamshire	20	363
Parkes	Stoke Poges	20	364
Royal Park Hotel	Regent's Park	1/4	365
Stafford	Stoke Park	26	366
Threadneedles	Stoke Park	30	367

IRELAND

Aberdeen Lodge	Portmarnock	8	374
Aghadoe Heights Hotel	Killarney	2	375
Ahernes	Youghal	2	376
Ard na Sidhe	Beaufort	6	377
Ardtara Country House	Moyola	10	378
Ashlee Lodge	Muskerry	Adj.	380
Athenaeum House Hotel	Waterford	2	381
Ballygarry House	Tralee	2	382
Bayview Hotel	East Cork	20	383
Brownes	Elm Park	2	384
Bushmills Inn Hotel	Royal Portrush	4	385
Butlers Town House	Elm Park	1	386
Cahernane House Hotel	Killarney	4	387
Caragh Lodge	Dooks	4	388
Castle Durrow	Abbeyleix	5	389
Culloden Estate and Spa	Royal Belfast	2 1/2	390
Dunbrody Country House	Faithlegg	4	392
Dunloe Castle	Dunloe	1/4	393
Fitzwilliam Hotel	Portmarnock	10	394
Glin Castle	Ballybunion	20	396
Gregans Castle	Lahinch	16	397
Halpin's Hotel	Kilkee	1/4	398
Hayfield Manor	Fota Island	20	399
Hunter's Hotel	Wicklow	3	400
Kilkenny Hibernian Hotel	Castlecomer	12	401
Killarney Royal Hotel	Killarney	2	402
King Sitric	Royal Dublin	2	403
Knockranny House Hotel	Westport	2	404
Lacken House	Mount Juliet	2	405
Longfield's	Elm Park	1	406
Lough Inagh Lodge Hotel	Connemara	30	407
Markree Castle	Strandhill	5	408
Maryborough House Hotel	Douglas	5	409
Merrion Hall	Portmarnock	8	410
Merrion Hotel	Portmarnock	8	411
Moy House	Lahinch	1	412
Mustard Seed At Echo Lodge	Adare Manor	8	413
Park Hotel Kenmare	Kenmare	Adj.	414
Perryville	Old Head	5	415
Ross Lake House Hotel	Oughterard	2	418
Sea View House Hotel	Bantry Park	1	419
St Clerans	Athenry	5	420
Ten Square	Royal Belfast	5	421
Tinakilly House	Wicklow	2	422
Wineport Lodge	Glasson	2 1/2	424

Many Best Loved hotels have partner offers with nearby golf clubs. Contact the hotels directly for details.

PET-FRIENDLY HOTELS

SCOTLAND

Airds Hotel	16
Archiestown Hotel	17
Ballathie House Hotel	18
Banchory Lodge	19
Boat Hotel	20
Bridge Hotel & Tackle Shop	22
Bunchrew House Hotel	23
Castleton House Hotel	25
Cavens Country House Hotel	26
Coul House Hotel	29
Craigellachie Hotel of Speyside	30
Cringletie House	31
Cromlix House	32
Culloden House	34
Dalhousie Castle & Spa	36
Darroch Learg	37
Dunain Park Hotel	38
Dunalastair Hotel	39
Enterkine Country House	41
Flodigarry Country House Hotel	42
Four Seasons Hotel	43
Garvock House Hotel	44
Glenapp Castle	46
Glenmorangie Highland Home	47
Greywalls	49
Hotel Eilean Iarmain	50
Inn at Ardgour	52
Inn At Lathones	53
Inverlochy Castle	54
Isle of Barra Hotel	55
Isle of Eriska	56
Kilcamb Lodge	57
Kinloch Lodge	58
Knight Residence	59
Knockinaam Lodge	60
Knockomie Hotel	61
Lodge - Daviot Mains	63
Mar Hall	64
Melfort Pier & Harbour	65
Melvin House Hotel	66
Old Manor Hotel	67
One Devonshire Gardens	68
Peat Inn	69
Prestonfield	71
Roman Camp Country House	72
Royal Marine Hotel	73
Scotsman	75
Stonefield Castle Hotel	76
Summer Isles	77
Taychreggan	78
Tigh an Eilean	79
Woodside Hotel	80

NORTH

Armathwaite Hall Hotel	88
Blue Lion	89
Broxton Hall	91
Crosby Lodge	93
Devonshire	95
Feversham Arms	97
General Tarleton Inn	98
Grange Hotel	100
Grants Hotel	101
Hob Green Hotel & Restaurant	103
Holbeck Ghyll Hotel & Spa	104
L'Enclume	107
Linthwaite House	109
Lovelady Shield	110
Matfen Hall	111
Miller Howe Hotel	113
Monk Fryston Hall	114
Pheasant Hotel	117
Quebecs	118
Red Lion Hotel & Restaurant	119
Samling	121
Studley Hotel	124
Swinton Park	126
Traddock	127
Vermont Hotel	129
Waren House Hotel	130
White Swan	131
Willington Hall	132
Yorke Arms	134

WALES

Bell at Skenfrith	143
Castle Hotel	146
Hotel Maes-y-Neuadd	148
Inn at the Elm Tree	149
Lake Country House	150
Lake Vyrnwy Hotel	151
Llangoed Hall	152
Llansantffraed Court Hotel	153
Parva Farmhouse Hotel and Restaurant	156
Penmaenuchaf Hall	159
Sychnant Pass House	160
Wolfscastle Country Hotel	162

MIDSHIRES

Brookhouse	175
Cockliffe Country House Hotel	180
Colwall Park Hotel	181
Cotswold House Hotel	183
Cottage in the Wood	184
Crown at Blockley	186
Dormy House	189
Elms	190
Fawsley Hall	191
Feathers	192
Fosse Manor	193
Grapevine Hotel	195
Greenway	196
Hoste Arms	197
Hotel Felix	199
Hotel on the Park	200
Kegworth House Hotel	201
Lace Market Hotel	202
Lamb at Burford	203
Langar Hall	204
Le Manoir Aux Quat' Saisons	205
Lords of the Manor	206
Lower Slaughter Manor	207
Mallory Court Hotel	208
Malt House	209
Meadowcroft Hotel	211
New Inn At Coln	212
Noel Arms	213
Nuthurst Grange	214
Old Parsonage	216
Old Vicarage Hotel & Restaurant	217
Painswick Hotel & Restaurant	218
Pear Tree at Purton	220
Shaven Crown	225
Stapleford Park	226
Stretton Hall	227
Swan	228
Swynford Paddocks	229
Thornbury Castle	230
Titchwell Manor Hotel	231
Unicorn Hotel	232
Westwood Country Hotel	234
Wild Duck	235
Wroxton House Hotel	236

WEST COUNTRY

Andrews on the Weir	244
At The Sign Of The Angel	245
Bovey Castle	249
Browns Hotel	250
Budock Vean	251
Castle at Taunton	252
Court Barn	254
Fowey Hotel	256
Gabriel Court Hotel	257
Garrack Hotel	258
Hell Bay	261
Holne Chase Hotel	262
Horn of Plenty	264
Hotel Riviera	265
Hunstrete House	266
Idle Rocks Hotel	267
Lewtrenchard Manor	269
Luttrell Arms	271
Metropole	272
Mill End Hotel	273
Mount Somerset	274
Port Gaverne Hotel	276
Prince Hall Hotel	277
Rose-In-Vale Country House Hotel	279
Royal Crescent Hotel	280
Ston Easton Park	281
Talland Bay Hotel	282
Tides Reach Hotel	283
Well House	285

SOUTH

Beech House Hotel	298
Bishopstrow House	299
Chase Lodge	301
Cliveden House	303
Cottage Hotel	304
Eastwell Manor	307
Esseborne Manor	308
Flackley Ash Hotel	309
Grasmere House	311
Hartwell House Hotel	312
Hintlesham Hall	313
Howard's House	315
Langshott Manor	317
Lord Bute	318
Montagu Arms Hotel	321
New Park Manor	322
Rye Lodge	328
Shelleys	329
Thatched Cottage Hotel	335
Three Lions	336

LONDON

Basil Street Hotel	349
Capital	352
Colonnade Town House	353
Draycott Hotel	357
Grim's Dyke Hotel	360
Montcalm Hotel	363

IRELAND

Aghadoe Heights Hotel	375
Ashlee Lodge	380
Castle Durrow Country House	389
Glin Castle	396
Killarney Royal Hotel	402
Lough Inagh Lodge Hotel	407
Park Hotel Kenmare	414
Rathsallagh House	417
Ross Lake House Hotel	418
Sea View House Hotel	419

Please contact hotels directly for any applicable restrictions or surcharges.

HOTELS WITH HELI-PADS

SCOTLAND

KEY TO HOTELS

Rosettes indicate the page number of the hotel, with the colour a rough guide to the price of a twin or double room.

- Up to £95 per night
- £96 – £145 per night
- £146 – £195 per night
- £196+ per night

Base map © MAPS IN MINUTES™ 2004
© Crown Copyright, Ordnance Survey 2004
Design and modification
© 2005 Best Loved Hotels of the World

ORKNEY ISLANDS

KIRKWALL

WICK

INVERNESS

ABERDEEN

BENBECULA

WESTERN ISLES

Outer Hebrides

Isle of Lewis

Isle of Skye

Isle of Barra

The Minch

The Little Minch

Pentland Firth

Moray Firth

NORTH SEA

NORTH
see pages
442 - 443

IRELAND
see pages
454 - 455

North Channel

MAP KEY

- Region border
- National border
- Motorways
- Major throughroutes
- Other roads
- Ferry routes
- River
- Urban area
- ✈ Airport
- Lake/Loch
- ▢ Capital
- PLYMOUTH
- ▢ LONDON Major town
- KING'S LYNN Minor town
- ▪ Braintree Other town
- Pwlheli
- ○ Mumbles Other settlement

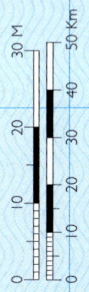

NORTH

KEY TO HOTELS

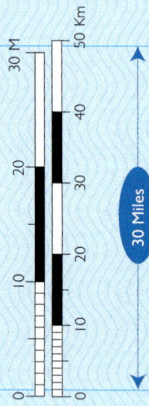

Rosettes indicate the page number of the hotel, with the colour a rough guide to the price of a twin or double room.

Up to £95 per night

£96 - £145 per night

£146 - £195 per night

£196+ per night

Base map © MAPS IN MINUTES™ 2004
© Crown Copyright, Ordnance Survey 2004
Design and modification
© 2005 Best Loved Hotels of the World

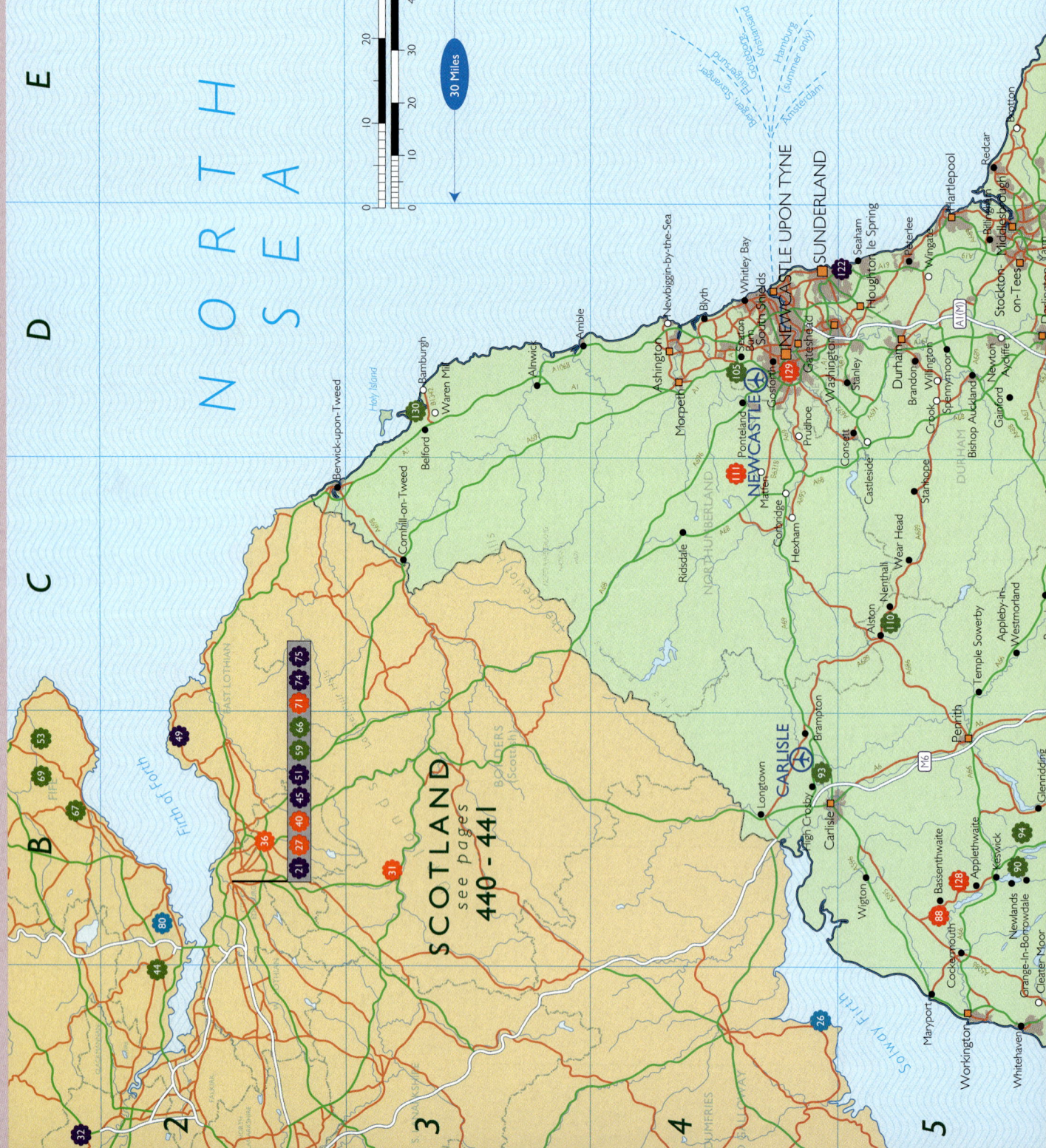

NORTH SEA

50 Km

30 Miles

30 M

SCOTLAND
see pages
440 - 441

Firth of Forth

EAST LOTHIAN

BORDERS
(Scottish)

Solway Firth

NORTHUMBERLAND

DURHAM

NEWCASTLE UPON TYNE

SUNDERLAND

CARLISLE

Berwick-upon-Tweed
Cornhill-on-Tweed
Belford
Bamburgh
Waren Mill
Holy Island
Alnwick
Amble
Newbiggin-by-the-Sea
Whitley Bay
South Shields
Blyth
Ashington
Morpeth
Ponteland
Gosforth
Prudhoe
Hexham
Corbridge
Ridsdale
Alston
Nenthall
Wear Head
Stanhope
Consett
Castleside
Durham
Stanley
Washington
Houghton le Spring
Seaham
Peterlee
Wingate
Hartlepool
Redcar
Middlesbrough
Stockton-on-Tees
Newton Aycliffe
Spennymoor
Bishop Auckland
Crook
Willington
Brandon
Gainford
Appleby-in-Westmorland
Temple Sowerby
Penrith
Brampton
Longtown
High Crosby
Carlisle
Wigton
Bassenthwaite
Applethwaite
Keswick
Glenridding
Newlands
Grange-In-Borrowdale
Cleator Moor
Cockermouth
Maryport
Workington
Whitehaven

130
105
129
111
122
93
110
94
90
128
88
32
80
44
26
53
69
67
49
36
27
40
45
51
59
66
71
74
75
21
31

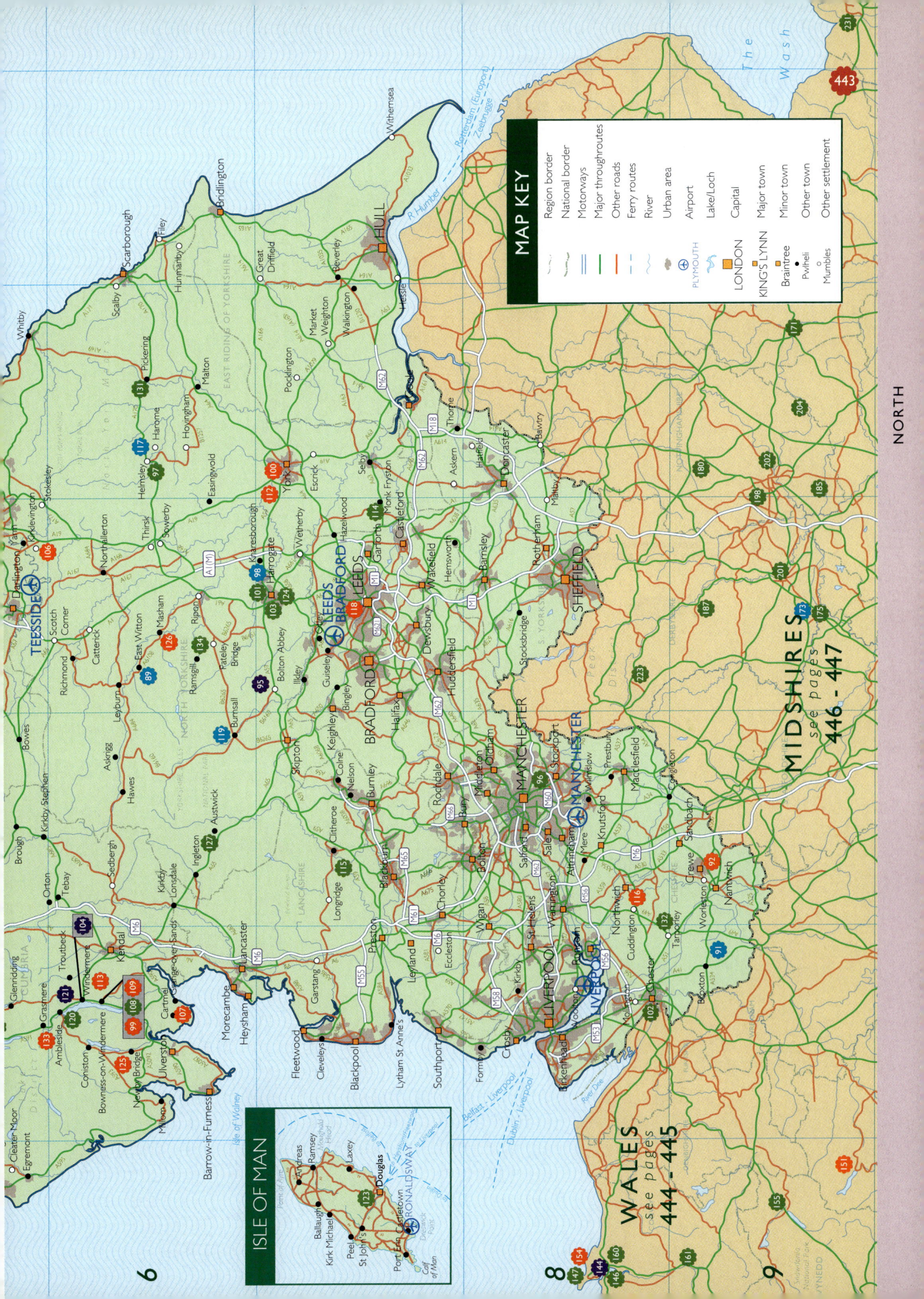

MAP KEY

- Region border
- National border
- Motorways
- Major throughroutes
- Other roads
- Ferry routes
- River
- Urban area
- Airport
- Lake/Loch
- Capital — LONDON
- Major town — KING'S LYNN
- Minor town — Braintree
- Other town — Pwllheli
- Other settlement — o Mumbles

PLYMOUTH

443

ISLE OF MAN

Point of Ayre
Bride
Andreas
Ramsey
Kirk Michael
Ballaugh
Laxey
Peel
St John's
Douglas
RONALDSWAY
Castletown
Port Erin
Port St Mary
Calf of Man

WALES
see pages
444 - 445

MIDSHIRES
see pages
446 - 447

6 **8** **9**

The Wash

R Humber

HULL
Bridlington
Scarborough
Whitby
Filey
Hunmanby
Great Driffield
Beverley
Market Weighton
Pocklington
Malton
Pickering
Helmsley
Easingwold
York
Selby
Doncaster
Thorne
Bawtry
Rotherham
SHEFFIELD
Barnsley
Wakefield
Dewsbury
Huddersfield
Halifax
BRADFORD
LEEDS
Harrogate
Ripon
Thirsk
Northallerton
Richmond
Catterick
TEESSIDE
Darlington
Stokesley
Leyburn
Hawes
Sedbergh
Kirkby Stephen
Brough
Orton
Tebay
Kendal
Windermere
Bowness-on-Windermere
Ambleside
Grasmere
Coniston
Ulverston
Barrow-in-Furness
Morecambe
Lancaster
Fleetwood
Cleveleys
Blackpool
Lytham St Anne's
Southport
Preston
Leyland
Chorley
Blackburn
Burnley
Nelson
Colne
Clitheroe
Skipton
Keighley
Ilkley
Bingley
Bolton Abbey
Settle
Ingleton
Kirkby Lonsdale
Longridge
Garstang
Formby
Crosby
LIVERPOOL
Birkenhead
Wigan
St Helens
Warrington
Widnes
Runcorn
Chester
Northwich
Crewe
Nantwich
Sandbach
Congleton
Macclesfield
Knutsford
Wilmslow
Stockport
MANCHESTER
Salford
Rochdale
Oldham
Bury
Middleton
Eccles

NORTH YORKSHIRE
EAST RIDING OF YORKSHIRE
SOUTH YORKSHIRE
WEST YORKSHIRE
LANCASHIRE
CUMBRIA
CHESHIRE
DERBYSHIRE

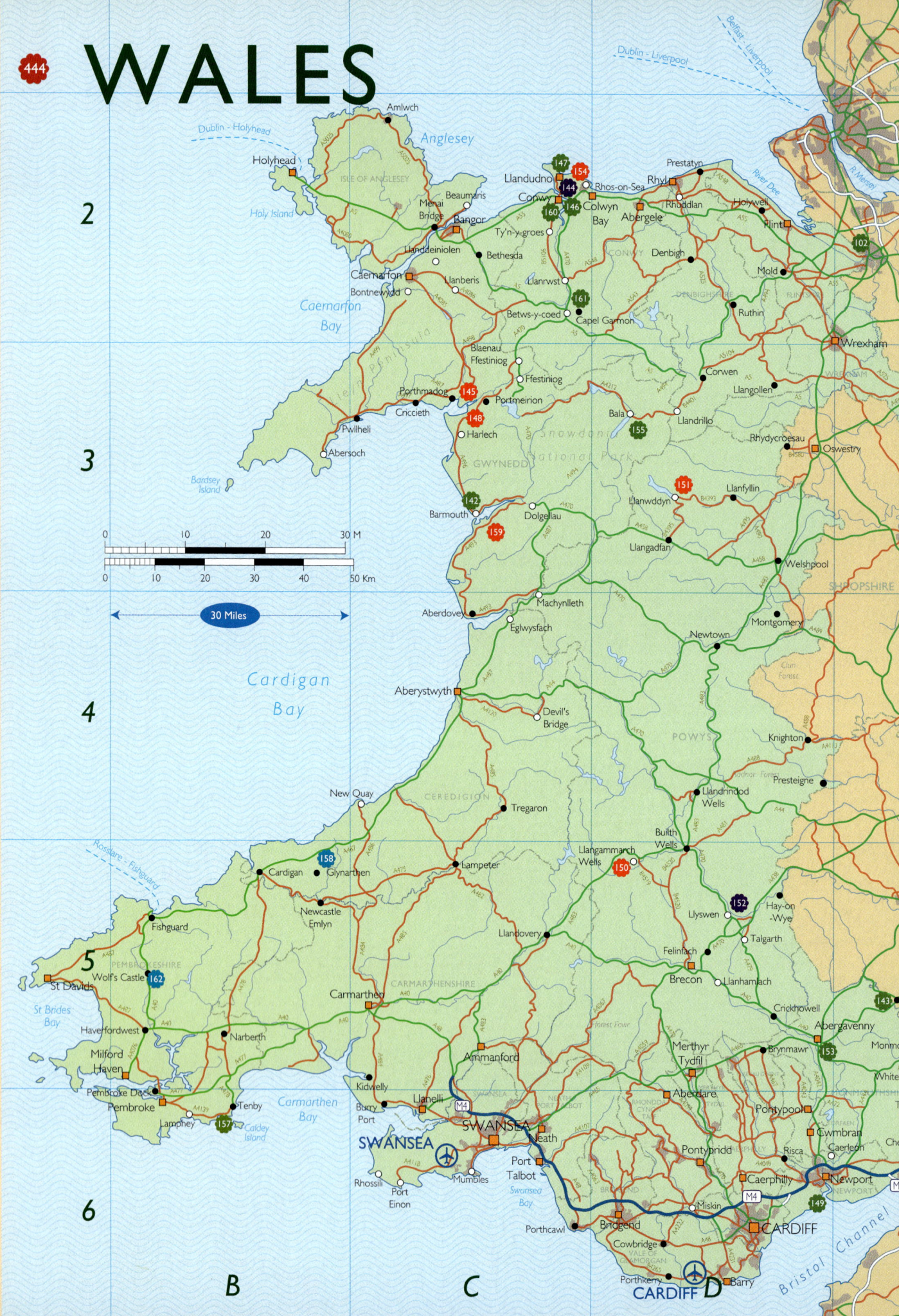

WALES

WALES

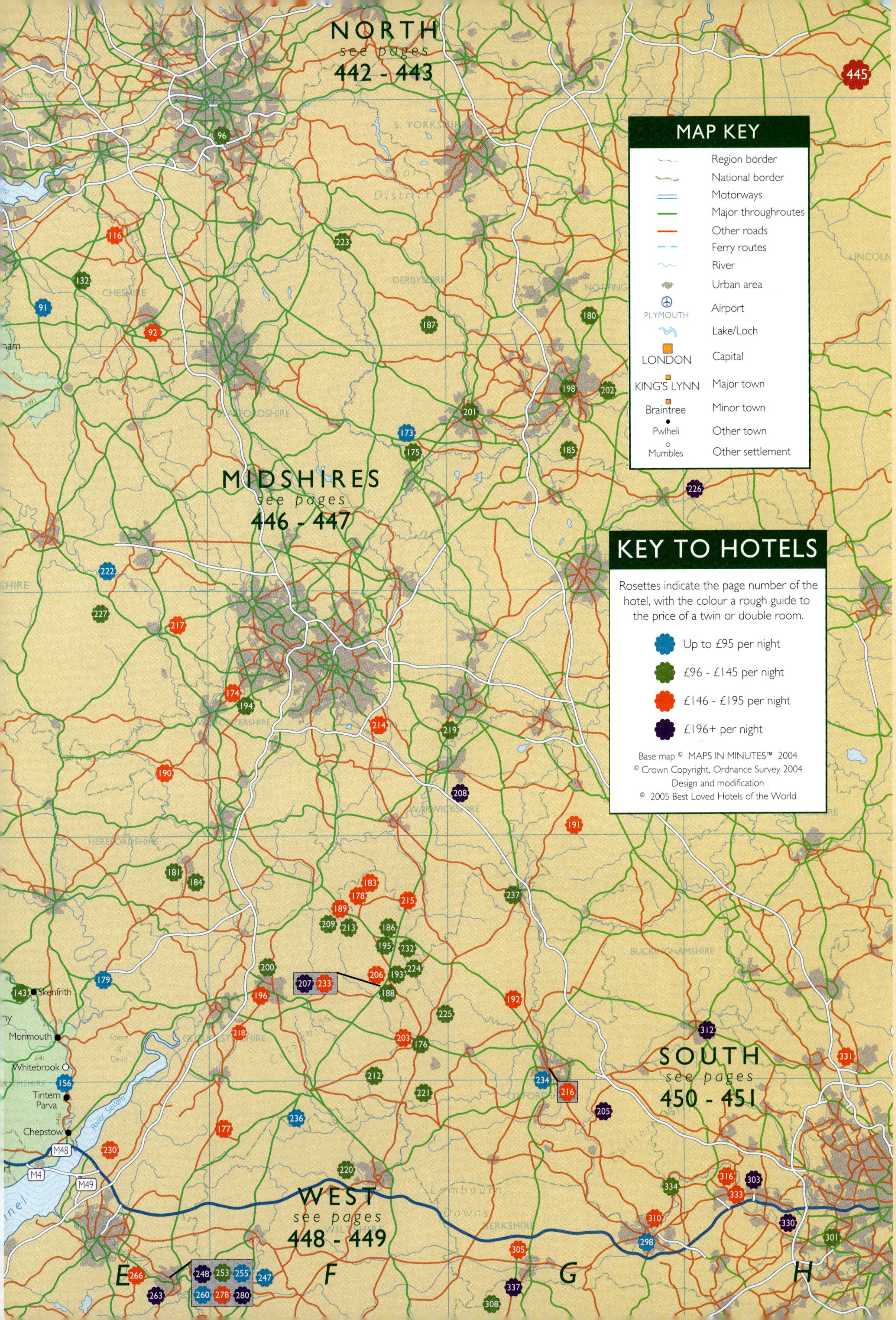

445

MAP KEY

	Region border
	National border
	Motorways
	Major throughroutes
	Other roads
	Ferry routes
	River
	Urban area
PLYMOUTH	Airport
	Lake/Loch
LONDON	Capital
KING'S LYNN	Major town
Braintree	Minor town
Pwlheli	Other town
Mumbles	Other settlement

KEY TO HOTELS

Rosettes indicate the page number of the hotel, with the colour a rough guide to the price of a twin or double room.

- Up to £95 per night
- £96 - £145 per night
- £146 - £195 per night
- £196+ per night

Base map © MAPS IN MINUTES™ 2004
© Crown Copyright, Ordnance Survey 2004
Design and modification
© 2005 Best Loved Hotels of the World

MIDSHIRES
see pages
446 - 447

SOUTH
see pages
450 - 451

WALES

S. YORKS
District
Derbyshire
CHESHIRE
LINCOLN
NOTTING
HEREFORDSHIRE
WARWICKSHIRE
GLOUCESTERSHIRE
BUCKINGHAMSHIRE
Forest of Dean
River Severn
BERKSHIRE
Downs

Skenfrith
Monmouth
Whitebrook
Tintem Parva
Chepstow

E   F   G   H

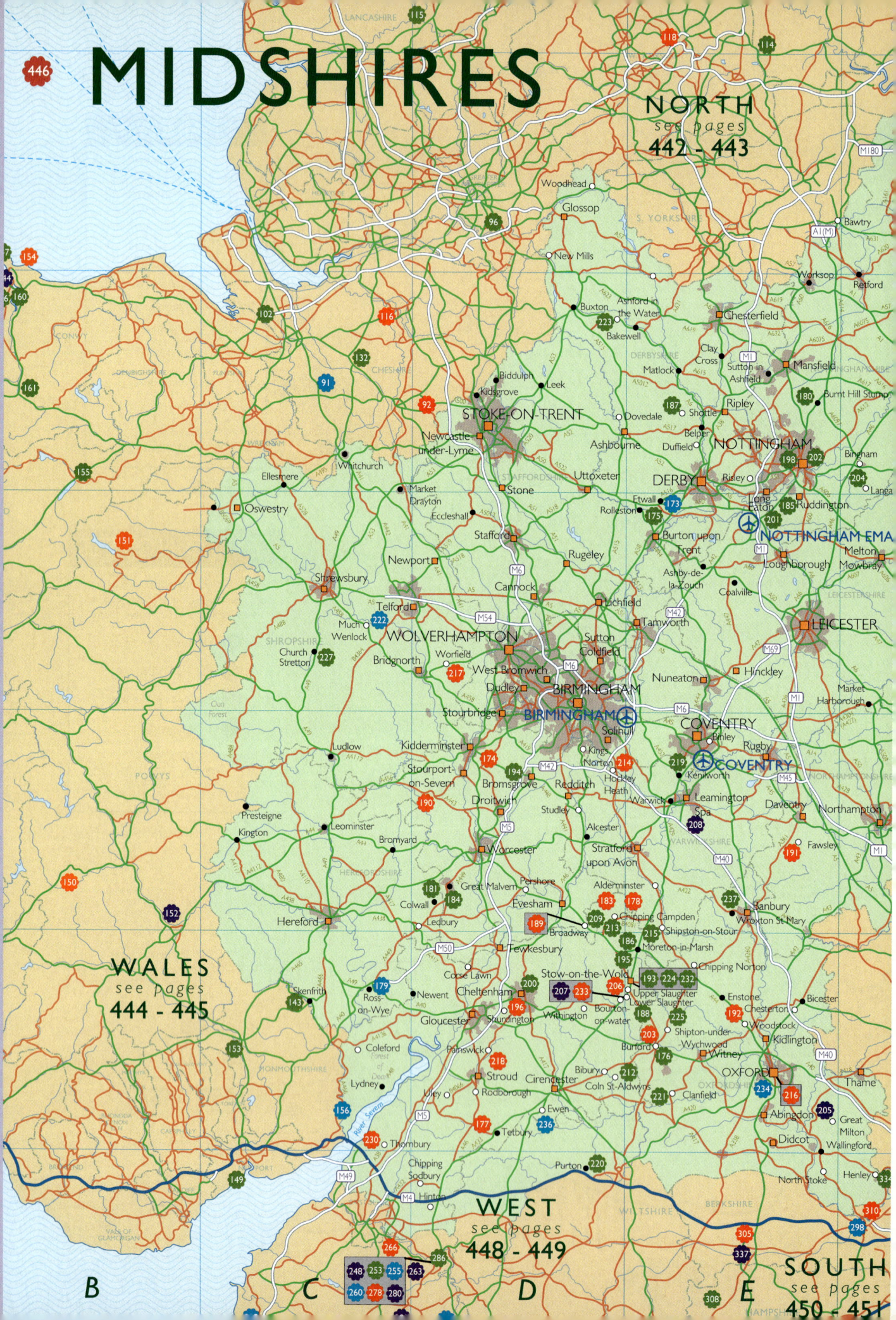

MIDSHIRES

NORTH
see pages
442 - 443

MIDSHIRES

WALES
see pages
444 - 445

WEST
see pages
448 - 449

SOUTH
see pages
450 - 451

Woodhead
Glossop
New Mills
Buxton
Ashford in the Water
Bakewell
Chesterford
Worksop
Retford
Bawtry
Clay Cross
Sutton in Ashfield
Mansfield
Matlock
Biddulph
Kidsgrove
Leek
STOKE-ON-TRENT
Newcastle-under-Lyme
Dovedale
Ashbourne
Shottle
Ripley
Burnt Hill Stump
Belper
Duffield
NOTTINGHAM
Whitchurch
Ellesmere
Oswestry
Market Drayton
Stone
Eccleshall
Uttoxeter
DERBY
Rolleston
Etwall
Burton upon Trent
Risley
Long Eaton
Ruddington
Bingham
Langar
NOTTINGHAM EMA
Melton Mowbray
Stafford
Ashby-de-la-Zouch
Coalville
Loughborough
Shrewsbury
Newport
Rugeley
Cannock
Lichfield
Tamworth
LEICESTER
Telford
Much Wenlock
WOLVERHAMPTON
Sutton Coldfield
Nuneaton
Hinckley
Market Harborough
Church Stretton
Bridgnorth
Worfield
West Bromwich
Dudley
BIRMINGHAM
BIRMINGHAM
Solihull
COVENTRY
COVENTRY
Binley
Rugby
Ludlow
Kidderminster
Stourbridge
Stourport-on-Severn
Bromsgrove
Droitwich
Redditch
Studley
King's Norton
Hockley Heath
Warwick
Kenilworth
Leamington Spa
Daventry
Northampton
Presteigne
Kington
Leominster
Bromyard
Worcester
Alcester
Stratford upon Avon
Fawsley
Hereford
Colwall
Great Malvern
Pershore
Evesham
Alderminster
Chipping Campden
Shipston-on-Stour
Banbury
Wroxton St Mary
Ledbury
Broadway
Moreton-in-Marsh
Chipping Norton
Skenfrith
Coose Lawn
Tewkesbury
Newent
Cheltenham
Stow-on-the-Wold
Upper Slaughter
Lower Slaughter
Bourton-on-water
Enstone
Chesterton
Woodstock
Bicester
Ross-on-Wye
Gloucester
Shurdington
Withington
Shipton-under-Wychwood
Witney
Kidlington
Coleford
Painswick
Burford
OXFORD
Thame
Lydney
Uley
Stroud
Rodborough
Bibury
Coln St-Aldwyns
Clanfield
Abingdon
Great Milton
Wallingford
Cirencester
Ewen
Tetbury
Didcot
Thornbury
Chipping Sodbury
Hinton
Purton
North Stoke
Henley

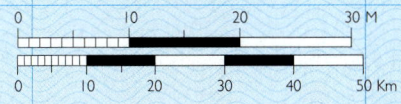

WEST

WALES
see pages
444 - 445

WEST COUNTRY

MAP KEY

Region border	
National border	
Motorways	
Major throughroutes	
Other roads	
Ferry routes	
River	
Urban area	
Airport	(PLYMOUTH)
Lake/Loch	
Capital	LONDON
Major town	KING'S LYNN
Minor town	Braintree
Other town	Pwlheli
Other settlement	Mumbles

KEY TO HOTELS

Rosettes indicate the page number of the hotel, with the colour a rough guide to the price of a twin or double room.

- Up to £95 per night
- £96 - £145 per night
- £146 - £195 per night
- £196+ per night

Base map © MAPS IN MINUTES™ 2004
© Crown Copyright, Ordnance Survey 2004
Design and modification
© 2005 Best Loved Hotels of the World

Skomer Island
Skokholm Island
St Bay

162

157

Carmarthen Bay

SWANSEA
Swansea Bay

Bristol

CELTIC SEA

Mount's Bay

Isles of Scilly 261 268

Lizard

Ilfracombe Lynton Lynmouth Porlock Minehe
Mortehoe Parracombe 244 Dun
Exford 271
Barnstaple Exmoor
Northam Dulverton Wivelsco
Bideford South Molton
Great Torrington Wivelsco
Burrington Tiverton Cullompton
Holsworthy Hatherleigh Crediton
Bude 254 Clauston Okehampton DEVON M5
Virginstow 273 Exeter
Tintagel Launceston Lewdown Chagford Moretonhampstead EXE
Lifton 269 Dartmoor 249 Bovey Tracey Exmouth
Port Isaac 276 Two Bridges 277 Dawlish
Padstow Rock 264 Tavistock Princetown Newton Abbot Teignmouth
272 Wadebridge Gulworthy 250 262 Kingsteignton
Bodmin Buckfastleigh Ashburton Torquay
Newquay NEWQUAY Bodmin Moor 259 Kingskerswell 257 Paignton
CORNWALL St Keyne PLYMOUTH South Brent Totnes Galmpton Brixham
Widegates 285 Saltash Ivybridge 246 Dartmouth
279 Mithian Tregrehan 287 Looe 282 Goveton Start Point
Truro St Austell 256 Fowey Kingsbridge 283 Salcombe
258 284 Mevagissey
St Ives 270 Portloe
Camborne Redruth St Mawes
Hayle 251 267
St Just Helston Falmouth
Penzance Mawnan Smith
Sennen

Santander (Summer only)
St Malo (winter only)
Roscoff

2 3 4 5

B C D

SOUTH
see pages
450 - 451

WEST COUNTRY

GLOUCESTERSHIRE

MONMOUTHSHIRE

WILTSHIRE

OXFORDSHIRE

BERKSHIRE

SOMERSET

DORSET

Forest of Dean

River Severn

Lambourn Down

Salisbury Plain

New Forest

Bristol Channel

ol Channel

ENGLISH CHANNEL

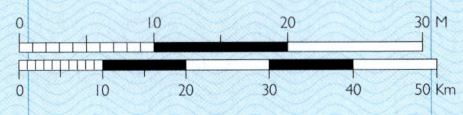

Lyme Bay

English Channel

ISLE OF WIGHT

Isle of Wight

The Solent

Guernsey and Jersey

Channel Islands

St Malo (summer only)

Cherbourg

VALE OF GLAMORGAN

BRISTOL

Avonmouth
Portishead
Clevedon
Nailsea
Yatton
Weston-super-Mare
Congresbury
Winscombe
Hunstrete
Bradford-on-Avon
Bath
Lacock
Cheddar
Radstock
Norton St Philip
Woolverton
Ston Easton
Frome
Wells
Shepton Mallet
Glastonbury
Street
Minehead
Dunster
Watchet
Burnham-on-Sea
Highbridge
Brent Knoll
Langford Budville
Taunton
Henlade
Hatch Beauchamp
Wellington
Bridgwater
Langport
Wincanton
Ilminster
Cricket Malherbie
Chard
Crewkerne
Yeovil
Honiton
Gittisham
Axminster
EXETER
Sidmouth
Budleigh Salterton
Seaton

179 143 153 156 149 230 177 198 196 218 212 220 236 177
213 195 232 193 224 206 207 233 188 225 203 176 234 216 205 192 449
305 337 308 315 311 336 322 335 304 321 318 320 300 325 326 306 299 315
248 253 255 260 278 280 286 263 245 266 247 289 281 252 274 275 265
290 271 B3227 B3224

M5 M32 M4 M49

E F G H

0 10 20 30 M
0 10 20 30 40 50 Km

30 Miles

A370 A38 A39 A37 A303 A35 A36 A361 A371

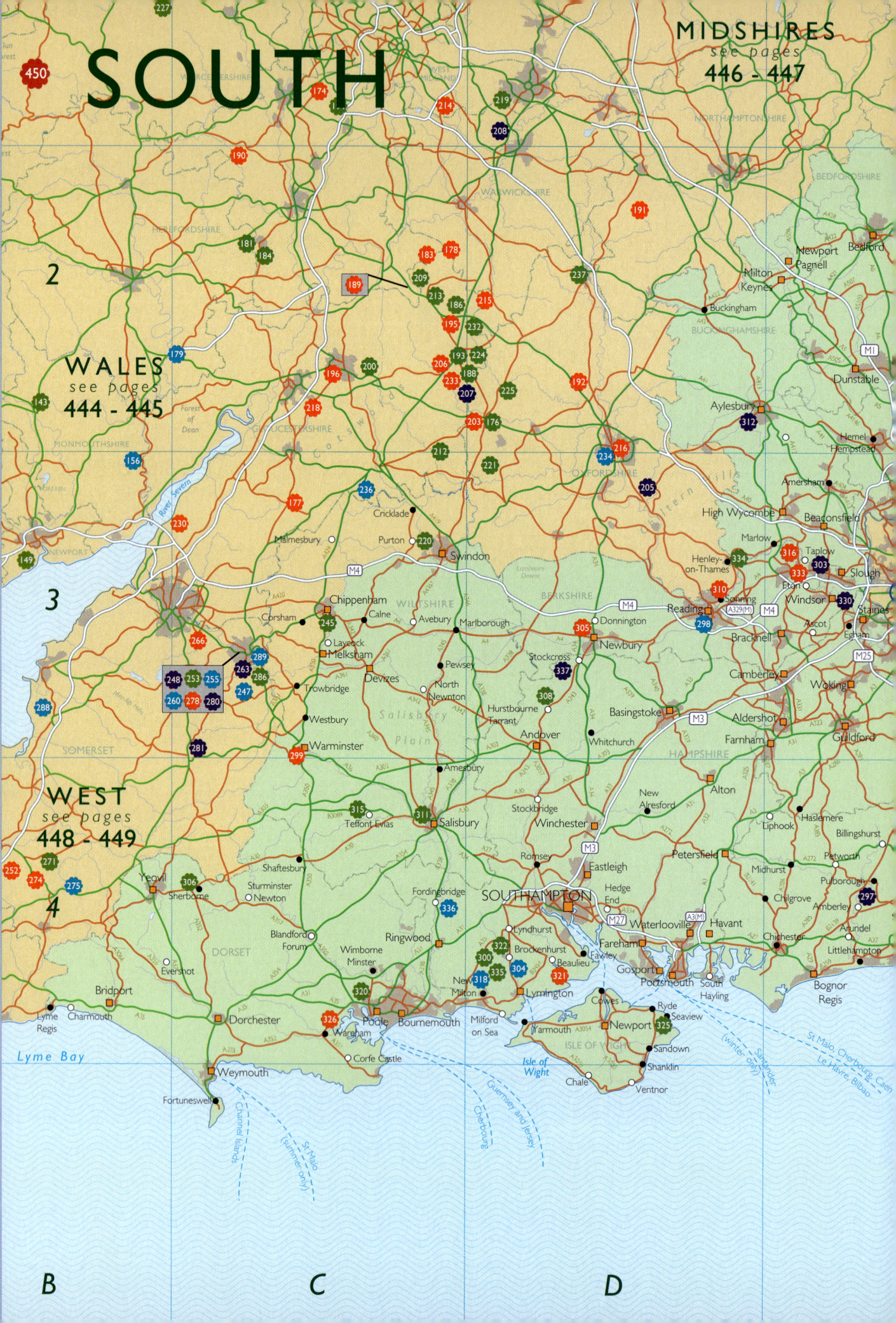

WALES
see pages
444 – 445

WEST
see pages
448 – 449

2

3

4

B   C   D

Newport Pagnell
Bedford
Milton Keynes
Buckingham
Dunstable
Aylesbury
Hemel Hempstead
Amersham
High Wycombe
Beaconsfield
Marlow
Taplow
Slough
Eton
Windsor
Staines
Egham
Ascot
Henley-on-Thames
Reading
Bracknell
Sonning
Camberley
Woking
Donnington
Newbury
Basingstoke
Aldershot
Farnham
Guildford
Stockcross
Whitchurch
Andover
Alton
New Alresford
Liphook
Haslemere
Billingshurst
Petersfield
Midhurst
Petworth
Stockbridge
Winchester
Pulborough
Amberley
Romsey
Eastleigh
Arundel
Littlehampton
Hedge End
Waterlooville
Havant
Chilgrove
Chichester
SOUTHAMPTON
Lyndhurst
Brockenhurst
Fareham
Fawley
Gosport
Portsmouth
South Hayling
Bognor Regis
Beaulieu
New Milton
Lymington
Cowes
Ryde
Seaview
Sandown
Shanklin
Milford on Sea
Yarmouth
Newport
Chale
Ventnor
Isle of Wight

Cricklade
Malmesbury
Purton
Swindon
Chippenham
Calne
Corsham
Avebury
Marlborough
Lacock
Melksham
Pewsey
Devizes
North Newnton
Hurstbourne Tarrant
Trowbridge
Westbury
Warminster
Amesbury
Teffont Evias
Salisbury
Shaftesbury
Sturminster Newton
Yeovil
Sherborne
Blandford Forum
Wimborne Minster
Ringwood
Fordingbridge
Evershot
Bridport
Lyme Regis
Charmouth
Dorchester
Poole
Bournemouth
Wareham
Corfe Castle
Weymouth
Fortuneswell

Lyme Bay

Monmouthshire
Herefordshire
Gloucestershire
Forest of Dean
Warwickshire
Northamptonshire
Bedfordshire
Buckinghamshire
Oxfordshire
Berkshire
Wiltshire
Hampshire
Somerset
Dorset

River Severn

St Malo, Cherbourg, Caen, Le Havre, Bilbao
St Malo (summer only)
Channel Islands
Guernsey and Jersey
Cherbourg
Lymington–Yarmouth (winter only)

MAP KEY

	Region border
	National border
	Motorways
	Major throughroutes
	Other roads
	Ferry routes
	River
	Urban area
PLYMOUTH	Airport
	Lake/Loch
LONDON	Capital
KING'S LYNN	Major town
Braintree	Minor town
Pwlheli	Other town
Mumbles	Other settlement

KEY TO HOTELS

Rosettes indicate the page number of the hotel, with the colour a rough guide to the price of a twin or double room.

- Up to £95 per night
- £96 - £145 per night
- £146 - £195 per night
- £196+ per night

Base map © MAPS IN MINUTES™ 2004
© Crown Copyright, Ordnance Survey 2004
Design and modification
© 2005 Best Loved Hotels of the World

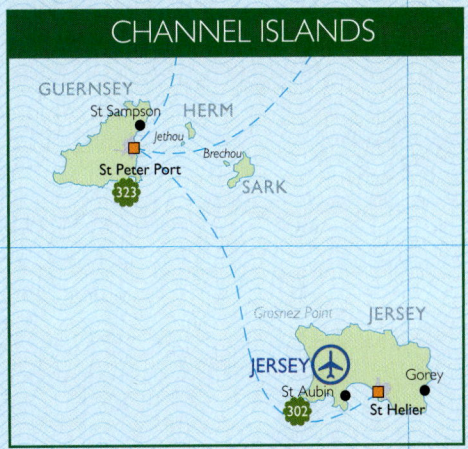

Map labels

CAMBRIDGESHIRE
SUFFOLK
211 199
229
228
313
Ipswich
Sudbury
Hintlesham
Biggleswade
Royston
Saffron Walden
Dedham
319
324
Harwich
Esbjerg, Ham
Hoek van Holland
Letchworth
STANSTED
Braintree
Colchester
ESSEX
Luton
LUTON
Stevenage
Bishop's Stortford
Witham
Clacton-on-Sea
Welwyn Garden City
Ware
331
Hatfield
Harlow
Chelmsford
Maldon
St Albans
Hoddesdon
Potters Bar
Watford
Chigwell
Brentwood
Rayleigh
Foulness Island
LONDON see pages 452-453
M25
Basildon
Southend-on-Sea
HEATHROW
Canvey Island
301
LONDON
Dartford
Tilbury
Gravesend
Sheerness
Minster
327
Swanley
Isle of Sheppey
Herne Bay
Margate
Epsom
Gillingham
Whitstable
Ramsgate
Leatherhead
Sittingbourne
Faversham
Caterham
Sevenoaks
North Downs
Canterbury
Dorking
Maidstone
Lenham
Deal
Reigate
Redhill
Oxted
338
317
Horley
Tonbridge
KENT
307
Dover
GATWICK
332
East Grinstead
Tunbridge Wells
Ashford
Oostende
Crawley
Turners Hill
Folkestone
Calais
Horsham
296
Cranbrook
Hythe
Channel Tunnel
Crowborough
Tenterden
New Romney
Boulogne
Cuckfield
Haywards Heath
Newick
Uckfield
Peamarsh
309
Rye
328
Ashington
Netherfield Hill
Battle
Hailsham
Storrington
Lewes
EAST SUSSEX
Hastings
329
Brighton
Hove
314
Bexhill
Worthing
Newhaven
Seaford
Eastbourne

ENGLISH CHANNEL

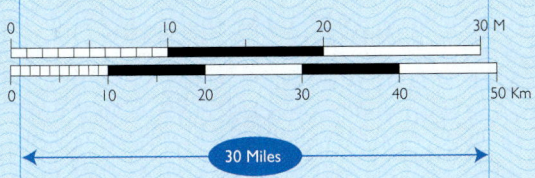

Scale
0   10   20   30 M
0   10   20   30   40   50 Km
30 Miles

CHANNEL ISLANDS

GUERNSEY
St Sampson
HERM
Jethou
Brechou
St Peter Port
323
SARK
Grosnez Point
JERSEY
JERSEY
St Aubin
302
St Helier
Gorey

E   F   G

LONDON

452

KEY TO HOTELS

Rosettes indicate the page number of the hotel, with the colour a rough guide to the price of a twin or double room.

- Up to £95 per night
- £96 - £145 per night
- £146 - £195 per night
- £196+ per night

Base map © MAPS IN MINUTES™ 2004
© Crown Copyright, Ordnance Survey 2004
Design and modification
© 2005 Best Loved Hotels of the World

KEY

- Parks & gardens
- Lakes & rivers
- Motorways
- Through routes
- Other important roads
- Canal
- Mainline railway station
- Underground station
- Tourist information centre
- Pier

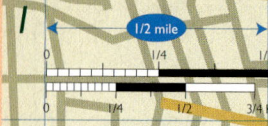

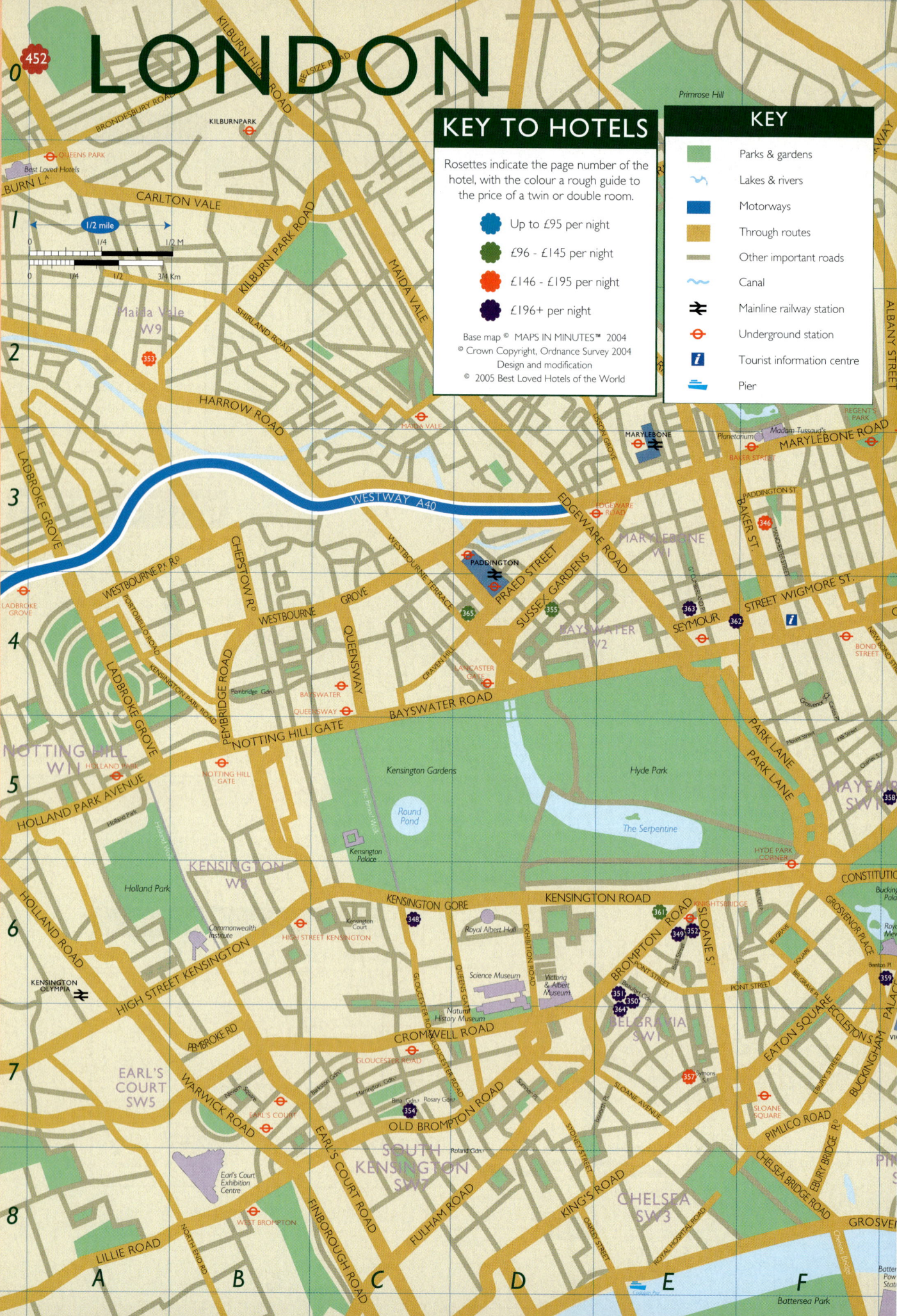

1/2 mile
0 1/4 1/2 M
0 1/4 1/2 3/4 Km

KILBURN HIGH ROAD · BELSIZE ROAD · PRIMROSE HILL · KILBURNPARK · QUEENS PARK · Best Loved Hotels · BURN LA · CARLTON VALE · KILBURN PARK ROAD · MAIDA VALE W9 · SHIRLAND ROAD · MAIDA VALE · HARROW ROAD · WESTWAY A40 · EDGWARE ROAD · MARYLEBONE · Planetarium · Madam Tussaud's · MARYLEBONE ROAD · BAKER STREET · PADDINGTON · PRAED STREET · SUSSEX GARDENS · BAYSWATER W2 · SEYMOUR · STREET WIGMORE ST · BOND STREET · NEW BOND STREET · LADBROKE GROVE · WESTBOURNE PK RD · CHEPSTOW RD · WESTBOURNE GROVE · QUEENSWAY · LANCASTER GATE · BAYSWATER ROAD · PARK LANE · MAYFAIR · PORTOBELLO ROAD · PEMBRIDGE RD · NOTTING HILL GATE · Kensington Gardens · Round Pond · Hyde Park · The Serpentine · HYDE PARK CORNER · NOTTING HILL W11 · HOLLAND PARK AVENUE · Holland Park · KENSINGTON W8 · Kensington Palace · KENSINGTON ROAD · KENSINGTON GORE · Royal Albert Hall · BROMPTON ROAD · KNIGHTSBRIDGE · SLOANE ST · GROSVENOR PLACE · CONSTITUTION · Buckingham Palace · HOLLAND ROAD · Commonwealth Institute · HIGH STREET KENSINGTON · Science Museum · Victoria & Albert Museum · BELGRAVIA SW1 · EATON SQUARE · KENSINGTON OLYMPIA · Natural History Museum · CROMWELL ROAD · PIMLICO ROAD · EARL'S COURT SW5 · WARWICK ROAD · GLOUCESTER ROAD · OLD BROMPTON ROAD · SLOANE AVENUE · SLOANE SQUARE · BUCKINGHAM PALACE RD · PEMBROKE RD · SOUTH KENSINGTON SW7 · KING'S ROAD · CHELSEA SW3 · CHELSEA BRIDGE ROAD · LILLIE ROAD · FINBOROUGH ROAD · EARL'S COURT ROAD · FULHAM ROAD · Earl's Court Exhibition Centre · WEST BROMPTON · Battersea Park

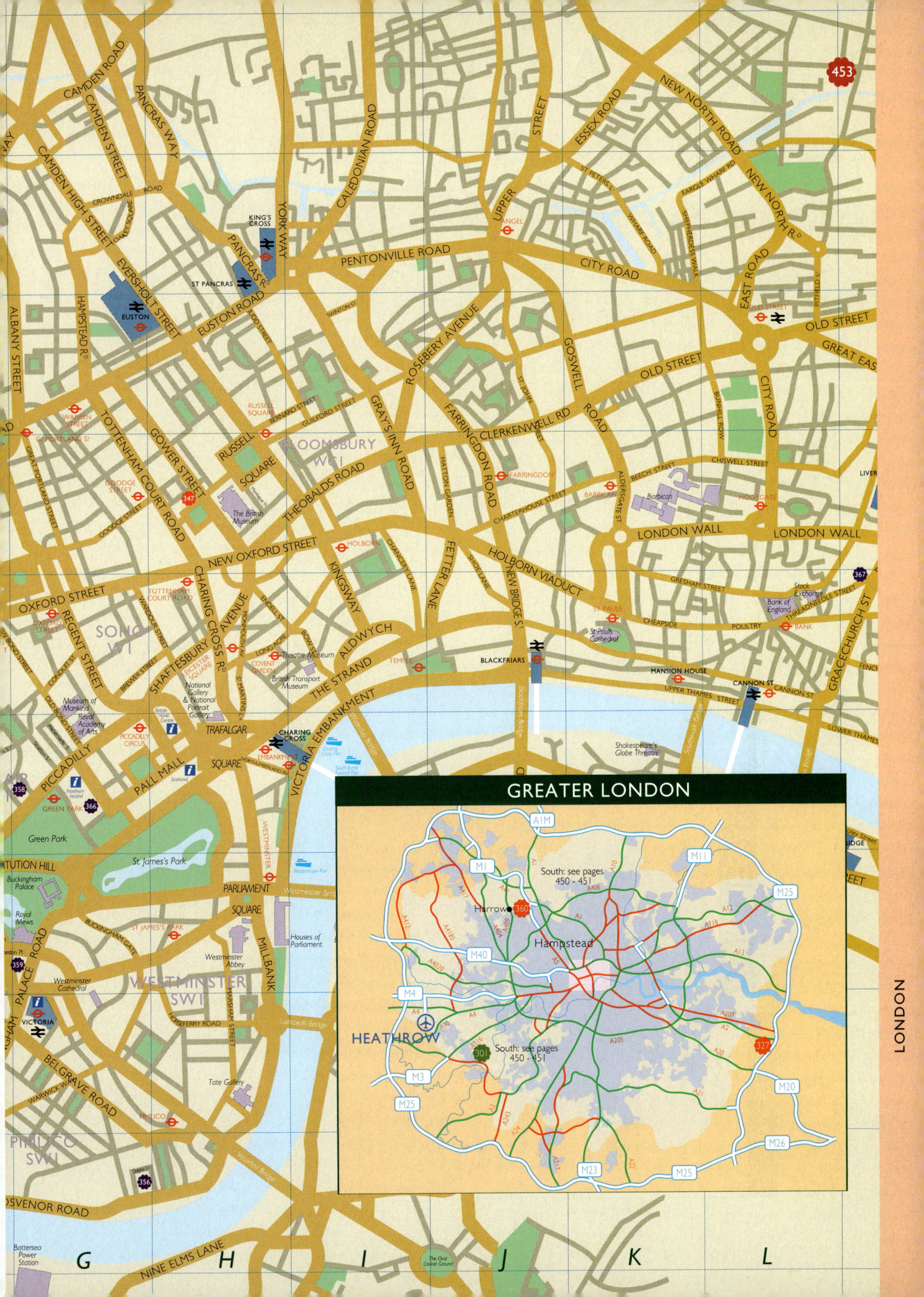
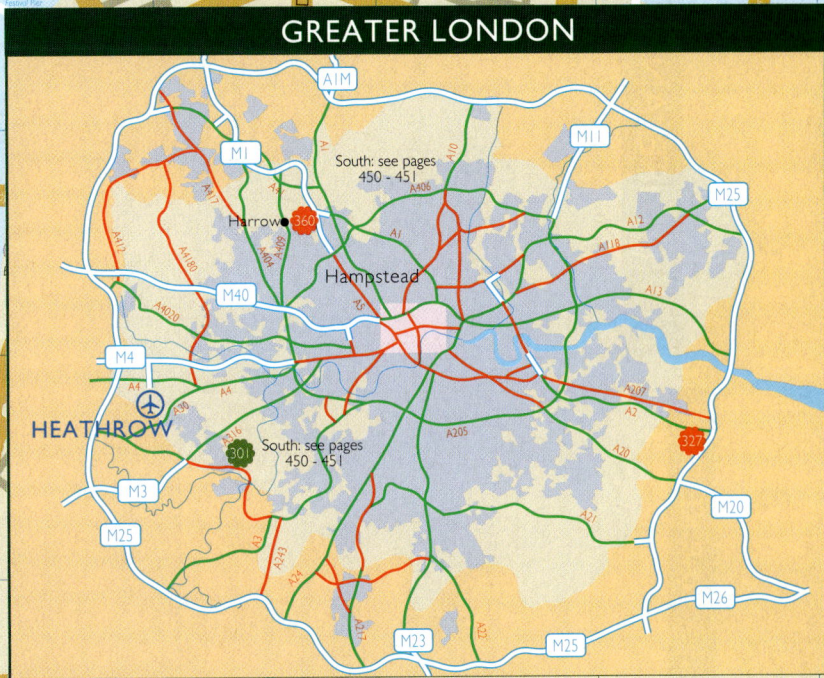

IRELAND

SCOTLAND
see pages
440 - 441

North Channel

MAP KEY

| Region border |
| National border |
| Motorways |
| Major throughroutes |
| Other roads |
| Ferry routes |
| River |
| Urban area |
| Airport |
| Lake/Loch |
| Capital |

PLYMOUTH
LONDON — Major town
KING'S LYNN — Minor town
Braintree — Other town
Pwllheli
o Mumbles — Other settlement

KEY (N. IRELAND)

Rosettes indicate the page number of the hotel, with the colour a rough guide to the price of a twin or double room.

- Up to £95 per night
- £96 - £145 per night
- £146 - £195 per night
- £196+ per night

Base map © MAPS IN MINUTES™ 2004
© Crown Copyright, Ordnance Survey Northern Ireland Permit No. NI 1675
© Government of Ireland, Ordnance Survey Ireland Design and modification
© 2005 Best Loved Hotels of the World

BELFAST INT'L
CITY OF DERRY
LONDONDERRY

Belfast
Bangor
Newtownards
Portaferry
Downpatrick
Lisburn
Ballynahinch
Newcastle
Annalong
Kilkeel
Carlingford
Warrenpoint
Newry
Castlewellan
Banbridge
Dromore
Portadown
Lurgan
Armagh
Keady
Castleblayney
Crossmaglen
Dundalk
Ardee
Navan
Trim
Kells
Drogheda
Balbriggan
Skerries
Rush

Larne
Whitehead
Carrickfergus
Ballyclare
Ballymena
Antrim
Crumlin
Holywood
Comber
Coalisland
Dungannon
Cookstown
Moneymore
Magherafelt
Maghera
Dungiven
Limavady
Coleraine
Portrush
Portstewart
Bushmills
Ballycastle
Cushendall
Ballymoney

Inishowen Head
Moville
Buncrana
Fahan
Milford
Rathmullan
Carndonagh
Strabane
Newtownstewart
Omagh
Newtownbutler
Lisnaskea
Enniskillen
Clones
Monaghan
Ballybay
Cootehill
Cavan
Ballyconnell
Belturbet
Cootehill
Ballinamore
Carrick-on-Shannon
Carrickmacross
Bailieborough
Cavan
Granard
Longford
Mullingar
Athlone
Glasson

Letterkenny
Ballybofey
Donegal
Ballyshannon
Bundoran
Sligo
Collooney
Ballysadare
Riverstown
Boyle
Ballaghaderreen
Castlerea
Roscommon
Swinford
Ballyhaunis
Kiltimagh
Claremorris
Ballinrobe
Cong
Ballinasloe
Tuam
Headford
Oughterard
Caherlistrane

Killybegs
Ballina
Castlebar
Westport
Newport
Belmullet
Bangor
Achill Island
Clare Island
Inishturk
Inishbofin
Inishark
Renvyle
Letterfrack
Cleggan
Clifden
Recess

Inishtrahull
Tory Island
Aran Island
Inishmurray
Clew Bay

Inishkea North
Inishkea South

454
46
60
385
378
390
421
408
424
379
418
404
407

M5
M2
M22
M1
M12

North Channel
Belfast · Liverpool
Lough Neagh
Lough Erne

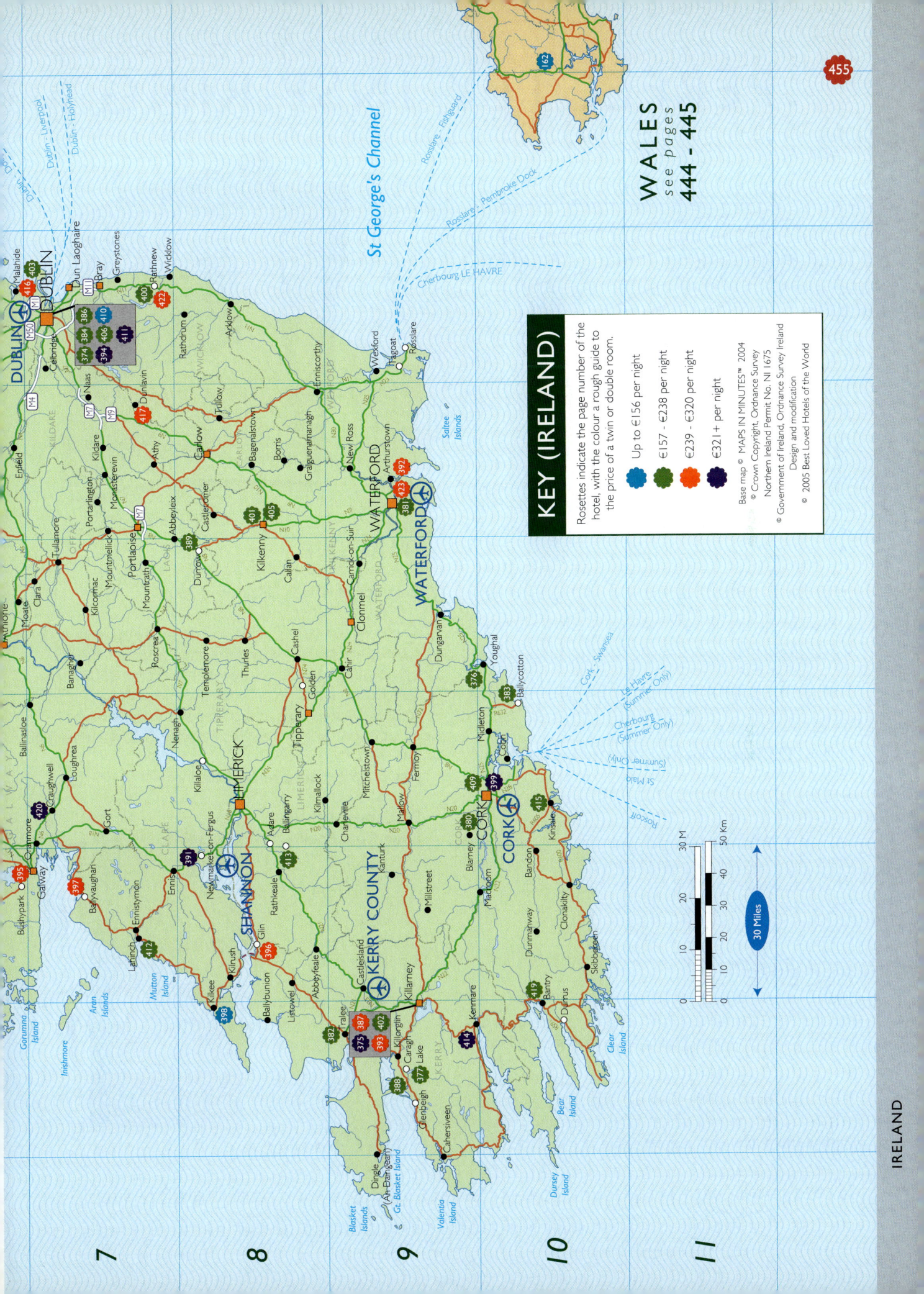

WALES
see pages
444 - 445

St George's Channel

Dublin - Liverpool
Dublin - Holyhead

Rosslare - Fishguard
Rosslare - Pembroke Dock
Cherbourg LE HAVRE

KEY (IRELAND)

Rosettes indicate the page number of the hotel, with the colour a rough guide to the price of a twin or double room.

- Up to €156 per night
- €157 - €238 per night
- €239 - €320 per night
- €321+ per night

Base map © MAPS IN MINUTES™ 2004
© Crown Copyright, Ordnance Survey
Northern Ireland Permit No. NI 1675
© Government of Ireland, Ordnance Survey Ireland
Design and modification
© 2005 Best Loved Hotels of the World

DUBLIN
Malahide 416 403
Dun Laoghaire
Bray
Greystones
Rathnew
Wicklow
400 422
Celbridge
374 384 406 410
394 411
Naas
Dunlavin
Arklow
417
Kildare
Athy
Rathdrum
Enniscorthy
Monasterevin
Bagenalstown
Borris
Carlow
Tullow
Graiguenamanagh
New Ross
Arthurstown
Wexford
Tagoat
Rosslare
Saltee Islands

Portarlington
Portlaoise
387
Mountmellick
Mountrath
Abbeyleix
Castlecomer
401 405
Durrow
Kilkenny
Callan
WATERFORD
423
381 392
Camac-on-Suir
Clonmel

Epfield
Tullamore
Clara
Moate
Kilcormac
Banagher
Roscrea
Templemore
Thurles
Cashel
Cahir
Golden
TIPPERARY
Dungarvan
Youghal
376
383 Ballycotton

Ballinasloe
Loughrea
Craughwell
420
Gort
Nenagh
Killaloe
LIMERICK
Adare
413
Ballingarry
Kilmallock
Charleville
Mallow
Fermoy
Mitchelstown
409 399
Midleton
Cobh
CORK 415
380
Blarney
Macroom
Bandon
Kinsale

Bushypark 395
Galway
397
Lahinch
Ennistymon
Ennis
291
Newmarket-on-Fergus
SHANNON
Glin
Rathkeale
Kanturk
Millstreet
KERRY COUNTY
Dunmanway
Clonakilty
Skibbereen

Kilkee
398
Kilrush
Ballybunion
396
Listowel
Abbeyfeale
Castleisland
Tralee 382 387 402
375 393
Killorglin
Killarney 414
Kenmare
419
Bantry
Durrus

Aran Islands
Inishmore
Mutton Island
412

Dingle
An Daingean
Gt. Blasket Island
388 377 Lake
Glenbeigh
Caherciveen
Valentia Island
Bear Island
Dursey Island
Clear Island

Le Havre (Summer Only)
Cherbourg (Summer Only)
St Malo (Summer Only)
Roscoff

30 M
50 Km
30 Miles
0 10 20 30 40

7
8
9
10
11

PERFECTLY INSPIRING

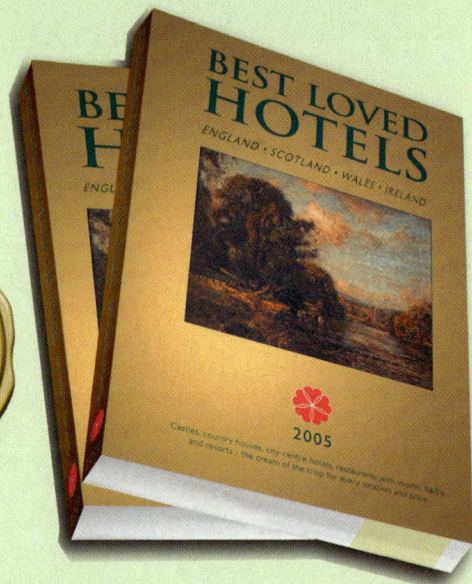

GIVE

Give your friends or family memories they'll cherish for a lifetime ... a great meal or a stay at a Best Loved Hotel. The **Best Loved Hotels Gift Voucher Package** includes

- The latest 456-page Best Loved Hotels - UK/Ireland full-colour directory, packed with enticing travel ideas

- £100 gift certificate valid for accommodation or dining

- One year's free membership in our Red Rosette Club

- All beautifully gift-wrapped with your special message and sent to the address of your choice

Only £149.95, including VAT, postage and packing. Already have a copy of the book? Vouchers alone are available in values of £50, £100, £150 and up.

Or, give a perfect present in pocket size - the **Little Gold Book Gift Voucher Package** for just £129.95, including VAT, postage and packing. Includes a £100 voucher, a year's membership in the Red Rosette Travel Club and a copy of Best Loved Hotels' Little Gold Book.

RECEIVE

Join the Red Rosette Club and keep up to date with all the news at Best Loved Hotels! Your membership includes

- £60 in vouchers for stays or meals at selected hotels
- Exclusive Red Rosette Club e-Newsletter
- Special offers and invitations from hotels and affiliates

Annual membership is a great value at just £9.95!

IMAGINE

Best Loved Hotels UK/Ireland 2005

The definitive large-format directory to inspire all your travel plans in the UK and Ireland. Features full-colour photos and editorial reviews of more than 350 hotels, detailed facts and ratings, culinary and regional guides, route planning maps and cross-referenced indexes. Includes one year's **free** Red Rosette Club membership!

Just £18.99 + postage and packing

Best Loved Hotels Little Gold Book

All the variety and imagination of Best Loved Hotels in a special pocket-sized format. Includes ratings and enticing special offers from nearly 300 member hotels - perfect for a short break or weekend getaway!

Just £8.99 + postage and packing

ORDERS/INFO: 0870 432 8700 (UK) OR +44 208 962 9555   E-MAIL ORDERS@BESTLOVED.COM

OR USE THE FREEPOST ORDER/INFORMATION FORM LOCATED IN THE BACK OF THIS BOOK

ORDER FORM

BOOKS, CLUB MEMBERSHIP & GIFTS

☐ I would like to order _____ copies of **Best Loved Hotels - UK/Ireland 2005** at £18.99 each + £4.50 P&P (Europe add £2; other countries add £8).

☐ I would like to order _____ copies of the **Best Loved Hotels Little Gold Book** at £8.99 each + £1.10 P&P (Europe add £1; other countries add £4).

The above include a year's free Red Rosette Club Membership.
To activate your membership, fill in the short questionnaire overleaf.

☐ I would like a year's membership in the **Red Rosette Club** only for £9.99, including VAT.

☐ I would like to order your **Best Loved Hotels Gift Voucher Package** for £149.95, including VAT and postage.

☐ I would like to order your **Little Gold Book Gift Voucher Package** for £129.95, including VAT and postage.

☐ Please add ☐ £50 ☐ £100 ☐ £150 ☐ £ _____ to my voucher.

Please advise recipients' names and address details separately if they differ from those listed below. Allow at least two weeks for delivery.

BILLING INFORMATION

☐ I enclose a cheque/postal order for £ _____ payable to **Best Loved Hotels**

☐ Please charge my Amex / Switch / Delta / MasterCard / Visa £ _____

Start Date: ☐☐/☐☐ or Switch issue number: ☐☐

Expiry Date: ☐☐/☐☐ My card number is:
☐☐☐☐☐☐☐☐☐☐☐☐☐☐☐☐

Signature ....

Title _____ First Name _____

Surname _____

Company _____

Address _____

Town _____ Postcode _____ Country _____

Tel _____ E-mail _____

Send to: Best Loved Hotels
Freepost LON 16342
London W10 4BR (UK only)

Orderline: 0870 432 8700 or +44 (0)20 8962 9555
Fax: 0870 432 8770 or +44 (0)20 8962 9550
E-mail: orders@bestlovedhotels.com

BLD05/OFI

ORDER FORM

BOOKS, CLUB MEMBERSHIP & GIFTS

☐ I would like to order _____ copies of **Best Loved Hotels - UK/Ireland 2005** at £18.99 each + £4.50 P&P (Europe add £2; other countries add £8).

☐ I would like to order _____ copies of the **Best Loved Hotels Little Gold Book** at £8.99 each + £1.10 P&P (Europe add £1; other countries add £4).

The above include a year's free Red Rosette Club Membership.
To activate your membership, fill in the short questionnaire overleaf.

☐ I would like a year's membership in the **Red Rosette Club** only for £9.99, including VAT.

☐ I would like to order your **Best Loved Hotels Gift Voucher Package** for £149.95, including VAT and postage.

☐ I would like to order your **Little Gold Book Gift Voucher Package** for £129.95, including VAT and postage.

☐ Please add ☐ £50 ☐ £100 ☐ £150 ☐ £ _____ to my voucher.

Please advise recipients' names and address details separately if they differ from those listed below. Allow at least two weeks for delivery.

BILLING INFORMATION

☐ I enclose a cheque/postal order for £ _____ payable to **Best Loved Hotels**

☐ Please charge my Amex / Switch / Delta / MasterCard / Visa £ _____

Start Date: ☐☐/☐☐ or Switch issue number: ☐☐

Expiry Date: ☐☐/☐☐ My card number is:
☐☐☐☐☐☐☐☐☐☐☐☐☐☐☐☐

Signature ....

Title _____ First Name _____

Surname _____

Company _____

Address _____

Town _____ Postcode _____ Country _____

Tel _____ E-mail _____

Send to: Best Loved Hotels
Freepost LON 16342
London W10 4BR (UK only)

Orderline: 0870 432 8700 or +44 (0)20 8962 9555
Fax: 0870 432 8770 or +44 (0)20 8962 9550
E-mail: orders@bestlovedhotels.com

BLD05/OFI

ORDER FORM

BOOKS, CLUB MEMBERSHIP & GIFTS

☐ I would like to order _____ copies of **Best Loved Hotels - UK/Ireland 2005** at £18.99 each + £4.50 P&P (Europe add £2; other countries add £8).

☐ I would like to order _____ copies of the **Best Loved Hotels Little Gold Book** at £8.99 each + £1.10 P&P (Europe add £1; other countries add £4).

The above include a year's free Red Rosette Club Membership.
To activate your membership, fill in the short questionnaire overleaf.

☐ I would like a year's membership in the **Red Rosette Club** only for £9.99, including VAT.

☐ I would like to order your **Best Loved Hotels Gift Voucher Package** for £149.95, including VAT and postage.

☐ I would like to order your **Little Gold Book Gift Voucher Package** for £129.95, including VAT and postage.

☐ Please add ☐ £50 ☐ £100 ☐ £150 ☐ £ _____ to my voucher.

Please advise recipients' names and address details separately if they differ from those listed below. Allow at least two weeks for delivery.

BILLING INFORMATION

☐ I enclose a cheque/postal order for £ _____ payable to **Best Loved Hotels**

☐ Please charge my Amex / Switch / Delta / MasterCard / Visa £ _____

Start Date: ☐☐/☐☐ or Switch issue number: ☐☐

Expiry Date: ☐☐/☐☐ My card number is:
☐☐☐☐☐☐☐☐☐☐☐☐☐☐☐☐

Signature ....

Title _____ First Name _____

Surname _____

Company _____

Address _____

Town _____ Postcode _____ Country _____

Tel _____ E-mail _____

Send to: Best Loved Hotels
Freepost LON 16342
London W10 4BR (UK only)

Orderline: 0870 432 8700 or +44 (0)20 8962 9555
Fax: 0870 432 8770 or +44 (0)20 8962 9550
Email: orders@bestlovedhotels.com

BLD05/OFI

RED ROSETTE CLUB
MEMBERSHIP
PROFILE

Keep up to date with all the news at Best Loved Hotels!

Your membership includes

- £60 in travel vouchers for selected Best Loved hotels, valid for stays or meals
- Exclusive Red Rosette Club e-Newsletter
- Special offers and invitations from selected hotels and our Red Rosette Club affiliates and sponsors

Activate your membership by filling in this short questionnaire.

Name _____

Address _____

E-mail address _____

Nationality _____

Spouse/Partner's Name _____

☐ I would like my partner's name on my membership card.

I/we have _____ children living at home.

While travelling and visiting hotels, I/we particularly enjoy...

	Always	Sometimes	Never
food and wine	☐	☐	☐
shopping/sightseeing	☐	☐	☐
theatre and concerts	☐	☐	☐
playing golf	☐	☐	☐
playing tennis	☐	☐	☐
spas/swimming	☐	☐	☐

I/we prefer a ☐ smoking ☐ non-smoking room.

Other comments or requests when booking hotels (e.g. twin beds or dietary requirements):

Please provide a username of 6-20 characters for your profile:

We will confirm your membership by post or e-mail, including your password.

From time to time we publish special offers, news and hotel updates as well as share your data with other reputable third parties. If you do not wish to receive third-party offers, tick here. ☐

RED ROSETTE CLUB
MEMBERSHIP
PROFILE

Keep up to date with all the news at Best Loved Hotels!

Your membership includes

- £60 in travel vouchers for selected Best Loved hotels, valid for stays or meals
- Exclusive Red Rosette Club e-Newsletter
- Special offers and invitations from selected hotels and our Red Rosette Club affiliates and sponsors

Activate your membership by filling in this short questionnaire.

Name _____

Address _____

E-mail address _____

Nationality _____

Spouse/Partner's Name _____

☐ I would like my partner's name on my membership card.

I/we have _____ children living at home.

While travelling and visiting hotels, I/we particularly enjoy...

	Always	Sometimes	Never
food and wine	☐	☐	☐
shopping/sightseeing	☐	☐	☐
theatre and concerts	☐	☐	☐
playing golf	☐	☐	☐
playing tennis	☐	☐	☐
spas/swimming	☐	☐	☐

I/we prefer a ☐ smoking ☐ non-smoking room.

Other comments or requests when booking hotels (e.g. twin beds or dietary requirements):

Please provide a username of 6-20 characters for your profile:

We will confirm your membership by post or e-mail, including your password.

From time to time we publish special offers, news and hotel updates as well as share your data with other reputable third parties. If you do not wish to receive third-party offers, tick here. ☐

RED ROSETTE CLUB
MEMBERSHIP
PROFILE

Keep up to date with all the news at Best Loved Hotels!

Your membership includes

- £60 in travel vouchers for selected Best Loved hotels, valid for stays or meals
- Exclusive Red Rosette Club e-Newsletter
- Special offers and invitations from selected hotels and our Red Rosette Club affiliates and sponsors

Activate your membership by filling in this short questionnaire.

Name _____

Address _____

E-mail address _____

Nationality _____

Spouse/Partner's Name _____

☐ I would like my partner's name on my membership card.

I/we have _____ children living at home.

While travelling and visiting hotels, I/we particularly enjoy...

	Always	Sometimes	Never
food and wine	☐	☐	☐
shopping/sightseeing	☐	☐	☐
theatre and concerts	☐	☐	☐
playing golf	☐	☐	☐
playing tennis	☐	☐	☐
spas/swimming	☐	☐	☐

I/we prefer a ☐ smoking ☐ non-smoking room.

Other comments or requests when booking hotels (e.g. twin beds or dietary requirements):

Please provide a username of 6-20 characters for your profile:

We will confirm your membership by post or e-mail, including your password.

From time to time we publish special offers, news and hotel updates as well as share your data with other reputable third parties. If you do not wish to receive third-party offers, tick here. ☐

BEST LOVED HOTELS

FREE BROCHURE SERVICE

Please send me full details on hotels with page numbers
circled opposite (maximum 10 hotels)

Name _____

Address _____

_____

City _____

Postcode _____ Country _____

Tel/Fax: _____

E-mail: _____

If returning this card from outside the UK, send to:

Best Loved Hotels
Suite 11, The Linen House, 253 Kilburn Lane
London W10 4BQ United Kingdom   BLD05/BR

16	42	68	101	127	160	193	219	252	278	310	336	375	401
17	43	69	102	128	161	194	220	253	279	311	337	376	402
18	44	70	103	129	162	195	221	254	280	312	338	377	403
19	45	71	104	130	170	196	222	255	281	313	346	378	404
20	46	72	105	131	171	197	223	256	282	314	347	379	405
21	47	73	106	132	172	198	224	257	283	315	348	380	406
22	48	74	107	133	173	199	225	258	284	316	349	381	407
23	49	75	108	134	174	200	226	259	285	317	350	382	408
24	50	76	109	142	175	201	227	260	286	318	351	383	409
25	51	77	110	143	176	202	228	261	287	319	352	384	410
26	52	78	111	144	177	203	229	262	288	320	353	385	411
27	53	79	112	145	178	204	230	263	289	321	354	386	412
28	54	80	113	146	179	205	231	264	296	322	355	387	413
29	55	88	114	147	180	206	232	265	297	323	356	388	414
30	56	89	115	148	181	207	233	266	298	324	357	389	415
31	57	90	116	149	182	208	234	267	299	325	358	390	416
32	58	91	117	150	183	209	235	268	300	326	359	391	417
33	59	92	118	151	184	210	236	269	301	327	360	392	418
34	60	93	119	152	185	211	244	270	302	328	361	393	419
35	61	94	120	153	186	212	245	271	303	329	362	394	420
36	62	95	121	154	187	213	246	272	304	330	363	395	421
37	63	96	122	155	188	214	247	273	305	331	364	396	422
38	64	97	123	156	189	215	248	274	306	332	365	397	423
39	65	98	124	157	190	216	249	275	307	333	366	398	424
40	66	99	125	158	191	217	250	276	308	334	367	399	
41	67	100	126	159	192	218	251	277	309	335	374	400	

BEST LOVED HOTELS

FREE BROCHURE SERVICE

Please send me full details on hotels with page numbers
circled opposite (maximum 10 hotels)

Name _____

Address _____

_____

City _____

Postcode _____ Country _____

Tel/Fax: _____

E-mail: _____

If returning this card from outside the UK, send to:

Best Loved Hotels
Suite 11, The Linen House, 253 Kilburn Lane
London W10 4BQ United Kingdom   BLD05/BR

16	42	68	101	127	160	193	219	252	278	310	336	375	401
17	43	69	102	128	161	194	220	253	279	311	337	376	402
18	44	70	103	129	162	195	221	254	280	312	338	377	403
19	45	71	104	130	170	196	222	255	281	313	346	378	404
20	46	72	105	131	171	197	223	256	282	314	347	379	405
21	47	73	106	132	172	198	224	257	283	315	348	380	406
22	48	74	107	133	173	199	225	258	284	316	349	381	407
23	49	75	108	134	174	200	226	259	285	317	350	382	408
24	50	76	109	142	175	201	227	260	286	318	351	383	409
25	51	77	110	143	176	202	228	261	287	319	352	384	410
26	52	78	111	144	177	203	229	262	288	320	353	385	411
27	53	79	112	145	178	204	230	263	289	321	354	386	412
28	54	80	113	146	179	205	231	264	296	322	355	387	413
29	55	88	114	147	180	206	232	265	297	323	356	388	414
30	56	89	115	148	181	207	233	266	298	324	357	389	415
31	57	90	116	149	182	208	234	267	299	325	358	390	416
32	58	91	117	150	183	209	235	268	300	326	359	391	417
33	59	92	118	151	184	210	236	269	301	327	360	392	418
34	60	93	119	152	185	211	244	270	302	328	361	393	419
35	61	94	120	153	186	212	245	271	303	329	362	394	420
36	62	95	121	154	187	213	246	272	304	330	363	395	421
37	63	96	122	155	188	214	247	273	305	331	364	396	422
38	64	97	123	156	189	215	248	274	306	332	365	397	423
39	65	98	124	157	190	216	249	275	307	333	366	398	424
40	66	99	125	158	191	217	250	276	308	334	367	399	
41	67	100	126	159	192	218	251	277	309	335	374	400	

GUEST SURVEY

Please tell us about your stay - the more
we know, the more reliable future editions
of Best Loved Hotels will be.

Hotel name _____

Name of guest(s) _____

Address _____

_____

_____

Postcode _____ Country _____

Tel/Fax _____

E-mail _____

Reason for your stay:

❑ Business   ❑ Conference

❑ Pleasure   ❑ Dining

How did you find your visit?

	Excellent	Good	Not Good	Poor
Public Rooms	❑	❑	❑	❑
Bedrooms	❑	❑	❑	❑
Restaurant/Food	❑	❑	❑	❑
Comfort	❑	❑	❑	❑
Facilities	❑	❑	❑	❑
Service	❑	❑	❑	❑
Courtesy/friendliness	❑	❑	❑	❑
Value for money	❑	❑	❑	❑

Additional comments:

_____

_____

_____

_____

_____

_____

Where are your own best-loved hotels?

In the UK ...

Name of hotel _____

Location _____

_____

In Europe ...

Name of hotel _____

Location _____

_____

In the rest of the world ...

Name of hotel _____

Location _____

BEST LOVED HOTELS
FREEPOST LON16342
LONDON
W10 4BR

No stamp
needed
in UK

BEST LOVED HOTELS
FREEPOST LON16342
LONDON
W10 4BR

No stamp
needed
in UK

BEST LOVED HOTELS
FREEPOST LON16342
LONDON
W10 4BR